Frommer's®

Provence & the Riviera

8th Edition

by Mary Novakovich
& Louise Simpson

au Enchante - nice to meet u
"au Enchante madame"
merci, merci beaucoup merci bien
au votre Sante - How to toast
Je M appelle my name is
Excusez-moi - Excuse me
excuse moi
Pardon.

WILEY

John Wiley & Sons, Inc.

Published by:
JOHN WILEY & SONS, INC.
111 River St.
Hoboken, NJ 07030-5774

Copyright © 2012 John Wiley & Sons, Inc., Hoboken, New Jersey. All rights reserved. No part of this publication may be reproduced, stored in a retrieval system or transmitted in any form or by any means, electronic, mechanical, photocopying, recording, scanning or otherwise, except as permitted under Sections 107 or 108 of the 1976 United States Copyright Act, without either the prior written permission of the Publisher, or authorization through payment of the appropriate per-copy fee to the Copyright Clearance Center, 222 Rosewood Drive, Danvers, MA 01923, 978/750-8400, fax 978/646-8600. Requests to the Publisher for permission should be addressed to the Permissions Department, John Wiley & Sons, Inc., 111 River Street, Hoboken, NJ 07030, 201/748-6011, fax 201/748-6008, or online at http://www.wiley.com/go/permissions.

Wiley and the Wiley logo are trademarks or registered trademarks of John Wiley & Sons, Inc. Frommer's is a trademark or registered trademark of Arthur Frommer. Used under license. All other trademarks are the property of their respective owners. John Wiley & Sons, Inc. is not associated with any product or vendor mentioned in this book.

ISBN 978-1-118-09604-8 (paper); ISBN 978-1-118-22364-2 (ebk); ISBN 978-1-118-24237-7 (ebk); ISBN 978-1-118-23688-8 (ebk)

Editor: Jennifer Polland
Production Editor: Erin Geile
Cartographer: Andrew Murphy
Photo Editor: Richard Fox
Production by Wiley Indianapolis Composition Services

Front Cover Photo: Wheat field and flowers in Provence, France ©Jelle van der Wolf / Alamy Images

Back Cover Photo: Sailing boats in the port of Saint-Tropez at the Cote d'Azur/ Provence ©E.D. Torial / Alamy Images

For information on our other products and services or to obtain technical support, please contact our Customer Care Department within the U.S. at 877/762-2974, outside the U.S. at 317/572-3993 or fax 317/572-4002.

Wiley also publishes its books in a variety of electronic formats. Some content that appears in print may not be available in electronic formats.

Manufactured in the United States of America

5 4 3 2 1

CONTENTS

4 LANGUEDOC-ROUSSILLON 59

5 PROVENCE 109

6 THE WESTERN CÔTE & INLAND VAR 188

7 THE FRENCH RIVIERA 230

8 PLANNING YOUR TRIP TO PROVENCE & THE RIVIERA 342

9 USEFUL TERMS & PHRASES 360

Index 367

LIST OF MAPS

ABOUT THE AUTHORS

Mary Novakovich is an award-winning travel writer and journalist and a member of the British Guild of Travel Writers. Based in Hertfordshire, England, she worked at the BBC for many years before going freelance in 1997. Since then she has written extensively about France, her articles appearing in The Independent newspapers, The Daily Telegraph, The Guardian, Le Monde, France magazine, and MSN Travel, among many others. She has been writing for Frommer's since 2009, and this, her first guidebook for the company, gave her the opportunity to focus on her two favorite regions of France: Provence and Languedoc-Roussillon.

Louise Simpson is a travel writer based in Southern France. Having studied French and Spanish at Cambridge University, she worked for a decade in London as a PR director for two leading travel PR agencies and as a writer for numerous U.K. newspapers and magazines including The Independent on Sunday, Vogue, Timesonline, and Financial Times. Since moving to Provence with her husband and two children, she has authored nine print and online travel guides to Southern France.

ACKNOWLEDGMENTS

I would like to thank Patricia de Pouzilhac, Mélody Raynaud, Valérie Gillet, Adam Batterbee, Michel Blanc, Fiona Quinn, as well as the many tourism officials in Languedoc-Roussillon and Provence whose help, insights, patience, kindness, and generosity were invaluable in the writing of this book.

—Mary Novakovich

This book would never have happened without the astute advice and understanding ear of Jennifer Polland, our editor on this project. Special thanks are due to my dear friend Anna Goldrein and to my husband, Jason, whose patient support made this book possible. Mary and I would like to give additional thanks to all those who have given their support over the course of this book including: Andrea Kahn, Marie-Claire Boudaud at Hôtel Martinez, and PR extraordinaire Martine Deloupy.

I would like to dedicate this book to my lifelong travel companions: Jason, Alexandra, and Charlie.

—Louise Simpson

HOW TO CONTACT US

In researching this book, we discovered many wonderful places—hotels, restaurants, shops, and more. We're sure you'll find others. Please tell us about them, so we can share the information with your fellow travelers in upcoming editions. If you were disappointed with a recommendation, we'd love to know that, too. Please write to:

Frommer's Provence & the Riviera, 8th Edition
John Wiley & Sons, Inc. • 111 River St. • Hoboken, NJ 07030-5774
frommersfeedback@wiley.com

ADVISORY & DISCLAIMER

Travel information can change quickly and unexpectedly, and we strongly advise you to confirm important details locally before traveling, including information on visas, health and safety, traffic and transport, accommodations, shopping, and eating out. We also encourage you to stay alert while traveling and to remain aware of your surroundings. Avoid civil disturbances, and keep a close eye on cameras, purses, wallets, and other valuables.

While we have endeavored to ensure that the information contained within this guide is accurate and up-to-date at the time of publication, we make no representations or warranties with respect to the accuracy or completeness of the contents of this work and specifically disclaim all warranties, including without limitation warranties of fitness for a particular purpose. We accept no responsibility or liability for any inaccuracy or errors or omissions, or for any inconvenience, loss, damage, costs, or expenses of any nature whatsoever incurred or suffered by anyone as a result of any advice or information contained in this guide.

The inclusion of a company, organization. or website in this guide as a service provider and/or potential source of further information does not mean that we endorse them or the information they provide. Be aware that information provided through some websites may be unreliable and can change without notice. Neither the publisher nor author shall be liable for any damages arising herefrom.

FROMMER'S STAR RATINGS, ICONS & ABBREVIATIONS

Every hotel, restaurant, and attraction listing in this guide has been ranked for quality, value, service, amenities, and special features using a **star-rating system.** In country, state, and regional guides, we also rate towns and regions to help you narrow down your choices and budget your time accordingly. Hotels and restaurants are rated on a scale of zero (recommended) to three stars (exceptional). Attractions, shopping, nightlife, towns, and regions are rated according to the following scale: zero stars (recommended), one star (highly recommended), two stars (very highly recommended), and three stars (must-see).

In addition to the star-rating system, we also use **seven feature icons** that point you to the great deals, in-the-know advice, and unique experiences that separate travelers from tourists. Throughout the book, look for:

- **special finds**—those places only insiders know about
- **fun facts**—details that make travelers more informed and their trips more fun
- **kids**—best bets for kids and advice for the whole family
- **special moments**—those experiences that memories are made of
- **overrated**—places or experiences not worth your time or money
- **insider tips**—great ways to save time and money
- **great values**—where to get the best deals

The following abbreviations are used for credit cards:

AE	American Express	**DISC**	Discover	**V**	Visa
DC	Diners Club	**MC**	MasterCard		

TRAVEL RESOURCES AT FROMMERS.COM

Frommer's travel resources don't end with this guide. Frommer's website, **www.frommers.com**, has travel information on more than 4,000 destinations. We update features regularly, giving you access to the most current trip-planning information and the best airfare, lodging, and car-rental bargains. You can also listen to podcasts, connect with other Frommers.com members through our active-reader forums, share your travel photos, read blogs from guidebook editors and fellow travelers, and much more.

1

THE BEST OF PROVENCE & THE RIVIERA

by Mary Novakovich & Louise Simpson

Provence and the Riviera evoke images of sun-drenched lavender groves, lush vineyards, and azure seas. The brilliant sunlight has seduced artists such as Vincent van Gogh and Pablo Picasso for more than a century. From the papal city of Avignon to the port city of Marseille, along the coast and beyond to Cannes and Nice, this is one of France's most enchanting regions. Provence and the Riviera are beautiful and culturally rich, offering everything from amazing art museums to fabulous beaches, Roman ruins, white-hot nightlife, and a distinctive cuisine that blends the best of the mountains and the sea.

Cities Vaucluse capital **Avignon** keeps visitors busy with medieval streets, Renaissance mansions, and Gothic palaces, while 18th-century Aix-en-Provence provides a lovely, flower-filled backdrop for the cafes once frequented by Cézanne and Zola. On the coast, bustling **Marseille** wows with a colorful assemblage of urban villages, beaches, and offshore islands. **Cannes,** capital of *the* film festival, takes over with palace hotels and Cistercian abbey islands. For old-school glamour, trace the pebbled shores to beautiful Belle Époque **Nice.**

Countryside The rocky outcrops of the Provençal countryside are studded with hilltop villages. Travel past vineyards and onto mountains such as **Mont Ventoux,** the 1,912m (6,273-ft.) thigh-killer cycled sometimes during the Tour de France. From here it's a picturesque drive to higgledy-piggledy **Gordes,** cascading elegantly down the hillside. For a flirt with the outdoors head to **Moustiers Sainte-Marie,** gateway to the **Gorges du Verdon.** These dramatic ravines offer breathtaking panoramas, especially when you're canoeing the twisting, cliff-lined waters.

Coast **St-Tropez's** beaches still attract bikinied crowds, but the Riviera's coastline is more than just bronzing bodies. Twenty-somethings flock to **St-Raphaël** for watersports in the shadow of the volcanic **Massif de l'Estérel.** While families invade nearby **Fréjus** with beach balls and ice cream, golfers head to **Toulon's** Dolce Frégate, one of Europe's prettiest golf courses. At the foot of the Massif des Maures, **Domaine du Rayol's** cascading Mediterranean gardens meet the turquoise sea in a blur of green.

Eating & Drinking Fertile soil, generous sunshine, and ample rain provide all the right ingredients for growing olives, peppers, tomatoes, garlic, herbs, and those cherished black diamonds, truffles. In **Menton,** France's lemon capital, treat yourself to tangy *tarte au citron.* Head west to Italian-influenced **Nice** for pizzalike *pissaladière* loaded with anchovies, black olives, and caramelized onions. **Cavaillon** loves its melons, while **Marseille** turns to the sea for saffron-infused *bouillabaisse.* For wine, sample rosé from the **Var** hills and reds from **Bandol.**

THE best TRAVEL EXPERIENCES

- **Partying in the Land of Festivals:** Provence hosts some 500 festivals with an astonishing 4,000 events. The ultimate example is the spectacular Cannes Film Festival in May. July and August are the busiest months, as Aix-en-Provence, Toulon, Juan-les-Pins, and Nice host jazz festivals, and Nîmes and Arles stage theater and dance performances. In mid-May, St-Tropez's riotous *bravades* (acts of defiance) honor the Roman saint Torpes (Tropez) in theory, but are really just an excuse for revelry. Many festivals have deep roots in Provençal folklore, honoring the bounty of earth and sea: the wine harvest in numerous villages, the rice harvest in the Camargue, and the cherry harvest in Céret. See "When to Go" in chapter 2.
- **Absorbing a Unique Lifestyle:** Provence and Languedoc share a uniquely Mediterranean lifestyle. Nothing could be more typical than a game of boules, or *pétanque,* played under shade trees on a hot afternoon in a Provençal village. This is a region that respects time-honored crafts; Picasso might have arrived here a painter, but he left a potter. And there are few finer things in life than to be invited into a Provençal kitchen—the heart of family life—and smell the aroma of herbs and wines cooking with the catch of the day. To walk in the gardens filled with vegetables, flowers, and fruit trees is reason enough to visit. Attend a harvest, not just of grapes, but perhaps of linden blossoms.
- **Dining & Drinking, Provence Style:** Many people flock to the south of France specifically to enjoy *cuisine provençale,* a Mediterranean mix of bold flavors with an emphasis on garlic, olive oil, and aromatic local herbs such as thyme and basil. The world's greatest *bouillabaisse* (fish stew) is made here, particularly in Marseille; Provençal lamb is among the best in France; and the local vegetables (such as asparagus, eggplant, tomatoes, and artichokes) fill the markets of France. The southern French version of fast food can be seen in classic Niçoise snacks such as *pan bagnat* (salade Niçoise in a giant bun) and *socca* (chickpea pancake). Regional wines are the perfect accompaniment, ranging from the warm, full-bodied Châteauneuf-du-Pape to the crisp whites of the vineyards of Cassis near Marseille.
- **Spending a Day in St-Rémy-de-Provence:** To wander St-Rémy's streets is to recapture Provence's essence, especially in its Vieille Ville (Old Town). After exploring its alleys, pause in one of its immaculate leafy squares, then search out an art gallery or two, and reward yourself with a painting and a memory. See "St-Rémy-de-Provence" in chapter 5.
- **Following in the Footsteps of the Great Artists:** Artists have been flocking to this region for centuries to capture its exceptional light. Most of these artists left

behind fabulous legacies. Perhaps it all began when Monet arrived with Renoir in 1883. In time, they were followed by others, including Bonnard in St-Tropez. Van Gogh arrived in Arles in 1888, and Gauguin showed up a few months later. The Fauves sought out this region, notably Matisse, whose masterpiece is his chapel at Vence. Not long afterward, Picasso arrived at Antibes. Deeply jealous of Picasso and Matisse, Chagall moved to Vence and was later infuriated that the street on which he lived was renamed avenue Henri-Matisse. He got over it and lived and painted on the Riviera until he died at 97.

- **Sunning & Swimming on the Riviera Beaches:** There are greater beaches but none more fabled, overcrowded though they are. Most of them are sandy, except beaches in Nice. These are shingled (covered with gravel or pebbles), but that doesn't stop the world from flocking to them. A beach mattress works just fine on the shingles, and umbrellas are for rent when you want to escape the relentless sun. Along the Riviera, topless sunbathing is de rigueur. Legend says it began with Brigitte Bardot, who pulled off her bra and said, "Let's wake up sleepy St-Trop." Nudist beaches also exist, notably at Cap d'Agde and Port Cros.
- **Breaking the Bank at Monte-Carlo:** Few other casinos can match the excitement generated at the Casino de Monte-Carlo. The world's wealthy flocked to Monaco when the casino was opened by Charles Garnier in 1878. But since 1891 much of the nonwealthy world has followed—even those who can't afford losses. During a 3-day gambling spree that year, Charles Deville Wells, an American, turned $400 into $40,000, an astonishing amount back then. His feat was immortalized in the song "The Man Who Broke the Bank at Monte-Carlo." Even if you do no more today than play the slot machines, a visit to this casino will be a highlight as you bask amid the extravagant decor and under the gilded rococo ceilings. (Some not as lucky as Wells have leaped to their deaths from the casino windows or the "Suicide Terrace.") See "Monaco" in chapter 7.
- **Cooling Down with an Ice Cream:** As temperatures rise in southern France, the lines outside ice-cream parlors grow longer and longer. Ice-cream making has become an art on the Riviera, where flavors range from tempting tiramisu to fragrant *jasmin* (jasmine) and from alcoholic Irish coffee to bizarre-sounding chewing gum. Ice-cream supremos include Barbarac (p. 214) in St-Tropez, where you can order an icy home delivery, and Fenocchio (p. 306) in Nice, where you can choose from more than 90 flavors.

THE best OFFBEAT EXPERIENCES

- **Exploring Massif des Calanques** (btw. Marseille and Cassis, Provence): At the old fishing port of Cassis, with its white cliffs and beaches that were a favorite of Fauvist painters, you can rent a boat and explore the *calanques,* small fiords along the rugged coast. Covered with gorse and heather, the white cliffs are the backdrop for this adventure. By car from Cassis, you can drive to the creek of Port Miou, with its rock quarries. To reach the Port Pin and En Vau creeks farther west, you must travel on foot (trails are well signposted). You can, however, take a boat excursion from Cassis. If you go on your own (not by boat), take a picnic and spend the day in these cool crystal waters. See "Exploring the Massif des Calanques" in chapter 5.

- **Driving to the top of Mont Ventoux:** The highest peak in Provence is the holy grail of cyclists eager to follow the tracks of Tour de France professionals. You can still see the race markings on the road as it winds its way to its barren 1,912m (6,273 ft.) peak. Along the way you'll pass cyclists doggedly tackling the twisting roads, their loved ones waiting by the side to photograph them in all their exhaustion. The views from the top make it all worthwhile. See "Mont Ventoux: King of the Mountains" in chapter 5.
- **Water Rambling in the Gorges** (Gorges du Verdon, Western Côte): This emerald-green canyon is the largest in Europe and the second largest in the world after America's Grand Canyon. One of the most unusual ways to explore the canyon is *aqua-rando* (water rambling), a mixture of floating and swimming in rapids that allows adventurous travelers to reach sections of the canyon that are inaccessible to rafts or hikers. See "Gorges du Verdon" in chapter 6.
- **Dancing with Wolves** (Mercantour National Park, French Riviera): Within an hour of the French Riviera's glittering coastline lies one of Europe's largest national parks, the 70,000-hectare (173,000-acre) Mercantour. In this sparsely populated paradise of gorges, waterfalls, and wild orchid meadows, you'll find wolves. Since their reappearance in 1992, there has been fierce debate between ecologists and shepherds. Listen to the divided opinions and see the wolf packs for yourself at **Scénoparc** in Saint-Martin Vésubie. See "Menton" in Chapter 7.

THE best ROMANTIC GETAWAYS

- **Les Baux-de-Provence** (Provence): Les Baux stands in a spectacular position on a promontory of sheer rock ravines. In the distance across the plain, you can view the Val d'Enfer (Valley of Hell). After a turbulent history, the town today is one of the great escapes for the French, who can gaze from their windows on the thousands of olive trees (many planted by the Greeks) that produce the best oil in France. Les Baux also has some of the country's grandest inns, notably **Oustau de Baumanière,** Les Baux-de-Provence (www.oustaudebaumaniere.com; ✆ **04-90-54-33-07**). After you and your loved one sample the ravioli with truffles, you'll understand why. See "Les Baux-de-Provence" in chapter 5.
- **Crillon-le-Brave** (Provence): This tiny hamlet at the foot of Mont Ventoux had a proud history from the 14th to the 17th centuries. But decline set in during the 19th century and the place was in ruins by the end of World War II. During the 1970s, however, life slowly started to creep back, and now it's the home of one of the most idyllic hotels in Provence. **Hôtel Crillon le Brave** (www.crillonlebrave.com; ✆ **04-90-65-61-61**) has created a hamlet within a hamlet, with its luxurious bedrooms housed in a cluster of 16th- and 17th-century buildings overlooking wide vistas of vineyards. See "Mont Ventoux" in chapter 5.
- **Roussillon** (Provence): At least 17 shades of ocher were used to create this exquisite hilltop village in the Luberon, best seen when bathed in the warm light of late afternoon. Less crowded than its overrun neighbor Gordes, Roussillon retains its Provençal charm and friendliness. Lose yourself in the romance of the Luberon at **Hostellerie Le Phébus & Spa** (www.lephebus.com; ✆ **04-86-60-80-12**), a luxurious retreat with glorious views of the ocher canyons of the Colorado Provençal de Rustrel. See "Roussillon" in chapter 5.

- **Îles d'Hyères** (Western Côte): If an off-the-record weekend is what you have in mind, there's no better spot than the "Îles d'Or," so-called because of the golden glow of the islands' rocks in the sun. This string of enchanting little islands is 39km (24 miles) southeast of the port of Toulon. The largest and westernmost island is Ile de Porquerolles, thickly covered with heather, eucalyptus, and exotic shrubs. Île de Port-Cros is hilly and mysterious, with spring-fed lush vegetation. The best spot for a romantic retreat is on this island—**Le Manoir** (http://hotelmanoirportcros.monsite-orange.fr/; ✆ **04-94-05-90-52**), an 18th-century colonial-style mansion set in a park. See "Îles d'Hyères" in chapter 6.
- **Grasse** (French Riviera): This back-country hideaway is the place to surprise loved ones with sweet-smelling gifts. You can also design your own perfume here. This perfumed town's shabby-chic character may not suit everyone, but a stay at **La Bastide St-Antoine** (www.jacques-chibois.com; ✆ **04-93-70-94-94**) should woo any cynics. Surrounded by parkland, this 200-year-old bastide lures diners with its Michelin-starred cuisine and 1,600-strong wine cellar. See "Grasse" in Chapter 7.
- **Peillon** (French Riviera): Located on a craggy mountaintop 19km (12 miles) northeast of Nice, this fortified medieval town is the least spoiled of the perched villages and still guards its medieval look, with covered alleys and extremely narrow streets. For a cozy hideaway, try the **Auberge de la Madone** (www.auberge-madone-peillon.com; ✆ **04-93-79-91-17**). Dinner for two on the terrace set among olive trees is the best way to start a romantic evening. See "Peillon" in chapter 7.
- **Saint-Jean-Cap-Ferrat** (French Riviera): With its Belle Époque palaces and legendary hotels dotted among its forested hills, this exclusive peninsula is the area of the Riviera that lives up to your imagination. Take a walk along promenade Maurice Rouvier past immaculate villas toward the earthy fishing harbor. The best place to combine luxury and romance is the **Grand Hôtel de Cap-Ferrat** (www.grand-hotel-cap-ferrat.com; ✆ **04-93-76-50-50**): the only hotel in southern France to be awarded the coveted "palace" label in 2011 under France's new hotel categorization system. See "Saint-Jean-Cap-Ferrat" in Chapter 7.

THE best BEACHES

- **Sète to Cap d'Agde** (Languedoc-Roussillon): If you want an alternative to the expensive beaches of the Côte d'Azur, you could do worse than the 18km (11 miles) of sand that connect these two towns east of Montpellier. In many stretches the facilities can be quite sparse, and you're unlikely to see magnums of champagne being splashed over expensive bikinis as you would in Saint-Tropez. But what you will see is enough space to stretch out, relax, and soak up the sun. See chapter 4.
- **Île de Porquerolles** (Western Côte): This island lies 15 minutes by ferry from the Giens peninsula east of Toulon. One of the Îles d'Hyères, Porquerolles is only 8.1km (5 miles) long and some 2.4km (1½ miles) across, and enjoys national park status. Its beaches, along the northern coast facing the mainland, get 275 days of sunshine annually. Several white-sand beaches stretch their way around the island; the best are Plage d'Argent, Plage de la Courtade, and Plage de Notre-Dame. See "Îles d'Hyères" in chapter 6.
- **Plages de Pampelonne** (St-Tropez, Western Côte): The Plages de Pampelonne in Ramatuelle are home to some of the world's most famous beaches. Where Plage

Tahiti and La Voile Rouge are notoriously hedonistic and brash, Club 55 retains a laid-back bohemian chic adored by A-listers and stylish travelers alike. See "Saint-Tropez" in chapter 6.

- **Plage Port Grimaud** (St-Tropez, Western Côte): This long golden-sand beach is set against the backdrop of the urban architect François Spoerry's *cité lacustre* (lakeside city), facing St-Tropez. Spoerry created this 98-hectare (247-acre) marine village inspired by an ancient fishing village. The world has since flocked to Port Grimaud and its beach. Some of the Riviera's most expensive yachts are tied up in the harbor. See "Saint-Tropez" in chapter 6.
- **Antibes & Juans-les-Pins** (French Riviera): Antibes and Juans-les-Pins are home to the French Riviera's best beaches. While other resorts along this coastline import sand to shore up their *plages,* this 25km (16-mile) coastal stretch has more than 48 natural golden sand beaches. Many have Blue-Flag eco-label status. See "Antibes & Juans-les-Pins" in chapter 7.
- **Cannes** (French Riviera): From the Palais des Festivals and west to Mandelieu, the beach at Cannes has real sand, not pebbles as in Nice. Along the promenade, called La Croisette, the golden sands are littered with sun beds and parasols rented at the beach concessions. The beach is actually divided into 32 sections; good choices are **Plage du Mourre Rouge** just east of Port Canto and **Plage du Midi** along boulevard du Midi just west of the Vieux Port. For beach recliners, parasols, and gastronomic restaurants, head to **Z-Plage** opposite the Hôtel Martinez or nearby **Vegaluna.** See "Cannes" in chapter 7.
- **Monte-Carlo Beach** (at the Monaco border, French Riviera): This private beach, once frequented by Princess Grace, is actually on French soil. Of all the Riviera's beaches, this is the most fashionable, even though its sands are imported. The beach is part of the ultrachic **Monte-Carlo Beach Hotel,** 22 av. Princesse-Grace (www.monte-carlo-beach.com; ✆ **04-93-28-66-66**). See "Monaco" in chapter 7.

THE best MARKETS

- **Uzès** (Languedoc-Roussillon): There are few more romantic settings for an outdoor market than the arcades of the medieval square in the heart of Uzès. The place aux Herbes teems every Saturday morning with stalls selling local produce and crafts, with more stalls filling the narrow side streets. See chapter 4.
- **St-Rémy-de-Provence** (Provence): This is the place to turn up on a Wednesday morning when the streets of the old town are crammed with scores of stalls. Sellers of local goat cheeses and *saucisson* (sausage) vie for attention with vendors of olive oil soap and other souvenirs of Provence. See chapter 5.
- **L'Isle-sur-la-Sorgue** (Provence): Sunday mornings are a busy time, as hundreds of stalls set up along the banks of the Sorgue River in this pretty Vaucluse town. As it's also the second-largest antiques center in France (after Paris), there's an enormous *brocante* market, too, where you can hunt for bargains among the bric-a-brac. See chapter 5.
- **Arles** (Provence): Be aware that the weekly market on Saturday can bring Arles to a standstill. As it's the largest market in Provence, this isn't so surprising. The boulevard des Lices throngs with stall after stall selling food and local (and not so local) crafts. See chapter 5.
- **Apt** (Provence): The capital of the Luberon area holds one of the most enjoyable markets in all of Provence. You'll see many of the same stallholders

at l'Isle-sur-la-Sorgue, but you might find it easier to get around Apt's wide streets and large main square. See chapter 5.

- **Antibes** (French Riviera): The daily covered market in Cours Masséna is a riot of Provençal produce and color. You find it hard to resist some of the stalls selling high-quality (if not particularly economical) olives and tapenade. See chapter 7.

THE best SMALL TOWNS

- **Uzès** (Languedoc-Roussillon): Uzès is a gem; with lofty towers and narrow streets, it feels like it belongs to a different era. Racine once lived here and was inspired by the town to write his only comedy, *Les Plaideurs.* Don't miss the delightful medieval heart of the city, the place aux Herbes. See chapter 4.
- **Pézenas** (Languedoc-Roussillon): Time has barely moved on in the medieval center of Pézenas, where Molière once called home. This pretty town in the Hérault Valley had been the seat of the Languedoc parliament in the 15th century. Even though its importance has waned in the intervening centuries, it's still as charming as ever. See chapter 4.
- **Roussillon** (Provence): Northeast of Gordes, Roussillon stands on a hilltop in the heart of ocher country, where the earth is a bright red. This ancient village has houses in every shade of burnt orange, dusty pink, and russet red—they take on a particular brilliance at sunset. Roussillon, however, is no longer the sleepy village described in Laurence Wylie's *Village in the Vaucluse,* yet it's still very beautiful. See chapter 5.
- **Mougins** (French Riviera): Only 8.1km (5 miles) north of Cannes, the once-fortified town of Mougins is about a thousand years old, and it's still a place to come enjoy the good life. Picasso chose a place nearby, Notre-Dame-de-Vie, to spend his last years. This hilltop town is known for its cuisine, with Michelin-starred chefs Sébastien Chambru at **Le Moulin de Mougins** (✆ **04-93-75-78-24;** www.moulindemougins.com) and Serge Gouloumès at **Le Mas Candille** (✆ **04-92-28-43-43;** www.lemascandille.com) vying for top position. See chapter 7.
- **Roquebrune-Cap-Martin** (French Riviera): This medieval hill village southwest of Menton is the finest along the Côte d'Azur. It has been extensively restored, and not even the souvenir shops can spoil its charm. Steep stairways and alleys lead up to its feudal castle crowning the village. But before heading here, take in rue Moncollet, flanked by houses from the Middle Ages. This castle, dating from the 10th century, is the oldest in France—in fact, it's the only Carolingian castle left standing. See chapter 7.

THE best CHATEAUX & PALACES

- **Château d'If** (off Marseille, Provence): One of France's most notorious fortresses, this was the famous state prison whose mysterious guest was the Man in the Iron Mask. Alexandre Dumas's *Count of Monte Cristo* made the legend famous around the world. It doesn't really matter that the story was apocryphal; people flock here because they believe it, just as they go to Verona, Italy, to see where Romeo and Juliet lived. The château was built by François I in 1524 as part of the defenses of Marseille. See chapter 5.

- **Palais des Papes** (Avignon, Provence): This was the seat of Avignon's brief golden age as the capital of Christendom. From 1352 to 1377, seven popes—all French—ruled here, a period dubbed "the Babylonian Captivity." They lived with pomp and circumstance. The Italian poet Petrarch denounced the palace as "the shame of mankind, a sink of vice." Even after Gregory XI was persuaded to return to Rome, some cardinals remained, electing their own pope or "anti-pope," who was finally expelled by force in 1403. See chapter 5.
- **Château de la Napoule** (Mandelieu, La Napoule, French Riviera): The Riviera's most eccentric château is also the most fascinating. This great medieval castle was purchased in 1919 by American sculptor Henry Clews, heir to a banking fortune. He lived, worked, and was buried here in 1937. In this castle, Clews created his own grotesque menagerie—scorpions, pelicans, gnomes, monkeys, lizards, whatever came to his tortured mind. See p. 231.
- **Les Grands Appartements du Palais** (Monte Carlo, Monaco, French Riviera): The world has known greater palaces, but this Italianate one on "the Rock" houses the man who presides over the tiny but incredibly rich principality of Monaco, Europe's second-smallest state. In 2011, this palace hosted the civil wedding celebrations for Prince Albert II and his bride Charlene Wittstock. When the prince is here, a flag flies. You can watch the changing of the guard every day at 11:55am. The throne room is decorated with paintings by Holbein, Bruegel, and others, and in one wing of the palace is a museum devoted to souvenirs of Napoleon. See p. 325.
- **Villa Kérylos** (Beaulieu-sur-Mer, French Riviera): This villa is a faithful reconstruction of an ancient Greek palace, built between 1902 and 1908 by the eccentric archaeologist Théodore Reinach. Designated a historic monument of France, with its white, yellow, and lavender Italian marble and its ivory and bronze copies of vases and mosaics, Kérylos is a visual knockout. See p. 313.
- **Villa Ephrussi de Rothschild** (Saint-Jean-Cap-Ferrat, French Riviera): This ornate pink Belle Époque palace and its immaculate gardens evoke the golden era of the Riviera. Baronne Ephrussi de Rothschild left a treasure-trove of art and artifacts to the Institut de France on her death in 1934. The Villa Ephrussi, the 1912 palace that contains these pieces, reveals what a woman with unlimited wealth and highly eclectic tastes can collect. It's all here: paintings by Carpaccio and other masters of the Venetian Renaissance; canvases by Sisley, Renoir, and Monet; Ming vases; Dresden porcelain; and more. An eccentric, she named her house after the ocean liner *Ile de France* and insisted that her 35 gardeners dress as sailors. See p. 311.

THE best MUSEUMS

- **Musée Fabre** (Montpellier, Languedoc-Roussillon): This extensive collection of Flemish, French, and Italian works from the 15th to the 18th centuries, as well as art from the 19th and 20th centuries, is housed in a handsome 19th-century mansion near the place de la Comédie. It's built around the private collection of Montpellier painter François-Xavier Fabre, which has been increasing steadily since the artist's death in 1837. Now the collections contain works by Poussin, Vernet, Bernini, Cabanel, Rubens, Courbet, and Dufy. See p. 88.
- **Musée de L'Annonciade** (St-Tropez, Western Côte): Few people come to St-Tropez for art. Yet this airy 16th-century chapel houses an impressive collection by 20th-century greats such as Bonnard, Dufy, Seurat, Utrillo, Vuillard, and Matisse.

You'll be able to view St-Tropez through the decades in works by Paul Signac, who installed himself in an art studio, La Hune, after stumbling across this little fishing village in 1892. Don't miss Aristide Maillol's nymph sculpture looking towards the port from the first floor of the museum. See p. 205.

- **Musée Picasso** (Antibes, French Riviera): After the bleak war years in Paris, Picasso returned to the Mediterranean in 1946. He didn't have a studio, so the curator of this museum offered him space. Picasso labored here for several months—it was one of his most creative periods. At the end of his stay, he astonished the curator by leaving his entire output on permanent loan to the museum, along with some 100 ceramics he produced at Vallauris. This museum reveals Picasso in an exuberant mood, as evoked by his fauns and goats in Cubist style, his still lifes of sea urchins, and his radiant *La Joie de Vivre*. See p. 266.
- **Fondation Maeght** (St-Paul-de-Vence, French Riviera): One of Europe's greatest modern art museums, this foundation is remarkable for its setting and its art alike. Built in 1964, the avant-garde building boasts a touch of fantasy, topped by two inverted domes. The colorful canvases radiate with the joy of life. All your favorites are likely to be here: Bonnard, Braque, Soulages, Chagall, Kandinsky, and more. A stunningly designed terraced garden is a setting for Calder murals, Hepworth sculptures, and the fanciful fountains and colorful mosaics of Miró. The courtyard is populated with Giacometti figures that look like gigantic emaciated chessmen. See p. 276.
- **Musée National Marc Chagall** (Nice, French Riviera): This Niçois museum houses the largest public collection of Marc Chagall's works. Set in the pretty Nice suburb of Cimiez, the austere building little prepares you for the fantastical world of violin-playing goats and horseback acrobats that greets you inside. Stained-glass windows in the auditorium take you on a tour of the creation of the world. After an initial donation of his *Message Biblique* series, the museum has gradually collated over 800 works by Chagall to give a more complete picture of his work from his time in Russia and prewar Paris to his war-time exile in the U.S., and finally to his return to France. See p. 292.
- **Musée des Beaux-Arts** (Nice, French Riviera): In the former home of the Ukrainian Princess Kotchoubey, the collection comes as an unexpected delight, with not only many Belle Époque paintings but also modern works, including an impressive number by Sisley, Braque, Degas, and Monet, plus Picasso ceramics. There's whimsy, too, especially in the sugar-sweet canvases by Jules Chéret, who died in Nice in 1932. Well represented also are the Van Loo family, a clan of Dutch descent whose members worked in Nice. The gallery of sculptors honors Rude, Rodin, and J. B. Carpeaux. See p. 102.

THE best CATHEDRALS & CHURCHES

- **Cathédrale St-Jean-Baptiste** (Perpignan, Languedoc-Roussillon): In 1324, Sancho of Aragón began this cathedral, but the consecration didn't come until its completion in 1509. Despite the different builders and architects over the decades, it emerged as one of Languedoc's most evocative cathedrals. The bell tower contains a great bell that dates from the 1400s. The single nave is typical of church construction in the Middle Ages and is enhanced by the altarpieces of the north chapels and the high altar, the work of the 1400s and the 1500s. See p. 68.

- **Cathédrale St-Just** (Narbonne, Languedoc-Roussillon): Though construction on this cathedral, begun in 1272, was never completed, it's an enduring landmark. Construction had to be halted 82 years later to prevent breaching the city's ancient ramparts to make room for the nave. In High Gothic style, the vaulting in the choir soars to 40m (131 ft.). Battlements and loopholes crown the towering arches of the apse. The cathedral's greatest treasure is the evocative *Tapestry of the Creation,* woven in silk and gold thread. See p. 78.
- **Cathédrale Notre-Dame-des-Doms** (Avignon, Provence): Next to the Palais des Papes, this was a luminous Romanesque structure before baroque artists took over. It was partially reconstructed from the 14th through the 17th century. In 1859, it was topped by a tall gilded statue of the Virgin, which earned it harsh criticism from many architectural critics. The cathedral houses the tombs of two popes, John XXII and Benedict XII. You'd think this cathedral would be more impressive because of its role in papal history, but it appears that far more time and money went into the construction of the papal palace. Nevertheless, the cathedral reigned during the heyday of Avignon. See p. 118.
- **Abbaye St-Victor** (Marseille, Provence): This is one of France's most ancient churches, believed to be built in the 5th century by St. John Cassian to honor St. Victor, a 3rd-century martyr. The church was destroyed by the Saracens, except for the crypt. In the 11th and 12th centuries, a fortified Gothic church was erected. In the crypt are pagan and early Christian sarcophagi; those depicting the convening of the Apostles and the Companions of St. Maurice are justly renowned. See p. 177.
- **Cathédrale Orthodoxe Russe St-Nicolas** (Nice, French Riviera): With its magnificent blue and gold onion-shaped domes and turrets, there's no more beautiful Russian Orthodox cathedral outside Russia than this. Built by the Russian royal family in honor of the 20-year-old Grand Duke Nicholas Alexandrovich, who died in Nice of tuberculosis, the cathedral dates from the Riviera's golden age, when everyone from Russian ballerinas to grand dukes visited the French Riviera. It was classified as one of France's *monuments historiques* in 1987. See p. 291.

THE best VINEYARDS

- **Château de Beaucastel,** 84350 Courthézon (© **04-90-70-41-00;** www.beaucastel.com): The Perrin brothers' vineyard is one of the top estates in Châteauneuf-du-Pape. But it's unusual in that it grows all 13 varieties of grape allowed within the Châteauneuf-du-Pape appellation. You can taste 10 vintages of their *grand vin* Château de Beaucastel, among many others, by appointment only.
- **Château de Simone,** 13590 Meyreuil (© **04-42-66-92-58;** www.chateau-simone.fr): This well-respected vintner lies less than .5km (1/3 mile) north of Aix-en-Provence. The vineyards surround a small 18th-century palace that might have been transported unchanged from *La Belle du bois dormant*. You can't visit the interior, but you can buy bottles of the recent crops of reds, rosés, and whites.
- **Château de Calissanne,** R.D. 10, 13680 Lançon-de-Provence (© **04-90-42-63-03;** www.calissanne.fr): On the premises is a substantial 18th-century white-stone manor house sporting very old terra-cotta tiles and a sense of the *ancien régime*. Even older is the Gallo-Roman *oppidum Constantine,* a sprawling ruined fortress

that you can visit if you obtain a special pass from the sales staff. The white, rosé, and red Côteaux d'Aix-en-Provence and the two grades of olive oil produced by the property are sold in an outbuilding. Advance reservations are vital.

- **Château d'Aquéria,** Route de Roquemaure, 30126 Tavel (✆ **04-66-50-04-56;** www.aqueria.com): Wines produced near the small Languedoc village of Tavel are considered some of the finest rosés in the world, which is not surprising considering this is where rosé was first created. An 18th-century château on the premises can be viewed only from the outside, and cellars and wine shops sell bottles of the famous pink wine.
- **Domaine de Fontavin,** 1468 rte. de la Plaine, 84350 Courthézon (✆ **04-90-70-72-14;** www.fontavin.com): Set 10km (6 miles) north of Carpentras, this is one of the leading producers of the heady, sweet dessert wine Muscat des Beaumes de Venise. As the organization here dates only from 1989, there's nothing particularly noteworthy in terms of architecture on-site. But oenophiles appreciate its proximity to some of the most legendary grapevines in the French-speaking world.
- **Château la Canorgue,** route du Pont Julien, 84480 Bonnieux (✆ **04-90-75-81-01;** chateaucanorgue.margan@wanadoo.fr): You might recognize this handsome château from Ridley Scott's 2006 romantic comedy *A Good Year,* as it stood in for the film's Château la Siroque. Jean-Pierre Margan and his family belong to one of a growing number of winemakers that work on strictly organic principles, forbidding the use of chemicals. You can buy the award-winning Côtes du Luberon reds, whites, and rosés directly from the château, which is on the D36 just north of Bonnieux, but some advance warning is appreciated.
- **Château de Pibarnon,** 410 chemin de la Croix des Signaux, 83740 La Cadière d'Azur (✆ **04-94-90-12-73;** www.pibarnon.fr): Some of the best of the rich red Bandol wines are produced here in an amphitheater of vineyards on top of the Colline du Télégraphe. The views are as seductive as the award-winning reds and rosés produced by Henri and Catherine de Saint-Victor and their family. Tastings are available Monday to Saturday (except during lunch), but advance warning is always welcome.

THE best LUXURY HOTELS

- **Villa Gallici** (Aix-en-Provence, Provence; www.villagallici.com; ✆ **04-42-23-29-23**): The first hotel in Aix-en-Provence to be awarded five stars is an impossibly romantic 19th-century villa set within lush gardens around an inviting swimming pool. The elegance of the 18th century has been recreated in sumptuous style, and dinner by candlelight under the plane trees is not to be missed. See p. 170.
- **Four Seasons Provence at Terre Blanche** (Tourrettes, Western Côte; www.fourseasons.com/provence; ✆ **04-94-39-90-00**): Not one but two 18-hole golf courses grace this plush resort in the Var countryside near Fayence. Nothing here is modest. The hotel offers suites which can accommodate four to eight guests each, and are spread around the landscaped grounds in terra-cotta villas. There are five summertime restaurants and a luxurious health club and spa boasting no fewer than three pools. See p. 228.
- **Château de la Messardière** (St-Tropez, Western Côte; www.messardiere.com; ✆ **04-94-56-76-00**): This fairy-tale 19th-century turreted château transports you to the Loire. The best feature of this five-star hotel is the magnificent view from the terrace through umbrella pines towards the Ramatuelle coastline. You can

browse art exhibitions in the hotel gallery, or lie back and enjoy the La Prairie and Cinq Mondes spa. See p. 207.

- **Hôtel du Cap-Eden-Roc** (Cap d'Antibes, French Riviera; www.hotel-du-cap-eden-roc.com; ✆ **04-93-61-39-01**): Looming large in F. Scott Fitzgerald's *Tender Is the Night,* this is the most stylish of the Côte's palaces, standing at the tip of the Cap d'Antibes peninsula in its own manicured garden. The hotel reflects the opulence of a bygone era and has catered to the rich and famous since it opened in 1870. See p. 267.
- **Palais de la Méditerranée** (Nice, French Riviera; www.palais.concorde-hotels.com; ✆ **04-92-14-77-00**): Since its reopening in 2004, this Art Deco palace has knocked its competitor Hôtel Negresco sideways. Josephine Baker performed at the hotel's theater in its heyday in nothing but a pair of high heels and a skirt of bananas. The theater is gone, but the casino has been restored to its 1930s splendor. Contemporary bedrooms are outfitted with luxurious extras from iPod docks to espresso coffee machines. See p. 295.
- **Grand Hôtel du Cap-Ferrat** (St-Jean-Cap-Ferrat, French Riviera; www.grand-hotel-cap-ferrat.com; ✆ **04-93-76-50-50**): The Grand Hôtel, built in 1908, competes with the Hôtel du Cap–Eden Roc as the Riviera's most opulent. Set in a well-manicured garden, it was once a winter haven for royalty. This pocket of posh has it all, including a private beach club with a heated seawater pool and a Michelin-starred restaurant. Following an extensive refurbishment, this hotel has become the first hotel in southern France to receive the coveted Palace label. See p. 311.
- **Hostellerie du Château de la Chèvre d'Or** (Eze, French Riviera; www.chevredor.com; ✆ **04-92-10-66-66**): In striking contrast to the palaces above, this gem lies in a medieval village 396m (1,300 ft.) above sea level. All its elegant rooms in this artistically converted medieval château open onto vistas of the Mediterranean. Everything here has a refreshingly rustic appeal rather than false glitter. See p. 317.
- **Hôtel de Paris** (Monte Carlo, Monaco, French Riviera; www.hoteldeparismontecarlo.com; ✆ **377-98-06-30-00**): The 19th-century aristocracy flocked here, and though Onassis, Sinatra, and Churchill long ago checked out, today's movers and shakers still pull up in limousines. This luxury palace houses two restaurants, the more celebrated of which is Alain Ducasse's Le Louis XV, the only restaurant in the region with three stars. Le Grill showcases Ligurian-Niçois cooking, a retractable roof, and a wraparound view of the sea. See p. 328.

THE best HOTEL BARGAINS

- **Hôtel Montmorency** (Carcassonne, Languedoc-Roussillon; www.hotelmontmorency.com; ✆ **04-68-11-96-70**): This hotel is only a few steps away from the entrance to the medieval Cité, yet it feels like a refuge with a swimming pool, Carita Spa, and imaginatively designed rooms. Somehow this comfortable place manages to combine the facilities of a four-star hotel with two-star prices. See p. 64.
- **Hôtel du Palais** (Montpellier, Languedoc-Roussillon; www.hoteldupalais-montpellier.fr; ✆ **04-67-60-47-38**): In the Old Town, in a labyrinth of narrow streets, this hotel dates from the late 18th century but has been modernized. The rooms are cozily arranged, and the hotel has a special French charm. It's one of the most historic hotels in town, and the bedrooms are relatively large. See p. 92.

- **Hôtel d'Arlatan** (Arles, Provence; www.hotel-arlatan.fr; ✆ **04-90-93-56-66**): At reasonable rates, you can stay in one of Provence's most charming cities at the former residence of the *comtes* d'Arlatan de Beaumont, built in the 15th century on the ruins of an old palace. Near the historic place du Forum, this small hotel has been run by the same family since 1920. See p. 133.
- **Hôtel Le Mouillage** (St-Tropez, Western Côte; www.hotelmouillage.fr; ✆ **04-94-97-53-19**): In the dizzyingly expensive resort town of St-Tropez, it's refreshing to find this reasonably priced boutique hotel. Stylish accommodations are scattered around a plant-filled terrace and pool where you'll be woken by the sound of a trickling garden fountain rather than the St-Trop party crowd. Free on-site parking is an added bonus. See p. 210.
- **Hôtel Villa La Tour** (Nice, French Riviera; www.villa-la-tour.com; ✆ **04-93-80-08-15**) is a former convent from the 18th century which has been converted into an atmospheric little hotel in the center of Nice, a 10-minute walk from the beach. Bedrooms, for the most part, open onto views of the Old Town, a few with balconies. A little roof garden is also open to guests. Its younger sister, Hôtel Villa Rivoli, is slightly more expensive, but worth every penny. See p. 299.
- **La Place Hôtel** (Antibes, French Riviera; www.la-place-hotel.com; ✆ **04-97-21-03-11**): A 5-minute walk from the *marché provençal* (marketplace), this well-run hotel is the best choice for central Antibes. With its tasteful contemporary decor and delicious French brasserie food, it has already made its name since opening in 2009. See p. 270.

THE best LUXURY RESTAURANTS

- **Le Jardin des Sens** (Montpellier, Languedoc-Roussillon; ✆ **04-99-58-38-38;** www.jardindessens.com): Twins Laurent and Jacques Pourcel set off a culinary storm in Montpellier, picking up two Michelin stars along the way. Both men know how to turn the bounty of Languedoc into meals sublime in flavor and texture. The results are often stunning, such as the fricassee of langoustines and lamb sweetbreads. See p. 90.
- **Christian Etienne** (Avignon, Provence; ✆ **04-90-86-16-50;** www.christian-etienne.fr): In a house as old as the nearby papal palace, Etienne reigns as Avignon's culinary star. A chef of imagination and discretion, he has a magical hand, reinterpreting and improving French cuisine. He keeps a short menu so that he can give special care and attention to each dish. See p. 123.
- **Oustau de Baumanière** (Les Baux-de-Provence, Provence; ✆ **04-90-54-33-07;** www.oustaudebaumaniere.com): This Relais & Châteaux occupies an old Provençal farmhouse. Founded in 1945 by the late Raymond Thuilier, the hotel's restaurant was once hailed as France's greatest. It might long ago have lost that lofty position, but it continues to tantalize today's palates. Thuilier's heirs carry on admirably as they reinvent and reinterpret some of the great *provençal* recipes. At the foot of a cliff, you dine in Renaissance charm, enjoying the bounty of Provence. See p. 141.
- **La Palme d'Or** (Cannes, French Riviera; ✆ **04-92-98-74-14**): The delectable cuisine here is no secret, as the restaurant has boasted two Michelin stars for the last 20 years. Chef Christian Sinicropi designs special menus for celebrity guests during the annual film festival. Robert De Niro liked his *Taxi Driver* dish (created

for the 2011 Film Festival Jury) so much that he took one of the handmade plates home as a souvenir. The restaurant defines elegance, with its private elevator and a pull-out shelf at each table, for ladies to rest their handbags. See p. 249.

- **Le Chantecler** (Nice, French Riviera; ✆ **04-93-16-64-00**): The most prestigious restaurant in Nice, and the most intensely cultivated, Chantecler has long been a training ground for the region's best Michelin-starred chefs. Currently in the hands of Jean-Denis Rieubland, this much-respected chef takes diners on a gastronomic voyage of French and Mediterranean flavors. Menus change almost weekly so you never know what's in store, but you can be assured of a memorable meal in this wood-paneled Regency dining room. See p. 301.
- **L'Aromate** (Nice, French Riviera; ✆ **04-93-62-98-24**): Since winning his first Michelin star in 2010, Mickaël Gracieux hasn't looked back. With its upbeat decor, his diminutive restaurant in central Nice has become a bastion of affordable gastronomy. His attention to detail combined with his sense of theatrical presentation has already won many Niçoise fans. See p. 302.
- **Joël Robuchon Monte-Carlo** (Monte Carlo, Monaco, French Riviera; ✆ **377-93-15-15-10**): Many critics hail Robuchon as the greatest chef in France. Emerging from retirement, he's become a star-studded culinary attraction in this chic principality, where his take on modern French cuisine is second to none. He seasons his delectable platters with "the perfumes of the Mediterranean." See p. 331.

THE best DINING DEALS

- **Tendances Lisita Restaurant** (Nîmes, Languedoc-Roussillon; ✆ **04-66-67-29-15**): In 2011, Olivier Douet joined the growing number of Michelin-starred chefs who have handed back their award and turned formerly expensive restaurants into more affordable brasseries. It certainly keeps the customer happy, as we now get an incredibly high standard of cooking for considerably less money. See p. 105.
- **Méli-Mélo** (Narbonne, Languedoc-Roussillon; ✆ **04-68-65-89-76**): The lavish interior of this restaurant (which doubles as an antiques shop) gives the false impression that you could end up spending a fortune. But what you'll find in this wonderfully quirky place is perfectly cooked dishes in a warm atmosphere. See p. 80.
- **La Mado** (Aix-en-Provence, Provence; ✆ **04-42-38-28-02**): Located beside the market in the bustling place des Prêcheurs, this ultramodern restaurant has a sleek interior, classy clientele, and elegant food—yet it's much more affordable than it seems. See p. 173.
- **Brasserie Tropézienne** (St-Tropez, Western Côte; ✆ **04-94-97-01-65**): Behind the Capitainerie du Port, this is one of St-Tropez's secret addresses. Locals have been thronging to this no-nonsense brasserie for almost 2 decades. With its tables spilling out onto the pavement, it's the perfect place for reasonably priced pasta, salads, and omelets. In the evening, the restaurant serves Asian cuisine. See p. 214.
- **Le Café de la Fontaine** (La Turbie, French Riviera; ✆ **04-93-28-52-79**): When a Michelin-starred chef decides to open an informal café-bistro, you can be sure that the quality of the ingredients will remain high. What is more challenging is to keep prices low, especially when your neighboring town is Monaco. Chef Bruno Cirino, who also runs the renowned Hostellerie Jérôme, manages to combine both with his hearty Provençal fare. See p. 319.

THE best SHOPPING BETS

- **Centre Sant-Vicens** (Perpignan, Languedoc-Roussillon; ✆ **04-68-50-02-18**): This region of France is next door to Catalonia, whose capital is Barcelona. This place is home to several merchants who sell various Catalan wares, with forceful geometric patterns in textiles, pottery, and furnishings. See p. 69.
- **Santons Fouque** (Aix-en-Provence, Provence; ✆ **04-42-26-33-38;** www.santons-fouque.com): Collectors from all over Europe and North America purchase *santons* (figures of saints) in Provence. You'll find the best ones here, cast in terra cotta, finished by hand, and decorated with an oil-based paint. The figures are from models made in the 1700s. See p. 170.
- **Alziari** (Nice, French Riviera; ✆ **04-93-85-76-92**): Established in 1868, Nicolas Alziari is the oldest olive manufacturer in Nice. As well as regional and flavored olive oils, there are numerous olive-infused products, from tapenades to face creams. There are two outlets in Nice: 318 bd. de la Madeleine (where you can visit the working olive mill) and 14 rue St-François de Paule. See p. 294.
- **Verrerie de Biot** (Biot, French Riviera; ✆ **04-93-65-03-00**): Biot is famed for its hand-blown glassware, and there's no better place to see them being produced than at this working glass-blowing factory. After you've watched red-hot molten blobs being blown into glassware of surprising beauty and complexity, you can head to the adjoining gallery where the one-of-a-kind collector pieces are for sale. See p. 272.

2

PROVENCE & THE RIVIERA IN DEPTH

by Mary Novakovich

France's most popular holiday destination is many things to many people. To some, it's a summertime playground of endless beaches and luxury hotels. Others delve into the region's rich history and revel in ancient Roman monuments and exquisite medieval villages. Landscapes take in dramatic gorges, vivid lavender fields, herb-scented hills, and wild expanses of marshy wetlands. Its sun-drenched way of life never stops luring visitors and locals alike.

PROVENCE & THE RIVIERA TODAY

Each resort on the **Riviera,** known as the Côte d'Azur (Blue Coast)—be it Beaulieu by the sea or eagle's-nest Eze—offers its unique flavor and special merits. Glitterati and eccentrics have always been attracted to this narrow strip, less than 200km (125 miles) long, between the Mediterranean and a trio of mountain ranges.

Tourism is the prime industry in Provence and the Riviera, with the majority of visitors clustering along the coast and leaving much of the vast hilly hinterland of Provence intact. Approximately five million people visit the Côte d'Azur in the summer months. While tourism brings employment to the area, it's mainly on a seasonal basis, with the summer months being the most crowded—reservations are imperative in July and August. Many of the villages turn into ghost towns in the winter months, reawakening briefly to celebrate Christmas in colorful Provençal style. The average summer temperature is 84°F (29°C); the average winter temperature, 55°F (13°C).

Popularity, overbuilding of the coast, and the summer hordes descending on such cities as Avignon have made the region less desirable in parts, especially if you're driving behind long lines of cars in summer heat. The disposition of its citizens is a bit taxed by the endless tourist pressure and tempers can easily flare.

Unlike the overbuilt Côte d'Azur, **Provence** still has vast pockets of rural area, and, yes, old men today still play a leisurely game of boules on a hot afternoon under the shade of trees. And although hordes of tourists flock to the region—especially in the summer—Provence still hasn't been irretrievably spoiled, as many claim. The vast hilly hinterland of Provence remains relatively intact.

Some of the vast migration to Provence has been good. Many villages in nostalgic decay and depopulation have been rescued by the arrival of craftspeople and artists, including potters and weavers, who have saved buildings from total collapse. Summer residents from Paris and Provence-loving foreigners have poured new energy, vitality, and money into this corner of France. The flip side to this, unfortunately, is the number of *maisons secondaires* (second homes) that are left empty for much of the year. This can create animosity between some permanent Provence residents and newcomers, particularly those from the capital, as it becomes harder for locals to remain in the villages and towns in which they were brought up.

Like the rest of the world, Provence suffered some of the effects of the recent global economic crises, but not nearly to the extent of some of its European neighbors. Although prices for food and accommodation have risen rapidly in recent years, the number of tourists continues to swell. One area that has grown in particular is business and conference travel, with cities such as Cannes and Marseille hosting major conferences for many months of the year. Foreign investment continues, with multinational corporations setting up offices in the region's business parks, such as Sophia Antipolis near Antibes, a sprawling technology park about 10km (6 miles) northwest of Antibes, where blue-chip companies including IBM, Hewlett Packard, and Accenture have opened offices. As a result, the income from high-tech businesses and services is rivaling the amount brought in by tourism.

Marseille is the largest port on the Mediterranean, receiving nearly 100 million tons annually as well as countless cruise ships. It has been deigned the 2013 European Capital of Culture and will host a year of cultural events along with its Provençal neighbors Aix-en-Provence, Arles, Aubagne, Gardanne, Istres, La Ciotat, Martigues, and Salon-de-Provence. The city has been busy refurbishing many of its major art galleries and museums, most of which won't be open until 2013. Major regeneration projects have been announced too, including turning part of the Vieux Port into one large traffic-free zone.

Although many perceive Provence to be idyllic, the region is not immune to tensions between different ethnic groups, which flare up occasionally, but not as frequently as in the impoverished suburbs of Paris, for example. There is also a large underclass of third-generation North Africans that finds it difficult to be integrated into mainstream French society. The French government invited people from its former North African colonies to rebuild the country after the devastation of World War II, but treatment of its immigrant population hasn't been fair over the decades. Provence has generally been a conservative area, and this attitude has been exploited from time to time by far-right xenophobic political parties. One thing that unites most Provençaux, however, is their dislike of France's unpopular president, Nicolas Sarkozy, who at press time was running for re-election in France's 2012 presidential election.

Neighboring **Languedoc** is another compelling region of France sending out its siren call. Much of the landscape, cuisine, lifestyle, and architecture of Languedoc is similar to Provence. Today, Languedoc-Roussillon consists of the eastern region along the coast and up towards the Cévennes mountains, stretching from Carcassonne to

DID YOU know?

- In the wake of the 1956 film at St-Tropez, *And God Created Woman* starring Brigitte Bardot, the first topless bathers were arrested. The police didn't know what to do with the women since they'd put Coca-Cola bottle caps over their nipples for modesty.
- The 1956 wedding of Grace Kelly and Prince Rainer attracted 600 guests, including some reporters disguised as cassocked priests and a few jewel thieves who robbed the princess's mother and a bridesmaid and made off with a Rembrandt and a Rubens. Fifty-five years later, in 2011, their son, Prince Albert, gave up his crown as the world's most eligible bachelor and finally got married. South African Olympic swimmer Charlene Wittstock formally entered the House of Grimaldi in a 2-day wedding at the Prince's Palace of Monaco. Almost 4,000 people watched the ceremonies outside the palace on giant screens.
- F. Scott Fitzgerald warned his editor, Maxwell Perkins, not to mention the Riviera in advertising copy: "Its very mention invokes a feeling of unreality and insubstantiality," he cautioned.
- The Cannes Film Festival, which was officially founded in 1946 and takes place every May, attracts more than 200,000 people, including film stars, directors and producers, and fans eager to spot celebrities. Over 4,000 journalists capture the celebrities and events.

Montpellier and taking in the area of Roussillon, which is French Catalonia. The capital, Montpellier, has one of the oldest universities in France as well as one of the youngest populations in France. The city continues to expand, with relatively new districts that were created in the 1980s and 1990s, such as the Corum, Antigone, and the Port Marianne neighborhood.

Like Provence, Languedoc has also experienced an influx of foreign buyers, although not nearly on the scale as seen in Provence. This has brought new dynamism to many of the smaller villages that were becoming depopulated.

Large numbers of locals as well as newcomers are involved in one of Languedoc's main industries: wine production. It's the world's largest wine region, and there isn't a single *département* that doesn't feature endless rows of vineyards. Languedoc used to have a reputation for producing vast quantities of inferior wine, but that has been changing in recent decades as winemakers focus more on quality.

LOOKING BACK AT PROVENCE & THE RIVIERA

Prehistory

During the Bronze Age, Provence was inhabited by primitive tribes whose art legacy began around 6000 B.C. in the form of etched pottery. By around 700 B.C., traders from Greek-speaking colonies in Greece and around the Aegean established colonies at Antipolis (Antibes), Nikaia (Nice), and Massilia (Marseille). Mediterranean wines, grains, and ceramics were exchanged, it's believed, for pewter and livestock from west-central France.

The Greeks even sailed up the Rhône Valley, trading with local Celtic and Ligurian tribes and generally influencing the culture with their more sophisticated ways. To them is credited the introduction of the grape and the olive, two foodstuffs that would play vital roles in the Provençal economy for millennia to come—and still do today.

Around 600 B.C., waves of migration from the Celtic north added to the non-Mediterranean population of Provence. The Celts allied and intermarried easily with the native Ligurians, and eventually formed a fierce force that to an increasing degree opposed the expansionistic efforts of Greek traders. In 218 B.C., some of the tribes supported Hannibal during his passage across the Alps and his destructive advance upon Rome, an alliance that Rome would severely punish several generations later. As the local forces faced off against Greek expansionism in the south, tensions grew to the point where the Greeks called on the rapidly emerging power of the Roman Empire to subdue the threat to their colonial power. The resulting genocides and annihilations committed by Rome helped define the future racial and cultural makeup of Provence for the next 2,000 years.

The Romans

In 125 B.C., thrusting northward and flexing his empire's muscles after some of its spectacular victories over the Carthaginians, Roman general Sextius massacred thousands of Celts and Ligurians on a battlefield at Egremont, a short distance north of Aix-en-Provence. This action was duplicated less than a quarter-century later, in 102 B.C. on an even larger scale, when the Roman general Marius massacred as many as 200,000 Teutonic, Celtic, and Ligurian tribespeople during their attempts at southward incursions. Ever after, Rome considered the Mediterranean coastline of what is today known as France as one of its most treasured provinces.

The Romans named their new possession *Provincia Transalpina,* a name that was later bastardized into "Provence." They established Narbonne as the region's administrative center, *Gallia Narbonensis.* By 49 B.C., Julius Caesar had conquered all of Gaul. But despite Roman influence throughout the rest of Europe, few other regions received as direct or as concentrated a dose of Romanization as Provence. Evidence of this remains in grandiose construction of amphitheaters, bathhouses, temples, and stadiums at sites that include Arles, Orange, Nîmes, Glanum (near St-Rémy-de-Provence), Fréjus, and Cimiez in Nice. **Pont du Gard** (p. 102)—a masterpiece of civic engineering and one of the most frequently photographed sites in France—was completed in 19 B.C. Ironically, Marseille, whose pedigree predated that of virtually every other Roman site in Provence, was bypassed during the explosion of Roman building because of its alliance with the losing side in the 49 B.C. civil war between Pompey and Julius Caesar.

Later, as the administration and the scope of the Roman Empire diminished, and the far reaches of the empire became frayed and tattered at the edges, *Provincia Narbonensis* remained staunchly Roman. Even after the empire's East-West schism, Provence remained staunchly Roman and a direct beneficiary of trade and attention from whomever happened to rule the empire at the time.

Rome's Collapse & the Early Middle Ages

As Rome's vast empire began to crumble, Provence seemed to rush headlong toward Christianization. Some of the earliest evidence of the spread of the inflammatory new

How Provence Got its Name

When the Romans ruled the region, they called it *Provincia Nostra* ("Our Province") or *Provincia* ("the Province"). Later, this name was adapted to the French "Provence"—the name of the region today.

religion can be viewed in Marseille at the oft-repaired remains of the **Abbaye St-Victor** (p. 177), founded in 413.

The preeminence of Arles as a centerpiece of Roman culture did not serve it well after the collapse of the empire. In 471, it was ransacked by the Visigoths, and a few years later, it and many of the other important settlements of Provence were sacked again by other barbarian hordes. From 600 to 800, the devastations were duplicated by Saracen (Moorish) navies from North Africa, and in rare instances, an occasional Viking raid along the valley of the Rhône.

Ironically, Charles Martel himself, one of the patriarchs of modern France, led his Frankish troops through Provence between 736 and 740 on destructive orgies of appalling brutality. In the aftermath of these recurrent catastrophes, local politics wavered between instability and anarchy as local warlords and feudal barons murdered their opponents, seized power, and were murdered in turn.

The only exception to the ongoing chaos was the brief ascendancy of the Merovingians around A.D. 500. But because their strongholds lay within what is now northeastern France, they didn't focus a lot of creative energy on Provence. Later, Charlemagne passed through Provence en route to Rome in 800, where he was crowned Emperor of the West by the Roman Pope. After Charlemagne's death, when his empire was split among three feuding grandsons, Provence was bequeathed to Lothair, the eldest of the three. Lothair placed his own son, Charles, on the throne of Provence, designating it as a kingdom in its own right. By 879, Provence was ruled jointly, though somewhat inefficiently, with Burgundy by the medieval ruler Boson, brother-in-law of Charles the Bald.

Medieval Provence

In 1032, with a capital established at Aix-en-Provence, the eastern half of Provence—the area east of the Rhône—became a member of the Holy Roman Empire, a loose configuration of duchies and kingdoms unified mainly by a shared fear and loathing of the Moors. The area west of the Rhône fell into the orbit of the Counts of Toulouse. Romanesque architecture, poetry, music, and verse flourished for a period of almost 300 years, a cultural high point that today represents a much-studied flowering of the troubadour and the beginnings of literature and popular entertainment as the world knows it today. Two of the most impressive examples of Romanesque architecture can be found at the Abbaye Notre-Dame de Sénanque near Gordes (p. 148) and Fréjus cathedral, Cité Episcopale (p. 220).

By around 1125, most of the power within Provence was controlled by the Counts of Toulouse and the Counts of Barcelona. Except for some political gaffes and a sense of regionalism, it appeared for a time that the Counts of Barcelona and the Counts of Toulouse might succeed at uniting their neighboring kingdoms. By 1246, control of Provence tipped in favor of the French kings, thanks to a series of politically motivated marriages between the family of St. Louis, the rulers of Barcelona, and royal residents of Provence. Today, the village of Barcelonnette (Alpes-de-Haute-Provence) derives its medieval name from the influence of those counts.

The strategic importance of Provence was obvious to the Paris-based kings. Construction of one of the most remarkable sites in southern France, the fortified town of **Aigues-Mortes** (p. 97), was commissioned by St. Louis as a bulwark against the Moors and other assorted interlopers. In 1248, he, along with a doomed army of soldiers, sailors, and priests, set sail from that city on the Seventh Crusade, only to die en route in Tunis of the plague.

In 1307, in one of the most bizarre political imbroglios of European history, a French-born pope, Clement V, fearful of the instability that prevailed within Rome, decided to move the official seat of the papacy to **Avignon** (p. 115). Here, surrounded by an army of courtiers, priests, and soldiers, and purveyors of luxury goods, it remained for 70 years under the protection of the kings of France and counts of Provence. Avignon became a vibrant and prosperous city that resembled a massive construction site throughout the entire process. The papacy was eventually moved back to Rome after violent politicking and even some armed conflicts between the papal factions. One of the most notable conflicts was the so-called War of the Eight Saints, waged between Florence and other Italian city-states and Pope Gregory XI and his band of mercenaries. Florence was excommunicated for her pains, and Pope Gregory's mercenaries massacred several thousand inhabitants of the Italian city of Cesena.

Plagues decimated the population of Provence beginning in 1348, with even more severe outbreaks of the disease beginning in 1375, killing off residents in staggering numbers. At the same time, extortion, plundering, and highway robbery by small-time feudal despots, including the rulers of the much-dreaded Les Baux-de-Provence, added to a general sense of confusion, unrest, and in many cases, despair.

In 1409, the University of Aix was founded as southern France's answer to the thriving University in Paris. In 1434, René of Anjou, former king of Naples, was designated count of an independent Provence, and in his new role fostered economic development and the arts. Shortly after René's death, his nephew and heir signed a pact with Paris-based Louis XI, who immediately annexed Provence into the orbit of the French monarchs.

Conflicts with Paris & Wars of Religion

Provence had always been fertile ground for the nurturing of offshoot religions. The Cathar heretics, whose strongholds had thrived most obviously in neighboring Languedoc but whose adherents also lived in Provence, were seen as a direct threat to the power of the French monarchs, and were violently obliterated. One of the most infamous massacres was in Béziers, when 7,000 people were burned alive in the church of La Madeleine in 1209.

In the 1500s, the Reformation changed the social fabric of Europe and the world forever. Influenced by the thriving community of Protestants under John Calvin, the number of Provence-based Huguenots (Protestants) grew in size and power. One of the most hotheaded of the Provençal sects included the Vaudois, spiritual descendants of the Cathars. Founded by a wealthy merchant, Valdès or Vaudès, from Lyon in the 1200s, the sect rejected the idea of an ecclesiastical hierarchy, preached the virtues of poverty, and denied the authenticity of the sacraments. All of this was greeted with something akin to horror by the established church. When the Vaudois responded to their persecutors by attacking several Catholic churches in 1545 near their stronghold in the Luberon hills, the armies of Renaissance king François the First massacred more than 3,000 of them over a 4-day period in April 1545, and sent another 600 into the galleys of the French navy as slaves.

Despite these repressions, Protestantism continued to flourish in the towns of Orange, Uzès, and especially Nîmes. During a 40-year period beginning around 1560, religious battles occurred with almost constant regularity throughout France. Chief of State Richelieu, whose personal obsession involved the unification of all aspects of French society into a form approved by Paris, eventually suppressed or destroyed Huguenot strongholds throughout France.

In 1720, a devastating plague was imported through the harbor of Marseille, killing what's conservatively estimated at 100,000 people in the process. Fields lay deserted, and cottage industries were abandoned in the process. Despite that and similar set-backs by the mid-1700s, Provence had become one of the wealthier regions of France. An aesthetic had developed that was distinct to the region, and which is today copied and emulated by decorators throughout the world, as noted in the majestic townhouses *(hôtels particuliers)* and country houses that are so prized today.

Some scholars argue that the revolutionary fervor that swept over France in May 1789 was greatly influenced by popular philosophers in Provence. One of the most articulate (and inflammatory) members of Paris's Etats-Généraux (the radical committee that helped inaugurate the French Revolution) was the Comte de Mirabeau, who was elected by the populace of Aix-en-Provence. In 1790 the Revolutionary government carved France and Provence into a labyrinth of political districts *(départements)* that shattered the country's medieval boundaries and political networks. In the process, the once-autonomous region of Provence was subdivided into three and later five subdivisions, an act that greatly hampered the region's sense of cohesion.

In 1792, a corps of volunteers from Marseille marched through the streets of Paris singing a call to arms that was later renamed "La Marseillaise" from its original title, "Battle Hymn of the Army of the Rhine." A year later, the emerging career of the Corsican general Napoleon Bonaparte received an enormous boost after he masterminded a victory at the siege of Toulon.

The 19th Century & the Rise of Tourism

Partly because of its strategic dominance of more than half of France's Mediterranean seaports, Provence gained enormous prosperity during the 19th century. The opening of the Suez Canal in 1869 and the expansion of French influence into Morocco, Algeria, Tunisia, and to some degree, Egypt, thrust the ports of Provence into worldwide prominence and helped to develop Marseille into one of the greatest seaports in the world. As it gained wealth, it also gained prestige that began to cement its status as an important region in France.

Tourism to the region also began to increase during this period, with the opening of a railway link that linked Provence with the rest of France in 1864. This train line encouraged increased travel and established a rapidly spreading reputation of Provence as a place to visit—a reputation that persists today. Part of the development of Nice and the Riviera into international resorts was the result of the unemployment caused by the phylloxera epidemic in Provençal vineyards and the collapse of the silkworm industry. Tourism was a logical answer to the economic deprivations of pestilence and economic dislocations of burgeoning industry. In 1822 the expatriate British colony in Nice helped to finance its namesake promenade. In 1830 Lord Brougham bought an estate in Cannes and invited his friends to escape from the fog,

The Route Napoleon

In 1815, Napoleon used a minor seaport near Cannes (Golfe-Juan) as the site of his return to France after his exile on Elba. The enthusiasm his armies received in Provence set a precedent for equivalent welcomes in other non-Provençal towns en route during his march to Paris and his short-lived return to power. The same year, he was defeated by Wellington at the Battle of Waterloo. The route he followed during his march upon Paris—the N85 through Dignes and Sisteron—has been known ever since as the Route Napoleon.

the cold, and the Victorian repressions of England. In 1860 the region around Nice, whose administration by the House of Savoy represented an anachronistic holdover from the feudal age, was fully integrated into France. A few years later, the ruler of one of the least prosperous territories of western Europe, Monaco, built the most opulent casino in the world. Thanks to the approval and patronage granted to the site by the wealthy aristocrats of the Belle Époque, profits came pouring in.

World War II

Provence was spared the destruction caused by World War I in northern France. During World War II, Provence and Languedoc were integrated into territory controlled by France's collaborationist Vichy government. In 1940, after Nazi-dominated North Africa fell to Allied forces, the Nazis retracted their pledge not to occupy the zones controlled by Vichy and moved into Provence with heavy artillery. In 1942, when the Nazis moved to confiscate the warships of the French navy, French saboteurs sank most of their Mediterranean fleet in the harbor at Toulon. Many martyrs were created by the conflicts all around them, most notably Jean Moulin, who has numerous streets named after him throughout Provence.

On August 15, 1944, Allied forces landed on the Provençal coast between St-Raphaël and St-Tropez to regain control of Europe from Nazi domination. All of Provence was liberated within 14 days of the landing, with some of the most dramatic of liberation scenes occurring in the center of Marseille, a site that was freed over a 6-day period between August 22 and 28, 1944.

The 20th Century & Modern Provence

Few other regions of the world have zoomed into the international consciousness the way Provence has since 1945. In 1947, Cannes initiated its role as film capital of Europe with its first-ever film festival, an event that would later grow to almost mythic proportions. Beginning around 1950, farming and industry were modernized to keep pace with technological developments in the rest of Europe. Tourism, which had been a recurrent theme in the region since the 19th-century days of the English expatriates in Nice, took a giant leap forward.

Beginning in the early 1950s, celebrity-watching seemed to go hand in hand with voyeurism and exhibitionism, as the Riviera's topless beaches caused a stir, and as stars such as Brigitte Bardot elevated St-Tropez to its continuing role as the sybaritic capital of the Riviera.

In 1953, Socialist politician Gaston Defferre, a pivotal figure in the region's politics, was elected mayor of Marseille, a post he held for the next 33 years. His ardent appeals for semi-autonomy of Provence finally came to fruition in 1981, 2 years

Football Champions

In 1993, Provençal pride swelled when Olympique de Marseille, a French football (soccer) team based in Marseilles, became the first French football team to win the UEFA Champions League Cup, formerly known as the European Cup. In both 2010 and 2011 Marseille became champions again, when the team won the Trophée des champions, a French football league trophy, 2 years in a row.

before his death, with the approval, under President François Mitterrand, of a limited form of self-government. To Defferre's chagrin, the culmination of his life's work—a degree of self-governing autonomy for Provence—helped to usher in right-wing opponents to a political landscape that had been dominated by leftist politics since before the turn of the 20th century.

Transit between Provence, Paris, and the rest of world was greatly facilitated in 1970 with the opening of the A6-A7 high-speed autoroute between the French capital and Marseille. Between 1970 and 1977, the year the Marseille metro was inaugurated, at least two major national parks (Parc Naturel Régional de Camargue and Parc Naturel Régional de Luberon) were created for the preservation of Provence's native ecology. In 1981, the high-speed *Train à Grande Vitesse* (TGV) was inaugurated between Paris and Marseille, with other branch lines opened in following years to other parts of France's Mediterranean coast.

Around 1985, Provence emerged as the national stronghold for anti-immigrant sentiments, perhaps in reaction to the thousands of non-French newcomers, legal and illegal, who have flooded into Provence from North and West Africa. This was exploited by the Front National (FN), the far-right political party led by Jean-Marie Le Pen, which touted an anti-immigration platform. The FN won the mayorship in three cities in Provence: Orange, Toulon, and Marignane. Although the FN had surprising political success in the 2002 national elections, its power eroded during that decade as factions formed within the party. Since then, France's left-wing Socialist party has returned with a vengeance, triumphing in the 2010 regional elections and taking over the French Senate in 2011. The FN is not a spent force, however, even if the former FN mayors in Provence have swapped parties for less extreme, albeit still ultra-conservative, alternatives.

ART & ARCHITECTURE

The sense of timelessness that permeates Provençal architecture has derived from ancient origins. Although Paleolithic remains and artifacts have been found in Provence, there's a lot less prehistoric art here than there is in such neighboring sites as Lascaux in the Dordogne. Despite that, excavations that include Terra Amata, just above the old port in Nice, have unearthed remnants of circular huts. Around 6000 B.C., during the Neolithic era, sheep and other livestock began to be domesticated, and **circular huts *(bories)*** were erected from flat stones laid on top of each other without mortar. None of the *bories* from that era survive, although many sociologists believe that the later development of rural farmhouses *(mas)* in Provence was affected by them. From around the same time, a series of dolmen—mysterious standing stones—and a scattered handful of rock carvings were poised on their ends and raised into vertical positions, for reasons that no one has ever really understood since.

Beginning in the 4th century B.C., for a period of around 400 years, Celtic tribes migrated into Provence, bringing with them an ease for carving rock with iron tools. Their greatest surviving tangible legacy includes a network of fortified ***oppidi*** **(fortresses on hilltops).** Greek mariners established ports at Antibes, St-Tropez, La Ciotat, Nice, and Hyères, which adopted many of the aesthetic preconceptions of the Greek world.

Provence was lavished by the **ancient Romans** with one of the ancient world's most comprehensive assortment of public buildings. The lessons derived from the Romans include the experienced use of the arch, the barrel vault (a technique that involved masonry where individual stones were so carefully cut that the use of mortar was unnecessary), and a primitive form of concrete. These technical accomplishments combined in a scale that's majestic even by today's standards. Examples of Roman architecture include the arenas of the **Amphithéâtre Romain** at Nîmes (p. 100) and the **Théâtre Antique/Amphithéâtre d'Arles** in Arles (p. 132); aqueducts, such as the **Pont du Gard** (p. 102), that are some of the finest examples of civil engineering anywhere in the ancient world; and triumphal arches at **Glanum** in St-Rémy-de-Provence (p. 144), the **Trophée d'Auguste** in La Turbie (p. 317), and the **Arc de Triomphe** in Orange (p. 110). Remains of ruined villas can still be seen at Vaison-la-Romaine. **Maison Carrée** (p. 102) in the center of Nîmes is the most copied monument, after the Parthenon in Athens and the Pantheon in Rome, in the ancient world.

Since Provence, because of its proximity to Rome, was Christianized before virtually any of the other regions of Gaul, Provence is honored with one of the oldest Christian basilicas in France, the **Abbaye St-Victor** in Marseille (p. 177). Inaugurated in the 400s, and enlarged and modified many times since, it's unique in France for its venerable age and its associations with the early Christian church.

The Dark Ages brought very little construction of note, but beginning around 1100 there was a revitalized interest in building, usually by monks from various religious orders. Consistent with the explosion of **Romanesque architecture** in Italy, floor plans of churches were usually laid out in a form that duplicated a cross, with soaring pillars and barrel vaulting, small, somewhat severe-looking windows, and facades that were allegorically sculpted with scenes of redemption, salvation, or punishment. The best examples of Provençal Romanesque can be visited at the **Cathédrale St-Sauveur** in Aix-en-Provence (p. 169); the **Eglise St-Trophime** in Arles (p. 130); and at the village churches of St-Rémy and Montmajour.

Beginning around 1250, Provence was depending more on artistic and architectural inspiration from such areas as Normandy, especially its **Gothic style.** Its larger window openings and more elaborate decoration derived from a more sophisticated use of pointed arches, ribbed vaulting, and flying buttresses. The sense of verticality that was the result of this was in direct contrast to the more horizontal and more rounded lines of the Romanesque. Provençal Gothic is most obvious in the newer part of Avignon's **Palais des Papes** (p. 120), the **Cathédrale St-Nazaire** at Béziers (p. 81), and the cloisters at the **Cité Episcopale** (p. 220) in Fréjus. Flamboyant Gothic, the final, most ornate, and, most decadent phase of the movement, can best be viewed in the facade of the **Cathédrale St-Sauveur** (p. 169) in Aix-en-Provence.

The most memorable aspect of architecture in Provence involves the **fortified towns and villages** that dot the region's landscapes. Testimonials to their residents' dogged determination to survive in the face of repeated sieges and attacks, they're often perched atop jagged hills or cliffs, meticulously crafted from chiseled blocks of stone, and are usually punctuated with crenelated battlements and/or a moat. Many have openings through which boiling oil or molten lead could be poured on attackers. The designs of many of them, including **Les Baux-de-Provence** (p. 139), Sisteron, and Tarascon, emerged spontaneously, after decades of brutish labor were expended. A handful of others, including the rigidly symmetrical quadrangle of **Aigues-Mortes** (p. 97), were commissioned (in this case, by Saint Louis himself) and elaborately designed before the first stone was laid. **Carcassonne** (p. 60), a fortified site in Languedoc built more or less in the same era, is less symmetrical than Aigues-Mortes but more impregnable.

So great was the fear of attack that many Provençal churches incorporated fortifications into their designs. In the event of attack, the church could provide physical as well as spiritual shelter from enemies, a fact that early medieval prelates used as a means of eliciting cheap or free labor from the corps of faithful that built them. Examples include the village church in **Saintes-Maries-de-la-Mer** (p. 136). The development of large-scale cannon in the 1400s made many of the above-mentioned fortifications obsolete, but by that time, defensive warfare had evolved so drastically that the fortress-style churches and towns of Provence were left intact, partly because they served a useful function, partly because they evoked the preoccupations and obsessions of earlier centuries.

In terms of painting and architecture, the **Renaissance** left two distinct legacies in Nice and Avignon. In Nice, beginning in the late 15th century, a school of design spearheaded by Louis Bréa produced a wide assortment of painted altarpieces. Because of the way they proliferate throughout the region around Nice, most notably within the village church at Lucéram, they were the most fashionable accessories at the time. During the same era, an equivalent school of painting flourished in Avignon, partly a result of the need to adorn the network of churches built a century earlier during the "Babylonian exile" of the papacy in Avignon. The leading artist of the era was Enguerrand Charonton (also known as "Quarton"). Completed in Avignon and later moved to Villeneuve, his *Coronation of the Virgin* is the best known painting from that era. A worthy colleague was Nicolas Froment, appointed painter to the court of King René. His most famous painting is *The Burning Bush,* which still adorns the interior of the cathedral at Aix. Charonton and Froment are today cited as the founders of the Avignon school of painting, which survived until the 1800s.

Beginning around 1650, artists began to abandon a reliance on purely religious subjects, opting instead for depictions of themes from antiquity or, in some cases, everyday secular subjects. The works of Pierre Puget, a Marseillais who is credited as the greatest sculptor ever produced by Provence, evoke the exalted drama of Bernini. His works are within museums throughout France, especially Paris, Toulon, and Marseille. A Dutch-born family of artists, the Van Loos, painted from bases in Aix and Nice during the 17th century, with some of their best works displayed today in the **Musée des Beaux-Arts** in Nice (p. 169).

During the 1800s, the newly moneyed of the industrial age showed off their wealth in elaborate architectural showcases. Public buildings and private villas were erected in styles that ranged from classical revival to what might be the most unusual of all, **neo-Byzantine.** A Provençal example of the latter includes the **Cathédrale de la**

THE great artists IN PROVENCE

- **Paul Cézanne** (1839–1906) was born in Aix, and spent large parts of his career depicting the terracotta roofs and verdant cypresses of Provence. One of his oft-repeated subjects was the Mont-Ste-Victoire.
- **Vincent van Gogh** (1853–1890) lived in Arles for several years, depicting starry heavens and fiercely vibrant landscapes before spending time in a mental hospital near St-Rémy.
- **Paul Signac** (1863–1935), a neo-Impressionist, retreated to the hamlet of St-Tropez around 1900, and established a mania for "Le Trop" that has existed ever since, attracting both **Matisse** and **Bonnard** for contemplative "paint-fests" within the region.
- **Auguste Renoir** (1841–1919) spent his final years near Cagnes-sur-Mer, painting and sculpting despite bouts of agonizing arthritis.
- **Henri Matisse** (b. 1869) lived at Cimiez, near Nice, and at Vence beginning in 1917, remaining here until his death in 1954.
- **Pablo Picasso** (1881–1973) came to Antibes in 1945, pouring out paintings during two of the most prolific and pivotal years of his many-faceted career. Later, he would be instrumental in reviving the pottery traditions at nearby Vallauris.
- **Marc Chagall** (1887–1985), master of the dreamlike power of artistic free association, moved to the Riviera and promptly created his acclaimed *Biblical Message*, now displayed in his namesake museum in Nice.
- Others who later flocked to the region included **Raoul Dufy** (1877–1953); **Georges Braque** (1882–1963); **Maurice de Vlaminck** (1876–1958); **Fernand Léger** (1881–1955), who has a namesake museum in Biot; and **Victor Vasarely** (1906–1997), whose works are exhibited in Gordes and Aix. Even **Jean Cocteau** (1889–1963), known for his frivolity in his earlier years, reached a more intense level of spirituality during his final years in Provence, as proven by frescoes he crafted on the walls of the Chapelle St-Pierre in Villefranche.

Major (p. 177) and the **Basilique Notre-Dame-de-la-Garde** (p. 177), both in Marseille. The **Casino de Monte-Carlo** (p. 334) and the **Hôtel de Paris** (p. 96) in Monte Carlo were lavished with gilded stucco and ornamentation. Charles Garnier himself, quintessential designer of the French Belle Époque, designed some aspects of the building boom in Monte Carlo. A few years later, the **Hôtel Negresco** (p. 295) in Nice captured the essence of the gilded age with elaborate Beaux Arts ornamentation. Later, around 1910, ostentatious construction continued in the form of the **Hotel Carlton** (p. 243) at Cannes.

At the same time that the great fortunes of Europe were changing the face of the Riviera with their upscale architecture, a core of devoted painters and aesthetes were influencing the way the world interpreted light and color. Under the streaming sunlight of Provence, they evolved their theories of luminosity and color. Several world-renowned impressionist artists flocked to Provence, and were inspired by its sunlight, colors, and natural beauty. These artists have left a rich heritage: Matisse in his chapel at Vence, Cocteau at Menton and Villefranche, Picasso at Antibes and seemingly everywhere else, Léger at Biot, Renoir at Cagnes, and Bonnard at Le Cannet. The best collection of all is at the **Fondation Maeght** (p. 276) in St-Paul-de-Vence. See "The Great Artists in Provence" box for more information on these artists.

No review of Provençal art and architecture would be complete without mention of the utilitarian rural architecture that is tenaciously associated with the primal appeal of the region itself. **Farmhouses *(mas)*** built as late as 1910 in many regions were directly influenced by the Middle Ages and their obsession with fortification and an ecological sensitivity to the rigors of the local climate. Thick masonry walls, undersized windows covered with shutters, and solid and stocky doors were all crafted from locally derived lumber, clay, mud, soil, and stone. North-facing walls were often designed with curved sides and without windows as a means of deflecting the harsh winds of the *mistral,* and roofs were pitched at low angles to reduce the possibility of tiles breaking loose from their fasteners and sliding off. Hinged shutters could be opened or closed as protection against heat, wind, and sun; chimneys were deliberately low and squat, never rising high enough to risk being demolished during windstorms. Evergreen cypress trees were usually planted as windbreaks on a farmhouse's north side; and deciduous broad-leaved trees such as sycamores provided midsummer shade to the south, but let in the warming sunshine in winter. The construction techniques for walls, made of coarsely chiseled stone and sometimes sheathed with stucco or plaster, were roughly equivalent to what had been developed 2,000 years previously by the Romans. Virtually every farmhouse and outbuilding in Provence was capped with rounded terra-cotta roof tiles *(tuiles romaines)* that derived both their name and their inspiration from equivalent materials used during the Roman conquest. Today, the boxy-looking old farmhouses, along with the olives, vines, and cypresses that traditionally surround them, are prized as valuable expressions of vernacular architecture.

Since World War II, a building boom has transformed many of the suburbs of such cities as Aix-en-Provence, Avignon, and Arles into urbanized landscapes with their attendant banality. Traffic congestion, especially noticeable during July and August, has diminished lots of the charm of roadside neighborhoods. As the need for holiday villas and housing for service personnel has risen, vast blocks of apartment houses, some stylish, some altogether ordinary, have been erected in more or less appealing ways. Many have at least tried to emulate the age-old Provençal farmhouse. A handful, however, including Le Corbusier's 1952 design for a massive apartment block in Marseille, the Unité d'Habitation at the **Hôtel Le Corbusier** (p. 182), and J. L. Sert's design for the Fondation Maeght museum of modern art (p. 276) at St-Paul-de-Vence, are cited for their intelligent application of age-old vernacular styles in bold new ways. British architect Norman Foster (creator of the Millau viaduct) continues to put his stamp on architecture in southern France, including the futuristic **Carré d'Art** in Nîmes and his project for the revamp of Marseille's Old Port.

Today, there is a thriving contemporary art scene in the region. Major modern art galleries in Marseille, Nice, and Nîmes, among others, showcase works from contemporary artists such as Yves Klein and Ben Vautier as well as lesser known emerging 21st-century artists. Young artists have started to flock to such places as St-Paul-de-Vence and Aix-en-Provence. They display their works in local galleries and art fairs. **Sm'art** (✆ **06-88-89-09-54;** www.salonsmart-aix.com) is a major contemporary and abstract art fair that showcases the works of emerging young artists from the region; it's held every June in Aix-en-Provence.

PROVENCE & THE RIVIERA IN LITERATURE, FILM & MUSIC

Books

Peter Mayle's hugely successful *A Year in Provence* (1989) and its two sequels, *Toujours Provence* (1992) and *Encore Provence* (2000), continue to sell more than 20 years after publication. This autobiography tells of Mayle's experiences in Provence; he captures the delight and frustration of the region, with visits to its markets, vineyards, goat races, and mushroom hunts.

Two Towns in Provence (1983), by M. F. K. Fisher, is by the author who practically invented food-based literary books. This memoir tells of the years she spent in France in the two towns of Aix-en-Provence and Marseille.

Vincent van Gogh—Letters from Provence (1995), by Martin Bailey, tells of the artist's last few years of life. Van Gogh's letters, a testimony of his struggle to survive and work here, are illustrated with his paintings, drawings, and facsimile letters.

A Pig in Provence: Good Food and Simple Pleasures in the South of France (2007), by Georgeanne Brennan, tells the story of how this cooking teacher and food author fell in love with Provence.

We've Always Had Paris . . . and Provence (2008) is by Patricia Wells, who was in the vanguard of the 1970s foodie movement. The book is filled with memorable scenes from her life in France, including her sojourns in Provence. Author Wells and her husband, Walter, bought and restored an 18th-century farmhouse with a vineyard in Provence. Wells is also the author of *The Provence Cookbook* (2004); for this volume, she toured little villages in Provence, picking up culinary tips from restaurateurs, farmers, winemakers, and others.

British actress Carol Drinkwater found success as a writer with her books about her new life as an olive farmer in Provence. Her books *The Olive Farm* (2002), *The Olive Season* (2006), and *The Olive Harvest* (2005) chronicle the ups and downs in turning a dilapidated house in the Var hills into a thriving organic olive farm.

Films

Few film-makers capture the essence of Provence more than Marcel Pagnol, who was born in Aubagne near Marseille and whose movies and books about Provençal village life continue to find new audiences. His novels *Jean de Florette* (1986) and *Manon des Sources* (1986) were adapted into box-office hits by Claude Berri in the 1980s and starred Gérard Depardieu, Emmanuelle Béart, and Daniel Auteuil. His gentle memoirs of his Provençal childhood, *La Gloire de Mon Père* (1990) and *Le Château de Ma Mère* (1990), were dreamily filmed by Yves Robert. His celebrated "Fanny trilogy" of films, *Marius, Fanny,* and *César,* evoke life in 1930s Marseille.

The lush Riviera setting is as much a star as Cary Grant and Grace Kelly in Alfred Hitchcock's *To Catch a Thief* (1955). The film was made in the months before Grace Kelly became the Princess of Monaco. Sadly, Princess Grace, on September 14, 1982, was killed in an automobile accident on the very same road as the film's famous chase scene and not far from where she had a cinematic picnic with Grant.

St-Tropez was never going to be the same after Roger Vadim cast a very young Brigitte Bardot in *Et Dieu . . . Créa la Femme (And God Created Woman)* in 1956. Soon after the film premiered, the previously simple fishing village of St-Tropez was changed forever as everyone flocked there for a slice of glitzy Riviera life.

That French Riviera glamour was captured time and time again in the long series of James Bond movies. From *Diamonds Are Forever* (1971) and *Never Say Never Again* (1983) to *Goldeneye* (1995), Bond often fights villains in sophisticated settings, like on an alluring Riviera beach or at the Monte Carlo casino.

A Good Year (2006), loosely based on a Peter Mayle novel of the same name, starred Russell Crowe, Marion Cotillard, and Albert Finney. It tells the story of a British investment broker who inherits his uncle's château and vineyard in Provence. He discovers a new laid-back lifestyle as he tries to renovate the estate to be sold. Every scene was shot within 8 minutes of the home in Provence where director/producer Ridley Scott lives.

Music

Music written about Provence includes Darius Milhaud's *Suite Provençale;* the opera *Mireille* by Charles Gounod based on Frédéric Mistral's poem *Mirèio;* Georges Bizet's *L'Arlésienne;* and the saxophone concerto *Tableaux de Provence,* composed by Paule Maurice.

A rare work of enchantment is *Renaissance en Provence—Traditional Music of South of France* by Terra Nova Consort, also available on a CD. Founded in 1988, the Terra Nova group explores ethnic influences in early music. In their CD, the artists emphasize the close cultural and linguistic ties between Provence and Spain. They combine passionate, gritty vocals with early guitars, viols, reeds, and percussion.

EATING & DRINKING

The Bounty of Provence & the Riviera

Because much of the allure of *provençale* cuisine derives from its raw ingredients, menus are likely to state the source of what you're about to consume. To see this wealth firsthand, head for any of the open-air markets where vast amounts of meat, cheese, produce, wine, and herbs are sold from simple stalls.

BREAD Almost as varied as the cheeses are the shapes and ingredients of the bread. You can buy it as long, thin *ficelles* that resemble baguettes, and as *gibassiers,* flavored with fruity olive oil and orange water. Choose from *pain aux olives,* with the flesh of the olive in the dough; *pain à l'anis,* aniseed bread; earthy *pain au levain,* sourdough bread; and one of the breads most associated with Provence, *fougasse,* a flatbread studded with olives and seasoned with herbs such as rosemary or thyme.

CHEESE In the south of France you could spend hours choosing among the varieties of *chèvre* (goat's cheese) alone. Looking for something esoteric? Ask for a *tomme de Camargue,* a firm but creamy cheese that combines milk from both goats and sheep and whose disclike surface is embedded with sprigs of rosemary. There's also Banon goat's cheese made in the hamlet of Banon in northeast Provence. During its fermentation, it's marinated in *eau-de-vie,* aged in clay pots on dried chestnut leaves, and wrapped with raffia string.

FRUITS & VEGETABLES Melons, especially from the town of Cavaillon, were so famous that in 1864, civic leaders opted to present a dozen perfect melons each year to the French novelist Alexandre Dumas *père* (father) as a sign of their ongoing respect. He later wrote that he hoped that the readers of Cavaillon would always find his books as charming as he found their melons. Apricots are delicious anywhere, but if they're from the slopes of the Roussillon, your menu will usually let you know.

Menton's lemons are so well regarded that they're celebrated in an annual festival. Provence's dry climate is perfect for the production of olives, an essential part of the region's cuisine; you'll find lots of olive oils as well. Juicy plump tomatoes, eggplant, zucchini, and peppers form the basis of that classic *provençale* dish, *ratatouille*. Small violet artichokes can be stuffed with bacon or served simply with a lemon butter sauce.

> **Impressions**
>
> **"The French spend as much of their income on their stomachs as the English do on their cars and stereo systems . . ."**
>
> **—Peter Mayle, *A Year in Provence* (1989)**

PASTRIES & SWEETS Southern France is expert at turning out *calissons,* diamond-shaped sweets concocted from almond paste; they invariably taste best when baked in Aix-en-Provence. More recipes exist for *nougat,* honey-sweetened chewy candy flavored with either almonds or pistachios, than anyone could possibly document. Carnival time in Nice usually means eating *ganses,* or *bugnes,* a deep-fried pastry flavored with orange and lemon and sprinkled with icing sugar. St-Tropez's contribution to Provence's culinary tradition is the indulgent *tarte tropézienne,* a rich cake made from brioche and filled liberally with French pastry cream *(crème pâtissière)* and butter cream.

The Provençal Menu

BULL Throughout the south, but especially in the flat wetlands and bull-raising terrain of the Camargue, look for the delicious stew *gardiane de taureau*. Marinated bull is cooked for hours in red wine, and served with *riz de Camargue*—rice from the lowlands of the delta of the Rhône.

CASSOULET & BOUILLABAISSE Head west to Languedoc's Carcassonne and Castelnaudary for the ultimate warming dish: cassoulet. It's a succulent mixture of slow-cooked white beans with duck, goose, sausages, and belly pork.

Bouillabaisse is Provence's most famous dish. It's hard to imagine that this was once a rough-and-tumble recipe used by local fishing folk to get rid of the least desirable portion of their catch. Traditionally, it combines a trio of fish cooked rapidly in bouillon and flavored with various seasonings. A chili-and-saffron paste called *rouille* sharpens the sauce, giving it an extra reddish color.

GAME If you're planning a trip to the south in autumn, you'll discover many game dishes on the menu. These include *perdreau* (partridge), *sanglier* (wild boar), *chevreuil* (venison), *faisan* (pheasant), and *lièvre* (hare). Often the meat will be marinated in herbs and wine, roasted, and served with vibrant red wine from the Rhône Valley.

GOOSE & DUCK The appreciation of foie gras has been elevated to something approaching a cult, and many dishes gain a noteworthy unctuousness when fried in *graisse d'oie* (goose fat). Thighs of both species are cooked in large quantities of their own fat to create tender *confits,* and the breast of ducks *(magrets)* are often grilled over charcoal or oak fires. Pâtés made from the byproducts of duck, and sometimes studded with truffles, figure high on most people's favorite appetizer list.

HEARTY STEWS A specialty remembered (sometimes fondly, sometimes not) from many Provençaux childhoods is *pieds et paquets,* a combination of mutton or lamb tripe and lambs' feet cooked with cured, unsmoked pork, garlic, wine, and tomatoes. This classic is much appreciated by adventurous gastronomes. An equally

> **Impressions**
>
> "Provençal cooking is based on garlic. The air in Provence is impregnated with the aroma of garlic, which makes it very healthful to breathe. Garlic is the main seasoning in bouillabaisse and in the principal sauces of the region. A sort of mayonnaise is made with it by crushing it in oil, and this is eaten with fish and snails. The lower classes in Provence often lunch on a crust of bread sprinkled with oil and rubbed with garlic."
>
> —Alexandre Dumas, *Grand Dictionnaire de Cuisine*

prized variation is a *gratin de pieds de porc aux truffes* (gratin of pigs' feet with truffles). *Civet de lapin* is wild rabbit stewed with herbs and red wine, with rabbit blood added to the stew at the last minute as a thickener. *Daube de boeuf à la provençale* is a combination of stewed beef marinated in garlic purée with red wine. *Bourride,* a spicy fish stew, is Languedoc's answer to the bouillabaisse of Provence.

VEGETARIAN DISHES Unlike in other parts of France, vegetarians need not go hungry in Provence; eggplant comes with basil-tomato sauce, and grilled vegetables are garnished with zucchini flowers (stuffed with a purée of zucchini and herbs, coated with batter, and deep-fried). Then there's *ratatouille,* the combination of eggplant, onions, peppers, and herbs slowly stewed in olive oil. The perfect accompaniment for any of these dishes is aïoli, the garlic-laced mayonnaise that's the appropriate foil for fish, grilled vegetables, and plain or toasted bread. Incidentally, aïoli can also refer to an entire meal composed of poached salt cod and vegetables.

Also look for specialties such as *pissaladière,* a Niçois pizzalike dish with anchovies, black olives, and onions; *socca,* a type of pancake made from chickpeas; mesclun, assorted wild greens that make divine salads; and *pistou,* soup enriched with a dollop of a *provençale* version of pesto.

Les Vins de Provence

In 1923, a distinguished Provençal landowner, Baron Le Roy de Boiseaumarie, inaugurated a series of quality controls from his lands near Châteauneuf-du-Pape. His efforts were instrumental in imposing standards on vintners and helped launch what later evolved into the national **Appellations d'Origine Contrôlées (A.O.C.).**

Despite the appeal of southern French wines as an accompaniment for strongly flavored foods such as anchovies, sardines, and bouillabaisse, the region has a lower percentage of wines that oenophiles call "great" than do more temperate regions. So pride is taken by vintners with lands in designated A.O.C. districts, and massive investments in recent years have helped elevate many of the region's vintages to earn international repute. Although it's no guarantee of quality, looking for A.O.C. labels is a beginning point for newcomers who want to distinguish prestigious vintages from ordinary *vin de table.*

Two of the best Provençal whites are the delicate Cassis near Marseille and the more forthright Palette near Aix-en-Provence. Bellet, a relatively small winegrowing district above Nice, produces excellent reds, whites, and rosés.

Particularly strong reds are Gigondas and Vacqueyras, whose alcohol content sometimes exceeds 13%. Names to look for are Côtes de Provence from the dry hills north of Toulon, Côtes du Rhône Villages, and Châteauneuf-du-Pape, the only wine in the world that's allowed to bear the crest of the long-ago popes of Avignon. Because of the vagaries of rainfall and the growing season, any bottle of this last wine might be composed of more than a dozen grapes from around the district. A memorable sweet wine from the Côtes du Rhône, favored by pastry chefs as a foil for their concoctions, is Beaumes de Venise.

The two most famous rosés of the south are Tavel in Languedoc, which is the birthplace of rosé, and Bandol, a worthy producer of which is Château Simone.

The vineyards of Languedoc-Roussillon, the largest in the world, represent more than a quarter of France's total acreage devoted to grapes. The fields around Nîmes, Béziers, and Narbonne produce wine that has been improving over the years. Aristocratic vintages from Roussillon include unusual sweet wines such as Banyuls and Muscat de Rivesaltes and the reds from villages on the eastern foothills of the Pyrénées, Côtes de Roussillon.

A cost-effective means of trying ordinary table wines is bringing your own container (usually a plastic jug sold on the premises or in hardware stores) to a large-scale producer. At bargain-basement prices, they'll use a gas pump–inspired nozzle to pump wine from enormous vats directly into your container. In a restaurant, such a vintage would be sold in a glass carafe or ceramic *pichet* at a low price. If you're driving through the vineyards and see one of the many signs announcing *vente au détail,* it means that you'll be able to buy estate-bottled wine by the bottle, invariably at lower prices than in retail wine shop. Look out also for signs saying *dégustation* if you're in the mood to taste some wines.

WHEN TO GO

Weather

In terms of weather, the most idyllic months for visiting the south of France are May and June. Though the sun is intense, it's not uncomfortable. Coastal waters have warmed up by then, so swimming is possible, and all the resorts have come alive but aren't yet overrun. The flowers and herbs in the countryside are at their peak, and driving conditions are ideal. In June, it remains light until around 10:30pm.

The most overcrowded times—also the hottest, in more ways than one—are July and August, when seemingly half of Paris shows up. Reservations are difficult to get, and space is tight on the popular beaches. Traffic jams become legendary.

September and early October are a good time to visit; temperatures have settled somewhat and the crowds have dispersed. Early September is often the time when villages will host festivals aimed at residents rather than tourists.

The Pleasure of Pastis

A traditional *provençale* meal usually begins with an aperitif of *pastis,* a translucent yellow liqueur that becomes cloudy when you add water or ice. Though the aniseed flavor may not appeal to everyone, it is the drink for a hot summer's day. It's scented with anise, fennel, mint, and licorice, but in the case of France's most popular brand name Ricard or its sweeter rival, Pernod, it contains some additional secret ingredients.

In November, the weather is often pleasant, especially at midday, though some of the restaurants and inns you'll want to visit will be closed. It's the month that many chefs and hoteliers elect to go on their own vacations after a summer of hard work.

If you don't mind the absence of sunbathing and beach life, winter could be a good time to show up. However, some resorts, like St-Tropez, become ghost towns when the cold weather comes, though Cannes, Nice, Monaco, and Menton remain active year-round. February is the time to visit Nice for the annual carnival, which lasts for much of the month.

The Mediterranean coast has the driest climate in France. Most rain falls in spring and autumn. Summers are comfortably dry—beneficial to humans but deadly to vegetation, which (unless it's irrigated) often dries and burns up in the parched months. This is the time when forest fires become a regular menace, and restrictions are often put in place in forested areas against people having picnics or even just walking on certain footpaths.

Provence dreads the *mistral* (a cold, violent wind from the French and Swiss Alps that roars south down the Rhône Valley). It most often blows in winter, sometimes for a few days, but sometimes for up to 2 weeks. Languedoc-Roussillon has its own, equally vicious, version called the *tramontane.* These winds can appear all too often during the spring and autumn months as well.

Average Temperature & Rainfall in Provence & the Riviera

MARSEILLE	JAN	FEB	MAR	APR	MAY	JUNE	JULY	AUG	SEPT	OCT	NOV	DEC
TEMP. (°F)	46	47	52	56	65	71	76	76	67	61	51	46
TEMP. (°C)	8	8	11	13	18	22	24	24	19	16	11	8
RAINFALL (IN.)	1.9	1.6	1.8	1.8	1.8	1.0	0.6	1.0	2.5	3.7	3.0	2.3
RAINFALL (CM)	4.8	4.1	4.6	4.6	4.6	2.5	1.5	2.5	6.4	9.4	7.6	5.8
NICE	**JAN**	**FEB**	**MAR**	**APR**	**MAY**	**JUNE**	**JULY**	**AUG**	**SEPT**	**OCT**	**NOV**	**DEC**
TEMP. (°F)	47	49	53	55	64	69	74	75	68	62	53	48
TEMP. (°C)	8	9	11	12	17	20	23	23	20	16	11	8
RAINFALL (IN.)	3.0	2.9	2.9	2.5	1.9	1.5	0.7	1.2	2.6	4.4	4.6	3.5
RAINFALL (CM)	7.6	7.4	7.4	6.4	4.8	3.8	1.8	3	6.6	11.2	11.7	8.9

HOLIDAYS In France, holidays are *jours fériés.* Shops and many businesses (banks and some museums and restaurants) close on holidays, but hotels and emergency services remain open. The main holidays include New Year's Day (Jan 1), Easter Sunday, Labor Day (May 1), V-E Day (May 8), Ascension Day (May 17, 2012), Pentecost (May 28, 2012), Bastille Day (July 14), Assumption of the Blessed Virgin (Aug 15), All Saints' Day (Nov 1), Armistice Day (Nov 11), and Christmas (Dec 25).

Calendar of Events

For an exhaustive list of events beyond those listed here, check http://events.frommers.com/, where you'll find a searchable, up-to-the-minute roster of what's happening in cities all over the world.

JANUARY

Route du Mimosas. Between January and March, towns all over the Var hold festivals to celebrate the canary-yellow mimosa flower. Events include flower battles, parades, and markets. For more information, visit the websites for Bormes-Les-Mimosas (www.bormeslesmimosas.com), Le Rayol-Canadel (www.lerayolcanadel.fr), Sainte-Maxime (www.ste-maxime.com), and Saint-Raphaël (www.saint-raphael.com). January to March.

Le Rallye de Monte-Carlo Historique. Check out the vintage cars lined up along the port for this vintage car rally, which takes place over a week at the end of January. It's a spin-off of the 5-day **Monte Carlo Rally** in which modern racecars compete to win on the streets of Monte Carlo. For more information on both races, call ACM at ✆ **377-93-15-26-00** (www.acm.mc). Late January.

FEBRUARY

Fête de la Chandeleur (Candlemas), Basilique St-Victor, Marseille. A celebration in honor of the arrival in Marseille of the three Marys. A procession brings the Black Virgin up from the crypt of the abbey. For more information, call ✆ **04-91-13-89-00.** Early February.

Nice Carnaval. This 2-week extravaganza of float processions, street music, fireworks, and masked balls dates back to the 13th century. The climax is the burning of King Carnaval in effigy, preceded by the *Bataille des Fleurs* (Flower Battle), during which members of opposing teams pelt one another with flowers. If you haven't booked in advance, you can buy tickets from temporary ticket booths 2 hours before each event. For more information about the carnival, call ✆ **08-92-70-74-07** (www.nicecarnaval.com). Mid-February to early March.

Fête du Citron, Menton. Expect processions of enormous edible citrus-laden floats—including such elaborate designs as a fruit-constructed Taj Mahal—at this 2-week festival. The best time to visit is towards the beginning of the festival, when the fruit is still in peak condition. For tickets and information, call ✆ **04-92-41-76-95** (www.feteducitron.com). Mid-February to early March.

MARCH

Procession des Pénitents (Procession of the Penitents). These marches are conducted in both **Arles** (✆ **04-90-18-41-20**) and **Collioure** (✆ **04-68-82-15-47**). Good Friday.

Procession du Christ Mort (Procession of the Dead Christ), Roquebrune-Cap-Martin. This fascinating religious procession takes place in the narrow medieval streets of Roquebrune village. For information, call Roquebrune-Cap-Martin tourist office at ✆ **04-93-35-62-87.** Good Friday.

La Féria de Pâques (Easter Bullfighting Festival), Arles. This is a major bullfighting event that includes not only appearances by the greatest matadors, but also *abrivados* (the ceremonial arrival of the bulls) and *bodegas* (wine stalls). For more information, call ✆ **04-90-18-41-20;** www.arlestourisme.com. Easter: April 6–9, 2012; March 29–April 1, 2013.

MAY

La Fête des Gardians (Camargue Cowboys' Festival), Arles. This event features a procession of Camargue cowboys through the streets of town. Activities feature various games involving bulls, including Courses Camarguaises, in which competitors have to snatch a rosette from between the horns of a bull. For information, call ✆ **04-90-18-41-20.** May 1.

Festival de Cannes. Movie madness transforms this city into the kingdom of the media deal, with daily melodramas acted out in cafes, on sidewalks, and in hotel lobbies. It's great for voyeurs. Reserve early and make a deposit. Admission to some of the prestigious films is by invitation only. There are box-office tickets for the less important films, which play 24 hours. For information, contact the Association Française du Festival International du Film, at ✆ **01-53-59-61-00** or www.festival-cannes.com. Mid-May.

Festival les Musiques d'Aujourd'hui, Marseille. This festival presents the works of young French and European composers in music and dance. For more information, call Experimental Music Groups of Marseille at ✆ **04-96-20-60-10** (www.gmem.org). Mid-May.

Expo Rose, Grasse. France's perfume capital is permeated with the smell of 50,000 cut roses for its annual rose festival. Don't leave without buying rose-infused chocolates or candles. For more information, call ✆ **04-93-36-66-66** (www.ville-grasse.fr/exporose). Mid-May.

Le Pélerinage des Gitans (Gypsies' Pilgrimage), Saintes-Maries-de-la-Mer. This festival is in memory of the three Marys for whom the town is named (Mary Magdalene, Mary Salome, and Mary Jacob). A model boat containing statues of the saints and a statue of Sainte-Sarah, patron saint of Gypsies, is taken to the seashore and blessed by the bishop. For more information, call ✆ **04-90-97-82-55** (www.saintesmaries.com). May 24–25.

Grand Prix de Monaco. Hundreds of Formula One cars race through the narrow streets and winding roads of Monaco in a surreal blend of high-tech machinery and period architecture. For more information, call ✆ **377-93-15-26-00** (www.acm.mc). Late May.

Fête de la Transhumance, St-Rémy-de-Provence. This event celebrates the ancient custom of shepherds presenting their flocks to the public before moving them to higher ground for summer. Several thousand sheep are paraded through the streets in a lively spectacle. For more information, call ✆ **04-90-92-05-22.** May to June.

JUNE

Festival de la St-Eloi, Maussane-les-Alpilles. For this festival, wagons are decorated and raced in the Carreto Ramado, followed by Mass, a procession in traditional dress, and a benediction. Special events are held and local produce and handicrafts are sold. For more information, call ✆ **04-90-54-33-60** (www.maussane.com). Mid-June.

Fête de la Musique, nationwide. This national festival marks the longest day of the year with music of all kinds in every town and village in the country. Musicians of all abilities perform wherever they can find a space, while proper stages are set up for performances by larger groups, orchestras, and choirs. June 21.

Fête de la Tarasque, Tarascon. The town relives St. Martha's victory over the dragon known as the Tarasque, which was believed to live in the Rhône in the 1st century. Celebrations include a procession of horsemen, an archery competition, historical events, a medieval tournament, a Tarasque procession, Novilladas (young bullfighters), and an orchestral concert with fireworks. For more information, call ✆ **04-90-91-03-52** (www.tarascon.org). Late June.

Feu de la St-Jean (St. John's Fire), Fontvieille. This event features folk troupes and Camargue cowboys who gather in front of the Château de Montauban. For more information, call ✆ **04-90-54-67-49.** Late June.

La Fête des Pêcheurs (Fishermen's Festival), Cassis. The local "Prud'hommes" (members of the elected industrial tribunal) walk in procession wearing traditional dress, and a Mass is held in honor of St. Peter, followed by a benediction. For information, call ✆ **08-92-25-98-92.** Late June.

Festival d'Aix, Aix-en-Provence. Concerts of classical music and choral singing are held in historic buildings, such as the Théâtre de l'Archevêché and the Hôtel Maynier d'Oppède. For more information, call ✆ **08-20-92-29-23** (www.festival-aix.com). Late June to late July.

Reconstitution Historique, Salon-de-Provence. This pageant held in honor of Nostradamus includes a cast of 700 in historical costume and is followed by a *son et lumière* (sound and light show) at the Château de l'Empéri. For more information, call ✆ **04-90-56-27-60.** Late June to early July.

Festival de Marseille Méditerranée, Marseilles. This festival features concerts and recitals of music and song from the entire Mediterranean region. Theater and dance are also presented, along with special exhibitions in the city's main museums. For more information, call ✆ **04-91-13-89-00.** Late June to late July.

JULY

St-Guilhem Music Season, St-Guilhem-le-Désert, Languedoc. This festival of baroque organ and choral music is held in a medieval monastery. For information, call ✆ **04-67-57-44-33** (www.saint-guilhem-le-desert.com). July.

Les Chorégies d'Orange, Orange. One of southern France's most important lyric festivals presents oratorios and choral works by master performers whose voices are amplified by the ancient acoustics of France's best-preserved Roman amphitheater. For more information, call ✆ **04-90-34-24-24** (www.choregies.asso.fr). Early July to early August.

14 Juillet (Bastille Day), nationwide. Celebrating the birth of modern-day France, the festivities in the south reach their peak in Nice with street fairs, pageants, fireworks, and feasts. The day begins with a parade down the promenade des Anglais and ends with fireworks along the beach. Similar celebrations also take place in Cannes, Arles, Aix, Marseille, and Avignon. Check with local tourist offices if you are in France on July 13, because some towns have their festivities on the eve of Bastille Day instead. July 14.

Riviera Jazz Festivals. July is the month for two of Europe's most successful jazz festivals. **Nice Jazz Festival** has a relaxed vibe with its three stages scattered around the beautiful Cimiez amphitheater and its gardens, while historic **Jazz à Juan** is held against a backdrop of the Pinède Gould's pine trees and the Mediterranean sea. Both vie for top position, attracting world-class entertainers. The 2011 lineup included Macy Gray and Keziah Jones in Nice and B.B. King and Santana in Juan-les-Pins. Reserve hotel rooms way in advance. For more information, call **Nice Jazz Festival** (✆ **08-92-68-36-22;** www.nicejazzfestival.fr) or **Jazz à Juan** (✆ **04-97-23-11-10;** www.jazzajuan.fr). Mid-July.

Festival d'Avignon. One of France's most prestigious theater events, this world-class festival has a reputation for exposing new talent to critical acclaim. The focus is usually on avant-garde works in theater, dance, and music by groups from around the world. Make hotel reservations early. For information, call ✆ **04-90-27-66-50** (www.festival-avignon.com). Last 3 weeks of July.

AUGUST

Fêtes Daudet, Fontvieille. At this festival, Mass said in Provençal is held on the avenue of pine trees. There's folk dancing outside Daudet's mill and a torchlight procession through the streets of town to the mill. For more information, call ✆ **04-90-54-67-49** (www.fontvieille-provence.com). Mid-August.

Féria de St-Rémy, St-Rémy-de-Provence. This event features a 4-day celebration of bulls with *abrivado* (the ceremonial arrival of the bulls) and *encierro* (the release of the bulls), branding, and Portuguese bull fighting (matadors on horseback). For more information, call ✆ **04-90-92-05-22.** Mid-August.

SEPTEMBER & OCTOBER

Féria des Prémices du Riz (Rice Harvest Festival), Arles. Bullfights are held in the amphitheater with leading matadors, and a procession of floats makes its way along boulevard des Lices. There are also traditional events with cowboys and women in regional costume. For more information, call ✆ **04-90-18-41-20.** Early September.

Fête des Olives, Mouriès. A Mass is held in honor of the green olive. There's a procession of groups in traditional costume, an olive tasting, and sales of regional produce. For more information, call ✆ **04-90-47-56-58** (www.mouries.com). Mid-September.

Perpignan Jazz Festival. World music and jazz musicians from everywhere jam in what many visitors consider Languedoc-Roussillon's most appealing season. For more information, call ✆ **04-68-51-13-14** (www.jazzebre.com). Late September to late October.

NOVEMBER

Marché aux Santons, Tarascon. Craftspeople from throughout Provence congregate in this medieval town to sell their *santons* (clay representations of saints). For more information, call ✆ **04-90-91-03-52.** Four days in late November.

DECEMBER

Fête des Bergers (Shepherds Festival), Istres. This festival features a procession of herds on their way to winter pastures. There are cowboys, a *carreto ramado* (livestock parade), a blessing of the horses, an all-night Provençal party with shepherds and Provençal storytellers, and folk troupes. For more information, call ✆ **04-42-55-50-00.** First weekend in December.

Foire de Noël. Hundreds of wooden chalets, bursting with all manner of Christmas ornaments and gifts, descend on southern France to herald in the Yuletide spirit. The best Christmas fairs are held in Cannes (Vieux Port), Monaco (Port Hercule), Aix-en-Provence (cours Mirabeau), and Avignon (place de l'Horloge). December.

Midnight Mass, Fontvieille. A traditional midnight Mass, including the *pastrage* ceremony, the presentation of a newborn lamb. A procession of folk troupes, Camargue cowboys, and women in traditional costume go from Daudet's mill to the church, followed by the presentation of the lamb. For more information, call ✆ **04-90-54-67-49** (www.fontvieille-provence.com). December 24.

Noël Provençal, Eglise St-Vincent, Les Baux-de-Provence. The procession of shepherds is followed by a traditional midnight Mass, including the *pastrage* ceremony, traditional songs, and performance of a nativity play. For more information, call ✆ **04-90-54-34-39.** December 24.

Fête de St-Sylvestre (New Year's Eve), nationwide. Along the Riviera, it's most boisterously celebrated in Nice's Vieille Ville around place Garibaldi. At midnight, the city explodes. Strangers kiss strangers, and place Masséna and the promenade des Anglais become virtual pedestrian malls. December 31.

LAY OF THE LAND

Between them, Provence and Languedoc-Roussillon encompass an astonishing array of landscapes. Mountain ranges include the peaks of the **Mercantour** national park and the **Préalpes** in northeastern Provence, the rolling hills of the **Luberon,** dramatic **Mont Ventoux** and the **Gorges du Verdon** in the center, and the limestone ridges of the Alpilles toward the west. The Massif Central tapers off in **Haut Languedoc** before flattening out on the way south. The **highlands** of the Corbières give a taste of the heights to come with the mighty **Pyrénées** that mark the border with Spain.

Coastal regions are just as captivating, as many are backed with massive cliffs such as the **Massif de l'Estérel** near Fréjus. The **calanques** near Marseille are a breathtaking sight, with rocky cliffs and narrow inlets. The Rhône delta is the home of the **Camargue,** a vast area of marshes and wetlands that has a haunting beauty of its own. Further west is the seemingly endless stretch of sand that is barely interrupted until it reaches the rocky **Côte Vermeille** and the Spanish border.

SUSTAINABLE TOURISM

In an age when environmental, ethical, and social concerns are becoming more important, the region of Provence and the Riviera is beginning to embrace sustainability and implement various green initiatives.

There is an excellent **public transportation system** in the region. The **rail network,** including high-speed TGV trains (*Train à Grande Vitesse,* meaning high-speed train) and local TER trains (Transport Express Régional), makes getting around the region quick and easy. There is also a widespread network of **buses,** which can take you to small towns that would otherwise be inaccessible via train.

Several cities also have modern, user-friendly public transportation systems. In **Nice,** in addition to offering over 40 bus and tram lines within the city limits, the city's public transportation organization, **Lignes d'Azur** (www.lignesdazur.com), offers public buses to nearly any destination along the Riviera for a mere 1 euro—an unbelievable bargain. **Marseille** has been expanding its metro system and has extended its network of trams and buses. **Montpellier** also offers a comprehensive tram system, in addition to buses that travel around the city and surrounding area.

Many cities in Provence, Languedoc-Roussillon, and the Riviera have set up **public bicycle-rental programs,** which allow people to rent bikes on a short-term basis, and then return these bikes to various stations around town—similar to the **Vélib'** bike scheme in Paris. These public bike-rental programs offer both locals and visitors a fast and inexpensive way to get around the cities; you'll find these bike-rental programs in Avignon, Montpellier, Marseille, Nice, and Perpignan. Alternatively, since many of the cities and towns in these regions are relatively small, many people choose to get around simply by walking.

Many hotels in Provence and the Riviera have undertaken measures to preserve the environment, and those that have are awarded with a green label; look for hotels with the certification of **Green Globe** (www.greenglobe.com), **La Clef Verte** (Green Key; www.laclefverte.org), or the European Eco-Label. These labels reward hotels that take a more environmental approach to water, energy, and waste, and raise environmental awareness among their guests. The **Hotel Martinez** (p. 243) and **Carlton** (p. 243) in Cannes, the **Palais de la Méditerranée** (p. 295) in Nice, and the **Hotel du Cap Eden-Roc** (p. 267) in Antibes have been certified as Green Globe properties for their environmental initiatives, including the use of eco-label cleaning products, locally sourced food in their restaurants, and recycling programs.

France is experiencing a huge growth in the organic farming of everything from vegetables to winemaking. Despite the fact that France is the biggest user of pesticides in Europe, more producers have opted for the organic approach to farming, and more **organic markets** are spring up all over the region. Look for signs saying BIO (organic) on products and in shops and restaurants.

However, despite all of these advances, France does still lag behind on some environmental issues, such as its heavy reliance on nuclear power and its use of pesticides on most of its farms. Still, Provence and the Riviera have made tremendous strides toward protecting the local environment.

Responsible tourism means leaving a destination in the same condition as you found it. You can do this by not dropping litter and recycling. Support the local economy and culture by shopping in smaller, neighborhood shops, and eating in local, family-run restaurants rather than big chain stores and restaurants. For more information and tips on responsible travel, see www.frommers.com/tips.

TOURS

An organized tour can provide good background information on the region and help you get your bearings. There are a number of different tour options on offer in Provence and the Riviera, including boat tours, bike tours, and walking tours. Many visitors are looking for more and more creative ways of getting to know the south of France. Whether you dream of learning to speak French or perfecting your French culinary skills, here are several ideas for exploring Provence and the Riviera in a different, more innovative, way.

Adventure Trips

BICYCLING Numerous companies in the U.S. and the U.K. run cycling tours in France. California-based **Backroads** (www.backroads.com) organizes tours of Provence and include stays in everything from Relais & Châteaux hotels to campgrounds. **Trek Travel** (www.trektravel.com) runs luxury cycling tours of Provence that can include Mont Ventoux if you're up to it. U.K.-based **Cycling for Softies** (www.cycling-for-softies.co.uk) does what its name implies and offers gentler cycling holidays. **Euro-Bike & Walking Tours** (www.eurobike.com) offers relatively moderate bike tours of Provence, including the area around Avignon and St-Rémy-de-Provence. **Belle France** (www.bellefrance.co.uk) offers a variety of tours ranging from cycling along the Canal du Midi to walking holidays along the Collioure coast.

Many of the local tourist offices are able to provide addresses, maps, and contacts for whatever a cyclist might need. In many cases, bikes can be rented within railway stations. Many hotels are able to help the cyclist too; look out for the ACCUEIL VELO sign. For general advice on biking in France, contact the **Fédération Française de Cyclotourisme** (www.ffct.org) or **Freewheeling France** (www.freewheelingfrance.com).

FISHING The Mediterranean provides a variety of fishing methods. You can line fish from the rocks along the coast or from small boats. Local fishermen often take visitors along when fishing in the sea for tuna. The rivers provide sea trout, speckled trout, and silver eel, and the sandy shores of the Camargue offer tiny shellfish. For more information on regulations and access to fishing areas, contact the **Fédération Française des Pêcheurs en Mer** (www.ffpm-national.com).

GOLF The area around Bouches-du-Rhône has many fine golf courses, with seven 18-hole courses, five 9-hole courses, and several practice courses in the Provence area. One excellent 18-hole course is **Golf de Marseille la Salette** (www.opengolf club.com).

Europe's largest golf travel company, **Golf Breaks** (www.golfbreaks.com) offers golfing holidays all over Provence and Languedoc, including the Four Seasons Terre Blanche and Dolce Frégate resorts. **Golf International, Inc.** (www.golfinternational.com) offers trips based in the historic hilltop village of Mougins, a 10-minute drive from Cannes. For more information on the options available, contact the **Fédération Française de Golf** (www.ffgolf.org).

HIKING The Bouches-du-Rhône area is a walker's heaven, whether you enjoy a leisurely stroll or a strenuous long-distance hike or even mountain climbing. Walking challenges include the wetlands of the Camargue, the semi-arid desert of La Crau, and the mountainous hills to the wild rocky inlets of the Calanques. Long-distance hiking paths, called **Sentiers de Grandes Randonnées (GRs),** join the area's major places of interest. GR6 starts in Tarascon, runs along the foot of the Luberon, and crosses the Alpilles. GR9 goes down the Luberon, passes Mont Ste-Victoire, and ends in Ste-Baume. GR98 is an alternative path linking Ste-Baume with the Calanques and ends in Marseille. GR51 links Marseille and Arles via La Crau. GR99A links GR9 to the highlands of the Var *département*. Spring and autumn are the best for hiking; many of the paths are closed in summer because of forest fires. Be sure to check with the *département* before you begin your walk.

Adventure Center (www.adventurecenter.com) offers hiking trips in the Luberon and the Alpilles as well as the Pyrénées. See also "Walking Tours" below.

HORSEBACK RIDING One of the best ways to see the wildlife, salt swamps, and marshlands of the Camargue or the hills of the Alpilles and Mont Ste-Victoire is on horseback. For more information, contact **Manade Saliérène** (www.manadesalierene.com) or the **Association Camarguaise de Tourisme Equestre (Camargue Equestrian Tourism Association;** www.parc-camargue.fr). **Equitours** (www.ridingtours.com) can arrange cross-country treks through Provence and the Camargue regions.

Boat Tours

Before the advent of the railways, many of the crops, building supplies, raw materials, and other products that sustained France were barged through a series of rivers, canals, and estuaries. Many of these are still graced with their old-fashioned locks and pumps, allowing shallow-draft barges easy passage through idyllic countryside. **Le Boat** (www.leboat.com) operates barges through the relatively narrow canals and locks of the Camargue, Languedoc, and Provence. Similarly, **European Waterways** (www.gobarging.com) runs luxury barge cruises along the waterways of the Canal du Midi, feeding passengers regional specialties and local wines along the way.

Food & Wine Trips

Food and wine are some of the premier reasons to visit Provence, so there are many food- and wine-themed tours in the region. **Arblaster & Clarke** (www.winetours.co.uk) offers gourmet experiences in the vineyards surrounding Les Baux-de-Provence, Aix-en-Provence, and Bandol. **Real Provence** (www.real-provence.com) hosts cooking classes in the heart of the Luberon, as well as tailor-made tours. **Provence Wine Tours** (www.provencewinetours.com) organizes wine and gourmet tours in Marseille, Aix-en-Provence, and the area around Bandol and Cassis. **Provence Cooking Tours** (www.provencecookingtours.com) offers tours of markets and vineyards around Avignon, Cassis, and Châteauneuf-du-Pape, among other regions.

Every year, American food writer **Patricia Wells** (www.patriciawells.com) hosts cooking classes in her 18th-century Provençal farmhouse for a select number of participants. The 5-day cooking program does not include lodging but does feature visits to markets, vineyards, and local restaurants as well as hands-on cooking lessons.

Guided Tours

Escorted tours are structured group tours, with a group leader. The price usually includes everything from airfare to hotels, meals, tours, admission costs, and local transportation, although there are often charges for excursions. American tour operators that lead escorted tours in Provence and the Riviera include **Globus** (www.globusandcosmos.com), which covers Avignon, Marseille, Aix-en-Provence, Oranges, Arles, among others, and **Trafalgar** (www.trafalgar.com), which includes tours of Provence and the Riviera among its many French destinations. **Tauck World Discovery** (✆ **800/788-7885;** www.tauck.com) provides first-class, escorted coach grand tours of Provence and the Riviera, as well as other general tours of regions within France.

Language Programs

A clearinghouse for information on French-language schools is **Lingua Service Worldwide** (www.linguaserviceworldwide.com). Its programs cover Antibes, Aix-en-Provence, Avignon, Cannes, Juan-les-Pins, Montpellier, and Nice. Courses can be long- or short-term, the latter with 20 language lessons per week. **Language in Provence** (www.languageinprovence.com) offers tailor-made courses in the Luberon countryside for all levels. **Parlons en Provence** (www.parlons-en-provence.com) is a family-run business that runs small classes for adults in St-Rémy-de-Provence. A wide range of courses and study programs is taught in Aix-en-Provence with **Languages Abroad** (www.languagesabroad.co.uk).

Working Trips

American students wishing to absorb French life can spend up to 3 months of the summer with **Work in France** (www.bunac.org). The organization arranges programs for students to gain work experience while improving their language skills. Seasonal work, mainly grape-picking during the wine harvest, is available for European Union citizens. It's physically demanding and not especially well paid, but you get food and lodging.

Walking Tours

Numerous companies operate walking holidays in Provence, ranging from easy guided walks to more challenging treks done independently. **Headwater** (www.headwater.com) offers guided walking tours in the countryside surrounding St-Tropez and independent walks through the Luberon, as well as cycling trips throughout Provence. **HF Holidays** (www.hfholidays.co.uk) has self-guided walks along the Calanques or guided walks through Provence's hilltop villages. **Belle France** (www.bellefrance.co.uk) takes hikers past the Cathar castles of Languedoc and along the coast of French Catalonia. **Ramblers Worldwide Holidays** (www.ramblersholidays.co.uk) hosts guided walks in the foothills of the Pyrénées and Carcassonne as well as explorations of Roman Provence, the gardens of the Riviera and villages of the Luberon. **Responsible Travel** (www.responsibletravel.com) organizes short holidays for small groups to stay in French homes, combining hiking through the Riviera countryside with cooking classes.

SUGGESTED PROVENCE & THE RIVIERA ITINERARIES

by Mary Novakovich

3

One of Europe's greatest pleasures is getting "lost" in Provence, the Riviera, and the Languedoc, wandering about at random, making new discoveries, and finding charming towns you may never find on a typical itinerary. Vibrant cities such as Marseille, Nice, and Montpellier beg to be explored, along with the mellow rolling hills of the Luberon and glittering coastal resorts such as Cannes, St-Tropez, and Juan-les-Pins. Medieval hilltop villages tower over timeless landscapes of world-class vineyards, lavender fields, and acres of vivid sunflowers. Ancient Rome is at your feet in the well-preserved arenas of Arles, Orange, and Nîmes, and the artistic centers of Avignon and Aix-en-Provence teem with the architectural splendors of the Renaissance.

Careful planning ahead of time can help you to see as much of these regions as possible without trying to cram in too much. Travel times can be cut considerably thanks to France's excellent road network, which leaves more time to meander along the quiet, secondary roads that take you into the hill towns. The region has an extensive public transportation system, with many of the towns and cities connected by train and/or bus. However, you might find that renting a car will be the best option if you want to explore some of the smaller villages.

THE REGIONS IN BRIEF

LANGUEDOC-ROUSSILLON Less frenetic and more affordable than Provence, Languedoc packs in a huge range of astonishing landscapes within its borders. Traditionally, at least since the Middle Ages, the dividing line between Provence and Languedoc has been the mighty Rhône. Even today the river marks the boundaries between the two regions—that of Provence-Côte d'Azur and that of Languedoc-Roussillon.

Its capital, **Montpellier,** is one of the most vibrant cities in France, with a younger-than-average population. A rich history and laid-back air permeate the Roman cities of **Nîmes** and **Narbonne,** while **Uzès** is simply one of the most delightful medieval towns in France. The vine-covered plains of Roussillon swiftly turn mountainous as they reach the peaks of the Pyrénées and everything takes on a Catalonian hue in **Perpignan, Céret,** and **Collioure. Carcassonne,** a marvelously preserved walled city with fortifications begun around A.D. 500, is one of the region's most popular sights.

PROVENCE Provence is more like Italy, its Mediterranean neighbor, than the rest of France. It's a land of gnarled olive trees, cypresses, and umbrella pines, with almond groves, fields of lavender, sunflowers, and *herbes de Provence,* plus countless vineyards. It's also home to the **Camargue,** the atmospheric marshy delta formed by two arms of the Rhône River. The mountains of the **Luberon** are dotted with pretty hilltop villages known as *villages perchés.* Premier destinations include **Aix-en-Provence,** associated with Cézanne; **Arles,** captured on canvas by van Gogh; **Avignon,** once the capital of Christendom during the 14th century; and **Marseille,** its busiest port. Its villages and small towns are a joy to explore, including **Les Baux-de-Provence, St-Rémy-de-Provence, Bonnieux,** and **Roussillon.**

THE WESTERN CÔTE & INLAND VAR People flock to this region to see the pastel-colored coastal village of **St-Tropez,** with its glamorous beach clubs and chic restaurants. But there is much more to this incredibly varied area: the rugged landscapes of inland Var culminating in the dramatic **Gorges du Verdon,** the bustling naval port of **Toulon,** the exquisite archipelago that makes up the **Îles d'Hyères,** and the oldest resort on the Côte d'Azur, **Hyères.** The neighboring towns of **Fréjus** and **St-Raphaël** draw families in search of Roman history combined with attractive beaches bordered by the rocky **Massif d'Estérel. Ste-Maxime** is just across the gulf from St-Tropez and an affordable option for those who want family-friendly Blue Flag (eco-label) beaches.

COTE D'AZUR (FRENCH RIVIERA) The chain of glittering coastal towns may have been overrun with tourists, but the names of its resorts still evoke glamour: **Cannes, Cap d'Antibes,** and **St-Jean-Cap-Ferrat.** July and August are the most crowded times, but spring and fall can be a delight. **Nice** is the most economical base for exploring the area. The principality of **Monaco** occupies less than a square mile. Don't expect sandy beaches—most are rocky. Glitterati and eccentrics have always been attracted to this strip of real estate, but so have dozens of artists and their patrons, who have left behind a landscape of world-class galleries and art museums.

PROVENCE IN 1 WEEK

A week will give you a tantalizing taste of Provence and undoubtedly will leave you wanting more. You can take in the highlights of the major cities—**Arles, Avignon, Aix-en-Provence,** and **Marseille**—as well as savor the beauty of the countryside. The villages in the **Luberon** are so evocative of Provence that it would be a shame to bypass them. The itinerary below is flexible: you can shorten stays in some of the towns and lengthen others. Some might want to spend more time in the large cities such as Aix or Marseille, while others prefer rural tranquillity.

The South of France

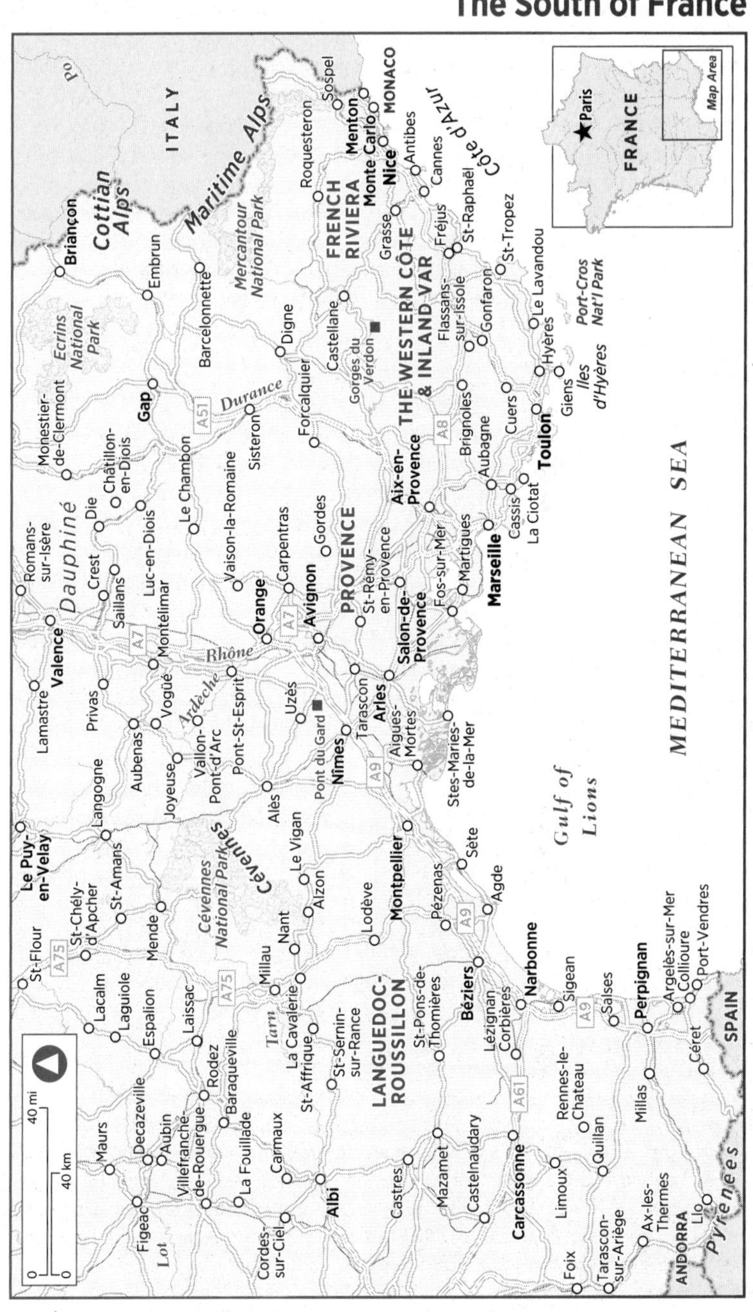

Day 1: Arles ★

Arles (p. 129) is packed with historical sights, but the city's compact size makes it easy to fit many of them within a day. Start with a walk through the old town that so enchanted van Gogh. Head to the **Théâtre Antique/Amphithéâtre** (**Les Arènes;** p. 132), where you can wander among the ruins of a Roman theater after taking a tour of the impressive arena. Stop at one of the cafes on **place du Forum,** ones of the liveliest squares in Arles. After lunch, visit the **Musée Départemental—Arles Antique** (p. 132), with one of the world's best collections of Roman and Christian sarcophagi. Try to visit the **Musée Réattu** (p. 132), an exciting mix of contemporary art and old masters. If you have time before its 7pm summer closing, also visit **Les Alyscamps** (p. 130), one of the world's best-known necropolises. Overnight in Arles.

Day 2: Les Baux-de-Provence ★ & St-Rémy-de-Provence ★★

Leave Arles on **day 2,** driving 19km (12 miles) northeast to the tiny village of **Les Baux-de-Provence** (p. 139) in the southern Alpilles. Arrive early to explore this medieval village and its evocative ruins, as large groups of tourists can soon overrun the place.

From Les Baux, drive 10km (7 miles) north to **St-Rémy-de-Provence** (p. 142), the birthplace of the French astrologer Nostradamus. It's one of the most pleasant towns in Provence, with a medieval old town full of galleries and shops encircled by a tree-shaded boulevard where cafes and restaurants tempt you to stop for lunch. In the afternoon, you can visit some of the town's major attractions, including the Roman ruins of **Glanum** (p. 144) and **Monastère de St-Paul-de-Mausole** (p. 144), the 12th-century monastery where van Gogh sought treatment and where he was inspired to paint some of his best works. Overnight in St-Rémy.

Day 3: Avignon ★★★

On **day 3**, drive 20km (12 miles) from St-Rémy-de-Provence to **Avignon**. Its old town encircled by medieval ramparts is full of fascinating sights, but pride of place goes to **Palais des Papes** (p. 120), the 14th-century home of the papacy. After a tour of the palace, take a leisurely wander through the old town before heading out to the **Pont St-Bénezet** (p. 120), Avignon's ancient bridge that now sits stranded halfway across the Rhône River. Try to catch some of the other sights in the afternoon, notably **Musée Angladon** (p. 118), with its splendid art collections, or the **Musée Calvet** (p. 118), with its collection of ancient silver displayed in an 18th-century town house. If you can make it here before 6pm, you can also see the **Musée Lapidaire** (p. 118), with some of the most intriguing Gallo-Roman sculptures in Provence. Overnight in Avignon.

Day 4: Nord Luberon ★★

On **day 4,** drive east from Avignon for 47km (29 miles) towards the Luberon village of **Bonnieux** (p. 152). You can use this pretty hilltop village as a base to explore the northern side of the Luberon. Along the way to Bonnieux, you can visit two of the best-known hilltop villages in the Luberon, **Gordes** (p. 147) and **Roussillon** (p. 150). If you have time, you can even drop by **Ménerbes** and

Provence in 1 Week

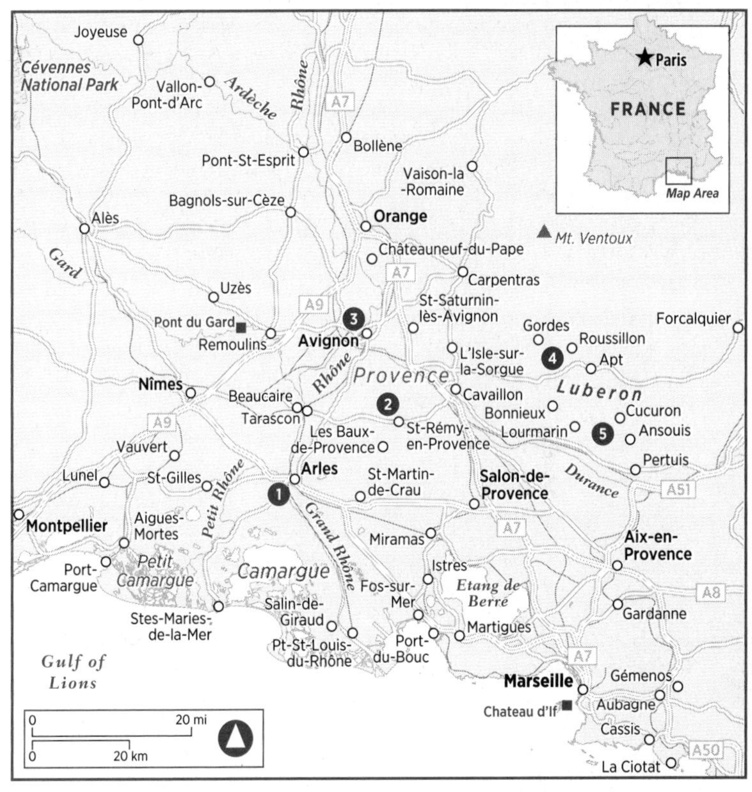

Lacoste, but save time for Bonnieux, which has wonderful views of the Petit Luberon from the top of the village. Overnight in Bonnieux.

Day 5: Sud Luberon ★★

The tour of the Luberon continues on **day 5,** as you drive 13km (8 miles) south toward **Lourmarin.** Take a tour of the **Château de Lourmarin** (p. 159), the first Renaissance château built in Provence, and stroll through the winding streets of this attractive market town. Later, drive the short distances to some of the pleasant neighboring towns, including **Cucuron** (p. 160), with its enormous tree-shaded reservoir in the center of the village; **Ansouis** (p. 161); and **La Tour d'Aigues** (p. 162). Overnight in Lourmarin.

Day 6: Aix-en-Provence ★★

On the morning of **day 6,** leave Lourmarin and head south 40km (25 miles) to this sophisticated university city. After checking into a hotel, walk along **cours Mirabeau** (p. 168), toward the old town, Viel Aix, a maze of narrow streets and tiny squares tucked into unexpected places. Have lunch in one of the cafes in

Viel Aix. After lunch, visit the main sights, including the **Atelier de Cézanne** (p. 169), the painter's studio just north of the old town. Other attractions worth a look include the city's main art gallery, **Musée Granet** (p. 169), and the **Cathédrale St-Sauveur** (p. 169). Overnight in Aix-en-Provence.

Day 7: Marseille ★★★

For your final day in Provence, head to bustling **Marseille,** France's oldest city. It's a 35km (22-mile) drive south of Aix-en-Provence. After checking into a hotel, spend the morning wandering the **Vieux Port** (p. 177), or Old Port, ducking in and out of its narrow streets. Cross the port to **Le Panier** (p. 176), one of Marseille's oldest and most authentic districts, and take the metro up to **cours Julien** (p. 177), one of the most vibrant parts of the city.

In the afternoon take a boat to the **Château d'If** (p. 179), an island that Alexandre Dumas used as a setting for his novel *The Count of Monte Cristo.* If you return to Marseille in time, visit the **Basilique St-Victor** (p. 177), exploring its early medieval crypt. Overnight in Marseille, one of France's great transportation hubs, with numerous rail and plane connections.

THE RIVIERA IN 2 WEEKS

With 2 weeks you can traverse the Côte d'Azur at a more relaxed pace. This tour begins in the west at **St-Tropez** and then takes you all the way east to **Menton,** on the border with Italy. Highlights include not only St-Tropez, but the chic resort of **Cannes,** bustling **Nice** (the capital of the Riviera), and elegant **Monaco.** You can take in stunning beaches along the way, but be sure to save some time to explore a few of the world's best galleries and museums—the Riviera has both in abundance.

Days 1 & 2: St-Tropez ★★

On **day 1,** arrive at the nearest rail station in St-Raphaël, making the rest of the journey to **St-Tropez** by boat or bus. For details, see p. 202. St-Tropez is all about beaches, the best of which include the Plage de la Bouillabaisse or Plage des Graniers. Following a day at the beach, drop into **Café de Paris** (p. 214) for a predinner drink. Enjoy a long, lingering dinner and take a stroll along the harborfront at night, inspecting the fleet of yachts from all over the world.

On **day 2,** before heading for another day at the beach, inspect the **Musée de l'Annonciade** (p. 205), the first of the modern art collections that opened on the Riviera in 1955. Do some boutique hopping before heading to Plage de Pampelonne. Spend your final evening in St-Tropez at the harborfront in the center of town.

Days 3 & 4: Cannes ★★★

On **day 3,** rent a car and drive east 83km (52 miles) along the coast to Cannes, site of the famous international film festival. After checking into your hotel, take a long walk along the **promenade de la Croisette** (p. 237) to see what the excitement is all about. Find a waterfront restaurant for lunch and then head for the beach—try **Plage de la Croisette,** extending between Vieux Port (Old Port) and Port Canto.

On the morning of **day 4,** take a ferryboat trip to **Île Ste-Marguerite** (p. 241), the most famous of the Lérins Islands, where the mysterious "Man in

The Riviera in 2 Weeks

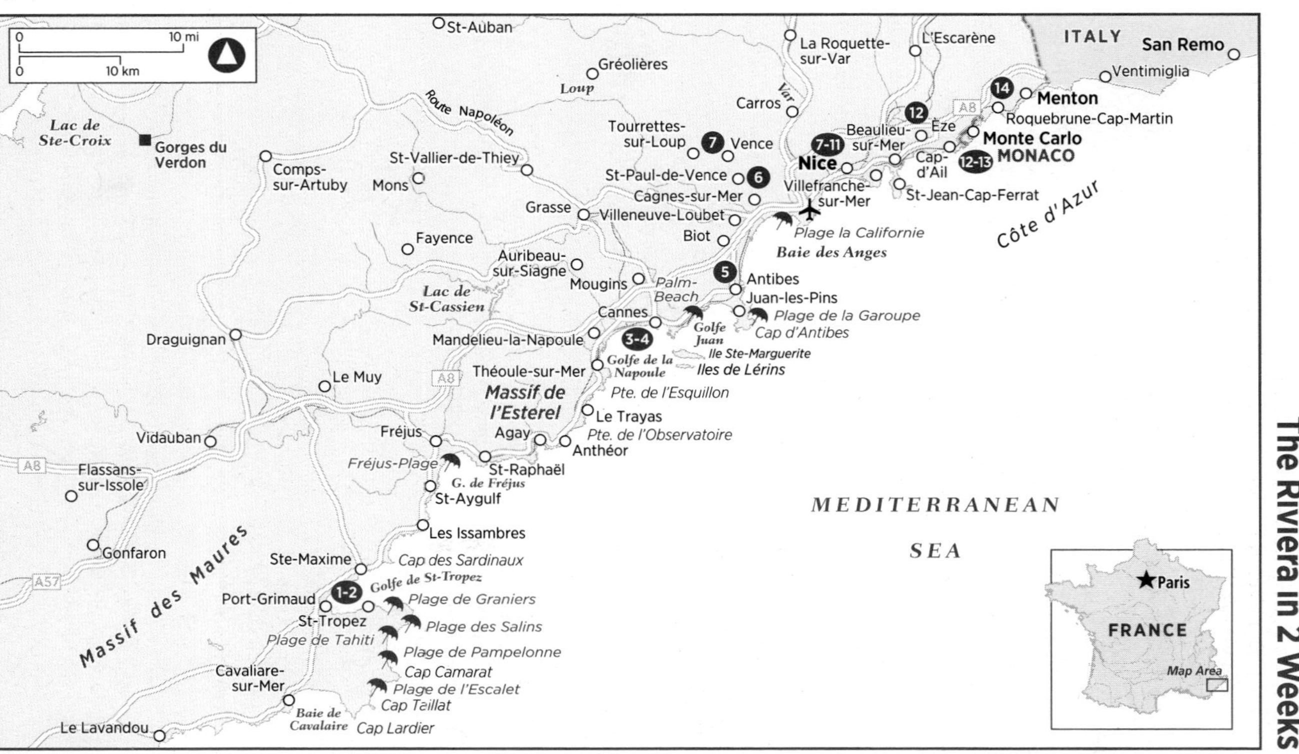

the Iron Mask" was held prisoner. You can spend all morning exploring the island and have lunch here. You can also visit the second major island, **Île St-Honorat** (p. 241), with its Abbaye de St-Honorat, or else return to Cannes for another afternoon at the beach. If you're a gambler, you can patronize one of the city's glittering casinos.

Day 5: Grasse ★★, Mougins ★ & Antibes ★★★

Leave Cannes on the morning of **day 5,** and drive north 18km (11 miles) to Grasse. This is the perfume capital of France, and you can visit its *parfumeries* (perfume factories); the best are **Fragonard** (p. 254) and **Molinard** (p. 255). Instead of lunching in Grasse, head back 10km (6 miles) on the road to Cannes, and stop in the village of **Mougins,** which was a favorite spot for Picasso, for lunch—Mougins has some of the best restaurants on the Riviera. (See the restaurant recommendations on p. 261.)

Head east toward the coast, and drive about 12km (7 miles) to Antibes. Picasso also lived here, as evidenced by the array of paintings he left to the **Musée Picasso** (p. 266), one of the greatest collections of his work. After seeing the museum, drive along the chic **Cap d'Antibes** (p. 265) to see how the very rich live and have done so ever since F. Scott Fitzgerald dramatized the resort strip in his novel, *Tender Is the Night.* Overnight in Antibes and wander through the winding streets of the old town, finding a typical seafood bistro.

Day 6: Biot ★ & St-Paul de Vence ★★

On **day 6,** leave Antibes in the morning, and drive north 8km (5 miles) to the town of Biot, which is celebrated for its beautiful pottery. (See shopping recommendations on p. 273.) While here, visit the **Musée National Fernand-Léger** (p. 273).

After lunch in town, head northeast 15km (9 miles) for a night in the hill town of **St-Paul de Vence.** After checking into your hotel, visit the **Fondation Maeght** (p. 276), the most famous—and the best—gallery of modern art on the Riviera, and one of Europe's finest museums. Spend the late afternoon or early evening wandering the town's cobblestone streets.

Days 7 & 8: Vence ★ & Nice ★★★

On the morning of **day 7,** drive 6km (4 miles) over to the neighboring hill town of Vence to see **Chapelle du Rosaire** (p. 280), the chapel that Henri Matisse designed and decorated between 1949 and 1951. He viewed it as his masterpiece. After an hour's visit, drive southeast 21km (13 miles) to Nice for a 3-night visit, part of which will be devoted to excursions.

After checking into a hotel in Nice, stroll through **Vieille Ville** (p. 224), the Old Town. Enjoy a snack of *socca,* a round pancake made with chickpea flour that's sold steaming hot by street vendors. Wander past the stalls at the colorful outdoor market in **cours Saleya,** then head for the **promenade des Anglais** (p. 287), the wide boulevard along the waterfront. You can spend at least an hour strolling, perhaps stopping at one of the grand cafes bordering the water for a Niçois lunch. In the afternoon, head for one of the beaches. Head back to the Old Town for dinner at a typical bistro.

On **day 8,** visit some important museums: start with the **Musée d'Art Moderne et d'Art Contemporain** (p. 290), one of the best modern art museums in the region, and then head to the **Musée des Beaux-Arts** (p. 291), devoted to the masters of the Second Empire and the Belle Époque era. In the afternoon, head for the suburb of **Cimiez** to see the **Musée Matisse** (p. 292). Return to Nice for the night, and see an opera or live music at one of Vieille Ville's many bars.

Day 9: Grande Corniche ★★★ & Moyenne Corniche ★★

On **day 9,** while still based in Nice, head out for the grandest drive in the south of France: the **Grande Corniche.** Built by Napoleon in 1806, this 32km (20 miles) stretch of road drives past blue seas, verdant landscape, and attractive towns, and takes about 3 hours to drive, although many motorists stop for a series of grand views, stretching the trip out to at least 5 hours.

From Nice, head east along avenue des Diables-Bleus. From points along the way, you can look down 450m (1,400 ft.) to Monaco, stop for panoramic views at Eze, and appreciate the highest point along the Grande Corniche: the **Trophée des Alps** (p. 317), a rock formation at 450m (1,500 ft.).

Stop for lunch in **Menton** before returning to Nice along the **Moyenne Corniche** or Middle Corniche, stretching 31km (19 miles). This superhighway, built during the 1920s, also runs from Nice to Menton and goes in and out of tunnels cut through mountains. Panoramic views, including some of Monaco, are possible to enjoy at many points along this grand highway. Return to Nice for the night.

Day 10: Villefranche-sur-Mer ★ & St-Jean-Cap-Ferrat ★

To save money because of its affordable hotels, you can still use Nice as your home base as you set out to see such highlights along the Riviera as Villefranche-sur-Mer and St-Jean-Cap-Ferrat on **day 10.** From Nice, drive 8km (5 miles) east to reach **Villefranche-sur-Mer.** Walk its vaulted **rue Obscure** (p. 308) and visit its 14th-century Romanesque **Chapelle St-Pierre** (p. 308), with frescoes painted by Jean Cocteau.

By late morning, leave Villefranche and head to posh **St-Jean-Cap-Ferrat,** a 15km (9-mile) promontory that lies 10km (6 miles) east of Nice. Here you will find one of the Côte d'Azur's most legendary villas, today the home of the art-stuffed **La Villa Ephrussi de Rothschild** (p. 311). Budget 2 hours for a visit and get in some beach time, perhaps at **Plage de la Paloma,** before returning to Nice for the night.

Day 11: Gorges du Loup

Again, with Nice as your hotel base, set out on **day 11** to see some of the most dramatic scenery in the mountains above the Côte d'Azur by visiting **Gorges du Loup** (p. 281). To get there, take a 13km (8-mile) drive filled with dramatic scenery such as waterfalls, rock spurs, and decaying castles.

For lunch, stop at the town of **Tourrettes-sur-Loup** (p. 274), which lies 29km (18 miles) west of Nice to wander its ancient streets and explore its many crafts studios. The best of these are showcased along the **Grand'Rue.** Return to Nice in the afternoon, hopefully in time for the beach. Spend your last night in Nice.

Days 12 & 13: Beaulieu-sur-Mer ★, Eze & Monaco ★★★

Leave Nice on **day 12,** heading east along the Lower Corniche, or Corniche Inférieure. First stop: the resort of **Beaulieu** 10km (6 miles) east of Nice (p. 313). The town opens onto the tranquil Baie des Fourmis, and you can walk its Boulevard Alsace-Lorraine lined with gardens. The seafront promenade is another idyllic place to stroll. The highlight of your visit will be **Villa Kérylos** (p. 313), a replica of an ancient Greek residence filled with art.

After a visit, continue along the coast to the village of **Eze,** lying 11km (7 miles) northeast of Nice. Have lunch and explore the medieval core of this old town, which is filled with shops, artisan studios, and art galleries. Visit the **Jardin d'Eze** (p. 317), which features cacti and offers panoramic views of the eastern Riviera.

From Eze, continue east to the principality of **Monaco,** 18km (11 miles) east of Nice, for a stopover of 2 nights. After checking into a hotel, head for **Le Café de Paris** (p. 332).

On **day 13,** set out to explore the attractions of this principality, witnessing the changing of the guard and visiting **Les Grands Appartements du Palais,** where Prince Albert rules the Monégasques. Allow 45 minutes or so to see **Jardin Exotique** (p. 324), filled with exotic plants. The other most visited attraction is the **Musée Océanographique de Monaco** (p. 325). If time remains, take in Prince Rainier III's **Collection de Voitures Anciennes** (old automobiles; p. 324). Spend yet another night in the principality, walking its seafront promenades before dinner.

Day 14: Roquebrune-Cap-Martin ★★ & Menton ★★

On **day 14,** your final day on the Riviera, continue along the Lower Corniche until you come to the resort of **Roquebrune-Cap-Martin.** You can explore the old village in 1½ hours. Stroll its covered streets, which are filled with crafts studios, art galleries, and souvenir shops or enjoy panoramic coastal views from the 10th-century Carolingian castle **Chateau de Roquebrune** (p. 336). After lunch, head to the coastline which lies 2km (1½ miles) west of the old village. Here you can take one of the great walks along the Riviera, a 3-hour trek along a coastal path, **Sentier Touristique** (p. 336).

After that, make your way to **Menton** for the night, a distance of 8km (5 miles) east of Monaco. After checking into a hotel, wander its old fishing town, and eat at a local bistro.

The following morning, drive back to Nice (26km/16 miles), the transportation hub of the Riviera.

PROVENCE & THE RIVIERA FOR FAMILIES

Provence and the Riviera offer many attractions that kids enjoy. Perhaps your main concern with having children along is pacing yourself with museum time. Our suggestion is to spend 2 days in Provence, exploring the two towns with the most appeal to families, **Avignon** and **Les Baux,** before tackling the three big resorts of the

Provence & the Riviera for Families

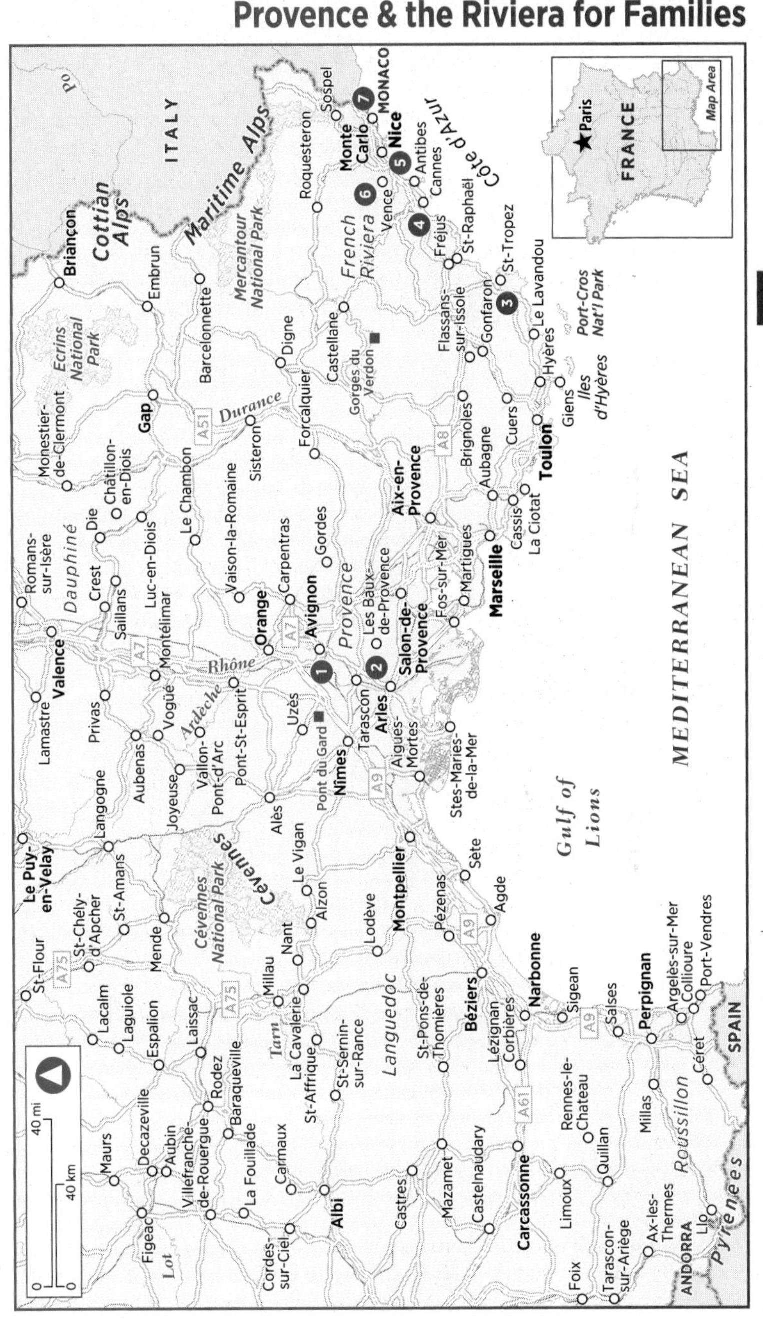

Riviera: **St-Tropez, Cannes,** and **Nice.** Because its hotels are the most affordable on the Riviera, you can spend 3 nights in Nice, using the resort as a base for exploring the two hill towns, **St-Paul-de-Vence** and **Vence,** with a final day reserved for **Monaco.**

Day 1: Avignon ★★★

The **TGV** (high-speed train) from Paris delivers you to the ancient papal city of Avignon in just 2 hours and 38 minutes. If you leave Paris early enough in the morning, you'll have a full day of sightseeing. First, head for the **pont St-Bénezet** (p. 120), the ancient bridge of Avignon, which inspired the old song, *"Sur le pont d'Avignon, l'on y danse, l'on y danse."* After a visit, take your family for a stroll within the ramparts of Avignon, followed by a 2-hour visit to the **Palais des Papes** (p. 122), the papal residence during the so-called period of "Babylonian Captivity," when a pope ruled in Avignon, as well as a rival pope in Rome.

After a lunch, take the kids to the **Musée Requien** (p. 120) for a visit to its herbarium with some 200,000 specimens gathered by botanists from around the globe. Afterwards, take them to **Rocher des Doms** (p. 116), the beautiful hilltop park with children's play areas, a cafe, duck pond, and minibikes to rent.

Day 2: Les Baux

On **day 2,** in a rented car from Avignon, drive southwest to Les Baux, where you can check into a hotel for the night. This bare rock spur, with ravines on each side, is fascinating to explore. You can wander at leisure, visiting the ruins of a fortified castle, even exploring the "ghost village" (often called "the dead village"). The ancient chateau holds special events for children during the summer, including battle reenactments and staged sword fights. After lunch, drive into the surrounding area to explore the gorge **Val d'Enfer** or "Valley of Hell" (p. 140). Return to Les Baux for the evening.

Day 3: St-Tropez ★★

From Les Baux drive southeast to the chic resort of **St-Tropez.** Although the image of St-Tropez is that of a decadent adult retreat, many French parents with children also vacation here. After checking into a hotel, head for the beach. The best sandy strips for families are those near town, including **Plage de la Bouillabaisse** and **Plage des Graniers.** You needn't return to town until later as you can enjoy lunch on the beach. After midafternoon, you can head back to the resort for a stroll along the yacht-clogged harbor and the waterfront. Overnight here.

Day 4: Cannes ★★

After driving east from St-Tropez to Cannes on **day 4,** check into a hotel and go for a stroll along the **promenade de la Croisette,** bordering the harbor. This is one of the grandest walks on the Riviera. After lunch, take one of the ferryboats leaving from the harbor for an afternoon visit to **Île Ste-Marguerite** (p. 241), where the "Man in the Iron Mask" was held. You can return to Cannes for some beach life at the **Plage de la Croisette** before dinner.

Day 5: Nice ★★★

On **day 5,** drive east from Cannes to this larger city, which has more of interest than any other town on the Riviera. It also makes the best base for exploring the hill towns or the resorts to its immediate east, including Monaco. After checking into a hotel for 3 nights, take the kids on the **Petit Train de Nice,** which will get them acquainted with the town. After a ride, take a long stroll along the **promenade des Anglais** (p. 287), the wide boulevard bordering the water, before heading into **Vieille Ville** (p. 290), or Old Town, for a lengthy stroll and a lunch at a typical Niçoise bistro. In the afternoon most kids will go along with you to visit Nice's two most important museums: **Musée d'Art Moderne et d'Art Contemporain** (p. 290) and the **Musée des Beaux-Arts** (p. 291). Or take them to the top of **Colline du Château** (by elevator if they don't want to walk) for panoramic views of the city and the coastline.

Day 6: St-Paul-de-Vence ★★ & Vence ★

While still based in Nice, on **day 6,** head for the Riviera's most beautiful hill town, **St-Paul-de-Vence,** 31km (19 miles) to the north. Kids will delight in spending the morning walking the streets of this historic hill town, especially **rue Grande** (p. 276). After lunch, head to **Fondation Maeght** (p. 276). Even if your child isn't an art lover, this museum is so daringly avant-garde that there will be something of intrigue here.

In the afternoon, drive to Vence to visit the **Chapelle du Rosaire** (p. 280), the chapel that Henri Matisse viewed as his masterpiece. Spend the remaining part of the afternoon exploring the old streets of Vence before returning to Nice.

Day 7: The Principality of Monaco ★

While still based in Nice, on **day 7,** your final day for the Riviera, head east for a distance of only 18km (11 miles). The tiny little country of Monaco was largely put on the map when Grace Kelly married Prince Rainier and went to live in this fairy-tale kingdom by the sea. Kids delight in watching the **changing of the guard** at **Les Grands Appartements du Palais** (p. 325), where Prince Albert lives. After a visit, take them for a walk through the **Jardin Exotique** (p. 324), known for its cacti collection, before lunch. One of the pizzerias in **Monaco-Ville** could be a good choice.

After lunch, you will still have time to visit the fascinating **Musée Océanographique de Monaco** (p. 325), filled with exotic creatures of the sea, as well as the **Collection de Voitures Anciennes** (p. 324), the antique-car collection that belonged to Prince Rainier.

Return to Nice for the night. Because it's the transportation hub of the Riviera, it will be relatively easy from here to get to where you are going next.

LANGUEDOC-ROUSSILLON IN 1 WEEK

The history-rich region of **Languedoc-Roussillon** contains some of the most fascinating terrain in all of France. This region has not only world-class tourist meccas, including the walled city of **Carcassonne,** but also the venerable university city of **Montpellier,** the capital of Languedoc, and the Roman city of **Nîmes,** with one of the best-preserved Roman amphitheaters in the world. Moving with a certain speed, you can take in the chief glories of these provinces in a week. As the distances between the major towns isn't especially great and the superhighways are spread out around the region, you can spend more time in some towns and cut out some of the others.

Day 1: Carcassonne ★

Carcassonne is a picture postcard of the Middle Ages and one of France's most-visited cities. After checking into a hotel, explore the walled city and visit the **Basilique St-Nazaire** (p. 63) and **Château Comtal** (p. 63). In the late afternoon, head down to the **Canal du Midi** (p. 62) and perhaps take a boat trip. You can also rent bicycles if you're in the mood for some gentle exercise along the canal towpath. Overnight in Carcassonne.

Day 2: Collioure ★★★ & the Côte Vermeille ★★

In a rented car from Carcassonne on **day 2,** head 156km (97 miles) to the charming **Côte Vermeille** village of **Collioure.** (You can either take this longer scenic route through the gorges and picturesque villages of the Corbières highlands, or take the A16 and the A9 straight to Collioure. This highway route will save you about 90 minutes but it will mean backtracking later.) Once you reach Collioure, check into your hotel and stroll around the narrow cobbled streets before having a swim in one of its pretty beaches tucked within the rocky cliffs. Overnight in Collioure.

Day 3: Narbonne ★ via Perpignan ★

On **day 3,** drive 30km (19 miles) north to Perpignan, the lively capital of French Catalonia. Walk around its historic core and visit **Castillet/Musée des Arts et Traditions Populaires Catalans** (p. 68). Either stop for lunch here in one of the busy squares or eat once you've driven the 64km (40 miles) to Narbonne. After checking into your hotel in Narbonne, stroll around the old town and along the Canal de la Robine. Visit its major monument, **Cathédrale St-Just** (p. 78), and the museums within the **Palais des Archevêques** (p. 78). Overnight in Narbonne.

Day 4: Montpellier ★★

On **day 4,** take the A9 east for 93km (58 miles) to the vibrant university city of Montpellier, the capital of Languedoc. You will use this as a base for the next 2 days to explore some of the neighboring towns. Check into a hotel before strolling through the **place de la Comédie** towards the **Musée Fabre** (p. 88), one of France's greatest provincial art galleries. Allow time for a long stroll along the 17th-century **promenade du Peyrou,** one of the great terraced parks of southwest France, as well as the **Jardin des Plantes** (p. 88). While walking through Montpellier's historic center, you might have spotted where you want to have dinner and popped in to make a reservation. Overnight in Montpellier.

Day 5: St-Guilhem-le-Désert ★★ & Sète ★

On **day 5,** you can decide how busy a day you want to have. You can explore more of Montpellier at leisure or perhaps visit one of its beaches, which are a short bus ride away. If you feel like venturing out of the city, you can drive 47km

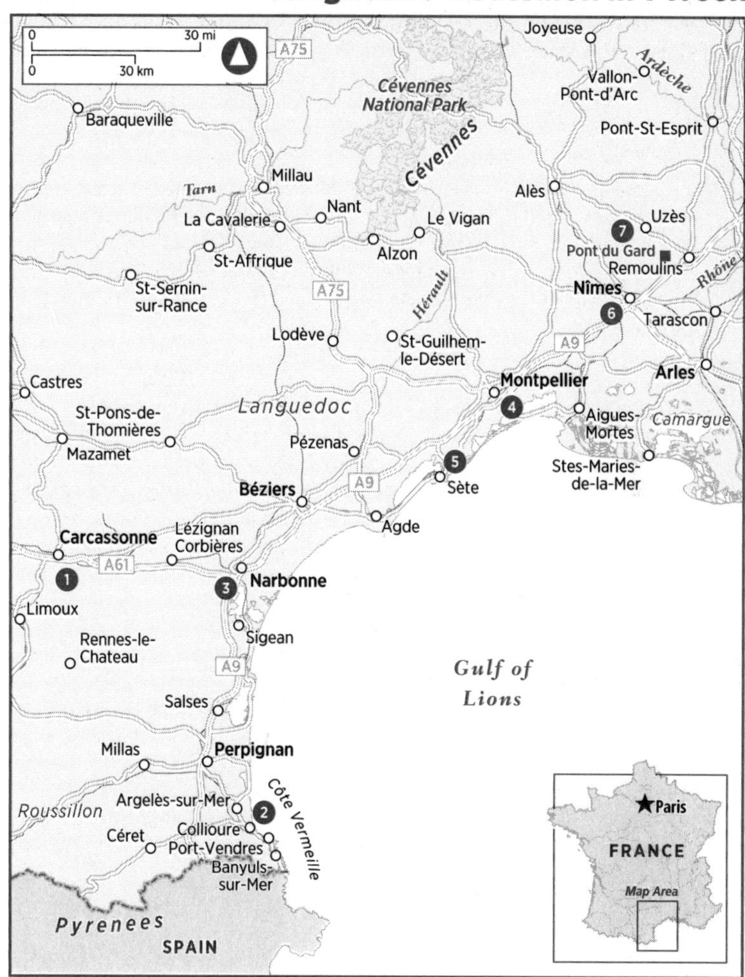

(29 miles) to the enchanting hilltop village of **St-Guilhem-le-Désert** (p. 94) to visit its 9th-century abbey, or you can drive 74km (46 miles) to the bustling port town of **Sète** (p. 95), whose quays are lined with dozens of restaurants serving the freshest seafood. On the way back to Montpellier, you can stop at the Etang de Thau village of **Bouzigues** for some of the best oysters in France. Overnight in Montpellier.

Day 6: Nîmes ★★★

On **day 6,** from Montpellier drive 52km (32miles) northeast to the ancient city of Nîmes, where you can check into a hotel for the night. Set out for a busy day of sightseeing, heading first for **Maison Carrée** (p. 102), one of the world's greatest Roman temples, and then visiting the **Amphithéâtre Romain** (p. 100).

In the afternoon, visit the **Carré d'Art/Musée d'Art Contemporain** (p. 100), then head to the beautiful gardens at **Jardin de la Fontaine** (p. 102) to take in views of Nîmes' Roman ruins. Try also to visit the city's largest museum, **Musée des Beaux-Arts** (p. 102), with its mammoth collection of French painting and sculpture from the 17th century to modern times.

Day 7: Uzès ★★★ & Pont du Gard

On your final day, **day 7,** drive 24km (15 miles) north from Nîmes to the beautiful medieval town of **Uzès.** If you've timed your week right, you might have turned up during its fabulous Saturday morning market. (If you did and you have a car, be prepared for parking difficulties.) Whatever day of the week, it's a delight to wander through the narrow streets of the old town, stopping for a lunch at the one of the restaurants in the place aux Herbes, one of the most splendid squares in France.

In the afternoon, drive 16km (10 miles) to the one of the greatest feats of Roman engineering, the **Pont du Gard** (p. 102). Most of it has been reconstructed, but its three levels of stone arches are a wonder to behold. You can have a picnic here with food bought from the Uzès market, or go for a swim in the Gardon River. Once you return to Uzès, it's not far from the large transport hubs of Nîmes and Avignon.

LANGUEDOC-ROUSSILLON

Languedoc, one of southern France's great old provinces, encompasses such cities as Montpellier (its capital), Nîmes, Carcassonne, and Narbonne. As neighboring Provence has become busier and more expensive, visitors are discovering the many charms and unspoiled landscapes of Languedoc. Vibrant Montpellier is home to a large university with a vast student population, making it one of the youngest cities in the country. Enchanting medieval market towns such as Uzès and Pézenas thrive by celebrating ancient crafts and traditions, their narrow streets filled with artisans' studios. Vineyards cover large expanses of the landscape—which is not surprising considering that Languedoc-Roussillon is the world's largest wine region.

The coast of Languedoc-Roussillon—from Montpellier to the Spanish frontier—has nowhere near the level of development of the Côte d'Azur. An almost-continuous strip of sand stretches west from the Rhône River and curves snakelike toward the Pyrénées, stopping at the rocky coves of the Côte Vermeille. Inland, the dramatic hills and peaks of the Haut Languedoc remain remote and undiscovered by the average tourist, while the forests and hills of the Corbières highlands attracts wine lovers on the trail of robust reds.

Ancient **Roussillon** is a small region bordering Spain and forming the Pyrénées-Orientales *département*. It includes the city of Perpignan and towns of Collioure and Céret within its borders. This is French Catalonia, symbolized by the towering snow-capped Pic du Canigou looming in the distance. The region is inspired as much by Barcelona in neighboring Spain as by Paris. Over its long and colorful history, it has known many rulers. Legally part of the French kingdom until 1258, it was surrendered to James I of Aragón, and until 1344 it was part of the ephemeral kingdom of Majorca, with Perpignan as the capital. By 1463, Roussillon was annexed to France again. Then Ferdinand of Aragón won it back, but by 1659 France had it once again. The bright yellow and red Catalan flag is everywhere, echoing the enormous pride residents have in their heritage, cuisine, and traditions—even if most people don't speak the language. Catalan, like many of France's regional languages, had been suppressed by Paris for more than 2 centuries, and as recently as the 1950s, schoolchildren were punished if they spoke it in class. Since 2007 it has been designated one of the official languages of Pyrénées-Orientales, and is visible on many of the street signs.

LANGUEDOC-ROUSSILLON: the world's largest winemaking region

One-quarter of France's wine production comes from the vineyards spread throughout the region of Languedoc-Roussillon. More than 250,000 hectares (618,000 acres) of vineyards cover some of the most diverse landscapes found in Europe. Its sheer scale makes it the largest single wine-producing region in the world. It used to be home to France's most basic wine, when quantity was prized over quality, but those days are disappearing.

More than 30 grape varieties are grown in wildly differing soils and climates, from the southernmost reaches of the Massif Central to the wide expanse of plains and flat coastal areas near the Mediterranean before heading towards the Pyrénées. Here you'll find reds, whites, rosés, sparkling wine, *vins doux naturels* (sweet fortified wines)—all of which show distinctive characteristics of their own region and history. The birth of rosé, for example, wasn't in the hills of Provence but in the Languedoc village of Tavel not far from Nîmes. And the small town of Limoux south of Carcassonne came up with a sparkling wine *(blanquette de Limoux)* more than a century before Champagne's monks discovered the secret of what made wine fizz. Incidentally, Limoux is also home to one of the liveliest February carnivals to be found in France.

Some of the popular wine appellations include:

Corbières, from the rugged landscape southeast of Carcassonne

Minervois, from the area around the Montagne Noire north of Carcassonne

Fitou, from just north of Perpignan

Faugères and **Saint-Chinian,** in the hills northwest of Béziers

Pic Saint-Loup, from north of Montpellier

Costières de Nîmes, from south of Nîmes and bordering the Petit Rhône River

Banyuls and **Rivesaltes,** two *vins doux naturels* that come from their respective villages south of Perpignan

Côtes du Roussillon, from the villages in the foothills of the Pyrénées

Like Provence and Roussillon, Languedoc has its own ancient language, Occitan. It, too, has just managed to survive official suppression over the centuries. Visitors are unlikely to hear it spoken nowadays, but many of the street names and signs are in both French and Occitan.

CARCASSONNE ★

797km (495 miles) SW of Paris; 150km (93 miles) SW of Montpellier

This great fortress city rises against the dramatic background of the Montagne Noire, the Black Mountain, to the north. Carcassonne captures a type of fairy-tale magic, evoking bold knights and fair damsels, but back in its heyday in the Middle Ages it was the target of assault by battering rams, catapults, flaming arrows, and more. Today, the city—which is a UNESCO World Heritage Site—is overrun with hordes of visitors and gift shops. However, the elusive charm of Carcassonne comes out in the evening, when day-trippers depart and floodlights bathe the ancient monuments.

Languedoc-Roussillon

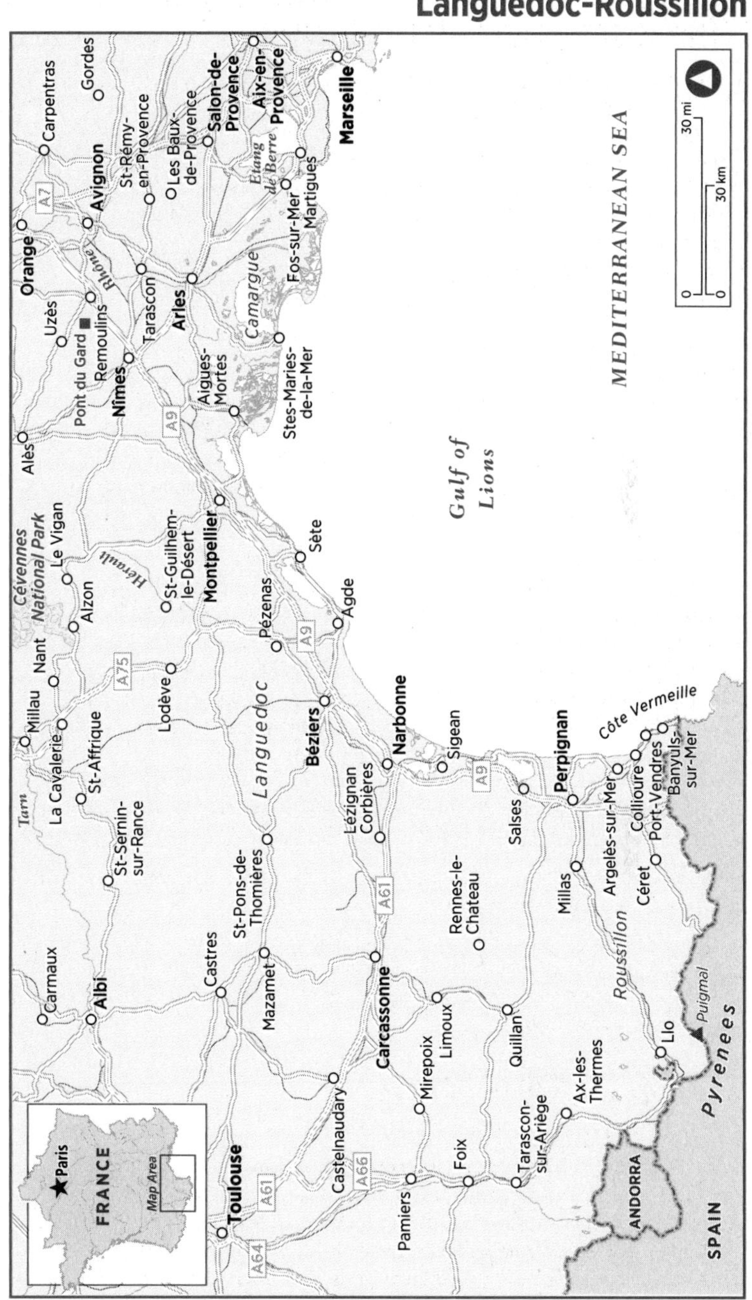

Carcassonne is also a major stop along the **Canal du Midi,** that marvel of engineering that runs for 240km (150 miles) from the Garonne River at Toulouse all the way to the Mediterranean Sea at Sète. A 17th-century minor noble, Pierre-Paul Riquet, became obsessed with the idea of linking the Atlantic and the Mediterranean and devoted decades of his life and all of his fortune to make his plan a reality. Unfortunately, he died just months before the canal was officially opened in 1681. Although the arrival of the railways in the 19th century eroded much of the canal traffic, nowadays it is one of the most pleasurable ways of exploring this part of France. Barge companies run independent or skippered cruises along the full length of the canal, or you can just take short circular jaunts from ports in Carcassonne and other towns along the route. Its wide towpaths make it popular for cyclists and walkers who appreciate the combination of flat terrain and plenty of scenic restaurant stops along the way.

Essentials

GETTING THERE Carcassonne's **airport** is 3km (2 miles) west of the city and has flights from destinations in the United Kingdom, Ireland, Belgium, and Portugal. Carcassonne is a major stop for **trains** between Toulouse and destinations south and east. Trains arrive from Toulouse, Montpellier, and Marseilles, among other destinations. For rail information, call ✆ **36-35,** or visit www.voyages-sncf.com. **Buses** to Carcassonne are mainly a local service. If you're **driving,** Carcassonne is on A61 southeast of Toulouse.

VISITOR INFORMATION The central **Office de Tourisme** is at 28 rue de Verdun (✆ **04-68-10-24-30;** fax 04-68-10-24-38; www.carcassonne-tourisme.com). There is also a smaller office at Porte Narbonnaise. The office has information on boat trips along the Canal du Midi, bike rentals, and more.

SPECIAL EVENTS The town's nightlife sparkles during its summer festivals. During the **Festival de Carcassonne** (✆ **04-68-11-59-15;** www.festivaldecarcassonne.com) in July, concerts, modern and classical dance, operas, and theater fill the city. Out of the 120 or so concerts, around 80 of them are free. On July 14, **Bastille Day,** France's second-largest fireworks display (after Paris's) lights up the skies over La Cité in a dramatic spectacle that looks as if the fortress is in flames.

Exploring La Cité

Carcassonne consists of two towns: the **Bastide St-Louis** (also known as the Ville Basse or Lower City) and the medieval **Cité.** The former is a pleasant grid of streets and squares, while the latter is among the major attractions in France. The fortifications consist of the inner and outer walls, a double line of ramparts. The Visigoths built the inner rampart in the 5th century. Clovis, king of the Franks, attacked it in 506 but failed to breach the fortifications. The Saracens overcame the city in 728, but Pepin the Short (father of Charlemagne) drove them out in 752.

The epic medieval poems *Chansons de Geste* tell the tale of the origin of the town's name. During a siege by Charlemagne, the populace of the city was starving and near surrender until a local noblewoman, Dame Carcas, reputedly gathered up the last of their wheat, stuffed it into the last remaining pig and threw the animal over the ramparts. The pig's stomach burst, scattering the wheat. Dame Carcas then ordered the trumpets sounded for a parley and cried, *"Carcas sonne!"* ("Carcas is calling!"). The Franks concluded that Carcassonne must have unlimited food supplies if its people were feeding precious grain to their pigs, and thus ended their siege. It's only a legend, of course, as Dame Carcas was the widow of a Saracen king and, being Muslim, would not have been likely to keep pigs.

Carcassonne's walls were further fortified during the crusades led by Simon de Montfort and Raymond Trencavel against the heretic Cathar sect. Those who survived the merciless assaults were allowed to build their bastide, a fortified town, in the **Ville Basse** below the citadel by the banks of the Aude River. They had to rebuild it in the 14th century when it was destroyed by England's Black Prince. By the mid-17th century the city had lost its position as a strategic frontier, and the ramparts were left to decay. In the 19th century, the builders of the Ville Basse began to remove the stone for use in new construction. As interest in the Middle Ages revived, the government ordered **Viollet-le-Duc** (who restored Notre-Dame in Paris) to repair and rebuild the walls. His reconstruction of the Cité, while maintaining medieval appearances, has been criticized over the decades as being too unreal, too Disney-like. However, this hasn't stopped millions of visitors from descending on La Cité to stroll around its cobbled streets and dine in its many restaurants.

In the highest elevation of the Cité, at the uppermost terminus of rue Principale (rue Cros Mayrevielle), you'll find the **Château Comtal,** place du Château (© **04-68-11-70-70**), a restored 12th-century fortress. It's open daily from 10am to 6:30pm April to September, and from 10am to 5pm October to March; entrance includes a 45-minute guided tour in French and occasionally in English. The cost is 8.50€ for adults, 5€ for students and ages 18 to 25, and free for children 17 and under. During the tour, you'll discover archaeological remnants discovered on-site, plus an explanation of the 19th-century restorations.

Another important monument in the fortifications is the **Basilique St-Nazaire ★**, La Cité (© **04-68-25-27-65**), dating from the 11th to the 14th centuries and containing some beautiful stained-glass windows and a pair of rose medallions. The nave is in the Romanesque style, and the choir and transept are Gothic. The 16th-century organ is one of the oldest in southwestern France. The 1266 tomb of Bishop Radulphe is well preserved. The cathedral is open in July and August daily 9am to 7pm, September to June daily 9am to noon and 1 to 5pm. Mass is celebrated on Sunday at 11am. Admission is free.

Shopping

Carcassonne has two distinct shopping areas. In the modern lower city, boutiques can be found along **rue de Verdun** as well in other streets such as **rue Albert Tomey** and **rue de la Liberté.** The main market is in **place Carnot** on Tuesday, Thursday, and Saturday mornings. In the walled medieval city, the streets are chock-full of tiny stores and boutiques; most sell gift items such as antiques and local arts and crafts.

In the Cité, a great store is **Comptoir des Vins et Terroirs,** 4 rue du Comte Roger (© **04-68-26-44-76**), where you'll find a wide selection of regional wines. Some antiques stores to visit are **Faye Henriette,** 4 place du Château (© **04-68-47-09-45**), for furniture; and **Antiquités Safi,** 26 rue Trivalle (© **04-68-25-60-51**), for paintings and art objects. (There is another branch in the lower town at 54 rue Verdun.)

Where to Stay

IN LA CITÉ

Best Western Hôtel Le Donjon This surprisingly reasonably priced three-star hotel, located right in the heart of La Cité, is composed of three buildings: le Donjon, le Comte Roger, and les Remparts, a former hotel with an unusual 13th-century staircase. Guest rooms are comfortable and somewhat spacious, and furnishings range from the functionally modern in the Remparts annex to the more romantic and voluptuous in the main Donjon building.

2 rue du Comte-Roger, 11000 Carcassonne. www.hotel-donjon.fr. ✆ **04-68-11-23-00.** Fax 04-68-25-06-60. 62 units. 105€–183€ double; 150€–403€ suite. AE, DC, MC, V. Parking 12€. **Amenities:** Restaurant; bar; room service. *In room:* A/C, TV, hair dryer, minibar, Wi-Fi (free).

Hôtel de la Cité ★★★ This luxurious five-star hotel, built on the site of a bishops' palace, is located within the walls of the city, adjoining the cathedral. Behind its vine-covered facade is a riot of neo-Gothic sumptuousness and wonderfully ornate interiors. Each room is individually designed, and many rooms are decorated with wooden paneling, frescoes, and tapestries. Several units have balconies or terraces with views of the secluded garden or of Carcassonne and its ramparts. Rooms are equipped with the modern amenities you would expect from a luxury hotel, as well as oversized marble bathrooms. The hotel is renowned for its Michelin-starred restaurant, **La Barbacane** (p. 65), and also runs a more affordable brasserie, Chez Saskia.

Place Auguste Pierre-Pont, 11000 Carcassonne. www.hoteldelacite.com. ✆ **04-68-71-98-71.** Fax 04-68-71-50-15. 67 units. 230€–545€ double; 445€–1,365€ suite. AE, DC, MC, V. Parking 21€ interior; 16€ exterior. Closed Jan–Mar. **Amenities:** 3 restaurants; bar; babysitting; pool (outdoor); room service. *In room:* A/C, TV/DVD, hair dryer, iPod dock, minibar, Wi-Fi (free).

Hôtel du Château ★ Along with its sister hotel, the **Montmorency** (see below), this three-star hotel is in an ideal location if you want to be near La Cité but away from the crowds. It's just steps away from the drawbridge, which means proximity to the best attractions, but with space for a restaurant with a terrace, an inviting swimming pool, a Carita Spa, and spacious grounds. The comfortable and cozy rooms have different themes and span several centuries; many are equipped with old beamed ceilings, deep red leather furniture, and upholstered walls. Some of the suites have their own terraces near the pool area.

2 rue Camille Saint-Saëns, 11000 Carcassonne. www.hotelduchateau.net. ✆ **04-68-11-38-38.** Fax 04-68-11-38-39. 16 units. 110€–200€ double; 190€–220€ suite. AE, DC, MC, V. Parking 10€. **Amenities:** Restaurant; bar; Jacuzzi; pool (outdoor); spa; room service. *In room:* A/C, TV, hair dryer, minibar, Wi-Fi (free).

Hôtel Montmorency Don't be deceived by this hotel's two-star rating: The Montmorency is a friendly, stylish, and comfortable hotel that offers excellent value. For one thing, guests have access to the excellent amenities in the Montmorency's sister property, **Hôtel du Château** (above), which includes its swimming pool and luxurious spa. There are two styles of guest rooms: contemporary rooms, which offer a vivid color palate and cutting-edge design, or country-style rooms, which are decorated with romantic floral motifs. Rooms have private terraces or balconies, as well as state-of-the-art bathrooms. And the location is great: You're only a few steps from La Cité.

11 rue Camille Saint-Saëns, 11000 Carcassonne. www.hotelmontmorency.com. ✆ **04-68-11-96-70.** Fax 04-68-11-96-79. 28 units. 65€–140€ double; 140€–300€ suite. AE, DC, MC, V. Parking 10€. **Amenities:** Restaurant; bar; room service; pool (outdoor); spa. *In room:* A/C, TV, hair dryer, minibar, Wi-Fi (free).

Trois Couronnes This three-star favorite is a good choice in Ville Basse, located south of the place Gambetta, and immediately west of the picturesque old bridge, Pont Vieux. It underwent a major refurbishment in 2009, which updated the decor in the guest rooms as well as the pool and bar areas. Rooms have a stylish simplicity, and many come with a balcony and views of the ramparts and the Aude River. The standard rooms are small and overlook the courtyard, so it's worth spending an extra 20€ for a view.

2 rue des Trois Couronnes, 11000 Carcassonne. www.hotel-destroiscouronnes.com. ✆ **04-68-25-36-10.** Fax 04-68-25-92-92. 68 units. 95€–145€ double; 200€–240€ suite. AE, DC, MC, V. Parking 9€. **Amenities:** Restaurant; bar; exercise room w/sauna; pool (indoor); room service; smoke-free rooms. *In room:* A/C, TV, hair dryer, minibar, Wi-Fi (free).

WHERE TO STAY NEARBY

Domaine d'Auriac ★★ Carcassonne's premier address for both food and lodging is this moss-covered 19th-century manor house about 2.5km (1½ miles) west of the Cité. It was built around 1880 as a cube-shape building, with three stone-sided annexes (site of many of the bedrooms) on the ruins of a medieval monastery. Each bedroom has lots of flowered fabrics, a range of decorative styles, and, in many cases, massive and sometimes sculpted ceiling beams. Part of the allure of this Relais & Châteaux member is in the well-crafted Michelin-starred meals served to guests and nonguests beside the pool on flowering terraces. Fixed-price menus, priced from 65€ to 160€, change several times each season.

Rte. de St-Hilaire, 11009 Carcassonne. www.domaine-d-auriac.com. ✆ **04-68-25-72-22.** Fax 04-68-47-35-54. 24 units. 150€–450€ double. AE, DC, MC, V. Free parking. Closed Jan–early Feb and second week of Nov. Take D104 W 2.5km (1½ miles) from Carcassonne. **Amenities:** 2 restaurants; bar; babysitting; golf course; pool (outdoor); room service; tennis court (lit). *In room:* A/C, TV, hair dryer, minibar, Wi-Fi (5€ per hr.).

Where to Eat

IN LA CITÉ

Bar à Vins TAPAS Tucked away in a large shaded garden in La Cité, this convivial tapas bar is a local favorite. Plates of tapas include Serrano ham, chorizo, Manchego cheese, and anchovies, while other dishes of tapenade, *boudin* (black pudding), and St-Marcellin cheese are served on wooden bread boards that make it easy to share. There's an excellent selection of wines available, too. During festival season, you'll see many of the performers having a postshow drink here, and on weekends, DJs play house and electronic music.

11 rue Porte-d'Aude. ✆ **04-68-25-71-24.** www.lebaravins.fr. Dishes from 4.50€. MC, V. Daily 9am–2am.

Comte Roger ★ FRENCH One of the classiest restaurants in La Cité, Comte Roger features elegant French cuisine, a cool contemporary dining room, and an attractive garden, where meals are served on warm days. Chef Pierre Mesa offers up his own take on classic Languedoc cuisine, with dishes such as a delicate trout mousse in fennel cream, or roasted duck breast with honey polenta and a sauce made of Banyuls wine.

14 rue St-Louis. ✆ **04-68-11-93-40.** www.comteroger.com. Reservations recommended. Main courses 18€–30€; fixed-price menu 36€–50€. AE, MC, V. July–Aug Tues–Sun noon–1:30pm; year-round Tues–Sat 7:30–9:30pm. Closed mid-Dec to mid-Jan.

La Barbacane ★ FRENCH Named after its medieval neighborhood, this Michelin-starred restaurant enjoys equal billing as its celebrated hotel, the Hôtel de la Cité. The elegant dining room is lined with wood paneling and stained-glass windows. The menu, crafted by noted chef Jérôme Ryon, is based on seasonal ingredients and varies according to the season. In the fall, for example, you might start with the autumn vegetables with truffles and seasoned toast, and then continue with the roasted wild turbot with caramelized walnuts or the Charolais beef filet stuffed with foie gras. Desserts, by pastry chef Régis Chanel, might include such delicate offerings as Toulouse violets in a crème brûlée and served with blackberry jelly, or a warm soufflé with apple sorbet and manzana liqueur.

In the Hôtel de la Cité (p. 64), place Auguste Pierre-Pont. ✆ **04-68-71-98-71.** www.hoteldelacite.com. Reservations required. Main courses 34€–80€; fixed-price menu 75€–160€. AE, DC, MC, V. Thurs–Mon 7:30–10pm. Closed Dec–Mar.

Restaurant Le Saint-Jean FRENCH This friendly bistro is an excellent budget option if you want to experience a fine Carcassonne cassoulet. Hearty dishes are served either in the modern interior or on the bustling terrace, with a view of Château Comtal. It's very popular with locals, so be sure to book a table ahead, even if only a few hours in advance. When the summertime festivals fill the streets, jazz and salsa bands play in the square in front.

1 place St-Jean. ✆ **04-68-47-42-43.** www.le-saint-jean.eu. Reservations recommended. Main courses 13€–24€; fixed-price menu 11€–24€. MC, V. Daily 9am–11pm (closed Tues in low season).

WHERE TO EAT NEARBY

Château St-Martin ★ FRENCH It's worth venturing to this 16th-century château at Montredon, 4km (2½ miles) northeast of Carcassonne, for excellent French food served in a charming country setting. The château is surrounded by a wooded park, and guests can dine either inside the cozy dining room or on the terrace, where you can enjoy lovely country views. The restaurant serves the superb cuisine of co-owners Jean-Claude and Jacqueline Rodriguez. Dishes might include sea bass with scallop mousseline, sole in tarragon, cassoulet Languedocien (made with pork, mutton, and goose or duck), or *bouillinade nouvelloise* (made with an assortment of seafood that includes scallops, sole, and turbot). On the premises are 15 simple but comfortable rooms (doubles 85€–120€); call ✆ **04-68-47-44-41** for information on rooms. The hotel is closed mid-November to mid-March.

Montredon, 11090 Carcassonne. ✆ **04-68-71-09-53.** Fax 04-68-25-46-55. www.chateausaintmartin.net. Reservations required. Fixed-price menu 33€–57€. AE, DC, MC, V. Thurs–Tues noon–1:30pm; Thurs–Sat and Mon–Tues 7:30–9:30pm. From La Cité, follow signs pointing to Stade Albert Domec 4km (2½ miles) northeast.

PERPIGNAN ★

904km (562 miles) SW of Paris; 369km (229 miles) NW of Marseille; 64km (40 miles) S of Narbonne

At Perpignan you might think you've crossed the border into Spain, for it was once Catalonia's second city after Barcelona. Even earlier it was the capital of the kingdom of Majorca. But when the Roussillon—the French part of Catalonia—was finally partitioned off, Perpignan became permanently French by the Treaty of the Pyrénées in 1659. A large portion of its population descends from Catalan refugees who fled Francoist Spain during its civil war in the 1930s. You'll still find some Catalan spoken here today.

Legend has it that Perpignan derives its name from Père Pinya, a plowman who followed the Têt River down the Pyrénées mountains to the site of the town today, where he cultivated the fertile soil while the river kept its promise to water the fields.

Today Perpignan is content to rest on its former glory. Its 120,000 residents enjoy the closeness of the Côte Catalane (the coastline of Catalonia, in neighboring Spain)

castelnaudary: BIRTHPLACE OF CASSOULET

Carcassonne and Toulouse, in the neighboring region of Midi-Pyrénées, might argue over who makes the best cassoulet, but even they can't deny that this rich dish didn't originate in either city but in a small town midway between the two: Castelnaudary.

Cassoulet is a staple of southwest France, a hearty stew of white beans, garlic, pork sausage, pork belly, and preserved duck legs, usually served in a rustic terra-cotta dish. It's said to have originated sometime in the 14th century in Castelnaudary, a small, sleepy town along the Canal du Midi, southeast of Toulouse. Legend has it that while the town was being besieged during the Hundred Years War, its defenders threw all of their remaining food into one pot to give them enough sustenance to carry on fighting. It obviously worked. Nowadays, the official ingredients of the dish are guarded by the Grande Confrérie du Cassoulet de Castelnaudary, a brotherhood of cassoulet lovers and chefs who dress in ceremonial robes during town festivals to celebrate, among other things, cassoulet.

Castelnaudary is a popular stop along the Canal du Midi, thanks to its large pleasure port. It's also home to several cassoulet factories where you can buy tins of this tasty dish, as well as takeout versions from local butchers. Arguments rage over the best restaurant to eat cassoulet, but it's worth trying **Le Tirou** at 90 av. Monseigneur de Langle (✆ **04-68-94-15-95;** www.letirou.com).

For information about Castelnaudary, contact the local **Office de Tourisme,** place de la République (✆ **04-68-23-05-73;** www.castelnaudary-tourisme.com).

and the mountains to the west. The pace is relaxed in the streets of the old town, where people gather in the cafes along the riverside place Arago.

Essentials

GETTING THERE **Perpignan-Rivesaltes airport** (✆ **04-68-52-60-70;** www.aeroport-perpignan.com; airport code PGF) has **flights** from Paris, Dublin, and London, as well as other U.K. cities such as Manchester and Southampton. Shuttle buses make the 5km (3 miles) journey into central Perpignan in 15 minutes. **Trains** arrive from Paris, Montpellier, Marseille, and Narbonne; for rail information and schedules, call ✆ **36-35,** or visit www.voyages-sncf.com. Perpignan is well connected to the region's towns by **bus,** which is operated by **CTPM** at 27 bd. Clemenceau (✆ **04-68-61-01-13;** www.ctpmperpignan.com). The city is also part of a bus network that charges only 1€ per journey, going as far south as Cerbère by the Spanish border. For more information, call ✆ **04-68-80-80-80,** or go to www.cg66.fr. If you're **driving** from the French Riviera, drive west along A9 to Perpignan.

VISITOR INFORMATION The **Office Municipal du Tourisme** is in the Palais des Congrès Georges Pompidou, place Armand Lanoux (✆ **04-68-66-30-30;** fax 04-68-66-30-26; www.perpignantourisme.com). There is also a tourist information office in place Arago.

SPECIAL EVENTS In the heat of July during a 4-week cultural binge, **Les Estivales** (✆ **04-68-66-33-54;** www.lesestivalesdelarchipel.org) causes the city to explode with music, dance, theater, and circus acts. Perpignan is host to one of the most widely discussed celebrations of photojournalism in the industry, the **Festival International du Photojournalisme** (✆ **04-68-62-38-00;** www.visapourlimage.com). Established in the late 1980s, it's also called **Le Visa pour l'Image.** From late August to mid-September, at least 10 sites of historic (usually medieval) interest are devoted to photojournalistic expositions from around the world as photographers and journalists descend on the city.

Exploring the Town

Castillet/Musée des Arts et Traditions Populaires Catalans ★ The Castillet is one of the chief sights of Perpignan. The machicolated and crenelated red-brick building from the 14th century is both a gateway and fortress. It houses the museum, also known as La Casa Pairal, which contains exhibitions of Catalan regional artifacts and folkloric items, including typical dress. Part of the charm of the Castillet derives from its bulky-looking tower, which you can climb for a good view of the town.

Place de Verdun. ✆ **04-68-35-42-05.** Admission 4€ adults, 2€ students and children 17 and under. May–Sept Wed–Mon 10am–6:30pm; Oct–Apr Wed–Mon 11am–5:30pm.

Cathédrale St-Jean-Baptiste ★ The cathedral dates from the 14th and 15th centuries and has an admirable nave and interesting 17th-century retables (altarpieces). Leaving through the south door, you'll find on the left a chapel with the *Devost-Christ (Devout Christ)*, a magnificent woodcarving depicting Jesus contorted with pain and suffering, his head, crowned with thorns, drooping on his chest. Sightseeing visits are discouraged during Sunday Mass.

Place Gambetta. ✆ **04-68-51-33-72.** Free admission. Daily 7:30am–6pm.

Palais des Rois de Majorque (Palace of the Kings of Majorca) ★ At the top of the town, the Spanish citadel encloses the Palace of the Kings of Majorca. The government has restored this structure, built in the 13th and 14th centuries, around a court encircled by arcades. You can see the old throne room, with its large fireplaces, and a square tower with a double gallery and a fine view of the Pyrénées. A free guided tour, in French only, departs four times a day if demand warrants it.

Rue des Archers. ✆ **04-68-34-48-29.** Admission 4€ adults, 2€ students, free for children 11 and under. June–Sept daily 10am–6pm; Oct–May daily 9am–5pm.

A MAJOR HISTORIC SITE NEARBY

Château de Salses ★ This important historic site is in the hamlet of Salses, 15km (9 miles) north of the city center. Since the days of the Romans, this fort has guarded the main road linking Spain and France. Ferdinand of Aragón erected a fort here in 1497 to protect the northern frontier of his kingdom. This Spanish-style fort, designed by Ferdinand himself, is a curious example of an Iberian structure in France. In the 17th century, it was modified by the French military engineer Vauban to look more like a château. After many changes of ownership, Salses fell to the forces of Louis XIII in September 1642, and its Spanish garrison left forever. Less than 2 decades later, Roussillon was incorporated into France.

Salses, 15km (9 miles) north of the center of Perpignan. ✆ **04-68-38-60-13.** Admission 7€ adults, 4.50€ ages 17–25, free for children 16 and under. Oct–May daily 10am–12:15pm and 2–5pm; June–Sept daily 9:30am–7pm. From Perpignan, follow signs to Narbonne and RN9.

PERPIGNAN'S beaches

Near Perpignan, there are 34km (21 miles) of wide sandy beaches from Port Bacarès in the north down to Argelès-sur-Mer in the south, at which point the smooth sand gives way to the rocky coast and inlets of the Côte Vermeille, which continues to Spain.

The closest beach to Perpignan is **Canet-en-Roussillon**, which you can reach in about 35 minutes; to get there, take the No. 1 bus, which leaves regularly from Perpignan's SNCF railway station. Other nearby beach resorts include **La Bacarès, Torreilles-Plage,** and **Sainte-Marie-Plage,** all of which can be reached by bus from Perpignan. A car would be more useful if you want to head further south to the sleepier resort of **St-Cyprien-Plage** and the biggest and buzziest of them all, **Argelès-Plage.** However, there is an excellent bicycle path that connects Canet with Argelès. For information about the coastal resorts, contact the Pyrénées-Orientales **Office de Tourisme,** 16 av. des Palmiers, Perpignan (✆ **04-68-51-52-53;** www.tourisme-pyreneesorientales.com).

Shopping

With its inviting storefronts and pedestrian streets, Perpignan is a good town for shopping. For one of the best selections of Catalan pottery, furniture, and carpets, and even a small inventory of antiques, visit the **Centre Sant-Vicens,** rue Sant-Vicens (✆ **04-68-50-02-18;** www.santvicens.fr), site of dozens of independent merchants. You'll find it 4km (2½ miles) southeast of the town center, following the signs pointing to Cabestany. In the town center, **La Maison Quinta,** 3 rue des Grande des Fabriques (✆ **04-68-34-41-62;** www.maison-quinta.com), sells Catalan-inspired items for home decorating.

Place République is where the main **food market** is on Wednesday, Saturday, and Sunday mornings as well as Friday afternoons. It's also worth a stroll down the lively **rue de la Poissonnerie,** where fish sellers vie for attention with delis and bars where the customers enjoy their morning glass of wine with a plate of Serrano ham.

Where to Stay

Hôtel de la Loge This beguiling little place dating from the 16th century has been renovated into a modern hotel. It's located right in the heart of town, near the Castillet and Loge de Mer, the town hall, from which it takes its name. The cozy rooms are attractively furnished, with a sense of warmth and hospitality. The bathrooms are small but adequate.

1 rue des Fabriques d'en Nabot, 66000 Perpignan. www.hoteldelaloge.fr. ✆ **04-68-34-41-02.** Fax 04-68-34-25-13. 22 units. 50€–70€ double; 65€–80€ triple. AE, MC, V. **Amenities:** Bar; smoke-free rooms. *In room:* A/C, TV, hair dryer, minibar (some), Wi-Fi (free).

Hôtel New Christina This modern three-star hotel is the only one in central Perpignan to have a swimming pool—that's quite an asset in one of France's hottest cities. Rooms are average size and simply furnished, but the combination of a rooftop swim and very friendly staff makes up for it.

51 cours Lassus, 66000 Perpignan. www.hotel-newchristina.com. ✆ **04-68-35-12-21.** Fax 04-68-35-67-01. 25 units. 93€–105€ double. MC, V. Parking 9€. **Amenities:** Bar; pool (outdoor); Jacuzzi (12€). *In room:* A/C, TV, hair dryer, minibar (some), Wi-Fi (free).

La Villa Duflot ★★ Tranquillity, style, and refinement reign in this four-star hotel that offers luxury for a very good value. Located in a suburb 4km (2½ miles) from Perpignan, La Villa Duflot is a Mediterranean-style dwelling surrounded by a park of pine, palm, and eucalyptus. You can sunbathe in the gardens surrounding the pool and order drinks from the outside bar. The good-sized rooms surround a patio planted with century-old olive trees. All are spacious and soundproof, with marble bathrooms and Art Deco interiors. The restaurant (below) is reason enough to stay.

Rond-Point Albert Donnezan, 66000 Perpignan. www.villa-duflot.com. ✆ **04-68-56-67-67.** Fax 04-68-56-54-05. 24 units. 150€–190€ double; 210€–275€ suite. AE, DC, MC, V. From the center of Perpignan, follow signs to Perthus-Le Boulou and A9, and travel 3km (1¾ miles) south. **Amenities:** Restaurant; 2 bars; babysitting; pool (outdoor); room service. *In room:* A/C, TV, hair dryer, minibar, Wi-Fi (free).

Where to Eat

L'Assiette Catalane CATALAN This boisterous restaurant is as Catalan as it comes, with rugby and flamenco posters, hand-painted ceramic plates, and antique farm implements covering the thick stone walls. Even the long, lively bar is inlaid with Iberian mosaics, and copies of works by Dalí and Picasso hang from the wall. Dishes include stuffed squid, *boles de picolat* (Catalan meatballs), and *pareillade* (mixed grill) of fish served on a hot slab of iron brought directly to your table.

9 rue de la République. ✆ **04-68-34-77-62.** www.assiettecatalane.com. Main courses 12€–18€; fixed-price dinner 16€–27€. AE, MC, V. Mon–Sat noon–2pm; Wed–Mon 7:15–10:30pm.

La Table MEDITERRANEAN Located down the street from the bustle of the fish market in a quiet lane, this restaurant serves up Mediterranean fare in a cozy atmosphere, with its stone walls and heavy ceiling beams. Its refined Mediterranean dishes include tuna tartare, turbot with summer truffles, grilled giant shrimps sautéed in cognac, and slow-roasted leg of lamb in a thyme crust. Tables spill out into the tiny lane on warm summer evenings.

5 rue de la Poissonnerie. ✆ **04-68-28-53-21.** www.latable-restaurant.com. Main courses 21€–32€; fixed-price dinner 25€–37€. MC, V. Tues–Sat noon–2pm and 7–11:30pm (10:30pm Thurs).

La Villa Duflot ★ FRENCH Slightly removed from the city center, André Duflot's top-notch chefs turn out dish after dish with remarkable skill. Try, for example, a salad of warm squid, a platter of fresh anchovies marinated in vinegar, excellent duck foie gras, or lasagna of foie gras with asparagus points. A wonderful dessert is chocolate cake with saffron-flavored cream sauce.

In La Villa Duflot (see above), Rond-Point Albert Donnezan, 66000 Perpignan. ✆ **04-68-56-67-67.** Fax 04-68-56-54-05. Reservations required. Main courses 19€–25€; Sat–Sun fixed-price menu 31€. AE, DC, MC, V. Daily noon–2pm and 8–11pm. From the center of Perpignan, follow signs to Perthus-Le Boulou and A9, and travel 3km (1¾ miles) south. Just before you reach A9, you'll see the hotel.

Le Calao CATALAN/TAPAS Lively yet ultramodern, this tapas bar offers up a wide array of tapas, including chorizo or razor clams, as well as more substantial Mediterranean dishes, including plates of brochettes that come with giant shrimp, duck, beef, or chicken.

48 rue des Augustins. ✆ **04-68-59-42-12.** www.lecalao.fr. Fixed-price dinner 18€–26€. MC, V. Tues–Sat noon–2pm and 7–10:30pm.

Perpignan After Dark

Perpignan's nightlife centers on its cafes, especially in the summer and during festivals. Evenings often begin with an aperitif and tapas at one of the bars in place Arago by the waterside. **Café Vienne** at no. 3 (✆ **04-68-34-80-00**) and **Brasserie l'Arago** at no. 1 (✆ **04-68-51-81-96**) are popular choices. The pedestrianized place de la Loge buzzes in the evenings when the outside terraces are full to bursting. Revelers flit between **Le Grand Café de la Bourse** at no. 2 (✆ **04-68-34-25-05**) and **Le France** (✆ **04-68-51-61-71**), directly opposite.

COLLIOURE ★★★ & THE CÔTE VERMEILLE ★★

929km (577 miles) SW of Paris; 27km (17 miles) SE of Perpignan

It's easy to see why the early-20th-century Fauvist painters were attracted to this rocky coastline dotted with vineyards, and to its charming port town of Collioure. The vivid blue-green of the Mediterranean, the clear azure skies, and the deep red sunsets that gave the coast its vermilion name inspired painters such as Matisse and Derain. Today, you can even follow their trail in Collioure's winding streets, where replicas of paintings, such as those depicting Matisse's views of Collioure and Derain's seascapes, are strategically placed right where the artists would have painted them, either on the nearest wall or on iron easels. Even if you're not a fan of art, it is difficult to resist the beauty of this port village. Its sloping, narrow streets, charming semifortified church, antique lighthouse, pretty beaches, and generally agreeable ambience make it an inviting place to visit. It's also a major center for the production of anchovies, which you can buy directly from the fishermen and producers in the port. Its market, on Wednesday and Sunday mornings, is one of the most picturesque in the region.

Essentials

GETTING THERE Collioure has frequent **train** and bus service, especially from Perpignan. For train information and schedules, call ✆ **36-35,** or visit www.voyages sncf.com. Collioure is also on the 1€ **bus** route that goes from Perpignan. Many visitors **drive** along the coastal road (RN114) leading to the Spanish border.

VISITOR INFORMATION The **Office de Tourisme** is on place du 18 Juin (✆ **04-68-82-15-47;** fax 04-68-82-46-29; www.collioure.com).

SPECIAL EVENTS Every August, the village celebrates the festival of its patron saint, **St. Vincent,** with 4 days of dancing, concerts, games, and competitions on the water. A bullfight and fireworks take place halfway through the festival.

Exploring the Town

The two curving ports sit on either side of the heavy masonry of the 13th-century **Château Royal,** place de 8 Mai 1945 (✆ **04-68-82-06-43**). It's of interest in its own right for its medieval fortifications and overall bulk, but it's also the home to a changing series of special (temporary) exhibitions. Entrance fees are 4€ for adults, 2€ for students and children ages 12 to 18, and free for children 11 and under. From June to September, the château is open daily 10am to 5:15pm (6:15pm July–Aug), and from October to May it is open daily 9am to 4:15pm.

The **Musée d'Art Moderne,** route de Port-Vendres (✆ **04-68-82-10-19**), is home to a collection of works by artists who painted here, including Picasso, Matisse, Dufy, Chagall, and Derain. It's open in July and August daily 10am to noon and 2 to 7pm, September to June Wednesday to Monday 10am to noon and 2 to 6pm. Admission is 2€ for adults, 1.50€ for children 12 to 16 and students, and free for children 11 and under.

Several companies run trips in colorful **fishing boats** along the coast, which can take anywhere from 15 minutes to 2 hours. The tourist office has details of fares and timetables.

Where to Stay

Casa Païral ★ This wonderfully tranquil family-operated hotel, located in a 150-year-old Catalan house, is just a short walk from the port. In the guest rooms, charming antiques blend with more modern pieces, with some rooms echoing the style of the 1930s or 1950s. The best doubles have *petit salons* and small balconies. On sunny days, guests can take a dip in the pool shaded by the luxuriant garden's century-old trees.

Impasse des Palmiers, 66190 Collioure. www.hotel-casa-pairal.com. ✆ **04-68-82-05-81.** Fax 04-68-82-52-10. 27 units. 89€–269€ double. AE, DC, MC, V. Parking 16€. Closed Nov–Mar. **Amenities:** Breakfast room; pool (outdoor); room service. *In room:* A/C, TV, hair dryer, minibar, Wi-Fi (free).

Hôtel le Relais des Trois Mas ★★ This four-star hotel offers fabulous views of Collioure and the bay beyond. Each of the individually decorated guest rooms is named after an artist who once lived in Collioure, with rooms dedicated to Picasso, Matisse, Dalí, and Derain. The rooms, which have spacious bathrooms with whirlpool baths, open onto views of the water. Even if you aren't a guest, you might want to have a meal in the Michelin-starred restaurant, La Balette (see review below).

Rte. de Port-Vendres, 66190 Collioure. www.relaisdes3mas.com. ✆ **04-68-82-05-07.** Fax 04-68-82-38-08. 23 units. 100€–220€ double; 190€–340€ suite. Half board available. AE, MC, V. Free parking. Closed Dec–Feb. **Amenities:** Restaurant; babysitting; pool (indoor); room service; sauna; Wi-Fi (free). *In room:* A/C, TV, hair dryer, minibar.

Hôtel Princes de Catalogne This relatively modern hotel is only 100m (328 yards) from the beach, and is run by a hardworking and cooperative staff. The simple yet contemporary guest rooms are surprisingly spacious for the price and location. The free parking the hotel offers can be a bit chaotic, so be prepared for double and triple parking at times.

Rue des Palmiers, 66190 Collioure. ✆ **04-68-98-30-00.** Fax 04-68-98-30-31. www.hotel-princes catalogne.com. 30 units. 55€–145€ double. AE, MC, V. Free parking. **Amenities:** Bar; room service. *In room:* A/C, TV, minibar, hair dryer; Wi-Fi (free).

Le Bon Port Built during the 1940s, this stucco-sided hotel perches beside the port, across the water from the town center, which is within a 5-minute walk. It offers comfortable, appealingly simple bedrooms with summery furniture, tiled floors, and flowered upholsteries. Accommodations are scattered among three separate buildings, the smallest of which is a two-unit cabana set beside the swimming pool. It's worth paying extra for a room with a private terrace.

12 rte. de Port-Vendres, 66190 Collioure. www.bon-port.com. ✆ **04-68-82-06-08.** Fax 04-68-82-54-97. 22 units. 79€–108€ double; 105€–135€ triple; 150€–180€ quad. MC, V. **Amenities:** Bar; babysitting; Internet (free); pool (outdoor). *In room:* A/C (in some), TV.

Where to Eat

La Balette FRENCH The harborside setting is as enticing as the inventive dishes served in this Michelin-starred restaurant, located in the Hôtel le Relais des Trois Mas. The creative cuisine pairs local ingredients with unexpected preparations: Collioure anchovies are turned into sushi, local fish are paired with creamy risotto, and roasted lamb is infused with fresh thyme and served over a rich chickpea purée.

Rte. de Port-Vendres. ✆ **04-68-82-05-07.** www.relaisdes3mas.com. Fixed-price dinner 39€–90€. AE, MC, V. Open daily noon–2pm and 7–10:30pm from Apr–Sept; closed all day Mon and lunchtimes Tues–Wed from Oct–Mar.

L'Arcade PIZZERIA This friendly pizzeria set under a canopy of plane trees in a charming little central square offers good food at a decent price. Pizzas are generous, with thin bases and plenty of Spanish-inspired toppings such as Serrano ham and chorizo. *Moules marinières* (mussels cooked in a white wine sauce) and grilled fish, among other dishes, are also on offer.

24 rue Vauban. ✆ **04-68-82-40-66.** Main courses 8.50€–22€; set menu 20€. MC, V. Daily noon–3pm and 7–10pm.

Le Puits CATALAN Named after its kitchen's now-sealed-off well *(le puits)* that used to provide water for houses nearby, this is a small-scale and charming restaurant that makes special efforts in its preparation of time-honored Catalan specialties. The dining room is accented with exposed beams and soft tones of red and orange, with an additional dozen seats lined up beside the all-pedestrian street in front. Come here for calamari stew prepared with Banyuls wine; stuffed mussels; and tuna steak in Catalan (tomatoes, onions, and peppers) sauce.

2 rue Arago. ✆ **04-68-82-06-24.** Reservations recommended. Main courses 17€–29€; fixed-price menus 17€–35€. MC, V. Daily 11:30am–3pm and 6:30–10:30pm (closed Thurs Oct–May).

Le Trémail CATALAN/SEAFOOD Set on a narrow, cobble-stoned alleyway in the oldest part of Collioure, this is a rustic and authentically Catalan restaurant. Surrounded by stone walls, hand-painted Spanish tiles, and dangling fishing nets, and located less than 18m (60 ft.) from the edge of the sea, the specialty here is grilled fish *(à la plancha)*, invariably served with olive oil and herb-enriched vinaigrette. Try the marinated anchovies with braised onions and peppers, and a succulent version of the day's catch.

16 bis, rue Mailly. ✆ **04-68-82-16-10.** Reservations recommended. Main courses 13€–28€; set menu 16€–35€. AE, DC, MC, V. Daily noon–3pm and 7–10pm (until 11pm June–Oct).

Neptune ★★★ FRENCH/CATALAN One of Collioure's best restaurants is easygoing and remarkably unpretentious. You'll find Neptune on the southeastern edge of town in a salmon-toned farmhouse facing the sea. Main courses change with the seasons but have included several versions of lobster, rack of suckling lamb with fresh thyme, and beef tenderloin in a rich Collioure red-wine sauce.

9 rte. de Porte-Vendres. ✆ **04-68-82-02-27.** www.leneptune-collioure.com. Reservations recommended. Main courses 21€–54€; fixed-price menus 38€–79€. AE, MC, V. Wed–Mon noon–2pm and 7:30–9pm.

Restaurant Can Pla CATALAN Hearty Catalan cuisine is served with great warmth in this hospitable and cozy restaurant with a lively terrace. Most things turn up on the grill, including large platters of crayfish, clams, squid, razor clams, and large shrimp, as well as meaty plates of grilled rabbit, lamb chops, and giant sausages.

7 rue Voltaire. ✆ **04-68-82-10-00.** Reservations recommended. Main courses 13€–44€; set menu 18€–33€. MC, V. Daily noon–2pm and 7–10pm.

Side Trips from Collioure

PORT-VENDRES

A 5-minute drive southeast from Collioure takes you to the bustling fishing port of Port-Vendres. You won't find the beauty of Collioure, although the houses clustering around the quayside are in typically southern French pastel shades of yellow and ocher, with terra-cotta tiles covering the rooftops. What you will find is an authentic slice of marine life, where fishing is still a major industry. You can see this firsthand at the Saturday morning market in the port, where stalls sell fish and seafood just off the boats. If you miss the Saturday market, visit the huge indoor seafood market at **Les Poissonneries de la Côte Catalane** (✆ **04-68-98-46-00;** www.cotecatalane.com) near the fish auction, La Criée, on the northern side of the port. Here you will find an enormous range of seafood, an excellent wine selection, an oyster bar, and a wide range of prepared seafood dishes including paella.

One of the best restaurants among the many lining the quay is **Le Chalut,** at No. 8 (✆ **04-68-82-00-91**). This friendly family-run business puts as much care into its 15€ menu as it does its oyster extravaganza for 95€. So you can enjoy mussels, whelks (sea snails), or Catalan cod in a Banyuls wine sauce without paying a fortune.

Port-Vendres was home to the renowned Scottish designer and architect **Charles Rennie Mackintosh** (1868–1928), who spent the last few years of his life living here—he said it was the happiest time in his life. Rather than join the painters in nearby Collioure, he stayed in Port-Vendres to capture the village in a series of watercolors. A permanent exhibition of his life is featured in the **Jardins du Dôme.** Opening times vary but are generally 3pm to 7pm Tuesday, Wednesday, and Friday; visit www.crmackintoshfrance.com for information.

The **Office de Tourisme** is at 1 quai François Joly (✆ **04-68-82-07-54;** www.port-vendres.com).

BANYULS-SUR-MER

Drive another 6km (4 miles) south from Port-Vendres and you quickly reach this pretty little seaside village, where the beach curves in one large arc in front of the waterside restaurants and bars. The sight of vineyard after vineyard clinging to vertiginous terraces will give you a clue as to how Banyulencs occupy themselves when not swimming or diving in the waters that were France's first marine reserve. Banyuls is home to a sweet wine that is usually drunk as an aperitif or with dessert, as well as fruity reds and whites. You can visit *caves* (vineyards) in the village, or have a tour and a tasting in the atmospheric cellars of **Cellier des Templiers,** a large cooperative of wine growers just outside the village on route des Mas Reig (✆ **04-68-98-36-92;** www.banyuls.com).

A visit to **Domaine St-Sébastien,** 10 av. du Fontaulé (✆ **04-68-88-30-14**), a nearby winery, starts with a boat ride along the Côte Vermeille before a tour of the cellars, followed by a wine tasting in the restaurant's panoramic dining room, and finally lunch in its olive tree-shaded garden. Banyuls is the birthplace of French sculptor **Aristide Maillol** (1861–1944); some of his works are placed around the village. His former house in the countryside outside Banyuls has been turned into a museum, where his sculptures celebrating the female form are on display along with temporary exhibitions of other artists' work. The museum, called the **Fondation Dina Vierny,** is at Vallée de la Roume (✆ **04-68-88-57-11;** www.musee-maillol.com).

Hôtel des Elmes, Plages des Elmes (✆ **04-68-88-03-12;** www.hotel-des-elmes.com), a three-star Logis de France hotel, is in an enviable location at the northern entrance to Banyuls, with its own stretch of beach right in front. Its good-size rooms are furnished in a cool, contemporary style, and some have balconies facing the sea; doubles range from 48€ to 129€. The hotel is home to a well-regarded restaurant called **La Littorine.**

The **Office de Tourisme** is at 4 av. de la République (✆ **04-68-88-31-58;** www.banyuls-sur-mer.com). They have information on guided tours of the village and the surrounding countryside, boat trips along the coast, scuba diving, as well as directions to the other beaches just south of the village.

CÉRET ★

875km (544 miles) SW of Paris; 34km (21 miles) SE of Perpignan

The attractive town of Céret is known for two things: cherries and Cubism. Located in the Vallespir Valley, its microclimate between the Pyrénées and the Mediterranean has given birth to countless cherry orchards that are somehow sheltered from the *tramontane,* the brutal wind of the Languedoc-Roussillon region. This unofficial cherry capital of France generally provides the first fruits of the spring. When the Catalan sculptor Manolo Hugué (1872–1945) came to live in Céret in 1910, it wasn't long before his artist friends followed—initially Picasso and Braque, and then later Matisse, Dufy, and Chagall. The town was also a place of refuge for those fleeing fascist Spain from the 1930s onwards. Today people are drawn here for its pleasantly bustling atmosphere: Cafes line the main boulevard, and the town hums with people and activity. This is a bit of a rarity in southern France, where the populations of many villages have dwindled as people departed for the cities.

Essentials

GETTING THERE Regular **buses** run from Perpignan to Céret, ending at rue du 19 Mars on the northwestern edge of the town; contact ✆ **04-68-80-80-80** or www.cg66.fr for schedules. If **driving,** take the A9 south from Perpignan before exiting at Le Boulou and heading west on the D115 towards Céret.

VISITOR INFORMATION The **Office de Tourisme** is at 1 av. Clemenceau (✆ **04-68-87-00-53;** www.ot-ceret.fr).

SPECIAL EVENTS Céret celebrates its Catalan soul every July with its 2-day **Féria.** The streets fill with music, dancing, food and wine stalls, as well as the bulls that are on their way to fight in the *corridas.* Later that same month is the **Festival de Sardanes,** 3 days of revelry when everyone pays homage to the traditional Catalan dance.

Exploring the Town

Tip: Ask at the tourist office for a map of the town showing where the artists drew their inspiration, with reproduction paintings marking the spot.

Musée d'Art Moderne de Céret The main attraction in Céret, this museum was created in 1950 from the legacy of all those artists who had lived or even just passed through the town. Natural light floating through the modern building illuminates vivid paintings by Picasso, Dufy, Gris, Chagall, Matisse, as well as temporary exhibitions.

8 bd. Maréchal Joffre, Céret. ✆ **04-68-87-27-76.** www.musee-ceret.com. Admission 8€ adults, 6€ students, free for children ages 11 and under; admission for just the permanent collection is 5.50€ for adults and 3.50€ students. Daily 10am–6pm (until 7pm July–Sept); closed Tuesday from October to April.

Where to Stay

Hôtel des Arcades This friendly family-run two-star hotel offers great value in a central location right in front of one of the town's ancient gateways. The rooms are basic but of a decent size and comfortable. Eight of the rooms have kitchenettes, which are ideal for weekly rentals. The hotel also hosts an exhibition of works by passing artists.

1 place Pablo Picasso, 66400 Céret. www.hotel-arcades-ceret.com. ✆ **04-68-87-12-30.** Fax 04-68-87-49-1044. 30 units. 49€–53€ double; 76€–82€ triple; 350€–415€ weekly rental for apts. MC, V. Parking 6€. **Amenities:** Breakfast room. *In room:* A/C (some), TV; kitchenettes (in apts).

Hôtel le Mas Trilles ★ Located about 4km (2½ miles) west of Céret is this relaxing hotel, set in a 17th-century Catalan manor house and surrounded by beautiful grounds near the Tech River. All of the elegantly furnished rooms have a private terrace or small patio, and the ones on the upper floors have enchanting views of the Pyrénées and the Pic du Canigou. Hammocks and lounge chairs are laid out invitingly in the garden for lazy days.

Le Pont de Reynès, 66400 Reynès. www.le-mas-trilles.com. ✆ **04-68-87-38-37.** Fax 04-68-87-42-62. 10 units. 93€–217€ double. MC, V. Free parking. Closed Nov–Easter. **Amenities:** Breakfast room; pool (outdoor, heated); room service. *In room:* TV, Wi-Fi (free).

Hôtel Vidal Formerly an 18th-century bishop's house, this handsome little hotel offers great charm and value, so don't be misled by its one-star status. Rooms are colorful and of a good size, with reproduction antiques. The ones overlooking the square can be a bit noisy, so ask for a room overlooking the courtyard in the back. Its restaurant, Del Bisbe, is excellent (see below).

4 place Soutine, 66400 Céret. www.hotelceret.com. ✆ **04-68-87-00-85.** Fax 04-68-87-62-33. 9 units. 40€ double. MC, V. **Amenities:** Restaurant.

Where to Eat

La Fontaine CATALAN/FRENCH Although it appears to be just an average French restaurant, La Fontaine is actually a pleasingly old-fashioned place that serves French classics with a few Catalan twists. You'll find Catalan meatballs and *pain à la catalane* (grilled bread with tomatoes, garlic mayonnaise, onions, and ham) on the menu, as well as solidly good plates of *confit de canard,* escargots, and roast lamb.

10 place des Neuf-Jets. ✆ **04-68-87-23-47.** Main courses 8.50€–14€; fixed-price menus 15€–19€. MC, V. Wed–Mon noon–2pm and 7:30–9pm.

Le Pied dans le Plat CATALAN/FRENCH Located in one of Céret's most pleasant squares, this cheerful restaurant offers a mix of Catalan and French dishes. So along with grilled duck breasts, carpaccio of scallops, or pan-fried foie gras, come plates of anchovies and Serrano ham with grilled peppers, spicy Catalan meatballs, and a rich cuttlefish stew. Meals are served either in the shady square, near the large fountain, or in the cozy stone–lined dining room.

9 place des Neuf-Jets. ✆ **04-68-87-17-65.** Main courses 12€–25€; fixed-price menus 20€–32€. MC, V. Daily 11:30am–3pm and 6:30–10:30pm.

Restaurant del Bisbe FRENCH The Hôtel Vidal's (see above) tree-shaded stone terrace is the lovely setting for the Restaurant del Bisbe. The attentive staff serves up uncomplicated but delicious French dishes. The menu is kept simple, which leaves time to devote care to dishes such as grilled scallops served with leeks, duck breast with Céret cherries, and roasted cod in a light garlic cream.

4 place Soutine, in the Hôtel Vidal. ✆ **04-68-87-00-85.** www.hotelceret.com. Main courses 13€–25€; set menu 18€–34€. MC, V. Sept–June Thurs–Mon noon–2pm and 7–10pm; Jul–Aug Thurs–Tues noon–2pm and 7–10pm.

NARBONNE ★

845km (525 miles) SW of Paris; 61km (38 miles) E of Carcassonne; 93km (58 miles) S of Montpellier

Medieval Narbonne was a port to rival Marseille in Roman days. It was the first town outside Italy to be colonized by the Romans, but the Mediterranean, now 8km (5 miles) away, left it high and dry. Its medieval heyday was followed by several centuries of natural disasters as well as the usual ravages of the plague. However, prosperity began to creep back to the area in the 19th century, when winemaking became an important part of the economy. That hasn't changed, as the wine industry today is what helps to keep this attractive town afloat. Too far from the sea to be considered a beach town (although there is a beachfront suburb, Narbonne-Plage), Narbonne attracts history buffs who come here to explore its rich historic sites and try to capture its glorious past. Some 50,000 Narbonnais enjoy the relaxed pace of life along the banks of the **Canal de la Robine,** an offshoot of the Canal du Midi, where boats lazily drift along the water. Its covered food market, **Les Halles,** is one of the best in the region to shop for seasonal local produce.

Essentials

GETTING THERE Narbonne is easily accessible via train from Perpignan, Toulouse, or Montpellier; you can also take the high-speed TGV directly from Paris to Narbonne; for **rail** information, call ✆ **36-35** or visit www.voyages-sncf.com. **Bus** service is minimal and geared toward resident travelers. If you're **driving,** Narbonne is at the junction of A61 and A9, easily accessible from either Toulouse or the Riviera.

VISITOR INFORMATION The **Office de Tourisme** is 31 rue Jean-Jaurès (✆ **04-68-65-15-60;** fax 04-68-65-59-12; www.narbonne-tourisme.com).

Exploring the Town

THE CENTRAL COMPLEX

The town's sights are concentrated in the medieval Vieille Ville (Old City), a massive central labyrinth of religious and civic buildings. You can pay 4€ for each attraction, but if you're planning to visit more than one site, it makes more sense to purchase a Pass Monuments et Musées, a combination ticket that is valid for 15 days and allows admittance to seven of the town's museums; the pass costs for 9€ for adults and 6€ for students and seniors. Entrance to any of the central museums is free for children 10 and under.

The neo-Gothic **Hôtel de Ville (Town Hall)** in the complex was reconstructed by Viollet-le-Duc, the 19th-century architect who refurbished Notre-Dame in Paris and Le Cité in Carcassonne. Directly in front of the Hôtel de Ville is a large expanse of exposed stone. This is a remnant of the **Via Domitia,** the vast road the Romans constructed around 118 B.C. to run from Italy to Spain.

Cathédrale St-Just ★★ The cathedral's construction began in 1272, but it was never finished. Only the transept and a choir were completed. The choir is 40m (130 ft.) high, built in the bold Gothic style of northern France. At each end of the transept are 59m (194-ft.) towers from 1480. The cathedral also holds an impressive collection of Flemish tapestries and is connected to the archbishop's palace by 14th- and 15th-century cloisters.

Place de l'Hôtel-de-Ville (enter on rue Gauthier). ✆ **04-68-09-30-65.** Free admission. June–Sept daily 10am–7pm; Oct–May daily 9am–noon and 2–6pm.

Donjon Gilles Aycelin A watchtower and prison in the late 13th century, it has a lofty observation platform with a view of the cathedral, the surrounding plain, and the Pyrénées. If you're up for it, take a hike up the steep steps of the watchtower for superb views.

Place de l'Hôtel de Ville. ✆ **04-68-90-30-30.** Admission 4€. Apr to mid-July Wed–Mon 10am–noon and 2–5pm; mid-July to Oct daily 10am–1pm and 2:30–6pm; Nov–Mar Wed–Mon 2–5pm.

Palais des Archevêques (Archbishop's Palace, or Vieux-Palais) This palace was conceived as part fortress, part pleasure residence. It has three military-style towers from the 13th and 14th centuries. The Old Palace on the right dates from the 12th century, and the so-called "New Palace" on the left dates from the 14th. It's said that the old, arthritic, and sometimes very overweight archbishops used to be hauled up the interior's monumental Louis XIII–style stairs on mules.

Today the once-private apartments of the former bishops contain three museums. The **Musée Archéologique ★** contains prehistoric artifacts, Bronze Age tools, 14th-century frescoes, and Greco-Roman amphorae. Several of the sarcophagi date from the 3rd century, and some of the mosaics are of pagan origin. The **Musée d'Art et d'Histoire** is located three floors above street level in the archbishop's once-private apartments (the rooms where Louis XII resided during his siege of Perpignan). Their coffered ceilings are enhanced with panels depicting the nine Muses. A Roman mosaic floor and 17th-century portraits are on display, as well as a collection of antique porcelain, enamels, and a portrait bust of Louis XIV. In the **Horreum Romain** is a labyrinth of underground passageways, similar to catacombs but without burial functions, dug by the Gallo-Romans and their successors for storage of food and supplies during times of siege.

Place de l'Hôtel de Ville. ✆ **04-68-90-30-65**. Admission 4€. Apr to mid-July Wed–Mon 10am–noon and 2–5pm; mid-July to Oct daily 10am–1pm and 2:30–6pm; Nov–Mar Wed–Mon 2–5pm.

MORE SIGHTS

Basilique St-Paul-Serge This early Gothic church was built on the site of a 4th-century necropolis. It has an elegant choir with fine Renaissance woodcarvings and ancient Christian sarcophagi. The chancel, from 1229, is admirable. The north door leads to the Paleo-Christian Cemetery, part of an early Christian burial ground.

Rue de l'Hôtel-Dieu. ✆ **04-68-32-68-98.** Free admission. Apr–Sept daily 9am–7pm; Oct–Mar daily 9am–noon and Mon–Sat 2–6pm.

Musée Lapidaire Located in the 13th-century Notre-Dame de Lamourguier, this museum contains an important collection of Roman artifacts—broken sculptures and Latin inscriptions—as well as relics of medieval buildings. While it has no major exhibits, it does offer a vast array of classical busts, Roman lintels, and ancient sarcophagi. You can enter with your general admission ticket to the museums of the archbishop's palace.

Place Lamourguier. ✆ **04-68-65-53-58.** Admission 4€. Apr to mid-July Wed–Mon 10am–noon and 2–5pm; mid-July to Oct daily 10am–1pm and 2:30–6pm; Nov–Mar Wed–Mon 2–5pm.

Where to Stay

Hôtel de France Just a few steps away from the large covered market of Les Halles, this friendly hotel is located on a quiet street that's still right near the town's main attractions. Housed in a 19th-century townhouse, this hotel offers decent-size rooms that are tastefully furnished in a traditional manner. The hotel offers very good value considering its great location in the town center.

6 rue Rossini, 11100 Narbonne. www.hotelnarbonne.com. ✆ **04-68-32-09-75.** Fax 04-68-65-50-30. 16 units. 55€–73€ double. MC, V. **Amenities:** Breakfast room. *In room:* A/C, TV, hair dryer, Wi-Fi (free).

Hôtel le Régent This charming little hotel has an unexpected bonus for a two-star hotel: a roof terrace with lounge chairs and lovely views stretching across the city and the surrounding countryside. The standard rooms are extremely basic in decor, so it's worth spending a bit extra for the room with a terrace or one of the two rooms that open onto the lovely garden.

13 rue Suffren, 11100 Narbonne. www.leregent-narbonne.com. ✆ **04-68-32-02-41.** Fax 04-68-65-50-43. 15 units. 40€–60€ double. MC, V. Parking 6€. **Amenities:** Rooftop terrace; breakfast room. *In room:* TV, Wi-Fi (free).

La Résidence For more than 40 years, this 19th-century converted townhouse has been welcoming guests to its central location near the Cathédrale St-Just. It has undergone regular renovations, which have brought more comfort to its elegant and spacious rooms. The style is simple, with pale tones and reproduction antiques. Its cozy bar is the scene for occasional wine tastings. Ask to see its "golden book" of guests' comments: You'll find everyone there from ex-presidents (François Mitterrand) to actors (Jean Marais).

6 rue du 1er Mai, 11100 Narbonne. www.hotelresidence.fr. ✆ **04-68-32-19-41.** Fax 04-68-65-51-82. 26 units. 80€–145€ double. AE, DC, MC, V. Parking 7.50€. Closed Jan–Mar. **Amenities:** Bar; breakfast room. *In room:* A/C, TV, hair dryer, minibar, Wi-Fi (free).

Where to Eat

Chez Bébelle FRENCH Chez Bébelle is one of the many cafes clustered around the food stalls of Les Halles, Narbonne's large covered market. But this one is different: As you order your meat dish from the limited menu, the owner booms the order through a megaphone to the nearest butcher, who then chucks the package over the heads of the diners. It's quite a spectacle, and very popular with locals, so book your table in the morning for lunch that day.

Les Halles, 1 bd. du Docteur Ferroul. ✆ **06-85-40-09-01.** Reservations required. Dishes 10€. No credit cards. Daily 6am–2pm.

La Table St-Crescent ★★ FRENCH This highly respected, Michelin-starred restaurant serves up exquisite dishes. Located east of town, in a complex of wine-tasting boutiques established by a local syndicate of growers, it's believed that the foundations of the building date from the 8th century, when the building was used as a small chapel. The menu changes seasonally, but the food remains fresh and delicious. You may find dishes such as slow-roasted pork shoulder with Iberian ham and a Parmesan tartlet, cuttlefish cannelloni with oysters, or macaroni stuffed with foie gras and artichokes.

In the Palais des Vins, 68 av. Général Leclerc, rte. de Perpignan. ✆ **04-68-41-37-37.** www.la-table-saint-crescent.com. Reservations recommended. Main courses 24€–41€; fixed-price dinner and Sun lunch 48€–79€. AE, DC, MC, V. Tues–Fri and Sun noon–1:30pm; Tues–Sat 8–9:30pm.

Méli-Mélo ★ FRENCH The name of this restaurant—which loosely translates to "hodge-podge"—suits it perfectly: It's a delightful mishmash of a lively bistro and a higgledy-piggledy antiques shop. From the dining room, you can see the wood-fired grill through a glass window, so you can watch your main course—perhaps brochettes of scallops or giant shrimp—cook while you enjoy a starter or a drink. After an evening spent in this genial atmosphere, you might be tempted to buy one of the antiques.

6 rue du Lion d'Or. ✆ **04-68-65-89-76.** Reservations recommended. Main courses 12€–28€; fixed-price dinner 18€–30€. MC, V. Mon–Sat 7:30–10pm.

Restaurant le Cottage FRENCH This friendly restaurant is tucked away in a tiny square, where the tables spill out in good weather. You'll find solid French staples, such as salad with goat cheese or *confit de canard,* on the menu, but if you're feeling more adventurous, opt to grill your own food on a *brasérade* (a table-top barbecue).

50 passage de l'Ancien Courrier. ✆ **04-68-49-30-47.** Main courses 15€–18€; fixed-price dinner and Sun lunch 40€–79€. MC, V. Tues–Sat noon–1:30pm and 7:30–10:30pm.

Restaurant l'Ecrevisse d'Alsace FRENCH This is one of Narbonne's most enjoyable restaurants. Despite the restaurant's name, the cuisine here isn't from Alsace-Lorraine, but is typical of southwestern France, with an extra focus on seafood: Dishes include sea perch baked whole in a bed of coarse sea salt or scallops tartare. The comfortable, English-style dining room has plenty of wood paneling and a glass-enclosed patio. It's located across from the train station.

1 av. Pierre Sémard. ✆ **04-68-65-10-24.** www.restaurant-narbonne.com. Reservations recommended. Main courses 14€–40€; fixed-price menus 20€–60€. AE, DC, MC, V. Thurs–Sat and Mon–Tues 11am–2pm and 6–11pm.

BÉZIERS ★

758km (471 miles) SW of Paris; 234km (145 miles) W of Marseille; 71km (44 miles) SW of Montpellier; 93km (58 miles) N of Perpignan

Because of its strategic position on the **Canal du Midi,** Béziers is a popular stop for the thousands of visitors who sail, hike, or cycle along this vast waterway. Béziers has had its share of tribulations in the course of its long history—it was the site of the Cathar Crusade that resulted in the deaths of thousands of heretic Cathars in the 13th century. But today Béziers focuses on other things, namely wine production from its many surrounding vineyards, as well as rugby and bullfighting. Its old town is an alluring maze of narrow winding streets that eventually lead to the plateau overlooking the Orb Valley, home of the impressive 13th-century Cathédrale St-Nazaire.

Essentials

GETTING THERE **Trains** from Paris, Barcelona, Montpellier, Sète, and Perpignan arrive at the SNCF station south of the town on boulevard de Verdun. For information and train schedules, call ✆ **36-35,** or visit www.voyages-sncf.com. **Buses** run in and around Béziers as well as to local beaches, including Valras-Plage. For bus information, call **Bus Occitan** at ✆ **04-67-28-36-41.** Béziers has a small **airport** 12km (8 miles) east of the city, which is connected by regular shuttle buses. Depending on the season, flights arrive from Beauvais near Paris, as well as destinations in the U.K., Scandinavia and Germany.

VISITOR INFORMATION The **Office de Tourisme** is at 1 bd. du Président Wilson (✆ **04-67-76-20-20;** fax 04-67-11-09-09; www.beziers-mediterranee.com).

SPECIAL EVENTS The city lights up every mid-August for the **Féria.** For 4 days, everyone joins in for street festivals, music, dancing, and, most importantly, bullfighting.

Exploring the Town

The magnificent **Cathédrale St-Nazaire** has been in its majestic position overlooking the Orb River since the 13th century, when it was rebuilt after the Albigensian crusade. Two austere fortified towers flank the enormous rosette window. To enter the stark interior, you can go through the cloister that eventually leads to the beautiful 14th-century gardens that belonged to the bishops, the **Jardin des Evêques.** The views of the river and the countryside beyond are captivating. The cathedral is open from 9am to 5:30pm in the summer and from 9am to noon and 2:30pm to 5:30pm in the winter; the cloister is open from 10am to 7pm May to September, and from 10am to noon and 2 to 5:30pm October to April.

Béziers pays homage to its favorite son, Canal du Midi inventor Pierre-Paul Riquet, with the **allées Paul-Riquet,** a long, tree-shaded esplanade on the edge of the old town. It's a pleasant place for a stroll past its many cafes, and it's also the bustling setting for the **Friday morning market.** At the bottom of the promenade is the romantic greenery of the **Plateau des Poètes.** Created in the 19th century in the "English" style, this tranquil spot offers cool lawns, mossy ponds, arbors, fountains, and sculptures.

Where to Stay

For a city of more than 72,000, Béziers is surprisingly lacking in accommodations. There is nothing above a three-star property, and many of the hotels are part of chains such as Mercure, Etap, and Formule 1.

Hôtel des Poètes Overlooking the peaceful expanse of the Plateau des Poètes is this friendly two-star hotel run by a particularly helpful owner. The rooms are quite basic, with simple Ikea-style furniture, and the showers could be a tight squeeze for some guests. But the welcome is warm, and there are even free bicycles you can borrow for leisurely rides along the Canal du Midi.

80 allées Paul Riquet, 34500 Béziers. www.hoteldespoetes.net. ✆ **04-67-76-38-66.** Fax 04-67-76-25-88. 14 units. 45€–85€ double. AE, MC, V. Parking (6€). **Amenities:** Breakfast room; bike rentals (free). *In room:* A/C, TV, hair dryer, Wi-Fi (free).

Hôtel Impérator It's hard to get more central than this handsome 19th-century three-star hotel located along the wide tree-shaded expanse of the allées Paul Riquet. The rooms are a bit on the old-fashioned side, and some have a few too many frills, but they're of a good size and the ones overlooking the busy street are soundproofed. A courtyard garden in the back is a delightful place to relax, and the staff is very pleasant.

28 allées Paul Riquet, 34500 Béziers. www.hotel-imperator.fr. ✆ **04-67-49-02-25.** Fax 04-67-28-67-28-92-50. 45 units. 65€–120€ double. AE, MC, V. Parking 10€. **Amenities:** Bar; breakfast room; room service. *In room:* A/C, TV, Wi-Fi (free).

Where to Eat

Chez Toi, Chez Moi 🎁 FRENCH This cozy and unpretentious restaurant near the cathedral is an absolute delight. While chef Sammy cooks in the kitchen with its wood-fired oven, Martine greets and serves guests. She'll cheerfully bring out tasty dishes such as *parmentier de canard* (slow-cooked duck with mashed potatoes), prime beef, or lamb chops grilled on the wood fire.

32 rue Viennet. ✆ **04-67-28-00-00.** Fixed-price dinner 14€. MC, V. Mon–Sat noon–2pm and 7–10pm.

Le Cep d'Or FRENCH Slightly more expensive than Chez Toi, Chez Moi but no less intimate is this perennial Béziers favorite. The friendly, efficient staff serves hearty dishes such as a delicious rabbit pie, chicken supreme with tiny shrimps, and grilled hake with creamy mashed potatoes.

7 rue Viennet. ✆ **04-67-49-28-09.** Fixed-price dinner 17€–22€. MC, V. Tues–Sat noon–2pm and 7–10pm.

Octopus ★ FRENCH One of Béziers' two restaurants with a Michelin star, Octopus serves up excellent French cuisine in an elegant, yet relaxed setting—diners can opt to sit in the sophisticated dining room or the charming courtyard patio. Award-winning chef Fabien Laurent concocts exquisite and innovative dishes, such as bergamot-flavored sole with artichoke chips, and squid or lamb sweetbreads with asparagus. If you're up for it, you can even order an entire roast suckling pig.

12 rue Boieldieu. ✆ **04-67-49-90-00.** www.restaurant-octopus.com. Main courses 28€–50€; fixed-price dinner 30€–90€. AE, MC, V. Daily noon–1:45pm and 7–9:45pm. Closed last 2 weeks of Aug and Dec 24–Jan 3.

PÉZENAS ★

734km (456 miles) SW of Paris; 39km (24 miles) S of Lodève; 24km (15 miles) NE of Béziers; 22km (13 miles N of Agde

This attractive town between Béziers and Montpellier was briefly home to Molière in the 17th century, and it won't let you forget it, especially during its summertime festival celebrating France's greatest playwright. Pézenas doesn't need the Molière connection, however, to entice you to visit its medieval- and Renaissance-era splendors. Medieval walls surround the old town, which is a maze of narrow, pedestrian streets filled with artisans' workshops, boutiques, and cafes. The newer part of town surrounding the center still dates from the 17th to the 19th century, so there's plenty of history to savor. Vineyards surround this part of the Languedocian plain, and numerous *caves* are happy to offer wine tastings. The Saturday market, which runs all day, is one of the biggest and liveliest in the region and includes a large number of stalls selling organic produce.

Essentials

GETTING THERE Local **buses** connect Pézenas with Béziers and St-Jean-de-Védas, which connects to Montpellier via a tramway; visit **www.herault-tranport.fr** for bus information. If you're **driving** from the north, take the A75; from the east or west, take the A9 and exit at Agde-Bessan.

THE agde TRIANGLE

An ancient market town, a seaside fishing port, and the world's largest nudist colony—these three distinctly different entities make up the towns of **Agde, Le Grau d'Agde,** and **Cap d'Agde,** respectively. Between the three, there's something for everyone.

Agde, which sits where the Canal du Midi crosses the Hérault River, was founded in Phoenician times. Its 12th-century **St-Etienne cathedral** looks more like a fortress than a church, with defensive walls 3m (10ft) thick. A walk up the belltower rewards you with views of the town and the surrounding vineyards. Agde is a relatively quiet place, with pleasant riverside cafes and an enormous **market** that takes over much of the town every Thursday. Its **Musée Agathois,** rue de la Fraternité (✆ **04-67-94-82-51**), recreates life in the town from prehistoric days to the present, and demonstrates the major role played by its long fishing tradition.

A few minutes' drive south along the Hérault River—or an even more enjoyable bicycle journey along the riverside path—takes you to **Le Grau d'Agde.** In contrast to the summertime madness that descends on its Cap d'Agde neighbor, Le Grau d'Agde is an old-fashioned fishing village with its own decent-size Mediterranean beach on one side and boats that offer leisurely cruises along the Hérault River. A little ferry takes you across the river to Plage de la Tamarissière, a wide stretch of beach in a protected area backed by pine groves.

In comparison with the simpler charms of Agde and Le Grau d'Agde, **Cap d'Agde** can look a little soulless. This modern resort's architecture is quite bland, lifted somewhat by the profusion of palm trees and brightly colored flowers. Contrary to what many people believe, its status as the world's largest nudist colony has little bearing on day-to-day life beyond the designated **Quartier Naturiste Cap d'Agde** (✆ **04-67-26-00-26;** www.agdenaturisme.com). In this clearly signposted area at the northeastern side of the resort, nudity is required on the beach and expected in the shops and restaurants. Those who arrive on foot at the compound's gate pay 5€ for entrance; motorists pay 10€. In the other three-quarters of Cap d'Agde, life goes on as in other French beach resorts, with marinas filled with sleek boats, watersports, beaches, and children's play areas, which include the **Aqualand** water theme park.

The **Office de Tourisme** in Agde is in rue Jean Roger (✆ **04-67-62-91-99;** www.ville-agde.fr). The office in Cap d'Agde is at Rond-point Bon Accueil (✆ **04-67-01-04-04;** www.capdagde.com).

VISITOR INFORMATION The **Office de Tourisme** is at place des Etats du Languedoc (✆ **04-67-98-36-40;** fax 04-67-98-96-80; www.pezenas-tourisme.fr).

SPECIAL EVENTS The **Molière festival** in June or July takes over the town with open-air productions, street theater, and fireworks. Pézenas also holds a major **carnival** in February to celebrate the last few days before Lent.

Exploring the Town

The greatest pleasure in Pézenas is strolling around the tangle of streets in the **old town,** where centuries collide in the richness of its architectural history. You never quite know when you're about to peer through an open doorway and see a Renaissance stone staircase swooping under vaulted ceilings. It was a substantial center of trade during the Middle Ages, when the reputation of the town's craftspeople was known all over the region. That tradition carries on, with today's generation of skilled artisans creating beautiful objects out of glass, wood, ceramics, and other materials. You can see their *ateliers* (workshops) as you wander through the narrow streets, and on warm days some will take their work outside. Street names hark back to the days when you could tell instantly what was being sold there: Impasse Fromagerie Vieille (Old Cheese Shop), for example, and rue Triperie Vieille (Old Tripe Shop) won't leave you in suspense for long.

The work of 17th-century playwright Jean-Baptiste Poquelin, better known as **Molière,** is celebrated in the cultural complex set up in the Hôtel Peyrat (which also houses the tourist office). **Scénovision** (✆ **04-67-98-35-39;** www.scenovision moliere.com; admission 7€) evokes life in the 17th century through 3D films and multimedia displays, giving a glimpse into the sights—and even the smells—of the time.

Where to Stay

There is an unusual lack of hotels in Pézenas, and the few hotels that exist are of inferior quality. The best bets are B&Bs, or *chambres d'hôtes,* listed below.

La DorDîne This small but charming B&B is located in an area that once was a 14th-century Jewish ghetto in the old town. Owners Véronique and Aurélien have transformed this 14th-century village house into a cozy *chambres d'hôtes* with atmospheric interior stone walls. Bear in mind that the room in the attic has a low ceiling, and two of the other rooms share a bathroom. Breakfast is a convivial affair, starring Véronique's homemade goodies. The couple also hosts wine-tasting evenings in the vaulted cellar, with local delicacies to go with neighborhood vintages.

9 rue des Litanies, 34120 Pézenas. www.ladordine.com. ✆ **04-67-90-34-81.** 5 units. 44€–54€ double. Rates include breakfast. MC, V. **Amenities:** Breakfast room. *In room:* TV, Wi-Fi (free).

Hôtel de Vigniamont ★ Book early to nab one of the five luxurious bedrooms in this handsome B&B set in a 17th-century *hôtel particulier* (an old mansion). The rooms wind their way up a stone staircase surrounding an interior courtyard, and the hotel has a roof terrace with chaise lounges. The individually designed rooms are immensely comfortable, stylish, and include such thoughtful touches as a small bottle of wine, water, and fresh fruit on arrival. Guests are invited to join the aperitif hour every evening, where you can share a drink and snacks with the bubbly hostess, Babette. If you're not feeling sociable, she'll send it to your room instead.

5 rue Massillon, 34120 Pézenas. www.hoteldevigniamont.com. ✆ **04-67-35-14-88** or 06-12-87-75-32. 5 units. 95€–120€ double; 140€ suite. Rates include breakfast. MC, V. **Amenities:** Breakfast room; bar; room service. *In room:* TV, hair dryer, Wi-Fi (free).

Villa Juliette It's only a few minutes' walk from the town center, but the peace and tranquillity behind the gates of this B&B make the town seem a world away. The airy, unfussy rooms have wrought-iron bedsteads, some with a canopy, others with views over the colorful gardens and the swimming pool.

6 chemin de la Faissine, 34120 Pézenas. www.villajuliette.com. ✆ **04-67-35-25-38** or 06-61-19-82-17. 5 units. 74€–99€ double; 149€–179€ suite. Rates include breakfast. MC, V. Free parking. **Amenities:** Breakfast room; pool (outdoor). *In room:* A/C, TV.

Where to Eat

L'Entre Pots ★ FRENCH Located in a converted warehouse, L'Entre Pots is one of the most attractive restaurants in Pézenas, with two elegant dining rooms as well as a little deli at the entrance. Menus depend on the season and what the chefs have been able to source from local suppliers. In the summer you might find grilled giant shrimp with a tomato-and-Parmesan risotto on the menu, while the spring menu may include tuna grilled with cuttlefish and chorizo. When the weather is warm, book ahead to secure a table in the romantic Italian-style courtyard.

8 av. Louis Montagne. ✆ **04-67-90-00-00.** www.restaurantentrepots.com. Reservations recommended. Fixed-price dinner 21€–29€. MC, V. Tues–Sat noon–1:30pm and 8–9:30pm.

Le Pré Saint-Jean ★ FRENCH This refined restaurant offers up excellent cuisine that takes advantage of some of the best southern French ingredients. Innovative dishes include saddle of rabbit with *chichoumeille,* a Languedoc dish of eggplant, tomatoes, and garlic; lamb sweetbreads with *girolle* mushrooms and lamb brochettes; and a fricassee of scallops and giant shrimp.

18 av. Maréchal Leclerc. ✆ **04-67-98-15-31.** www.restaurant-leprestjean.fr. Reservations recommended. Main courses 16€–26€; fixed-price dinner 25€–45€. MC, V. Tues–Sun noon–2pm; Tues–Sat 7:30–10pm (closed Thurs evening Sept–June).

Mamita MEDITERRANEAN/TAPAS This cozy tapas restaurant, located in the old town, offers friendly service and a cheerful setting in its dining room with stone-vaulted ceilings. Enjoy tapas of grilled mussels and plates of Serrano ham or more substantial main courses, including sea bass or cuttlefish *à la plancha* (grilled), or slow-cooked lamb shank that falls off the bone.

10 rue Mercière. ✆ **04-67-93-49-75.** Tapas from 5€; main courses 15€–34€. No credit cards. Tues–Sun noon–2pm; Tues–Sat 7:30–10pm (closed Thurs evening Sept–June).

LODÈVE ★

695km (432 miles) SW of Paris; 98km (61 miles) SW of Alès; 63km (39 miles) N of Béziers; 60km (37 miles) S of Millau.

Drive north of Pézenas for less than half an hour and you soon feel that you've left the heat of the Languedoc behind. Forested hills and gorges start to appear, telling you that you're very close to the dramatic landscapes of the Parc Régional du Haut Languedoc. Lodève is at the confluence of two rivers, the Lergue and the Soulondre. It has a history that stretches back to Roman days when Nero used to mint his coins here. Its next shot at prosperity came during the Middle Ages when it was a center for the woolen cloth industry. Nowadays Lodève benefits from its proximity to **Lac du Salagou,** an enormous man-made lake 10km (6 miles) south that is the water-sports and outdoor-pursuits playground of this part of the Languedoc. Hiking and cycling trails abound throughout the vivid ocher landscape, and the aquatics center on the lake is the place to rent small boats and windsurfing boards.

Essentials

GETTING THERE **Buses** arrive from Montpellier and Clermont l'Hérault to the **gare routière** (bus station) beside the tourist office; visit www.herault-transport.fr

for bus information. If you're **driving,** take the A75 south from Paris or north from Montpellier.

VISITOR INFORMATION The **Office de Tourisme** is at 7 place de la République (✆ **04-67-88-86-44;** fax 04-67-88-07-56; www.lodeve.com).

Exploring the Town

Lodève isn't very big (about 7,000 people), but it packs in a few sights. Its most arresting is the **Cathédrale Saint-Fulcran** in place de l'Hôtel de Ville, which has 6th-century foundations but was built mainly during the 13th and 14th centuries. It's an impressive example of Gothic architecture, with a large chancel and, in a side chapel, the final resting place for 84 bishops of Lodève. The church makes a magnificent backdrop for the choral concerts that are held throughout the year.

The 16th- to 17th-century mansion formerly belonging to the Cardinal de Fleury has since become home to Lodève's main museum, **Musée Fleury,** at square Georges Auric (✆ **04-67-88-86-10**). Within this handsome building are two distinct collections: one displaying the archaeological history of Lodève, the other exhibiting works by artists including Braque, Dufy, Soutine, and Léger, as well as temporary exhibitions. Admission is 7€ adults; 5.50€ students; free for children 11 and under. It's open Tuesday through Sunday 10am to 6pm.

Just 8km (5 miles) east of Lodève is a wonderfully preserved marvel of the Middle Ages: the 12th-century **Prieuré St-Michel de Grandmont** (✆ **04-67-44-09-31;** www.prieure-grandmont.fr). Although it is worth coming here just to see the priory's beautifully stark architecture and cloisters, the main reason to visit is to explore the 35 hectares (86 acres) of surrounding parkland, where you'll find a series of ***dolmens,*** megalithic tombs dating from 2,000 B.C. On a clear day you can even see the Mediterranean coastline from the top of the hill. The priory is also a popular place for summertime events, including concerts, markets, and organized walks through the hills. Guided visits cost 6.20€ adults and 3.80€ children. It's open daily 10am to 3pm January to May; 10am to 4pm October to December; and 10am to 5pm June to September.

Where to Stay

Hôtel de la Paix This hotel has been run by five generations of the same family since the 19th century. Styles vary throughout the spacious rooms, with some rooms decorated in bright southern French colors and others in muted contemporary tones. The Moroccan-style courtyard garden is a pleasant place to relax, particularly when it's warm enough to swim. It also has a highly regarded restaurant (see Restaurant de la Paix below).

11 bd. Montalangue, 34700 Lodève. www.hotel-dela-paix.com. ✆ **04-67-44-07-46.** Fax 04-67-44-30-47. 23 units. 55€–78€ double; 80€–150€ suite. MC, V. Parking 8€. **Amenities:** Restaurant; bar; pool (outdoor); Wi-Fi (free). *In room:* A/C (some), TV, hair dryer. Closed Feb and last 2 weeks of Nov.

Hôtel du Nord This simple yet friendly two-star hotel is a favorite with hikers who use Lodève as a base to explore the countryside. Rooms are functional but clean, and some have mezzanine levels and kitchenettes that can sleep up to five people. On warm days, breakfast is served on the large courtyard terrace.

18 bd. de la Liberté. www.hotellodeve.com. ✆ **04-67-44-10-08.** Fax 04-67-44-92-78. 25 units. 49€–60€ double; 63€–130€ triples and suite. MC, V. Parking 9€. **Amenities:** Breakfast room; Wi-Fi (free). *In room:* A/C, TV, kitchenette (in some).

Where to Eat

Le Petit Sommelier FRENCH A pleasingly old-fashioned Parisian bistro has somehow landed in Lodève. The atmosphere is convivial, both in the cozy interior and on the lively terrace, as French classics such as *confit de canard,* grilled steak, or thyme-encrusted lamb are served. But southern flavors creep in, too, with mussels in a Banyuls wine sauce or *supions* in parsley (mini-squid-like creatures found in the Mediterranean).

Place de la République, 34700 Lodève. ✆ **04-67-44-05-39.** Main courses 18€–26€. MC, V. Tues, Wed–Sun noon–2pm; Thurs–Sat 7–9pm.

Restaurant de la Paix FRENCH The Hôtel de la Paix's elegant dining room attracts people from all over the area, especially wine aficionados eager to try the large selection of regional vintages. But the menu is enough of a draw on its own: Try a delicious crème brûlée made with Roquefort cheese, squid in a saffron sauce with a garlicky chili paste, or leg of lamb in a light mint sauce. On warm evenings and at lunch, meals are served in the colorful Moroccan-style courtyard garden beside the pool.

11 bd. Montalangue, 34700 Lodève. ✆ **04-67-44-07-46.** Reservations recommended. Main courses 14€–18€; fixed-price dinner 25€–50€. MC, V. Sept–June Wed and Fri–Sun noon–2pm, Tues–Sun 7:30–10pm; July–Aug daily noon–2pm and 7:30–10pm. Closed 3 weeks in Mar and 2 weeks in Oct.

MONTPELLIER ★★

758km (471 miles) SW of Paris; 161km (100 miles) NW of Marseille; 50km (31 miles) SW of Nîmes

The capital of Languedoc, the medieval university city of Montpellier is renowned for its medical school, founded in the 13th century. Nostradamus qualified as a doctor here, and Rabelais studied at the school. Petrarch came to Montpellier in 1317 and stayed for 7 years. Today Montpellier is one of southern France's most dynamic and fastest-growing cities, and it continues to expand, particularly in its business district of Port Marianne. The city's handsome old town, also known as Ecusson, has tree-flanked promenades, ancient monuments, and winding medieval lanes that lead to small squares filled with numerous cafes. Its population is one of the youngest in France, thanks to the large number of students who give the city a lively feel. It's also just a short bus ride from the Mediterranean, where the beaches at Palavas-les-Flots, Maguelone, and Carnon are ringed with wetlands and flocks of pink flamingoes.

Essentials

GETTING THERE **Montpellier Méditerranée Airport** (www.montpellier.aeroport.fr) is 11km (7 miles) southeast from the center and has flights from Paris, Great Britain, Spain, Germany, and North Africa, among other destinations. **Trains** arrive regularly from Avignon, Marseille, Toulouse, Perpignan, and other towns. The city is on the TGV line that goes from Paris to Perpignan and eventually to Barcelona. The St-Roch SNCF station is a few minutes' walk south of the old town. For rail information, call ✆ **36-35,** or visit www.voyages-sncf.com. Regular shuttle buses connect the airport with the city center.

Montpellier has an efficient **tramway** system that continues to expand. Visit www.montpellier-agglo.com/tam for details. The **bus station** is at 1 rue du Grand St-Jean

(✆ **04-67-92-01-43**), with buses covering most of the towns in the Hérault region. Visit www.herault-transport.fr for timetables.

If you're **driving,** Montpellier is off the A9.

VISITOR INFORMATION The **Office de Tourisme** is at 30 allée Jean de Latte de Tassigny (✆ **04-67-60-60-60;** fax 04-67-60-60-61; www.ot-montpellier.fr). Ask for details about the Montpellier City Card, which gives discounts and/or free entry to many of the city's sights and public transport. The tourist office also organizes English-language guided tours of the old town, including visits to private mansions and other sights that are normally closed to the general public.

SPECIAL EVENTS From late June to early July, **Montpellier Danse** attracts leading dancers from around the world for a festival of dance. For tickets, contact **Montpellier Danse,** 18 rue Ste-Ursule (✆ **08-00-60-07-40** or 04-67-60-83-60; www.montpellierdanse.com). During July's **Festival de Radio France et Montpellier** (✆ **04-67-02-02-01;** www.festivalradiofrancemontpellier.com), you can see classical music, world music, jazz, and electronic music.

Exploring the Town

Scores of cafes and restaurants fill the many squares of Montpellier, but the largest is **place de la Comédie,** with its opulent 18th-century opera house and fountain of the Three Graces. It's the living room of Montpellier where people gather to chat and people-watch. At its easternmost end, you will often find market stalls set up throughout the week selling seasonal organic produce.

The **Jardin des Plantes,** boulevard Henri IV (✆ **04-67-63-43-22;** www.jardindesplantes.univ-montp1.fr), which opened in 1593, is the oldest botanical garden in France. Shaded by trees and filled with exotic plants, it's a delightful place for a cooling walk on a hot summer's day. It's reached from boulevard Henri IV. Admission is free. It's open June to September, Tuesday to Sunday from noon to 8pm, and October to May, Tuesday to Sunday from noon to 6pm.

The town's greatest attraction is **Musée Fabre ★★**, 2 rue Montpelliéret (✆ **04-67-14-83-00;** http://museefabre.montpellier-agglo.com), one of France's great provincial art museums. The collection originated when Napoleon sent Montpellier an exhibition of the Royal Academy in 1802. François-Xavier Fabre, a Montpellier painter, contributed its most important works in 1825. After Fabre's death, other paintings from his collection were donated to the gallery. Several were his own creations, but the more significant works were ones he had acquired—including Poussin's *Venus and Adonis.* The museum continued to grow and now has an extensive collection of Flemish, French, and Italian works from the 15th to the 20th centuries, including works by Courbet, Dufy, and de Staël. One of the most riveting works is Jean-Antoine Houdon's life-size sculpture of Voltaire. Admission is 6€ for adults and 4€ for students and youths ages 7 to 20, free for children 6 and under. Admission is free for everyone on the first Sunday of every month.

Nearby is the town's spiritual centerpiece, the **Cathédrale St-Pierre,** on place St-Pierre (✆ **04-67-66-04-12**), founded in 1364. It suffered badly in centuries of religious wars and revolutions, and for a long time after 1795 it wasn't a cathedral at all, but was occupied by a medical school. Its greatest architectural achievement is its unusual canopied porch, supported by two conical turrets. The best artworks inside are 17th-century canvases in the transepts—notably the work of a Huguenot, Montpellier-born Sébastien Bourdon, who painted himself among the "heathen" in

Montpellier

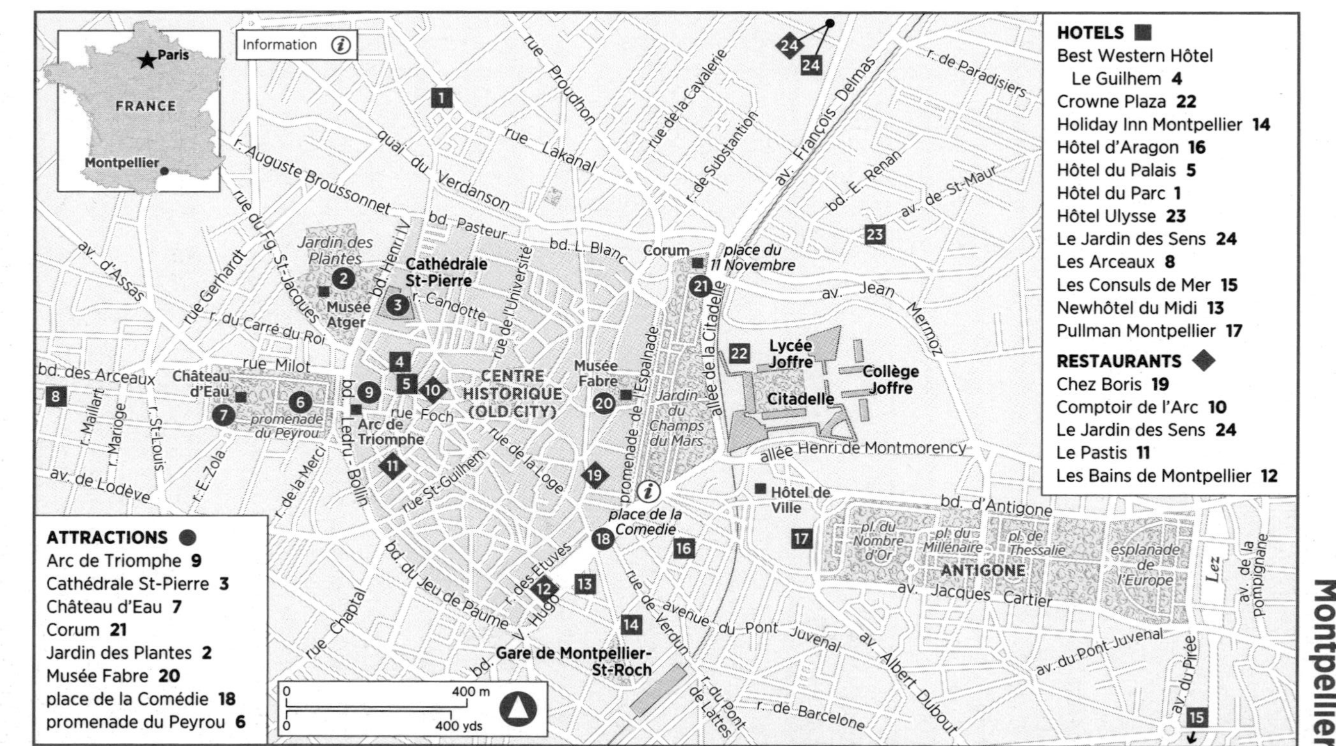

The Fall of Simon Magnus. Also moving is Jean Troy's *Healing of the Paralytic*. The church can be visited daily from 9am to noon and 2 to 7pm.

Take a leisurely stroll along the 17th-century **promenade du Peyrou ★★**, a terraced park with views of the Cévennes. This is a broad esplanade constructed at the loftiest point of Montpellier. Opposite the entrance is an **Arc de Triomphe,** erected in 1691 to celebrate the victories of Louis XIV. In the center of the promenade is an equestrian statue of Louis XIV and, at the end, the **Château d'Eau,** a pavilion with Corinthian columns that serves as a monument to 18th-century classicism. Water is brought here by a conduit, nearly 14km (8¾ miles) long, and an aqueduct.

Shopping

At the southeastern end of **place de la Comédie** is the ultramodern **Polygone** shopping center, site of more than 120 independent boutiques. For traditional regional delicacies, visit **Pâtisserie aux Gourmets,** 2 rue Clos-René (✆ **04-67-58-57-04**), or visit **Pâtisserie Scholler,** 121 av. Lodève (✆ **04-67-75-71-55**), for a plentiful supply of Ecusson de Montpellier (almond cream with Grand Marnier wrapped in chocolate).

Where to Stay

IN MONTPELLIER

Expensive

Crowne Plaza ★★ Opened in 2011, the four-star Crowne Plaza hotel is Montpellier's newest high-end chain hotel. Located just outside of the old city walls, near the Corum convention center and the Musée Fabre, the Crowne Plaza is right near the city's main attractions but far enough removed from the sometimes rowdy streets to ensure a peaceful night's sleep. Each floor in this modern hotel is inspired by a different continent—for example, you'll see Chinese lanterns on the floor devoted to Asia and zebra prints on the floor devoted to Africa. Guest rooms are spacious and modern, with bright splashes of color, sleek contemporary furniture, and internationally inspired design elements.

190 rue d'Argencourt, 34000 Montpellier. www.crowneplaza.com/montpellier. ✆ **04-67-72-22-22.** Fax 04-67-72-44-64. 142 units. 225€–250€ double; 450€ suite. AE, DC, MC, V. Parking 11€. **Amenities:** Restaurant; bar; concierge; exercise room; pool (outdoor); room service; smoke-free rooms. *In room:* A/C, TV, hair dryer, minibar, Wi-Fi (free).

Le Jardin des Sens ★★★ The boutique hotel owned by Montpellier's Michelin-starred twin chefs, Jacques and Laurent Pourcel, is an attractive four-star hotel about a mile north of the old town. Its stylish guests rooms, including two suites, have been designed in cutting-edge yet refined style. One of the suites has a private terrace and its own pool, but all guests can relax in the pool and the Jacuzzi set within the pretty gardens.

11 av. St-Lazare. www.jardindessens.com. ✆ **04-99-58-38-38.** Fax 04-99-58-38-39. 15 units. 170€–280€ double; 310€–480€ suite. AE, DC, MC, V. Free parking. **Amenities:** Bar; restaurant; room service; swimming pool (outdoor). *In room:* A/C, TV, hair dryer, minibar, Wi-Fi (free).

Pullman Montpellier ★ A few minutes away from the place de la Comédie is this ultramodern, ultracomfortable hotel. Most of the top floor is taken up by a swimming pool and a panoramic restaurant, which offers great views over Montpellier. Extensive renovations have given this business hotel a sleek, contemporary look, with splashes of bold colors and king-size beds. You enter via the Polygone shopping center, so be sure to ask staff how to get back in at night when the center is closed.

1 rue des Pertuisanes, 3400 Montpellier. www.pullmanhotels.com. ✆ **04-67-99-72-72.** Fax 04-67-65-17-50. 89 units. 220€–240€ double; 480€ suite. AE, DC, MC, V. **Amenities:** Restaurant; bar; pool (outdoor); fitness center; room service; Wi-Fi (free). *In room:* A/C, TV, hair dryer.

Moderate

Best Western Hôtel Le Guilhem ★ Two 16th-century houses make up this pleasantly quiet hotel on a back street in the old town. Each room is furnished and decorated in an individual style, with more than a hint of Laura Ashley design in the striped wallpaper and flowery bed spreads. Although they aren't particularly large, they are tastefully furnished and comfortable. The luxury room is under an atmospheric stone ceiling with direct access to the secluded garden.

18 rue Jean-Jacques-Rousseau, 34000 Montpellier. www.leguilhem.com. ✆ **800/528-1234** or 04-67-52-90-90. Fax 04-67-60-67-67. 36 units. 96€–139€ double; 158€–192€ junior suite. AE, DC, MC, V. Parking 8€ in nearby garage. **Amenities:** Room service. *In room:* A/C, TV, hair dryer, minibar, Wi-Fi (free).

Holiday Inn Montpellier In the heart of Montpellier, this 1898 monument adjacent to the train station stands behind an entrance with a soaring portal set into a stone facade. But behind the grand stone facade, beware that some of the rooms here have become shabby and run down. Still, it may be worth staying here for its central location and its lovely outdoor swimming pool. Ask for a room overlooking the gardens, as the ones facing the street can get noisy in the evenings.

3 rue Clos-René, 34000 Montpellier. www.holidayinn-montpellier.com. ✆ **04-67-12-32-32.** Fax 04-67-92-13-02. 80 units. 110€–215€ double. AE, DC, MC, V. Parking 12€. **Amenities:** Restaurant; bar; exercise room; pool (outdoor); room service. *In room:* A/C, TV, fridge, hair dryer, Wi-Fi (payable).

Hôtel d'Aragon ★ Tucked away in a peaceful street off the place de la Comédie is this friendly hotel in a 19th-century townhouse. There's a literary air in the elegant rooms, each of which is named after a famous writer. The rooms are of a good size, with classic furniture and modern amenities, including the free use of a netbook computer.

10 rue Baudin, 34000 Montpellier. www.hotel-aragon.fr. ✆ **04-67-10-70-00.** Fax 04-67-10-70-01. 12 units. 92€–139€ double. AE, MC, V. **Amenities:** Breakfast room; Wi-Fi (free). *In room:* A/C, TV, hair dryer, minibar, netbook, Wi-Fi (free).

Newhôtel du Midi ★ This grand old place on the place de la Comédie is right beside the opera house, and it's a favorite among visiting artists. Its recent refurbishment has done wonders, bringing much-needed style and elegance to this venerable old building. Furnishings in the airy rooms are traditional, with the occasional quirky touch in the decor in the public rooms.

22 bd. Victor Hugo, 34000 Montpellier. www.new-hotel.com. ✆ **04-67-92-69-61.** Fax 04-67-92-73-63. 44 units. 155€–180€ double. AE, MC, V. **Amenities:** Restaurant; bar; room service. *In room:* A/C, TV, hair dryer, minibar, Wi-Fi (17€/day).

Les Consuls de Mer This place, located in the growing commercial district of Port Marianne, combines the services of a hotel with the freedom of having your own apartment. Run by Madame Vacances rentals, Les Consuls de Mer offers modern studios and apartments with one or two bedrooms for either short- or long-term stays. (Prices drop considerably for longer-term stays, making this a popular option with students.) The shallow rooftop pool and sun terrace are very welcome in hot weather.

The tram stop is directly outside the entrance, and it's about a 10-minute ride to the place de la Comédie.

455 av. Professeur Etienne Antonelli, 34070 Montpellier. www.madamevacances.co.uk. ✆ **04-79-65-07-65.** Fax 04-79-65-08-08. 118 units. 93€–104€ double; 119€–124€ quad; 199€ sleeping 6. MC, V. **Amenities:** Restaurant; pool (outdoor); whirlpool; sauna. *In room:* A/C, TV, kitchen, Wi-Fi (free).

Inexpensive

Hôtel du Palais ★ This hotel in the heart of a neighborhood loaded with antiques dealers offers great value. Built in the late 18th century, Hôtel du Palais is in the center of Montpellier, amid a labyrinth of narrow streets. Its decor features lots of fabrics, big curtains, faux marble finishes, and a sometimes an overly enthusiastic use of stenciling on the walls. But the guest rooms are relatively large and appealing, thanks to thoughtful placement of antique reproductions and good maintenance.

3 rue du Palais, 34000 Montpellier. www.hoteldupalais-montpellier.fr. ✆ **04-67-60-47-38.** Fax 04-67-60-40-23. 26 units. 75€–90€ double. MC, V. Parking 8€. **Amenities:** Room service. *In room:* A/C, TV, hair dryer, minibar, Wi-Fi (free).

Hôtel du Parc One of the town's more charming moderately priced hostelries, this cozy hotel is near the Palais des Congrès. The rooms in this 18th-century residence have been individually decorated in a style far above the average two-star hotel. A garden and flowering terrace are available for breakfast outside.

8 rue Achille-Bégé, 34000 Montpellier. www.hotelduparc-montpellier.com. ✆ **04-67-41-16-49.** Fax 04-67-54-10-05. 19 units. 55€–93€ double; 100€ triple. AE, MC, V. Free parking. **Amenities:** Breakfast room; room service. *In room:* A/C, TV, hair dryer, minibar, Wi-Fi (free).

Hôtel Ulysse The owners have worked hard to make this simple hotel as stylish as possible. Each of the individually decorated guest rooms weaves in wrought-iron elements—whether it's in the form of a headboard, night tables, or light fixtures. The comfortable yet simple rooms have fully equipped bathrooms. The hotel is within a 15-minute walk north of Montpellier's center.

338 av. de St-Maur, 34000 Montpellier. www.hotel-ulysse.fr. ✆ **04-67-02-02-30.** Fax 04-67-02-16-50. 24 units. 80€–110€ double. AE, MC, V. Parking 7€. **Amenities:** Room service. *In room:* TV, hair dryer, minibar, Wi-Fi (free).

Les Arceaux A hotel has stood at this prime location, right off the promenade du Peyrou, since the late 1800s. The smallish rooms are simply but pleasantly furnished, each in a different color, and each with a compact bathroom. Ask for the Côté Jardin room, which opens directly onto the garden. The on-site bar, which also opens onto a garden, serves simple platters.

33–35 bd. des Arceaux, 34000 Montpellier. www.hoteldesarceaux.com. ✆ **04-67-92-03-03.** Fax 04-67-92-05-09. 18 units. 65€–105€ double. AE, MC, V. **Amenities:** Bar; room service. *In room:* A/C (in some), TV, minibar, Wi-Fi (free).

WHERE TO STAY NEAR MONTPELLIER

Demeure des Brousses ★★ This 18th-century country house stands in a large, impressive park about a 10-minute drive from the heart of Montpellier. A tranquil choice, it has been skillfully converted for guests. Rooms range from medium-size to spacious, each individually decorated with 19th-century style. Public rooms are decorated like those of a gracious French country house, including loads of antiques, making this an intimate retreat.

538 rue du Mas de Brousse, 34000 Montpellier. www.demeure-des-brousses.com. ✆ **04-67-65-77-66.** Fax 04-67-22-22-17. 17 units. 75€–175€ double. AE, DC, MC, V. Free parking. Take D-172E 3km (2 miles) east of the town center. **Amenities:** Restaurant; bar; bikes; room service. *In room:* A/C, TV, hair dryer, Wi-Fi (free).

Where to Eat

EXPENSIVE

Le Jardin des Sens ★★★ FRENCH This is one of the great restaurants of southern France, with two Michelin stars. The chefs, twins Laurent and Jacques Pourcel, imaginatively plunder the rich bounty of Languedoc. A starter may be ravioli stuffed with duck foie gras and mushrooms, floating in chicken bouillon fortified with truffles. Main courses include flash-fried filets of red mullet, roasted sea bass with an artichoke and potato cake, and Corsican leg of lamb roasted in garlic with fondant potatoes and mushrooms.

11 av. St-Lazare. ✆ **04-99-58-38-38.** Fax 04-99-58-38-39. www.jardindessens.com. Reservations required. Main courses 45€–80€; fixed-price dinners 83€–170€. AE, MC, V. Tues and Thurs–Sat noon–2pm and 7:30–10pm; Mon and Wed 7:30–10pm. Closed 2 weeks in Jan.

MODERATE

Le Pastis ★ MODERN FRENCH This cozy restaurant near the church of St. Anne is an intimate spot with stone interior walls and an innovative menu. Dishes change with the season and depend on what the chef can get fresh from the market, but the menu may include such dishes as tartlets of snails with wild garlic, broad beans, and chorizo; pork belly with a mustard crust; and stir-fried cuttlefish and clams. They take great pride in their wine cellar, which features the best of the local vineyards.

3 rue Terral. ✆ **04-67-66-37-26.** www.le-pastis.fr. Reservations recommended. Fixed-price dinner 28€–33€. AE, MC, V. Wed–Sat noon–2pm and 7:30–10pm.

Les Bains de Montpellier ★ 🎁 MEDITERRANEAN It's hard to find a more enchanting setting for a restaurant than these former city baths, which date from the 18th century. Century-old palm trees shade the tables in the inner courtyard, while another plush dining area has been created in what used to be the shower booths. The regional seasonal menu changes regularly, but can include a carpaccio of octopus or sea bream; veal chops from the Aveyron; or the catch of the day, simply grilled with olive oil and sea salt. On Saturdays, live jazz adds to the ambience of the champagne and wine bar.

6 rue Richelieu. ✆ **04-67-60-70-87.** www.les-bains-de-montpellier.com. Reservations recommended. Main courses 21€–27€; fixed-price lunch 21€, dinner 38€–48€. AE, MC, V. Tues–Sat noon–2pm and 7:30–10:30pm.

INEXPENSIVE

Chez Boris FRENCH Meat is king in this lively restaurant along the tree-shaded boulevard off the place de la Comédie. This is where to get the best burgers, including horse, the best cuts of beef, as well as steak tartare and luscious beef carpaccio. The quality is outstanding, and the service is friendly and efficient. However, it might not be the place to take your vegetarian friends.

17 bd. Sarrail. ✆ **04-67-02-82-38.** Main courses 14€–24€. MC, V. Daily noon–2pm and 7:30–10pm.

Comptoir de l'Arc FRENCH/TAPAS Located in the corner of one of the loveliest squares in Montpellier, place de la Canourgue, this convivial tapas bar/restaurant is as good a place for an aperitif as it is for a full dinner. Start with a drink and some tapas, such as mini-squid salad with smoked paprika or sweet and sour shrimps, and then tuck into prime rib skewers or veal *à la parmigiana* with buffalo mozzarella.

2 rue de l'Hôtel de Ville. ✆ **04-67-60-30-79.** Tapas from 4€; main courses 14€–22€. MC, V. Daily noon–11pm.

Montpellier After Dark

The traffic-free streets around the church of **St-Roch**—namely, **rue des Teissiers, four des Flammes, rue de la Fontaine,** and **plan d'Agde**—buzz with cafes and bars, and overflow with people having late-night drinks and dinner.

The theater at **Le Corum** (✆ **04-67-61-67-61**) is the place for plays, dance recitals, operas, and classical concerts. It's in the Palais des Congrès, esplanade Charles-de-Gaulle. For ticket information and schedules, contact the Corum or the **Opéra Comédie,** place de la Comédie (✆ **04-67-60-19-80**).

Rockstore, 20 rue de Verdun (✆ **04-67-06-80-00;** www.rockstore.fr), is a Montpellier institution you can't miss, thanks to the back end of a red Cadillac sticking out over the entrance. It's a huge venue, with separate rooms to watch indie bands or dance to DJs. Over the years it's played host to Radiohead, Faith No More, The Kills, and countless other non-French bands on their European tour. For excellent jazz and blues, check out **JAM,** 100 rue Ferdinand-de-Lesseps (✆ **04-67-58-30-30;** www.lejam.com). Regular concerts attract jazz enthusiasts from miles around, and serious students come to study at the jazz music school attached.

A Side Trip from Montpellier

ST-GUILHEM-LE-DÉSERT ★★

Designated as a UNESCO World Heritage Site and one of the *Plus Beaux Villages de France* (the most beautiful villages in France), this tiny exquisite village is well worth a day trip from Montpellier. Fewer than 300 people live in the medieval houses that tumble down cobble-stoned lanes encircled by a wooded ravine within the dramatic Gorges de l'Hérault. The central square, **place de la Liberté,** has one of the largest and widest plane trees in France, which shelter several cafe tables.

The main attraction, in addition to the general beauty of the village, is the **11th-century abbey** that sits on the site of the 9th-century monastery founded by Guilhem, Charlemagne's counselor. Guilhem returned from Rome in 800 with three pieces of wood believed to be relics of the Cross, which were stored in the abbey. Soon the abbey became a place of pilgrimage as well as a stopping point for pilgrims on the route of Santiago de Compostela. Today, the abbey contains Guilhem's tomb. After exploring the beautiful abbey, with its seven large arches over the vaulted apse, stop in the tranquil cloisters. Some of the sculptures from the cloisters are on display in the Cloisters Museum in New York. The cultivated plots within the gardens beyond the cloisters are a testament to the work done by the monks over the centuries. Admission is free. The abbey is opening daily from 8am to 6pm (until 6:30pm July–Aug). The cloisters are closed from noon to 2pm weekdays and 11am to 2:30pm Sunday.

The **Musée du Village,** at 15 rue Chapelle des Pénitents (✆ **04-67-57-77-07;** www.museestguilhem.fr), is an enchanting little place located in the owners' 12th-century house. The museum recreates 19th-century provincial life with some of its exhibits, including an incredible scale model of the village populated entirely by *santons,* tiny ceramic figurines made by the proprietor. A *salon de thé* (tea room) at the back of the house has glorious views over the village and the gorge. Admission is 4€, free for children.

If you choose to spend the night here, the best place to stay is **Le Guilhaume d'Orange,** 2 av. Guilhaume d'Orange (✆ **04-67-57-24-53;** www.guilhaume dorange.com). Its 10 rooms are prettily furnished with antiques, and cost from 66€ to 99€ a night. Its restaurant serves local seasonal dishes on its panoramic terrace; menus start from 20€.

The **Office de Tourisme** is at the foot of the village at 2 rue Font du Portal (✆ **04-67-57-44-33;** www.saint-guilhem-le-desert.com).

SÈTE ★

787km (489 miles) S of Paris; 48km (30 miles) NW of Béziers; 63km (39 miles) SW of Lodève; 35km (22 miles) SE of Montpellier.

Sète, the deepest port in the Mediterranean, is in the process of change. Once cheerfully scruffy, with its focus firmly on the fishing industry, it has been busy expanding, regenerating, and generally smartening itself up. Its sea soul is still there, but it's acquired a new gloss. Sète was built on a limestone rock on the slopes of Mont Saint-Clair, with a 25km-long (16-mile) spit of sand connecting it westward to Cap d'Agde and eastward to the mainland via bridges. It's a city of canals lined with mainly 19th-century pastel-colored buildings. Inevitably it gets compared to Venice, but so does anywhere with a canal or two. Sète doesn't pretend to be anything other than what it is: a bustling, thriving fishing port with some of the best seafood in France.

Sète is on the southwestern edge of the Etang de Thau, an enormous lagoon that is the breeding ground for countless beds of mussels, oysters, and whelks. These end up on the plates of Sète's quayside restaurants, as well as in the villages on the northern side of the *étang,* namely Bouzigues, Mèze, and Marseillan.

The road from Sète to Cap d'Agde used to be one of the best drives along France's Mediterranean coast, with nothing but 18km (11 miles) of practically empty beach and the vivid blue of the sea. Unfortunately, because of coastal erosion, the road has been moved inland to offer some protection to the coast. Now the road is punctuated by a series of parking lots in front of each individual beach, separated by a windbreaker of tall grasses. Some of the magic has gone, but the beaches are still wide, windswept, and nearly empty—it's a far cry from the huddled bodies wedged along the crowded sands of the Côte d'Azur.

Essentials

GETTING THERE **Trains** arrive regularly from Montpellier, and Sète is on the TGV line that runs from Paris to Perpignan. For information and train schedules, call ✆ **36-35,** or visit www.voyages-sncf.com. The **Totem bus** network (✆ **04-67-74-21-06;** www.cars-bassin-thau.com) operates within Sète and connects it to the other towns along the coast and on the Etang de Thau. If you're **driving,** Sète is off the A9.

VISITOR INFORMATION The **Office de Tourisme** is at 60 grand rue Mario Roustan (✆ **04-99-04-71-71;** fax 04-67-46-17-54; www.tourisme-sete.com).

SPECIAL EVENTS Every August, the people of Sète pay homage to their patron saint with the **Fêtes de la Saint-Louis,** which includes 6 days of nonstop music, dancing, fireworks, and, that favorite Sétois pastime, water-jousting tournaments on the canal.

Exploring the Town

Most of the pleasure of being in Sète comes from strolling along the canals, where smaller boats vie for space with the huge fishing trawlers that supply the town's restaurants with plentiful seafood. The **Canal Royal** is the setting for the wonderfully zany Sétoise tradition of water jousting tournaments, *les joutes nautiques,* which take place all summer long. Two opposing teams ride in gondola-style boats, with members taking turns to try to knock their opponents off one by one using long lances. There are night-time versions, too, and even one for children.

Two of Sète's most famous sons have museums devoted to them. The **Espace Georges Brassens,** at 67 bd. Camille Blanc (✆ **04-99-04-76-26**), sits on a hill overlooking the evocative mariners' cemetery where the great singer rests. Inside the modern glass gallery are multimedia exhibitions recalling the life and career of the influential singer-songwriter who was a great friend of Jacques Brel; admission is 5€ for adults, and 2€ for students and children over 10. The **Musée Paul Valéry** is also near the top of Mont St-Clair, at 148 rue François Desnoyer (✆ **04-99-04-76-16**). Along with exhibitions celebrating the poet, it contains a sizeable collection of art as well as displays chronicling the history of life in Sète; admission for the permanent collection is 7€ adults, 2€ children ages 10 to 18, and children 9 and under are free.

One of the most dramatic sights in Sète is the **Théâtre de la Mer,** route de al Corniche (✆ **04-67-74-98-86**), an 18th-century citadel that has been converted to an open-air amphitheater. Concerts, plays, and recitals are performed throughout the summer, with the Mediterranean as its enchanting backdrop.

Sète's nearest beach is less than 2km (1 mile) east of the Vieux Port (old port) at **La Corniche.** Its 1960s architecture leaves much to be desired, but it doesn't detract from the large expanse of beach that eventually stretches all the way to Cap d'Agde.

Where to Stay

Grand Hôtel ★ Unlike many hotels that presume to call themselves grand, this one suits its name. This venerable Belle Époque hotel overlooks the intersection of two canals, which means lovely waterside views for a good number of the rooms. The guest rooms are bright, spacious, and comfortable, and are decorated with modern furniture and some exotic touches. The rooms are located off the large central atrium where breakfast is served. It also has a restaurant, Quai 17 (see review below).

17 quai Maréchal de Lattre de Tassigny, 34200 Sète. www.legrandhotelsete.com. ✆ **04-67-74-71-77.** Fax 04-67-74-29-27. 43 units. 85€–230€ double. AE, DC, MC, V. Parking 9€. **Amenities:** Restaurant; bar; room service. *In room:* A/C (some), TV, minibar, Wi-Fi (free).

Hôtel de Paris ★ Only a few years ago, this central hotel was a shabby two-star property that was best avoided. One total renovation later, and it's a funky, friendly, imaginative boutique hotel where the bar and restaurant have become a major draw for young locals. Its innovative rooms are based on themes, including wood, glass, stone, or colors. The red room, for example, has giant red lips for a headboard, while the metal room has lots of metallic elements and furniture. The internal courtyard leads to the tranquil confines of the well-equipped spa.

2 rue Frédéric Mistral, 34200 Sète. www.hoteldeparis-sete.com. ✆ **04-67-18-00-18.** Fax 04-13-33-70-84. 36 units. 95€–135€ double; 125€–270€ suite. MC, V. Parking 8€. **Amenities:** Restaurant; bar; spa; whirlpool; room service. *In room:* A/C, TV, hair dryer, Wi-Fi (free).

Where to Eat

Les Demoiselles Dupuy SEAFOOD This Sétoise institution is an unpretentious place at the furthest end of the quayside restaurants—all the way down to the fish auction, La Criée. It's worth the walk to savor the freshest plates of mussels, oysters, squid, sardines, and, one of their specialties, paella. You can also buy shellfish from them directly.

4 quai Maximin Licciardi. ✆ **04-67-74-03-46.** Main courses 13€–19€. MC, V. Daily noon–2pm and 7:30–10pm.

Quai 17 ★ MEDITERRANEAN It's not surprising that Sète's best hotel should serve top-class cuisine in its canalside restaurant. Nor is it surprising that local seafood ends up on menu, including oysters from the Etang de Thau, lobster risotto, grilled sea bream, and the restaurant's own version of bouillabaisse with turbot and red mullet.

17 quai Maréchal de Lattre de Tassigny. ✆ **04-67-53-81-13.** Reservations recommended. Main courses 20€–40€; fixed-price menus 19€–47€; children's menu 13€. AE, DC, MC, V. Mon–Fri noon–2pm; Mon–Sat 7–9pm.

AIGUES-MORTES ★

750km (466 miles) SW of Paris; 63km (39 miles) NE of Sète; 40km (25 miles) E of Nîmes; 48km (30 miles) SW of Arles

Aigues-Mortes, the town of the "dead waters," is the main destination within the **Petite Camargue.** This expanse of wetlands, salt marshes, and lagoons is the smaller neighbor of the larger **Parc Naturel Régional de Camargue** to the east in Provence. In the middle of this marshy landscape is one of France's best-preserved walled towns, a medieval wonder that has changed little over the centuries. Aigues-Mortes stands on four navigable canals 6km (4 miles) from the sea, although it was once a thriving port that served as the departure point for one of the Crusades. Now the coast is a series of purpose-built beach resorts, including **Le Grau-du-Roi** and **Port Camargue,** which teem with sun worshippers in the summer months. As you drive south from Aigues-Mortes to the coast you pass the evocative sight of the **Salins du Midi,** an enormous salt works that is part of the Camargue's important sea-salt industry.

Essentials

GETTING THERE **Trains** and **buses** connect Aigues-Mortes to Montpellier and Nîmes. For information and train schedules, call ✆ **36-35,** or visit www.voyagessncf.com. For **bus** information, visit the Gard *département* transport website at www.edgard-transport.fr. The town does not have a bus station, only a bus stop. If you're **driving** to Aigues-Mortes, take D979 south from Gallargues, or A9 from Montpellier or Nîmes.

VISITOR INFORMATION The **Office de Tourisme** is at place St-Louis (✆ **04-66-53-73-00;** fax 04-66-53-65-94; www.ot-aiguesmortes.fr).

SPECIAL EVENTS Every August, Aigues-Mortes puts on its medieval finery to celebrate the **Fête de St-Louis.** Three days of parades, dances, jousting tournaments, and fireworks culminate in a reenactment of St. Louis's departure on the seventh Crusade.

Exploring the Town

The main allure in Aigues-Mortes is the town itself. The Middle Ages still permeates virtually every building, rampart, and cobble-stoned street, and the town is still enclosed by **ramparts ★★** that were constructed between 1272 and 1300. The **Tour de Constance ★★** (✆ **04-66-53-61-55**), which looks out on the marshes, is a model medieval castle. At the top, which you can reach by elevator, a panoramic view unfolds. Admission to the tower is 7€ for adults, 4.50€ for ages 18 to 25, and free for children 17 and under.

The city's religious centerpiece is the **Eglise Notre-Dame des Sablons,** rue Jean-Jaurès. Constructed of wood in 1183, it was rebuilt in stone in 1246 in the ogival style. Its modern stained-glass windows were installed in 1980 as replacements for the badly damaged originals. The church is open May to September daily from 8:30am–6pm, and October to April 10am–5pm.

The waterways and wetlands of the **Petite Camargue** can be explored in many ways: You can join a jeep safari, canoe, kayak, cycle, ride on a paddle steamer, or just put your hiking boots on and wander along the trails that are inaccessible by car. Your reward is the sight of flocks of flamingoes and other birdlife, white Camargue horses, and herds of Camargue bulls. Just make sure to cover yourself with plenty of mosquito repellent.

Where to Stay

Hostellerie des Remparts Located at the foot of the Tour de Constance, this handsome 18th-century hotel underwent a major overhaul in 2011, which gave it a fresh, modern feel. Guest rooms have an elegant simplicity, with a neutral color palette and unfussy furnishings. The friendly staff will go out of their way to help make your stay comfortable. The restaurant, which is on the large front terrace on warm days, fills up quickly; the 28€ menu includes a "lasagne" of scallops with artichokes and sun-dried tomatoes, and sea bream stuffed with fennel and flambéed in pastis.

6 place Anatole-France, 30220 Aigues-Mortes. www.remparts-aiguesmortes.fr. ✆ **04-66-53-82-77.** Fax 04-66-53-73-77. 12 units. 60€–180€ double; 190€–410€ suites. AE, MC, V. **Amenities:** Restaurant; bar; room service. *In room:* A/C, TV, Wi-Fi (free).

Hôtel St-Louis This inn near place St-Louis offers small but comfortably furnished bedrooms, each with a compact bathroom. The peaceful tree-shaded garden is a romantic place to relax or have breakfast. The restaurant serves local favorite dishes, including skewers of Camargue beef, for 29€.

10 rue Amiral-Courbet, 30220 Aigues-Mortes. www.lesaintlouis.fr. ✆ **04-66-53-72-68.** Fax 04-66-53-75-92. 22 units. 79€–102€ double. AE, MC, V. Parking 12€. Closed Jan to mid-Mar. **Amenities:** Restaurant; bar; room service. *In room:* A/C, TV, minibar.

Les Arcades ★ This charming hotel makes imaginative and quirky use of its 16th-century interiors. Each room is named after a Camargue bird, and most of the good-size rooms have large painting of various local water fowl. It's a cute touch that complements the exposed ceiling beams and simple country furniture. There's a small swimming pool on the sun terrace, which is a welcome treat. The restaurant is a popular local choice, with menus for 35€ and 45€. Local ingredients figure prominently, featuring oysters from the Etang de Thau near Sète; ravioli with foie gras and mushrooms; and grilled Camargue bull steaks.

23 bd. Gambetta, 30220 Aigues-Mortes. www.les-arcades.fr. ✆ **04-66-53-81-13.** Fax 04-66-53-75-46. 9 units. 98€–150€ double. AE, MC, V. Free parking. **Amenities:** Restaurant; pool (outdoor). *In room:* A/C, TV, hair dryer, Wi-Fi (free).

Villa Mazarin ★★ The most luxurious of Aigues-Mortes's hotels is this sumptuous 15th-century manor house within the ramparts. Spacious, regal rooms evoke the 17th century in design but have 21st-century comforts, with king-size beds and modern bathrooms. Some of the rooms have terraces and balconies overlooking the colorful gardens in the tranquil inner courtyard. The dining room is adorned with dark red beams and medieval-style murals; the restaurant menu features regional flavors, such as veal from Aveyron served with truffle gnocchi, or succulent twice-roasted lamb.

35 bd. Gambetta, 30220 Aigues-Mortes. ✆ **04-66-73-90-48.** Fax 04-66-73-90-49. 16 units. 120€–260€ double. AE, MC, V. **Amenities:** Restaurant; bar; pool (indoor); spa; gym; room service. *In room:* A/C, TV, hair dryer, Wi-Fi (free).

Where to Eat

See also the restaurants at Villa Mazarin, Les Arcades, Hostellerie des Remparts, and Hôtel St-Louis (above).

La Camargue ★ FRENCH The oldest restaurant in Aigues-Mortes is a convivial place with a romantic courtyard garden and an interior that dazzles you with its colors. The decor suits the lively atmosphere, which includes regular performances by Gypsy musicians. This is the place to try *gardiane de taureau,* a wonderfully rich stew of Camargue bull that's cooked for hours in red wine and served with red Camargue rice.

19 rue de la République. ✆ **04-66-53-86-1388.** www.restaurantlacamargue.com. Main courses 16€–23€; fixed-price dinner 32€. MC, V. Daily noon–2pm and 7:30–10pm.

Le Dit Vin MEDITERRANEAN/TAPAS It's fiesta time at this tapas bar/restaurant, where live music on weekends adds to the general buzz. The red-hued interior is a successful combination of rusticity and class, while the shaded courtyard garden is the place to be on warm summer evenings. Have a taste of the sea with a plate of Bouzigues oysters, or try their *petite bouillabaisse* of red mullet, monkfish, and scallops.

6 rue du 4 Septembre. ✆ **04-66-53-52-76.** www.restoleditvin.com. Main courses 19€–23€. MC, V. Daily 10am–10pm.

NÎMES ★★★

708km (440 miles) S of Paris; 43km (27 miles) W of Avignon

Roman history pervades this sunny, relaxed city that feels more Provençal than Languedocian in its outlook and physical appearance. The city, which is in the ancient Roman Via Domitia that runs from Italy to Spain, grew to prominence during the reign of Caesar Augustus (27 B.C.–A.D. 14). Today it possesses one of the best-preserved Roman amphitheaters in the world and a near-perfect Roman temple. There's a touch of Spain, too, in the celebrations surrounding the *corridas* (bullfights)

> **Your Lucky Ticket**
>
> If you want to see all of the city's monuments and museums, consider buying a **combined ticket** to the Roman arena, the Maison Carrée, and the Tour Magne. They cost 9.90€ (7.60€ reduced), are valid for 3 days, and are sold at the ticket counter of all three attractions. It provides access for a 3-day period to all the cultural sites described below. There are also combined tickets to the Roman arena in Nîmes, the amphitheater in Orange, and the Château des Baux in Les Baux-de-Provence. See www.arenes-nimes.com for details.

at the arena and the flamenco festivals. And the modern world has crept in, too, in the form of some of the most innovative architecture and design seen in the past 20 years.

Essentials

GETTING THERE Flights from Great Britain, Spain, and Italy arrive at the **airport** 15km (9 miles) south of the town, which is connected by shuttle bus to the city center. Nîmes lies on the main **rail** line between Paris and Perpignan, and also has trains from Marseille and Montpellier. For train information and schedules, call ✆ **36-35,** or visit www.voyages-sncf.com. Regional **buses** are operated by **Edgard** (✆ **08-10-33-42-73;** www.edgard-transport.fr), which runs buses between Nîmes and Avignon, Montpellier, Arles, Uzès, and other local towns. If you're **driving,** take A7 south from Lyon to the town of Orange and connect to A9 into Nîmes.

VISITOR INFORMATION The **Office de Tourisme** is at 6 rue Auguste (✆ **04-66-58-38-00;** fax 04-66-58-38-01; www.ot-nimes.fr).

SPECIAL EVENTS Nîmes is busy with festivals for most of the year, starting with January's **Flamenco Festival.** The Roman amphitheater lights up for most of July and August during the **Festival de Nîmes,** when pop and classical concerts are staged. But the big event is the springtime **Féria de Pentecôte,** 6 days of nonstop music, dancing, parades, and, of course, bullfights in the arena.

Exploring the City

THE TOP SIGHTS

Amphithéâtre Romain ★★★ The elliptically shaped amphitheater is a better-preserved twin of the one at Arles and is far more complete than the Colosseum of Rome. It's two stories high, each floor having 60 arches, and was built of stones fitted together without mortar. One of the best-preserved arenas from ancient times, it once held around 24,000 spectators who came to see gladiatorial combats and wolf or boar hunts. Today it's used for everything from concerts to bullfights.

Place des Arènes. ✆ **04-66-21-82-56.** www.arenes-nimes.com. Admission 7.80€ adults, 5.90€ students and children 7–17, free for children 6 and under. Daily 9:30am–5pm Nov–Feb, 9am–6pm Mar and Oct, 9am–6:30pm Apr–May and Sept, 9am–7pm June, 9am–8pm July–Aug.

Carré d'Art/Musée d'Art Contemporain Across the square stands the modern-day twin of the Maison Carrée (below), a sophisticated exhibition space that contains a collection of nearly 400 works of contemporary art, as well as a library, bookshop, and restaurant (see Le Ciel de Nîmes, below). The understated design by

Nîmes

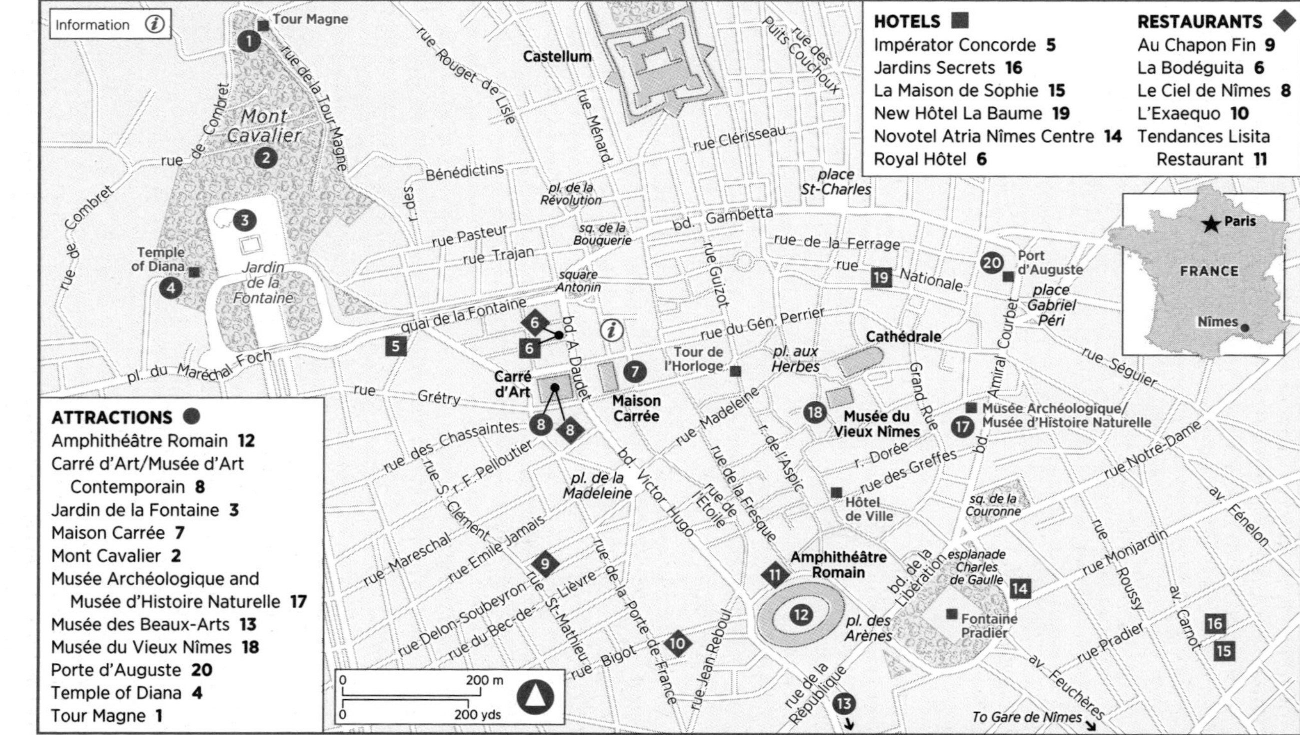
Information
Tour Magne
Castellum
Mont Cavalier
HOTELS
Impérator Concorde 5
Jardins Secrets 16
La Maison de Sophie 15
New Hôtel La Baume 19
Novotel Atria Nîmes Centre 14
Royal Hôtel 6
RESTAURANTS
Au Chapon Fin 9
La Bodéguita 6
Le Ciel de Nîmes 8
L'Exaequo 10
Tendances Lisita Restaurant 11
place St-Charles
Paris
FRANCE
Nîmes
Temple of Diana
Jardin de la Fontaine
Port d'Auguste
place Gabriel Péri
Cathédrale
Tour de l'Horloge
pl. aux Herbes
Carré d'Art
Maison Carrée
Musée du Vieux Nîmes
Musée Archéologique/
Musée d'Histoire Naturelle
pl. de la Madeleine
Hôtel de Ville
sq. de la Couronne
Amphithéâtre Romain
esplanade Charles de Gaulle
pl. des Arènes
Fontaine Pradier
To Gare de Nîmes
ATTRACTIONS
Amphithéâtre Romain 12
Carré d'Art/Musée d'Art Contemporain 8
Jardin de la Fontaine 3
Maison Carrée 7
Mont Cavalier 2
Musée Archéologique and Musée d'Histoire Naturelle 17
Musée des Beaux-Arts 13
Musée du Vieux Nîmes 18
Porte d'Auguste 20
Temple of Diana 4
Tour Magne 1
0 200 m
0 200 yds

British architect Norman Foster (who created the Millau viaduct) was inspired by the ancient monument opposite. The museum's permanent expositions are often supplemented with temporary exhibits of contemporary art.

16 place de la Maison Carrée. ✆ **04-66-76-35-70.** http://carreartmusee.nimes.fr. Free admission to the permanent exhibitions; temporary exhibition admission 5€ adults, 3.70€ students and children 14 and under. Tues–Sun 10am–6pm.

Maison Carrée ★★ The pride of Nîmes, this is one of the most beautiful, and singularly best-preserved Roman temples of Europe. It was built during the reign of Caesar Augustus in the 1st century A.D. Set on a raised platform with tall Corinthian columns, this so-called "square house" is more rectangular in shape. A changing roster of cultural and art exhibits is presented inside.

Place de la Maison Carrée. ✆ **04-66-21-82-56.** www.arenes-nimes.com. Admission 4.50€ adults, 3.70€ students and children 7–17, free for children 6 and under. Daily 10am–1pm and 2–4:30pm Nov–Feb, 10am–6pm Mar and Oct (closed 1–2pm in Oct), 10am–6:30pm Apr–May and Sept, 10am–7pm June, 10am–8pm July–Aug.

Musée des Beaux-Arts The city's largest museum—and the second largest in the Languedoc-Roussillon region—contains French paintings and sculptures from the 17th to the 20th centuries, as well as Flemish, Dutch, and Italian works from the 15th to the 18th centuries. You can't miss the giant Roman mosaic in the atrium.

Rue Cité-Foulc. ✆ **04-66-67-38-21.** Free admission to the permanent exhibitions; temporary exhibition admission 8€ adults, 5€ students and children 16 and under. Tues–Sun 10am–6pm.

MORE SIGHTS

One of the most beautiful gardens in France, **Jardin de la Fontaine ★★**, at the end of quai de la Fontaine, was laid out in the 18th century, using the ruins of a Roman shrine as a centerpiece. It was planted with rows of chestnuts and elms, adorned with statuary and urns, and intersected by grottoes and canals. Within the garden are the ruined **Temple of Diane ★** and the remains of some Roman baths. Over the park, within a 10-minute walk north of the town center, is **Mont Cavalier,** a low, rocky hill on top of which rises the sturdy bulk of the **Tour Magne ★**, the city's oldest Roman monument. It offers a panoramic view over Nîmes and its environs and is worth the climb up the narrow stone stairs. You can walk up it for 2.70€ adults, 2.30€ students and children aged 7 to 17, and free for children 6 and under.

If time allows, visit the **Musée du Vieux-Nîmes,** place aux Herbes (✆ **04-66-76-73-70**), housed in a 17th-century former bishops' palace and rich in antiques, porcelain, and everyday objects from the 18th and 19th centuries. Admission is free, but temporary exhibitions cost 5€ for adults, 3.70€ students and children 16 and under.

One of the city's busiest thoroughfares, **boulevard de l'Amiral-Courbet,** leads to the **Porte d'Auguste** (also known as the Porte d'Arles)—the remains of a gate built by the Romans during the reign of Augustus. About 45m (150 ft.) to the south are the **Musée d'Histoire Naturelle** (✆ **04-66-76-73-45**) and the **Musée Archéologique ★** (✆ **04-66-76-74-80**), in the same building at 13 bis bd. l'Amiral-Courbet. Admission is free, but temporary exhibitions cost 5€ for adults, 3.70€ students and children 16 and under. Hours are Tuesday to Sunday 10am to 6pm.

A FAMOUS ROMAN BRIDGE

Outside the city, 23km (14 miles) northeast, the **Pont du Gard ★**, now a UNESCO World Heritage Site, spans the Gardon River. The aqueduct was the highest in the

Roman world and is constructed of huge stones fitted together without mortar. Although most of it has been reconstructed, it stands as one of the region's most vivid reminders of its ancient glory. Consisting of three tiers of arches arranged into gracefully symmetrical patterns, it dates from about 40 to 60 B.C. Abandoned by the 6th century, it fell into ruin until major reconstruction projects started in the 19th century. To visit it, take N86 from Nîmes to a point 3km (1¾ miles) from the village of Remoulins, where signs are posted.

The Pont du Gard has a museum (✆ **08-20-90-33-30;** www.pontdugard.fr), with exhibiting detailing the bridge's construction, its function throughout the Middle Ages, and insights into the architectural genius of ancient Rome. There's also a restaurant, cafe, and several gift shops. The Pont du Gard site is open all year round, but the "discovery areas," including the museum, are closed Monday morning. It's free to visit the Pont du Gard, but you have to pay to use the closest parking lot. A daily rate of 15€ covers up to five people and includes visits to the museum and temporary exhibits.

Shopping

Head to the center of town and **rue du Général-Perrier, rue des Marchands, rue du Chapitre,** and the pedestrian **rue de l'Aspic** and **rue de la Madeleine** for boutiques of all budgets. **Les Halles,** the large, covered food market in rue Général Perrier, is open daily until 1pm for your fix of delicious local produce. A huge all-day Monday market takes place in the parking lot of the **Stade des Costières,** site of most of the town's football (soccer) matches, adjacent to the southern edge of the boulevard *périphérique* that encircles Nîmes. Here you'll find clothing and flower stalls alongside food sellers. The **organic farmers' market** sets up every Friday from 7am to 1pm on avenue Jean-Jaurès south of the Jardins de la Fontaine.

Where to Stay

EXPENSIVE

Impérator Concorde This quaint four-star hotel is in an excellent location near the Jardins de la Fontaine, with most of the city's major attractions within walking distance. The old-fashioned rooms vary substantially in size, but they all have traditional French furniture, floral furnishings, and wallpaper. Ask for a room that looks out over the pretty courtyard garden where meals are served in good weather.

Quai de la Fontaine, 30900 Nîmes. www.hotel-imperator.com. ✆ **04-66-21-90-30.** Fax 04-66-67-70-25. 60 units. 155€–290€ double; 255€–330€ suite. AE, DC, MC, V. Parking 20€. **Amenities:** Restaurant; bar; babysitting; room service. *In room:* A/C, TV, hair dryer, minibar, Wi-Fi (free).

Jardins Secrets ★★★ The discreet gold-plated sign outside the gate gives little clue to the lush greenery within the garden walls of this four-star haven. This is one of the region's most beautiful and sumptuous hotels, with splendidly opulent rooms decked out in 18th-century style clustering around private cloisters, gardens, and the swimming pool. If rare cases of bad weather keep you from dozing under the lemon trees in the jasmine-scented garden, relax in one of the five salons (including two music rooms with pianos at the guests' disposal) and enjoy breakfast in the large country kitchen. The well-equipped spa harks back to Roman times, with atmospheric arches and columns.

3 rue Gaston Maruéjols, 30000 Nîmes. www.jardinssecrets.net. ✆ **04-66-84-82-64.** Fax 04-66-84-27-47. 14 units. 195€–295€ double; 350€–410€ suite. AE, DC, MC, V. Parking 20€. **Amenities:** Breakfast room; pool (outdoor); spa. *In room:* A/C, TV, hair dryer, Wi-Fi (free).

MODERATE

La Maison de Sophie Built in 1901, this charming little hotel resembles a small Venetian *palazzo,* with a scattering of marble columns in the entrance area, and with Art Deco touches, such as stained glass. The lovely garden is loaded with old-species roses and irises, and features a swimming pool. The rooms aren't particularly luxurious, but each has a balcony and a small bathroom.

31 av. Carnot, 30000 Nîmes. http://hotel_lamaisondesoph.monsite-orange.fr. ✆ **04-66-70-96-10.** Fax 04-66-36-00-47. 7 units. 150€–230€ double; 290€ suite. AE, MC, V. Parking 10€. **Amenities:** Breakfast room; pool (outdoor). *In room:* A/C, TV, Wi-Fi (free).

New Hôtel La Baume The magnificent stone staircase ornamenting the interior courtyard is an impressive sight when you first enter this 17th-century townhouse. In contrast to the stately entrance, the rooms are modern, somewhat small, and quite plain, usually decorated in tones of soft reds, oranges, and ochers. But the open-air patio is welcoming, and the hotel is in a central location by the pedestrianized district.

21 rue Nationale, 30000 Nîmes. www.new-hotel.com. ✆ **04-66-76-28-42.** Fax 04-66-76-28-45. 34 units. 140€–170€. AE, DC, MC, V. **Amenities:** Bar; room service. *In room:* A/C, TV, hair dryer, minibar, Wi-Fi (17€).

Novotel Atria Nîmes Centre This chain hotel occupies a desirable spot in the heart of Nîmes very close to the ancient arena. Its six floors wrap around a carefully landscaped inner courtyard. Each room contains a double bed, a sofa (which converts into a single bed), a well-equipped bathroom, and a wide writing desk, all of which suits its predominantly business clientele.

5 bd. de Prague, 30000 Nîmes. www.accor-hotels.com. ✆ **04-66-76-56-56.** Fax 04-66-76-56-59. 119 units. 125€–165€ double; 180€ suite. AE, DC, MC, V. Parking 11€. **Amenities:** Restaurant; bar; room service. *In room:* A/C, TV, minibar, Wi-Fi (free).

INEXPENSIVE

Royal Hôtel This friendly, welcoming hotel in a handsome 19th-century building is steps away from the Maison Carrée. Rooms vary in size, but all have tastefully simple furnishings with a scattering of antiques. Some have balconies that look out over the funky place d'Assas, a wide plaza created in 1989 that is filled with cutting-edge contemporary art and restaurants. The Spanish theme runs deeply at the Royal: Art celebrating the féria (bullfighting festivals) decorates the walls and the restaurant offers excellent tapas. (See La Bodéguita below.)

3 bd. Alphonse Daudet, 30000 Nîmes. ✆ **04-66-58-28-27.** Fax 04-66-58-28-28. www.royalhotel-nimes.com. 21 units. 50€–98€ double; 110€–160€ family room. AE, MC, V. **Amenities:** Restaurant; bar; Wi-Fi (free). *In room:* A/C, TV.

Where to Eat

EXPENSIVE

Alexandre ★★ TRADITIONAL FRENCH Two-Michelin–starred chef Michel Kayser oversees this elegant yet rustic domain located 8km (5 miles) south of the center. Chef Kayser adheres to classic French tradition, yet makes subtle improvements to his dishes. Menu items that delight the palate include courgette flowers stuffed with truffle mousse; roasted pigeon breast with baby vegetables; and Kayser's own version of *brandade de morue,* a local specialty with salted cod that's been poached and puréed. Be sure to try the selection of goat cheeses from the region.

Rte. de l'Aéroport de Garons. ✆ **04-66-70-08-99.** www.michelkayser.com. Reservations recommended. Main courses 44€–66€; fixed-price menus 46€–134€. AE, DC, MC, V. Wed–Sun noon–1:30pm;

Wed-Sat 8-9:30pm. Closed 2 weeks in Feb-Mar. From town center, take rue de la République southwest to av. Jean-Jaurès; then head south and follow signs to the airport (toward Garons).

MODERATE

La Bodéguita SPANISH The Royal Hotel's tapas restaurant is hugely popular among the smart set of Nîmes, attracted to its prime spot on the place d'Assas. You get tapas favorites such as octopus salad and *albondigas* (meatballs, but with a Greek twist), and the Nîmois *brandade de morue* turns up stuffed into red peppers. More substantial dishes include generous portions of organic bull steaks.

3 bd. Alphonse Daudet, 30000 Nîmes. © **04-66-58-28-29.** Fixed-price dinner 22€-34€. MC, V. Mon-Fri noon-2pm; daily 8-11pm (closed Mon in winter).

L'Exaequo FRENCH It's easy to forget the bustle of Nîmes when sitting in the shaded courtyard garden at L'Exaequo. In this tranquil spot you can enjoy French dishes with an Asian twist. Monkfish fritters come with a curry sauce, for example, and pan-fried scallops are served with Thai vegetables.

11 rue Bigot. © **04-66-21-71-96.** Fixed-price dinner 22€-34€. MC, V. Mon-Fri noon-2pm and 8-10pm; Sat 8-10pm.

Tendances Lisita Restaurant ★ FRENCH/BRASSERIE Among the throng of cafes and restaurants outside the Roman amphitheater, this brasserie stands out. In 2011, Chef Olivier Douet took the brave step of closing his Michelin-starred Lisita restaurant and turning it into a much more reasonably priced brasserie. While dining in the huge covered terrace or elegant indoor dining room, feast on such creations as scallop risotto or filet of local bull with creamed garlic. Of course, the deliberate decision to forego such things as tablecloths and a high staff-to-customer ratio means that Michelin won't be handing out the stars, but that's good news for diners who don't want to spend a fortune on an excellent meal.

2 bd. des Arènes. © **04-66-67-29-15.** www.lelisita.com. Reservations recommended. Main courses 22€-29€; fixed-price menus 23€-28€. AE, DC, MC, V. Tues-Sat noon-1:30pm and 7-9:30pm.

INEXPENSIVE

Au Chapon Fin MEDITERRANEAN Good hearty grilled foods are on offer at this friendly restaurant with a lovely rooftop terrace. Start with the marinated sardines, deep-fried camembert, or zucchini fritters, before moving on to generous portions of steak, mixed grilled meats, or leg of lamb.

3 rue du Château-Fadaise. © **04-66-67-34-73.** www.chaponfin-restaurant-nimes.com. Main courses 10€-16€; fixed-price dinner 28€. MC, V. Mon-Fri noon-2pm; Mon-Sat 7:30-10pm.

Le Ciel de Nîmes MEDITERRANEAN One of the loveliest views of Nîmes can be had at the open-air restaurant on top of the Carré d'Art. Head here for lunch or an aperitif (it closes at 6pm) and enjoy beautifully presented plates of roasted monkfish tails with a tomato tart, or tagliatelle with cep mushrooms and foie gras.

Place de la Maison Carrée, 3rd floor. © **04-66-36-71-70.** www.lecieldenimes.fr. Main courses 12€-17€; fixed-price lunch 23€-28€. MC, V. May-Sept Tues-Sun 10am-6pm; Oct-Apr Fri-Sat evenings only.

Nîmes After Dark

Once warm weather hits, all sorts of activities take place at the arena, including concerts and theater under the stars. The Office de Tourisme has a complete listing, and tickets are available at the Nîmes branch of **FNAC,** La Coupoule des Halles, 22 bd. Gambetta (© **08-25-02-00-20**), a multimedia chain store that sells books,

CDs, DVDs, electronics, and concert tickets. Tickets for cultural events such as symphonic or chamber-music concerts, theater, and opera performances are sold through **Le Théâtre de Nîmes,** 1 place de la Calade (✆ **04-66-36-65-10;** www.theatredenimes.com).

Streets to explore on virtually any night of the week include **place d'Assas** and **place de la Maison Carrée.** A popular spot is the **Zinc Cafe,** 13 rue de l'Agau (✆ **09-53-96-94-50**), formerly the Haddock Café, which now attracts a youngish crowd on the hunt for late-night tapas and some live music.

UZÈS ★★

682km (424 miles) S of Paris; 39km (24 miles) W of Avignon; 51km (32 miles) NW of Arles

Set on a limestone plateau amid the scented *garrigues,* the herb-covered scrubland countryside along the foot of the ancient Massif Central, Uzès is one of the loveliest villages in the Languedoc. It's the home of the lords of Uzès, the first duchy of France, whose members can trace their ancestry back to Charlemagne and who still reside in the ducal palace of Le Duché. The poet and dramatist Jean Racine lived here in 1661, sent by his family to stay with an uncle, the vicar general of Uzès. Racine has since been followed by numerous French luminaries who have discovered the pleasures of having a second home in Uzès and the surrounding Uzège region where they can live relatively unobtrusively.

In 2008, Uzès was officially designated a *ville d'art et d'histoire* (a town of art and history), both of which are apparent as you wander through the medieval streets. Artists and craftspeople have set up their workshops and studios throughout the town, where they work with ceramics, stone, wrought iron, and painted furniture. It adds up to create a pleasant and quietly affluent atmosphere.

Essentials

GETTING THERE As Uzès has no train station, **train** passengers must get off at Avignon or Nîmes. For rail schedules and information, call ✆ **36-35,** or visit www.voyages-sncf.com. **Buses** also connect Uzès to Avignon and Nîmes. For bus information, contact the **Gare Routière d'Uzès,** avenue de la Libération, through the tourist office (✆ **04-66-22-68-88**). By **car** from Avignon, take N100 west to the intersection with D981, following the signs northwest into Uzès.

VISITOR INFORMATION The **Office de Tourisme** is in the Chapelle des Capucins, place Albert-1er (✆ **04-66-22-68-88;** fax 04-66-22-95-19; www.uzes-tourisme.com).

SPECIAL EVENTS July's **Nuits Musicales d'Uzès** draws musicians of many stripes and talents from all over the world to a series of musical concerts performed at various venues throughout the town. Tickets for these events, along with announcements of concerts, are available at the tourist office. For 2 days in the middle of January, the **truffle festival** attracts more than 10,000 to the place aux Herbes for tastings and a truffle market, and the local restaurants join in by offering special truffle-based menus. Uzès' Saturday morning market is one of the finest in the region.

Exploring the Town

In the old part of town, every building is worth a moment or two of consideration. The central **place aux Herbes** is one of the prettiest and atmospheric squares in all of southern France, its medieval stone arcades housing cafes, restaurants, and shops. This is where the Saturday market begins before it meanders along the outlying streets. The **Jardin Médiéval,** impasse Port Royal (✆ **04-66-22-38-21**), stands between two 12th-century towers and is an evocative trip into the past when herbs were the only medicine. Tours of the garden end with a refreshing herbal drink, and cost 4€ for adults and 2€ for students. The **Cathédrale St-Théodorit,** place de l'Evêché (✆ **04-66-22-13-26**), still uses its original 17th-century organ, a remarkable instrument of 2,772 pipes. If you're lucky enough to be here during the last 2 weeks of July, you can attend organ concerts of the Nuits Musicales d'Uzès festival (see above). Adjacent is the circular six-story **Tour Fenestrelle,** all that remains of the original 12th-century cathedral that was burned down by the Huguenots. It's closed to the public, but you can see how the exterior resembles the Leaning Tower of Pisa.

Le Duché This palace is a massive conglomeration of styles, the result of nearly continuous expansion in direct correlation to the rising wealth and power of the duke and duchess. Large segments of the compound are occupied by the Duc and Duchesse de Crussol d'Uzès and cannot be visited. You can, however, climb the winding staircase in the square 11th-century Tour Bermonde for a sweeping view over the countryside from its elevated terrace. Whether or not this is worth the steep entrance fee is debatable. The 11th-century cellar contains casks of wine from the surrounding vineyards. Tours of the site end with a *dégustation* of the reds and rosés of the Cuvée Ducale. The building's showcase apartments include a dining room with Louis XIII and Renaissance furnishings, a great hall (Le Grand Hall) done in the style of Louis XV, a large library that includes family memoirs, and the 15th-century Chapelle Gothique. Visits are usually part of an obligatory French-language tour, but you can follow the commentary with an English-language pamphlet.

Place du Duché. ✆ **04-66-22-18-96.** www.uzes.fr. Admission 17€ adults, 13€ students and teens 12–16, 6€ children 7–11, free for children 6 and under. Tower only 6€ adults and children. Price reduced to 10€ on Sat Apr–June and Oct. Sept–June daily 10am–noon and 2–6pm; July–Aug daily 10am–12:30pm and 2–6:30pm.

Where to Stay

Au Quinze ★ You know you're in for something special when you enter this charming B&B, housed in an 18th-century mansion, through the stone vaulted entrance hall and stroll past the country kitchen. Belgian couple Carole and Jean-Pierre are wonderful hosts. The large rooms are romantically styled with wrought-iron canopies and fireplaces. One studio is also available just across from the main house; it has a fully equipped kitchen, although the bathroom is less up-to-date than the others. You won't want to leave the magical shaded garden, with a swimming pool set against the stone walls in the corner.

15 rue de la Grande Bourgade, 30700 Uzès. www.auquinze.com. ✆ **04-66-57-29-26** (cellphone 06-84-09-11-07). 4 units. 85€–180€ double. MC, V. **Amenities:** Breakfast room; pool (outdoor); Wi-Fi (free). *In room:* TV, hair dryer.

Hostellerie Provençale ★ Just a few steps away from the place aux Herbes is this charming hotel run by a friendly, welcoming staff. Rooms are spacious and prettily decorated in French country style; many have exposed beams, terra-cotta floors, and stone walls. Head up to the roof terrace for views across town. The restaurant, La Parenthèse, is worth a visit (see below).

1-3 rue de la Grande Bourgade, 30700 Uzès. www.hostellerieprovencale.com. ✆ **04-66-22-11-06.** Fax 04-66-75-01-03. 35 units. 95€–145€ double. AE, MC, V. Parking 10€. **Amenities:** Restaurant; bar; room service. *In room:* A/C, TV, hair dryer, minibar, Wi-Fi (free).

Le Patio de Violette Less than a 10-minute drive from the town center brings you to this modern villa in the Uzège countryside. Many of the airy rooms come with patios and pleasing views of the distant hills, as well as the gardens surrounding the swimming pool. Decor is contemporary and uncluttered, with large comfortable beds.

Quartier de Mayac, Chemin de Trinquelaïgues, 30700 Uzès. www.patiodeviolette.com. ✆ **04-66-01-09-83.** Fax 04-66-59-33-61. 25 units. 60€–140€ double. MC, V. Free parking. **Amenities:** Restaurant; bar; pool (outdoor); Wi-Fi (free). *In room:* A/C, TV, hair dryer.

Where to Eat

Le Parenthèse FRENCH This restaurant, in the Hostellerie Provençale hotel, specializes in using local, fresh ingredients. The menu changes based on the season and what's fresh at the market, but inventive dishes might include calf's liver glazed with a raspberry vinaigrette, giant shrimp roasted in lime and ginger, or a saddle of rabbit with an especially hot mustard sauce. On warm days, meals are served on the third-floor terrace.

1-3 rue de la Grande Bourgade. ✆ **04-66-22-41-20.** Reservations recommended. Main courses 18€; set menu 32€. AE, MC, V. Wed–Sun noon–2pm and 7–9pm. Closed mid-Feb to mid-Mar.

Les Terroirs MEDITERRANEAN/TAPAS Right in the center of place aux Herbes is this convivial bistro and its lively terrace. The trio of tapas is a good way to start, with a generous portion of hummus, tabbouleh, and octopus *à la provençale*. Main courses include beef or scallop carpaccio, as well as salads with goat's cheese, artichokes, and tapenade, among other fresh and well-presented dishes. It's a popular spot, so it's worth booking even a few hours beforehand. There's also a deli inside the restaurant if you want high-quality olive oil, tapenade, and other French products to take home.

5 place aux Herbes. ✆ **04-66-03-41-90.** Reservations recommended. Main courses 8.70€–14€. MC, V. Daily noon–2pm and 7–10pm (closes at 6pm Nov–Mar).

Le Zanelli PIZZERIA/ITALIAN This cheerful Italian restaurant offers good value and a buzzing atmosphere in the heart of the old town. There's a good selection of pizzas as well as a wider than expected range of pasta, meat, and shrimp dishes on offer. You might want to book a bit in advance if you want to eat on the terrace.

3 place Nicolas Froment. ✆ **04-66-03-01-93.** Reservations recommended. Main courses 7.50€–17€. MC, V. Thurs–Mon noon–2pm and 7–9:30pm (also Wed July–Aug). Closed Nov.

Myou MEDITERRANEAN/PROVENÇAL When the bustle of place aux Herbes gets to be too much, it can be bliss to stop in this relaxed restaurant near the church of St-Etienne. Flavors from neighboring Provence permeate the menu, featuring dishes like sautéed duck with black olives or filet of bream with Provençal herbs.

1 place St-Etienne. ✆ **04-66-22-59-28.** Main courses 14€–23€; set menus 20€–26€. MC, V. Tues–Sun noon–2:30pm and 7:30–9:30pm.

PROVENCE

by Mary Novakovich

Provence has been called a bridge between the past and the present, where yesterday blends with today. The Greeks and Romans filled the landscape with Hellenic theaters, Roman baths, amphitheaters, and triumphal arches. These were followed in medieval times by Romanesque fortresses and Gothic cathedrals. Provence's light and landscapes inspired Cézanne, van Gogh, and many other artists to paint some of their most celebrated works. Despite the changes over the years, the bone-chilling wind known as the mistral still howls through the broad-leaved plane trees.

The region is bounded on the west by the Rhône, on the northeast by the Alps, and on the south by the Mediterranean. The subsequent chapters will focus on the part of Provence known as the French Riviera or Côte d'Azur.

ORANGE ★★

658km (409 miles) S of Paris; 55km (34 miles) NE of Nîmes; 26km (16 miles) S of Avignon

Founded in 35 B.C. as Aurisio, Orange gets its name from the days when it was a dependency of the Dutch House of Orange-Nassau. Overlooking the Valley of the Rhône, Orange tempts visitors with Europe's third-largest extant triumphal arch and a well-preserved Roman theater. Louis XIV, who toyed with the idea of moving the theater to Versailles, said, "It is the finest wall in my kingdom." Orange's attractive squares make this town of 30,000 a pleasant place for a stroll.

The town is also within the Châteauneuf-du-Pape wine appellation, making it a magnet for wine connoisseurs. Many *caves* (vineyards) are spread throughout the district, most of which offer *dégustations* (wine tastings).

Essentials

GETTING THERE **Trains** to Orange arrive from Avignon and Marseille, among other places. From the Gare de Lyon Paris, you can catch a TGV train to Orange. For rail information, call ✆ **36-35,** or visit www.voyages sncf.com. For information on bus routes, contact the **gare routière** (✆ **04-90-34-15-59**), cours Pourtoules, behind the Théâtre Antique. If you're **driving** from Paris, take A6 south to Lyon, then A7 to Orange.

VISITOR INFORMATION The **Office de Tourisme** is at 5 cours Aristide-Briand (✆ **04-90-34-70-88;** fax 04-90-34-99-62; www.otorange.fr).

SPECIAL EVENTS From early July to early August, a drama, dance, and music festival called **Les Chorégies d'Orange** takes place at the Théâtre Antique, one of the most evocative ancient theaters in Europe. For information or tickets, contact the office, 18 place Silvain, adjacent to the theater (✆ **04-90-34-24-24;** fax 04-90-11-04-04; www.choregies.com).

Exploring the Town

In the southern part of town, the carefully restored **Théâtre Antique ★★★**, rue Madeleine Roch (✆ **04-90-51-17-60;** www.theatre-antique.com), dates from the days of Augustus. Built into the side of a hill, it once held 8,000 spectators in tiered seats. You can see how the theater has been used through the ages in an imaginative series of films shown in the depths of the structure. The theater is nearly 105m (345 ft.) long and 38m (125 ft.) high, making it a compelling backdrop for evening concerts, plays, and opera productions. It's open daily in January, February, November, and December from 9:30am to 4:30pm; March and October from 9:30am to 5:30pm; April, May, and September 9am to 6pm; and June to August 9am to 7pm. Admission is 8€ for adults, 6€ for students and children 17 and under.

West of the theater stood a huge temple that formed one of the greatest buildings in the empire. Across the street, the **Musée d'Art et d'Histoire,** place du Théâtre-Antique (✆ **04-90-51-17-60**), displays fragments of the temple. Your ticket to the theater also admits you to the museum, which is open daily April through September 9:30am to 7pm, and October to March 9am to 5:30pm.

Even older than the theater is the **Arc de Triomphe ★**, on avenue de l'Arc-de-Triomphe. It has decayed, but its decorations and other elements are fairly well preserved. Built to honor the conquering legions of Caesar, it rises 22m (72 ft.) and is nearly 21m (69 ft.) wide. Composed of a trio of arches held up by Corinthian columns, it was used as a dungeon in the Middle Ages.

Before leaving Orange, head for the park **Colline St-Eutrope,** adjacent to the Théâtre Antique, for a view of the valley and its mulberry plantations.

Where to Stay

Best Western Hôtel Arène Kulm ★ This friendly three-star hotel in the center of the historic district is in a quiet square shaded by plane trees. Guest rooms are furnished in a stripped-down version of Provençal decor, and the well-equipped executive rooms have large walk-in showers. A whole floor of "ecological" rooms has been designed for guests with allergies to carpets and other offending fabrics. A small outdoor pool was added in 2011 to go with the indoor whirlpool in the fitness center.

Place de Langes, 84100 Orange. www.hotel-arene.fr. ✆ **04-90-11-40-40.** Fax 04-90-11-40-45. 35 units. 82€–145€ double; 125€–160€ triple; 170€ junior suite. AE, MC, V. Parking 8€. **Amenities:** 2 restaurants; 2 pools (1 indoor and 1 outdoor); room service; Wi-Fi (free). *In room:* A/C, TV, hair dryer, minibar, Wi-Fi (in executive rooms only; free).

L'Apropos 🎁 Hidden behind heavy gates on one of Orange's busiest streets is a haven of comfort and style. Housed in a former *hôtel particulier* (mansion) that dates from 1860, this luxurious B&B offers five plush guest rooms that are bright and spacious. The only room that isn't a suite has a large private terrace. The property also has two cozy salons, a tapas restaurant, and beautifully landscaped gardens surrounding a swimming pool.

Provence

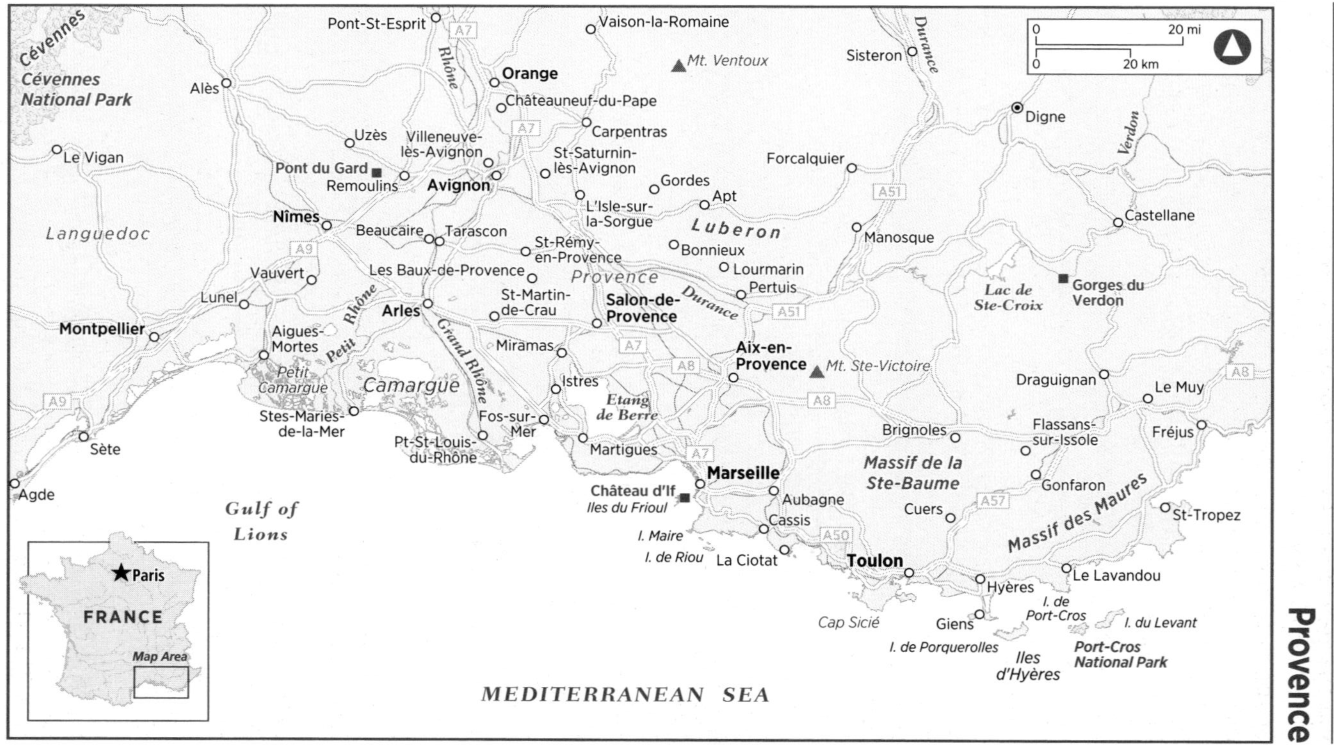

Cévennes
Cévennes National Park
Le Vigan
Alès
Languedoc
Pont-St-Esprit
Rhône
Orange
Châteauneuf-du-Pape
Vaison-la-Romaine
Mt. Ventoux
Uzès
Villeneuve-lès-Avignon
Pont du Gard
Remoulins
Avignon
Carpentras
St-Saturnin-lès-Avignon
Gordes
Apt
L'Isle-sur-la-Sorgue
Luberon
Nîmes
Beaucaire
Tarascon
St-Rémy-en-Provence
Bonnieux
Lourmarin
Les Baux-de-Provence
Provence
Pertuis
Vauvert
Lunel
Arles
St-Martin-de-Crau
Salon-de-Provence
Durance
Montpellier
Aigues-Mortes
Petit Rhône
Grand Rhône
Miramas
Aix-en-Provence
Mt. Ste-Victoire
Petit Camargue
Camargue
Istres
Etang de Berre
Stes-Maries-de-la-Mer
Fos-sur-Mer
Pt-St-Louis-du-Rhône
Martigues
Sète
Agde
Marseille
Château d'If
Iles du Frioul
Aubagne
Cassis
I. Maire
I. de Riou
La Ciotat
Toulon
Gulf of Lions
MEDITERRANEAN SEA
Sisteron
Durance
Digne
Verdon
Forcalquier
Manosque
Castellane
Lac de Ste-Croix
Gorges du Verdon
Draguignan
Le Muy
Fréjus
Brignoles
Flassans-sur-Issole
Gonfaron
Massif de la Ste-Baume
Massif des Maures
Cuers
St-Tropez
Le Lavandou
Hyères
I. de Port-Cros
I. du Levant
Cap Sicié
Giens
I. de Porquerolles
Iles d'Hyères
Port-Cros National Park
A7
A9
A51
A8
A50
A57
0
20 mi
20 km
Paris
FRANCE
Map Area

15 av. Frédéric Mistral, 84100 Orange. www.lapropos.com. ✆ **04-90-34-54-91** (cellphone 06-10-33-06-32). 5 units. 110€-135€ double; 195€-245€ suite, including breakfast. AE, MC, V. Secure parking. **Amenities:** Restaurant; bar; pool (outdoor, heated); solarium. *In room:* A/C, TV, hair dryer, Wi-Fi (free).

Park Inn by Radisson The well-managed hotel in a 1980s building has wings that curve around a landscaped courtyard. Its well-furnished rooms are arranged around a series of gardens, the largest containing a pool. Rooms have compact modern bathrooms. The poolside restaurant serves fixed-price menus.

80 rte. de Caderousse, 84100 Orange. www.parkinn.com. ✆ **04-90-34-24-10.** Fax 04-90-34-85-48. 99 units. 89€-140€ double. AE, MC, V. Free parking. Drive .8km (½ mile) west of the city center, following directions to Caderousse. **Amenities:** Restaurant; bar; pool (outdoor); room service. *In room:* A/C, TV, hair dryer, minibar, Wi-Fi (free).

Villa Aurenjo A 10-minute walk from the Roman theater takes you to an elegant and quirky 18th-century *chambres d'hôtes* (B&B) set within a grove of olive and sycamore trees. Its five rooms are inspired by Van Gogh in their color and style, with charming touches like pleasingly old-fashioned roll-top tubs. Large rooms open onto the terrace or garden.

121 rue François Chambovet, 84100 Orange. www.villa-aurenjo.com. ✆ **04-90-11-10-00** (cellphone 06-62-67-03-30). 5 units. 100€-210€ double; 190€-260€ suite. Rates include breakfast. MC, V. Parking. **Amenities:** Pool (outdoor); tennis; sauna. *In room:* TV, Wi-Fi (free).

Where to Eat

Le Parvis ☺ TRADITIONAL FRENCH One of the best restaurants in the area, Le Parvis offers a changing menu that changes seasonally and takes advantage of the region's fresh produce. Chef Jean-Michel Béringier offers such delicious dishes as red mullet grilled with rosemary and roasted guinea fowl with celeriac. There is also a children's menu.

55 cours Pourtoules. ✆ **04-90-34-82-00.** Reservations required. Main courses 17€-23€; fixed-price menu 25€-42€; children's menu 12€. MC, V. Tues-Sun noon-2:30pm; Tues-Sat 7:30-9:15pm. Closed mid-Nov to early Dec and mid-Jan-early Feb.

Where to Stay & Eat Nearby

Château de Rochegude ★★ This Relais & Châteaux turreted castle stands at the edge of a hill, surrounded by vineyards and 10 hectares (25 acres) of parkland. Each room is done in Provençal style, with fabrics and furniture influenced by the region's 18th- and 19th-century traditions. As befits a château, rooms come in many shapes and sizes, and some are quite spacious.

The restaurant here offers excellent food and service. You can enjoy meals in the stately dining room, barbecue by the pool, and refreshments on the sunny terraces. Fixed-price lunches cost from 26€, fixed-price dinners 39€ to 89€.

Place du Château 26790 Rochegude. www.chateauderochegude.com. ✆ **04-75-97-21-10.** Fax 04-75-04-89-87. 25 units. 170€-430€ double; 350€-540€ suite. AE, DC, MC, V. Free parking. Closed Nov. Take D976 13km (8 miles) north of Orange, following signs toward Gap and Rochegude. **Amenities:** Restaurant; bar; pool (outdoor); room service; tennis court. *In room:* A/C, TV, minibar, Wi-Fi (free).

CHÂTEAUNEUF-DU-PAPE

671km (417 miles) S of Paris; 19km (12 miles) N of Avignon; 13km (8 miles) S of Orange

Near Provence's northern border, Châteauneuf-du-Pape was built as the Castel Gandolfo, the summer home of the French popes of Avignon, during the 14th-century

Orange

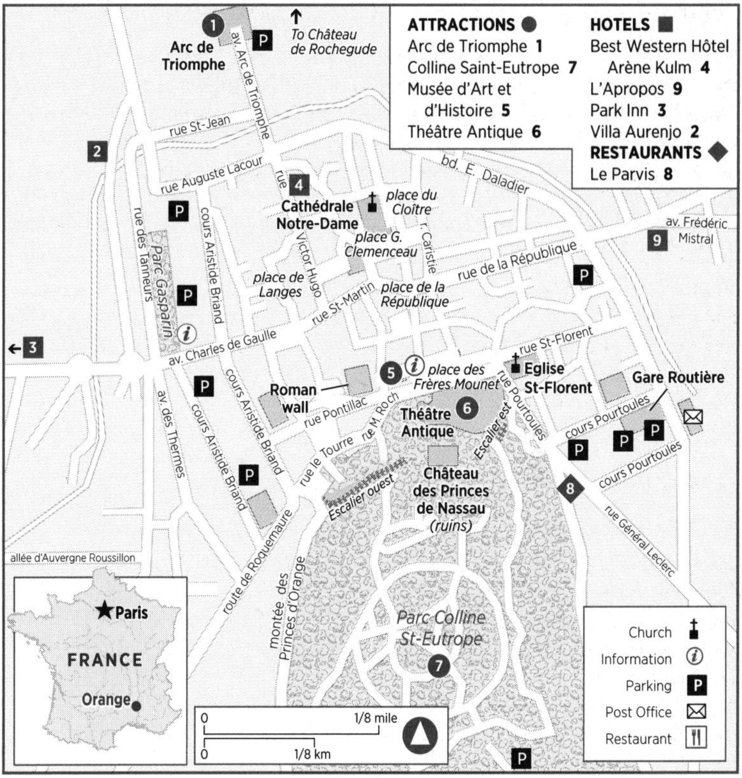

ATTRACTIONS ●
Arc de Triomphe **1**
Colline Saint-Eutrope **7**
Musée d'Art et d'Histoire **5**
Théâtre Antique **6**

HOTELS ■
Best Western Hôtel Arène Kulm **4**
L'Apropos **9**
Park Inn **3**
Villa Aurenjo **2**

RESTAURANTS ◆
Le Parvis **8**

reign of Pope John XXII. Today the castle ruins overlook the vast acres of vineyards planted by the popes, the start of a regional industry that today produces some of the world's best reds as well as excellent white wines.

Essentials

GETTING THERE To reach Châteauneuf-du-Pape, take one of the regular **buses** from Avignon (p. 115), a journey of less than 30 minutes. Châteauneuf does not have a bus station; you are deposited and picked up at place de la Bascule, behind the post office. The tourist office (see below) is the best source for schedules and information about bus access.

If you're **driving** from Avignon, head north on A7 to the intersection with Route 17, and continue northwest following the signs into Châteauneuf-du-Pape.

VISITOR INFORMATION The **Office de Tourisme** is at place du Portail (✆ **04-90-83-71-08;** www.ccpro.fr).

SPECIAL EVENTS Since the Middle Ages, the annual **Fête de la Véraison** has been held in early August (see below). The village also takes part in the **Floraisons Musicales,** a music festival that travels throughout Provence and will pitch up in Châteauneuf-du-Pape for several dates in June and July.

Wine Lure & Lore

The local wines are distinctive in their blending of 13 varieties of grapes, grown on vines surrounded by stones that reflect heat onto them during the day and keep them warm in the cool night. As a result, the wines produced in the district's vineyards are among the most potent in France. The region played a central role in the initiation of the Appellation d'Origine Contrôlée, France's strict quality-control system. The late Baron Le Roy de Boiseaumarie, the most distinguished of the local vintners, initiated geographical boundaries and minimum standards for the production of wines given the Châteauneuf-du-Pape label. In 1923, local producers won exclusive rights to market their Côtes du Rhônes under that label, and thus paved the way for other regions to identify and protect their distinctive wines. You'll see a plaque devoted to his memory in the town's place de la Renaissance.

A useful source is **La Vinadéa,** or Maison des Vins, 8 rue Maréchal Foch (**© 04-90-83-70-69;** www.vinadea.com), a promotion house set up by the winemakers' Fédération des Syndicats de Producteurs. It's open for wine tastings and sales daily.

Touring & Tasting the Wines

A map posted in place du Portail (but called place de la Fontaine by just about everyone) pinpoints 22 wineries open for touring and tasting. One of the best known is **Clos des Papes,** avenue Pierre de Luxembourg, in the town center (**© 04-90-83-70-13;** www.clos-des-papes.fr), where Paul-Vincent Avril is the fourth generation of winemakers to produce top-class wine.

The town's museum devotes all its exhibition space to winemaking. The **Musée du Vin,** avenue Pierre de Luxembourg (**© 04-90-83-70-07;** www.brotte.com), contains the history and artifacts of local wine production, including a 16th-century wine press, winemakers' tools, barrel-making equipment, and a tasting cellar. It's open daily from April to September from 9am to 1pm and 2 to 7pm, and October to March from 9am to noon and 2 to 6pm. Admission and tastings are free.

A WINE FESTIVAL During 3 days in early August, the village hosts the annual **Fête de la Véraison ★**, a medieval fair. It includes tasting stalls set up by local winemakers, actors impersonating Provençaux troubadours, merchants selling locally made handicrafts, concerts, a gala dinner, and a torchlight parade. If you attend, you can drink all the wine you want for the price of a *verre de la véraison.* This souvenir glass, filled on demand at any vintner who participates, costs only a few euros and is sold at strategically positioned kiosks around town.

Wine & Chocolate

If you're a fan of wine and chocolate, visit Vin Chocolat & Compagnie, a chocolate and wine showroom on the Route d'Avignon (© 04-90-83-54-71; www.vin-chocolat-castelain.com), about 3km (2 miles) south of town. In these show rooms, chocolate-maker Bernard Castelain demonstrates how he produces Bouchons de Châteauneuf-du-Pape, dark chocolate *(ganache)* flavored with a distilled version of the wine produced in local vineyards *(vieux marc de Châteauneuf).* Children and adults can make their own chocolate to see how their creations compare to the company's best-selling Palets des Papes and Picholines.

Where to Stay & Eat

Hostellerie du Château des Fines-Roches ★★ This manor house located on a hill looks as if it has been around since the Middle Ages, but it was actually built in the late 19th century. Named for the smooth rocks (*fines roches*) found in the soil of the nearby vineyards, the château devotes its huge cellars to the storage of thousands of bottles of local wines. The guest rooms on the upper floors of this charming hotel include Provençal styling with a scattering of antiques. The views from the terrace stretch as far as Avignon's Palais des Papes and the Alpilles mountains. The restaurant serves finely crafted dishes, including *barigoule* (stew) of crayfish tails with artichokes and filet of bull from the Camargue marinated in strong red wine. The wine list, naturally, focuses on local vintages.

Rte. de Sorgues, 84230 Châteauneuf-du-Pape. www.chateaufinesroches.com. ✆ **04-90-83-70-23.** Fax 04-90-83-78-42. 11 units. 109€–315€ double. MC, V. Free parking. Closed Nov. From the center of town, drive 3km (2 miles) south, following the signs to Avignon. **Amenities:** Restaurant; bar; pool (outdoor); room service. *In room:* A/C, TV, hair dryer, minibar, Wi-Fi (free).

La Garbure This Logis de France hotel is in the heart of the village, offering simple yet stylish rooms. The restaurant, which spills out onto tables near the village's central square, offers a menu that is far grander than its rustic surroundings would suggest. Dishes could include langoustine ravioli, braised beef cheeks in red wine, or duck stuffed with girolle mushrooms.

3 rue Joseph Ducos, 84230 Châteauneuf-du-Pape. www.la-garbure.com. ✆ **04-90-83-75-08.** Fax 04-90-83-52-34. 8 units. 76€–92€ double. MC, V. Restaurant: fixed-price menus 26€–55€. **Amenities:** Restaurant; bar; garage parking; Wi-Fi (free). *In room:* A/C, TV, hair dryer.

La Sommellerie ★ Formerly a 17th-century farm building, La Sommellerie is a relaxing and comfortable hotel located just outside the village. The Provençal-style bedrooms overlook the pool, gardens, vineyards, or surrounding hills. The restaurant makes the most of local game and seasonal produce, serving truffled risotto and its own version of bouillabaisse.

Rte. de Roquemaure D17, 84230 Châteauneuf-du-Pape. www.la-sommellerie.fr. ✆ **04-90-83-50-00.** Fax 04-90-83-51-85. 16 units. 75€–123€ double; 99€–182€ suites. Restaurant menus start at 31€. AE, MC, V. Free parking. **Amenities:** Restaurant; bar; pool (outdoor); Wi-Fi (free). *In room:* A/C, TV, hair dryer.

AVIGNON ★★★

684km (425 miles) S of Paris; 80km (50 miles) NW of Aix-en-Provence; 106km (66 miles) NW of Marseille

Once the heart of Christendom, medieval Avignon invites you to meander its elegant cobblestones in the shadow of the world's largest Gothic palace, the 14th-century Palais des Papes. Nowadays papal fervor has been replaced by an upbeat, arty vibe that peaks during July's wildly theatrical Festival d'Avignon. But the capital of the Vaucluse region throngs year-round too, in squares and museums, on bustling cafe terraces, and atop the ruins of one of the world's most serenaded bridges, the Pont d'Avignon.

Things to Do Avignon's 4.3km (2⅔ miles) of ramparts embrace one of Europe's culture centers. Discover monumental Cistercian and Gothic architecture inside the **Palais des Papes,** the 14th-century headquarters of schismatic cardinals who very nearly destroyed papal authority in Rome. Then whistle "Sur le Pont d'Avignon" on the very bridge the kitschy song was written about. Admire medieval treasures at the **Musée du Petit Palais,** then relax with locals amid historic water wheels, cafes, and bookshops on **Rue des Teinturiers.**

Relaxation Stroll through the **Rocher des Doms,** the hilltop gardens that are the site of the city's oldest settlement. Perched over the Rhône River, the lush gardens include landscaped terraces and a shaded duck pond. A free ferry shuttles across the Rhône to **Ile de la Barthelasse,** Europe's largest river island and home to the municipal swimming pool, campsites, restaurants, and small organic farms.

Restaurants & Dining This is Provence, the land of juicy tomatoes, lemons, rosemary, and thyme. Avignon is nestled into the vine-clad **Bouches-du-Rhône** region, and you can drink down all that glorious food with delicious, locally produced wines. **Place de l'Horloge** is littered in brasseries, while **Hiély Lucullus,** on rue de la République, has been serving dishes like beef with truffles since 1938. Gastronomes can head to the covered market at **Les Halles** for Saturday-morning cooking lessons with the city's finest chefs.

Nightlife & Entertainment Avignon's nightlife is all about roaming its narrow, softly lighted streets, stopping as soon as you hear the locals' accents warming the airwaves on a cafe terrace. **Place de l'Horloge,** watched over by its ornate clock tower, is awash in cafes and bars. Opera lovers catch a concert in the gracious 19th-century environs of the **Opéra Théâtre.** If film's your genre, the quaint art house **Utopia Manutention** cinema is snuggled into a nook below the papal palace.

Essentials

GETTING THERE **Flights** from Paris, and from British destinations such as London, Southampton, Exeter, and Birmingham arrive at **Aéroport Avignon-Caumont** (✆ **04-90-81-51-51**), 8km (5 miles) southeast of Avignon. Check www.tcra.fr for exact times and fares. Taxis from the airport to the center cost about 20€; call ✆ **04-90-82-20-20** to order a taxi. **Trains** arrive regularly from Paris, Marseille, and Arles.

From Paris, TGV **trains** from Gare de Lyon take about 3 hours and 30 minutes. Trains arrive frequently from Marseille (70 min.) and from Arles (20 min.). For train information, call ✆ **36-35,** or visit www.voyages-sncf.com.

The **bus station (gare routière)** is at 5 av. Monclar (✆ **04-90-82-07-35**). The main routes connect to Arles (trip time 1½ hr.) and Marseille (trip time 2 hr.).

If you're **driving** from Paris, take A6 south to Lyon, then A7 south to Avignon. To explore the area by **bike,** go to **Provence Bike,** 52 av. St-Ruf (✆ **04-90-27-92-61;** www.provence-bike.com), which rents all sorts of bikes as well as motorcycles and scooters. ***Note:*** Avignon also has a municipal bicycle-hire scheme, which allows you to rent a bike from one of the stations dotted through the city.

VISITOR INFORMATION The **Office de Tourisme** is at 41 cours Jean-Jaurès (✆ **04-32-74-32-74;** fax 04-90-82-95-03; www.avignon-tourisme.com). Ask for a free **Avignon Passion tourist pass,** which gives discounts on the major sights once you've paid for the first one.

SPECIAL EVENTS The biggest celebration is the **Festival d'Avignon,** which takes over most of July. The festival, one of the largest in France, focuses on theater, dance, and music. Part of the fun is the nightly revelry in the streets. Tickets cost 5€ to 40€. Prices for rooms and meals skyrocket, so make reservations far in advance. For information, contact the **Bureau du Festival,** Espace Saint-Louis, 20 rue du

Avignon

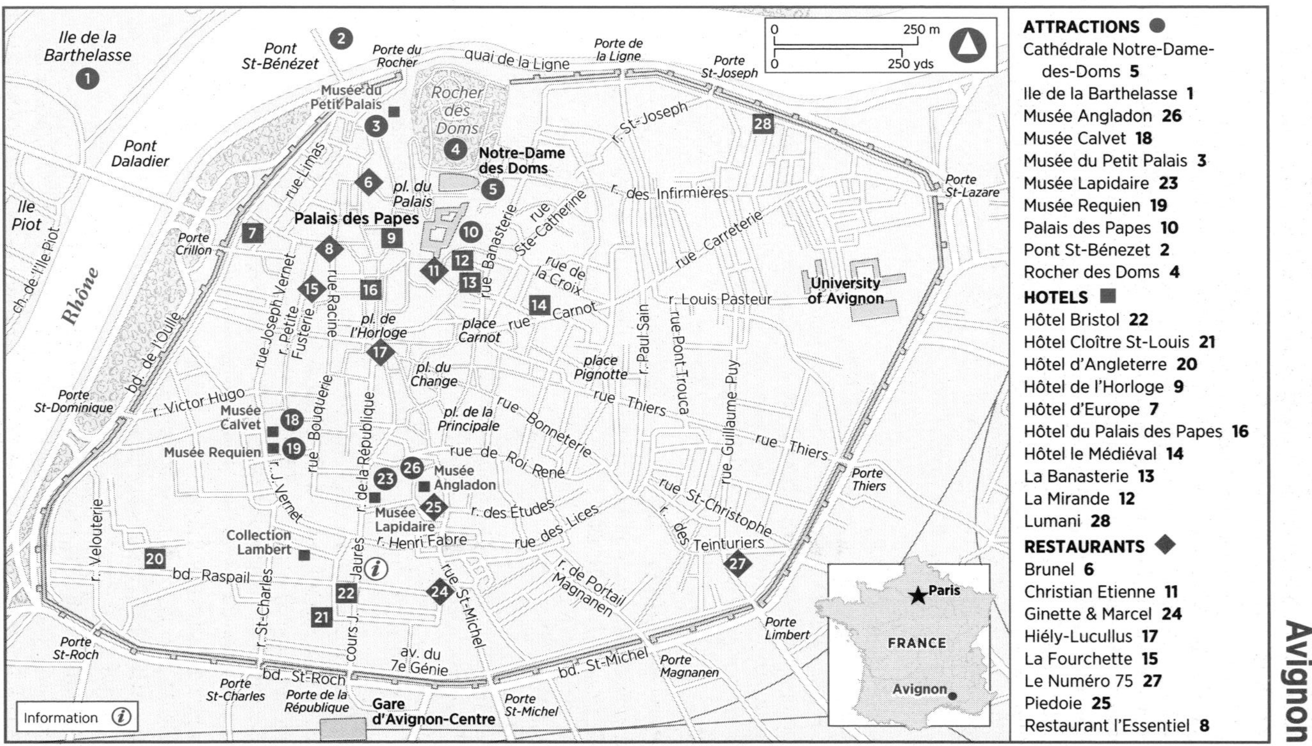
ATTRACTIONS
Cathédrale Notre-Dame-des-Doms 5
Ile de la Barthelasse 1
Musée Angladon 26
Musée Calvet 18
Musée du Petit Palais 3
Musée Lapidaire 23
Musée Requien 19
Palais des Papes 10
Pont St-Bénezet 2
Rocher des Doms 4
HOTELS
Hôtel Bristol 22
Hôtel Cloître St-Louis 21
Hôtel d'Angleterre 20
Hôtel de l'Horloge 9
Hôtel d'Europe 7
Hôtel du Palais des Papes 16
Hôtel le Médiéval 14
La Banasterie 13
La Mirande 12
Lumani 28
RESTAURANTS
Brunel 6
Christian Etienne 11
Ginette & Marcel 24
Hiély-Lucullus 17
La Fourchette 15
Le Numéro 75 27
Piedoie 25
Restaurant l'Essentiel 8
0
250 m
250 yds
Ile de la Barthelasse
Pont St-Bénezet
Porte du Rocher
quai de la Ligne
Porte de la Ligne
Porte St-Joseph
Musée du Petit Palais
Rocher des Doms
Pont Daladier
Notre-Dame des Doms
pl. du Palais
Palais des Papes
Ile Piot
ch. de l'Ile Piot
Rhône
Porte Crillon
rue Limas
r. St-Joseph
r. des Infirmières
Porte St-Lazare
rue Ste-Catherine
rue Banasterie
rue Carreterie
rue de la Croix
rue Carnot
University of Avignon
r. Louis Pasteur
rue Joseph Vernet
r. Petite Fusterie
rue Racine
pl. de l'Horloge
place Carnot
r. Paul Sain
rue Pont Trouca
rue Guillaume Puy
bd. de l'Oulle
place Pignotte
pl. du Change
Porte St-Dominique
r. Victor Hugo
Musée Calvet
Musée Requien
rue Bouquerie
r. de la République
pl. de la Principale
rue Bonneterie
rue Thiers
Porte Thiers
rue de Roi René
Musée Angladon
r. J. Vernet
Musée Lapidaire
r. des Études
rue des Lices
rue St-Christophe
r. des Teinturiers
r. Velouterie
Collection Lambert
r. Henri Fabre
bd. Raspail
r. St-Charles
cours J. Jaurès
rue St-Michel
r. de Portail Magnanen
Porte Limbert
Paris
FRANCE
Avignon
Porte St-Roch
av. du 7e Génie
bd. St-Michel
Porte Magnanen
Porte St-Charles
bd. St-Roch
Porte de la République
Gare d'Avignon-Centre
Porte St-Michel
Information

portail Boquier, 84000 Avignon (✆ **04-90-27-66-50;** www.festival-avignon.com). At roughly the same time is the festival's offshoot, **Avignon OFF,** which fills the streets with hundreds of acts (✆ **04-90-85-13-08;** www.avignonleoff.com).

Exploring the Town

Avignon's main attraction is the **Palais des Papes** (see review below), the 14th-century headquarters of cardinals who very nearly destroyed papal authority in Rome, but the city has many other wonderful attractions to explore.

Cathédrale Notre-Dame-des-Doms ★ Near the Palais des Papes is this 12th-century cathedral, containing the flamboyant Gothic tomb of a few apostate popes. Crowning the top is a gilded statue of the Virgin from the 19th century. From the cathedral, enter the promenade du Rocher-des-Doms and its garden to enjoy the view across the Rhône to Villeneuve-lès-Avignon.

Place du Palais des Papes. ✆ **04-90-86-81-01.** Free admission. Daily 8am–9pm; hours may vary according to religious ceremonies.

Musée Angladon ★ This enchanting museum, opened in 1995, contains the magnificent art collection of Jacques Doucet, renowned Parisian haute couture designer. Doucet cultivated a number of young artists, among them Picasso, Braque, Max Jacob, Marcel Duchamp, and Guillaume Apollinaire, and began to collect their early works. For decades, Doucet's heirs kept the treasure-trove a relative secret and lived in quiet splendor amid canvases by Cézanne, Sisley, Derain, Degas, and Modigliani. Today you can wander through Doucet's former abode, which is also filled with rare antiques and art objects that include 16th-century Buddhas and Louis XVI chairs designed by Jacob. Doucet died in 1929 at the age of 76, his own fortune so diminished that his nephew paid for his funeral. But his rich legacy lives on here.

5 rue Laboureur. ✆ **04-90-82-29-03.** www.angladon.com. Admission 6€ adults, 3€ students; 1.50€ children 7–14. Tues–Sun 1–6pm. Closed Tues in winter.

Musée Calvet ★ This museum in an 18th-century mansion features the works of Vernet, David, Corot, Manet, and Soutine, plus a collection of ancient silverware. Look out for Bruegel the Younger's *Le Cortège Nuptial (The Bridal Procession),* a copy of Bosch's *Adoration of the Magi,* plus sculptures by Camille Claudel.

65 rue Joseph-Vernet. ✆ **04-90-86-33-84.** www.musee-calvet.org. Admission 6€ adults, 3€ students, free for children 12 and under. Wed–Mon 10am–1pm and 2–6pm.

Musée du Petit Palais This was the palace where the first two Avignon popes lived until the construction of the Palais des Papes. It holds an important collection of paintings from the Italian schools of the 13th to 16th centuries, including works from Florence, Venice, Siena, and Lombardy. Salons display 15th-century paintings done in Avignon, and several galleries are devoted to Roman and Gothic sculptures.

Place du Palais des Papes. ✆ **04-90-86-44-58.** Admission 6€ adults, 3€ students, free for children 12 and under. June–Sept Wed–Mon 10am–6pm; Oct–May Wed–Mon 10am–1pm and 2–6pm.

Musée Lapidaire ★ Behind a baroque facade, a 17th-century Jesuit church has been turned into an intriguing museum of mainly Gallo-Roman sculptures. In the museum you can trace the history of the various civilizations that have cultivated Provence. Some of the exhibitions are frightening, including the statue of a man-eating monster discovered at Noves called *Tarasque.* Fascinating Greco-Roman statues are on exhibition, including a magnificent copy of Praxiteles' ***Apollo the Python Killer*** ★. A large number of ancient sarcophagi and funerary art is also on show.

Palais des Papes

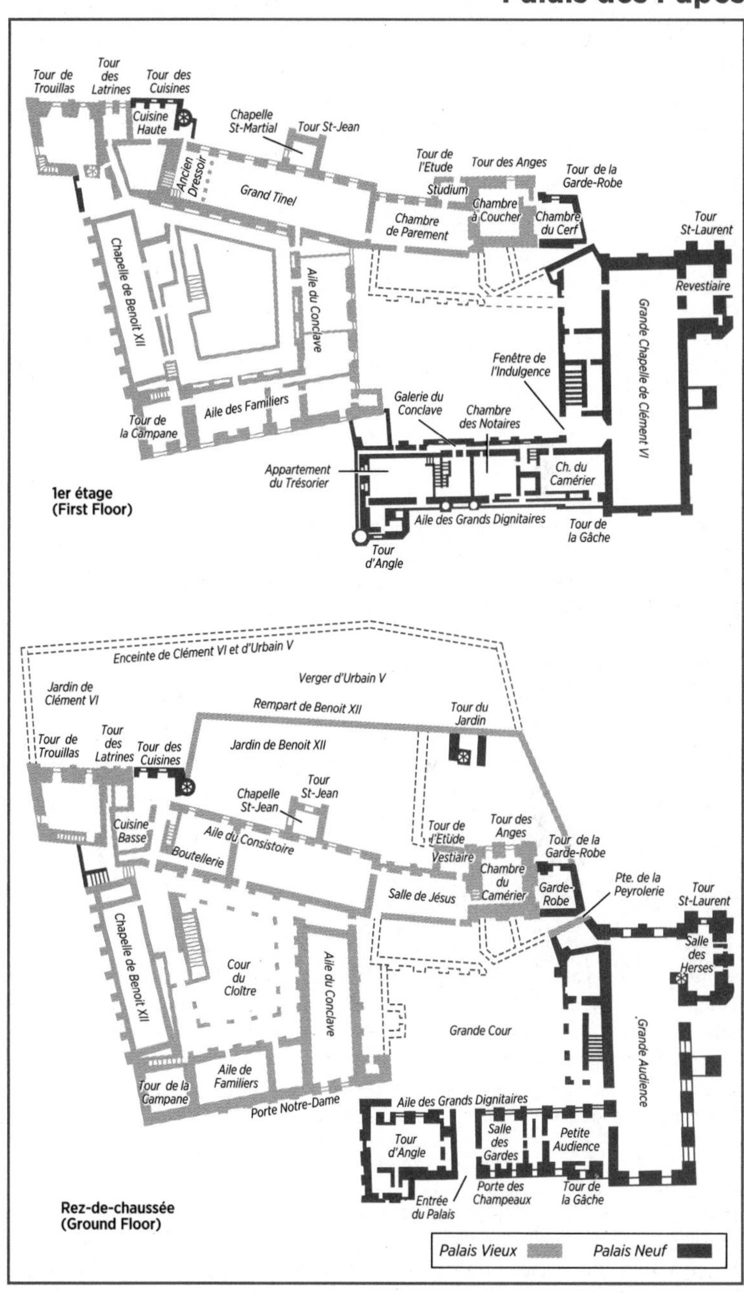
Tour de Trouillas
Tour des Latrines
Tour des Cuisines
Cuisine Haute
Chapelle St-Martial
Tour St-Jean
Ancien Dressoir
Grand Tinel
Tour de l'Etude
Studium
Tour des Anges
Tour de la Garde-Robe
Chambre à Coucher
Chambre du Cerf
Chambre de Parement
Tour St-Laurent
Revestiaire
Chapelle de Benoit XII
Aile du Conclave
Grande Chapelle de Clément VI
Fenêtre de l'Indulgence
Galerie du Conclave
Chambre des Notaires
Tour de la Campane
Aile des Familiers
Appartement du Trésorier
Ch. du Camérier
Aile des Grands Dignitaires
Tour de la Gâche
Tour d'Angle
1er étage (First Floor)
Enceinte de Clément VI et d'Urbain V
Jardin de Clément VI
Verger d'Urbain V
Rempart de Benoit XII
Tour du Jardin
Tour de Trouillas
Tour des Latrines
Tour des Cuisines
Jardin de Benoit XII
Tour St-Jean
Chapelle St-Jean
Cuisine Basse
Aile du Consistoire
Boutellerie
Tour de l'Etude
Tour des Anges
Vestiaire
Tour de la Garde-Robe
Chambre du Camérier
Garde-Robe
Salle de Jésus
Pte. de la Peyrolerie
Tour St-Laurent
Salle des Herses
Chapelle de Benoit XII
Cour du Cloître
Aile du Conclave
Grande Cour
Grande Audience
Tour de la Campane
Aile de Familiers
Porte Notre-Dame
Aile des Grands Dignitaires
Tour d'Angle
Salle des Gardes
Petite Audience
Entrée du Palais
Porte des Champeaux
Tour de la Gâche
Rez-de-chaussée (Ground Floor)
Palais Vieux
Palais Neuf

65 rue de la République. ✆ **04-90-85-75-38.** Admission 2€ adults, 1€ students, free for children 12 and under. Wed-Mon 10am-noon and 2-6pm.

Musée Requien This offbeat museum can easily take up an hour of your time. Located next to the Musée Calvet, it was named after the naturalist Esprit Requien (1788–1851), who was largely responsible for the nucleus of the collection. The museum houses one of the most important natural history libraries in France but is most often visited for its herbarium ★, containing some 200,000 specimens gathered by botanists from around the world.

67 rue Joseph-Vernet. ✆ **04-90-82-43-51.** www.museum-avignon.org. Free admission. Tues-Sat 9am-noon and 2-6pm.

Palais des Papes ★★★ Dominating Avignon from a hill is one of the most famous (or notorious, depending on your point of view) palaces in the Christian world. Headquarters of a schismatic group of cardinals who came close to toppling the authority of the popes in Rome, it is part fortress, part showplace. In 1309, Pope Clement V fled to Avignon to escape political infighting in Rome. His successor, John XXII, chose to stay in Avignon. The third Avignon pope, Benedict XII, was the one responsible for the construction of this magnificent palace. Avignon became, for a time, the Vatican of the north. During the period, dubbed "the Babylonian Captivity" by Rome, the popes held extravagant court in the palace; art and culture flourished, as did prostitution and vice. When Gregory XI was persuaded to return to Rome in 1376, Avignon elected its own rival pope, and the Great Schism split the Christian world. The real struggle, of course, was about the wealth and power of the papacy. The reign of Avignon's antipopes finally ended in 1417 with the election of Martin V in Rome, and the papal court here was disbanded.

Chapelle St-Jean is known for its beautiful frescoes, attributed to the school of Matteo Giovanetti and painted between 1345 and 1348. The frescoes present scenes from the life of John the Baptist and John the Evangelist. More Giovanetti frescoes can be seen above the Chapelle St-Jean in the **Chapelle St-Martial.** The frescoes here depict the miracles of St. Martial, patron saint of Limousin.

Grand Tinel (Banquet Hall) is about 41m (135 ft.) long and 9m (30 ft.) wide, and the pope's table stood on the southern side. The **pope's bedroom** is on the first floor of the Tour des Anges. Its walls are entirely decorated in tempera with foliage on which birds and squirrels perch; bird cages are painted in the recesses of the windows. In a secular vein, the **Studium (Stag Room)**—study of Clement VI—was frescoed in 1343 with hunting scenes. Added under the same Clement, who had a taste for grandeur, the **Grande Audience (Great Audience Hall)** contains frescoes of the prophets; these are also attributed to Giovanetti and were painted in 1352.

Self-guided tours in English, using a hand-held audio device, are available anytime during opening hours and are included in the price.

Place du Palais des Papes. ✆ **04-90-27-50-00.** www.palais-des-papes.com. Admission (including tour with guide or recording) 8.50€–11€ adults, 7€–8.50€ seniors and students, free for children 7 and under. Daily Mar 1-14 9am-6:30pm, Mar 15-June 9am-7pm, July 9am-8pm, Aug 9am-9pm, Sept 1-15 9am-8pm, Sept 16-Nov 1 9am-7pm, Nov 2-Feb 9:30am-5:45pm.

Pont St-Bénezet ★★ This ancient bridge, which was immortalized in the song *"Sur le pont d'Avignon, l'on y danse, l'on y danse,"* was far too narrow to dance upon, as the rhyme suggests. More likely locals danced on the riverbank below it—*sous le pont.* Spanning the Rhône and connecting Avignon with Villeneuve-lès-Avignon, the bridge is now a ruin, with only 4 of its original 22 arches. The bridge was built between 1177 and 1185 and suffered various disasters. (In 1669, half of it fell into the river.) On one of the piers is the two-story **Chapelle St-Nicolas**—one story in Romanesque style, the other in Gothic. A visit to the small chapel on the bridge is part of the overall admission fee.

Rue Ferruce. ✆ **04-90-27-51-16.** Admission 4€–4.50€ adults, 3€–3.50€ seniors and students, free for children 7 and under. Daily Nov–Mar 9:30am–5:45pm, Apr–June and Oct 9am–6pm, Aug 9am–9pm; July and Sept 9am–8pm.

Shopping

Pick up high-quality lavender products at **Pure Lavande**, 61 rue de la Grande Fusterie (✆ **04-90-14-70-05;** www.lavandeandco.fr). Its natural ingredients come from the lavender estate at Château du Bois in Haute Provence. **Souleiado,** 19 rue Joseph Vernet (✆ **04-90-86-47-67**), which means "first ray of sunshine after a storm," offers clothing that is inspired by traditional Provençal costumes, as well as traditional Provençal fabrics, which you can buy by the meter. **Hervé Baume,** 19 rue Petite Fusterie (✆ **04-90-86-37-66**), specializes in upmarket garden furniture and antiques. **Jaffier-Parsi,** 42 rue des Fourbisseurs (✆ **04-90-86-08-85**), is known for its copper saucepans from the Norman town of Villedieu-les-Poêles, which has been making them since the Middle Ages. If you're seeking a new perspective on Provençal pottery, go to **Terre è Provence,** 26 rue de la République (✆ **04-90-85-56-45**), where you can pick up wonderful kitsch, such as terra-cotta plates decorated with three-dimensional cicadas.

Most markets in Avignon are open from 6am to 1pm. The biggest covered market with 40 different merchants is **Les Halles,** place Pie, open Tuesday to Sunday. Try to catch the free cooking lesson given by local chefs every Saturday at 11am (except Aug). The **flower market** is on place des Carmes on Saturday, and the **flea market** is in the same place on Sunday.

Where to Stay

VERY EXPENSIVE

La Mirande ★★★ This opulent five-star hotel is tucked behind the Palais des Papes in a former cardinal's palace. It's sumptuous but unstuffy. The exquisitely decorated and comfortable guest rooms evoke the splendor of the 18th century, with hand-printed fabrics lining the walls. Try to find time for the afternoon tea served daily within the glass-covered interior courtyard, or the whisky-tasting sessions in the Napoleon III salon. The delightfully old-fashioned basement kitchen doubles as a cooking school for people of all levels and ages. The Michelin-starred restaurant serves finely crafted yet unpretentious seasonal dishes served either in the Renaissance dining room or on the vast shaded terrace overlooking the Palais des Papes.

4 place de l'Amirande, 84000 Avignon. www.la-mirande.fr. ✆ **04-90-85-93-93.** Fax 04-90-86-26-85. 20 units. 330€–616€ double; 450€–1,419€ suite. AE, DC, MC, V. Parking 22€. **Amenities:** Restaurant; bar; babysitting; room service. *In room:* A/C, TV, hair dryer, minibar, Wi-Fi (free).

EXPENSIVE

Hôtel Cloître St-Louis ★ This hotel is in a former Jesuit school built in the 1580s. Much of the original premises remains, including the baroque facade, the wraparound arcades, and the soaring ceiling vaults. Guest rooms are more functional and can look quite austere. Rooms range from medium-size to spacious, and some have sliding glass doors overlooking the patio. A chief bonus is the outdoor pool.

20 rue du Portail Boquier, 84000 Avignon. www.cloitre-saint-louis.com. ✆ **04-90-27-55-55.** Fax 04-90-82-24-01. 80 units. 210€–320€ double. AE, DC, MC, V. Parking 12€–15€. **Amenities:** Restaurant; bar; pool (outdoor); room service; Wi-Fi (free). *In room:* A/C, TV, hair dryer, minibar.

Hôtel d'Europe ★★★ In operation since 1799, this deluxe hotel is almost the equal of La Mirande (see above). The grand hall and salons contain antiques, and the good-size guest rooms have handsome decor and period furnishings. Guest rooms are spacious and comfortable, and are decorated with period furniture, such as antique wooden wardrobes. Two suites are on the roof, with views of the Palais des Papes. The restaurant, which specializes in traditional French and *provençale* cuisine, has a Michelin star.

12 place Crillon, 84000 Avignon. www.heurope.com. ✆ **04-90-14-76-76.** Fax 04-90-14-76-71. 44 units. 210€–540€ double; 720€–880€ suite. AE, DC, MC, V. Parking 15€. **Amenities:** Restaurant; bar; babysitting; room service. *In room:* A/C, TV, hair dryer, minibar, Wi-Fi (free).

MODERATE

Hôtel Bristol In the center of Avignon, on one of the principal streets leading to the place de l'Horloge and the Palais des Papes, the Bristol is one of the town's better bets. A traditional hotel, it offers comfortably furnished, well-maintained rooms, most with twin beds. Though it's not the most atmospheric place, it offers good, solid value.

44 cours Jean-Jaurès, 84000 Avignon. www.bristol-hotel-avignon.com. ✆ **04-90-16-48-48.** Fax 04-90-86-22-72. 67 units. 86€–153€ double; 143€–222€ suite. AE, DC, MC, V. Parking 11€. **Amenities:** Bar; room service. *In room:* A/C, TV, hair dryer, minibar.

Hôtel de l'Horloge You're in the center of the action on place de l'Horloge in this elegant 19th-century hotel—though you'll still get a good night's sleep due to its excellent soundproofing. The spacious rooms are uncluttered, with iron bedsteads and contemporary fabrics and colors. Ask for one of the five rooms with a private terrace.

1 rue Félicien David, 84000 Avignon. www.hotel-avignon-horloge.com. ✆ **04-90-16-42-00.** Fax 04-90-82-17-32. 66 units. 115€–210€ double. AE, MC, V. **Amenities:** Breakfast room. *In room:* A/C, TV, hair dryer, minibar, Wi-Fi (free).

Hôtel du Palais des Papes From the twin terraces of this hotel, you can enjoy views of the clock tower (overlooking the place de l'Horloge) and the Palais des Papes. Few other hotels are able to boast construction that was completed in series between the 15th century and the 1920s. You access the three floors via a corkscrew stone staircase that, in addition to exposed stone walls, massive ceiling beams, and wrought-iron bedsteads, evokes a modern twist on the Middle Ages.

3 place du Palais, 84000 Avignon. www.hotel-avignon.com. ✆ **04-90-86-04-13.** Fax 04-90-27-91-17. 27 units. 68€–133€ double. AE, MC, V. Parking 8€ per night in nearby municipal parking lot. **Amenities:** Restaurant; bar. *In room:* A/C (in some), TV, Wi-Fi (free).

La Banasterie ★ Parisian owners Françoise and Jean-Michel operate one of the most stylish B&Bs in Avignon in a building that preserves the stone walls and architectural details of another age. The hosts share a devotion to *chocolat:* All of the individually decorated bedrooms are named for famous types of different chocolates, and excellent hot cocoa in the evening and fine chocolates on your pillow round out the day. In the center of town, the B&B lies on a hard-to-find side street by the Palais des Papes.

11 rue de la Banasterie, 84000 Avignon. www.labanasterie.com. ✆ **06-87-72-96-36.** 5 units. 100€ double; 170€ suite. Rates include continental breakfast. No credit cards. **Amenities:** Breakfast room. *In room:* A/C, TV, hair dryer, Wi-Fi (free).

Lumani ★ 🎁 Artist-owners Elisabeth and Jean have restored this 1800s manor house and decorated it with style. Each room has a distinct personality and is decorated with taste and comfort in mind. Old architectural features are blended with modern comfort, and the lovely courtyard is shaded by centuries-old plane trees. Dining is available by reservation only, costing 30€ per person, with a minimum of six diners required.

37 rue du Rempart St-Lazare, 84000 Avignon. www.avignon-lumani.com. ✆ **03-90-82-94-11.** 5 units. 90€–170€ double. MC, V. **Amenities:** Dining room. *In room:* No phone.

INEXPENSIVE

Hôtel d'Angleterre This Art Deco structure has the advantage of being located inside the city ramparts. Built in 1929 of gray stone, it emulates the style that local builders imagined was characteristic of English houses. The rooms are small but comfortably furnished, and guests can use the large private terrace overlooking a rare thing within Avignon's ramparts: a free and secure parking lot.

29 bd. Raspail, 84000 Avignon. www.hoteldangleterre.fr. ✆ **04-90-86-34-31.** Fax 04-90-86-86-74. 38 units. 50€–85€ double. AE, MC, V. Free parking. Closed mid-Dec–mid-Jan. *In room:* A/C, TV, Wi-Fi (free).

Hôtel le Médiéval About 3 blocks south of the Palais des Papes, this town house from the late 1600s is uncomplicated and well maintained. Under beamed ceilings, the comfortable guest rooms are medium-size to spacious. Most peaceful are the units that overlook the inner courtyard. Those that overlook a congested medieval street corner might be noisier, but they have a rough-and-ready charm of their own.

15 rue Petite Saunerie, 84000 Avignon. www.hotelmedieval.com. ✆ **04-90-86-11-06.** Fax 04-90-82-08-64. 35 units. 62€–93€ double. MC, V. Closed mid-Dec–early Feb. **Amenities:** Room service. *In room:* A/C, TV, hair dryer, Wi-Fi (free).

Where to Eat

EXPENSIVE

Christian Etienne ★★★ PROVENÇALE The stone house containing this Michelin-starred restaurant was built in 1180, around the same time as the Palais des Papes (which happens to be next door). The dining room contains early-16th-century frescoes honoring the marriage of Anne de Bretagne to the French king in 1491. Owner Christian Etienne pays homage to his native Provence's abundance and offers an array of high-quality dishes that change with the seasons. The fixed-price menus, which change seasonally, focus on different themes, including one devoted entirely to lobster. In summer, look for the "tomato" menu, while in winter you might find the "truffle" menu, which features the region's black diamond, truffles. There is an extensive wine list, which spotlights many Côtes du Rhône wines.

10 rue Mons. ✆ **04-90-86-16-50.** www.christian-etienne.fr. Reservations required. Main courses 28€–45€; fixed-price lunch 31€, dinner 65€–125€. AE, DC, MC, V. Tues–Sat noon–1:15pm and 7:30–9:15pm. Closed first 2 weeks in Aug and mid-Dec–early Jan.

Hiély Lucullus ★★ FRENCH This place is formidable competition for Christian Etienne (see above) as Avignon's most outstanding restaurant. The Belle Époque decor enhances the grand cuisine. Market-fresh products go into such innovative dishes as crayfish-stuffed ravioli flavored with sage and served with pumpkin sauce, filet of venison with tangy honey sauce, and escalope of sautéed foie gras on toasted rye bread. Lots of fresh fish is imported daily and cooked to perfection. There is an extensive wine list, which includes Châteauneuf-du-Pape and Côtes du Rhône wines.

5 rue de la République. ✆ **04-90-86-17-07.** www.hiely-lucullus.com. Reservations required. Main courses 25€-40€; fixed-price menu 29€-59€. AE, MC, V. Daily noon-2pm and 7-10pm.

MODERATE

Brunel PROVENÇALE This flower-filled restaurant is in the heart of Avignon. The managing Brunel family offers such superb dishes such as monkfish with anise-flavored butter, confit of lamb couscous, and tuna steak with coulis of capers and onions. Artichoke hearts accompany grilled John Dory, and the pigs' feet are sublime.

46 rue de la Balance. ✆ **04-90-85-24-83.** Reservations required. Main courses 13€-20€ lunch, 28€-35€ dinner; fixed-price menu 28€-33€. AE, MC, V. Tues-Sat noon-1:30pm and 7:30-9pm (also Mon in July). Closed first 2 weeks in Aug and mid-Dec-early Jan.

La Fourchette ★ FRENCH This bistro's two airy dining rooms have large bay windows that flood the inside with light. The menu offers creative cooking, with such starters as fresh sardines flavored with citrus, ravioli filled with haddock, or parfait of chicken livers with spinach tart and confit of onions. For a main course, try the monkfish stew with endive or daube of beef with gratin of macaroni.

17 rue Racine. ✆ **04-90-85-20-93.** Fixed-price lunch 26€-28€, dinner 32€. MC, V. Mon-Fri noon-2pm and 7:30-9:30pm. Closed 3 weeks in Aug.

Le Numéro 75 ★★ FRENCH Centrally located on a narrow street that connects with rue des Teinturiers, this restaurant occupies what was once the 19th-century private home of distiller Jules Pernod, creator of the anisette liqueur that bears his name today. Within a contemporary dining room that opens onto a restful garden studded with century-old trees, you'll appreciate the flavorful but unpretentious cuisine of Chef Robert Brunel. The menu is tailored every day to a limited array of dishes made from very fresh ingredients that change with the seasons. The finest examples include such dishes as a grilled fish platter, a crème brûlée of gooseliver, and a poached filet of sea bass with artichoke hearts.

75 rue Guillaume Puy. ✆ **04-90-27-16-00.** www.numero75.com. Reservations recommended. Fixed-price lunch 17€; fixed-price dinner 33€. MC, V. May-June and Aug-Oct Mon-Sat noon-2pm and 8-10pm; Nov-Apr Mon-Fri noon-2pm, Tues-Sat noon-10pm; July daily noon-2pm and 8-10pm.

Piedoie ★ MODERN FRENCH In an intimate yellow-and-ocher-colored dining room behind the city ramparts, this place is the creative statement of its namesake, Thierry Piedoie. Menu items change with the seasons, but are likely to include a warm tartlet of asparagus tips and Serrano ham; a platter with smoked Scottish salmon, black Provençal olives, and herb salad; and sweetbreads with glazed ginger and lemon.

26 rue des Trois-Faucons. ✆ **04-90-86-51-53.** www.restaurant-gastronomique-avignon.fr. Reservations recommended. Main courses 23€; fixed-price menus 17€-49€ lunch, 25€-49€ dinner. MC, V. Thurs-Sun and Tues noon-1:30pm and 7:15-9:30pm. Closed 2 weeks in Feb and 2 weeks in Nov.

Restaurant l'Essentiel ★ FRENCH Book ahead to get a table in the cozy courtyard of this elegant 17th-century town house near the Palais des Papes. Its innovative dishes include ballotine of rabbit and grilled gambas with escalope of bass, and its 29€ price-fixed dinner menu is of particularly good value for the quality of cooking you get in return.

2 rue Petite Fusterie. ✆ **04-90-85-87-12.** www.restaurantlessentiel.com. Reservations recommended. Fixed-price lunch 17€, dinner 29€-41€. MC, V. Mon-Tues and Thurs-Sat 11:30am-2pm and 7:30-10pm.

INEXPENSIVE

Ginette & Marcel ★ FRENCH Located in place des Corps Saints, one of Avignon's friendliest squares, Ginette & Marcel offers French fare in a setting that looks like an old-fashioned *épicerie* (grocery store). The cafe specializes in tartines, large slabs of toasted country bread covered in anything from goat's cheese to cold meats, and is a delightful place for lunch.

25 place des Corps Saints. ✆ **04-90-85-58-70.** Tartines 4€-6€. MC, V. Daily 11:30am-11:30pm.

Where to Stay & Eat Nearby

Auberge de Cassagne ★★ A member of the Small Luxury Hotels of the World group, Auberge de Cassagne is an enchanting five-star Provençal *bastide* (country house) set in a large park. The country-style rooms, most of which are connected by the pleasant, tree-studded inner courtyard, feature fine Provençal linens. The cuisine is exceptionally good, featuring dishes such as lobster tail in zucchini flowers, smoked scallops, and braised pigeon with Jerusalem artichokes. You can enjoy your meals in an elegantly rustic dining room or at a table in the garden.

450 allée de Cassagne, 84130 Le Pontet-Avignon. www.aubergedecassagne.com. ✆ **04-90-31-04-18.** Fax 04-90-32-25-09. 43 units. 169€-425€ double; 448€-850€ suite. AE, DC, MC, V. Free parking. **Amenities:** Restaurant; babysitting; bar; spa w/hot tub and sauna; 2 pools (indoor and outdoor); room service. *In room:* A/C, TV, hair dryer, minibar, Wi-Fi (free).

Avignon After Dark

The dance-club standby is **Les Ambassadeurs,** 27 rue Bancasse (✆ **04-90-86-31-55**), particularly for those in their 30s and upwards. You'll find a younger crowd at **Red Zone,** 27 rue Carnot (✆ **04-90-27-02-44;** www.redzonebar.com), during its themed DJ nights. For live music on Friday nights, head to **Zinzolin,** 22 rue des Teinturiers (✆ **04-90-82-41-55;** www.lezinzolin.fr), which doubles as a restaurant. **Bokao's Café,** 9 bis quai St-Lazare (✆ **04-90-82-47-95;** www.bokaos.fr), is a restaurant and disco just outside the city walls. **Le Cid,** 11 place de l'Horloge (✆ **04-90-82-30-38;** www.lecidcafe.com), is the buzziest bar on the street and attracts a friendly gay/straight clientele long after the rest of the neighboring bars have closed. **L'Esclave,** 12 rue de Limas (✆ **04-90-85-14-91;** www.esclavebar.com), is the city's main gay bar and disco, which has club nights Monday to Saturday.

A Side Trip from Avignon: Villeneuve-lès-Avignon ★

The modern world is impinging on Avignon, but across the Rhône, the Middle Ages slumber on. When the popes lived in exile at Avignon, cardinals built palaces across the river in what is now the region of Languedoc. Villeneuve-lès-Avignon (also spelled Villeneuve-lez-Avignon) lies just across the Rhône from Avignon and is easiest to reach on bus no. 11, which crosses the **pont Daladier.** The **Office de Tourisme** is at 1 place Charles David (✆ **04-90-25-61-33;** fax 04-90-25-91-55; www.tourisme-villeneuvelezavignon.fr).

Cardinal Arnaud de Via founded the **Eglise Notre-Dame,** place Meissonier (✆ **04-90-25-46-24**), in 1333. Other than its architecture, the church's most popular attraction is an antique copy (by an unknown sculptor) of Enguerrand Quarton's *Pietà*, the original of which is in the Louvre. The church is open daily April to September 10am to 12:30pm and 2 to 6:30pm, and October to March 10am to noon and 2 to 5pm. Admission is free.

EXPLORING THE TOWN

Chartreuse du Val-de-Bénédiction Inside France's largest Carthusian monastery, built in 1352, you'll find a church, three cloisters, rows of cells that housed the medieval monks, and rooms depicting aspects of their daily lives. Part of the complex is devoted to a workshop (the Centre National d'Ecritures et du Spectacle) for painters and writers, who live in the cells rent-free for up to a year to pursue their craft. Photo and art exhibits take place throughout the year. Pope Innocent VI (whose tomb you can view) founded this charterhouse, which became the country's most powerful. The 12th-century graveyard cloister is lined with cells where the fathers prayed and meditated.

Rue de la République. ✆ **04-90-15-24-24.** www.chartreuse.org. Admission 7.50€ adults, 6€ students, free for children 17 and under. Mon–Fri 9:30am–5pm; Sat–Sun 10am–5pm.

Tour Philippe le Bel Philippe the Fair constructed this tower in the 13th century, when Villeneuve became a French possession; it served as a gateway to the kingdom. With stamina, you can climb to the top for a view of Avignon and the Rhône Valley.

Rue Montée-de-la-Tour. ✆ **04-32-70-08-57.** Admission 2.20€ adults, free for children 17 and under. Apr–Sept daily 10am–12:30pm and 2–6pm; Mar and Oct–Nov Tues–Sun 10am–noon and 2–7pm.

WHERE TO STAY IN VILLENEUVE-LÈS-AVIGNON

Best Western La Magnaneraie ★★ One of the most charming accommodations in the region is this 15th-century country house on a hectare of gardens. Tastefully renovated, the place is furnished with antiques and good reproductions. Many guests who arrive for only a night remain for many days to enjoy the good food and atmosphere, garden, tennis court, and landscaped pool. Menu items might include zucchini flowers stuffed with mushroom and cream purée, a pastry of foie gras and truffles, and croustillant of red snapper with basil and olive oil.

37 rue Camp-Bataille, 30400 Villeneuve-lès-Avignon. www.hostellerie-la-magnaneraie.com. ✆ **04-90-25-11-11.** Fax 04-90-25-46-37. 30 units. 121€–261€ double; 233€–472€ suite. AE, DC, MC, V. parking 10€. **Amenities:** Restaurant; bar; babysitting; pool (outdoor); room service; tennis court (lit). *In room:* A/C, TV, hair dryer, minibar, Wi-Fi (free).

Hôtel de l'Atelier The name of this 16th-century house (which translates as "the workshop") derives from the weaving machines that produced fabrics here during the 1950s. The style is romantic and nostalgic, with handsome antique furnishings. On warm days, breakfast is served in the delightful rear garden in the shadow of fruit trees. The inglenook fireplace in the lounge blazes on cold winter nights.

5 rue de la Foire, 30400 Villeneuve-lès-Avignon.www.hoteldelatelier.com. ✆ **04-90-25-01-84.** Fax 04-13-33-71-41. 23 units. 69€–144€ double; 109€–174€ triple. MC, V. Parking 9€ in nearby garage; book in advance. **Amenities:** Room service. *In room:* TV, hair dryer, Wi-Fi (free).

Le Prieuré ★★★ This five-star Relais & Chateaux property was converted from a 1322 cardinal's residence. Roger Mille purchased it in 1943, and since then it has been run by three generations of his family. Adjacent to the village church, it has an ivy-covered stone exterior, with green shutters, a tiled roof, and rustic but lush public rooms. Rooms are contemporary in style and plush in comfort, with some opening out onto the rose-scented landscaped gardens. The choice of bedrooms includes those in the main house (the old priory), which are a bit small but filled with antique charm; or those in the modern annex by the swimming pool, which are much more spacious and offer better views. The gastronomic restaurant focuses on local flavors and produce, featuring Costières roasted pigeon or slow-cooked veal hock.

7 place du Chapitre, 30400 Villeneuve-lès-Avignon. www.leprieure.com. ✆ **04-90-15-90-15.** Fax 04-90-25-45-39. 26 units. 185€–335€ double; 350€–560€ suite. AE, DC, MC, V. Free parking. **Amenities:** Restaurant; bar; babysitting; concierge; pool (outdoor); 2 tennis courts (lit). *In room:* A/C, TV, hair dryer, minibar, Wi-Fi (free).

L'ISLE-SUR-LA-SORGUE ★

693km (430 miles) S of Paris; 23km (14 miles) E of Avignon; 34km (21 miles) W of Apt

France's second-largest antiques center (after Paris) stretches across five branches of the Sorgue River and a network of canals. Inevitably some call it the Venice of Provence, but L'Isle-sur-la-Sorgue doesn't need this fatuous comparison to draw visitors to its flower-filled riverside restaurants and winding streets of the old town. It used to be a hive of industry, with its water wheels powering the work of silk weavers, tanners, and grain and oil millers. Nowadays the giant moss-covered wheels are purely decorative, adding a picturesque note to the general attractiveness of this bustling town.

Antiques shops are everywhere, and on Sunday morning the town heaves with one of the region's largest weekly markets. *Brocante* (second-hand goods) dealers squeeze in alongside the scores of stalls selling local produce and Provençal souvenirs. You're in luck if you're in town on the first Sunday in August, when a floating market takes over the river. Fishermen and their wives make a colorful sight as they dress up in period costume to sell their wares.

Essentials

GETTING THERE Trains arrive from Avignon and Cavaillon to the **SNCF train** station on avenue Julien Guigue on the southwest corner of the town. For rail schedules and information, call ✆ **36-35,** or visit www.voyages-sncf.com. For direct bookings, call ✆ **04-90-82-56-29. Buses** from Avignon, Apt, Fontaine-de-Vaucluse, Cavaillon, Carpentras, Marseille, and Aix-en-Provence stop at Pont Gambetta near the post office (✆ **04-90-38-15-58**). By **car** from Avignon, take D900 east following signs for Apt.

VISITOR INFORMATION The **Office de Tourisme** is in place de la Liberté (✆ **04-90-38-04-78;** www.oti-delasorgue.fr).

SPECIAL EVENTS For more than 50 years, the **Féerie Nautique** has been one of the most magical spectacles in town. This lively river carnival takes place on the last Saturday and Sunday in July, when dozens of brightly lit floats meander along the Sorgue in a torchlight procession accompanied by music.

Exploring the Town

The most pleasurable way to explore L'Isle-sur-la-Sorgue is simply to stroll along the waterside streets and avenues, passing the old mills and the tempting antiques shops. Just beside the tourism office is the 17th-century **Notre-Dame-des-Anges,** with its splendid baroque interior and church organ that has been declared a national monument.

Campredon—Centre d'Art The birthplace of the French poet and Resistance fighter René Char, this handsome 18th-century mansion pays homage to the poet with an exhibition space. Two of the floors host large-scale exhibitions of artists with an association to Char, while the upper floor has the poet's personal belongings and his writing desk.

20 rue du Docteur Tallet. ✆ **04-90-38-17-41.** Admission 6€. Tues–Sun 10am–1pm and 2:30–6:30pm.

Musée du Jouet et de la Poupée Ancienne This curious museum houses the private doll collection of one Madame Huguette Jeanselme. Hundreds of dolls from 1880 to 1920 in remarkably superb condition form an enchanting display.

20 rue Carnot. ✆ **04-90-20-97-31.** Admission 3.50€. Daily 10am–7pm.

Where to Stay

Hôtel Best Western Domaine de la Petite Isle A 5-minute drive from town takes you to this relaxing three-star hotel surrounded by lush gardens and two swimming pools. The rooms are modern and comfortable, with some opening into the gardens. The in-house restaurant focuses on southern French cuisine, offering filet of sea bass and slow-roasted lamb shoulder with thyme and rosemary.

871 rte d'Apt. www.domainedelapetiteisle.com. ✆ **04-90-38-40-40.** Fax 04-90-20-84-74. 50 units. 79€–148€ double; 149€–260€ suite/studio. AE, DC, MC, V. Free parking. **Amenities:** Restaurant; bar; babysitting; 2 pools (outdoor); room service; smoke-free rooms. *In room:* A/C, TV, hair dryer, kitchenette (in some), minibar, Wi-Fi (free).

La Maison sur la Sorgue ★ 🎁 Hidden behind an unassuming door is this delightful B&B, which is located in an 18th-century *hôtel particulier* (private mansion). The rooms are decorated in various complementing colors and the decor has been inspired by the owners' travels. The rooms have nice personal touches: Some have large roll-top baths and a terrace, and one room even has a private loggia overlooking the market and the river.

6 rue Rose Goudard. www.lamaisonsurlasorgue.com. ✆ **04-90-20-74-86.** Fax 04-90-20-72-66. 4 units. 240€–330€ double, including breakfast. MC, V. **Amenities:** Pool (outdoor); parking (15€). *In room:* A/C, hair dryer, Wi-Fi (payable).

Where to Eat

La Prévôté PROVENÇALE/MEDITERRANEAN Located in a 17th-century convent, this restaurant is one of the most refined in the old town. During warm days, plates of ravioli with lobster and scallops and roasted veal with truffles are served in its pretty interior courtyard. The restaurant also has five individually designed and elegant rooms, which cost 120€–200€ for a double room.

4 rue Jean-Jacques Rousseau. ✆ **04-90-38-57-29.** Fax 04-90-38-57-29. www.la-prevote.fr. Main courses 25€–29€; fixed-price menus 39€–70€. AE, MC, V. Thurs–Mon noon–2pm and 7–10pm. Hotel and restaurant closed mid-Nov–early Dec.

La Table de Ninou PROVENÇALE This relaxed riverside restaurant offers Provençal favorites such as *boeuf en daube* (slow-cooked beef stew) and *pieds et paquets à la provençale* (lamb trotters and tripe parcels). Its *plateau provençal,* with terrine of rabbit and marinated anchovies, is a tasty introduction to the local cuisine.

22 bis quai Rouget de l'Isle. ✆ **04-90-38-48-13.** Main courses from 11€; fixed-price menus from 17€. MC, V. Tues–Sun noon–2pm and 7–10pm. Closed mid-Nov to mid-Mar.

Le Vivier FRENCH The cuisine is as exquisite as the setting in this Michelin-starred restaurant on the river. Start with the poached eggs with asparagus and morel mushrooms or the smoked eel and foie gras terrine, followed by the pigeon in puff pastry with porcini mushrooms and foie gras, or swordfish steak with squid-ink risotto.

800 cours Fernande Peyre. ✆ **04-90-38-52-80.** www.levivier-restaurant.com. Fixed-price lunch 30€, dinner 48€–75€. AE, MC, V. Tues–Thurs noon–2pm and 7–10pm; Fri–Sat 7–10pm; Sun noon–2pm.

mont ventoux: KING OF THE MOUNTAINS

The formidable summit of **Mont Ventoux** can be visible all over the valleys of the Rhône, Durance, and Luberon. Its 1,912m (6,273ft) peak makes it the highest in Provence, and one of the most legendary. Even when the snow finally melts sometime in May, its barren upper reaches give it a ghostly look as it looms over the horizon.

From time to time, the ascent to Mont Ventoux forms one of the most punishing stages of the **Tour de France.** It was here in 1967 that British cyclist Tommy Simpson died from heart failure on a particularly scorching day. You can see the memorial to Simpson just above the tree line, although you may choose not to believe his supposed last words: "Put me back on the bloody bike." Regardless of the risks, cyclists from all around the world come to Mont Ventoux to tackle its steep, twisting roads. All along the route, friends and families wait by the roadside to get the perfect photograph before driving to the top to greet the exhausted cyclist with cheers and a badly needed drink. It's an exciting sight, even if you're merely an onlooker. It can get quite festive at the top, too, especially when the market stalls selling local produce have been set up.

There's also a restaurant called **Le Vendran** (✆ **04-90-60-29-25**), on the D974 100m (328 ft.) from the summit, that has been serving customers since the 19th century, its staff battling through thick snow for half the year. They can't close during the winter, however, as Mont Ventoux forms part of the Mont Serein ski resort.

To get the full experience of Mont Ventoux, take the D974 that winds through thick forests (carefully passing the cyclists) and hair-raising bends. The drive to the top rewards you with views that reach as far as Mont Blanc in the Alps, as well as the Rhône valley and the Luberon.

The best hotel in the area is the welcoming **Hôtel Crillon le Brave,** place de l'Eglise, Crillon le Brave (✆ **04-90-65-61-61;** fax 04-90-65-62-86; www.crillonlebrave.com). This exquisite Relais & Chateaux hotel is set within a cluster of seven 16th- and 17th-century stone houses in an ancient hilltop hamlet about 40km (25 miles) northeast of Avignon. The property feels utterly peaceful, with its glorious views of vineyards, olive groves, and Mont Ventoux—you can see these spectacular views from the rooms and the golden stone terraces surrounding the swimming pool. Elegant simplicity is the rule for the rooms, with pale furniture, whitewashed beams, terra-cotta floors, and supremely comfortable mattresses. Superb meals are served under a stone vaulted ceiling in an inviting dining room, with the emphasis on local specialties such as Provençal leg of lamb cooked slowly in the fireplace. Its 32 rooms and suites are air-conditioned, with TVs, minibars, and free Wi-Fi. Doubles cost 250€ to 780€ per night.

ARLES ★

724km (450 miles) S of Paris; 35km (22 miles) SW of Avignon; 89km (55 miles) NW of Marseille

Sometimes called the soul of Provence, this town on the Rhône attracts art lovers, archaeologists, historians, and pilgrims on the route to Santiago de Compostela. To the delight of visitors, many of the luminous vistas of van Gogh's paintings remain. The painter left Paris for Arles in 1888—the same year he cut off part of his left ear—and painted some of his most celebrated works here, including *Starry Night over the Rhône, Café Terrace on the Place du Forum,* and *Sunflowers.*

The Greeks are said to have founded Arles in the 6th century B.C., although there is evidence of a previous Celtic settlement. Julius Caesar established a Roman colony here; Constantine the Great named it the second capital of his empire in A.D. 306, when it was known as "the little Rome of the Gauls." Arles was incorporated into France in 1481. The town makes a rewarding visit, with first-rate museums, excellent restaurants, and summer festivals. Its Saturday food market, which takes over boulevard des Lices, is the largest in Provence.

Essentials

GETTING THERE Frequent **trains** connect Arles and Avignon (20 min.), Marseille (50 min.), and Nîmes (20 min.). For rail schedules and information, call ✆ **36-35,** or visit www.voyages-sncf.com. Several **buses** a day make the trip from Aix-en-Provence. For bus information, call ✆ **08-10-00-08-16.** If **driving,** head south along D570 from Avignon.

VISITOR INFORMATION The **Office de Tourisme** is on boulevard des Lices opposite the intersection with rue Jean-Jaurès (✆ **04-90-18-41-20;** fax 04-90-18-41-29; www.arlestourisme.com). Here you can buy one of the **tourist passes**, such as the *pass avantage* and the *pass liberté,* that offer entry to museums and monuments for a flat rate. These offer considerable savings and are worth buying if you want to see more than one attraction.

SPECIAL EVENTS The major festivals in Arles include the **Easter Féria,** which opens the bullfighting season in France; **Les Rencontres d'Arles** (www.rencontres-arles.com), a major international photography festival which runs from June to September; and **rice festivals** in September. The biggest festival is the **Fêtes d'Arles** (www.fetes-arles.com) in early July, which features 4 days of costumed parades and bullfights in the ancient arena.

Exploring the Town

Arles is full of Roman monuments. **Place du Forum,** shaded by trees, is around the old Roman forum. The Café de Nuit, immortalized by van Gogh, once stood on this square. You can spot two Corinthian columns and fragments from a temple at the corner of the Hôtel Nord-Pinus. Three blocks south is **place de la République** with its 15m-tall (50-ft.) obelisk made of blue porphyry. On the north is the **Hôtel de Ville (town hall),** which dates from 1676 and is made from the plans of Jules Hardouin-Mansart, the architect who designed the palace at Versailles.

Eglise St-Trophime ★ This church is noted for its 12th-century portal, one of the finest achievements of the southern Romanesque style. Frederick Barbarossa was crowned king of Arles here in 1178. The cloister, in Gothic and Romanesque styles, is noted for its medieval carvings.

East side of place de la République. ✆ **04-90-96-07-38.** Free admission to church; cloister 3.50€ adults, 2.60€ students and children 12–18, free for children 11 and under. Church open daily but closed 12–2pm and during services. Cloister Nov–Feb daily 10am–5pm; Mar–Apr and Oct daily 9am–6pm; May–Sept daily 9am–7pm. Closed Jan 1, May 1, Nov 1, and Dec 25.

Les Alyscamps ★ This is one of the most famous necropolises of the western world. Its fame began when Genesius, a Roman civil servant, refused to write down an edict calling for persecution of Christians. For this, he was beheaded in 250; later

Arles

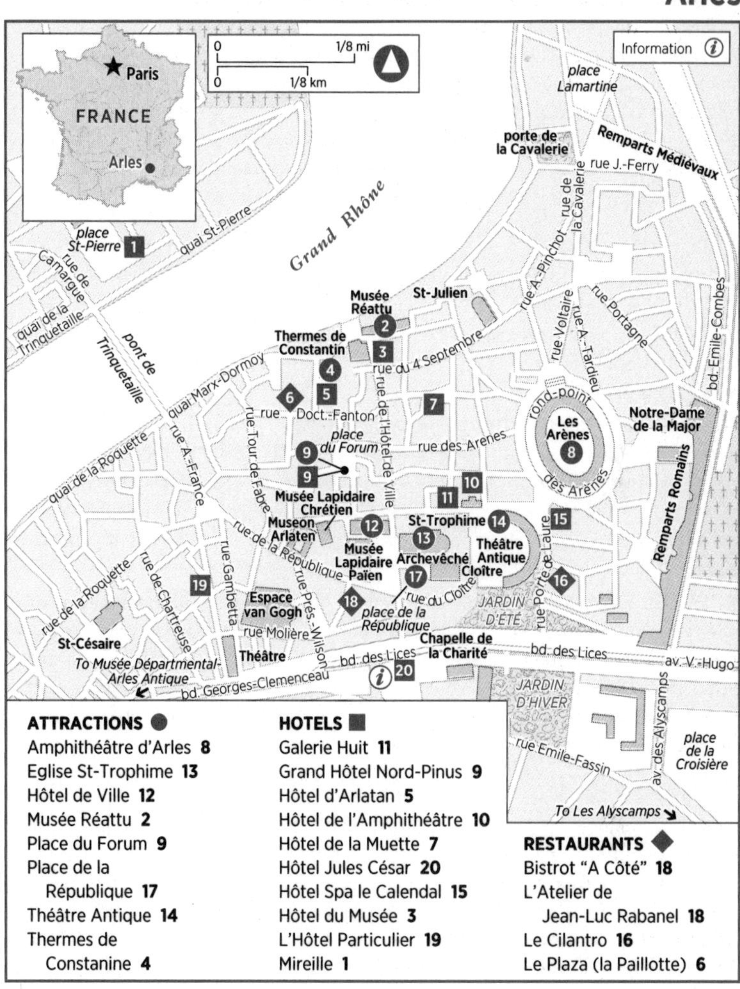

he was made a saint when it was said that miracles began to happen on this site. In time, as the fame of Les Alyscamps spread throughout the Christian world, more of the faithful wanted to be buried here. Dante even mentioned it in his *Inferno*.

In the Middle Ages, 19 churches and chapels occupied this site. After the Renaissance, the graveyard was desecrated. Tombs were removed and stones were taken to construct other buildings. For an evocative experience, walk down L'Allée des Sarcophages, where 80 generations have been buried over 2,000 years. The lane is lined with sarcophagi under tall poplar trees.

Rue Pierre-Renaudel. ✆ **04-90-49-36-87.** Admission 3.50€ adults, 2.60€ children 12–18, free for children 11 and under. Nov–Feb daily 10am–noon and 2–5pm; Mar–Apr and Oct daily 9am–noon and 2–6pm; May–Sept daily 9am–7pm. Closed Jan 1, May 1, Nov 1, and Dec 25.

Musée Départemental—Arles Antique ★★ Less than a kilometer (½ mile) south of town within a modern setting built in 1995, you'll find one of the world's most famous collections of Roman Christian sarcophagi, plus a rich ensemble of sculptures, mosaics, and inscriptions from the Augustinian period to the 6th century. Detailed models show the region's ancient monuments as they existed in the past.

Presqu'île du Cirque Romain. ✆ **04-90-18-88-88.** www.arles-antique.cg13.fr. Admission 6€ adults, 4.50€ students and children 17 and under. Wed-Mon 10am-6pm. Closed Jan 1, May 1, Nov 1, and Dec 25.

Musée Réattu ★ This collection, which belonged to the local painter Jacques Réattu (1760–1833), is an eclectic mix of old masters and contemporary art. Housed in the former Grand Priory of the Knights of Malta, it's worth the price of admission just to see the salon filled with portraits of Picasso by some of the world's best photographers. Picasso himself donated 57 of his drawings.

10 rue du Grand-Prieuré. ✆ **04-90-49-37-58.** www.museereattu.arles.fr. Admission 7€ adults, 5€ students and children 12-18, free for children 11 and under. Free admission on the first Sun of the month. Jul-Sept Tues-Sun 10am-7pm; Jan-June 10am-12:30pm and 2-6:30pm.

Théâtre Antique/Amphithéâtre d'Arles ★★ These are the city's two great classical monuments. The Roman theater, begun by Augustus in the 1st century, was mostly destroyed and only two Corinthian columns remain. Here the *Venus of Arles* was discovered in 1651. A copy of a masterpiece of Hellenistic statuary, it was broken into three pieces and armless when discovered. Arles offered it to Louis XIV, who had it restored, and today it is in the Louvre. The stones and statues strewn about the garden make it a popular place for French youngsters practicing the sport of *parkour,* or free running, as they leap from pillar to column.

Nearby, and also built in the 1st century, the amphitheater seats almost 12,000 and hosts bullfights and other major events. For a good view, you can climb the three towers that remain from medieval times when the amphitheater was turned into a fortress. The stone steps are uneven and much of the masonry is worn down, which could be a problem for people with limited mobility.

Théâtre Antique: Rue du Cloître. Amphitheater: Rond-pont des Arènes. ✆ **04-90-49-36-74.** Combined ticket 6€ adults, 4.50€ students and children 18 and under. May-Sept daily 9am-7pm; Mar-Apr and Oct daily 9am-6pm; Nov-Feb daily 10am-5pm.

Thermes de Constantin Near the banks of the Rhône is the entrance to 4th-century Roman baths, which have been partially restored with characteristic bands of brickwork. The baths or thermae are all that remain of a once grand imperial palace that stood here, Palais Constantin. Dating from Constantine's era, the ruins of the baths measure 45 to 98m (148–322 ft.). You enter by the tepidarium (tepid room) and then proceed through the caldarium (hot room), with its remaining hypocaust (heated floors).

Rue du Grande Prieuré. ✆ **04-90-49-36-74.** 3€ adults, 2.20€ children. May-Sept daily 9am-noon and 2-7pm; Mar-Apr and Oct daily 9am-noon and 2-6pm; Nov-Feb daily 1-5pm.

Where to Stay

VERY EXPENSIVE

L'Hôtel Particulier ★★ Occupying an 18th-century pavilion, Arles's only five-star hotel was the last of the grand private town houses built in the center of town. Behind its monumental gate are ancient yew trees and a courtyard with teak lounges and a limestone-built lap pool. Guests congregate here for morning coffee or the first aperitif of the evening. Each bedroom is decorated individually and elegantly in creamy tones with gold accents, giving the rooms a bright, clean look.

4 rue de la Monnaie, 13200 Arles. www.hotel-particulier.com. ✆ **04-90-52-51-40.** Fax 04-90-96-16-70. 15 units. 239€–319€ double; 289€–429€ suite. AE, MC, V. Parking 19€. **Amenities:** Restaurant; small pool (outdoor); room service; spa. *In room:* A/C, TV, minibar, hair dryer, Wi-Fi (in some; free).

EXPENSIVE

Grand Hôtel Nord-Pinus ★ Occupying a town house on a tree-lined square in the heart of Arles, this charming Provençal hotel has public rooms filled with antiques and an ornate staircase with wrought-iron balustrades. Guest rooms are glamorous, even theatrical; they come in a range of shapes, sizes, and decors, and are filled with rich upholsteries, wrought-iron accents, and draperies arranged artfully beside oversize French doors. Other rooms are more restrained and classic in their design. The suite has its own private terrace. Many bullfighters and artists have stayed here—their photographs and posters decorate the public areas.

14 place du Forum, 13200 Arles. www.nord-pinus.com. ✆ **04-90-93-44-44.** Fax 04-90-93-34-00. 26 units. 170€–345€ double; 570€ suite. AE, DC, MC, V. Parking 17€. **Amenities:** Restaurant; bar; room service. *In room:* AC, TV, hair dryer, Wi-Fi (free).

Hôtel Jules César This 17th-century Carmelite convent is now a stately four-star hotel. Although it's located on a busy street, most rooms face the unspoiled cloister and the gardens surrounding the pool—you'll wake to the scent of roses and the sounds of birds singing. The decor is luxurious, with antique Provençal furnishings. The interior rooms are the most tranquil and the darkest, though enlivened by bright fabrics. The rooms in the modern extensions are comfortable but lack character.

9 bd. des Lices, 13631 Arles. www.hotel-julescesar.fr. ✆ **04-90-52-52-52.** Fax 04-90-52-52-53. 58 units. 160€–250€ double; 300€–385€ suite. AE, DC, MC, V. Parking 13€. Closed Nov–Mar. **Amenities:** Restaurant; bar; pool (outdoor); babysitting; room service. *In room:* TV, hair dryer, minibar.

MODERATE

Galerie Huit ★ There's more than a touch of Italy in this sumptuous and friendly B&B run by English expatriate Julia de Bierre. Her historic town house, which originated in the 16th century, combines an art gallery with five refined and comfortable rooms. The Marco Polo suite, which includes a kitchen and dining area, beautifully echoes 18th-century Venice in its opulent decor. Breakfast is served either in the authentic Arlésienne kitchen or the pretty courtyard garden.

8 rue de la Calade, 13200 Arles. www.galeriehuit.com. ✆ **04-90-97-77-93.** 5 units. 85€–150€ double; 220€–310€ suite. Rates include breakfast. MC, V. **Amenities:** Breakfast room. *In room:* TV, hair dryer, Wi-Fi (free).

Hôtel d'Arlatan ★★ Near place du Forum, this hotel occupies the former residence of the *comtes* d'Arlatan de Beaumont and has been managed by the same family since 1920. It was built in the 15th century on the ruins of an old palace begun by Constantine—in fact, one of the walls is from the 4th century. Rooms are furnished with Provençal antiques and reproductions, and some have stone walls and prettily painted beamed ceilings. The most appealing rooms overlook the garden and the pool.

26 rue du Sauvage, 13100 Arles. www.hotel-arlatan.fr. ✆ **04-90-93-56-66.** Fax 04-90-49-68-45. 41 units. 85€–157€ double; 177€–247€ suite. AE, MC, V. Parking 13€–16€. Closed Nov 15–Mar. **Amenities:** Bar; babysitting; heated pool (outdoor); Wi-Fi. *In room:* A/C, TV, minibar.

Hotel de l'Amphithéâtre Built in the 1600s, this hotel is ideally situated midway between the ancient Roman amphitheater and the Roman theater. The antique atmosphere is filled with hand-hewn ceiling beams, reproductions of Provençal furniture, and soft lighting. Some bedrooms feature sweeping views out over Arles. If you opt for the rooftop Belvedere Suite, you'll be rewarded with 360-degree views over the town.

5-7 rue Diderot, 13200 Arles. www.hotelamphitheatre.fr. ✆ **04-90-96-10-30.** Fax 04-90-93-98-69. 30 units. 56€–136€ double, triple, or quad; 126€–156€ suite. AE, DC, MC, V. Parking 6€. **Amenities:** Babysitting. *In room:* A/C, TV, fridge, hair dryer, Wi-Fi (free).

Hôtel Spa le Calendal ★ Ancient Roman history buffs may want to stay in this hotel for its **Aux Bains du Calendal** spa (www.spa-arles.com), which is inspired by the ancient Roman baths, with its concept of a caldarium (hot bath), frigidarium (cold bath), and tepidarium (warm bath). Housed in a room with a vaulted ceiling, the spa overlooks the Roman amphitheater. When you're not relaxing under the water jets in the spa pool, you can enjoy the comforts of the Provençal-style rooms, most of which have views of the hotel's luxurious garden. The restaurant in the garden is open for lunch from Easter till November and specializes in organic local ingredients.

5 rue Porte de Laure, 13200 Arles. www.lecalendal.com. ✆ **04-90-96-11-89.** Fax 04-90-96-05-84. 38 units. 109€–159€ double, triple or quad. AE, MC, V. **Amenities:** Restaurant; babysitting; Jacuzzi; spa. *In room:* A/C, TV, hair dryer, Wi-Fi (free).

Mireille ★ On the right bank of the Rhône River on the outskirts of Arles, this charming hotel is an oasis of tranquillity. Set in two joined houses, it features a poolside terrace lined with mulberry trees. Spacious bedrooms are warmly decorated in typical Provençal style with bright fabrics. On-site is a little shop selling quality products of Provence, such as tapenade, *herbes de provence,* regional wines, and jams.

2 place St-Pierre at Trinquetaille, 13200 Arles. www.hotel-mireille.com. ✆ **04-90-93-70-74.** Fax 04-90-93-87-28. 34 units. 89€–150€ double. AE, DC, MC, V. **Amenities:** Restaurant; bar; pool (outdoor); room service. *In room:* A/C, TV, hair dryer, Wi-Fi (free).

INEXPENSIVE

Hôtel de la Muette This Logis de France hotel occupies an old manor house that originated in the 12th century. Within its ancient stone walls are good-size rooms decorated either in bright Provençal colors or more muted contemporary tones. It's extremely good value for the money considering its central location, a short walk from the ancient Roman arena.

15 rue des Suisses, 13200 Arles. www.hotel-muette.com. ✆ **04-90-96-15-39.** Fax 04-90-49-73-16. 18 units. 54€–90€ double, triple or quad. AE, MC, V. Parking 8€. **Amenities:** Breakfast room. *In room:* TV, fridge, hair dryer, minibar, Wi-Fi (free).

Hotel du Musée Another good budget option, this family-run 17th-century hotel is across from the Musée Réattu and the Thermes de Constantin. Rooms are simply furnished with Provençal fabrics and antique reproductions, and the courtyard garden is a delightful place for breakfast.

11 rue du Grand Prieuré, 13200 Arles. www.hoteldumusee.com. ✆ **04-90-93-88-88.** Fax 04-90-49-98-15. 28 units. 58€–70€ double; 110€–130€ quad. MC, V. Parking 10€. **Amenities:** Breakfast room. *In room:* A/C, TV, hair dryer, Wi-Fi (free).

Where to Eat

EXPENSIVE

L'Atelier de Jean-Luc Rabanel ★★★ MEDITERRANEAN Chef Jean Luc Rabanel harvests ingredients from his organic garden right before cooking to create an original and personalized cuisine that has won him two Michelin stars. His exquisite dishes change constantly and freely borrow flavors from the Far East, but the focus remains on local produce such as asparagus, artichokes, sardines, and zucchini flowers.

7 rue des Carmes. ✆ **04-90-91-07-69.** www.rabanel.com. Reservations required. Fixed-price lunch 45€–85€, dinner 85€–150€. AE, MC, V. Wed–Sun noon–2pm and 7–9pm.

Le Cilantro FRENCH Located near the amphitheater, Arles's other Michelin-starred restaurant puts an international spin on its top-class local ingredients. During the week, its affordable *idées de chef* menu (25€–30€) is dictated by what's available in the market and is a delicious way to savor the best of the current season. The a la carte menu includes foie gras with truffles, slow-cooked lamb, and an innovative vegetarian option.

31 rue Porte de Laure. ✆ **04-90-18-25-05.** www.restaurantcilantro.com. Reservations recommended. Main courses 29€–39€; fixed-price dinner 25€–99€. MC, V. Sept–June Tues–Fri noon–2pm and 7–10:30pm; Jul–Aug Mon–Fri noon–2pm and Tues–Sat 7–10:30pm.

MODERATE

Bistrot "A Côté" ★★ FRENCH Jean-Luc Rabanel offers a more affordable version of his Atelier (see above) in this next-door bistro. The emphasis, though, is still on fresh, local ingredients in everything from their breakfasts to tapas. Dishes could include warm potato salad with anchovies, smoked herrings, guinea fowl encrusted in salt, or shellfish risotto.

7 rue des Carmes. ✆ **04-90-91-07-69.** www.bistro-acote.com. Tapas from 6€; main courses from 18€. Daily 9am–midnight.

Le Plaza (la Paillotte) PROVENÇALE Tucked behind the bustling place du Forum is this cozy restaurant in the relatively quiet rue du Docteur Fanton. The menus offer good value, featuring a flaky pie of asparagus and chorizo, roast cod with leeks, filet of bull cooked in its own parcel, or lobster and crab in pastry.

28 rue du Docteur Fanton. ✆ **04-90-96-33-15.** Main courses from 14€; fixed-price dinner 20€–33€. MC, V. Thurs–Tues noon–1:30pm and 7–9:30pm. Closed Thurs Dec–Feb.

Bullfighting

Bullfighting is alive and well in the Camargue. For obvious reasons, many people consider bullfighting cruel and shocking, but the spectacle is an authentic local experience. Bullfighting first arrived in France from Spain in 1701, and the first *corrida* (bullfight) in Arles was staged in 1853 after the Roman arena was restored.

The course camarguaise is the gentler form of the event, in which white-clad participants known as *raseteurs* rush at the bulls in an attempt to grab the ribbons that have been tied to the horns. The bulls are not killed, and injuries are rare. The Spanish-style *corrida,* on the other hand, is a considerably crueler affair and results in the ritual killing of the bull. After decorated barbs are stuck into the bull's back, the matador begins his elegant dance with the creature, ideally culminating in a single stab to the heart. The matador doesn't always succeed, though, as fatal injuries are not unheard of. The bull is then butchered and eaten.

Although some minor bullfights occur in July and August in small arenas in the Camargue, the best ones are staged in Arles, notably in the July festival and during the Easter *féria* (fair). Bullfighting is also popular in neighboring Languedoc, notably in Nîmes and Béziers.

Arles After Dark

The bars and cafes in the **place du Forum,** especially **Le Bistrot d'Arlésien,** are the best places for pre- and postdinner drinks and snacks. Don't be tempted to stray into the nearby Café de Nuit, which stands on the spot of the cafe immortalized by van Gogh. It's purely a tourist trap now. **Le Cargo de Nuit,** 7 av. Sadi-Carnot (✆ **04-90-49-55-99;** www.cargodenuit.com), is the place for live music and clubbing. The lineup includes anything from soul and jazz to French rock and hip-hop.

SAINTES-MARIES-DE-LA-MER

778km (483 miles) S of Paris; 129km 80 miles) E of Marseille; 67km (41 miles) S of Nîmes

Saintes-Maries-de-la-Mer is the largest town in the Camargue, an alluvial plain inhabited by wild white horses, black bulls, lagoons, salt marshes, wetlands, and seriously ferocious mosquitoes. There are numerous cattle ranches and cowboys *(gardians)* that tend to the herds of bulls that roam through the area (see "*Les Gardians* of the Camargue," below.) It's a strange landscape, desolate but with a haunting beauty—quite unlike anything else you will see in France. This most fragile ecosystem in France has been a national park since 1970. Flora and fauna abound where the delta of the Rhône River empties into the Mediterranean. The area is known for its colonies of pink flamingos *(flamants roses)* who share living quarters with some 400 other bird species, including ibises, egrets, kingfishers, owls, wild ducks, and swans.

Saintes-Maries buzzes in the summer and is a popular beach resort filled with French families enjoying the long coastline filled with beaches. The old town, which feels more Spanish than French, is comprised of squares and alleyways that fan out from the central Romanesque church. You can climb the church's bell tower for views of the Mediterranean and surrounding marshland. The many cafes, restaurants, bars shops, and street musicians keep things very lively, made even more vibrant by its large Gypsy population, which swells several times over during the annual Gypsy festival every May 24 and 25. (See "Special Events," below.)

Essentials

GETTING THERE Regular **buses** from Arles arrive at place Mireille north of the church. Saintes-Marie-de-la-Mer is best reached by **car.** From Arles, take D750 for 38km (24 miles) south.

VISITOR INFORMATION The **Office de Tourisme** is at 5 av. Van Gogh near the seafront (✆ **04-90-97-82-3955;** fax 04-90-97-71-15; www.saintesmaries.com).

SPECIAL EVENTS Since the 16th century, Gypsies from around the world have been gathering here every May for their **annual pilgrimage** to honor their patron saint, Sarah. According to legend, she was the servant who arrived on these shores with Mary Magdalene and several other Marys (hence the name of the town) after they were banished from Palestine. Their relics are said to be in the church. The festival is marked by music, dancing, religious processions, Masses, and a blessing of the Gypsies. It's an immensely colorful spectacle that completely takes over the town, so don't assume you'll find last-minute accommodations and expect plenty of traffic clogging up all of the roads. A slightly smaller version of the festival happens on October 22 and 23.

Exploring the Area

The Camargue is best explored by **bike, horse,** or **jeep,** or on the water in a **boat,** canoe, or paddle steamer. A camarguais horse can take you into the interior, through waters and marshlands to places where the black bulls graze and wild birds nest. You'll find two to three dozen stables (depending on the time of year) along the highway from Arles to Stes-Maries. The rides are so easy that they're recommended even for those who have never been on a horse before. **Cabanes de Cacharel** (© **04-90-97-84-10;** www.camargueacheval.com) offers excursions for all levels as well as rides on a horse-drawn carriage.

Bicycle hire is easy to arrange, either through **Vélo Saintois** in rue de la République (© **04-90-74-56**) or **Le Vélociste** in place Mireille (© **04-90-83-26**).

Bird-watchers must visit the bird sanctuary at **Parc Ornithologique de Pont de Gau** (© **04-90-97-82-62;** www.parcornithologique.com), where they can wander the nature trails through 60 hectares (148 acres) of natural marshes to spy on pink flamingoes and many other species of beautiful fauna. It's open daily 9am to sunset; admission is 7€ for adults and 4€ for children aged 4 to 10.

LES GARDIENS of the camargue

The waterlogged flatlands encompassing the Grand and Petit Rhône were scorned by conventional farmers throughout the centuries because of their high salt content and root-rotting murk. However, the area was considered a fit grazing ground for the local black-pelted longhorn cattle, so a breed of cowboys evolved on these surreal flatlands. These French cowboys, known as *les gardiens,* take care of the cattle that survive amid the flamingos, ticks, hawks, snakes, and mosquitoes of the hot, salty wetlands.

The tradition of *les gardiens* originated in the 1600s, when local monasteries began to disintegrate and large tracts of cheap land were bought by private owners. Wearing their traditional garb of leather pants and wide-rimmed black hats, the *gardiens* present a fascinating picture as they ride through the marshlands on their sturdy horses. Once the *gardiens* lived in distinctive, single-story *cabanes* with thatched roofs and without windows; bulls' horns were positioned above the entrance to drive away evil spirits.

An ally in the business of tending cattle is the strong, heavy-tailed Camargue horse, probably a descendant of Arabian stallions brought here by Moorish invaders after the collapse of the Roman Empire. Brown or black at birth, these horses develop a white coat, usually after their fourth year. Traditionally, they were left to fend for themselves during the stifling summers and bone-chilling winters without sheltered stables.

Today, in the world of modern tourism, the *gardiens* have become living symbols of an antique tradition that hasn't changed much—the cattle still run semiwild, identified by the brand of their *manadier,* or owner. Although there are fewer *gardiens* now than in the past, there are some ranches that allow you to visit and watch them at work. They include **Manade des Baumelles** (© **04-90-97-84-37;** www.manade-des-baumelles.com) and **Manade Saint-Antoine** (© **06-10-66-02-12;** www.manadesaintantoine.com); both of these ranches allow visitors to spend time exploring the Camargue with the *gardiens,* as well as offering lunches and dinners.

Where to Stay

Hôtel le Galoubet Away from the bustle of the town but still within walking distance of the center is this comfortable, friendly three-star hotel. Rooms are brightly furnished in Provençal colors of yellows, pinks, and whites. Several rooms on the first floor have a balcony with lovely views overlooking the marshy countryside, but not all have bathtubs. On warm days, breakfast is served on the pretty patio beside the swimming pool.

Rte. de Cacharel, Saintes-Marie-de-la-Mer. www.hotelgaloubet.com. ✆ **04-90-97-82-17.** Fax 04-90-97-71-20. 20 units. 64€–91€ double; 89€–111€ triple. MC, V. Free parking. **Amenities:** Restaurant; bar; pool (outdoor). *In room:* A/C, TV, hair dryer, minibar, Wi-Fi (free).

L'Auberge Cavalière ★ A few minutes' drive north of Saintes-Maries will take you to this tranquil four-star resort set on a series of small islands that are surrounded by marshland and connected by wooden walkways. Most of the guest rooms are set within individual thatched-roof white *cabanes,* the traditional abodes of the Camargue cowboys. Rooms feel rustic yet luxurious, and are decorated with upscale Provençal furnishings and beamed ceilings. The resort offers yoga classes by the water and tours of the area by horseback. Light, delicious Mediterranean and camarguaise dishes are served in the Grande Cabane restaurant; fixed-price menus cost 32€ and 42€.

Rte. d'Arles D570, 13460 Saintes-Maries-de-la-Mer. www.aubergecavaliere.com. ✆ **04-90-97-88-88.** Fax 04-90-97-84-07. 42 units. 140€–195€ double; 180€–240€ triple. Half board available. AE, MC, V. Free parking. **Amenities:** Restaurant; bar; babysitting; pool (outdoor); room service. *In room:* A/C, TV, hair dryer, minibar, Wi-Fi (free).

Mas de Calabrun ★ The only sounds you will hear if you stay here will be the occasional whinny of the Mas de Calabrun's horses in the nearby stables. This welcoming three-star hotel is based in a single-story *mas* (a traditional Provençal farmhouse) surrounding the large swimming pool, just 5km (3½ miles) from Saintes-Maries. Guests can explore the property's 3 hectares (7 acres) of grounds and wetlands on one of the hotel's gentle horses. Its newly renovated rooms are comfortable, airy, and spacious, some with more ranch motifs than others. (One bathroom has amusing stable doors rather than conventional ones, with a bath carved from a giant slab of slate.) The restaurant serves simple yet refined dishes, such as spring vegetables and sheep's cheese in a delicate phyllo pastry, or duck confit with a creamy mash for 30€, including some wine.

Rte. de Cacharel D85, Saintes-Marie-de-la-Mer. www.mas-de-calabrun.fr. ✆ **04-90-97-82-21.** Fax 04-90-97-60-26. 30 units. 130€–160€ double. Half board available. AE, MC, V. Free parking. **Amenities:** Restaurant; bar; pool (outdoor); Jacuzzi. *In room:* A/C, TV, hair dryer, minibar, Wi-Fi (free).

Where to Eat

See also the restaurants at l'**Auberge Cavalière** and **Mas de Calabrun** (above).

Bistrot Chez Fanneù FRENCH This funky bistro is an appealing place for lunch away from the more touristy restaurants lining the old town's streets. Choose from generous salads including chicken Caesar or goat's cheese, or *galettes* (savory crêpes) filled with ham, egg, and melted cheese. Or try a taste of North Africa with a *brick,* a fried phyllo pastry parcel filled with sun-dried tomatoes and goat's cheese on a bed of salad.

6 place des Remparts. ✆ **04-90-97-87-39.** Dishes 5€–13€. MC, V. Daily noon–6pm (also Fri 7–10pm Jul–Aug).

Casa Romàna PROVENÇALE High-quality Camargue bull figures prominently in this convivial restaurant in the heart of the old town. But the regional menu goes beyond *steak de taureau* or *daube de taureau;* there are plenty of Mediterranean fish dishes to choose from, too, including large platters of *fruits de mer,* sea bream, and sole *à la meunière.*

6 rue Joseph Roumanille. ✆ **04-90-97-83-33.** Fixed-price dinner 17€–20€. MC, V. Wed–Sun noon–2pm; Tues–Sun 7–9pm.

LES BAUX-DE-PROVENCE ★

715km (444 miles) S of Paris; 19km (12 miles) NE of Arles; 80km (50 miles) N of Marseille

Cardinal Richelieu called Les Baux-de-Provence a "nesting place for eagles." In its lonely position high on a windswept plateau overlooking the southern Alpilles, Les Baux seems to be part of the mysterious, shadowy rock formations themselves.

Once it was the citadel of the powerful seigneurs of Les Baux, who ruled with an iron fist and sent their conquering armies as far as Albania. In medieval times, the flourishing culture of Les Baux attracted troubadours from all over Europe to the "court of love." Later, it was ruled by the notorious "Scourge of Provence," Raymond de Turenne, who sent his men throughout the land to kidnap people. If a victim's friends and family could not pay ransom, the poor wretch was forced to walk a gangplank over the cliff's edge.

When Les Baux became a Protestant stronghold in the 17th century, Richelieu, fed up with its constant rebellion against Louis XIII, commanded his armies in 1632 to destroy the "eagle's nest." Today the castle and ramparts are a mere shell, though you can see remains of great Renaissance mansions.

Time your visit to Les Baux carefully. It's difficult to find a quiet time of year (apart from the depths of winter), as it's a firm fixture on tourist bus tours of Provence. Either arrive first thing in the morning or late in the afternoon when the tour groups have left.

Essentials

GETTING THERE There is no rail or bus service; by **train,** most passengers get off at Arles. Taxis in Arles (✆ **06-80-27-60-92**) will take you to Les Baux for around 30€; be sure to agree upon the fare in advance. Les Baux is best reached by **car.** From Arles, take the express highway N570 northeast until you reach the turnoff for a secondary road (D17), which will lead you northeast to Fontvieille. From here, follow the signs east into Les Baux. Parking can be difficult and expensive. In high season, be prepared to park quite a distance from the low end of the village.

VISITOR INFORMATION The **Office de Tourisme** (✆ **04-90-54-34-39;** fax 04-90-54-51-15; www.lesbauxdeprovence.com) is on Maison du Roy, near the northern entrance to the old town.

Exploring the Area

Les Baux has two different characters: the inhabited and carefully preserved medieval village and the evocative ruins of its fortress, the "dead" village. Visitors enter the city through the 19th-century **Port Mage,** but in medieval times, the monumental Porte d'Eyguières was the only entrance to the fortified city.

From place St-Vincent are sweeping views over the Vallon de la Fontaine. This is the site of the 12th-century **Eglise St-Vincent,** with its beautiful campanile. The stained-glass windows were a gift from Prince Rainier of Monaco, in his capacity as the marquis des Baux. They are modern, based on designs of the French artist Max Ingrand. The church is open April to October daily from 9am to 6:30pm, November to March daily 10am to 5:30pm. The **Yves Brayer Museum,** at the intersection of rue de la Calade and rue de l'Eglise (✆ **04-90-54-36-99**), holds a collection of the works of Yves Brayer (1907–90), a figurative painter and Les Baux's most famous native son. (He's buried in the village cemetery.) He painted scenes of Italy, of Morocco, and, in Spain, of many bullfights, working mainly in shades of red, ocher, and black. Brayer also decorated the restored 17th-century **Chapelle des Pénitents Blancs,** which stands close to the Church of St. Vincent, with frescoes of the Annunciation, the Nativity, and Christ in Majesty. The museum, housed in the handsome 16th-century Hôtel de Porcelet, is open April to September daily from 10am to 12:30pm and 2 to 6:30pm; off-season hours are Wednesday to Monday from 10am to 12:30pm and 2 to 5:30pm (closed Jan–Feb). Admission is 5€ for adults, and 3€ for students and children 12 and under.

The 16th-century **Hôtel de Manville,** rue Frédéric-Mistral, functions today as the *mairie* (town hall). Only its courtyard is open to visitors. The ancient town hall on place Louis Jou now contains the **Musée des Santons** (✆ **04-90-54-34-39**), a charming collection of the terra-cotta crèche figures so popular in Provence. It's open April to October daily from 9am to 7pm, November to March daily from 9am to 5pm, and admission is free. In the Renaissance-era Hôtel Jean-de-Brion, rue Frédéric-Mistral (✆ **04-90-69-88-03** or 90-54-34-17), is the **Fondation Louis Jou,** which can be visited only by a guided tour arranged in advance. It has paintings, engravings, and personal belongings of Louis Jou, the Spanish artist who moved to this mansion in Les Baux in 1939.

Château des Baux The grounds of the château encompass a complex of evocative, mostly ruined buildings, which were carved out of the rocky mountain peak. Also called *la ville morte* (the "dead village") or La Citadelle, the Château des Baux is at the upper (northern) end of Les Baux. It's accessible via the rue du Château, at the Hôtel de la Tour du Brau, which contains a small archaeological and lapidary museum. Inside the compound is the ruined château des Baux with its tower-shaped *donjon* and surrounding ramparts, and the two towers, Tour Paravelle and Tour Sarrasine. The collection of replicated medieval siege engines was built from the original plans. The ruined chapel of St-Blaise houses a little museum devoted to the olive. The site of the former castle covers an area at least five times that of the present village of Les Baux. As you stand here you can look out over the *Val d'Enfer* (Valley of Hell), the dramatic and jagged gorge that sits below Les Baux. Vineyards and olive groves fill the valley, looking little different from how it was in ancient times.

North end of Les Baux, via the rue de Château. ✆ **04-90-54-55-56.** www.chateau-baux-provence.com. Admission 8€ adults, 6.50€ students and children ages 7–17, 23€ family. July–Aug daily 9am–8:30pm; Sept–Oct daily 9:30am–6pm; Nov–Feb daily 9:30am–5pm; Mar–June daily 9:30am–6:30pm.

Where to Stay & Eat

EXPENSIVE

La Cabro d'Or ★★★ Some of the most comfortable accommodations in the region are in these five low-slung stone buildings owned by the same family that owns Oustau de Baumanière (see below). The original building, a farmhouse, dates from the 18th century. The rooms in this five-star hotel are rustically stylish, and decorated in an upmarket Provençal style. Some open out onto their own private terrace, and others have sweeping views over the countryside.

The hotel's Michelin-starred restaurant is flanked by a vine-covered terrace with views of a pond, garden, and a rocky and barren landscape that has been compared to the surface of the moon. The cuisine is sublime—light and flavorful, with an emphasis on fresh produce. Specialties include scampi ravioli, spit-roasted lamb, and sea bass grilled *à la plancha*. Fixed-price menus cost 75€ to 115€.

Rte. d'Arles, 13520 Les Baux. www.lacabrodor.com. ✆ **04-90-54-33-21.** Fax 04-90-54-45-98. 21 units. 170€–370€ double; 340€–530€ suite. AE, DC, MC, V. Free parking. Closed mid-Nov to mid-Dec. **Amenities:** Restaurant; bar; babysitting; pool (outdoor); 2 tennis courts (lit). *In room:* A/C, TV, hair dryer, minibar, Wi-Fi (free).

La Riboto de Taven ★ Although this place, located in a 19th-century *mas* (farmhouse) just outside the medieval village, began as a restaurant, today it is also a charming small hotel. The Novi family has expanded the premises to include six rooms within the thick walls of the main house, including two suites that have been carved into the grottoes at the far end of the garden.

Known for its flawless cuisine and market-fresh ingredients, this is one of the great restaurants of the area. Strong flavors and the heady perfumes of Provençal herbs characterize Chef Jean-Pierre Novi's cuisine. The menu changes virtually every day and always features a tasteful use of local ingredients and produce. The restaurant is only open for dinner, and the fixed-price menu is 56€.

Le Val d'Enfer, 13520 Les Baux. www.riboto-de-taven.fr. ✆ **04-90-54-34-23.** Fax 04-90-54-38-88. 6 units. 180€–200€ double; 230€–300€ suite. Children 9 and under are not allowed. AE, MC, V. Closed Nov–Jan. **Amenities:** Restaurant; bar; pool (outdoor). *In room:* A/C, TV, hair dryer, minibar, Wi-Fi (free).

Oustau de Baumanière ★★★ This five-star Relais & Châteaux property is one of southern France's legendary hotels. Raymond Thuilier bought the 14th-century farmhouse in 1945 and, by the 1950s it was a rendezvous point for the glitterati. The spacious rooms are spread out over three different buildings, with decor ranging from plush contemporary to classic Provençal. No two units are alike, although all contain large sitting areas. In the stone-vaulted dining room of the two-Michelin–starred restaurant, the chef serves French specialties such as frogs' legs with a Parmesan cappuccino, grilled turbot with vegetables from the kitchen garden, and milk-fed leg of lamb with anchovies. Fixed-price menus cost 155€ to 180€.

Rte. d'Arles, 13520 Les Baux. www.oustaudebaumaniere.com. ✆ **04-90-54-33-07.** Fax 04-90-54-40-46. 30 units. 205€–440€ double; 325€–625€ suite. AE, DC, MC, V. Free parking. Closed early Jan–early Mar and early Nov–mid-Dec. Restaurant closed Wed all day and Thurs at lunch Oct–Mar. **Amenities:** Restaurant; babysitting; pool (outdoor); room service. *In room:* A/C, TV, hair dryer, minibar, Wi-Fi (free).

MODERATE

La Benvengudo ★ In a quiet location about 1.5km (1 mile) south of town, this *auberge* is a 19th-century farmhouse surrounded by sculptured shrubbery, towering trees, and parasol pines. The property has an outdoor pool, a tennis court, and a terrace filled with the scent of lavender and thyme. About half the rooms are in the original building, above the restaurant, and the rest are in an attractive stone-sided annex. All are sunny and well maintained, and each has a private terrace or balcony.

Vallon de l'Arcoule, rte. d'Arles, 13520 Les Baux. www.benvengudo.com. ✆ **04-90-54-32-54.** Fax 04-90-54-42-58. 27 units. 105€–205€ double; 155€–370€ suite. AE, MC, V. Parking 13€. Closed Nov–Mar 15. Take RD78 for 1.5km (1 mile) southwest of Les Baux, following signs to Arles. **Amenities:** Restaurant; babysitting; pool (outdoor); room service; tennis court (lit). *In room:* A/C, TV, hair dryer, Wi-Fi (in some; free).

Le Mas d'Aigret ★ 🎁 Tucked away behind an olive grove at the foot of Les Baux is this welcoming hotel that offers convenience and comfort at very reasonable prices.

The two-story Provençal *mas* (farmhouse) is only a few minutes' walk from the village, yet it's surrounded by expansive gardens with a sweeping terrace and an inviting swimming pool. All but two of the rooms have a balcony or terrace, and are furnished in classic Provençal style. Look out for the atmospheric stone rooms that have been cut into the ancient rock face. The restaurant is set in a stone dining room and a tree-shaded garden terrace.

D27, 13520 Les Baux. www.masdaigret.com. ✆ **04-90-54-20-00.** Fax 04-90-54-44-00. 16 units. 120€–240€ double. MC, V. Free parking. **Amenities:** Restaurant; pool (outdoor). *In room:* A/C, TV, hair dryer, Wi-Fi (free).

Mas de L'Oulivié ★★ This complex of traditional Provençal buildings capped with terra-cotta roofs is 1.6km (about a mile) from town. Lounges have beamed ceilings, terra-cotta floor tiles, and comfortable furnishings. The high-ceilinged bedrooms of varying sizes have casement doors that open onto the garden.

13520 Les Baux de Provence. www.masdeloulivie.com. ✆ **04-90-54-35-78.** Fax 04-90-54-44-31. 27 units. 130€–305€ double; 490€ suite. AE, DC, MC, V. Closed Nov to early Mar. **Amenities:** Restaurant; bar; babysitting; pool (outdoor); tennis court (lit). *In room:* A/C, TV, hair dryer, minibar, internet (free).

INEXPENSIVE

Hostellerie de la Reine Jeanne In the heart of the village, this warm, well-scrubbed inn is the best bargain in Les Baux. You enter through a typical French bistro. All the guest rooms are spartan but comfortable, and three have terraces. Bathrooms are cramped and relatively modest.

Grand-Rue, 13520 Les Baux. www.la-reinejeanne.com. ✆ **04-90-54-32-06.** Fax 04-90-54-32-33. 10 units. 56€–70€ double; 100€ apt for 4. AE, MC, V. Closed for 2 weeks in Jan and 2 weeks in Nov. **Amenities:** Restaurant; bar; room service. *In room:* A/C, TV.

ST-RÉMY-DE-PROVENCE ★★

705km (438 miles) S of Paris; 26km (16 miles) NE of Arles; 19km (12 miles) S of Avignon; 13km (8 miles) N of Les Baux

Even though tourists have long since discovered St-Rémy-de-Provence, it hasn't eroded the charms of this delightful market town at the foot of the Alpilles mountain range. The medieval streets of the Vieille Ville (Old Town) jumble together to form a maze filled with upscale boutiques and pretty shops stocking Provençal products. Plane trees shade the cafes and restaurants along the wide boulevard that circles the old town. History is everywhere, from the Renaissance architecture to the Roman ruins south of the town, giving the town a sense of timelessness.

Nostradamus, the French physician/astrologer, was born here in 1503, and you can still see the remains of his birthplace in rue Hoche. Van Gogh was another famous resident, when he came to St-Rémy in 1889 for psychiatric help after a disastrous period in Arles; he committed himself to an asylum here after cutting off his left ear. Between moods of despair, van Gogh painted such works as *Olive Trees* and *Cypresses*. You can follow the paths he took to see how the landscapes of the Alpilles inspired some of his best-known paintings.

Essentials

GETTING THERE St-Rémy has no train station but has regular buses from Avignon. For bus information, call ✆ **04-90-82-07-35.** If you're **driving,** head south from Avignon along D571.

St-Rémy-de-Provence

FRANCE
Paris
St-Rémy-de-Provence
0 1/8 mi
0 1/8 km
To Domaine de Valmouriane
chemin de Montplaisir
av. Albert Schweitzer
chemin de St-Bernard
Arielade
LES MAGNANARELLES
av. du Maréchal Juin
av. du Dix-Neuf Mars 1962
place du Général de Gaulle
av. Maréchal de Lattre
av. Félix Gras
chemin de Ranjarde
L'AUTIN
av. Gabriel St-René Taillandier
av. Louis Mistral
Arène Barnier
av. Charles Mauron
rue Bertrand Dauvin
Musée des Aromes
Stade du Sans Souci
blvd. Gambetta
ch. des Figuières Folles
Musée Archéologique
rue du Parage
Musée des Alpilles
SANS SOUCI
ch. de Barrielle
av. Albert Gleizes
Carnot
Fontaine Nostradamus
blvd. Marceau
rue
Mirabeau
To Le Château des Alpilles & Mas de Cornud
av. Fauconnet
Eglise St-Martin
rue Lafayette
av. de la Liberation
LE ROUGADOU
blvd. Victor Hugo
chemin de St-Joseph
rue Etienne Astier
chemin de la Combette
Office de Tourisme
ch. de la l'Oratoire
av. Durand Maillane
ST-JOSEPH
chemin du Souvenir Francais
av. Pasteur
av. Jean de Servières
Cimetière
ch. de la Combette
ch. de la Croix d'Arles
Canal des Alpilles
av. Pierre Barbier
QUATRE CANTONS
chemin Gaulois
av. Joseph d'Arbaud
av. Folco de Baroncelli
av. J. Baltus
D5
av. Marius Girard
av. Marius Gasquet
chemin du Tor Blanc
av. Antoine de Salle
av. Vincent van Gogh
av. Edgar-le-Roy
Guadre du Barrage
Monastère de St-Paul-de-Mausolée
chemin des Carrieres
Information
ATTRACTIONS
Glanum 12
Monastère de St-Paule-de-Mausole 11
HOTELS
Hôtel de l'Image 6
Hôtel du Soleil 8
Hôtel Gounod 5
Hôtel le Vallon de Valrugues 9
Hôtel Sous les Figuiers 2
Hostellerie le Chalet Fleurie 1
Le Mas des Carrassins 10
RESTAURANTS
La Maison Jaune 4
Le Bistrot Découverte 7
Le Cigalon 3

5 PROVENCE | St-Rémy-de-Provence

VISITOR INFORMATION The **Office de Tourisme** is on place Jean-Jaurès (✆ **04-90-92-05-22;** fax 04-90-92-38-52; www.saintremy-de-provence.com).

SPECIAL EVENTS Every spring on the first Monday after Pentecost, the whole town is taken over by the **Fête de la Transhumance,** which re-enacts the ancient ritual of taking sheep from their winter pastures to their summer grasses. It's an incredible sight to see several thousand sheep being herded through the streets. St-Rémy has one of the liveliest markets in Provence, which takes place every Wednesday and takes up the whole southeastern side of the old town.

Exploring the Town

The cloisters of the asylum at the 12th-century **Monastère de St-Paul-de-Mausole ★★**, avenue Edgar-le-Roy (✆ **04-90-92-77-00**), were made famous by the paintings of Vincent van Gogh, who was a patient here from 1889 to 1890. Visitors can tour a replica of van Gogh's cell and a treatment room, which manage to convey the painful isolation in which he produced the *Starry Night* and other paintings that established his genius and appeal only after his death. Most moving is the self-guided walking tour that uses homespun placards of his artworks to mark the spots in which he painted them. It's wonderfully peaceful in the Romanesque chapel and the cloisters, with their circular arches and columns and beautifully carved capitals. The cloisters are open April to September daily 9:30am to 7pm, and October to December and February to March daily 10:15am to 5pm. Admission is 4€ adults, and 3€ students and children 12 to 16. It's free for kids 11 and under. Adjacent to the church, you'll see a commemorative bust of van Gogh.

Glanum ★ A Gallo-Roman settlement thrived here during the final days of the Roman Empire. Its monuments include a triumphal arch from the time of Julius Caesar, along with a cenotaph called the Mausolée des Jules. Garlanded with sculptured fruits and flowers, the arch dates from 20 B.C. and is the oldest in Provence. The mausoleum was raised to honor the grandsons of Augustus and is the only extant monument of its type. In the area are entire streets and foundations of private residences from the 1st-century town, plus some remains from a Gallo-Greek town of the 2nd century B.C.

Av. Vincent-van-Gogh. ✆ **04-90-92-23-79.** Admission 7€ adults, 5.50€ students and ages 18–25, free for children 17 and under. Apr–Aug daily 10am–6:30pm; Sept–Mar Tues–Sun 10:30am–5pm. From St-Rémy, take D5 1.5km (1 mile) south, following signs to LES ANTIQUES.

Where to Stay

EXPENSIVE

Domaine de Valmouriane ★★ This country-house hotel occupies a century-old farmhouse set on rocky, sun-flooded land. The charming rooms are individually decorated with antiques, flowered upholsteries, and wood furniture. A sense of nostalgia for bygone eras and tremendous charm permeates throughout. Several of the rooms have a private terrace. The hotel also runs a well-regarded cooking school, with classes held in English as well as French.

Petite rte. des Baux (D27), 13210 St-Rémy-de-Provence. www.valmouriane.com. ✆ **04-90-92-44-62.** Fax 04-90-92-37-32. 145€–320€ double; 250€–340€ suite. AE, MC, V. From St-Rémy, drive 5km (3 miles) from the center, following the signs to Beaucaire/Tarascon, and then, after reaching the D27, follow signs to Les Baux. **Amenities:** Restaurant; bar/tearoom; babysitting; Jacuzzi; pool (outdoor); tennis court (lit); Wi-Fi (free). *In room:* A/C, CD player, hair dryer, minibar.

Hôtel le Vallon de Valrugues ★★★ Just outside the town center is this luxurious five-star hotel surrounded by lush parkland. Rooms are elegant, airy, and spacious, and some have a small terrace overlooking the gardens or the Alpilles. The Michelin-starred restaurant's terrace is as appealing as its cuisine, which is winning praise for innovative light dishes, such as John Dory with truffles. Fixed-price menus are 58€ to 98€. There is also a bistro for more informal meals.

Chemin de Canto Cigalo, 13210 St-Rémy-de-Provence. www.vallondevalrugues.com. ✆ **04-90-92-04-40.** Fax 04-90-92-44-01. 52 units. 190€–310€ double; 250€–1,200€ suite. AE, MC, V. Closed mid-Jan to mid-Feb. **Amenities:** Restaurant; bar; babysitting; pool (outdoor); spa; shuttle bus; room service; 2 tennis courts (lit). *In room:* A/C, TV, hair dryer, minibar, Wi-Fi (free).

Le Château des Alpilles ★★★ For luxury and refinement, this is the only château in the area that can equal Vallon de Valrugues (see above). It sits in the center of a tree-studded park 2km (1¼ miles) from the center of St-Rémy. The Pichot family built it in 1827, and it has since housed Chateaubriand and other luminaries. The rooms combine an antique setting with plush upholstery, rich carpeting, and vibrant colors, with a garden graced with majestic magnolias. Whimsical accessories grace each guest room, such as a pair of porcelain panthers flanking one of the mantels, and travertine-trimmed bathtubs. The rooms are housed within the main house, as well as in a former chapel, an old farmhouse, and a charming converted wash house.

Rte. de Rougadou, 13210 St-Rémy-de-Provence. www.chateaudesalpilles.com. ✆ **04-90-92-03-33.** Fax 04-90-92-45-17. 24 units. 190€–286€ double; 265€–560€ suite. AE, DC, MC, V. Closed early Jan to mid-Mar. **Amenities:** Restaurant; bar; pool (outdoor); room service. *In room:* A/C, TV, hair dryer, minibar.

Hôtel de l'Image ★★★ It's hard to get more central than this welcoming four-star hotel right on the main boulevard in the heart of town. What used to be the town cinema is now a chic haven dedicated to photography, with original works exhibited throughout. The style is contemporary without being coldly minimalist, with many of the rooms looking out over the hectare (2½ acres) of luxuriant gardens as well as heart-stopping views of the Alpilles beyond. If you really want to treat yourself, book La Cabane, a suite that includes its own private tree house overlooking the garden. The hotel restaurant, Le Provence, adds a fresh modern twist to Provençal cuisine, and there is also a funky poolside sushi bar.

36 bd. Victor Hugo, 13210 St-Rémy-de-Provence. www.hoteldelimage.com. ✆ **04-90-92-51-50.** Fax 04-90-92-43-52. 30 units. 165€–380€ double; 300€–600€ suite. AE, DC, MC, V. Free parking. Closed Nov–Mar. **Amenities:** Restaurant; bar; pool (outdoor); room service. *In room:* A/C, TV, hair dryer, Wi-Fi (free).

Mas de Cornud The setting is a severely dignified, carefully renovated Provençal farmhouse built 250 years ago. Accommodations are cozy, high ceilinged, and charming, with many yards of cheerful fabrics, a whimsical sense of nostalgia, and antique ceiling beams. The on-site cooking school can sometimes result in the participants filling the hotel to capacity. These week-long sessions occur during 4 weeks scattered throughout the year.

Petite rte. De Baux, 13210 St-Rémy-de-Provence. www.mascornud.com. ✆ **04-90-92-39-32.** Fax 04-90-92-55-99. 7 units. 155€–240€ double. Rates include breakfast. No credit cards. Closed Nov–Mar. From St-Rémy, follow D99 to the D27 and then D31, following the signs to Mas de Cornud, driving 3km (2 miles) west of St-Rémy. **Amenities:** Restaurant; bar; babysitting; pool (outdoor). *In room:* A/C, Wi-Fi (free).

MODERATE

Hôtel Gounod ★ St-Rémy's oldest hotel is named in honor of composer Charles Gounod, who composed his opera *Mireille* here in 1863. Its ornate rooms hark back to the 19th century, some painted in particularly vivid colors. As the standard rooms can be a bit small, ask for a "charming" room which includes a private terrace or balcony overlooking the secluded garden and swimming pool. The hotel is within a stone's throw of St-Rémy's excellent Wednesday market.

Place de la République, 13210 St-Rémy-de-Provence. www.hotel-gounod.com. ✆ **04-90-92-06-14.** Fax 04-90-92-56-54. 34 units. 100€–210€ double. AE, MC, V. Closed Nov–Mar. **Amenities:** Restaurant; bar; pool (outdoor); room service. *In room:* A/C, TV, hair dryer, Wi-Fi (free).

Le Mas des Carassins ★ Van Gogh and Nostradamus used to walk by the front door of this property, on which the present *mas* was constructed in the mid-1880s southwest of the town. It is surrounded by fountains and gardens planted with century-old olive trees, lavender, rosemary, bay trees, and thyme. Each bedroom is beautifully decorated, the beds often with wrought-iron canopies, and some with stone walls. Rooms open onto views of the gardens or the distant Alpilles. The public areas are furnished in the style of a typical upmarket Provençal private home, great for lingering or reading. Excellent Provençale and Mediterranean cuisine is served in the restaurant.

1 Chemin Gaulois, 13210 St-Rémy-de-Provence. www.masdescarassins.com. ✆ **04-90-92-15-48.** Fax 04-90-92-63-47. 14 units. 99€–187€ double; 186€–220€ suite. MC, V. **Amenities:** Restaurant; bar; room service. *In room:* A/C, TV, hair dryer, minibar.

INEXPENSIVE

Hostellerie le Chalet Fleuri Just a few minutes' walk from the old town is this delightful Logis de France three-star hotel set within pretty gardens surrounding a swimming pool. The rooms are brightly and simply furnished but of a decent size, and the owners are especially pleasant and friendly. It's very good value if you want a central location with a pool.

15 av. Frédéric Mistral, 13210 St-Rémy de Provence. www.hotel-lechaletfleuri.com. ✆ **04-90-92-03-62.** 12 units. 64€–115€ double. AE, MC, V. Free parking. **Amenities:** Breakfast room; pool (outdoor). *In room:* TV, hair dryer, Wi-Fi (free).

Hôtel du Soleil In 1965, a private home was converted into this amiable, unpretentious hotel, set in a garden with grand trees and a wrought-iron gazebo, located south of the town center. Inside, the ceiling beams and Provençal accessories evoke the region around you. Guest rooms are simple but convenient, with tasteful furnishings and small bathrooms. There are also three apartments with kitchens.

35 av. Pasteur, 13210 St-Rémy-de-Provence. www.hotelsoleil.com. ✆ **04-90-92-00-63.** Fax 04-90-92-61-07. 27 units. 69€–88€ double; 98€–150€ apt. AE, DC, MC, V. Free parking. Closed mid-Nov to early Mar. **Amenities:** Bar; pool (outdoor); room service. *In room:* TV, hair dryer, kitchens (in some), Wi-Fi (free).

Hôtel Sous les Figuiers Serenity rules in this elegant hotel "under the fig tree," as the name suggests. They've even banned televisions, but style more than makes up for it. Its comfortable rooms are decorated in a rustic Provençal style; be sure to ask for one with a terrace, as only three don't have one. A small pool provides some respite from the Provençal summertime heat.

3 av. Taillandier, 13210 St-Rémy de Provence. www.hotel-charme-provence.com. ✆ **04-90-92-03-62.** 14 units. 77€–168€ double. MC, V. Free parking. **Amenities:** Breakfast room; pool (outdoor). *In room:* A/C, hair dryer, Wi-Fi (free).

Where to Eat

La Maison Jaune FRENCH/PROVENÇALE Strangely, for the only Michelin-starred restaurant in the town center, things can be hit and miss here. The setting, in an 18th-century building with a large shaded terrace in the Vieille Ville, makes for a lovely dining experience. However, the service and, indeed, the food can be inconsistent. On good days, expect dishes of braised artichokes in vinaigrette or grilled loin of lamb with a garlic confit.

15 rue Carnot. ✆ **04-90-92-56-14.** www.lamaisonjaune.info. Reservations required. Fixed-price menu 36€-66€. MC, V. Sun noon-1:30pm; Wed-Sat 7:30-9pm. Closed Nov-Jan.

Le Bistrot Découverte PROVENÇALE Be sure to get a table on the terrace at this lively restaurant on the main boulevard. The menu pays equal attention to meat and fish dishes, including a creamy risotto with scallops and giant shrimp, grilled squid, or a filet of Camargue bull.

8 bd. Victor Hugo. ✆ **04-90-92-34-49.** www.bistrotdecouverte.com. Main courses 14€-28€; fixed-price menus 16€-30€. MC, V. Tues-Sun noon-2pm; Mon-Sat 7-10pm. Closed mid-Feb to mid-Mar.

Le Cigalon ★ PROVENÇALE This convivial restaurant specializes in grilled fish, but it also likes to do its own version of surf 'n' turf with its *assiette terre et mer*: grilled scallops served with grilled steak and a salad of tomatoes, Emmenthal cheese, cured ham, and a very Provençal *pistou*. The service and atmosphere are friendly, but the prices for bottles of wine can be a bit steep.

8 bd. Marceau. ✆ **04-32-62-03-82.** Main courses 13€-24€; fixed-price menus 19€-38€. MC, V. Tues-Sun noon-2pm; Tues-Sat 7:30-9:30pm. Closed Dec-Feb.

GORDES

713km (443 miles) SE of Paris; 35km (22 miles) E of Avignon; 16km (10 miles) NE of Cavaillon; 64km (40 miles) N of the Marseille airport

The majestic sight of Gordes's ancient stone houses rising in tiers above the Imergue Valley is one of the enduring images of Provence. Yet the village's beauty has made it a victim of its own success, with busloads of tourists crowding the cobblestone streets even outside the high season of July and August. Combined with its popularity among the members of Paris's media elite, who have bought second homes here over the years, it's hard to shake off the feeling that this undeniably pretty village has lost its soul somewhere along the way. Expect a higher than usual markup in the local restaurants and shops, as well as long waits to get into the parking lots during the summer.

Essentials

GETTING THERE Gordes has no rail station. **Trains** arrive at nearby Cavaillon, where taxis wait at the railway station; the trip into Gordes costs around 25€. For rail information and schedules in Cavaillon, call ✆ **36-35,** or visit www.voyages-sncf.com. There are no local buses. By **car** from Avignon, take Route 100 east to the intersection to D2, at which point you head north following the signs into Gordes. Parts of the village are closed to cars, but large paying parking lots are along the edges.

VISITOR INFORMATION The **Office de Tourisme** is in the Salle des Gardes du Château, place du Château (✆ **04-90-72-02-75;** www.gordes-village.com).

Exploring the Town

Dominating the skyline, the **Château de Gordes** is a 12th-century fortress with crenelated bastions and round towers in each of its four corners. This is home to the **Musée Pol Mara** (✆ **04-90-72-02-75**), site of a collection of works by the 20th-century Belgian painter Pol Mora, who was a resident of Gordes. An impressive

Renaissance stone spiral staircase leads to the collection, which covers three floors and ends in the magnificent interior of the town hall reception room. It's open daily from 10am to noon and 2 to 6pm. Adults pay 4€ admission; students and youths aged 13 to 17 pay 3€; entrance is free for children 12 and under.

A hidden side to Gordes is revealed in the **Caves du Palais Saint-Firmin** (✆ **04-90-72-02-75;** www.caves-saint-firmin.com). This large underground network of cellars, mills, vats, and stone caves dating from the 11th century reveals how much activity went on at subterranean level when land above ground was so scarce. It's open Wednesday to Monday 10am to 6pm. Admission is 5€ adults, 4€ students, and 15€ for families, including an audio guide.

Some 4km (2½ miles) south of the village, surrounded by a rocky, arid landscape that supports only gnarled oaks and wild herbs, stands the **Moulin des Bouillons,** route de St-Pantaléon (✆ **04-90-72-22-11**), an olive-oil mill so ancient it was mentioned in the 1st-century writings of Pliny the Elder. It's now owned by the stained-glass artist Frédérique Duran, and its interior still has the original Roman floors and the base of the olive press. The complex is open Wednesday to Monday from 10am to noon and 2 to 6pm. A ticket granting admission to the mill costs 5€ adults and 3.50€ ages 10 and under. Within the same site is the **Musée du Verre et du Vitrail,** which showcases stained glass and glass art over the centuries and whose collection has been growing steadily since its inception in 1975. A combined ticket of 7.50€ or 5.50€ gets you into both museums.

Reconstructed *bories* make up the **Village des Bories,** Les Savournins (✆ **04-90-72-03-48**), 3km (2 miles) southwest of town. These structures are composed of thin layers of stone that spiral upward into a dome without the use of mortar. They look as if they have been around since Neolithic times, but most of the buildings were constructed in the 18th and 19th centuries, if not later. They were generally thought to be used by shepherds as a shelter and place to store tools. To get here, take D15, veering right beyond a fork at D2. A sign marks another right turn toward the village, where you must park and walk 45 minutes to visit the site. The village is open daily from 9am to dusk. Admission is 6€ for adults and 4€ for children aged 12 to 17. *Bories* can be found throughout the Provençal countryside and can be encountered for free on walks through farmland.

Founded in 1148, the **Abbaye Notre-Dame de Sénanque ★**, a Cistercian monastery 4km (2½ miles) north of Gordes on D15/D177 (✆ **04-90-72-05-72;** www.senanque.fr), sits in isolation surrounded by lavender fields. It was abandoned during the Revolution, reopened in the 19th century, closed again in 1969, and reopened yet again (by the Cistercians) in 1988. The influential 20th-century writer and Catholic theologian Thomas Merton can be counted among those who found

Lavender Fields Photo Op

In the height of summer, the area around the tranquil **Abbaye Notre-Dame de Sénanque** (✆ **04-90-72-05-72; www.senanque.fr**) is engulfed by a carpet of purple, perfumed lavender, rendering it one of the most photographed sites in Provence. **Visiting the Abbaye de Sénanque in bloom** is possibly the most clichéd summer activity in Provence. But that doesn't make the seas of lavender surrounding the 12th-century Cistercian monastery any less breathtaking. It's a great memory.

peace here. Individuals can visit only with a guide. Admission costs 7€ for adults, 5€ for students, and 3€ for persons ages 6 to 18; it's free for children 5 and under. Be aware that this is a working monastery, not merely a tourist site. You can attend any of five Masses per day, buy religious souvenirs and texts in the gift shop, and generally marvel at a medieval setting brought back to life.

Where to Stay

Hôtel Le Gordos Set within a prosperous-looking residential neighborhood about a kilometer (½ mile) southwest of the town center, this hotel was established in the early 1990s within the stone-sided shell of a several-hundred-year-old Provençal *mas*. Surrounded by shrubbery and capped with terra-cotta tiles, it's a less expensive version of its plusher sibling, La Bastide de Gordes & Spa (see below). Inside is a smooth and seamlessly comfortable decor that's light, airy, and traditional. Bedrooms are simple but appealing, with lots of sunlight and pale colors.

Rte. de Cavaillon, 84220 Gordes. www.hotel-le-gordos.com. ✆ **04-90-72-00-75.** Fax 04-90-72-07-00. 19 units. 124€–290€ double. AE, MC, V. Free parking. Closed Mar. From the center of Gordes, follow the signs to Cavaillon and travel 1km (½ mile) southwest. **Amenities:** Babysitting; pool (outdoor); tennis court (lit), Wi-Fi (free). *In room:* A/C, TV, hair dryer.

Hôtel Les Bories ★★★ This modern hotel clad in rough stone is built around the core of an old Provençal *mas*. It takes advantage of its hillside setting, offering vistas from the dining terrace, outdoor pool and terrace, glass-fronted lobby, and indoor pool. The decor was inspired by high-tech Milanese design, with streamlined furniture, tile floors, and Oriental rugs in public spaces and the spacious guest rooms alike. Chef Pascal Ginoux's inventive cooking has given the hotel restaurant a Michelin star, with such dishes as simply grilled turbot and roasted wild boar.

Rte. de l'Abbaye de Sénanque, 84220 Gordes. ✆ **04-90-72-00-51.** Fax 04-90-72-01-22. www.hotellesbories.com. 33 units. 200€–438€ double; 510€–820€ suite. Fixed-price dinner 57€–92€. AE, DC, MC, V. Closed Jan–Feb. From town, drive 2.4km (1½ miles) north, following the signs to Abbaye de Sénanque or Venasque. **Amenities:** Restaurant; bar; babysitting; health club w/Jacuzzi; 2 pools (indoor and outdoor). *In room:* A/C, TV, hair dryer, minibar, Wi-Fi (free).

La Bastide de Gordes & Spa ★★★ This 16th-century five-star hotel is in an enviable location right in the village. While the facade looks over the busy street, the back of the hotel tumbles down the hillside in several levels, giving guests superb views from the gardens, panoramic terrace, and swimming pool. Bedrooms are luxurious and tasteful, with antique and reproduction furnishings and soft colors. Try to get one of the bedrooms with a view of the valley rather than the village. Known for its inventive and creative cuisine, the on-site restaurant, Olivier Bouzon, is a worthy choice even if you're not a guest of the hotel. Dishes include whole roasted sea bream with risotto and fava beans, and rack of lamb with thyme and pesto-infused vegetables. The fixed-price dinner menu is 68€.

Le Village, 84220 Gordes. www.bastide-de-gordes.com. ✆ **04-90-72-12-12.** Fax 04-90-72-05-20. 41 units. 180€–460€ double; 300€–870€ suite. AE, MC, V. Free parking. Closed Jan to mid-Feb. **Amenities:** Restaurant; bar; babysitting; health club and spa; 2 pools (outdoor); room service. *In room:* A/C, TV, hair dryer, minibar, Wi-Fi (free).

La Clé des Champs ★ Nine kilometers (5½ miles) east of Gordes, La Clé des Champs (formerly known as Le Mas de Garrigon) occupies a gracious building that was custom-built in 1979, using antique materials. Each room is uniquely decorated in mainly white tones, with accents of bright colors and cool terra-cotta floors. All rooms have private terraces that open onto views of the Luberon. Dinner can be arranged on request; simply let the owners know in the morning.

Rte. de St. Saturnin d'Apt, 84220 Gordes. www.masdegarrigon-provence.com. ✆ **04-90-05-63-22.** Fax 04-90-05-70-01. 9 units. 92€-182€ double. AE, MC, V. Free parking. From Gordes, follow the signs to St-Saturnin d'Apt. **Amenities:** Restaurant (for hotel guests only); pool (outdoor); room service; Wi-Fi (free). *In room:* A/C, TV, minibar.

Le Mas du Loriot ★ This tranquil hotel sits on the southern slopes of Monts du Vaucluse in the heart of Luberon Regional Nature Park, between Gordes and Roussillon. The simply furnished rooms are on the ground floor, all but one with a south-facing private terrace that takes advantage of the views of the Luberon mountains. Groves of lavender and pine trees surround the swimming pool in the lush gardens. Dinner can be arranged on Monday, Wednesday, and Friday for 32€.

Rte. de Joucas, 84220 Murs-en-Provence (8km/5m E of Gordes). ✆ **04-90-72-62-62.** www.masduloriot.com. 8 units. 60€-145€ double. MC, V. Closed Nov-Mar. **Amenities:** Restaurant; bar; pool (outdoor). *In room:* TV, hair dryer, minibar, Wi-Fi (in some; free).

Where to Eat

See also the restaurants at **La Bastide de Gordes** and **Hôtel Les Bories** (above).

Le Mas Tourteron PROVENÇALE On the outskirts of the village of Les Imberts, this restaurant occupies an 18th-century Provençal *mas* surrounded by cherry trees and vines. It has a sun-flooded dining room, with additional seating that spills over into the garden. The menu is based on fresh ingredients and includes cuttlefish salad with seasonal vegetables, roast leg lamb with mustard and honey, and guinea fowl crusted with Provençal herbs.

Chemin de St-Blaise, Les Imberts. ✆ **04-90-72-00-16.** Reservations required. www.mastourteron.com. Fixed-price menu 51€. MC, V. Daily 7:30-9:30pm; Sun noon-2pm. Closed Jan-Feb. Take D2 for 6km (4 miles) southwest of Gordes.

ROUSSILLON & BONNIEUX ★

These villages are so close to each other that you can visit both in a long morning or afternoon.

Roussillon

45km (28 miles) E of Avignon; 10km (6 miles) E of Gordes

Color—at least 17 shades of ocher, to be more precise—has proven to be this village's lifeblood. The area's rich deposits of ocher have been valued ever since Roman times; beginning in the late 1700s, Roussillon's ocher powders were shipped around the world from Marseille. Though the mining industry has dried up, hordes of artists and visitors still flock here to marvel at and be inspired by the gorgeous ranges of the vibrant warm tones. It does get very busy during the summer, but, unlike other popular villages in the Luberon, it hasn't given over completely to the tourist dollar.

ESSENTIALS

GETTING THERE No trains or buses service Roussillon, apart from a small bus that takes you to the Saturday morning market at Apt. To **drive** from Avignon, drive east on N7 to D973, and then to D22. Finally, turn north on D149 and follow the signs to Roussillon. The trip takes about 45 minutes.

VISITOR INFORMATION The **Office de Tourisme** is on place de la Poste (✆ **04-90-05-60-25;** www.roussillon-provence.com).

EXPLORING THE TOWN

Take time to explore the narrow, steep streets, soaking in the rusts, reds, and ochers of the stone used in the construction of the houses. From the **Castrum,** at the high point along rue de l'Eglise, you'll see a magnificent vista. Face north and gaze across the Vaucluse plateau and to Mont Ventoux. Turn south to see the Coulon valley and the Grand Luberon.

You can reach the **old ocher quarries,** with their exposed, sunburned rocks, by taking a 40-minute scenic walk east of the village. Paths to the quarries start at the tourist office (see "Essentials," above). The huge red cliffs of **Chaussée des Géants** comprise another panorama. To view them, take the path southeast of the tourist office. The walk is about 45 minutes and includes a great look back at Roussillon.

WHERE TO STAY

Hostellerie Le Phébus & Spa ★★★ This five-star Relais & Chateaux hotel between Roussillon and Gordes is an absolute delight from arrival to (very reluctant) departure. Formerly a stone farmhouse overlooking the ocher hills surrounding Roussillon, this is now a complex of luxurious rooms and suites, many with a terrace and some with a private pool. The airy, spacious rooms are furnished in rich, soft fabrics, flowing linens and agreeably overstuffed sofas. The well-equipped on-site Carita Spa offers a range of high-quality spa treatments, including facials and massages. The hotel's Michelin-starred restaurant, headed by Provençal native Xavier Mathieu, is refined without being pretentious, much like the hotel itself. Mathieu presents high-class versions of Provençal dishes, like *soupe au pistou* (vegetable soup); *daube* (a type of stew) with oxtail and beef cheeks; and slow-cooked lamb served in a delicate pastry.

Rte. de Murs, 84220 Joucas. www.lephebus.com. ✆ **04-86-60-80-12.** Fax 04-90-05-73-61. 24 units. 210€–355€ double; 335€–655€ suites. Fixed-price menus 49€–130€. AE, DC, MC, V. Closed mid-Oct to mid-Apr. **Amenities:** Restaurant; bar; babysitting; gym; helipad; pool (outdoor); spa; tennis. *In room:* A/C, TV, minibar, Wi-Fi (free).

Le Clos de la Glycine Oodles of charm and a central location make this stylish three-star hotel the best bet if you want to stay in the heart of the village. Rooms are pleasingly old-fashioned and feature Provençal furnishings, with wrought-iron bedsteads and bleached white antique reproductions. Many rooms come with private terraces with astounding views of the ocher-colored countryside. The hotel also has a highly regarded restaurant, David (see below).

Place de la Poste, 84200 Roussillon. www.luberon-hotel.com. ✆ **04-90-05-60-13.** Fax 04-90-05-75-80. 9 units. 105€–175€ double; 155€–270€ suite/apt. AE, MC, V. **Amenities:** Restaurant; bar; Wi-Fi. *In room:* A/C, TV, minibar.

Le Mas de la Tour The history of this *mas* on the outskirts of town dates back some 800 years. It has been renovated to add modern amenities, including a large enticing pool. The rooms run the gamut from matchbox-size to palatial. The smaller ones have exterior entrances, and the larger ones have bathtubs and terraces.

Rte. de Tarachole, 84400 Gargas. www.mas-de-la-tour.com. ✆ **04-90-74-12-10.** Fax 04-90-04-83-67. 32 units. 58€–127€ double. MC, V. Closed Oct to early May. From Gargas, drive 3km (2 miles) south, following the signs to Apt. **Amenities:** Restaurant; bar; pool (outdoor). *In room:* TV, Wi-Fi (free).

WHERE TO EAT

David PROVENÇALE This popular restaurant offers an airy dining area and panoramic views of the red cliffs and hills of the Vaucluse. The restaurant serves up innovative dishes, such as lobster salad with baby spinach and mozzarella, asparagus with soft-boiled egg and cured ham, and caramelized rack of suckling pig.

Place de la Poste. ✆ **04-90-05-60-13.** Reservations recommended. Main courses 31€; fixed-price menus 35€–55€. AE, MC, V. Thurs–Sun and Tues 12:30–2pm; Mon–Tues, Thurs, and Sat 7:30–9pm. Closed mid-Nov to mid-Dec.

Le Bistro de Roussillon PROVENÇALE This bustling bistro has one intimate dining room and two terraces—one with a vista of valley and hills and the other facing the square. The menu varies from salads with goat's cheese in phyllo pastry to veal casserole in a mushroom sauce and poached filet of sea bass with shallots and rice.

Place de la Mairie. ✆ **04-90-05-74-45.** Main courses 14€; fixed-price menu 25€. MC, V. Daily noon–3pm and 7–9pm. Closed Nov.

L'Ocrier FRENCH/PIZZA Although this place looks like a tourist trap, it is actually a lively bistro full of no-nonsense dishes served by friendly staff. It's a good place for an affordable lunch if you want good-quality pizzas, pastas, plates of *provençale* charcuterie, and French staples such as steak tartare and omelets.

Av. Burlière. ✆ **04-90-05-79-53.** Main courses 9.50€–16€; fixed-price menus 14€–20€. MC, V. Daily noon–9pm.

Bonnieux

11km (7 miles) S of Roussillon; 45km (28 miles) N of Aix-en-Provence

This romantic hilltop village, nestled in the heart of the Petit Luberon, commands views of nearby Roussillon and the whole Coulon Valley. Strategically located between Spain and Italy, Bonnieux has had a bloody history of raids and battles since its beginnings in Roman times, when it stood closer to the valley floor. To better defend itself, the town was moved farther up the hill during the 1200s, when it also received sturdy ramparts and sentry towers. In the 16th century, Bonnieux grew into a Catholic stronghold and often found itself surrounded by Protestants who were suspicious and jealous of its thriving economy. Since its streets were lined with mansion after mansion belonging to prominent bishops, allegations swirled around that the town received particular "favors" to bolster its standing. Envy and zeal got the best of the Protestants, and they eventually laid siege to the town, killing approximately 3,000 of the 4,000 inhabitants. Even though Bonnieux is the largest hill town in the area, its population never truly recovered and continues to hover around 1,500.

ESSENTIALS

GETTING THERE There is no train or bus service. From Roussillon, **drive** south along D149 directly to Bonnieux. The trip takes about 15 minutes.

VISITOR INFORMATION The **Office de Tourisme** is at 7 place Carnot (**✆ 04-90-75-91-90**).

EXPLORING THE TOWN

Start at the summit of this steep village with the **Vieille Eglise (Old Church)** and its cemetery. The grounds of stately cedars surrounding this Romanesque church, which dates from the 1100s, provide the best vantage point from which to view the valley's hill towns. Farther down the incline is the **Musée de la Boulangerie,** 12 rue de la République (**✆ 04-90-75-88-34**), dedicated to the art of French breadmaking.

Exhibits show all stages of the process, from planting and harvesting the grain to the final mixers and ovens that turn the flour, water, salt, and yeast mixture into warm, crusty loaves. The museum is open Wednesday to Monday 10am to 12:30 and 2:30 to 6pm from April to June and September to October, and from 10am to 1pm and 2 to 6pm July and August. Admission is 3.50€ for adults and 1.50€ for seniors and students (free for those 12 and under).

At the lower extreme of town, clearly signposted from the center, is the **Eglise Neuve (New Church),** from the late 1800s. Its four beautiful panels from the Old Church date from the 1500s and are painted in the brightly colored German style to show the intensity of the Passion of Christ. It's open daily from 9am to 7pm.

WHERE TO STAY

Auberge de l'Aiguebrun Come here to relax in one of the most tranquil settings in Provence and soak up that special, surreal sunlight. Artists and lovers seek out this remarkable 19th-century manor house enclosed by the Luberon hills and a mountain river. The intimate guest rooms that look out over the river or hills are individually decorated in the Provençal style. In the public rooms, attention is lovingly paid to every detail, from the crackling fire on cooler evenings to the soft and classical music wafting from room to room. The hotel also has a superb restaurant with its own garden; it's open Thursday to Monday (closed Wed at lunchtime).

Domaine de la Tour, D943, 84480 Bonnieux. www.aubergedelaiguebrun.fr. ✆ **04-90-04-47-00.** Fax 04-90-04-47-01. 140€–290€ double. MC, V. Free parking. Closed Nov–Mar. From town, drive 6km (4 miles) southeast, following the signs to Lourmarin. **Amenities:** Restaurant; bar; babysitting; pool (outdoor). *In room:* A/C, TV, hair dryer, Wi-Fi (free).

La Bastide de Capelongue ★★★ Housed in a Provençal farmhouse just outside Bonnieux and surrounded by beautifully landscaped gardens, this sophisticated hotel is a peaceful spot. The bedrooms are elegant, and some have terraces or balconies. The hotel also offers fully equipped apartments in its neighboring La Ferme de Capelongue. The hotel's restaurant is one of the most renowned in the area—chef Edouard Loubet has rightfully earned his two Michelin stars. Herbs and vegetables from the kitchen garden are used for creative dishes, including grilled Alpilles pigeon with rocket *jus* and a tartlet of offal decorated with flowers from chives.

Chemin des Cabanes, Les Claparèdes, 84480 Bonnieux. www.capelongue.com. ✆ **04-89-01-56-52.** 17 units. 190€–380€ double; weekly rates at La Ferme 695€–3,850€. AE, DC, MC, V. **Amenities:** Restaurant; bar; pool (outdoor); room service. *In room:* A/C, TV, hair dryer, minibar, Wi-Fi (in some; free).

La Bouquière Barcelona native Angel and his Parisian wife Françoise have been running this delightful countryside B&B for more than 20 years, turning it into one of the most relaxing corners of Provence. Furnishings are simple but comfortable, with heavy beamed ceilings and whitewashed walls. Each of the rooms has its own little garden area under shady trellises, and the huge garden tumbles towards the swimming pool with captivating views of the forest-clad hills.

Chemin des Gardiols, 84480 Bonnieux. www.labouquiere.com. ✆ **04-90-75-87-17.** 4 units. 78€–120€ double, including breakfast. No credit cards. Free parking. **Amenities:** Pool (outdoor). *In room:* TV, Wi-Fi (free).

Le Clos du Buis ★ Set within a garden centered on a copse of small trees *(les buis),* this small-scale hotel is housed within a late-18th-century stone-fronted Mediterranean-style villa. Bedrooms are colorful and comfortable, often with rough-hewn ceiling beams and sweeping views over the Luberon countryside. A summer kitchen by the outdoor pool is available if you want to do your own cooking.

Rue Victor Hugo, 84480 Bonnieux. www.leclosdubuis.fr. ✆ **04-90-75-88-48.** Fax 04-90-75-88-57. 8 units. 92€–132€ double. MC, V. parking. **Amenities:** Restaurant; pool (outdoor); Wi-Fi (free). *In room:* A/C, TV.

WHERE TO EAT

L'Arôme PROVENÇALE Come to this welcoming restaurant, housed in a building with a 14th-century stone-vaulted ceiling, for innovative Provençale cuisine with a few twists. There's thyme-infused lamb shoulder and simply grilled bream with fresh-from-the-market vegetables. Or try the Pyrénées' famous Bigorre pork, which is cooked for 8 hours and effortlessly melts in the mouth.

2 rue Lucien Blanc, 84480 Bonnieux. ✆ **04-90-75-88-62.** www.larome-restaurant.com. Reservations recommended. Main courses 20€–35€; fixed-price menus 29€ and 41€. MC, V. Thurs 12:30–1:45pm and Fri–Tues 12:30–1:45pm and 7:30–9:45pm. Closed Jan–Mar.

Le Fournil PROVENÇALE This restaurant occupies the premises of a cave, which opens onto a small-scale square graced with a 12th-century fountain. The

lacoste: A FIGHT FOR ITS SOUL

The hilltop Luberon village of Lacoste, approximately 7km (4 miles) east of Bonnieux, has seen its fair share of controversy over the centuries, not least because it was the former home of the **Marquis de Sade.** The 18th-century libertine lived in the Château de Lacoste at the top the village, and used it as a refuge when he was on the run from charges of blasphemy and abusive sexual behavior. But he had to flee the château itself when his employees complained of being badly mistreated by their master. The celebrated marquis, who gave us the term *sadism,* eventually died in a lunatic asylum. The château subsequently became a victim of revolutionary zeal in 1789 and was all but destroyed.

Its ruins formed a haunting part of the picturesque landscape of the Luberon, its outline clearly visible for miles around. It looked ready to crumble into nothing when, in 2001, fashion mogul **Pierre Cardin** bought what was left of the château and set about restoring it with a similar zeal that brought its destruction. That's when Lacoste's latest controversy started. Cardin wasn't satisfied with simply restoring the château; he proceeded to buy more than 40 of the village houses and renovate them. He launched the **Festival de Lacoste** (www.festivaldelacoste.com), which puts on opera, concerts, and theater productions every summer in the open-air stage beside the château. His stated intention was to turn this pretty little village into a cultural St-Tropez, but without the showbiz side. He wanted to restore its "truth."

The villagers, meanwhile, felt that Lacoste's spirit was being drained as they watched Cardin buy one house after another. They complain that the restored buildings are used less now than they were when the village was supposedly dying. When Cardin's friends and artists from the festival aren't around, the houses are boarded up and silent.

Controversy aside, Lacoste is worth a stop to admire the village's ancient stone houses and take the cobbled path that leads to the sculpture-strewn garden surrounding Cardin's château. The works of modern art that Cardin has been collecting over the years have since blended in with the glorious views of the Luberon countryside you can see from the top of the hill. In the lower town, the **Café de France** (✆ **04-90-75-82-25**) serves simple lunches on its panoramic terrace and also rents four rooms for 65€ a night.

menu varies with the season and the inspiration of the chefs, but might include ravioli with artichokes and gambas, roasted veal with shallot confit, and whatever the catch of the day might be.

5 place Carnot, 84480 Bonnieux. © **04-90-75-83-62.** Reservations recommended. Main courses 23€; fixed-price lunch 22€–27€, dinner 44€–48€. MC, V. Apr–Sept Wed–Fri and Sun noon–2pm, Tues–Sun 7–10pm; Oct to late Nov, late Dec to mid-Jan, and mid-Feb–Mar Wed–Sun 12:30–1:45pm and 7:30–9:45pm.

APT

52km (32 miles) W of Avignon; 52km (32 miles) N of Aix-en-Provence; 726km (451 miles) S of Paris

Known as *Colonia Apta Julia,* this was an important Gallo-Roman city and today is a bustling market town. Ignore the modern industrial area and head for the Vieille Ville (Old Town) to capture the beauty of Apt. Here you can walk long, narrow streets that wind between old houses, where every nook and cranny offers something waiting to be discovered.

Apt is known for its wines—it's a region of the Rhône Valley where the grapes that go into Côtes du Luberon and Côtes du Ventoux wines are grown. It is also known for its basket- and wickerwork and has been a producer of hats since the 17th century. Others know it as the capital of *fruits confits,* the crystallized fruit so beloved in Provence.

The old Roman city faded into history and was eventually deserted and covered by silt from the river and the hillsides. Roman remains are still buried around 5 to 10m (16–33 ft.) below the current town. But you can still see one of the best-preserved relics of Roman times—the **Pont Julien,** a three-arched bridge more than 2,000 years old spanning the Calavon River 8km (5 miles) west of Apt.

Essentials

GETTING THERE Apt has no railway station. **Buses** from Avignon (trip time 75 min.) drop passengers in a parking lot beside the **Route de Digne** (© **04-90-74-20-21**), at the eastern periphery of town. The best way to reach Apt is by **driving;** follow the N100 east from Avignon.

VISITOR INFORMATION The **Office de Tourism** is at 20 av. Philippe de Girard (© **04-90-74-03-18;** www.luberon-apt.fr).

SPECIAL EVENTS Apt is the main base for the annual **Luberon Jazz Festival** (www.luberonjazz.net), which takes place in May and attracts musicians from all over France for a week of concerts.

Exploring the Town

The best time to visit Apt is for its Saturday-morning market centered on **place de la Bouquerie,** voted one of the 100 most appealing village markets in France. The streets are packed with market stalls and temporary shops. Lavender growers, purveyors of goat cheese, potters, local beekeepers, and craftspeople invade the town to peddle their wares. The Tour de l'Horloge, dating from the 1500s and straddling the rue des Marchands, is a particularly active area for the Saturday market. On market days, the town fills with jazz musicians, barrel-organ players, and other street performers.

Cathédrale Ste-Anne This major monument is known for its ancient two-level crypt. According to legend, the bones of the legendary Ste-Anne, mother of the Virgin Mary, were miraculously discovered in this crypt in the 8th century, resulting in the

wine, truffles & corkscrews IN MÉNERBES

Ménerbes is another hilltop village that has found itself on the list of Les Plus Beaux Villages de France (the Most Beautiful Villages in France). It also found itself under siege by countless tourists looking for the house that Peter Mayle immortalized in his 1989 book *A Year in Provence.* Mayle has since moved on elsewhere, but Ménerbes is still on the tourist trail, even if the frenzy has died down somewhat.

As with many Luberon villages, the town is built on a hill, with the best views at the top. At the top of the medieval village is the place de l'Horloge, a charming square with a simple bell tower topped with a wrought-iron cage. In this place the **Maison de la Truffe et du Vin du Luberon** (✆ **04-90-72-38-27;** www.vin-truffe-luberon.com) pays tribute to wine and truffles, with its wine cellar, museum, laboratory, restaurant, and library—all housed in a building that dates from the 17th century. Here, you can discover the history of wine production in the region while sampling some of the local wines; you can also purchase bottles at vineyard prices. Similarly, there are demonstrations on how truffles—those elusive, expensive, and delicious tubers—make their journey from oak forests to the dinner plate. Taste them for yourself in the restaurant set in a splendid garden with views of the Luberon.

Outside Ménerbes, on the D103 heading towards Cavaillon, is an unusual museum: the **Musée du Tire-Bouchon** (✆ **04-90-72-41-58;** www.domaine-citadelle.com). This museum houses a unique collection of more than 1,200 corkscrews dating from the 17th century to the present day. The exhibits show how the humble corkscrew has developed over the centuries, from the first steel ones forged by hand to modern designer contraptions that are a triumph of style over substance. It's open from April to September Monday to Friday 9am to noon and 2pm to 7pm, and Saturday to Sunday 10am to noon and 2pm to 7pm; from October to March Monday to Friday 9am to noon and 2pm to 5pm. Admission is 4€. The museum is run by Yves and Alexis Rousset-Rouard who own the neighboring **Domaine de la Citadelle,** where you can visit the cellars or take a tour of the vineyard.

building of the cathedral. Her life is depicted in a beautiful set of 14th-century stained-glass windows at the end of the apse. Her shroud is also displayed among the reliquaries of the treasury. Scholars speculate that Anne was not the biblical figure, but a dim memory of the primeval Pan-European mother goddess sometimes known as Ana or Anna Perenna to the Romans.

In the 13th century, the present church was enlarged, and in the 18th century the floor was raised and the broken-barrel vault turned into a higher arched vault. The oldest part of the cathedral is the tower crypt, which still has both a funerary monument honoring a priest in the time of Apia Julia and Carolingian flagstones. The church and treasury are filled with rare ecclesiastical artifacts. In the chapel of St. John the Baptist is an early Christian marble sarcophagus from the Pyrenees. Among the treasures in the sacristy are 11th- and 12th-century manuscripts, elaborate vestments, and an 11th-century Arab standard brought back from the First Crusade. The nave is adorned with scenes from the life of Christ, painted by Pierre and Christophe Delpech in the 18th century.

Vieille Ville. ✆ **04-90-04-85-44.** www.apt-cathedrale.com. Free admission. Mon–Fri noon–2:30pm and 3–6pm; Sun 2:30–6pm. Ask the caretaker for entrance to the sacristy.

Hôtel Colin d'Albertas The lavish 17th-century baroque interior of this building contains some of the most spectacular plaster- and stuccowork in the region and is a museum in its own right.

Rue de la République. ✆ **04-90-74-02-40.** Tours 5€ adults. July–Aug Thurs only 11am–4pm.

Musée de l'Aventure Industrielle Apt's agricultural, artisanal, and industrial roots are showcased in what used to be the Marliagues candied fruit factory. Exhibits show how the town profited by its production of *fruits confits,* its extraction of ocher, and the glazed earthenware known as *faïence.*

Place du Postel. ✆ **04-90-74-95-30.** Admission 4€ adults, 2€ students, free for children 15 and under. Mon and Wed–Sat 10am–noon and 2–5:30pm Oct–May; Mon and Wed–Sat 10am–noon and 3–6:30pm, Sun 3–7pm June–Sept.

Shopping

If you want to take home prettily packaged boxes of *fruits confits* (candied fruits), try **Confiserie Marcel Richaud,** 112 quai de la Liberté (✆ **04-90-74-43-50**) or **Confiserie Le Coulon Jean Ceccon,** 24 quai de la Liberté (✆ **04-90-74-21-90**).

Where to Stay

Domaine des Andéols ★★ This hyperupscale country inn gleams with a chic modern feel, and includes Mies van der Rohe leather lounges, Andy Warhol serigraphs, and an overall decor that's about as high design as you're likely to find anywhere. Owners Olivier and Patrizia Massart have gathered paintings, furniture, and sculpture from their global travels to decorate their nine stone-sided houses. Each bedroom has its own kitchenette. Two of the units include private outdoor pools of their own. Just 10 minutes north of Apt, it's surrounded by lakes, gardens, and orchards.

Les Andéols, 84490 Saint-Saturnin-lès-Apt. www.domaine-des-andeols.com. ✆ **04-90-75-50-63.** Fax 04-90-75-43-22. 9 units. 260€–375€ junior house; 350€–850€ privilege/superior house; 650€–725€ prestige house with private pool. AE, MC, V. Free parking. **Amenities:** Restaurant; 2 pools (indoor and outdoor); room service; sauna. *In room:* TV, hair dryer, minibar, Wi-Fi (free).

Le Couvent Apt's most charming hotel is right in the heart of the old town. Parisian refugees Laurent and Marie Pierrepont have converted this 17th-century convent into a stylish and tranquil retreat with the occasional quirk. (Laurent loves music, so expect to hear strains of Mozart in the bathroom.) The large rooms are elegantly furnished, and feature different themes based on color schemes, including chocolate, ocher, and sienna. The secluded garden is an inviting place to relax; there's a decent-size pool. The breakfast has restored original vaulted ceilings.

36 rue Louis Rousset, 84400 Apt. www.loucouvent.com. ✆ **04-90-04-55-36** (cellphone 06-08-90-15-88). 6 units. 95€–125€ double. Rates include breakfast. DC, MC, V. **Amenities:** Breakfast room; pool (outdoor). *In room:* TV, hair dryer, Wi-Fi (free).

Relais de Roquefure Lying 6km (3½ miles) southwest of the center, this Logis de France country hotel offers good food and a good night's sleep, all at a fair price. Rooms are brightly furnished in Provençal colors and fabrics, and some open directly into the garden and the pool area. The north-facing rooms have dramatic views of Mont Ventoux.

Quartier de Roquefure, Along N100, 84400 Apt. www.relaisderoquefure.com. ✆ **04-90-04-88-88.** Fax 04-90-74-14-86. 16 units. 64€–118€ double; half board 134€–190€ double. MC, V. Closed Dec–Jan. **Amenities:** Restaurant; bar; pool (outdoor). *In room:* TV, hair dryer, Wi-Fi (free).

Outdoors in Luberon Regional Nature Park

Apt is located within the vast **Luberon Regional Nature Park,** which has been named a biosphere reserve by UNESCO. The area covers 1,200 sq. km (463 sq. miles), encompassing numerous villages, thick forests, and many long-distance walking paths known as *sentiers de grandes randonnées,* or GRs.

The **information office** for the park is in an 18th-century house in Apt, La Maison du Parc at 60 place Jean-Jaurès (✆ **04-90-04-42-00**). The office provides maps, details of hiking trails in the park, and other outdoor activities in the area, including cycling, which is one of the most popular pursuits in the region. Otherwise, the tourist office in Apt (see above) will provide information as well as useful maps. Much of the land in the Luberon area is privately owned, but trails in the park are open to the public. On-site is a small **museum of geology.** Admission is free, and it's open May to October Monday to Saturday from 8:30am to noon, and the rest of the year Monday to Friday from 1:30 to 6pm. Buses can be sporadic, so it's best to explore the area by car or on foot.

Where to Eat

Auberge de la Loube ★ PROVENÇALE This century-old domain, located in the rolling hills of the Luberon, features the delicious cuisine of Provençal chef and entrepreneur Maurice de la Loube. Monsieur de la Loube's starters are flavorful and varied—poached asparagus in vinaigrette, braised artichokes, tapenade, *brandade de morue* (a creamy dip made of salted cod), and eggplant "caviar"—and are presented in a creative way. These starters may be carried to your table in a wicker basket and laid out with fanfare on your table. Main courses are succulent and generous, especially the house specialty of perfectly roasted local lamb.

Quartier de la Loube, Buoux. ✆ **04-90-74-19-58.** Reservations recommended. Main courses 18€; fixed-price menus 23€–33€. No credit cards. Tues–Wed and Fri–Sun noon–1:30pm and 7–9:30pm. Closed Jan–Feb. Located 8km (4½ miles) south of Apt; from Apt, follow signs to Buoux.

Thym te Voilà ★ PROVENÇALE/FUSION World cuisine blends harmoniously with Provençal produce in this sophisticated, friendly restaurant in the old town. Chef Nicolas likes to experiment and spice things up a bit, giving braised beef the Moroccan treatment, turning salmon into a curry, and serving Thai sausages with vermicelli. The vegetarian lasagna made of zucchini is given more depth with a healthy dose of tapenade.

59 place St-Martin, 84400 Apt. ✆ **04-90-74-28-25.** http://thymtevoila.free.fr. Main courses 11€; fixed-price menus 19€–30€. MC, V. Tues–Sat noon–2pm; Thurs–Sat 7–9:30pm.

LOURMARIN & SUD LUBERON

19km (12 miles) south of Apt; 37km (23 miles) east of Aix-en-Provence; 32km (20 miles) east of Cavaillon.

Residents of the southern part of the Luberon maintain that their side is less spoiled, not quite as overrun with tourists, and offers a more authentic slice of Provençal life than the northern area. The area does have a more relaxed air, and fewer obvious signs of overtourism. That said, Lourmarin can be just as busy as Gordes in high season, especially during its excellent Friday morning market. And it, too, has its share of second-home owners who disappear after the summer. But the village, with its delightful squares, fountains, historic belfries, lively cafes, and artisanal boutiques, remains one of the pleasant spots in the Luberon and deserves its membership in the Les Plus Beaux Villages de France association.

Essentials

GETTING THERE Buses to and from the nearest transport hub of Pertuis are infrequent. For bus information, call ✆ **08-91-02-40-25.** If you're **driving,** Lourmarin is on the D943 if you're coming from Apt.

VISITOR INFORMATION The **Office de Tourisme** is at place Henri Barthélémy (✆ **04-90-68-10-77;** www.lourmarin.com). The tourist office organizes **literary walks** that trace the steps of two of Lourmarin's illustrious former residents, writers **Albert Camus** and **Henri Bosco,** both of whom are buried there.

SPECIAL EVENTS The Chateau de Lourmarin is the magical setting for the **Festival Musiques d'Eté,** when classic concerts and jazz performances are held in the grounds from June to August (✆ **04-90-68-15-23;** www.chateau-de-lourmarin.com).

Exploring the Area

The **Château de Lourmarin** (✆ **04-90-68-15-23;** www.chateau-de-lourmarin.com) was the first Renaissance chateau to be built in Provence, and it's a magnificent sight that dominates the village. Originally a 12th-century fortress, it was extended into the Château Vieux (Old Chateau) in the 15th century. The Renaissance wing (Château Neuf), added in the 16th century, contains some of the most impressive rooms, with wonderfully elaborate fireplaces and a grand stone staircase. This is where you can see the living areas, including dining rooms, bedrooms, and the music room, which is reserved for the use of visiting music students. The surrounding landscaped

driving LES ROUTES DE LA LAVANDE

Lavender has played a major role in this region for hundreds of years. When it was part of the Roman Empire, Provence produced lavender flowers to scent the public baths. In the Middle Ages, villages burned piles of the plant in the streets in an effort to fight disease. But it was during the Renaissance that the current industry took root, linked to the Medicis, who padded their wealth with trade in the distillation of the flower's essential oils.

Lavender production covers many regions in Provence, and the Luberon in particular. A drive through the region is most scenic just before the June/July harvest, when the countryside is a purplish hue from the blossoms of the lavender plants, spread out in seemingly endless rows. Not only can you take in the sight and scent of the flowers, but you can also tour the distilleries and farms. Some of these are open only during summer when the year's harvest is undergoing distillation. Those that are open year-round offer tours. They also sell the plants, essential oils, dried flowers, perfumes, honey, and herbal teas.

In the hamlet of **Les Agnels** just south of Apt, the Agnel family has been running a lavender distillery since 1957. The business has since expanded to include a wellness center with a lavender-scented indoor pool and spa. You can buy their products at their boutique after taking a guided tour of the distillery. The distillery is located at rte. de Buoux D113, Les Agnels (✆ **04-90-04-77-00;** www.lesagnels.com); it's open Monday to Friday 10am to 6pm.

gardens and olive groves add to the beauty of the place. Daily hours are 10am to 6pm in July and August; 10:30am to noon and 2:30pm to 5:30pm May, June, and September; 10:30am to 11:30am and 2:30pm to 4:30pm March, April, and October; and 10:30am to 11:30am and 2:30 to 4pm February, November, and December. In January, the chateau is open Saturday and Sunday 2:30pm to 4pm. Admission is 6€ adults, 3.50€ students, 2.50€ children 10 and over, and free for those 9 and under.

Where to Stay

Hôtel Bastide de Lourmarin ★ Located just outside the center of Lourmarin, this stylish hotel features innovative rooms based on different themes. Soft muslin billows over the canopy in the Romantique room, while Indian artifacts decorate the Orientale room. You get to sleep in the round in La Ronde amid some ultramodern designs. Le Bastidon, the restaurant overlooking the pool and the gardens, serves refined Mediterranean fare, such as grilled squid, mussels, or beef stew with goat cheese potatoes; a three-course meal costs 34€.

Rte. de Cucuron, 84160 Lourmarin.www.hotelbastide.com. ✆ **04-90-07-00-70.** Fax 04-90-68-89-48. 19 units. 85€–220€ double; 250€–305€ suite. AE, MC, V. Free parking. Closed Jan–Feb. **Amenities:** Restaurant; bar; pool (outdoor); room service. *In room:* A/C, TV, hair dryer, minibar, Wi-Fi (free).

Mas de Guilles ★★ Glorious views of the Luberon await in this peaceful 17th-century Provençal *mas* located 1.5km (1 mile) outside Lourmarin. Rooms are elegant, airy, and spacious; many have patios looking over the Luberon mountains, which adds to the general air of tranquillity in this welcoming hotel. The 3 hectares (7 acres) of beautifully landscaped gardens invite leisurely strolls. Breakfast is served on the enormous patio overlooking the hills, as is dinner on balmy evenings. The Mediterranean menu features roasted red mullet with tomatoes and aubergines and carpaccio of scallops with pistachio oil.

Rte. des Vaugines, 84160 Lourmarin. www.guilles.com. ✆ **04-90-68-30-55.** Fax 04-90-68-37-41. 28 units. 76€–188€ double; 204€–240€ suite. AE, MC, V. Free parking. Closed Nov–Mar. **Amenities:** Restaurant; bar; boutique; pool (outdoor); tennis. *In room:* TV, hair dryer, minibar, Wi-Fi (free).

Where to Eat

See also the restaurants at **Hôtel Bastide de Lourmarin** and **Mas de Guilles** (above).

La Récréation PROVENÇALE This convivial, classy restaurant in the heart of the village specializes in local organic ingredients. The sheltered terrace is a wonderful setting for dishes such as duck breast with the Honey of a Thousand Flowers, Camargue bull stew with Lourmarin wine, and lamb shoulder with green olives.

15 av. Philippe de Girard, 84160 Lourmarin. ✆ **04-90-68-23-73.** Main courses 11€–246€; fixed-price menus 27€–34€ dinner. MC, V. Thurs–Tues noon–2pm and 7:30–9:30pm. Closed mid-Nov–mid-Dec and early Jan–early Feb.

Side Trips from Lourmarin

Hilltop villages, vineyards, verdant valleys, and ancient châteaux characterize the region of Sud Luberon, located north of the Durance River. It's best to explore this area by car, since Pertuis (see below) is the only town with substantial transport links.

CUCURON

25km (15 miles) SE of Apt; 39km (24 miles) E of Cavaillon; 8km (5 miles) east of Lourmarin

Movie fans might already know Cucuron from the many films that have been shot here. Location managers can't resist the combination of a panorama of terra-cotta rooftops, an 11th-century dungeon, ramparts, stone gateways, and an air of ancient peace. They are also drawn to the **Etang,** an enormous reservoir picturesquely shaded by 200-year-old plane trees and the setting for the Tuesday morning market (as well as not-to-be-missed night markets during the summer). While the village appeared in Jean-Paul Rappaneau's 1995 adventure *Le Hussar sur le Toit,* the Etang itself had a starring role in Ridley Scott's 2006 romantic comedy *A Good Year.*

Cafes and restaurants surround the Etang, notably the Michelin-starred **La Petite Maison** (**✆ 04-90-68-21-99;** www.lapetitemaisondecucuron.com). Top-quality dishes are served within its secluded garden, including caramelized sweetbreads, roasted pigeon, and tuna tartare; menus start from 40€. A considerably more affordable alternative—with lovely views of the Etang—is next door at the **Bar de l'Etang** (**✆ 04-90-77-23-11**). It might attract tourists but it's not particularly touristy; it's just a down-to-earth cafe serving good omelets and other French staples at decent prices. The **Hôtel de l'Etang** (**✆ 04-90-77-21-25;** www.hoteldeletang.com) is a two-star Logis de France hotel in a bright-yellow building right beside the Etang. Its six rooms are simply furnished but you can't beat the location; doubles range from 70€ to 120€.

The **Office de Tourisme** is in rue Léonce Brieugne (**✆ 04-90-77-28-37;** www.cucuron-luberon.com). They have information on local walking routes as well as details for visits to local olive farms.

PERTUIS

23km (14 miles) N of Aix-en-Provence; 36km (22 miles) S of Apt; 76km (47 miles) SE of Avignon

Pertuis is the largest town in the area, and the only one with decent links to public transportation as well as a substantial shopping district. **Trains** arrive from Marseille and Aix-en-Provence to the SNCF station just south of the town, and buses come into the **gare routière** in place Garcin near the town center. The ancient central quarter is the site for the busy Friday morning market in **place Mirabeau.** Stalls are set up in full view of the remains of the 13th-century fortified **château,** whose dungeon and clock tower are symbols of the town.

One of the area's most renowned restaurants is **Le Boulevard,** 50 bd. Pécout (**✆ 04-90-09-69-31;** www.restaurant-leboulevard.com), where organic local ingredients are served in a cozy setting. Chef Pierre Bontoux prepares Provençal specialties, including stuffed zucchini flowers and roasted loin of lamb, with many of his dishes featuring Pertuis's own variety of potato; menus start at 28€. Bontoux also holds Saturday morning cooking classes.

Just east of Pertuis is the **Best Western Sévan Parc Hôtel** on route de la Bastidonne (**✆ 04-90-79-19-30;** www.sevanparchotel.com), a friendly family hotel set within 3 hectares (7 acres) of landscaped gardens. It's like a minivillage, with two swimming pools, plenty of sporting activities, and two restaurants: l'Olivier serves French specialties and La Paillote serves Tex-Mex. Doubles range from 102€ to 163€.

The **Office de Tourisme** is in the château's dungeon in place Mirabeau (**✆ 04-90-79-15-56;** www.tourismepertuis.fr). They have information on bicycle rentals as well as visits to local vineyards.

ANSOUIS

35km (22 miles) N of Aix-en-Provence; 79km (49 miles) SE of Avignon; 63km (39 miles) N of Marseille

Ansouis is another of the numerous Provençal villages that has officially been designated one of the most beautiful in France. Unlike many hilltop villages in the Luberon, Ansouis manages to avoid the worst of the *mistral* winds thanks to its southern situation. This makes it very pleasant to leisurely wander through its ancient and pretty cobblestoned streets.

Its **medieval château** (✆ **06-84-62-64-34;** www.chateauansouis.fr; admission 8€) had been in the same family since its inception in the 12th century until it was sold in 2008. Now it's run by the Rousset-Rivière family, who give guided tours of their magnificent home. Mme Rousset-Rivière explains how the castle had been modified since its beginnings in a thoroughly enjoyable tour of the salons, kitchen, bedrooms, and gardens.

The **Musée Extraordinaire** (✆ **04-90-02-82-64;** admission 3.50€) is an unusual museum that pays homage to sea life. Scuba diver and artist Georges Mazoyer has combined his artworks with his finds from his travels to create a series of interesting exhibits dedicated to underwater life. The highlight is a blue grotto made of coral. Sculptures, corals, fossils, and glass creations form a vivid display in a medieval setting. It's just on the right side of kitsch.

Accommodation is scarce in the village, but there is a charming *chambres d'hôtes* (bed and breakfast). **Un Patio en Luberon,** rue du Grand Four (www.unpatioen luberon.com; ✆ **04-90-09-94-25**), has five romantic rooms in a 16th-century auberge for 70€ to 80€ a night, including breakfast. They also serve evening meals with advance notice.

Ansouis doesn't have a tourism office of its own, but you can get information from the office at La Tour d'Aigues (below) or at **www.ansouis.fr**.

LA TOUR D'AIGUES

29km (18 miles) N of Aix-en-Provence; 35km (22 miles) S of Apt; 81km (50 miles) SE of Avignon

This tiny village overlooking the banks of the Eze River sprang up around an 11th-century priory and tower. Nowadays, it focuses on producing excellent Côtes du Luberon and harvesting fruit from its numerous orchards. La Tour d'Aigues's main claim to fame, however, is the **Renaissance château** (www.chateau-latourdaigues.com; admission 4.50€), which stands in ruins overlooking the village. The château dates back to medieval times, but fires and uprisings during the French Revolution caused much damage to the structure. Fortunately, the impressive gateway and other parts of the château still stand. These form an evocative backdrop to numerous events and festivals held in the vast courtyard, notably the August jazz festival. A visit to the château includes constantly changing exhibitions as well as the 18th-century earthenware on display in the **Musée des Faïences.** The **Office de Tourisme** is located in the château (✆ **04-90-07-50-29;** www.sourireduluberon.com).

Less than a 10-minute drive northwest is one of the Luberon's favorite water playgrounds, the **Etang de la Bonde.** It's a popular spot for swimming, fishing, and boating. It's also the idyllic setting for the **Restaurant du Lac** (✆ **04-90-09-14-10;** www.restaurantdulac.eu), a superior restaurant with a panoramic terrace on the lakeside. The light cuisine focuses on the best seasonal products from the region. You can put yourself in chef Philippe Sublet's hands and go for the six-course surprise menu for 55€.

SALON-DE-PROVENCE

47km (29 miles) SE of Avignon; 37km (23 miles) NW of Aix-en-Provence; 53km (33 miles) NW of Marseille

The hometown of Nostradamus is located between Aix-en-Provence and Avignon, and is often overlooked by tourists on their way to Salon-de-Provence's better-known neighbors. It's their loss, as it's an attractive town of tree-shaded boulevards and medieval squares, with an air of quiet affluence.

The town originated as a hilltop fortress centering on Château de l'Empéri. During the Middle Ages its economy relied on tanneries and fields of saffron. In the 15th century it began to prosper, thanks to its native black olives, which were used to make soap by the 19th century. As the soap factories multiplied, its owners turned their wealth into handsome mansions that now give the town an elegant appearance. At its height there were 14 factories; now there are only two, both of which are open to visitors (see "Shopping," below). More recently, Salon-de-Provence became home to the French Air Force's officer training school.

Salon-de-Provence was the also birthplace of Adam de Craponne (1527–76), creator of the Canal de Craponne that diverted water from the Durance River in order to irrigate the otherwise arid region of Crau. The town is an excellent base for exploring the countryside around the canal and along the Durance valley, as well as routes around the region's enormous inland lagoon, the Etang de Berre.

Essentials

GETTING THERE Regular **trains** arrive from Avignon and Marseille, with less frequent service from Aix-en-Provence. For more information, call ✆ **36-35,** or visit www.voyages-sncf.com. From Aix-en-Provence, daily **buses** make the trip to downtown Salon de Provence's place Morgan; for bus information, call ✆ **08-91-02-40-25.** If you're **driving,** Salon-de-Provence is strategically located at the junction of highways connecting Avignon with Aix-en-Provence (N7), and Marseille with Arles and Nîmes (N113), as well as the A7 and A54 autoroutes.

VISITOR INFORMATION The **Office de Tourisme** is at 56 cours Gimon (✆ **04-90-56-27-60;** www.visitsalondeprovence.com). Ask about the **Pass Avantages Séjour**, which gives discounts on entry to attractions as well as some boutiques. The tourist office also organizes free guided tours called **Flâneries** that take visitors behind the scenes of local attractions during the spring and summer.

SPECIAL EVENTS The Chateau de l'Empéri is the enchanting backdrop for the summertime **Musique à l'Empéri** festival of classical music (✆ **04-90-56-00-82;** www.festival-salon.fr). For almost 2 weeks in July and August, the medieval courtyard of the Château de l'Empéri hosts world-renowned orchestras and soloists. The town's streets become the stage for October's **Salon Public** festival, when actors and circus performers put on shows all around Salon-de-Provence.

Exploring the Town

Salon-de-Provence's unofficial mascot is **Fontaine Moussue** on the place Crousillat just outside the Porte de l'Horloge. Covered by a thick mound of moss and resembling a giant mushroom, this much-photographed fountain dates from the 16th century. It is surrounded by plane trees planted to commemorate events over the centuries. One was planted in 1799 to mark the end of the Revolution; another was planted in 1919 to mark the end of World War I.

Château de l'Empéri This 10th-century château is surrounded by ancient circular walls. You can enter through the 17th-century Porte de l'Horloge or the Porte Bourg Neuf. The château is one of the most beautiful in Provence, with its courtyards, towers, and walls. Once this was the residence of the archbishops of Arles, lords of Salon. Both François I, in 1516, and Marie de Médici, in 1600, visited and stayed here. From 1831, it was used as a barracks and was severely damaged in an earthquake in 1909, but over the years it has been gradually and attractively restored.

The château houses the **Musée de Art et d'Histoire Militaire,** with a collection of more than 20,000 artifacts, including military uniforms, weapons, waxwork figures, and military flags. The museum covers the era from Louis XIV, the Sun King, up to France's entry into World War I.

Montée du Puech. ✆ **04-90-44-72-80.** Admission 4.50€ adults, 3€ seniors Wed–Mon 10am–noon and 2–6pm.

Musée Grévin de la Provence In this wax museum, lifelike tableaux attempt to re-create 2,600 years of the history of Provence. That history is displayed in part in the exhibition of some 15 historical paintings, one of which depicts the fabled marriage of Gyptis and Protis. Their marriage sealed the union of the Phocaeans with the Celtic-Ligurians. The exhibits go up to the 20th century, including scenes from Marcel Pagnol's films set in Provence.

Place des Centuries. ✆ **04-90-56-36-30.** Admission 4.50€ adults, 3€ seniors. Mon–Fri 9am–noon; daily 2–6pm.

Musée Nostradamus Nostradamus (1503–66), who was born in St-Rémy-de-Provence, spent the last 19 years of his life at this little house close to the château. It's now a museum devoted to him and his enigmatic predictions of the future, with his history told in English-language audio guides. After training as a doctor in Montpellier, Nostradamus treated plague victims in Lyon and Aix. He married a woman from Salon in 1547 and settled here, where he studied astrology, published almanacs, and invented new recipes for cosmetics. Written in the future tense, his *Centuries* in rhyming quatrains was published in 1555, bringing him instant celebrity. Nostradamus is buried in the 14th-century Eglise St-Laurent, which lies just to the north of the town center.

11 rue Nostradamus. ✆ **04-90-56-64-31.** Admission 4.50€ adults, 3€ seniors. Mon–Fri 9am–noon; daily 2–6pm.

Shopping

Both of the remaining soap factories in Salon-de-Provence are open for visits; you can also pick up high-quality soap products in their on-site boutiques. At **Marius Fabre,** 148 avenue Paul Bourret (✆ **04-90-53-24-77;** www.marius-fabre.fr), four generations of the same family have been making soap since 1900, and this history is shown in its attractive museum in addition to tours of its artisan factory. Open times vary, but are generally Monday to Friday 8:30am to noon and 1:30 to 5:30pm; admission is 3.50€ to both museum and factory, or 2.50€ for just the museum. **Savonnerie Rampal,** 71 rue Félix Pyat (✆ **04-90-56-07-28;** www.rampal-latour.com), is slightly closer to the town center and also features a boutique stocking an enormous range of natural and organic products. Boutique open hours are Monday to Friday 8am to noon and 2 to 6pm. Tours need to be arranged in advance.

Where to Stay

Abbaye de Sainte-Croix ★★★ All is tranquil at this 12th-century converted monastery about 5km (3 miles) north of the city center. This four-star Relais & Châteaux hotel sits in luxurious gardens behind thick stone walls, where the scent of lavender wafts from the estate's groves. Once the living quarters of Benedictine monks, the elegant rooms blend medieval grandeur with modern comfort; they still retain the original arches and vaults, but have modern amenities. Many of the rooms have private terraces, and most have glorious views of the surrounding hills. On warm days, meals are taken on the large terrace with sweeping views of the countryside. Its restaurant is one of the best in the area (see below).

Val de Cuech, 13300 Salon de Provence. www.hotels-provence.com. ✆ **04-90-56-24-55.** Fax 04-90-56-31-12. 25 units. 149€–404€ double; 270€–545€ suite. AE, DC, MC, V. Free parking. Closed Nov to mid-Mar. **Amenities:** Restaurant; bar; babysitting; pool (outdoor); room service; Wi-Fi (free). *In room:* A/C, TV, hair dryer, minibar.

Grand Hôtel de la Poste It's hard to find a more central or economical hotel than this converted 19th-century coach house. Its soundproofed rooms look out over the historic clock tower and the Fontaine Moussue in place Crousillat. The style is simple yet comfortable, and the hotel's friendly and helpful owners are in the process of updating many of the rooms to give them a more boutique-hotel look.

1 rue des Frères Kennedy, 13300 Salon de Provence. www.ghpsalon.com. ✆ **04-90-56-01-94.** Fax 04-90-56-20-77. 23 units. 47€–75€ double, triple, and quad. MC, V. Limited parking 5.50€. **Amenities:** Breakfast room. *In room:* A/C, TV, hair dryer, Wi-Fi (free).

Le Mas des Vergers Located just 4km (2½ miles) north of Salon-de-Provence, this peaceful 19th-century *mas* B&B is surrounded by orchards and vast gardens that invite lazy afternoons. The large rooms, some with fridges and microwaves, are brightly furnished with Provençal fabrics, antiques, and cool tiled floors. Some have private terraces and their own entrances.

Chemin de la Miette, 13300 Salon de Provence. http://lemasdesvergers.free.fr. ✆ **04-90-59-64-81** (cellphone 06-73-26-39-56). 5 units. 792€ double; 89€ triple, including breakfast and welcome drink. MC, V. Free parking. **Amenities:** Breakfast room; barbecue; internet (free); pool (outdoor). *In room:* TV; fridge (in some); microwave (in some).

Le Mas du Soleil This 1850s stone farmhouse inn is a 5-minute walk from the center of town. An upper floor contains 10 well-maintained bedrooms with traditional Provençal furniture. Each has a bay window overlooking the garden and terrace or a private patio. The hotel also has a renowned restaurant (see below).

38 chemin St-Côme, Salon de Provence. www.lemasdusoleil.com. ✆ **04-90-56-06-53.** Fax 04-90-56-21-52. 10 units. 108€–280€ double. AE, DC, MC, V. Free parking. **Amenities:** Restaurant; bar; pool (outdoor); room service; Wi-Fi (free). *In room:* A/C, TV, hair dryer.

Where to Eat

Abbaye de Sainte-Croix ★★★ FRENCH/PROVENÇALE In the hotel of the same name (see above), this restaurant serves refined cuisine in impossibly romantic surroundings. When inclement weather forces guests inside from the enormous panoramic terrace with views of surrounding hills, the same vista is appreciated under the beamed ceilings of the elegant dining room. The food is of a high standard but not fussy; menus change with the seasons but can include such exquisite combinations as an oyster tartare with scallop carpaccio or slow-cooked pigeon with duck foie gras. If you're lucky, your dessert might be raspberry with white chocolate and a sorbet made of basil and lime.

Val de Cuech, 13300 Salon de Provence. ✆ **04-90-56-24-55.** www.hotels-provence.com. Reservations recommended. Main courses 34€–76€; fixed-price menus 75€–109€ dinner. AE, MC, V. Tues–Sun noon–2pm; Wed–Mon 7:30–9pm in high season; other times vary.

Café des Arts ★ FRENCH This Salon-de-Provence institution has been a popular meeting place since Frédéric Mistral used to visit. Classic bistro dishes are served in agreeable surroundings under the shade of the plane trees on the terrace, with the occasional Far Eastern ingredient to spice things up. Choose from large portions of salmon tartare to start before carrying on with lamb brochettes with sun-dried tomatoes.

20 place Crousillat, 13300 Salon de Provence. ✆ **04-90-56-00-07.** www.cafedesarts-restaurant.fr. Main courses 13€–16€. MC, V. Daily noon–2pm; Tues–Sat 7:30–9:30pm.

La Case à Palabres ★ FRENCH Part informal restaurant, part *épicerie* (grocery store), and part events space, La Case à Palabres fits it all into a small, convivial space. The emphasis is on local organic ingredients, such as plates of charcuterie consisting of beef from nearby St-Martin-de-Crau and pork from Ventoux served with Lamanon goat cheese.

44 rue Pontis, 13300 Salon de Provence. ✆ **04-90-56-43-21.** www.lacaseapalabres.fr. Main courses 8.50€–15€. MC, V. Tues–Wed 11am–7pm; Thurs–Fri 11am–11pm; Sat 11am–midnight.

Le Mas du Soleil ★ PROVENÇALE/MEDITERRANEAN The critically acclaimed cuisine of Francis Robin changes according to the season and the availability of the ingredients. Expect inventive *provençale* cuisine, such as ratatouille with grilled red mullet, or rabbit terrine infused with Provençal herbs. Lobster fans may opt for the *menu homard,* which features lobster cooked in four different ways. Set inside the hotel of the same name (see above), meals are served in a dining room overlooking the swimming pool and garden.

38 chemin St-Côme, 13300 Salon de Provence. ✆ **04-90-56-06-53.** www.lemasdusoleil.com. Reservations recommended. Main courses 22€–37€; fixed-price menus 33€–87€. AE, DC, MC, V. Tues–Sun noon–2pm; Tues–Sat 7:30–9:30pm.

L'Endroit ★ FRENCH The medieval walls of the Château de l'Empéri provide an atmospheric backdrop for this classy family-run restaurant. Creative dishes include roasted quail or guinea fowl, along with rich plates of beef filet Rossini, served in the cozy ambience of its secluded terrace.

20 Montée André Viallat, 13300 Salon de Provence. ✆ **04-42-86-85-32.** www.lendroit13300.fr. Main courses 15€–25€; fixed-price menus 21€–27€. MC, V. Mon–Sat noon–2:30pm and 7:30–10:30pm.

AIX-EN-PROVENCE ★★

755km (469 miles) S of Paris; 80km (50 miles) SE of Avignon; 32km (20 miles) N of Marseille; 175km (109 miles) W of Nice

Beautiful, fountain-filled Aix-en-Provence invites you to step back in time. Vestiges of the Roman city are still visible at the Thermes Sextius spa, while Gothic cloisters can be admired at the Cathédrale St-Sauveur. The Mazarin quarter's grid layout conceals sumptuous neoclassical houses whose graceful facades have long inspired writers and artists; it's a living tableau as colorful as any painting. Aix's university suffuses the city with intellectual energy—students soak up the sun amid bustling Provençal markets and tree-shaded terraces.

Things to Do Stroll **cours Mirabeau,** where fountains ripple and waiters waltz between the tables where Emile Zola and Paul Cézanne once sat. Or lose yourself amid the 18th-century mansions of the **Mazarin quarter,** where muscular *atlantes* (statues of Greek gods) support intricate, wrought-iron balconies. At his last workshop, **Atelier de Cézanne,** the artist's coat still hangs on the wall.

Aix-en-Provence

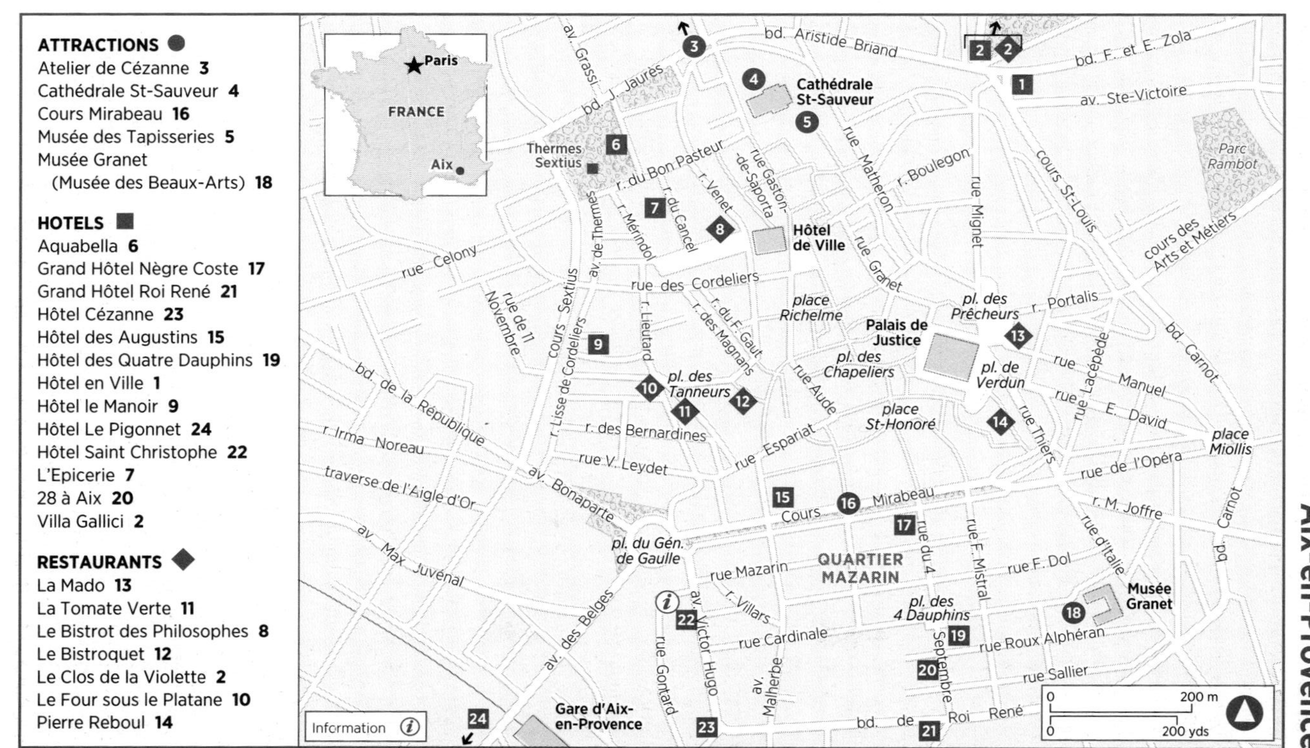

Nightlife & Entertainment Sophistication is the name of the game in Aix, where a highbrow crowd flocks to the Grand Théâtre de Provence for top-quality classical music performances. On weekends, however, beer and cocktails rule for Aix's large student population, who colonize bars along rue de la Verrerie. This narrow, cobblestoned street is also a jazz hot spot. At Le Scat Club, DJs and live bands entertain into the wee hours.

Restaurants & Dining Sun-ripened tomatoes, olives, peppers, almonds, and herbs fresh from the surrounding Provençal hillsides are signature ingredients in Aixoise cuisine. Cours Mirabeau has its fair share of Belle Époque brasseries. On a balmy evening, head to place des Cardeurs for a laid-back meal on a restaurant terrace. Whatever you eat, save room for calisson d'Aix—the city's tear-shaped almond cake, supposedly invented in 1473 by Good King René to win the affection of his inexperienced wife.

Active Pursuits The Montagne Ste-Victoire, Aix's iconic limestone backdrop, cries out to be explored. Hike along its stony paths to the rhythm of cicadas, past sun-baked olive groves and emerald cypress trees. The mountain inspired more than 60 of Cézanne's works, and its contrasting colors make you feel as though you're roaming through an oil painting. When you can walk no more, soak at Thermes Sextius, a natural spa in Aix's Centre Ville, which has been soothing tired muscles since the Roman days.

Essentials

GETTING THERE Regular **trains** arrive daily from Marseille, Nice, and Cannes to the SNCF station, and fast TGV trains arrive at Vitrolles, 5.5km (3½ miles) west of Aix. Shuttle buses connect the two train stations, as well as Marseille airport. For more information, call ✆ **36-35,** or visit www.voyages-sncf.com. **Buses** arrive regularly from Marseille, Avignon, and Nice. For more information, call ✆ **08-91-02-40-25** or go to www.lepilote.com. If you're **driving** from Avignon or other points north, take A7 south to RN7 and follow it into town. From Marseille and points south, take A51 north into town.

To explore the region by bike, head for **La Rotondo,** 2 av. Des Belges (✆ **04-42-26-78-92**), a short walk northeast of the cours Mirabeau. Here you can rent 10-speed racing bikes or more durable mountain bikes for 20€ per day.

VISITOR INFORMATION The **Office de Tourisme** is at 300 avenue Giuseppe Verdi (✆ **04-42-16-11-61;** fax 04-42-16-11-62; www.aixenprovencetourism.com). Here you can find out about passes that save money on the city's attractions and museums.

SPECIAL EVENTS Summer festivals showcase music, opera, and dance, including **Festival International d'Art Lyrique** (✆ **04-34-08-02-17;** www.festival-aix.com), which attracts musicians from all over the world for 3 weeks in July. Most of the concerts take place in the 17th-century courtyard of the Théâtre de l'Archevêché. Its fringe offshoot, **Festival Côté Cour** (✆ **06-83-60-19-80;** www.festival-cotecour.org), showcases new voices in jazz, world music, and opera.

Exploring the City

Aix's main thoroughfare, **cours Mirabeau,** is one of Europe's most beautiful. Plane trees stretch across the street like umbrellas, shading it from the hot Provençal sun and filtering the light into shadows that play on the rococo fountains below. Shops and sidewalk cafes line one side of the street; sandstone *hôtels particuliers* (mansions) from the 17th and 18th centuries fill the other. The street begins at the 1860 fountain on place de la Libération, which honors Mirabeau, the revolutionary and statesman. A ring of streets, including boulevard Carnot and cours Sextius, circles the heart of the old quarter (Viel Aix).

Atelier de Cézanne Paul Cézanne, the major forerunner of Cubism, immortalized the countryside nearby Aix. It's worth the 15-minute uphill walk north of town to take in the atmosphere of the great painter's final studio. Repaired in 1970, it remains much as Cézanne left it in 1906, his coat and hat hanging on the wall. The beautiful gardens surrounding the house are worth exploring.

9 av. Paul-Cézanne. ✆ **04-42-21-06-53.** www.atelier-cezanne.com. Admission 5.50€ adults, 2€ students and children 13–25, free for those 12 and under. Apr–June and Sept daily 10am–noon and 2–6pm (tours in English at 5pm); July–Aug daily 10am–6pm (tours in English at 5pm); Oct–Mar daily 10am–noon and 2–5pm (tours in English at 4pm). Closed Jan 1, May 1, and Dec 25.

Cathédrale St-Sauveur ★ The cathedral of Aix is dedicated to Christ under the title St-Sauveur (Holy Savior or Redeemer). Its baptistery dates from the 4th and 5th centuries, and the complex as a whole has seen many additions. It contains a 15th-century Nicolas Froment triptych, *The Burning Bush*. One side depicts the Virgin and Child, the other, Good King René and his second wife, Jeanne de Laval.

Place des Martyrs de la Résistance. ✆ **04-42-23-45-65.** www.cathedrale-aix.net. Free admission. Daily 8am–noon and 2–6pm. Mass Sun 10:30am and 7pm, weekdays 8am.

Musée des Tapisseries ★ Three series of tapestries from the 17th and 18th centuries line the gilded walls of this former archbishop's palace. The prelates decorated the palace with *The History of Don Quixote*, by Natoire; *The Russian Games*, by Le Prince; and *The Grotesques*, by Monnoyer. The museum also exhibits rare furnishings from the 17th and 18th centuries.

28 place des Martyrs de la Résistance. ✆ **04-42-23-09-91.** Admission 3.20€. Mid-Apr to mid-Oct Wed–Mon 10am–6pm; mid-Oct to Dec and Feb to mid-Apr Wed–Mon 1:30–5pm.

Musée Granet (Musée des Beaux-Arts) Seven centuries of art are displayed in this stately 17th-century former center of the Knights of Malta. Its permanent collection contains works by Van Dyck, Rubens, Rigaud, and Rembrandt; portraits by Pierre and François Puget; and a *Jupiter and Thetis* by Ingres. Ingres also did an 1807 portrait of the museum's namesake, François Marius Granet, whose own works abound. Cézanne has a place of honor with nine paintings, and the sculpture gallery is particularly striking.

Place St-Jean-de-Malte (up rue Cardinale). ✆ **04-42-52-88-32.** www.museegranet-aixenprovence.fr. Admission 4€ adults, free for ages 24 and under. June–Sept Tues–Sun 10am–7pm; Oct–May daily noon–6pm. Closed Jan 1, May 1 and Dec 25.

Shopping

Viel Aix fills with markets every Tuesday, Thursday, and Saturday. Food stalls take over place des Pêcheurs and place de la Madeleine, while a flower market sets up in front of the town hill. Clothing stalls spread out into cours Mirabeau on Saturdays.

For an excellent selection of art objects and fabrics inspired by the traditions of Provence, head to **Les Olivades,** 15 rue Marius-Reinaud (✆ **04-42-38-33-66**). It sells fabrics, shirts for women and men, fashionable dresses, and table linens.

Opened more than a century ago, **Béchard,** 12 cours Mirabeau (✆ **04-42-26-06-78**), is the most celebrated bakery in town. It takes its work so seriously that it refers to its underground kitchens as a *laboratoire* (laboratory).

Founded in 1934, **Santons Fouque,** 65 cours Gambetta (✆ **04-42-26-33-38;** www.santons-fouque.com), stocks the largest assortment of *santons* (terra-cotta figurines of "little saints") in Aix. More than 1,900 figurines are created in terra cotta, finished by hand, and painted according to 18th-century models. Each of the trades practiced in medieval Provence is represented, including shoemakers, barrel makers, coppersmiths, and ironsmiths, all poised to welcome the newborn Jesus.

Where to Stay

VERY EXPENSIVE

Villa Gallici ★★★ Less than a 10-minute walk from the town center, this sumptuous and romantic villa is Aix's first five-star hotel. The 3 hectares (7 acres) of lavender-scented Florentine gardens surrounding this 19th-century Provençal mansion induce utter tranquillity. Rich fabrics and antique furnishings evoke the 18th century in the elaborate yet extremely comfortable rooms and salons. Each room is different, with some featuring a private terrace or garden. On warm evenings, dinner is served by candlelight under the plane trees in the garden, where finely crafted dishes might include *brandade* (creamed, smoked cod) or a rich risotto with crab and chorizo.

Av. de la Violette (impasse des Grands Pins), 13100 Aix-en-Provence. www.villagallici.com. ✆ **04-42-23-29-23.** Fax 04-42-96-30-45. 22 units. 230€–690€ double; 430€–945€ suite. AE, DC, MC, V. Free parking. Closed Jan and Dec 20–26. **Amenities:** Restaurant; bar; babysitting; pool (outdoor); room service. *In room:* A/C, TV, hair dryer, minibar, Wi-Fi (free).

EXPENSIVE

Hôtel Cézanne ★★ Aix's first boutique hotel features light-filled rooms and suites that pay tribute to the paintings of Cézanne. The bedrooms are spacious, innovative, and up-to-date, and offer nice amenities, like king-size beds, "tropical" showers, and free cold drinks in the minibar. Breakfast, which consists of smoked salmon and champagne, can be served in your room until noon.

40 av. Victor-Hugo, 13100 Aix-en-Provence. www.hotelaix.com. ✆ **04-42-91-11-11.** Fax 04-42-91-11-10. 55 units. 240€–385€ double; 460€–545€ junior suite. Parking on request. AE, MC, V. **Amenities:** Bar; babysitting; room service. *In room:* A/C, TV, minibar, Wi-Fi (free).

Hôtel Le Pigonnet ★★ Recently awarded its fifth star, this pink-sided Provençal mansion on the edge of town is surrounded by gardens and memories of Paul Cézanne, who used to visit. In fact, you can see Mont Ste-Victoire from the hotel's terrace. The high-ceilinged bedrooms are elegantly furnished in a modern style. Breakfast is served on a colonnaded veranda overlooking a reflecting pool in the courtyard.

5 av. du Pigonnet, 13090 Aix-en-Provence. www.hotelpigonnet.com. ✆ **04-42-59-02-90.** Fax 04-42-59-47-77. 49 units. 125€–375€ double; 340€–530€ junior suite. AE, DC, MC, V. Free parking. **Amenities:** Restaurant; bar; babysitting; spa; exercise room; pool (outdoor); room service. *In room:* A/C, TV, hair dryer, minibar, Wi-Fi (free).

28 à Aix ★★ This exquisite B&B is set in a restored 17th-century mansion in the heart of the Mazarin quarter. With its voluptuous little garden out back, it's like living in a jewel box. Some rooms have flowing canopies, fireplaces, large sofas, and state-of-the-art bathrooms; ask for the one with the private terrace.

28 rue du 4 Septembre, 13100 Aix-en-Provence. www.28-a-aix.com. ✆ **04-42-54-82-01.** 4 units. 220€–500€ double. Rates include breakfast. MC, V. Parking 20€. **Amenities:** Breakfast lounge; room service. *In room:* A/C, TV, hair dryer, minibar, Wi-Fi (free).

MODERATE

Aquabella The ancient world blends with modern times smoothly in this three-star hotel on the edge of the old town. Remnants of Aix's medieval ramparts jut alongside the large pool in the pleasant garden, and an ancient Roman thermal spring supplies the next-door Sextius Thermes spa. Rooms are decorated in a stripped-down Provençal style, with white wood, and pale shades of blue and beige. Ask for a room overlooking the garden, which also has a pretty restaurant on a shaded terrace.

2 rue des Etuves, 13100 Aix-en-Provence. www.aquabella.fr. ✆ **04-42-99-15-00.** Fax 04-42-99-15-01. 110 units. 175€–205€ double; 235€ suite. AE, DC, MC, V. Parking 10€. **Amenities:** Restaurant; bar; pool (outdoor); room service; spa. *In room:* A/C, TV, hair dryer, minibar, Wi-Fi (free).

Grand Hôtel Nègre Coste This hotel, located in an 18th-century former town house, is very popular with the musicians who take part in Aix's summer festivals. Flowers cascade from *jardinières,* and 18th-century carvings surround the windows. A wide staircase, marble portrait busts, and a Provençal armoire grace the interior. The medium-size soundproof rooms contain antiques, and the higher floors overlook cours Mirabeau or the old town.

33 cours Mirabeau, 13100 Aix-en-Provence. www.hotelnegrecoste.com. ✆ **04-42-27-74-22.** Fax 04-42-26-80-93. 37 units. 90€–145€ double; 185€ apt. AE, MC, V. Parking 10€. **Amenities:** Room service; free internet in reception. *In room:* A/C, TV, hair dryer, minibar, Wi-Fi (free).

Grand Hôtel Roi René ★ This four-star hotel touts a central location, comfortable rooms, and a swimming pool—a rarity in central Aix. Rooms are bright with contemporary furnishings and are decorated in neutral tones; some have a private terrace overlooking the flower-filled garden and pool.

24 bd. Du Roi-René, 13100 Aix-en-Provence. www.mgallery.com. ✆ **04-42-37-61-00.** Fax 04-42-37-61-11. 134 units. 155€–175€ double; 220€–240€ junior suite; 310€ suite. Parking 16€. AE, DC, MC, V. **Amenities:** Restaurant; bar; pool (outdoor); babysitting; room service. *In room:* A/C, TV, hair dryer, minibar, Wi-Fi (free).

Hôtel des Augustins ★ Converted from the 12th-century Grands Augustins Convent, this hotel has been beautifully restored, with vaulted ceilings, stained-glass windows, stone walls, terra-cotta floors, and Louis XIII furnishings. Guest rooms are spacious and soundproof; two have terraces. They possess a severe kind of monastic dignity, with dark-grained wooden furniture and high ceilings.

3 rue de la Masse, 13100 Aix-en-Provence. www.hotel-augustins.com. ✆ **04-42-27-28-59.** Fax 04-42-26-74-87. 29 units. 99€–250€ double. AE, MC, V. **Amenities:** Breakfast room. *In room:* A/C, TV, minibar, Wi-Fi (free).

Hôtel des Quatre Dauphins This 18th-century town house is just steps away from place des Quatre Dauphins and a few minutes from the cours Mirabeau. Some original motifs have survived through frequent modernizations. The medium-size rooms are in simplified Provençal style, some with painted ceiling beams and casement windows overlooking the street.

54 rue Roux-Alphéran, 13100 Aix-en-Provence. www.lesquatredauphins.fr. ✆ **04-42-38-16-39.** Fax 04-42-38-60-19. 13 units. 95€–130€ double. MC, V. **Amenities:** Breakfast room. *In room:* A/C, TV, Wi-Fi (free).

Hôtel Saint Christophe Built in 1936, this friendly two-star hotel heavily features Art Deco elements. Centrally located near the cours Mirabeau, the hotel features rooms of varying sizes and styles: Some rooms are decorated with old-style Provençal furnishings, while others mix in Art Deco pieces (like geometric headboards), and others offer a more a more contemporary look. Ask for a room with a private terrace.

2 av. Victor Hugo, 13100 Aix-en-Provence. www.hotel-saintchristophe.com. ✆ **04-42-26-01-24.** Fax 04-42-38-53-17. 67 units. 92€–174€ double. AE, DC, MC, V. Parking 12€. **Amenities:** Restaurant; bar. *In room:* A/C, TV, minibar, Wi-Fi (free).

L'Epicerie An old-fashioned French grocery store, in an 18th-century building in the old town, has been converted to this utterly charming B&B. Its five rooms and suites have different themes, ranging from elaborate Art Deco to classic Provençal style. Breakfast is taken either on the long table in the mock *épicerie* or in the delightful courtyard garden.

12 rue du Cancel, 13100 Aix-en-Provence. www.unechambreenville.eu. ✆ **06-08-38-38-68.** 5 units. 100€ double; 120€–130€ suite, including breakfast. MC, V. **Amenities:** Garden. *In room:* A/C, TV, Wi-Fi (free).

INEXPENSIVE

Hôtel en Ville You're in the thick of things in this modern hotel on a very busy intersection in the old town. Luckily the rooms are soundproofed, and many have little patios that offer a bit of respite from the bustle below. The style might be too minimalist chic for some, and there is little privacy in how some of the bathrooms are laid out, but staff members are exceptionally welcoming and helpful.

2 place Bellegarde, 13100 Aix-en-Provence. www.hotelenville.fr. ✆ **04-42-63-34-16.** Fax 04-42-96-10-22. 10 units. 65€–90€ double. MC, V. Parking 13€. **Amenities:** Restaurant. *In room:* A/C, TV, minibar, Wi-Fi (free).

Hôtel Le Manoir One of the best economy options in the heart of the old city of Aix is Hôtel Le Manoir, located in a converted abbey with a private garden. The original cloister dated from the 14th century, but it was reconstructed in the 16th century and became Hôtel le Manoir in 1970. The bedrooms are pleasingly old-fashioned, with antique wardrobes and some with beamed ceilings. Breakfast is served under a vaulted cloister.

8 rue d'Entrecasteaux, 13100 Aix-en-Provence. www.hotelmanoir.com. ✆ **04-42-26-27-20.** Fax 04-42-27-17-97. 40 units. 67€–87€ double; 93€–100€ triple; 117€ quad. AE, MC, V. Free parking. Closed Jan. **Amenities:** Breakfast room; Wi-Fi in reception (1 hr. free). *In room:* TV.

Where to Eat

EXPENSIVE

Le Clos de la Violette ★★★ MODERN FRENCH This innovative and elegant Michelin-starred restaurant near **Villa Gallici** (see above) offers stylish seasonal dishes that highlight the flavors of Provence. Dishes might include monkfish carpaccio, poached lobster, braised bream with a crab tart, or thyme-infused lamb with goat cheese gnocchi.

10 av. de la Violette. ✆ **04-42-23-30-71.** www.closdelaviolette.fr. Reservations recommended. Main courses 47€–49€; fixed-price menu 50€–130€. AE, MC, V. Tues–Sat noon–1:30pm and 7:30–9:30pm. Closed mid-Feb–early Mar and first half of Aug.

Pierre Reboul ★★ MODERN FRENCH In the heart of the old town, this modern restaurant specializes in the innovative cuisine of Michelin-starred chef Pierre Reboul. He likes to give classics an inventive twist, coming up with such dishes as pan-fried foie gras with apple and passion fruit, or a dessert of strawberry macaroon with olive oil and basil.

11 Petite Rue St. Jean. ✆ **04-42-20-58-26.** www.restaurant-pierre-reboul.com. Reservations required. Fixed-price menu 39€, 81€, and 120€. AE, DC, MC, V. Tues–Sat noon–1:30pm and 7:30–9:30pm.

MODERATE

La Mado ★ MEDITERRANEAN/SUSHI In complete contrast with the colorful market on its doorstep, inside La Mado it's ultracool and modern, with the clientele to match. The choice of French dishes on offer is almost overwhelming, and the adjoining sushi bar offers fresh seafood. Fish dishes range from a monkfish *osso buco* in a sea urchin cream sauce to sea bass tartare with wasabi. Meat and pasta choices are equally tantalizing: slow-cooked wild boar with tagliatelle, or penne with smoked salmon and caviar.

4 place des Prêcheurs. ✆ **04-42-38-28-02.** www.lamado-aix.com. Main courses 11€–33€. MC, V. 7pm–2am.

La Tomate Verte PROVENÇALE The boss's mother, Claudette, is firmly in charge of the menu in this classy bistro down one of the old town's atmospheric narrow streets. She is especially proud of her specialties, including a *tarte tatin* of green tomatoes, as well as her innovative take on bouillabaisse.

15 rue des Tanneurs. ✆ **04-42-60-04-58.** www.latomateverte.com. Main courses 20€; fixed-price lunch 14€–19€, dinner 27€–30€. MC, V. Tues–Sat noon–2pm and 7–10:30pm.

Le Bistroquet ★ FRENCH Cozy little place Ramus, in the old town, has seen many restaurants come and go in recent years, but Le Bistroquet seems to have found a winning formula, both in its lively main restaurant and its tapas bar opposite. Although some dishes are Asian-influenced, like stir-fried giant shrimp with Chinese noodles, French flavors dominate the menu, with items like grilled duck breast and saddle of lamb with an herb crust.

27 place Ramus. ✆ **04-42-26-75-55.** www.lebistroquet.fr. Main courses 15€–27€; fixed-price lunch 15€, dinner 27€–37€. MC, V. Daily noon–2pm and 7–10:30pm.

Le Bistrot des Philosophes FRENCH This bistro is a cut above the many restaurants whose terraces crowd into the place des Cardeurs. The starters are composed of clean, fresh flavors—try the iced melon gazpacho or sea bream tartare. Meat lovers can opt for a whole duck breast with morello cherries, rib of beef, or pork filet with tapenade and polenta.

20 place des Cardeurs. ✆ **04-42-21-64-25.** Main courses 17€–49€; fixed-price lunch 20€. MC, V. Daily noon–2pm and 7–10pm.

INEXPENSIVE

Le Four sous le Platane PIZZA As the name suggests, plane trees shade this lively restaurant that serves some of the best pizzas in Aix. Regional flavors mix freely with Italian favorites, resulting in such toppings as St-Marcellin cheese with tapenade and a Corsican version with *figatelli* (pork liver sausage) and *brousse* (creamy ewe's milk cheese). The salads, risotto, and gnocchi dishes are of an equally high standard.

31 rue de la Couronne. ✆ **04-42-26-07-71.** Pizzas, salads, pasta 12€–18€. MC, V. Mon–Sat noon–2:30pm; daily 7–11:30pm.

Aix After Dark

While the cours Mirabeau is still a magnet for strollers and people in search of a late-night drink, many of the bars, including Les Deux Garçons, merely trade on their history to pull in the tourists. One of the best bets on Mirabeau is **La Bastide du Cours** at no. 41–47 (✆ **04-42-26-10-06;** www.bastideducours.com), with its lively and cozy terrace. It also rents out 11 luxurious rooms from 145€–400€. Nearby at No. 29 is the champagne and vodka bar at **La Belle Epoque** (✆ **04-42-27-65-66;** www.labelleepoqueaixenprovence.com), the place to lounge languidly with a cocktail until 2am.

Much of the student population hangs out along **rue de la Verrerie.** Beer drinkers pack **O'Shannon** Irish pub at no. 30 (✆ **04-42-23-31-63**), where it can get raucous during happy hour and when major sporting events are on television. **Le Scat Club** at no. 11 (✆ **04-42-23-00-23;** http://scatclub.free.fr/scatnet) used to be known as a jazz club, but its live music has broadened over the years to include rock, soul, and funk in one of its rooms, and DJs in the other.

MARSEILLE ★★★

771km (479 miles) S of Paris; 187km (116 miles) SW of Nice; 31km (19 miles) S of Aix-en-Provence

Marseille, France's oldest city, has been a gateway to Europe since the Phoenicians landed in 600 B.C. Today it's a bustling trading port where Provençal traditions meet exotic influences from North Africa and the Middle East, revealed in spice-infused markets and stately 19th-century thoroughfares. Beacons to city life are also visible in state-of-the-art skyscrapers at the Docks and Le Corbusier's revolutionary 1950s Cité Radieuse apartments. The city is a cultural hub, and it will be the European Capital of Culture in 2013. Marseille is first and foremost a coastal city, however, and its 35 miles of chalky-white creeks called *calanques* await those who crave relaxation.

Things to Do Stroll Marseille's **Vieux Port,** where fishing boats bob and cafes clink with cutlery as foodies tuck into saffron-tinted, fish-thick *bouillabaisse.* Scale **Le Panier**'s steep cobbles to explore medieval streets where waves of immigrants have settled for centuries. A climb up to the gilded **Basilique Notre-Dame-de-la-Garde** rewards you with dizzying coastal panoramas. Across the waves, the **Ile d'If** beckons with seagulls, salamanders, and the eerie Renaissance château where the Count of Monte Cristo was held in Alexandre Dumas's novel.

Nightlife & Entertainment Throngs of people gravitate toward the **Vieux Port's** wine bars, jazz cellars, and mainstream clubs. Watch top-class opera at the Canebière's colonnaded **Opéra de Marseille.** Dress down (in cool labels, *bien-sûr*) for a night in the up-and-coming Belle de Mai district, where **La Friche** (a converted tobacco factory) programs some of the hippest electro and rock concerts outside Paris. On balmy nights, pick up a mojito and drink in the sunset along the **Prado's** beachside bars.

Restaurants & Dining Centuries of immigration lend Marseille's cuisine an international flavor, so follow your nose along **rue Longue-des-Capucins,** past stands of steaming Armenian pizzas, Moroccan lamb, spicy olives, and Chinese noodles. Remember, though, this *is* Provence—a region blessed with herbs, sun-ripened vegetables, and, in Marseille's case, fresh seafood—so sample the day's catches around the **Vieux Port.**

Relaxation When the city gets too much, sail from the Vieux Port to the **Frioul** islands, to relax and swim, with little else but wild thyme, sand, and lizards for company. The sea breeze also blows your stress away in Marseille's **Massif des Calanques**—weather-worn limestone pinnacles that conceal sandy beaches accessible by foot or by boat. They are perfect for a soothing dip on a sunny day.

Marseille

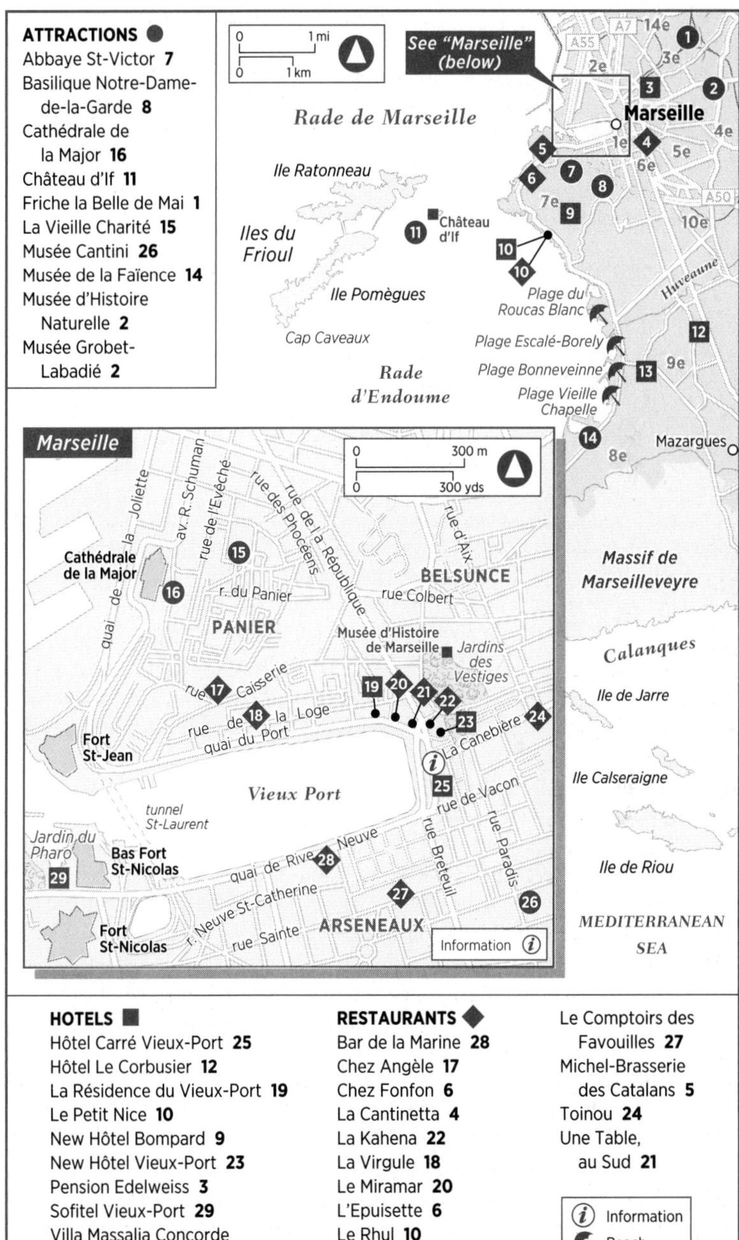
ATTRACTIONS
Abbaye St-Victor 7
Basilique Notre-Dame-de-la-Garde 8
Cathédrale de la Major 16
Château d'If 11
Friche la Belle de Mai 1
La Vieille Charité 15
Musée Cantini 26
Musée de la Faïence 14
Musée d'Histoire Naturelle 2
Musée Grobet-Labadié 2
See "Marseille" (below)
Rade de Marseille
Ile Ratonneau
Iles du Frioul
Château d'If
Ile Pomègues
Cap Caveaux
Rade d'Endoume
Plage du Roucas Blanc
Plage Escalé-Borely
Plage Bonneveinne
Plage Vieille Chapelle
Mazargues
Huveaune
Massif de Marseilleveyre
Calanques
Ile de Jarre
Ile Calseraigne
Ile de Riou
MEDITERRANEAN SEA
Marseille
quai de la Joliette
av. R. Schuman
rue de l'Evêché
rue des Phocéens
rue de la République
rue d'Aix
Cathédrale de la Major
BELSUNCE
r. du Panier
rue Colbert
PANIER
Musée d'Histoire de Marseille
Jardins des Vestiges
rue Caisserie
rue de la Loge
quai du Port
La Canebière
Fort St-Jean
Vieux Port
tunnel St-Laurent
rue de Vacon
Jardin du Pharo
Bas Fort St-Nicolas
quai de Rive Neuve
rue Breteuil
rue Paradis
r. Neuve St-Catherine
ARSENEAUX
rue Sainte
Fort St-Nicolas
Information
HOTELS
Hôtel Carré Vieux-Port 25
Hôtel Le Corbusier 12
La Résidence du Vieux-Port 19
Le Petit Nice 10
New Hôtel Bompard 9
New Hôtel Vieux-Port 23
Pension Edelweiss 3
Sofitel Vieux-Port 29
Villa Massalia Concorde Marseille 13
RESTAURANTS
Bar de la Marine 28
Chez Angèle 17
Chez Fonfon 6
La Cantinetta 4
La Kahena 22
La Virgule 18
Le Miramar 20
L'Epuisette 6
Le Rhul 10
Les Arcenaulx 27
Le Comptoirs des Favouilles 27
Michel-Brasserie des Catalans 5
Toinou 24
Une Table, au Sud 21
Information
Beach

European Capital of Culture

In 2013, Marseille will be the European Capital of Culture and the focus of countless artistic and cultural events throughout the year. It shares the honor with its neighbors Aix-en-Provence, Arles, Aubagne, Gardanne, Istres, La Ciotat, Martigues, and Salon-de-Provence. In the meantime, some of the city's museums are closed while undergoing major refurbishment in time for 2013. The Vieux Port will get a revamp over the next few years, too, courtesy of British architect Norman Foster, who designed the Millau viaduct and the Carré d'Art in Nîmes.

Essentials

GETTING THERE The **airport** (✆ **04-42-14-14-14;** www.mrsairport.com), 27km (17 miles) northwest of the city center, receives international flights from all over Europe. From the airport, shuttles *(navettes)* make the trip to Marseille's St-Charles rail station, near the Vieux Port, for 8.50€.

Marseille has **train** connections from all over Europe, with especially good connections to and from Italy. The city is the terminus for the TGV, which departs daily from Paris's Gare de Lyon (trip time 3 hr.). For information, call ✆ **36-35,** or visit www.voyages-sncf.com. **Buses** serve the Gare Routière, place Victor Hugo (✆ **04-91-08-16-40**), adjacent to the St-Charles railway station. Marseille has frequent bus connections to Avignon and Aix-en-Provence, among other towns.

If **driving** from Paris, follow A6 south to Lyon, then continue south along A7 to Marseille. The drive takes about 7 hours. From Provence, take A7 south to Marseille.

VISITOR INFORMATION The **Office de Tourisme** is at 4 la Canebière (✆ **08-26-50-05-00;** fax 04-91-13-89-20; www.marseille-tourisme.com; Métro: Vieux Port).

GETTING AROUND Marseille's public transportation system consists of a network of **Métro** lines, **buses,** and two **tram** lines, run by RTM, 6 rue des Fabres (✆ **04-91-91-92-10;** www.rtm.fr). Tickets, sold at all bus and Métro stations, are good for 1 hour, costing 1.50€. You can buy tickets on the tram or bus or at a Métro entrance. You can get different passes, including a **spécial visite** for 5€, which gives you unlimited travel for 24 hours.

SPECIAL EVENTS Festivals happen all year round in Marseille, taking in everything from extreme sports to the world *pétanque* championships. The **Festival de Marseille** (www.festivaldemarseille.com) takes place every June and July and brings together an eclectic program of music, dance, and contemporary theater. The **jazz festival** in July (www.festival-jazz-cinq-continents.com) takes over the Palais Longchamp, the massive gardens that surround the city's canal. June's **Fête du Panier** draws everyone to the ancient quarter to mark the start of summer with dancing and fireworks, while maritime life is celebrated every July during the **Fête de St-Pierre,** the patron saint of fishermen.

Exploring the City

Marseille is divided into 16 arrondissements that fan out from the **Vieux Port.** North of the port is the oldest district in the city, **Le Panier,** a maze of hilly cobblestoned streets that has a strong sense of neighborhood identity. Further north are **Les Docks,** which are in the process of being regenerated. **La Canebière,** the wide boulevard that divides the city east-west, is lined with shops and cafes. South is the artsy area of **cours Julien,** with its lively cafes, music venues, shops, picturesque fountains and pools, children's play areas, and miniwaterways. La Canebière winds down to the **Vieux Port ★**, dominated by the massive neoclassical forts of St-Jean and St-Nicholas. The port is filled with fishing boats and yachts and is ringed with seafood restaurants.

Motorists can continue along to the **corniche Président-J.-F.-Kennedy,** a promenade running for about 5km (3 miles) along the sea. You pass villas and gardens along the way and have a good view of the Mediterranean. To the north, the **Port Moderne** (also known as "La Joliette") is a man-made labyrinth of nautical engineering. Its construction began in 1844, and a century later, the Germans destroyed it. Today it's one of the Mediterranean's busiest ports.

THE TOP ATTRACTIONS

Abbaye St-Victor ★ This semifortified basilica was built above a crypt from the 5th century, when St. John Cassian was believed to have founded the church and abbey. You can visit the crypt, which also reflects work done in the 10th and 11th centuries.

Place St-Victor. ✆ **04-96-11-22-60.** www.saintvictor.net. Admission to crypt 2€. Church and crypt daily 9am–7pm. Head west along quai de Rive-Neuve (near the Gare du Vieux Port). Métro: Vieux Port.

Basilique Notre-Dame-de-la-Garde This landmark church crowns a limestone rock overlooking the southern side of the Vieux Port. It was built in the Romanesque-Byzantine style popular in the 19th century and topped by a 9m (30-ft.) gilded statue of the Virgin. Visitors come for the view—best at sunset—from its terrace. Spread out before you are the city, the islands, and the sea.

Rue Fort-du-Sanctuaire. ✆ **04-91-13-40-80.** www.notredamedelagarde.com. Free admission. Daily 7am–7pm. Métro: Vieux Port.

Cathédrale de la Major This was one of the largest cathedrals (some 135m/443 ft. long) built in Europe in the 19th century. It has mosaic floors and red-and-white marble banners, and the exterior is done in a mixture of Romanesque and Byzantine styles. This vast pile has almost swallowed its 12th-century Romanesque predecessor, built on the ruins of a temple of Diana.

Place de la Major. ✆ **04-91-90-53-57.** Free admission. Hours vary. Métro: Vieux Port.

Friche la Belle de Mai This is an offbeat attraction, a government-sponsored artists' building in a converted tobacco factory by the train station. From the visual arts to the digital arts, the center is a never-ending spectacle of painting, theater, dance, music, and film. About 60 houses of art are located here, with about 400 professional artists in all fields participating.

41 rue Jobin. ✆ **04-95-04-95-04.** www.lafriche.org. Free admission. Mon–Sat 10am–noon and 1–6pm. Bus: 49B to Belle de Mai Maternité (get off at Jobin/Pautrier).

La Vieille Charité Formerly a hospice built in the 17th century, this venue became a cultural center in 1986. Today it is a poetry center and it also houses two museums: the Museum of African, Oceanic and Native American Art, and the Museum of Mediterranean Archaeology, both of which curve around a large airy courtyard.

2 rue de la Charité. ✆ **04-95-14-58-80.** www.vieille-charite-marseille.org. Admission to museums 3€, 5€ for special exhibitions. Oct–May Tues–Sun 10am–5pm; June–Sept Tues–Sun 11am–6pm.

Musée Cantini The temporary exhibitions of contemporary art here are often as good as the permanent collection housed in this 17th-century mansion. This museum is devoted to modern art, with masterpieces by Picasso, Derain, Ernst, Bacon, Balthus, and others. It also owns a selection of works by important young international artists.

19 rue Grignan. ✆ **04-91-54-77-75.** Admission 3€ for permanent collection, 5€ for special exhibitions, free Sun 10am–noon. Oct–May Tues–Sun 10am–5pm; June–Sept Tues–Sun 11am–6pm.

Musée de la Faïence This museum contains one of the largest collections of porcelain in France. Its collections date from Neolithic times to the present. Especially numerous are the delicate and richly ornate ceramics that graced the tables of local landowners during the 18th and 19th centuries. The museum is about 5km (3 miles) south of the center of Marseille, in a stately manor house (Château Pastré) that was built by a local ship owner in 1864.

Château Pastré, 157 av. de Montredon. ✆ **04-91-72-43-47.** Admission for permanent collection 3€, 5€ for temporary exhibits. June–Sept Tues–Sun 10am–6pm; Oct–May Tues–Sun 10am–5pm.

Musée d'Histoire Naturelle This museum lies in the right wing of the Palais Longchamp and offers a parade of the fossilized remains of the animals of Provence. The museum illustrates 400 million years of the region's natural history in its exhibits, including a safari section that shows the diversity of animals throughout the world. Of special interest to botany lovers is a gallery showcasing regional flora and fauna. On the lowest level, a Mediterranean aquarium is devoted to fish from five oceans.

Palais Longchamp. ✆ **04-91-14-59-50.** www.museum-marseille.org. Admission 2€ or 4€ depending on the exhibition; free Sun 10am–noon. Tues–Sun 10am–5pm.

EXPLORING THE massif des calanques

You can visit the **Massif des Calanques,** a wild and rugged terrain, from either Marseille or Cassis. This craggy coastline lies between the two ports, directly south of Marseille and to the west of Cassis. With its highest peak at 555m (1,850 ft.), the *calanques* stretch for some 20km (12 miles) of dazzling limestone whiteness. One of France's great natural beauties, the Massif des Calanques was turned into a national park in 2011. As the *calanques* are located within Marseille's city limits, they have become Europe's first national park to be located in an urban area.

Exactly what is a *calanque?* The word comes from the Provençal *cala,* meaning "steep slopes." Nature has cut coastal valleys into solid rock, creating steep inlets called *calanques.* Most of these gorges extend less than a kilometer inland from the Mediterranean. They're similar to fiords, created by glaciers, but these gorges have been created by the raging sea. The needlelike rocks and cliff faces overhanging the sea attract rock climbers and deep-sea divers.

The highlight of the Massif des Calanques is **Sormiou,** with its beach, seafood eateries, and small harbor. Sormiou is separated from another small but enchanting settlement at Morgiou by **Cap Morgiou,** which offers a panoramic belvedere with splendid views of both the *calanques* and the eastern side of the massif (the land mass). The **Morgiou** has tiny inlets for swimming.

Musée Grobet-Labadié ★ This collection, bequeathed to the city in 1919, includes Louis XV and Louis XVI furniture, as well as an outstanding collection of medieval Burgundian and Provençal sculpture. Other exhibits showcase 17th-century Gobelin tapestries; 15th- to 19th-century German, Italian, French, and Flemish paintings; and 16th- and 17th-century Italian and French faïence.

140 bd. Longchamp. ✆ **04-91-62-21-82.** Admission for permanent collection 3€ and 5€ for temporary exhibits. June–Sept Tues–Sun 11am–6pm; Oct–May Tues–Sun 10am–5pm. Métro: Cinq av. Longchamp.

PANORAMIC VIEWS

Although the architecture of the **Basilique Notre-Dame-de-la-Garde** (see above) shows France's Gilded Age at its most evocative, visitors come here not so much for the church as for the view—best appreciated at sunset—from its terrace. The church is open daily from 7am to 7pm.

Another panoramic view is from **Parc du Pharo,** a promontory facing the entrance to the Vieux Port. Most people visit this park to escape the urban congestion of Marseille, but if you're in the mood for some history, check out the gray stone facade of the **Château du Pharo** (✆ **04-91-14-64-95**). Built in the 1860s by Napoleon III for his empress, Eugénie (who is reputed not to have liked it and seldom visited), it's owned and maintained by the city of Marseille as a convention center and—less frequently—as a concert hall. The building has no regular hours, but if nothing is going on, you can enter the lobby and ask for a quick glance at the Salon Eugénie.

A Day at the Beach

Bus no. 83 leaves from the Vieux Port heading for the public beaches outside Marseille. This bus takes you to **Plage du Prado** and **Plage de la Corniche,** the best bets for swimming and sunning. The sands are a bit gray and sometimes rocky, but the beaches are wide and the water is generally clear. These beaches are set against a scenic backdrop of the cliffs of Marseille.

Boating to Château d'If ★★

From quai des Belges at the Vieux Port, you can take a 20-minute motorboat ride to **Château d'If** for 10€ round-trip. Boats leave every 30 to 45 minutes, depending on the season. For information, contact the **Frioul If Express,** quai des Belges (✆ **04-91-46-54-65;** www.frioul-if-express.com). On the sparsely vegetated island of Château d'If (✆ **04-91-59-02-30** for information), François I built a fortress to defend Marseille. The site later housed a prison, where carvings by Huguenot prisoners can still be seen. Alexandre Dumas used the château as a setting for the fictional adventures of *The Count of Monte Cristo.* The château is open Tuesday to Sunday from 9am to 5:30pm (until 6:30pm Apr–Sept). Adults pay 5€ to enter the island or 3.50€ for ages 18 to 25; it's free for those 17 and under.

Shopping

Marseille's plentiful markets are colorful spectacles teeming with the region's bounty. The daily morning **fish market** (quai des Belges, Vieux Port) is a riot of sounds and smells. The **Marché aux Puces** (av. du Cap-Pinède, bus 36 from Vieux Port) is the place to haggle over bric-a-brac and the occasional affordable antique.

ART & ANTIQUES There are several arts and antiques shops on rue Edmond Rostand in the **Quartier des Antiquaires** (www.antiquairesmarseille.com), selling everything from antique furniture, china, and *objets d'art* to vintage electric guitars.

FASHION Marseille's fashion center is found along **cours Julien,** with dozens of boutiques and ateliers. Much of the clothing reflects North African influences, although a vast array of French styles are for sale as well. For hats, **Felio,** 4 place Gabriel-Péri (✆ **04-91-90-32-67**), offers large-brimmed numbers that would've thrilled ladies of the Belle Époque or guests at a stylish 1920s wedding inspired by Lanvin. It also carries a selection of *casquettes Marseillaises* (flat caps developed for men as protection from the sun) and berets.

FOLKLORE & SOUVENIRS Especially popular are ***santons*** (clay crèche figurines). The best place for acquiring these is just above the Vieux Port, behind the Théâtre National de la Criée. At **Ateliers Marcel Carbonel,** 47 rue Neuve-Ste-Catherine (✆ **04-91-54-26-58;** www.santonsmarcelcarbonel.com), more than 600 figures, available in half a dozen sizes, sell at prices beginning at 10€.

Among the souvenir shops lining the Vieux Port is **Au Savon de Marseille,** 106 quai du Port (✆ **04-91-90-12-73**), where you can pick up cream-colored or pale-green bars of the city's local soap, **savon de Marseille.** Infused with a healthy dollop of olive oil, it's known for its kindness to skin dried out by the sun and *mistral*. A large selection is available at **La Savonnerie du Sérail,** 50 bd. Anatole de la Forge (✆ **04-91-98-28-25;** www.savon-leserail.com). **Place aux Huiles** at 2 place Daviel (✆ **04-91-90-05-55**) has olive oil for tasting as well as for the skin.

FOOD & CHOCOLATE Since medieval times, Marseille has thrived on the legend of Les Trois Maries—three saints named Mary who, assisted by awakened-from-the-dead St. Lazarus, reportedly came ashore at a point near Marseille to Christianize ancient Provence. In commemoration of their voyage, small boat-shaped cookies called ***les navettes*** are flavored with secret ingredients (that include orange zest, orange-flower water, and sugar), and are forever associated with Marseille. You can find them throughout the city, notably at **Le Four des Navettes,** 136 rue Sainte (✆ **04-91-33-32-12;** www.fourdesnavettes.com), which has been in operation since 1791.

Give your taste buds a real jolt at **La Maison du Pastis** at 108 quai du Port (✆ **04-91-90-86-77**). There are 75 types of pastis and absinthe on offer, all of which are available for tasting before you buy.

Where to Stay

VERY EXPENSIVE

Le Petit Nice ★★★ This luxurious residence opened in 1917 when the Passédat family joined two villas in a secluded area below the street paralleling the beach. Rooms in the main house are modern and even avant-garde—four units were inspired by Cubism. The spacious Marina Wing offers rooms decorated in antique style, opening onto sea views. The glass-enclosed restaurant, which has a view of the shore and the rocky islands off the coast, was Marseille's first restaurant to be awarded three Michelin stars. The emphasis is on the freshest seafood, including line-caught bass and bream and Breton lobster; menus run from 85€ to 270€.

Corniche Président-J.-F.-Kennedy/Anse-de-Maldormé, 13007 Marseille. www.petitnice-passedat.com. ✆ **04-91-59-25-92.** Fax 04-91-59-28-08. 16 units. 195€–640€ double; 610€–1,090€ suite. AE, DC, MC, V. Free parking. Métro: Vieux Port. **Amenities:** Restaurant; bar; babysitting; bikes; pool (outdoor). *In room:* A/C, TV, hair dryer, minibar, Wi-Fi (free).

Sofitel Marseille Vieux Port ★★★ Marseille's first five-star hotel is a glistening, modern palace standing above the embankments of the old port. The style is sleek, sophisticated, and supremely comfortable, with plush leather furniture and thick duvets. Many of the generous-size rooms have panoramic views of the Vieux Port, as well as a private terrace. The large, uncluttered marble bathrooms sport deluxe showers. The hi-tech So Spa has breathtaking views over the port. The top-floor restaurant, Les Trois Forts, adds a hint of fusion in its refined French dishes.

36 bd. Charles-Livon, 13007 Marseille. www.sofitel.com. ✆ **04-91-15-59-00.** Fax 04-91-15-59-50. 134 units. 200€–550€ double; 650€–1,900€ suite. AE, DC, MC, V. Parking 18€. **Amenities:** Restaurant; bar; pool (outdoor, heated); room service; spa; babysitting. *In room:* A/C, TV, hair dryer, minibar; Wi-Fi (free).

EXPENSIVE

La Résidence du Vieux Port This welcoming four-star hotel, located directly beside the harbor, pays homage to the 1950s in its space-age design, yet it feels completely modern. The hotel recently underwent a major renovation, which updated all of the guest rooms and public spaces, converting them into a stylish abode. All the rooms have balconies with wonderful views of the port.

18 quai du Port, 13002 Marseille.www.hotel-residence-marseille.com. ✆ **04-91-91-91-22.** Fax 04-91-56-60-88. 50 units. 180€–290€ double. AE, MC, V. Parking 9€. **Amenities:** Cafe; bar; room service. *In room:* A/C, TV, hair dryer, minibar; Wi-Fi (free).

New Hôtel Vieux-Port Located close to the port, this hotel lies in a six-story, turn-of-the-20th-century building. It offers comfortable rooms and a hardworking, English-speaking staff, although you might balk at the high charges for extras, like in-room Internet. Rooms that overlook the port are outfitted in a traditional way with the occasional exotic furnishing; the more contemporary-looking accommodations look out over the commercial neighborhood nearby.

3 bis rue Reine-Elisabeth, 13001 Marseille. www.new-hotel.com. ✆ **04-91-99-23-23.** Fax 04-91-90-76-24. 42 units. 160€–260€ double. AE, DC, MC, V. Parking 12€. **Amenities:** Bar; room service. *In room:* A/C, TV, hair dryer, minibar; Wi-Fi (17€).

Villa Massalia Concorde Marseille ★ Near the Borély racetrack and Parc Chanot, this hotel lies in an upmarket residential district of the city. Its elegant modern design showcases such materials as real oak, feather bedding, and leather. It is close to several sandy beaches for those who can tear themselves away from the indoor/outdoor heated pool. The hotel is elegantly and warmly decorated with fine natural materials. Bedrooms are sleek and modern, with all the latest gadgets.

17 place Louis Bonnefon, 13008 Marseille. www.marseille.concorde-hotels.com. ✆ **04-91-72-90-00.** Fax 04-91-72-90-01. 140 units. 164€–325€ double; 305€–690€ suite. AE, DC, MC, V. **Amenities:** Restaurant; bar; pool (outdoor); room service. *In room:* A/C, TV, hair dryer, minibar, Wi-Fi (free).

MODERATE

Hôtel Carré Vieux Port This handsome three-star hotel is just steps away from the Vieux Port and offers great value for its location. Rooms are elegant in their simplicity, if a bit small, but the bathrooms are up-to-date in their design. It also has facilities for making coffee and tea in the rooms, which is still a rarity in French hotels. Staff members are friendly and welcoming.

6 rue Beauvau, 13001 Marseille. www.hvpm.fr. ✆ **04-91-33-02-33.** Fax 04-91-33-21-24. 49 units. 97€–103€ double; 115€ triple. AE, MC, V. **Amenities:** Bar; babysitting; room service. *In room:* A/C, TV, hair dryer, minibar, Wi-Fi (free).

New Hôtel Bompard This tranquil retreat, built after World War II, lies atop a cliff along the corniche, about 3km (2 miles) east of the Vieux Port. A Provençal *mas* in the garden holds four large rooms that are more luxurious and atmospheric than those in the main building. Furnishings are contemporary, uncluttered, and comfortable. Ask for one of the rooms with a private terrace.

2 rue des Flots Bleus, 13007 Marseille. www.new-hotel.com. ✆ **04-91-99-22-22.** Fax 04-91-31-02-14. 51 units. 95€–149€ standard double; 145€–215€ Provençal *mas* double. AE, DC, MC, V. Free parking. Bus: 61 or 83. **Amenities:** Restaurant; bar; pool (outdoor); room service. *In room:* A/C, TV, hair dryer, minibar, Wi-Fi (free).

INEXPENSIVE

Hôtel Le Corbusier Fans of modernism won't mind traveling some distance from central Marseille to stay in Le Corbusier's radical Unité d'Habitation (also known as La Cité Radieuse). This multifunctional, nine-story building built in 1952 combines shops and apartments with a hotel on its third and fourth floors. Rooms can be small and spartan for some tastes, but others will revel in staying in one of the world's best-known examples of modernist design.

On the 3rd and 4th floors of Le Cité Radieuse, 280 bd. Michelet, 13008 Marseille. www.hotellecorbusier.com. ✆ **04-91-16-78-00.** 21 units. 69€–135€ double. MC, V. Bus: 21. **Amenities:** Restaurant; bar; exercise room; wading pool. *In room:* A/C, TV, fridge.

Pension Edelweiss 🎁 You get a very warm welcome in this homey B&B close to St-Charles train station. Its four large rooms are brightly decorated with flea-market furniture that evokes different eras. All have either a balcony or a terrace overlooking the courtyard garden. The owners will even arrange an evening meal if booked in advance.

6 rue Lafayette, 13001 Marseille.www.pension-edelweiss.fr. ✆ **09-51-23-35-11.** Fax 09-51-23-35-11. 4 units. 75€–90€ double, including breakfast. MC, V. **Amenities:** Room service. *In room:* A/C (in some), TV, hair dryer, Wi-Fi (free).

Where to Eat

VERY EXPENSIVE

Une Table, au Sud ★★ MODERN PROVENÇALE Michelin-starred chef Lionel Lévy serves some of the city's most creative cuisine in this discreet restaurant overlooking the Vieux Port. The menu changes each month, depending on what ingredients are in season. Try Chef Lévy's signature dish, Bouille-Abaisse, a milk-shake inspired by the fish dish.

1 quai du Port. ✆ **04-91-90-63-53.** www.unetableausud.com. Reservations recommended. Fixed-price dinner 71€–127€. AE, MC, V. Tues–Thurs noon–2pm and 7:30–10:30pm; Fri–Sat noon–2pm and 7:30pm–midnight. Closed Aug and Dec 21–26. Métro: Vieux Port.

EXPENSIVE

See also the restaurants at **Sofitel Vieux Port** and **Le Petit Nice** (see both above).

Chez Fonfon ★ PROVENÇALE/FRENCH This Port du Vallon des Auffes institution specializes in *bouillabaisse,* but also serves all kinds of fish, sometimes grilled and sometimes baked in a salt crust. Start with the Fonfon seafood platter for the freshest oysters, mussels, whelks, and shrimps.

140 rue du Vallon des Auffes, Port du Vallon des Auffes. ✆ **04-91-52-14-38.** www.chez-fonfon.com. Reservations recommended. Main courses 26€–47€; fixed-price menus 42€–55€. AE, DC, MC, V. Tues–Sat noon–1:45pm; Mon–Sat 7:15–9:45pm. Closed 2 weeks in Jan. Métro: Vieux Port.

L'Epuisette ★ PROVENÇALE/MEDITERRANEAN Guillaume Sourrieu heads this Michelin-starred restaurant overlooking the fishing port of Vallon des Auffes, half a mile from the center of Marseille. As diners gaze on sea views, they can enjoy such dishes as sea urchin risotto, lobster tagine, or a slow-cooked spiced shoulder of lamb. You can also get a delicious bouillabaisse here—try it, and you'll understand why Dumas, Zola, and Stendhal smacked their lips over this succulent dish.

Vallon des Auffes, 13007 Marseille. ✆ **04-91-52-17-82.** www.l-epuisette.com. Reservations recommended. Main courses 42€–60€. MC, V. Tues–Sat noon–2pm and 7:30–10:30pm. Closed Aug.

Le Miramar ★★ SEAFOOD Bouillabaisse aficionados flock to this classic quayside restaurant, a founding member of the Marseille bouillabaisse charter that specifies exactly what goes into this often debased dish. Actually, it's two dishes, a saffron-tinted soup followed by the fish poached in the soup. It's eaten with *une rouille,* a sauce of red chilies, garlic, olive oil, egg yolk, and cayenne. The version served here involves lots of labor and just as much seafood. Every third Thursday of the month, chef Christian Buffa holds a course on how to make this celebrated dish.

12 quai du Port. ✆ **04-91-91-10-40.** www.bouillabaisse.com. Reservations recommended. Main courses from 30€; bouillabaisse from 58€ per person (minimum 2). AE, DC, MC, V. Tues–Sat noon–2:30pm and 7–10pm.

Michel-Brasserie des Catalans ★ SEAFOOD Although it's decorated with shellacked lobsters and starfish, this restaurant, located just beyond the Parc du Pharo and next to the Vieux Port, serves a fine bouillabaisse. It also offers a good *bourride* (fish stew with aïoli). The waiter brings you an array of fresh fish from which you make your selection.

6 rue des Catalans, 13007 Marseille. ✆ **04-91-52-30-63.** www.restaurant-michel.com. Reservations recommended. Main courses 33€–55€. AE, MC, V. Daily noon–1:30pm and 8–9:30pm. Bus: 81 or 83.

MODERATE

La Virgule SEAFOOD Chef Lionel Lévy, owner of Une Table, au Sud (see above), was so annoyed about people missing out the comma in the restaurant name that he called his informal bistro version La Virgule, which means comma. Along with the fish of the day and fried calamari with ratatouille, you'll find delicious plates of risotto made with Parma ham and mushrooms, seasonal vegetables, and of course seafood.

27 rue de la Loge, 13002 Marseille. ✆ **04-91-90-91-11.** http://lavirgule.marseille.free.fr. Main courses 14€–23€; fixed-price menu 25€. MC, V. Tues–Sat noon–2pm and 7–10pm; Sun noon–2pm.

Le Rhul ★★ SEAFOOD Since 1948, this restaurant, about 3km (2 miles) east of the Vieux Port, has been offering two versions of bouillabaisse that continue to wow gastronomes as they take in the views of the sea. Its owner Alex Galligani, was another one of the founders of the Marseille bouillabaisse charter, so you can count on superb flavors with the *bouillabaisse de pêcheur* served here. The *bouillabaisse homard* has lobster as well. The restaurant also doubles as a three-star hotel, with pretty rooms for 100€ to 160€.

269 Corniche Président-J.-F.-Kennedy. ✆ **04-91-52-01-77.** www.lerhul.fr. Reservations recommended. Main courses 19€–28€; bouillabaisse 45€. MC, V. Daily noon–2:30pm and 8–10pm. Métro: Vieux Port, then take bus for 3km (2 miles) east.

Les Arcenaulx ★ PROVENÇALE The navies of Louis XIV built these stone warehouses near the Vieux Port; today they house this restaurant, bookstores, and a gourmet boutique, all run by the sisters Simone and Jeanne Laffitte. Along with their version of bouillabaisse, they serve the catch of the day; a light soup of crab, giant shrimp, and scallops; steak tartare; and a filet of beef with flash-fried foie gras.

25 cours d'Estienne d'Orves. ✆ **04-91-59-80-30.** www.les-arcenaulx.com. Reservations recommended. Main courses 17€–48€; fixed-price dinner 59€. AE, MC, V. Mon–Sat noon–2pm and 8–11pm. Métro: Vieux Port.

Toinou SEAFOOD In a massive building overshadowing every other structure nearby, this landmark restaurant serves more shellfish than any other restaurant in

Marseille. Inside, a display of more than 40 species of shellfish is laid out for inspection. Dining rooms are on three floors, served by a waitstaff who are very entrenched in their Marseillais accents and demeanors. Don't come here unless you're really fond of shellfish, any species of which can be served raw or cooked.

3 cours St-Louis, 13001 Marseille. ✆ **04-91-54-08-79.** www.toinou.com. Reservations recommended. Main courses 15€–33€; fixed-price shellfish platter for two 42€. DC, MC, V. Daily 11:30am–11pm. Métro: Vieux Port.

INEXPENSIVE

Bar de la Marine PROVENÇALE This restaurant-bar was the inspiration for Marcel Pagnol's Marseille film trilogy and also featured in Richard Curtis's 2003 soppy romantic comedy *Love Actually*—two reasons why you'd think this place would be a tourist trap of the worst sort. You'd be wrong, however, as its kitchen turns out tasty and cheap plates of grilled sardines, octopus salad, and whatever fish landed in the nets that day. Locals vastly outnumber tourists, and it's also one of the most popular places in the city for an aperitif or after-dinner drink.

15 quai de Rive Neuve, 13007 Marseille. ✆ **04-91-54-95-42.** Main courses 12€–18€. MC, V. Mon–Sat 7:30am–2am; Sun 5pm–midnight. Métro: Vieux Port.

Chez Angèle PIZZA This small and unpretentious restaurant on the edge of Le Panier is reported to be the oldest pizzeria in Marseille. Pizzas and calzones are generous and the welcome is friendly as you choose between seafood starters such as octopus salad or smoked salmon and red mullet.

50 rue Caisserie, 13002 Marseille. ✆ **04-91-90-63-35.** Pizzas 13€–18€. MC, V. Mon–Sat noon–2:30pm; Sun–Fri 7:30–11:30pm. Closed mid-July–mid-Aug. Métro: Vieux Port.

La Cantinetta 🎁 ITALIAN Head out to the cours Julien district for innovative Italian cuisine, preferably at a table in the delightful interior courtyard. Most of the pasta and risotto dishes are dictated by what organic produce the chefs can get their hands on, and the ingredients and presentation are top notch. Dishes usually include *spaghetti alla vongole* (spaghetti with clams) and large salads of arugula, Parmesan, and *bresaola* (dried salted beef).

24 cours Julien, 13006 Marseille. ✆ **04-91-48-10-48.** Main courses 11€–19€. Reservations recommended. MC, V. Tues–Sat noon–1:45pm and 7:45–10:30pm. Métro: Notre-Dame du Mont.

La Kahena TUNISIAN This busy Tunisian restaurant near the Vieux Port is an enclave of savory North African aromas: minced or grilled lamb, tomatoes, eggplant, herbs, and couscous. The menu lists nine varieties of couscous, including versions with lamb, chicken, fish, the spicy sausage known as merguez, plus a "complete" version that includes a little bit of everything (except the fish).

2 rue de la République. ✆ **04-91-90-61-93.** Main courses 10€–18€. MC, V. Daily noon–2:30pm and 7:30–11pm. Métro: Vieux Port.

Le Comptoir des Favouilles PROVENÇALE On the opposite side of the building from Les Arcenaulx, this restaurant occupies a former dorm for prisoners who were forced to row the ornamental barges of Louis XIV during his inspections of Marseille's harbor. Provençale dishes include succulent baked sea bass prepared simply and a delicious combination of saltwater crayfish with foie gras.

44 rue Sainte. ✆ **04-96-11-03-11.** Reservations recommended. Main courses 12€–19€. AE, MC, V. Mon–Fri noon–2:30pm; Mon–Sat 7:30–10:30pm. Métro: Vieux Port.

Marseille After Dark

Clubs in Marseille can come and go with dizzying speed, but there are certain areas that are always hopping. The cafes along the **Vieux Port** are a good place to start, as the streets are always lively and are reasonably safe at night. Just south of the port on cours d'Estienne d'Orves is **Le Polikarpov** at No. 24 (✆ **04-91-52-70-30;** http://lepolikarpov.com), which calls itself Marseille's smallest vodka bar. When its youngish drinkers aren't sipping vodka on the outdoor terrace, they're inside on weekend nights dancing to techno.

Cocktails flow at **Comptoir Carmine,** 134 quai du Vieux Port (✆ **04-91-31-93-89;** www.restaurant-carmine.com), Thursday to Sunday evenings—this elegant bar beside Carmine restaurant is a popular spot for after-work drinks that have a way of carrying on into the night. It's a similar scene to nearby **Le Crystal** at No. 148 (✆ **04-91-91-57-96**), where the food plays a secondary role to thumping electro dance.

Trolley Bus, 24 quai de Rive-Neuve (✆ **04-91-54-30-45;** www.letrolley.com) has been packing in people for its live gigs and DJ nights since 1989. Housed in a 17th-century arsenal on the port, the club's four dance floors are atmospherically lit under stone vaulted ceilings as the young crowd chooses between techno, retro '80s, goth, or metal music.

If you find yourself in cours Julien on a Thursday, drop by **Oogie Lifestore** at no. 55 (✆ **04-91-53-10-70**). It's a concept store that crams in a weekly club night, restaurant, boutique, and even a hair salon. Nearby is **La Dame Noire,** 30 place Notre-Dame du Mont, another hypertrendy spot for electro music and cocktails.

Marseille's premier gay bar is **MP Bar,** 10 rue Beauvau (✆ **04-91-33-64-79**), open Tuesday to Sunday 7pm to 3am. An equally valid option is the **New Can Can,** 3–5 rue Sénac (✆ **04-91-48-59-76;** www.newcancan.com), a broad and sprawling bar-and-disco venue that is more mixed than strictly gay. It is open Thursday to Sunday 11pm until dawn. Cover charge is free except on Friday and Saturday nights. On Friday it's free until midnight. On Saturday a 15€ entrance is charged.

CASSIS

800km (497 miles) S of Paris; 51km (32 miles) SE of Aix-en-Provence; 30km (18 miles) E of Marseille

Despite its popularity, this fishing port remains one of the least spoiled towns along France's Mediterranean coast. Urban sprawl hasn't been able to take hold on the village, thanks to the imposing cliffs and *calanques* that surround it. Although it can become quite choked during the summer, it's still a delight to visit outside the months of July and August. Its 12 surrounding vineyards produce the highly regarded Cassis appellation, focusing on delicious dry fruity whites. They're the perfect accompaniment to the fresh seafood served in the many pastel-colored cafes and restaurants lining the port.

Essentials

GETTING THERE **Trains** that run from Marseille to Hyères stop at Cassis, whose SNCF station is 3km outside of town and is serviced by regular shuttle buses. For information, call ✆ **36-35,** or visit www.voyages-sncf.com. **Buses** run from Marseille until the early evening; call **08-20-82-14-00** for details. If you're **driving,** take the scenic D559 that winds through dramatic landscapes of rocky hills; it's about a 35-minute drive from Marseille. Parking in Cassis can be difficult in the summer and during its weekly Wednesday market. The best bet is to park in the Parking des Gorguettes at the northern entrance to the town and take the shuttle bus. Parking is free but the shuttle costs 1€. Parking by the port is considerably more expensive.

VISITOR INFORMATION The **Office de Tourisme** is at quai des Moulins (✆ **04-42-01-67-83;** fax 04-42-01-28-31; www.ot-cassis.com).

SPECIAL EVENTS The **Fête de St-Jean, de la Mer et des Pêcheurs** is a 3-day celebration of the sea that takes place in late June. Parades, dancing, massive picnic lunches, and bouts of water jousting bring even more color to the lively port. The **wine festival** on the last Sunday in September brings the area's winemakers to the village for a day of tastings, dancing, and processions.

Exploring the Town

A medieval castle built in 1381 by the counts of Les Baux-de-Provence hovers the eastern side of Cassis, but all you can do is admire its exterior as it's closed to the public. **Chateau de Cassis** (www.chateaudecassis.com) now functions as a very expensive luxury B&B, with rooms starting at 290€.

Cassis is popular with hikers keen to explore the chalk cliffs and the rocky inlets of the *calanques* to the west and the imposing **Cap Canaille** to the east, one of Europe's highest cliffs. Walking maps (available in town) show paths for all levels of hiker. Some lead to sheltered beaches, such as at **Port-Pin,** an hour's walk away. Others are more challenging, such as the steep descent to the shingle beach at **En-Vau.** Bear in mind that the paths will be off limits during times of strong winds, and be aware of the dangers of forest fires during dry summer months when smoking is not permitted on the paths.

Boat trips exploring the *calanques* run regularly from the port, ranging from 45-minute cruises for 13€ to 90-minute jaunts that take in eight calanques for 19€ (✆ **06-86-55-86-70;** www.calanques-cassis.com). Nocturnal cruises run during July and August, which include a sound-and-light show. And you don't have to hike or sail to enjoy the main Blue Flag (eco-labeled) beach at Cassis, which is right in front of the port.

Where to Stay

Hôtel Best Western La Rade Less than a 10-minute walk from the port is this comfortable three-star hotel with glorious views of the sea and the *calanques*. Rooms are on the small side, but are airy and decorated in cool neutral tones; many have balconies or terraces with panoramic sea views. Book ahead for parking as, like most hotels in Cassis with a parking lot, there aren't enough spaces for all the guests, so it fills up quickly.

1 av. Des Dardanelles, rte des Calanques, 13260 Cassis. www.hotel-cassis.com. ✆ **04-42-01-02-97.** Fax 04-42-01-01-32. 28 units. 95€–169€ double; 189€–225€ suite. AE, MC, V. Parking 15€. **Amenities:** Bar; pool (outdoor); room service. *In room:* A/C, TV, hair dryer, Internet (free).

Le Jardin d'Emile Color is everywhere in this peaceful old hotel by the Plage du Bestouan. The rooms are decked out in deep shades of blue, green, red, or yellow, but the light coming off the sea brightens things up. Most of the rooms have terraces that look out over either the lush gardens or the sea and Cap Canaille.

Plage du Bestouan, 13260 Cassis. www.lejardindemile.com. ✆ **04-42-01-80-55.** Fax 04-42-01-80-70. 7 units. 109€–139€ double. AE, MC, V. Free parking. **Amenities:** Restaurant; bar; room service. *In room:* A/C, TV, hair dryer, Wi-Fi (free).

Where to Eat

La Fleur de Thym ★ PROVENÇALE This mother-and-son operation turns out finely crafted family recipes in this cozy restaurant located in a little side street off the port. The focus is on seafood, not surprisingly, with a bouillabaisse of monkfish and mussels or a gratin of scallops and langoustines. Meat isn't ignored though, with a *mille-feuille* of beef and foie gras and that old Marseillais favorite, *pieds et paquets* (a slow-cooked dish of lambs' feet served with parcels of lamb tripe stuffed with bacon and herbs).

5 rue Lamartine. ✆ **04-42-01-23-03.** www.fleurdethym.com. MC, V. Main courses from 24€; fixed-price menu 29€–42€. Daily 7–10pm. Closed Jan.

La Poissonnerie ★ SEAFOOD Five generations of the same family have been serving fresh fish in this busy quayside restaurant, which doubles as a fish shop in the morning. The menu depends on the catch of the day, and little more than herbs and olive oil are allowed to go near plates of scorpion fish, gilthead bream, sea bass, and the little Provençal squid called *supion*.

6 quai Barthélémy. ✆ **04-42-01-71-56.** Main courses from 15€; fixed-price menu 20€–30€. Cash only. Feb–May and Oct–Dec Tues–Sun noon–1:30pm; June–Sep Tues–Sat noon–1:30pm and 7:45–9:45pm. Closed Jan.

6 THE WESTERN CÔTE & INLAND VAR

by Louise Simpson

Stretching from the historic naval town of Toulon to family-friendly Saint-Raphaël, the Western Côte coastline straddles the Mediterranean Sea and encompasses several charming towns. In the center of this coastline is the pastel-painted fishing village of Saint-Tropez. All summer long, the St-Trop peninsula is crowded with A-listers and designer-clad wannabe starlets lounging on superyachts or parading along Ramatuelle's golden beaches. Families head to the middle-class resorts of Sainte-Maxime and Saint-Raphaël with their Blue Flag beaches and reasonably priced accommodations. In this region of opposites, world champions windsurf on the Giens Peninsula as fishermen darn sardine nets in Sanary-sur-Mer. Ancient and modern lie cheek by jowl in Roman Fréjus, where its 1st century A.D. amphitheater now has a 21st-century glass-paneled counterpart designed by Jean-Michel Wilmotte.

Behind the glittering coastline lies the little-visited 6,000-sq.-km (2,316-sq.-mile) region of the **Var,** known for its cut flowers, honey, and chestnuts. When you've had enough of lying on the beach, head inland to mimosa-strewn hilltop villages such as Grimaud and Bormes-Les-Mimosas, or organize a hiking tour along the red volcanic Esterel hills. Further inland, a forested landscape dominates, dotted by time-worn hamlets. The new millennium has brought a creeping sophistication to the sleepy inland Var with Michelin-starred restaurants and luxury hotels. Straddling the border with the Alpes de Haute-Provence is the Verdon Nature Reserve, home to limestone peaks and an Alpine climate; here lies Europe's largest canyon, the staggering emerald-colored Gorges du Verdon. Because the Var is more seasonal and several degrees cooler than the year-round Alpes-Maritimes, many designer boutiques, restaurants, and hotels close from November to March, leaving the locals to hibernate in peace. From January to March, towns all over the Var celebrate the arrival of spring with canary-yellow mimosa flower festivals.

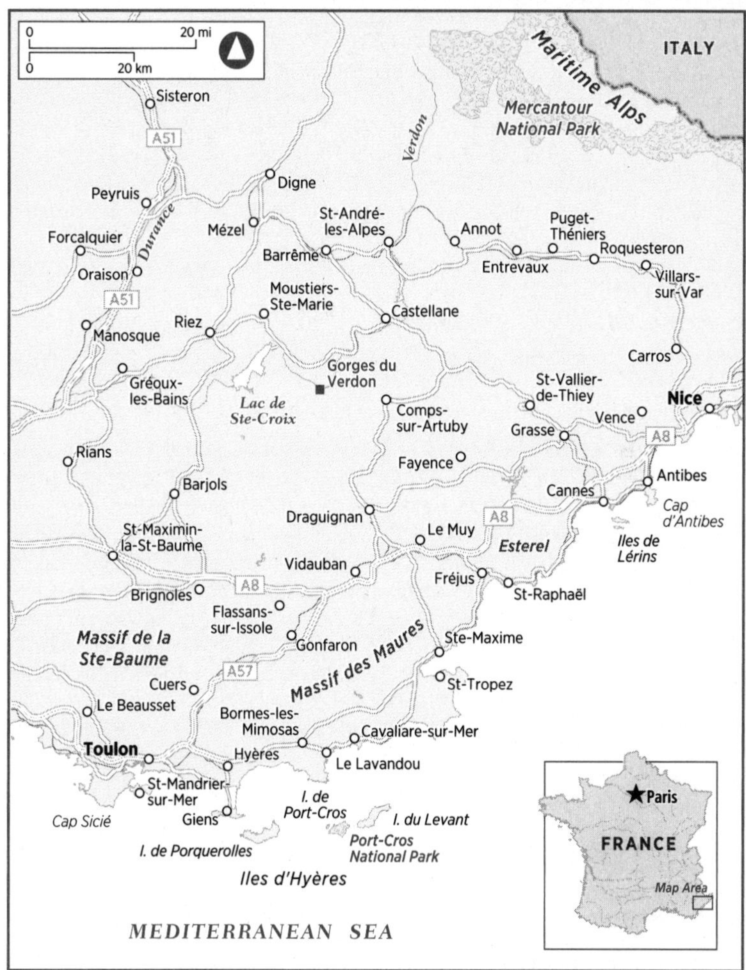

GORGES DU VERDON ★★★

Trigance: 72km (45 miles) S of Digne-les-Bains, 20km (12 miles) W of Castellane, 43km (27 miles) NW of Draguignan, 85km (53 miles) E of Manosque; La-Palud-sur-Verdon: 64km (40 miles) S of Digne-les-Bains, 25km (16 miles) W of Castellane, 60km (37 miles) NW of Draguignan, 66km (41 miles) E of Manosque

No trip to the Var would be complete without a trip to see this spectacular limestone ravine up to 700m (2,300 ft.) deep. Nicknamed the "God of the Green Waters," the canyon is known for its emerald color, which it gets from its high fluorine content. Three main tributaries (the Jabron, Artuby, and Colostre) join to form the canyon's rapid waters, although five dams forming five retention lakes have tamed its tempestuousness over the years. The Verdon Gorges form the largest canyon in Europe and the second largest in the world, after America's Grand Canyon. Straddling the border between the Var and the Alpes de Haute-Provence, these hollowed-out limestone gorges meander for 21km (13 miles) from Pont de Soleils to Pont du Galetas. From Pont de Galetas, you'll see pedalos and canoes floating from the watersports haven of Lac de Sainte-Croix towards the gorges' mouth. Vertiginous roads wind along both rims of the canyon; among the best viewpoints to stretch your legs and take a drink are at La Mescla on the southern rim or Point Sublime on the northern rim. Between Rougon and Castellane, the road dips down to the gorges—ideal for stopping to dip your toes into the ice-cold rapids. The canyon enjoys an Alpine climate, so you'll need a sweater for cooler summer nights.

Essentials

GETTING THERE From Cannes, follow the A8 west towards Fréjus. Take exit 36 for Le Muy, and continue on D54 and then D955 for Montferrat. From there, continue on D955 past Comps-sur-Artuby, then head west along D71 until you reach the canyon.

VISITOR INFORMATION Information about how best to take advantage of the region's natural beauty and sporting options, as well as information on events, is available from the tourist offices of the three largest settlements around the canyon: **Castellane** (✆ **04-92-83-61-14;** www.castellane.org), **Moustiers Sainte-Marie** (✆ **04-92-74-67-84;** www.moustiers.fr), and **Esparron de Verdon** (✆ **04-92-77-15-97;** www.esparrondeverdon.com; open mostly in midsummer).

Exploring the Area

The Verdon canyon lies in the middle of the **Parc Naturel Régional du Verdon** (www.parcduverdon.fr). Created in 1997 and thus one of France's newest nature reserves, this park has more than 700km (450 miles) of walking trails and bridle paths, and is yours to explore on foot, on horseback, or by mountain bike. In the wilder reaches of the park, above the tree line, the limestone peaks are home to chamois, wild goats, marmots, and some spectacular birds, including golden eagles and lammergeier vultures. You'll find gentler country with tidy patchworks of green and purple lavender fields on the sunny Valensole plateau, while sheep pastures and green oak woods surround Artuby.

Whistle-Stop Tour

A useful stopover in the Haut Var on the way to the gorges is **Tourtour.** Since Gordon Ramsay proclaimed it as one of his favorite French villages in 2007, this village has mushroomed with restaurants so that it now offers myriad dining options, from Moroccan to crepes. The pick of the bunch is **La Table** (✆ **04-94-70-55-95;** www.latable.fr): a delightful, family-run French restaurant with a shady terrace for summer dining. View seekers will love the **Bastide de Tourtour** (✆ **04-98-10-54-20;** www.bastidedetourtour.com); the interior decor is rather fusty, but gazing down on three Côte d'Azur regions over an evening drink in the loggia (Prestige Rooms only) leaves an indelible memory. Don't miss the troglodyte caves hewn into the cliff face in the nearby village of Villecroze.

Make time to visit the **Musée de Préhistoire des Gorges du Verdon** (© **04-92-74-09-59;** www.museeprehistoire.com), on the Route de Montmeyan near Quinson. Designed in the 1990s by British architect Norman Foster, this contemporary-looking museum houses ancient exhibits spanning almost half a million years of human history. There's a themed trail (the trail takes about 2 hr.) from the museum to the Baume Bonne grotto, where many of the exhibits were found. The cave was discovered in 1946; a viewing platform lets you see its walls and floor, where archaeologists are still at work, and you can go by boat deeper into the flooded parts of the cave. Further along the trail is an "archaeological village" where you can try your hand at living Stone Age–style—grinding grain by hand, chipping flints, and trying to light a fire by rubbing two sticks together.

Outdoor Pursuits

You can explore the canyon with guided hikes from the **Bureau des Guides,** La-Palud-sur-Verdon (© **04-92-77-30-50;** www.escalade-verdon.fr). Canoeing and kayaking are available through the **Aqua Viva Est** in Castellane (© **04-92-83-75-74;** www.aquavivaest.com), and the **Club Nautique,** Esparron (© **04-92-77-15-25**). Rafting trips, canyoning, and *aqua-rando* (water rambling) are conducted by **Aboard Rafting** (© **04-92-83-76-11;** www.aboard-rafting.com) in Castellane. All three of these organizations operate in full swing between May and early September. The rest of the year, they operate with skeleton staffs, usually via answering machine and fax. If you haven't booked in advance, you can just head to Pont de Galetas on Lac de Sainte-Croix, where you'll find plenty of pedalos for rent.

Where to Stay

Popular stopovers for people who are exploring the gorges include **Castellane,** with its streets that are crammed with shops selling outdoor equipment; **Trigance,** dominated by its medieval castle–turned-hotel; and **Moustiers Sainte-Marie,** famed for its pottery and for Alain Ducasse. Cheap hotels and B&Bs are underwhelming in the region, but there are some excellent campsites near Castellane. For the district's poshest hotel, look no further than the **Bastide de Moustiers** (see below).

EXPENSIVE

Bastide de Moustiers ★★★ Very near the Gorges du Verdon, in the village of Moustiers-Sainte-Marie, Alain Ducasse, arguably hailed as the world's greatest chef, has opened this informal inn of charm and grace. The property once belonged to a master potter, and the country house is filled with the celebrated Moustiers earthenware. The inn is surrounded by tree-studded grounds covering 4 hectares (10 acres). Aided by local artisans, the inn has been beautifully restored and each room individually designed. Accommodations are filled with the rewards of Ducasse's antiques-hunting expeditions. Bathrooms are luxurious—Chambre Coquelicot, for example, has a Philippe Starck–designed bath. My favorite rooms are the light-infused Chambre Blanche and the diminutive Chambre Pigeonnier, based in the ancient dovecote.

Even if you're not staying here, consider making a reservation for a meal here. The aroma of *provençale* flavors emerge from the Michelin-starred kitchen, and much homegrown produce is used, including provisions from the inn's own vegetable garden. Fixed-price menus range from 58€ to 72€.

Chemin de Quinson, 04360 Moustiers-Sainte-Marie. www.bastide-moustiers.com. © **04-92-70-47-47.** Fax 04-92-70-47-48. 12 units. 195€–375€ double; 335€–405€ suite. AE, DC, MC, V. **Amenities:** Restaurant; bar; pool (outdoor); room service. *In room:* A/C, TV/DVD, hair dryer, minibar.

A Worthwhile Detour

The beautiful Moulin du Château (✆ 04-92-74-02-47; www.moulin-du-chateau.com) in St-Laurent du Verdon is worth a detour. This ancient olive mill–turned-hotel provides one of the best stopovers on the way to the Verdon Gorges. In summertime, organic suppers are served to guests outside beneath the shade of a nettle tree.

MODERATE

Château de Trigance ★ Rising on a rocky spur above a hamlet of fewer than 120 full-time inhabitants, this three-star hotel occupies the core of a 9th- and 10th-century fortress. Over the last 50 years, the Hartmann and Thomas families have added various wings to transform the castle ruins into this 10-room hotel. The best feature is the arms and weapons room–turned–dining room with its dry-stone, Saracen-vaulted ceiling. Here guests feast on heavy meaty fare such as foie gras and beef fillet, although lighter fish dishes are available. Menus cost 27€ to 50€. Medieval touches adorn the bedrooms, including the archaic and lumpy baldachin-style beds. A parking lot near the entrance of the hotel saves you the arduous hike up the medieval-looking steps that were once the only route of access.

Route du Château, 83840 Trigance, Var. www.chateau-de-trigance.fr. ✆ **04-94-76-91-18.** Fax 04-94-85-68-99. 10 units. 117€–177€ double; 197€ junior suite. AE, DC, MC, V. Free parking. Closed Nov–Mar. **Amenities:** Restaurant; bar; room service. *In room:* TV.

Hôtel du Grand Canyon de Verdon This hotel is set on a rocky outcropping above the canyon precipice, vertiginously close to the edge, and exists only because of the foresight of the present owner's grandfather. In 1946, on holiday in Provence from his home in the foggy northern French province of Pas de Calais, he fell in love with the site, opened a brasserie, and secured permission to build a hotel here. In 1982, his grandson, Georges Fortini, erected the present two-story hotel. Sadly, such natural advantages are let down by the basic accommodation and patchy service. With its glassed-in restaurant overlooking a 322m (1,075-ft) drop to the canyon bottom, you come here for the views alone.

Falaise des Cavaliers, 83630 Aiguines. www.hotel-canyon-verdon.com. ✆ **04-94-76-91-31.** Fax 04-94-76-92-29. 13 units. 125€–135€ double. Rates include half board. AE, MC, V. Closed Oct to mid-Apr. **Amenities:** Restaurant; bar. *In room:* TV, hair dryer.

INEXPENSIVE

Auberge Point-Sublime This hotel offers simple, unpretentious rooms, each with congenially battered, old-fashioned (but not antique) furniture. Bedrooms are small, although each has a comfortable mattress, plus a somewhat cramped bathroom. You do get views over the gorge and a convenient location, opposite the popular viewpoint, Point Sublime. The restaurant serves excellent *provençale* fixed-price meals. Specialties are a goat cheese-and-thyme omelet, lamb stew, and fig-flavored crème brûlée. Weekend stays require half board.

RD952, 04120 Rougon. ✆ **04-92-83-60-35/69-15.** Fax 04-92-83-74-31. 13 units. 60€–65€ double. 60€–63€ per person for half board (based on 2 people). MC, V. Closed Oct–Mar. **Amenities:** Restaurant; bar. *In room:* TV.

Camping Les Collines de Castellane In the middle of the Verdon Nature Reserve and close to the gorges lies this reasonably priced campsite. As well as a huge swimming pool, the campsite has a restaurant, bar, and grocery store. You don't have to stay in a tent, though, as there are chalets and mobile homes with adequate kitchens for four to six people; you'll need to bring your own bed linen. Themed evenings and sporting entertainments are on hand, such as football matches and volleyball. The campsite is just outside the village of La Garde near Castellane.

04120 Castellane. www.rcn-campings.fr. ✆ **04-92-83-68-96.** 160 tent pitches; 30 chalets/mobile homes. Tent pitches from 19€, chalets/mobile homes 39€–148€. MC, V. Parking. **Amenities:** Restaurant; games (football, volleyball, boules), pool and paddling pool; tennis. *In room* (chalets and mobile homes): Kitchen.

Hôtel Le Vieil Amandier At the edge of town, this hotel offers clean, uncomplicated guest rooms and a dining room with straightforward but thoughtfully prepared cuisine. Half the rooms face the pool and get southern light; the remainder are just as comfortable but without views. The largest is the rustic and woodsy no. 6; nos. 3 and 4 are more Provençal, and the others are blandly international. There's a pleasant, unpretentious restaurant where lunch and dinner are served daily.

Montée de Saint-Roch, 83840 Trigance. http://levieilamandier.free.fr. ✆ **04-94-76-92-92.** Fax 04-94-85-68-65. 12 units. 61€–99€ double. AE, DC, MC, V. Free parking. Closed mid-Oct to Mar. **Amenities:** Restaurant; bar; pool (outdoor); spa. *In room:* TV, hair dryer.

Where to Eat

Many of the inns recommended above are also the finest places to dine—notably the sophisticated Michelin-starred **Bastide de Moustiers** and the **Auberge Point-Sublime** for rustic Provençal fare. Another excellent dining option is the earthy **Auberge du Teillon** (✆ **04-92-83-60-88;** www.auberge-teillon.com) in the tiny village of La Garde near Castellane.

Les Santons ★ FRENCH/PROVENÇALE One of the region's most charming restaurants occupies a stone-sided, 12th-century house adjacent to the village church. The cozy dining room filled with 19th-century paintings and antique pottery holds fewer than 20 seats. A terrace with flowering plants doubles the seating space during clement weather. Examples of the fare include homemade noodles studded with truffles and chunks of foie gras and Sisteron lamb roasted with honey and spices and served with an herb-scented ratatouille and *gratin dauphinoise* (potatoes with grated cheese).

Place de l'Eglise, 04360 Moustiers-Ste-Marie. ✆ **04-92-74-66-48.** www.lessantons.com. Reservations recommended. Main courses 19€–27€; fixed-price menu 26€. AE, MC, V. July–Aug noon–2pm; Wed–Sun noon–2pm and 7:30–9:30pm; Sept to mid-Nov and mid-Feb to June Mon noon–2pm; Wed–Sun noon–2pm and 7:30–9:30pm.

TOULON

835km (519 miles) S of Paris; 127km (79 miles) SW of Cannes; 68km (42 miles) E of Marseille

This fortress and modern town is the principal naval base of France—the headquarters of the Mediterranean fleet, with hundreds of sailors wandering the streets. The Var's capital, Toulon has cleaned up its act considerably since the demise of the Front National–led council, but it's still not the most attractive place to spend precious holiday time. Aside from the port with its boat trips, the real reason to come here is to take the cable car up **Mont Faron** with its zoo and far-reaching coastline views. Avoid the port area and the rue d'Alger at night.

Essentials

GETTING THERE **Trains** arrive from Marseille every 5 to 30 minutes (trip time 1 hr.); the one-way fare is 11€. Trains also arrive frequently from Nice (trip time 1 hr., 45 min.) and Cannes (trip time 80 min.). For information, call ✆ **36-35,** or visit www.voyages-sncf.com.

Three **buses** per day arrive from Aix-en-Provence (trip time 1 hr., 15 min.); the fare is about 10€ one-way. For information, call **Sodetrav** (✆ **08-25-00-06-50**). If you're **driving** from Marseille, take A50 east to Toulon. When you arrive, park your car underground at place de la Liberté; then go along boulevard de Strasbourg, turning right into rue Berthelot: This will take you into the pedestrian zone in the core of the old city, centered on the rue d'Alger.

GETTING AROUND A municipal **bus** system serves the town. A bus map is available at the tourist office. Buses depart from the main terminal on place de l'Europe next to the train station. Intercity bus tickets cost 1.40€. For information, call **Le Réseau Mistral** at ✆ **04-94-03-87-03.**

VISITOR INFORMATION The **Office de Tourisme** is at 12 place Louis Blanc (✆ **04-94-18-53-00;** fax 04-94-18-53-08; www.toulontourisme.com).

Exploring the Town

In **Vieux Toulon,** between the harbor and boulevard de Strasbourg (the main axis of town), are many remains of the port's former days. A colorful food market, conducted Tuesday to Sunday from 7:30am to 12:30pm, **Le Marché du Cours Lafayette** spills onto the streets around cours Lafayette. Also in old Toulon is the **Cathédrale Ste-Marie-Majeure** (also known as Sainte-Marie-de-la-Seds; ✆ **04-94-92-28-91**), built in the Romanesque style in the 11th and 12th centuries, and expanded in the 17th. The badly lit nave is Gothic; the belfry and facade are from the 18th century. It's open daily from 7:30am to noon and 2:30 to 7pm.

In contrast to the cathedral, tall modern buildings line quai Cronstadt, opening onto **Vieille Darse,** where you'll find cafes and restaurants galore. On the facade of the **Hôtel de Ville (Town Hall)** in Toulon port, look for the ***Atlantes,*** two male figures sculpted by famous 17th-century sculptor Pierre Puget. Recovered from the former town hall, which was destroyed in World War II, these figures have been cleverly recycled as columns to support the modern town hall's balcony.

Musée de la Marine, place Monsenergue, Quai de Norfolk (✆ **04-22-42-02-01;** www.musee-marine.fr), contains figureheads and impressive ship models. It's open 10am to 6pm daily July and August, and Wednesday through Monday September through June. Admission is 5.50€ for adults, 4€ for students, and free for ages 17 and under.

Musée d'Art, 113 bd. du Maréchal-Leclerc (✆ **04-94-36-81-00**), displays works from the 16th century to the present, including Provençal, New Realist, and Minimalist artworks, as well as photographs by Cartier-Bresson. It's open Tuesday to Sunday noon to 6pm; admission is free.

If you're staying in the southeastern suburb of Le Mourillon, it's worth a visit to the **Musée des Arts Asiatiques,** 169 Littoral Frédéric Mistral (✆ **04-94-36-83-10**), an Asian arts museum housed in Villa Jules Verne, named after the writer who spent many summers there. It's open Tuesday to Sunday noon to 6pm; admission is free.

PANORAMAS & VIEWS

After you've wandered around the town center, I'd suggest taking a drive an hour or two before sunset along the **corniche du Mont-Faron.** This scenic boulevard along the lower slopes of Mont Faron affords views of the busy port, the town, the cliffs, and, in the distance, the Mediterranean.

Earlier in the day, consider boarding a **téléphérique** (cable car; ✆ **04-94-92-68-25**), just off boulevard de L'Amiral Vence. It operates from May to September daily

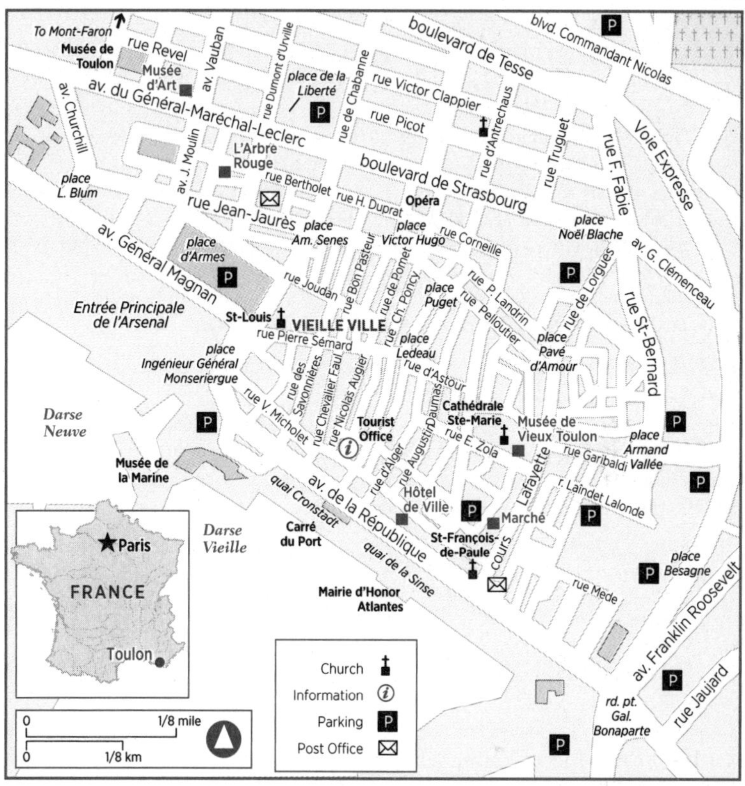

from 10am to 7pm (8pm in peak season), and from October to April Tuesday to Sunday 10am to 12:15pm and 2 to 6pm. The cable car is closed mid-November to mid-February, and in the case of strong winds. The round-trip costs 6.70€ for adults, 4.70€ for children 4 to 10 years old. At the top, enjoy the view and then visit the **Memorial** (✆ **04-94-88-08-09**), which documents the Allied landings in Provence in 1944, among other events. It's open Tuesday to Sunday from May to September 10am to 1pm and 2 to 6:30pm; from October to April, hours those same days are 10am to 1pm and 2 to 5:30pm. Admission is 3.80€ for adults, 1.55€ for children 8 to 16. There's also a zoo dedicated to wild cats. It's open daily from 10am to 5:30pm (later in peak season) and tickets cost 9€ for adults, 5.50€ for children 4 to 10 years.

Where to Stay

Best Western La Corniche ★ An attractive three-star hotel near the town's beaches, La Corniche offers a pleasant staff, comfortable accommodations, and an interior garden. Those at the front have sea views and loggias, and are more expensive. Rooms are decorated in a contemporary Provençal style. You'll find this place in Toulon's chicest suburb Le Mourillon, with its cafes, boutiques, and daily food market. The hotel shares a private beach with the Restaurant Le Lido.

Sanary-sur-Mer

Frugal visitors are fleeing the high prices of the St-Trop peninsula and heading for Sanary-sur-Mer (www.sanarysurmer.com), a tiny fishing village west of Toulon. Wednesday is market day at Sanary, as 300 vendors hawk their wares, selling everything from strawberries to foie gras. Drop in at portside Le Mac' Sym's, 10 quai de Gaulle (✆ 04-94-74-45-34), a popular all-day-dining restaurant and bar with a relaxed vibe. Not far from the Jardin Exotique-Zoo, Les Saveurs de Suzon, 1532 chemin de la Chapelle Sainte-Trinide (✆ 04-94-34-72-74), is the place to gaze at Bandol vineyards over a plate of stuffed squid and a glass or two of rosé (owner Corinne only opens on weekend evenings). For a hotel, check out three-star Hotel Synaya, 92 chemin Olive (✆ 04-94-74-10-50), a quiet hotel with pool, close to Portissol beach and a 10-minute walk from the port. Double bedrooms range from 90€ to 145€ per night.

17 Littoral Frédéric-Mistral (at Le Mourillon), 83000 Toulon. www.bestwestern-hotelcorniche.com. ✆ **04-94-41-35-12.** Fax 04-94-41-24-58. 23 units. 109€–150€ double. AE, DC, MC, V. Parking 12€. **Amenities:** Bar; room service. *In room:* A/C, TV, hair dryer, minibar, Wi-Fi (free).

Where to Eat

L'Arbre Rouge ★ SOUTHERN FRENCH The cuisine here is memorable, and the restaurant is the finest for miles. It's in the town center, in a nondescript building whose thick walls hint at its age. The menu changes with the seasons, but traditional favorites include foie gras *mi-cuit* (semi-preserved) and steak with morel mushrooms.

25 rue de la Comédie (ancienne rue Denfert-Rochereau). ✆ **04-94-92-28-58.** Reservations recommended. Main courses 14€–22€; fixed-price lunch 18€, dinner 27€. AE, MC, V. Mon–Fri noon–2:30pm; Fri–Sat 7:30–9:30pm. Closed first 2 weeks of Sept. Bus: 1 or 21.

Toulon After Dark

The temporary home of thousands of sailors is bound to have a nightlife scene that's earthier, and a bit raunchier, than those of equivalent-size towns elsewhere. A rough-and-ready bar for stiff drinks, live music, and a complete lack of pretension is **Le Bar 113,** 113 av. de l'infanterie de Marine (✆ **04-94-03-42-41;** www.le113cafe.com). At **Bar à Thym,** 32 bd. Cunéo (✆ **04-94-41-90-10;** www.barathym.com), everybody enjoys drinking beer, gossiping, and listening to live music.

Toulon is also home to one of the region's best-known gay discos, **Boy's Paradise,** 1 bd. Pierre-Toesca (✆ **04-94-09-35-90;** www.boysparadise83.com), near the train station. It's open from midnight during the week and from 11pm on Friday and Saturday nights. Adjacent to the port is the gay hot spot **Bar La Lampa,** 117 quai de la Sinse, Port de Toulon (✆ **04-94-03-06-09**), where tapas and live music accompany lots of beer and wine or whiskey.

HYÈRES ★

852km (529 miles) S of Paris; 100km (62 miles) SE of Aix-en-Provence; 122km (76 miles) SW of Cannes; 18km (11 miles) E of Toulon

Temperate and palm-filled Hyères is lost in time. The oldest resort along the Côte d'Azur was once frequented by the likes of Queen Victoria, Napoleon, Leo Tolstoy, and Robert Louis Stevenson. It has changed so little from its pre-WWII heyday that many French film directors, including Jean-Luc Godard (*Pierrot le Fou*) and François Truffaut, who shot his last film here (*Vivement Dimanche,* released as *Confidentially Yours* in the U.S.), have used it as locations for period pieces. Today it lives off its past glory and its memories, but still provides the perfect base for trips to the Îles d'Or and for overnight stops next to Toulon-Hyères airport.

The cobbled streets of the Vieille Ville (Old City), which lies 5km (3 miles) inland from the sea on a hill, are worth a visit with their plethora of health food shops and 19th-century villas. Stop off at the busy morning market in place Massillon before hiking uphill to the Mediterranean gardens of **Parc Saint-Bernard,** where you'll find staggering views over the Var coast and the equally staggering Cubist Villa Noailles.

The full name of the town is Hyères-les-Palmier, as it is known for its production of palm trees. Believe it or not, many of these trees are exported to the Middle East.

Essentials

GETTING THERE **Flights** from Paris arrive at Toulon-Hyères airport (✆ **08-25-01-83-87;** www.toulon-hyeres.aeroport.fr), which lies between the town center and the beach. Rail connections are fairly easy, as Hyères lies on the main Nice-Lyon-Paris line. Nine local **trains** a day connect Hyères with Toulon. For information, call ✆ **36-35,** or visit www.voyages-sncf.com.

Hyères does not have a bus station, only a bus stop. Bus information is available from **Sodetrav** (✆ **08-25-00-06-50**).

If you're **driving,** A570 from Hyères joins the southwest-bound A57 towards Toulon turning into the A50 towards Marseille and points north and west; A57 goes northeast to join A8, the autoroute between Nice and Aix-en-Provence.

VISITOR INFORMATION Contact the **Office de Tourisme,** 3 av. Ambroise Thomas, Hyères (✆ **04-94-01-84-50;** www.hyeres-tourisme.com) for information.

Exploring the Town

Although a small town, Hyères has three parks of note: **Parc Olbius Riquier,** with its mini-zoo, pony rides, and wandering peacocks; **Parc Sainte Claire,** the former home of American writer Edith Wharton; and **Parc Saint-Bernard.**

On a steep hill (Montée de Noailles) above Hyères, Parc Saint-Bernard is the perfect place to relax on benches shaded by olive trees and pines. Charles and Marie-Laure de Noailles, great patrons of the arts, commissioned a modern Cubist-style villa here in 1924 and brought in garden designer Gabriel Guevrekian, who created an extensive garden in the shape of an isosceles triangle, pointing away from the end of the villa. The **Villa Noailles** (✆ **04-98-08-01-98;** www.villanoailles-hyeres.com) played a role in nurturing the avant-garde artists of the Jazz Age, including Jean Cocteau and Man Ray, who made a film here in 1929. The villa is open throughout the year Wednesday to Sunday 1 to 6pm for changing fashion and photography exhibitions (check the website or phone in advance) and for its Fashion and Photography Festival in late April to May. Even if you can't go inside, the gardens are worth visiting for the incredible views alone. Above the villa are the ruins of a medieval castle destroyed by Henri IV. The park is open year-round daily from 8am to 6:30pm. The land lying between the city and the sea is unattractive, and the beaches are a bit polluted; but swimming is possible, notably at **Hyères-Plage.**

Port d'Hyères has a yacht marina. We find the parks and old town more interesting than the beachfront.

Heading into town from the beach, go along the wide **avenue Gambetta** shaded by double rows of palms. At the end of Gambetta, continue along rue du Portalet to **place Massillon,** the beginning of the Old Town and the site of many good terrace cafe-restaurants. The 12th-century **Tour St-Blaise (Tour des Templiers),** which stands on the square, was once a command post of the Knights Templar.

Above place Massillon is a warren of intriguing old streets climbing the hillside. Many are cobblestoned and bordered by stone walls, with an abundance of flowers in summer. Look for the medieval arched *portes.* Most of the Vieille Ville houses have been restored, often painted in lovely pastels with contrasting shutters and doors.

Parts of the 12th-century ramparts have survived, although most of them have been torn down. A trio of lovely old towers has survived from the north curtain wall. All that remains of the south "curtain wall" are Porte Baruc and **Porte-St-Paul,** next to the Collegiate Church, **L'Eglise Saint-Paul,** place St-Paul (✆ **04-94-01-84-50**).

Where to Stay

Hôtel du Soleil This pretty two-star hotel lies on a steep hill close to the Park Saint-Bernard and Villa Noailles. With foundations dating back to the 11th century, this boxy-looking *bastide* (Provençal house) has been softened over the years with a sheathing of ivy. The interiors have been kept up-to-date with frequent modernizations. Bedrooms are cozy, if somewhat cramped, with contemporary furniture and casement windows; from the back are views of the sea, and in front are views of upscale villas on a nearby hill. Bedrooms aren't air-conditioned, but thick walls help to guard against the heat. Breakfast is the only meal served, although several places to eat (including the Bistrot de Marius, below) are within a 3-minute walk.

Rue du Rempart (place Clemenceau), 83400 Hyères. www.hoteldusoleil.com. ✆ **04-94-65-16-26.** Fax 04-94-35-46-00. 20 units. 50€–105€ double. AE, DC, MC, V. **Amenities:** Breakfast room. *In room:* TV, Wi-Fi (free).

Ibis Thalassa This hotel is located on the eastern edge of the land bridge that stretches between the French mainland and the Giens peninsula. Designed in a horseshoe shape, with the open end of the U facing the beach, the hotel emphasizes resort life. Guest rooms are a decent size and decorated in a standardized format that includes a writing table; some have an additional single bed and a patio. Bathrooms are motel standard and tidy. Another Ibis hotel is located downtown. The thalassotherapy spa is next door with its indoor swimming pool and fitness room.

Allée de la Mer, La Capte, 83400 Hyères-Plage. www.thalassa.com. ✆ **04-94-58-00-94.** Fax 04-94-58-09-35. 95 units. 75€–139€ double. AE, DC, MC, V. **Amenities:** Restaurant; bar; health club and spa; pool (outdoor). *In room:* A/C, TV, hair dryer, Wi-Fi (free).

Where to Eat

Bistrot de Marius PROVENÇALE/SEAFOOD Set almost adjacent to the Tour des Templiers, this restaurant serves the tastiest Provençal food in town. With foundations dating back to the 13th century, this bistro has a trio of dining rooms (one is upstairs) with exposed stone and paneling, and a sense of historical charm. Fish, especially grilled sea bass, monkfish, dorado, and tuna, are specialties here, along with mussels and oysters. Sauce choices include *marchand de vin* (a red wine–based sauce), lemon butter, and basil-flavored vinaigrette.

1 place Massillon. ✆ **04-94-35-88-38.** Reservations recommended. Main courses 9.50€–46€; fixed-price menus 19€–32€. AE, DC, MC, V. Wed–Sun noon–2:30pm and 7–10:30pm (daily July–Aug). Closed Nov.

Le Jardin MODERN MEDITERRANEAN Set directly across the street from the town hall *(mairie)* of Hyères, this restaurant takes gardening, and its name, seriously. During most of the year, the retractable roof remains open to night breezes, as outdoor tables showcase the venerable plantings of a mature garden ringed with crab apple, orange, and palm trees. The London-trained owner, Mr. Cheval, speaks perfect English, and welcomes a young and young-at-heart crowd who keep the place convivial. The varied menu can include everything from a succulent steak tartare to a Lebanese mezze (a selection of small dishes) and a genuinely wonderful version of octopus stew cooked in red wine *(daube de pulpe)*.

19 av. Joseph Clotis. ✆ **04-94-35-24-12.** Reservations recommended. Main courses 13€–19€. AE, MC, V. Apr–Oct daily noon–11pm; Nov–Mar Mon–Sat noon–2:30pm, Fri–Sat noon–11pm. Closed mid-Dec to mid-Jan.

ÎLES D'HYERES ★★

39km (24 miles) SE of Toulon; 119km (74 miles) SW of Cannes

Enclosing the southern boundary of the Hyères anchorage is a little group of islands renowned for their outstanding beauty. During the Renaissance they were called the "Îles d'Or," from the golden glow sometimes given off by the rocks in the sunlight. Nothing in the islands today will remind you of the turbulent time when they were attacked by pirates and Turkish galleys, or even of the Allied landings here in World War II.

Mass tourism has arrived on these sun-baked islands, with some of the tackiness that goes with it. Yet the outlawing of cars for nonresidents has helped to guard their tranquillity. Thousands of midsummer day-trippers arrive, often with children, for a day of sun, sand, and people-watching. By sunset, the day-trippers are gone, leaving the islands in peace.

Which island is the most appealing? Île des Porquerolles and Île de Port-Cros—both of which are largely devoted to national parks—are the most beautiful. Thinking of heading to Le Levant? You might want to steer clear—only 25% of the island is accessible to visitors, as three-quarters of it belongs to the French army, and it is used frequently for testing missiles.

Note: Héliopolis, a section of Île du Levant, is home to the oldest nudist colony in Europe. Islanders and visitors go *au naturel* on the beaches. Many of the more daring visitors also don't wear a lot of clothing in the village.

Essentials

GETTING TO ÎLE DE PORQUEROLLES Ferryboats leave from several points along the Côte d'Azur. The most frequent, convenient, and shortest trip is from La Tour Fondue on the peninsula of Giens, a 32km (20-mile) drive east of Toulon. Depending on the season, there are 6 to 20 departures a day. The round-trip fare for the 15-minute crossing is 17€ for adults and 15€ for children ages 4 to 10. For information, call the **Transports du Littoral Varois,** La Tour Fondue, 83400 Giens (✆ **04-94-58-21-81;** www.tlv-tvm.com). The next-best option is the **ferryboat** from Toulon (✆ **04-94-46-24-65;** www.lesbateliersdelarade.com), but only between May and August. Other options available from April to September involve taking one of the

How to Best Explore Île de Porquerolles

One of the best ways to explore the island of Porquerolles is by bike. A good place to rent cycles is at L'Indien (© 04-94-58-30-39 or 06-07-38-44-67; www.lindien.fr) in place d'Armes. You can also hire jet-skis and day boats here.

ferries maintained by the **Compagnie Maritime des Vedettes Îles d'Or & Le Corsaire** (© **04-94-71-01-02;** www.vedettesilesdor.fr). Their ferryboats offer crossings from either of *Les Gares Maritimes* (ferryboat terminals) in Le Lavandou and Cavalaire.

GETTING TO ÎLE DE PORT-CROS The most popular ferry route to the island is the 35-minute crossing that departs from Hyères several times daily, depending on the season. (Oct–Mar, there are only four crossings per week.) Round-trip fares cost 25€ for adults and 22€ for children 4 to 10. For more information, contact **Transports du Littoral Varois** (© **04-94-58-21-81;** www.tlv-tvm.com). Alternatively, you can take the boat from Le Lavandou. For information, contact the **Compagnie Maritime des Vedettes** (© **04-94-71-01-02;** www.vedettesilesdor.fr). Round-trip fares cost 26€ for adults and 21€ for children 4 to 11. The same company also offers crossings to Port-Cros from Cavalaire, but only between April and September; round-trip tickets cost 30€ for adults and 24€ for children 4 to 11.

GETTING TO ÎLE DU LEVANT Ferries depart from Hyères several times daily, depending on the season (Oct–Mar, there are only four crossings per week). Round-trip fares cost 25€ for adults and 22€ for children 4 to 10. For more information, contact **Transports du Littoral Varois** (© **04-94-58-21-81;** www.tlv-tvm.com). Alternatively, you can go from Le Lavandou. For information, contact the **Compagnie Maritime des Vedettes** (© **04-94-71-01-02;** www.vedettesilesdor.fr).

VISITOR INFORMATION Other than temporary, summer-only kiosks without phones that distribute brochures and advice near the ferry docks in Porquerolles and Port-Cros, the islands do not operate tourist bureaus. The offices in Hyères and Toulon try to fill in the gaps. Contact the **Hyères Office de Tourisme,** 3 av. Ambroise Thomas, Hyères (© **04-94-01-84-50**), or the **Toulon Office de Tourisme,** 12 place Louis Blanc (© **04-94-18-53-00;** fax 04-94-18-53-08; www.toulon tourisme.com).

Île de Porquerolles ★★

This is the largest and westernmost of the Îles d'Hyères. It has a rugged south coast, but the north strand, facing the mainland, is made up of sandy beaches bordered by heather, scented myrtles, and pine trees. The island is about 8km (5 miles) long and 3km (2 miles) wide, and is 5km (3 miles) from the mainland.

The population is less than 400. The island is said to receive 275 days of sunshine annually. It's a land of rocky capes, pine forests twisted by the *mistral,* sun-drenched vineyards, and pale-ocher houses. The hot spots—if any—are the cafes around **place d'Armes,** where everybody gathers.

The island has had a violent history of raids, attacks, and occupation by everybody from the Dutch, English, and Turks to the Spaniards. Ten forts, some in ruins, testify to a violent past. The most ancient is **Fort Ste-Agathe,** built in 1531 by François I. In time it was a penal colony and a retirement center for soldiers of the colonial wars.

The French government purchased the largest hunk of the island in 1971 and turned it into a national park and botanical garden.

WHERE TO STAY & EAT

Hôtel et Résidence Les Medes ★ In the center of the village is this tranquil three-star choice set in a large private garden with a sun deck. Furnishings here are refreshingly modern. Each room and studio has a kitchenette, so it's a convenient place for those wanting to combine restaurant service with self-catering. There are also larger apartments for two to four guests and duplexes for up to six guests. Many of the accommodations contain bunk beds for children. The more desirable units at the back of the hotel have private terraces opening onto the hotel garden. The location is 400m (1,312 ft.) from Courtade Beach and only a short walk from the wharf. Guests gather in the lounge with its bar, fireplace, library, and free Wi-Fi. As well as a popular on-site restaurant, the hotel now has a pool area complete with waterfall. Reduced rates are available for stays of 1 week or longer.

Rue de la Douane, 83400 Porquerolles. www.hotel-les-medes.fr. ✆ **04-94-12-41-24.** Fax 04-94-58-32-49. 30 units. 67€–209€ double; 122€–434€ apt/duplex. MC, V. Closed early Nov–late Dec. **Amenities:** Restaurant; bar; pool; Wi-Fi (free). *In room:* A/C, TV, phone; kitchenette.

Mas du Langoustier ★★ In the midst of a 40-hectare (99-acre) park overlooking a pine-ringed bay, this four-star hotel is set in one of the most enchanted places in Southern France. With such natural advantages, it's a pity that service standards and attention to detail are not as reliable as they should be. Employees greet guests in a covered wagon by the jetty. Guest rooms done in antique Provençal style are the most elegantly decorated on the island. You can drink and dine on the terraces in the more informal **La Pinède** (meals here are included in the half board) or inside the bay-windowed Michelin-starred restaurant **L'Olivier** (meals here are in supplement to the half board). Should you visit just for a meal here, don't miss out on sunset cocktails on the terrace.

83400 Porquerolles. www.langoustier.com. ✆ **04-94-58-30-09.** Fax 04-94-58-36-02. 50 units. 180€–290€ double; 280€–350€ suite. Rates include half board. MC, V. Closed late Sept to late Apr. **Amenities:** 2 restaurants; bar; pool (outdoor); room service. *In room:* A/C, TV, minibar.

Île de Port-Cros ★★★

Lush subtropical vegetation reminiscent of the Caribbean makes this a green paradise, 5km (3 miles) long and 2km (1¼ miles) wide. The most mountainous of the archipelago, Port-Cros has been a French national park since 1963. A fire in 1892 devastated the island, which now abounds with pine forests and ilexes. Birders flock here to observe nearly 100 different species. Day-trippers can explore the many marked trails. The most popular and scenic is ***sentier botanique;*** the more adventurous and athletic take the 10km (6-mile) ***circuit historique*** (bring a packed lunch). Divers follow a 274m (900-ft.) trail from Plage de la Palud to the rocky islet of Rascas, where a plastic guide sheet identifies the underwater flora. Thousands of pleasure craft call here annually, which does little to help the island's fragile environment.

WHERE TO STAY & EAT

With its Caribbean-like ambience, a reliable place to dine on fish is the beachside **La Trinquette** (✆ **04-94-05-93-75;** www.restaurant-trinquette-port-cros.fr).

Le Manoir ★ This is the only bona fide hotel on the island, but despite lack of competition, its owners work hard to make their guests as comfortable as possible. Originally, it functioned as the grandiose home of the family that owned the entire island. Today, the three-star hotel consists of an 18th-century architectural core, plus an annex that contains most of the guest rooms. Accommodations are simple, and bathrooms come equipped with tub/shower combinations. Some rooms have air-conditioning, but rooms don't have televisions. The restaurant serves peppered prawns with artichokes, several seasoned meats, and fresh local fish with baby vegetables, as well as regional goat cheese and velvety mousses. A fixed-price menu costs 56€.

83400 Ile de Port-Cros. http://hotelmanoirportcros.monsite-orange.fr. ✆ **04-94-05-90-52.** Fax 04-94-05-90-89. 22 units. 160€–205€ double; 200€–255€ suite. MC, V. Closed Oct–Apr. **Amenities:** Restaurant; bar; pool (outdoor); room service. *In room:* A/C, hair dryer.

SAINT-TROPEZ ★★

874km (543 miles) S of Paris; 76km (47 miles) SW of Cannes

Pastel-painted Saint-Tropez has two faces. In summer, it's the ultimate celebrity-studded playground whose narrow streets are chockablock with chic shops and restaurants, where day-trippers mingle with the rich, the famous, and the designer-clad. In winter, this north-facing fishing village shuts down to all but the loyal townsfolk brave enough to face the bitter *mistral* wind. It's worth a visit just to ogle the superyachts backed into the picturesque quayside harbor or gaze towards the Alps from the 17th-century citadel. Even though summertime often comes with a large price tag, savvy visitors can enjoy St-Trop without maxing out the credit card.

Beaches Near the town center, the golden sands and shallow waters of **Plage de la Bouillabaisse** and **Plage des Graniers** are ideal for families. The daring **Plage des Salins** and **Plage de Pampelonne** are where the beautiful folk go to burnish their tans under striped parasols. For hedonistic exhibitionism, head to **Tahiti Beach,** on the north end of Pampelonne. Or step over the scantily clad bronzing bodies on **Coco Beach,** a favorite with gay men.

Things to Do St. Tropez's **port** is a requisite stop, a pretty place where luxury yachts bob rhythmically on the shimmering water. Here, don't miss the tiny fish market behind **Porte de la Poissonnerie,** resplendent in mosaics and marble; or the **Ponche** quarters, where fishermen and artists once inhabited narrow, pastel streets. Don't miss the Riviera's best collections of post-Impressionist masters at **Musée de l'Annonciade.**

Eating & Drinking **Place des Lices,** where locals sip pastis and play *pétanques* in the balmy shade of plane trees, is lined with cafes selling France's ubiquitous *steak-frites.* This is also the lair of **La Tarte Tropézienne,** the patisserie that invented St-Trop's famed sticky bun (with the same name as the shop)—a glorious sponge cake filled with orange blossom–infused cream custard. For lip-smacking Mediterranean cuisine and more than 300 wine references, indulge at top chef Alain Ducasse's exclusive **Spoon Byblos.**

Nightlife & Entertainment Start your soirée sipping crisp rosé at **Café Sénéquier,** the venerably stylish epicenter of nightlife around the port. Dress to the nines for a boogie at **Le Papagayo,** one of the largest nightclubs in town. Bump into celebrities at Hôtel Byblos' **Les Caves du Roy,** or order a bottle to share between friends at the all-chromed, all-mirrored **Le VIP Room;** this Parisian outpost is self-consciously trendy but serious fun.

Essentials

GETTING THERE The nearest **rail** station is in St-Raphaël, a neighboring resort, so if you travel here by train, you'll have to finish your journey by boat, bus, or car.

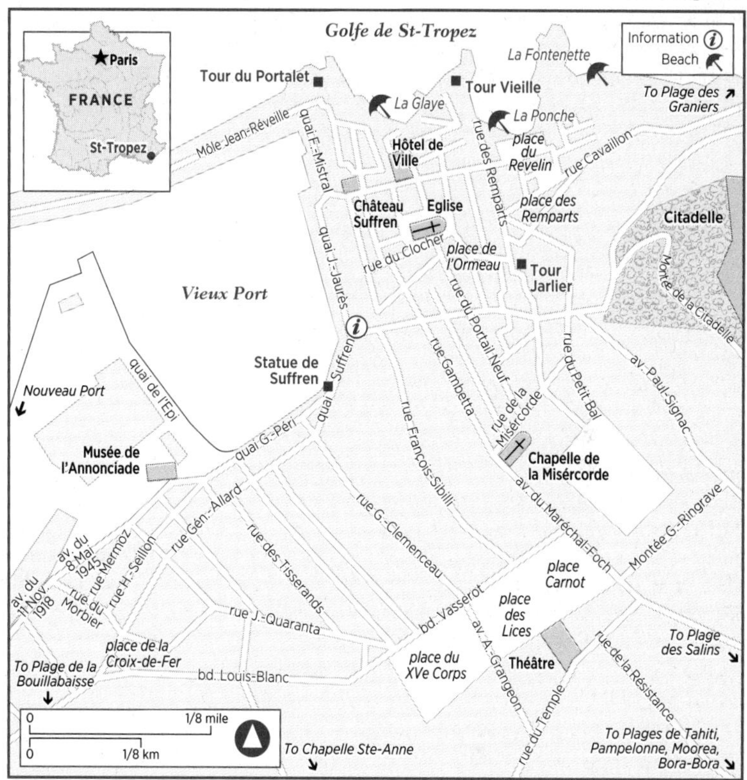

By far the quickest way to get to St-Tropez is by **boat.** There is a service from St-Raphaël to St-Tropez that runs daily from June to September (Oct–May Tues and Sat mornings only). **Boats** leave the Gare Maritime de St-Raphaël in Vieux Port (✆ **04-94-95-17-46**) for St-Tropez (trip time 1 hr.). The one-way fare is 14€. There is also the **Trans Côte d'Azur** (✆ **04-92-98-71-30;** www.trans-cote-azur.com) boat service, which takes 1¼ hours from Cannes for 42€, and 2½ hours from Nice for 56€. There are once-a-day departures to both destinations from Tuesday to Sunday July to mid-September, and Tuesday, Thursday, Saturday, and Sunday in June and late September. There is also a Monday departure in peak season from Cannes. Daily **Bâteaux Verts** (✆ **04-94-49-29-39**) boats ply between Sainte-Maxime and St-Tropez; there are departures every 15 to 20 minutes from 8am until midnight in peak season. The journey takes just 15 minutes. From April to October, there are also daily services from Port Grimaud, Les Marines de Cogolin, and Les Issambres.

The cheapest way to get to St-Tropez is by **bus. VarLib** buses depart from St-Raphaël bus station, 100 rue Victor Hugo (✆ **04-94-44-52-70**), for St-Tropez. The trip takes 1½ to 2¼ hours, depending on the bus and the traffic (which during midsummer is usually horrendous). Buses also run direct from Toulon-Hyères Airport and Nice Airport.

Hilltop Villages

When you're bored of sunbathing, head inland to discover hilltop views, medieval stone-built houses, and pretty squares shaded by linden trees where you can savor rosé wine. The *villages perchés* of Ramatuelle, Grimaud, and Gassin are all within striking distance of St-Tropez. Further along the coastline towards Hyères, Bormes-les-Mimosas, famed for its canary-yellow mimosa flowers, is worth a stop.

If you're **driving** from Cannes, take the A8 motorway before cutting south at exit 38 onto the D37 towards Fréjus, then briefly on the D98b around Fréjus before reaching the D1098 that takes you all the way to Sainte-Maxime, then the N98 to Port Grimaud and finally the D98a into St-Tropez. If you drive, note that parking in St-Tropez is very difficult, especially in summer. You can park in the **Parking des Lices** (✆ **04-94-97-34-46**), beneath place des Lices; enter on avenue Paul-Roussel. Many visitors with expensive cars prefer this lot, because it's more secure than any other. **Parking du Port,** avenue Charles de Gaulle, stands at the waterfront. Every municipal engineer in St-Tropez has worked hard to funnel incoming traffic toward either of these two underground garages.

VISITOR INFORMATION The **Office de Tourisme** is on quai Jean-Jaurès (✆ **04-94-97-45-21;** fax 04-94-97-82-66; www.ot-saint-tropez.com).

SPECIAL EVENTS Many towns in Provence have a ***bravade*** ("act of defiance") in their event calendar. Arguably the biggest and best is the one that takes place in St-Tropez in May, in celebration of the Tropezian army who protected the port from invaders during the Renaissance. Men dress up in old-fashioned military uniforms and women in Provençal costumes to march through the streets firing muskets, playing whistles, and banging drums. St-Tropez's tourist season finishes with the **Voiles de Saint Tropez** yacht festival in late September to early October. For more information on both events, call ✆ **08-92-68-48-28** or visit www.ot-saint-tropez.com.

Exploring the Town

Near the junction of quai Suffren and quai Jean-Jaurès stands the bronze **Statue de Suffren,** paying tribute to Vice-Admiral Pierre André de Suffren. This St-Tropez native became one of the greatest sailors of the 18th-century France, though he's largely forgotten today. In the Vieille Ville, one of the most interesting streets is **rue de la Miséricorde.** It's lined with boutiques set in stone houses. This street evokes medieval St-Tropez better than any other in town. At the corner of rue Gambetta is the **Chapelle de la Miséricorde,** with a blue, green, and gold tile roof.

Three kilometers (2 miles) east of St-Tropez, **Port Grimaud ★** makes an interesting outing. From St-Tropez, drive 4km (2½ miles) west on D98A, and then 1.5km (1 mile) north on D559 to the Port Grimaud exit. If you approach the village at dusk, when it's bathed in Riviera pastels, it looks like a hamlet from the 16th century. But this is a mirage. Port Grimaud is the dream of its promoter, François Spoerry, who carved it out of marshland and dug canals. Flanking these canals, fingers of land extend from the square to the sea. The homes are Provençal style, many with Italianate window arches. Boat owners can anchor at their doorsteps. One newspaper called the port "the most magnificent fake since Disneyland." Most shops and restaurants in Port Grimaud are closed between October and March.

Musée de l'Annonciade (Musée St-Tropez) ★★★ Near the harbor, this museum occupies the former chapel of the Annonciade. It houses one of the Riviera's finest art collections of post-Impressionist masters. Many of the artists, including Paul Signac, depicted the port of St-Tropez. The collection includes such works as van Dongen's *In the Plaza, Women at the Balustrade,* and paintings and sculpture by Bonnard, Matisse, Braque, Dufy, Utrillo, Seurat, Derain, and Maillol.

Place Grammont. ✆ **04-94-17-84-10.** Admission 5€ adults, 3€ children 12–17; free children 11 and under. July–Sept daily 10am–noon and 2–6pm; Oct–June Wed–Mon 10am–noon and 2–6pm.

Outdoor Pursuits

BICYCLING & MOTORSCOOTERING One of the best outfitters is **Rolling Bikes,** 14 av. Général Leclerc (✆ **04-94-97-09-39;** www.rolling-bikes.com). Deposits, depending on the model, range from 950€ to 3,500€. Rentals are for 24 hours: Scooter rentals cost from 40€ to 60€, and motorcycles rent for 120€.

BOATING The highly recommended **Suncap Company,** Passage du Port (✆ **04-94-97-11-23;** www.suncap.fr), rents boats from 12m (39 ft.) long. All rentals come with a captain at the helm. Prices begin at 3,000€ per day.

GOLF The nearest golf course, at the edge of Ste-Maxime, across the bay, is the **Golf Club de Beauvallon,** boulevard des Collines (✆ **04-94-96-16-98;** www.golf-club-de-beauvallon.com), a popular 18-hole course. Greens fees are 75€ per person. Sprawling over a rocky, vertiginous landscape that requires a golf cart and a lot of exertion is the Don Harradine–designed **Golf de Ste-Maxime,** route du Débarquement, Ste-Maxime (✆ **04-94-55-02-02**). It welcomes nonguests; phone to reserve tee times. Greens fees cost 66€ to 75€ for 18 holes per person, and 47€ to 53€ for 9 holes.

TENNIS Anyone who phones in advance can use the eight courts (artificial grass or "Quick," a form of concrete) at the **Tennis-Club de St-Tropez,** route des Plages (✆ **04-94-97-15-52**), less than a kilometer (about ½ mile) from the resort's center. Open year-round, the courts rent for 20€ per hour for green set or 25€ per hour for clay, from 9am to 8pm.

A Day at the Beach

The hottest Riviera beaches are in St-Tropez. One of the most daring beaches is the 9.5km (6-mile) long **Plage de Pampelonne.** This is the most outrageous, the sexiest, and the most exhibitionist (not for children) of the beaches of St-Tropez. At Pampelonne, about 35 businesses are on a 4.8km (3-mile) stretch, located about 10km (6¼ miles) from St-Tropez. Famous hedonistic spots along Pampelonne include the cash-only club **La Voile Rouge** (✆ **04-94-79-84-34**), which features bawdy spring break–style entertainment. Also thriving are the idyllic **Club 55,** boulevard Patch (✆ **04-94-55-55-55**), and the ultramodern **Nikki Beach** (✆ **04-94-79-82-04;** www.nikkibeach.com/sttropez). Maintained by an American from Miami, Nikki Beach is hip, frenetic, and about as Floridian a venue as you're likely to find in the south of France.

Notoriously decadent **Plage de Tahiti** occupies the north end of the 5.5km-long (3½-mile) Pampelonne, lined with concessions, cafes, and restaurants. It's a strip of golden sand long favored by hedonistic exhibitionists wearing next to nothing (or nothing) and cruising shamelessly. If you ever wanted to go topless, this is the place to do it.

The best beaches for families are closest to the center, including the **Plage de la Bouillabaisse** and **Plage des Graniers. Plage des Jumeaux** (✆ **04-94-55-21-80;** www.plagedesjumeaux.com) is another active beach, drawing many families with young kids because it has playground equipment. **Marine Air Sport** (✆ **04-94-97-89-19;** www.marine-air-sport.com) rents boats; **Sun Force** (✆ **04-94-79-90-11;** www.sunforce.fr) rents jet skis, scooters, water-skiing equipment, and boats.

Gay men tend to gravitate to **Coco Beach** in Ramatuelle, about 6.5km (4 miles) from the center of St-Tropez.

Shopping

St-Tropez is dense with stylish shops tucked in out-of-the-way corners of the Old Town. Big names include **Hermès** in place Georges Grammont, next to the Musée de l'Annonciade (✆ **04-94-97-04-29**) and **Dior** (✆ **04-98-12-67-67**), which moved into new premises on place de la Garonne in 2011.

Rue François Sibilli is the most designer-conscious street: It's home to **Giorgio Armani** at no. 44 (✆ **04-94-19-35-53**), **Louis Vuitton** (✆ **04-94-55-40-36**), and Southern French fashion label **Façonnable** at no. 6 (✆ **04-94-97-44-95**).

Rue Gambetta is lined with upmarket clothing shops, including **DVF** at no. 15 (✆ **04-94-96-68-30**), **Vilebrequin** at no. 24 (✆ **04-94-97-62-04**) for fashionable swimming trunks, and **Tartine et Chocolat** at no. 3 (✆ **04-94-43-88-96**) for immaculate kids' clothes. At no. 40 (✆ **06-11-80-12-42**) is an art gallery filled with the vibrant collages of renowned Hungarian-born artist **Ivan Hor,** who has spent the last 4 decades in St-Tropez with his wife and fellow artist Valérie Pons—you can find her charming childlike paintings at Ivan Hor's second shop at 20 rue des Remparts.

Take a quick coffee break at **place des Lices** before exploring its shops. Here, you'll find **Terre et Mer** (✆ **04-94-55-57-78**), the perfect place to stock up on white-linen clothes to channel St-Tropez summer chic, **BCBG Max Azria** (✆ **04-94-97-63-91;** www.bcbgmaxazriagroup.com) for a last-minute evening ensemble; and **Swarovski** (✆ **04-94-56-40-89;** www.swarovski.com) for crystal jewelry.

Hat makers Oska and Imogen Truffaux have brought their award-winning handwoven hats to St-Tropez all the way from Ecuador. At **Truffaux,** 5 rue Ste-Anne (✆ **06-69-55-86-54;** www.truffaux.com), Panama hats, fedoras, and trilbys are fitted to your head in the shop with the help of the on-site steamer.

Le Palais du Cigares, 20 quai de L'Epi (✆ **04-94-97-79-05**), just near the Capitainerie, houses a good selection of cigars and whiskeys, while **Cave Jeroboam**

Supermarket Sweep

If you're renting an apartment or plan to do some cooking on your own, you'll want to stop in at a local supermarket. Most supermarkets in central St-Tropez are open 7 days a week, with a lunchtime closure during winter. The major supermarkets are **Monoprix,** 9 av. Général Leclerc (www.monoprix.fr); **Petit Casino,** rue Général Allard and 13 rue des Commerçants; and **SPAR,** place des Lices (www.spar.fr).

in place de la Croix de Fer (✆ **04-94-49-17-54**) is the best place for stocking up on champagne.

An **outdoor market** with food, clothes, and *brocante* (second-hand goods) takes place on Tuesday and Saturday mornings on place des Lices. This is one of the best Provençal markets in the south of France, with more than 100 vendors selling everything from tableware to homemade bread. The fish, vegetable, and flower market is down a tiled alley (place aux Herbes) behind the tourist office. It operates daily 8am to noon in summer and Tuesday to Sunday 8am to noon in winter.

Where to Stay

St-Tropez is famous for its eye-popping hotel prices. If you're looking for a bargain, it's best to stay out of season—prices double to quadruple for the summer season. Cheap summertime accommodation does exist in the two- and three-star category but you should be prepared for simple furnishings.

Another anomaly of St-Tropez is the huge variety of room sizes and bathrooms, even within the same room category. The reason is that many hotels (from Hôtel Byblos to La Ponche) are constructed from the amalgamation of historic village houses. Some standard rooms can be 50% larger than others and some standard bathrooms offer bath and shower where others offer just a small shower. Where appropriate, you'll find recommendations for individual room numbers and descriptions to help your choices.

VERY EXPENSIVE

Château de la Messardière ★★★ Reminiscent of a fairytale Loire castle, this 19th-century turreted château with 25 acres of beautifully landscaped gardens is one of St-Tropez's most popular five-star hotels. The uninspiring interior design of some bedrooms and the garish yellow entrance hall don't live up to the exceptional beauty of the surroundings. However, any shortfalls are swiftly forgotten over dinner on the terrace gazing down upon umbrella pines towards the magnificent Ramatuelle coastline. There are 12 categories of rooms, from Small Room to Park Suite. All have comfortable beds, while renovated rooms offer both bath and shower. A crescent of West Indies–styled bedrooms with high white-beamed ceilings curve around the mosaic-tiled outdoor pool. Contemporary mosaics also decorate a second indoor pool next to the La Prairie and Cinq Mondes spa—arguably the best spa in St-Tropez. Welcoming staff and a well-run shuttle bus to the place des Lices and to a private beach complete the picture.

Route de Tahiti, 83990 St-Tropez. www.messardiere.com. ✆ **04-94-56-76-00.** Fax 04-94-56-76-01. 118 units. 260€–920€ double; from 660€ suite. AE, DC, MC, V. Free parking (covered parking 30€). Closed Nov to week before Easter. **Amenities:** 2 restaurants; bar; art gallery; babysitting; spa; 2 pools (outdoor and indoor); room service. *In room:* A/C, TV, hair dryer, minibar, Wi-Fi (free).

Hôtel Byblos ★★★ You know you've arrived at St-Tropez's most famous hotel when you spot the numerous Bentleys and Ferraris parked outside. Hôtel Byblos is perfect for the party crowd who appreciate its celebrity-spotting ambience and its easy entry into the hotel's stellar nightclub, Les Caves du Roy (p. 215). Painted in the shades of Provence, its trademark multicolored village houses curve around a central courtyard with a swimming pool and bar. It's filled with beautiful and rare details, like carved woodwork, marquetry floors, and a Persian-rug ceiling. The hotel oozes luxury, from famed chef Alain Ducasse's restaurant, Spoon Byblos (p. 212), to the Sisley spa. Rooms vary in size from medium to spacious, and many have high ceilings and antiques or reproductions. The smallest Classic rooms can be surprisingly generous—no. 519 has a small terrace. My favorite Deluxe suite is no. 611, with its Asian-inspired decor and two balconies offering sea and pool views. Suites in the stylish Hameau annex are more private, but can be noisy due to their proximity to the nightclub.

Av. Paul Signac, 83990 St-Tropez. www.byblos.com. ✆ **04-94-56-68-00.** Fax 04-94-56-68-01. 91 units, 410€–990€ double; from 650€ suite. AE, DC, MC, V. Parking 30€. Closed mid-Oct to mid-Apr. **Amenities:** 2 restaurants; 2 bars; babysitting; concierge; health club and spa; pool (outdoor); room service. *In room:* A/C, TV, hair dryer, minibar, Wi-Fi (free).

Hôtel La Résidence de la Pinède ★★★ This is possibly the only four-star hotel in the world that makes its five-star competitors look like a good value. It attracts a more reserved clientele than rival Hôtel Byblos with its palatial accommodations, glorious beach, and its restaurant, La Vague d'Or, the only two-star Michelin restaurant in St-Tropez. Offering postcard views over the bay of St-Tropez, this Small Leading Hotels of the World hotel was built in the 1950s around a rustic stone-sided tower once used to store olives. Jean-Claude and Nicole Delion are the owners of this luxurious place on the seaside, as well as its sister hotel, **La Réserve** (p. 218) in Beaulieu-sur-Mer. The airy, spacious rooms open onto balconies or terraces with sea views. The stylish but offhand staff seems constantly overburdened.

Plage de la Bouillabaisse, 83990 St-Tropez. www.residencepinede.com. ✆ **04-94-55-91-00.** Fax 04-94-97-73-64. 39 units. 395€–965€ double; 800€ suite. AE, DC, MC, V. Free parking. Closed early Oct to April. **Amenities:** 2 restaurants; bar; babysitting; pool (outdoor); private beach; room service. *In room:* A/C, TV, hair dryer, minibar, Wi-Fi (free).

Hôtel Le Yaca ★ This four-star hotel embodies *la dolce vita.* Built in 1722 off a narrow street in the old part of town, this was the first hotel in St-Tropez. Colette lived for a few weeks here in 1927, and before that it was the temporary address of pre-Impressionists such as Paul Signac. The high-ceilinged reception area and many of the rooms overlook a flower-filled inner courtyard. Each of the small to medium-size rooms has a comfortable bed, utilitarian furniture, and high ceilings, and most have a roomy bathroom. Those on the upper level have terra-cotta tiles and massive ceiling timbers. Located a 5-minute walk away on avenue Paul Signac, the Yaca has a sister hotel, Le Y, that takes the overflow of summer guests from Easter to August.

1 bd. d'Aumale, 83900 St-Tropez. www.hotel-le-yaca.fr. ✆ **04-94-55-81-00.** Fax 04-94-97-58-50. 28 units. 275€–795€ double; 795€–1,695€ suite. AE, DC, MC, V. Parking 25€. **Amenities:** Restaurant; bar; babysitting; pool (outdoor); room service. *In room:* A/C, TV, hair dryer, minibar, Wi-Fi (free).

Hôtel Villa Belrose ★★★ 🎁 Small-scale and luxe, Hôtel Villa Belrose is set within a sloping garden in Gassin, an upscale residential neighborhood within a 10-minute drive northwest of St-Tropez. It was built in 1997 in a peachy replica of a Florentine villa, with views that sweep from most of the bedrooms out over the gulf of St-Tropez. Guest rooms are lavishly and opulently accessorized with fine linens and lots of upscale toiletries in the bathrooms. Standard rooms fall midway along the spectrum of being either cozy or cramped, depending on your point of view. Superior rooms are twice the size of standard rooms, so it's worth paying extra for the size upgrade. In many cases, glass doors open onto private terraces, a well-landscaped garden, and magnificently ethereal views. Much of the establishment's identity derives from its elegant Michelin-starred restaurant, open daily for lunch and dinner to nonresidents with reservations in advance. Chef Thierry Thiercelin creates Mediterranean cuisine that's as chic as St-Tropez itself.

Gassin, St-Tropez. www.villabelrose.com. ✆ **04-94-55-97-97.** Fax 04-94-55-97-98. 40 units. 390€–850€ double; 1,200€–2,500€ suite. AE, DC, MC, V. Free outdoor parking; indoor parking 30€. Closed Nov to the week before Easter. **Amenities:** 2 restaurants; babysitting; spa; pool (outdoor); room service. *In room:* A/C, TV, hair dryer, minibar, Wi-Fi (free).

La Réserve Ramatuelle ★★★ This secret hideaway with a deluxe spa right near St-Tropez attracts the glitterati to its precincts. All the accommodations are gorgeously ultramodern. As well as rooms and suites, there are 11 villas, each with its own pool set in landscaped gardens. The five-star property opens onto views of the Mediterranean as far as the eye can see. A hedonistic atmosphere permeates the place; the 4-day rejuvenation program at the spa is the height of sybaritic indulgence. There's a 3-night minimum stay policy.

Chemin de la Quessine, 83350 Ramatuelle. www.lareserve-ramatuelle.com. ✆ **04-94-44-94-44.** Fax 04-94-44-94-45. 23 units, 12 villas. 550€–980€ double; 1,050€ suite; from 15,000€ villa for 1 week. AE, DC, MC, V. Free parking. **Amenities:** Restaurant; bar; concierge; health club and spa; 2 pools (indoor and outdoor); room service. *In room:* A/C, TV, hair dryer, minibar, Wi-Fi (free).

Pan Deï Palais ★★★ For privacy in a central location, you can't beat Pan Deï Palais. With only 12 bedrooms, it feels more like a decadent private house than a hotel—indeed, it's frequently rented out by well-heeled families for exclusive use. The Indian-inspired decor is set beside the pool with its thatched-roof pool beds and Indian umbrellas. Bedrooms vary from small to spacious. All feature dark sculpted woods, brightly colored throws over pristine white linen, Indonesian rugs, and Bulgari bathroom products. It's worth splashing out on a Prestige room that is twice the size of the rather small Standard rooms. The base of the pool lifts up on summer evenings to make room for the outdoor Asian restaurant (external visitors are allowed access to the hotel from 7pm only). There's even a miniature Valmont spa and *hammam.*

52 rue Gambetta, 83990 St-Tropez. www.pandei.com. ✆ **04-94-17-71-71.** 12 units. 195€–1,155€ double; from 560€ suite. AE, DC, MC, V. Parking 32€. **Amenities:** Restaurant; bar; babysitting; spa; pool (outdoor); room service. *In room:* A/C, TV, hair dryer, minibar, Wi-Fi (free).

EXPENSIVE

The popular **Hôtel La Mistralée** (www.hotel-mistralee.com), on avenue du Général Leclerc, is due to reopen in summer 2012 after a change of ownership.

Hôtel La Maison Blanche ★ Originally designed as a private villa late in the 19th century, this small and elegant government-rated four-star hotel enjoys a superbly convenient location directly beside the most visible square in St-Tropez, the place des Lices. Charming details include the in-house bar that serves only champagne and an 18th-century fountain that was found on-site. The rooms are comfortable and stylish, but have limited views. Apart from its champagne bar, the hotel provides no other luxury amenities such as restaurant, pool, or spa. In light of the resources of St-Tropez that lie in virtually every direction, no one seems to mind.

Place des Lices, 83990 St-Tropez. www.hotellamaisonblanche.com. ✆ **04-94-97-52-66.** Fax 04-94-97-89-23. 9 units. 180€–460€ double; 350€–890€ suite. Extra bed 60€–90€. AE, DC, MC, V. Parking 30€. **Amenities:** Champagne bar. *In room:* A/C, TV, hair dryer, Wi-Fi (free).

Hôtel La Ponche ★★ Overlooking the port, this cozy family-run four-star hotel has long been a favorite of ours. It's the most discreet, most charming, and least flashy establishment in town, yet numerous celebrities from Brigitte Bardot to Jack Nicholson have passed through its doors over the years—each room is named after a famous guest. Rooms are well equipped and open onto sea views. Sun-colored walls with subtle lighting lend a homey feeling. Despite its miniature shower room, my favorite room is Romy Schneider, with its large terrace with views over the citadel, the sea, and the rooftops of St-Tropez. The largest standard rooms are nos. 10, 15, and 16. In a neighboring annex, there are also two junior suites (nos. 18 and 19) that offer mini-kitchenettes. The canvas-covered restaurant may seem old-fashioned, but the food is delicious and the sea views are fine.

3 rue des Remparts, 83990 St-Tropez. www.laponche.com. ✆ **04-94-97-02-53.** Fax 04-94-97-78-61. 18 units. 185€–510€ double; 260€–655€ suite. AE, MC, V. Parking 20€. Closed Nov to mid-Feb. **Amenities:** Restaurant; bar; babysitting. *In room:* A/C, TV, hair dryer, minibar, Wi-Fi (free).

La Bastide de St-Tropez ★★★ Near the landmark place des Lices, this tile-roofed replica of a Provençal manor house is home to an opulent Relais & Châteaux hotel. A monumental staircase leads from a sun-filled living room to the upper floors. The guest rooms are named according to their individual decor: Rose of Bengal, Fuchsia, or Tangerine Dawn. Each has a terrace or private garden, and some have Jacuzzis. Several are quite small. The soft beds under fine quilting with matching draperies are among the most luxurious in St-Tropez. The well-appointed bathrooms have deluxe toiletries. The hotel is noted for its restaurant, L'Olivier. This hotel has its own yacht, *San Lorenzo* 72, which you can hire for the day.

Rte. des Carles, 83990 St-Tropez. www.bastide-saint-tropez.com. ✆ **04-94-55-82-55.** Fax 04-94-97-21-71. 26 units. 250€–550€ double; 335€–850€ suite. AE, DC, MC, V. Free parking. Closed Jan. **Amenities:** Restaurant; bar; babysitting; pool (outdoor); room service; yacht. *In room:* A/C, TV, hair dryer, minibar, Wi-Fi (free).

Pastis Hotel-St-Tropez ★★ Two expat Brits, John and Pauline Larkin, have taken a portside Provençal house and transformed it into a chic little inn. They have decorated it in a sophisticated eclectic style, even including their collection of framed albums of the Sex Pistols and the Rolling Stones. The courtyard pool is the focal point for socializing guests sipping aperitifs. The rooms are also furnished in an eclectic mix, and each unit comes with a spacious bathroom as well as a balcony or breakfast terrace. Some accommodations are large enough for extra beds or cots. Indian rugs, Chinese armoires, and beds adorned with Provençal *boutis* (quilts) enhance the warm, intimate ambience. Although the hotel doesn't have a restaurant, the staff prepares breakfast and light lunches for guests. Best-selling author Peter Mayle, whose writings have drawn thousands to visit Provence, occasionally drops by this boutique hotel.

61 av. du Général Leclerc. 83990 St-Tropez. www.pastis-st-tropez.com. ✆ **04-98-12-56-50.** Fax 04-94-96-99-82. 9 units. 175€–600€ double. AE, MC, V. Free parking. **Amenities:** Pool (outdoor). *In room:* A/C, TV.

MODERATE

Hôtel des Lices ★ This modern hotel, just off place des Lices, is a consistently reliable bet. The contemporary Provençal rooms are tranquil and comfortable, overlooking either the outdoor pool or the small private garden; their rates vary widely according to season, size, and view. There's even a three-bedroom villa that sleeps up to seven people. Breakfast is the only meal served, although lunchtime snacks are provided beside the pool.

135 av. Augustin-Grangeon, 83993 St-Tropez. www.hoteldeslices.com. ✆ **04-94-97-28-28.** Fax 04-94-97-59-52. 42 units. 130€–270€ double; 260€–400€ suite. AE, MC, V. Free parking. Closed mid-Nov to mid-Dec. **Amenities:** Restaurant; bar; babysitting; pool (outdoor). *In room:* A/C, TV, Wi-Fi (free).

Hôtel Le Mouillage ★★ Overlooking Bouillabaisse beach, this three-star boutique hotel offers the best *rapport-qualité-prix* (quality-to-price ratio) along the

St-Trop peninsula. Charming owners Jean-Claude and Pascale Pepino have a flair for interior design: rooms with private terraces are decorated around southern themes. There are trickling fountains beside the pool and on the verdant terrace with its rattan sofas. Copious breakfasts and free on-site parking are bonuses.

Port du Pilon, 83993 St-Tropez. www.hotelmouillage.fr. ✆ **04-94-97-53-19.** 10 units. 100€–280€ double; 200€–450€ suite. AE, MC, V. Free parking. Closed mid-Nov to mid-Dec and Jan. **Amenities:** Bar; pool (outdoor). *In room:* A/C, TV, minibar, safe, Wi-Fi (free).

Hôtel Sube If you want to be right on the port in a perfect ship- and celebrity-watching location, this three-star hotel fits the bill. It's directly over the Café de Paris bar in the center of a shopping arcade. The two-story bar has a beamed ceiling and a glass front, allowing for a great view of the harbor. Breakfast is served here in the mornings, while mojitos and margaritas are the most popular evening tipples. The bedroom decor is tired and bedspreads need updating, but the bathrooms are clean. The more expensive units have scenic views of the port.

15 quai de Suffren, 83900 St-Tropez. www.hotelsube.net. ✆ **04-94-97-30-04.** Fax 04-94-54-89-09. 28 units. 140€–320€ double. AE, MC, V. Parking nearby 30€. **Amenities:** Cafe; bar. *In room:* A/C, TV.

INEXPENSIVE

Hôtel Les Palmiers The best thing about this inexpensive hotel is its location overlooking the place des Lices. Bedrooms are clean, but plainly furnished. Priced according to size, smaller rooms represent the best value. The bamboo-lined courtyard is the perfect place to laze around on chocolate-colored sofas over summertime drinks. There's limited free parking; otherwise you'll need to park in one of the public car parks nearby.

24–26 bd. Vasserot (overlooking place des Lices), 83900 St-Tropez. www.hotel-les-palmiers.com. ✆ **04-94-97-01-61.** Fax 04-94-97-10-02. 25 units. 75€–240€ double. AE, MC, V. Free parking (5 places only). **Amenities:** Outdoor bar. *In room:* A/C, TV, minibar, Wi-Fi (free).

Hôtel Lou Cagnard ★ This pleasant roadside inn, with a tile roof and green shutters, offers quiet rooms in the rear overlooking the gravel courtyard. Monsieur and Madame Yvon are the hardworking owners, explaining to newcomers the translation of the name of their hotel (*Lou Cagnard,* in Provençal dialect, means "The hot, burning sun"). They extend a warm welcome to their guests. Although nothing is grand about the bedrooms, they are comfortable, with fine mattresses and well-maintained bathrooms with adequate shelf space. Not all rooms have air-conditioning, so it's worth checking this when booking. This hotel is a bargain in pricey St-Trop. A 5-minute walk from the place des Lices, the hotel has a large on-site car park.

18 av. Paul-Roussel, 83990 St-Tropez. www.hotel-lou-cagnard.com. ✆ **04-94-97-04-24.** Fax 04-94-97-09-44. 19 units. 58€–148€ double. MC, V. Free parking. Closed Nov–Dec 26. **Amenities:** Lounge. *In room:* A/C (except 4 rooms), TV, Wi-Fi (free).

Where to Eat

For Michelin-starred extravagance, head to **Hôtel La Résidence de la Pinède** (p. 208) or **Hôtel Villa Belrose** (p. 208). As a general guideline, many top restaurants and hotels open from Easter to the Voiles de Saint Tropez yacht show at the end of September.

You can grab a quick continental breakfast (that's usually cheaper than hotel breakfasts) of *pain-au-chocolat,* freshly squeezed orange juice, and a coffee at a cafe along the port, where you can watch the yachts, or in the place des Lices. Cafes on the town-center side of the place des Lices get the morning sunshine. From Tuesday to

Saturday, you'll be able to watch the food and flower market in full flow as you eat. This square is also a good place to stock up on picnic items or grab a cheap snack. At the **Petit Marché** permanent stalls, you'll find spit roast chickens, paella, salads, and prepared dishes, while nearby **Delices des Lices** sells panini and salads, and **Aroma** offers take-away pizzas. For dessert, pop into **La Tarte Tropézienne** to buy the eponymously named custard-filled tart beloved by Brigitte Bardot.

EXPENSIVE

Auberge des Maures PROVENÇALE Gaze upon murals of lavender fields as you dine at this idyllic restaurant that's been open since 1931. The seating capacity doubles when the roof is rolled away in good weather and tables are set up in the garden with views of the moon, stars, splashing fountains, and ornamental shrubbery. The interior decor changes with the seasons—our Easter-time visit timed with a festive display of newly hatched chicks. The hardworking staff in the kitchen are on display as they churn out unashamedly traditional Provençal dishes. Menu items include grilled versions of many kinds of fresh fish and meat, and often taste best when preceded with starters such as *panache provençale,* with piled deep-fried zucchini blossoms; hearts of artichoke *barigoule* (cooked in a mushroom sauce); and a medley of *petits farcis* (stuffed vegetables).

4 rue du Docteur Boutin. ✆ **04-94-97-01-50.** www.aubergedesmaures.fr. Reservations recommended. Main courses 40€–60€; fixed-price menu 52€. AE, DC, MC, V. Daily 7:30pm–1am. Closed Nov–Mar.

Spoon Byblos ★★ FRENCH/INTERNATIONAL This is one of the many entrepreneurial statements by Alain Ducasse, considered by some to be the world's greatest chef—or at least the most acclaimed. The cuisine here draws special inspiration from the food of Catalonia, Andalusia, Lebanon, Greece, and Italy; Byblos also offers more than 300 wines from around the world. Background music ranges from hip-hop to the hits of the '70s. The restaurant opens onto a circular bar made of blue-tinted glass and polished stainless steel. It's all terribly fashionable, although you may grow a bit weary of its self-conscious sense of chic after an hour or two within its ultradesigned premises. Dig into shellfish ravioli in a spicy tomato syrup, followed by roasted John Dory. Romantics may like to share dishes designed for two such as the oven-baked sea bream, pan-fried Black Angus beef, or the Nutella éclair. You may top off a meal with the chef's favorite cheesecake. Valet parking is available in July and August.

In the Hôtel Byblos (p. 207), av. Maréchal Foch. ✆ **04-94-56-68-20.** www.byblos.com. Reservations required. Main courses 25€–49€; fixed-price menu 86€. AE, DC, MC, V. Daily 8pm–12:30am. Closed Nov–Mar.

Villa Romana ★★ INTERNATIONAL/ITALIAN This is where the St-Tropez party scene breaks for dinner; it's behind place des Lices, close to the nightclub Les Caves du Roy. The Italian cuisine here hardly ranks with the best you've ever had, but watching the (often scantily clad) patrons makes for the most amusing dinner in town. The place looks like Hugh Hefner designed it for his Playboy Mansion. Tycoons, wannabes, tabloid celebrities, and yachties look up as each new diner enters. The international menu is designed to cater to the full range of diners' pockets, from cash-strapped starlets to billionaires. When we went, the caviar served with cold blini was an eye-wateringly expensive disappointment. We think your best bet is to stick with pizzas and homemade pastas. In summer wear your skimpiest attire (that goes for men and women alike). A free shuttle service will pick you up from your hotel and will even drop you back home or at the nightclub of your choice.

Joseph & the Golden Feast

The St-Tropez dining scene has had a shake-up since the retirement of famous Dutch restaurateur Joseph. His mini-empire of restaurants was split up during 2010 and 2011: Restaurant L'Escale (see below, formerly known as Le Quai Joseph) has been sold to Alp'Azur Hôtels (www.alpazurhotels.com). On the corner of rue Sibille, the reins of Le Grand Joseph (✆ 04-94-97-01-66; www.grand-joseph-saint-tropez.com) have been passed to Joseph's sister. This popular restaurant may no longer be the class act it once was, but it's still an essential fixture on the St-Tropez scene for a pre- or post-dinner cocktail while listening to DJ Remy mixing '80s music with R&B.

Chemin des Conquettes (near the corner of av. Paul Roussel, a short walk southwest of place des Lices). ✆ **04-94-97-15-50.** Reservations required. Main courses 36€–3,000€; pizzas/pasta 20€–35€. MC, V. Easter to early Oct daily 8–2am.

Restaurant L'Escale ★ SEAFOOD You dine with sand beneath your toes (the floor is covered with a layer of golden sand) at this stylish portside restaurant. Beige suede chairs, huge silver candlesticks, and vases of lilies add to the chic decor. The menu focuses on grilled fish and seafood. Service is prompt and the fish is fresh. What more could you ask for?

Quai Jean-Jaurès. ✆ **04-94-9700-63.** Main courses 22€–55€; fixed-priced menu 39€. MC, V. Daily noon–2pm and 7pm–10pm.

MODERATE

Chez Fuchs—Le Bistrot d'Olivier ★★ FRENCH Taken over 3 years ago by Olivier Fuchs, this family-run restaurant is in its second generation of business. Beyond the modest entrance bar filled with locals, you'll come across a classic French setting of wooden beams, white-clothed tables, and shelves of wine bottles and glasses. French bistro food at its best is served here: High-quality ingredients are sourced, from the Ramon Pena sardines to the Breton lobster. We usually opt for the daily specials. The wine list is strong on wines from Burgundy and the Rhone valley, as well as Provence.

9 rue de la Citadelle. ✆ **04-94-97-10-11.** Reservations recommended. Main courses 13€–26€. MC, V. Daily 7:30--10pm. Closed Nov–Mar.

Le Bistro ★ MEDITERRANEAN/JAPANESE This popular local hangout is one of the few restaurants that stays open all year around. From the colorful wooden bar and antique suitcases at the entrance to the more formal dining rooms with their Japanese-inspired decor, this restaurant fuses influences from around the globe. You can choose between Mediterranean pasta, fish, and meat dishes, or Japanese sashimi and sushi rolls. Live DJs light up this venue all summer long.

3 place des Lices. ✆ **04-94-97-11-33.** www.bistrot-saint-tropez.com. Main courses 13€–70€; fixed-price menus 18€–35€. MC, V. Daily noon–2:30pm and 7:30–11pm.

Le Girelier PROVENÇALE Chefs David Didelot and Laurent Simon run a smooth ship at this long-standing portside restaurant, whose blue-and-white color scheme has become a trademark. The menu includes seafood platters and whole grilled fish. We'd recommend the mussels and chips or the 17€ lunchtime *plat du jour.* Make sure you book a table in advance overlooking the port (after all, that's what you're paying for). The wine list focuses on Provence. Owner Annie Famose took over

Ice Cream Stop

The best place in St-Tropez to grab an ice cream is Barbarac, 2 Général Allard (✆ 04-94-97-67-83). Tiramisu, Nutella, and Cookies (with whole mini-chocolate cookies inside) are just some of the flavors that might take your fancy. If you're staying nearby, you can even have ice cream home-delivered.

neighboring portside restaurant Le Quai in 2010.

Quai Jean-Jaurès. ✆ **04-94-97-03-87.** Reservations recommended. Main courses 17€–59€; fixed-price menu 25€–39€. AE, DC, MC, V. Daily noon–midnight. Closed Nov–Mar.

Salama ★★ MOROCCAN The smell of incense greets you in this Moorish oasis in central St-Tropez. There are two dining rooms: The first is darkly rich with stone walls and red wall hangings, the second is lighter with a glass ceiling and Moroccan lamps hanging from a tree between the white-clothed tables. The Moroccan food won't disappoint, with signature dishes like lamb tagine with prunes and almonds, and meatballs and egg tagine. Ice creams are from the celebrated Tropézienne ice cream supremo *Barbarac*. If you're feeling daring, try the *Boukha* (fig liqueur). They also serve their own minty version of a mojito, La Salama.

1 rue des Tisserands. ✆ **04-94-97-59-62.** www.restaurant-salama.com. Main courses 21€–31€. MC, V. Daily 7:30–10pm. Closed Nov–Mar.

INEXPENSIVE

Brasserie Tropézienne ★ MEDITERRANEAN Run by Alsace-born Pascal, this reasonably priced brasserie is one of St-Tropez's hidden gems. Locals have been flocking here to dine on simple pasta, steaks, salads, and omelets for almost 2 decades. With tables spilling out onto the pavement, you'll find it on a quiet street behind the Capitainerie du Port. In the evenings, the same venue serves Asian cuisine.

10 rue Henri Seillon. ✆ **04-94-97-01-65.** Main courses 5€–20€. MC, V. Daily noon–4pm and 7pm–3am.

St-Tropez After Dark

Start the evening with a glass of champagne at the summertime Champagne Bar in the courtyard of the chic **Hôtel La Maison Blanche** (✆ **04-94-97-52-66**) in place des Lices.

Below the Hôtel Sube, the **Café de Paris,** quai Suffren (✆ **04-94-97-00-56;** www.cafedeparis.fr), is one of the most popular hangouts. Outside, you'll find tables lining the pedestrianized harbor, while inside you'll find mirrored walls, Parisian bench seating, and a long zinc bar. The crowd is irreverent and animated.

The reporter Leslie Maitland aptly captured the crowd attracted to nearby **Café Sénéquier,** quai Suffren (✆ **04-94-97-20-20**): "What else can one do but gawk at a tall, well-dressed young woman who appears *comme il faut* at Sénéquier's with a large white rat perched upon her shoulder, with which she occasionally exchanges little kisses, while casually chatting with her friends." Look for its trademark red tables and chairs.

Le Bar du Port, quai Suffren, adjacent to the Café de Paris (✆ **04-94-97-00-54**), attracts a consistently young clientele. Expect lots of table hopping, stylishly skimpy clothing, recorded music that may make you want to get up and dance, and insights into what's really going on in the minds of French 20-somethings.

An informal place to grab a beer is **Kelly's Irish Pub,** quai F. Mistral, at the eastern end of the Vieux Port (✆ **04-94-54-89-11**), which draws a mostly foreign crowd.

On the lobby level of the Hôtel Byblos (p. 207), **Les Caves du Roy,** avenue Paul-Signac (✆ **04-94-56-68-00;** www.lescavesduroy.com), is the most self-consciously chic and celebrity-studded nightclub in St-Tropez—and the most famous club in France. Entrance is free, but drink prices begin at a whopping 18€. It's open nightly from Easter to late September from 11:30pm until dawn. **Le Papagayo,** in the Résidence du Port (✆ **04-94-97-95-95;** www.papagayo-st-tropez.com), is one of the largest nightclubs in town and so often has the shortest queue. The decor was inspired by the psychedelic 1960s.

Around the corner from Le Papagayo is a club whose upscale male and female patrons may be equally at home in Les Caves du Roy: **Le VIP Room,** in the Résidence du Port (✆ **06-38-83-83-83;** www.viproom.fr). This celeb-spotting club is all steel, chrome, mirrors, and glass. Expect an active bar area, dance floor, and the kind of social posturing and preening that can be amusing—or not.

Le Pigeonnier, 11 rue de la Ponche (✆ **04-94-96-76-69**), rocks, rolls, and welcomes a crowd that's mostly gay or lesbian, and between 20 and 50. Most of the socializing revolves around the long, narrow bar, where patrons from all over Europe seem to enjoy chit-chat. There's also a dance floor.

SAINTE-MAXIME

24km (15 miles) SW of St-Raphaël; 61km (38 miles) SW of Cannes

Ste-Maxime is just across the gulf from glitzy St-Tropez, but its atmosphere is much less decadent. Endless **Blue Flag** (eco-labeled) beaches, kids' play areas, watersports, and affordable accommodations make this mimosa-strewn seaside resort a desirable option for young families. Surrounded by the red cliffs of the Massif des Maures, the town is protected from harsh weather. The wide stretches of sand and calm waters lure travelers to spend their days basking in the sun and dining out along cafe-lined promenades. Sadly, the main coastal route into St-Tropez runs along the seafront in Sainte-Maxime—avoid this traffic-laden road by opting for the **Bâteaux Verts** that offer a 15-minute boat service straight into central St-Tropez.

Essentials

GETTING THERE Access to the nearest **railway** station is at St-Raphaël. For information about the **buses** that run frequently between St-Raphaël and Ste-Maxime, and from Ste-Maxime on to St-Tropez, call **VarLib** (✆ **04-94-24-60-00;** www.varlib.fr). One-way passage between Ste-Maxime and either St-Raphaël or St-Tropez costs around 2€ per person.

The best way of getting from Ste-Maxime to St-Tropez is by boat. If you're headed to Ste-Maxime from St-Tropez (except Jan to mid-Feb and Nov to mid-Dec), a daily ferryboat service (transit time: 15 min.) costs 7€ per person, each way. For information about these boats, contact **Les Bâteaux Verts,** 14 quai Léon-Condroyer (✆ **04-94-49-29-39;** www.bateauxverts.com).

If you're **driving** from Cannes, take the A8 motorway before cutting south at exit 38 onto the D37 towards Fréjus, then briefly on the D98b around Fréjus before reaching the D1098 that takes you all the way to Sainte-Maxime.

VISITOR INFORMATION The Office de Tourisme is on 1 promenade Simon-Lorière (✆ **04-94-55-75-55;** www.ste-maxime.com).

SPECIAL EVENTS From January to March, Sainte-Maxime joins other towns across the Var in celebrating mimosa, the canary-yellow member of the acacia family that arrived in southern France in the 19th century. Events include flower battles, carnival parades, markets, and "Miss Mimosa" competitions. For more information on the Mimosa Festival, visit www.ste-maxime.com.

Exploring the Town

Start with the 16th-century **La Tour Carrée** at place des Aliziers. It was originally a defensive structure; today it's home to the **Musée des Traditions Locales,** place de l'Eglise (✆ **04-94-96-70-30**), with exhibits on the area's history and tradition. The museum is open Wednesday to Sunday from 10am to noon and 3 to 6pm (until 7pm July–Aug). Admission is 2.30€ for adults and 0.75€ for children 11 and under.

Facing the tower is the **Eglise Ste-Maxime,** place des Aliziers (✆ **04-94-49-06-67**), with a marble altar from the former Carthusian monastery of La Verne in the Massif des Maures. The choir stalls date from the 15th century.

Ste-Maxime is known for its numerous markets. There's a **covered market** selling fruit, vegetables, fish, and flowers that takes place in rue Fernand Bessy (near place du Marché). It's open every morning (and 4:30–8pm Mon–Sat) in summer and Tuesday to Sunday mornings from mid-September to May. On Monday morning, a **Provençal market** is held around avenue Georges Pompidou; on Thursday morning, a **food and crafts market** is held on and around place du Marché; on Friday morning (8am–noon), vendors sell a variety of **knickknacks** on place Jean-Mermoz. In the pedestrian streets of the old town, an **arts-and-crafts fair** takes place daily in summer from 5 to 11pm.

Outside town are several worthy sights. About 10km (6 miles) north in the Parc Saint-Donat on the road to Muy (Rte. de Muy) is the **Musée du Phonographe et de la Musique Méchanique** (✆ **04-94-96-50-52**). This extensive display of audio equipment is the result of one woman's 40-year obsession. Sometimes owner Danielle Munsch gives personal tours. In the museum is one of Edison's original "talking machines" and an audiovisual pantograph used to teach foreign languages in 1913. The museum is open Easter to late September only, Wednesday to Sunday 10am to noon. During July and August, it's also open from 4 to 6:30pm. Admission is 3€ for adults and 1.50€ for children 5 to 12 years.

Families can also enjoy a water-based fun day at **Aqualand** (✆ **04-94-55-54-54;** www.aqualand.fr), a water park on route Plan de la Tour, CD25, Sainte-Maxime.

Outdoor Pursuits

BICYCLING A great way to explore Ste-Maxime is on two wheels with some wind in your hair. Consider visiting **Rent Bike,** 13 rue Magali (✆ **04-94-43-98-07**), which rents bikes and mopeds. Mountain bikes are 12€ per day, with a 150€ deposit; mopeds are 37€, with a 760€ deposit.

HIKING If you're a nature lover, you'll find panoramic views along many hiking trails that wind along the coast or into the mountains, reaching an altitude of 120m (400 ft.). The tourist office has maps and guides, or you can head for the Sentier du Littoral (Chemin des Douaniers), a trail that meanders along the coast toward Fréjus/Saint-Raphaël and has access to the sea at almost all points along the way.

HORSEBACK RIDING Set in the Massif des Maures countryside near Sainte-Maxime, **Les Poneys du Verderet** (✆ **06-83-34-87-66;** www.leverderet.ffe.com) is a great place to go horse-back riding. Highly qualified instructor Valérie Lacaze offers pony rides and lessons for adults and kids. You'll need to wear long trousers and sturdy shoes.

A Day at the Beach

Beaches are the main attraction here in Ste-Maxime. Of the four nearby, two are an easy walk from the town center. Across the road from the casino is **Plage du Centre Ville**—we advise avoiding it because of the fumes from the nearby roadway, the narrow sands, and the hordes of sunbathers. A better bet is **Plage de la Croisette,** a wider, nominally less congested expanse that's a 2-minute walk west of Plage du Centre Ville. The most appealing beaches are the Blue Flag **Plage de la Nartelle** and the adjacent **Plage des Eléphants,** with broad expanses of clean, fine-textured light-beige sand about 2km (1¼ miles) east of town. Both beaches were involved in the 1944 Provence landings, while Plage des Eléphants was immortalized in Sainte-Maxime resident Jean de Brunhoff's "Babar's Travels." To reach them, follow signs along the coastal road pointing to Les Issambres and Fréjus. Here you can rent a mattress for sunbathing from any of several concessionaires for around 10€ to 15€, depending on the beach. Another Blue Flag beach is **Plage de la Garonette.**

Where to Stay

Although hotels are less expensive here than in the neighboring towns, you may find that you must pay for half board in July and August. Most places are closed in winter, but May, June, and September are great times to find a good deal.

Check out Ste-Maxime's chicest hotel and beach club: the legendary **Le Beauvallon** (✆ **04-94-55-78-88;** www.lebeauvallon.com). It was scheduled to reopen in spring 2012 after a multimillion-euro renovation that included the relocation from London's Hyde Park of the Pavilion—a steel-and-glass events space that was originally commissioned for the Serpentine Gallery.

MODERATE

Best Western Hôtel Montfleuri ★★ Our favorite hotel in Sainte-Maxime, this three-star hotel on a hillside in a quiet residential neighborhood opens onto a superb view of the Gulf of St-Tropez. The large guest rooms have fine linen, twin or double beds, and a small bathroom. The rooms have even been fitted with their own Nespresso coffee machines. All of the accommodations facing the ocean have their own private terraces. "Family cooking" *provençale* style is served in the restaurant overlooking the verdant garden and swimming pool. Friendly service completes the picture.

3 av. Montfleuri, 83120 Ste-Maxime. www.montfleuri.com. ✆ **04-94-55-75-10.** Fax 04-94-49-25-07. 32 units. 45€–235€ double; 100€–295€ suite. AE, DC, MC, V. Parking 15€–18€. Closed mid-Nov to mid-Dec and early Jan to Feb. **Amenities:** Restaurant; bar; pool (outdoor). *In room:* A/C, TV, hair dryer, minibar, Wi-Fi (free).

Hôtel La Croisette ★ This charming 1950s hotel is surrounded by its own lush garden and has an intimate aura, lying 200m (656 ft.) from the beach. Room rates vary according to view—those with a balcony and sea view are most expensive; those that open onto the garden are less. For the best views, ask for a room on the upper floors. Homey and cozy, they are decorated in a provincial southern style; the tiled bathrooms are tidy. Maintenance here is high quality, although service can be hit and miss. If La Croisette is full, its sister hotel **Les Santolines** (✆ **04-94-96-31-34**) has Provençal rooms curved around a pretty central garden and pool. The beach is just opposite Les Santolines, but it's a 10-minute walk along a traffic-laden road into town.

2 bd. des Romarins, 83120 Ste-Maxime. www.hotel-la-croisette.com. ✆ **04-94-96-17-75.** Fax 04-94-96-52-40. 19 units. 80€–174€ double. AE, MC, V. Closed mid-Oct to mid-Apr. **Amenities:** Bar; pool (outdoor). *In room:* A/C, TV, minibar, Wi-Fi (free).

Hôtellerie de la Poste ★ Its central location, welcoming staff, and reasonable prices ensure guests keep coming back to this three-star Logis de France hotel. The interiors are cool and comfortable, with a quiet lounge and bar. The bedrooms are decorated with contemporary furnishings, and some rooms have sea views. Breakfast and summertime lunches are served on the terrace near the small outdoor pool. Restaurants, shopping, and the beach (Plage du Centre Ville) are all within a 5-minute walk.

11 bd. Frédéric-Mistral, 83123 Ste-Maxime. www.hotelleriedusoleil.com. ✆ **04-94-96-18-33.** Fax 04-94-55-58-63. 28 units. 70€–190€ double; from 120€ suite. AE, DC, MC, V. Covered parking 15€. Closed 2 weeks in Dec. **Amenities:** Bar; babysitting; pool (outdoor). *In room:* A/C, TV, hair dryer, minibar, Wi-Fi (3€ per hr.).

INEXPENSIVE

Hôtel Le Chardon Bleu Offering surprisingly low prices for the St-Trop peninsula, Le Chardon Bleu is close to the pedestrianized town center and just 10m (33 ft.) from the beach. This two-star hotel has a garden where you can enjoy the aroma of the flowers. The well-maintained rooms are comfortable and inviting, though the furnishings are standard; all rooms have small balconies. Bathrooms are tiled and compact.

29 rue de Verdun, 83120 Ste-Maxime. www.hotelduchardonbleu.com. ✆ **04-94-55-52-22.** Fax 04-94-43-90-89. 23 units. 49€–95€ double; triple rooms from 75€; quadruple rooms from 85€. AE, DC, MC, V. **Amenities:** Lounge. *In room:* A/C, TV, fridge.

Where to Eat

La Gruppi FRENCH/PROVENÇALE Earthy and amusing (La Gruppi is the Provençal word for a miniature trough used to feed barnyard animals), this bay-windowed restaurant has thrived on the seafront promenade ever since the 1960s. The deluxe version of the establishment's savory bouillabaisse must be ordered a day in advance; otherwise, you get a simplified version, which the chefs refer to as a *soupe de poisson*. Other menu items include herbed and roasted lamb from Sisteron, and all the vegetarian bounty of Provence. If you opt for fish, a staff member will carry a basket filled with the best of the day's catch for your inspection and advise you on their respective merits.

82 av. Charles-de-Gaulle. ✆ **04-94-96-03-61.** Reservations recommended. Main courses 25€–40€; fixed-price menus 26€–37€. AE, MC, V. Tues and Thurs–Sun noon–2pm; daily 7–11pm. Closed 2 weeks in Dec.

La Réserve ★ FRENCH In its third generation of business, La Réserve has a strong local following who keep coming back for its French bistro cuisine. With its flower-patterned cushions and menus hanging from a large tree trunk in the middle of the room, the decoration of this centrally located restaurant transports diners to the Provençal countryside. Specialties from different French regions include *fondue bourguignonne* (meat fondue from Burgundy), *homard du vivier* (pick-your-own lobster), and bouillabaisse.

8 place Victor Hugo. ✆ **04-94-96-18-32.** Reservations recommended. Fixed-price menus 21€ and 29€. AE, MC, V. Daily noon–2pm and 7–10pm (until 10:30pm May–Sept).

FRÉJUS ★

3km (2 miles) W of St-Raphaël; 14km (8¾ miles) NE of St-Tropez

Halfway between St-Tropez and Cannes, Fréjus is popular with families due to its numerous sandy beaches and its dramatic backdrop of the red-hued Esterel mountain range. This, much like its neighboring town Saint-Raphaël, is a laid-back, affordable seaside resort.

Gaul's oldest Roman city, Fréjus is chockablock with impressive ancient remains. Fréjus was founded by Julius Caesar in 49 B.C. as Forum Julii; later, under Augustus's rule, it became a key naval base. The warships with which Augustus defeated Antony and Cleopatra at the battle at Actium were built here in 31 B.C. Remnants from Roman times still stand in the Vieille Ville, including Roman gateways and ramparts, as well as parts of an aqueduct, an amphitheater, and a theater. You can spot a double-headed Hermes (now the emblem of Fréjus) at the **Musée Archéologique** and visit some of France's oldest ecclesiastical buildings in the **Cité Episcopale.**

The pretty old town is also home to various well-priced art galleries, following a successful local government makeover that replaced dodgy bars with subsidized artists' studios. Today it's a thriving art community.

Essentials

GETTING THERE From the main station at St-Raphaël, several **trains** a day arrive at a small train station in Fréjus on rue Martin-Bidouré. Call ✆ **36-35,** or visit www.voyages-sncf.com. The beach is a shorter walk (about 15 min.) from the St-Raphaël station than from the Fréjus station.

AggloBus (✆ **04-94-53-78-46**), which functions in cooperation with **Estérel Bus,** operates routes throughout Provence and the Riviera, including a bus service into Fréjus from St-Raphaël every 30 minutes or so. Buses arrive at the **Fréjus Gare Routière,** place Paul-Vernet (✆ **04-94-83-87-63**), at the east end of the town center. One-way tickets cost 1.10€.

If you're **driving,** to reach Fréjus from Nice or Cannes, take the A8 before cutting south at exit 38 on the D37. From St-Raphaël, take the D1098 west to Fréjus.

GETTING AROUND Rent bicycles from **Cycles Patrick Béraud,** 7 rond-point de la Gendarmerie Nationale/337 rue de Triberg (✆ **04-94-51-20-20;** www.cycles beraud.fr). Expect to pay 10€ to 15€, plus a security deposit.

VISITOR INFORMATION The **Office de Tourisme** is at Le Florus II, 249 rue Jean-Jaurès (✆ **04-94-51-83-83;** www.frejus.fr).

SPECIAL EVENTS The **Fête des Plantes** is held annually in the park of the Villa Aurélienne (see below) during a 3-day period in late March and April. For information, call ✆ **04-94-51-83-83.**

Exploring the Town

THE TOP SIGHTS

If you want to visit several sites in the area, you can purchase a **Fréjus Pass** for 4.60€ for adults or 3.10€ for ages 12 to 18; it's free for ages 11 and under.

The best preserved of the Roman ruins is the **Amphithéâtre (Les Arènes)** ★, rue Henri-Vadon (✆ **04-94-51-34-31**). In Roman times, it held up to 10,000 spectators. The upper levels of the galleries have been reconstructed with the same greenish stone used to create the original building. Today it's used as a venue for rock concerts. ***Note:*** The amphitheater is currently closed for an extensive renovation, but is slated to reopen in late 2012.

A half kilometer (⅓ mile) north of town on avenue du Théâtre-Romain, the **Théâtre Romain Philippe Léotard** (✆ **04-94-53-58-75**), not to be confused with the amphitheater, is largely in ruins. However, one wall and a few of the lower sections remain and are used as a backdrop for a summertime theater festival. The theater is open Tuesday to Sunday 9:30am to 12:30pm and 2 to 5pm (until 6pm April–Sept). Admission is 2€ for all ages. Northwest of the theater, you can see a few soaring arches as they follow the coastal road leading to Cannes. These are the remaining pieces of the 40km (25-mile) aqueduct that once brought fresh water to Fréjus's water tower.

Cité Episcopale ★★★ The town's most frequently visited site is its fortified cathedral in the heart of the Vieille Ville. At its center is the **Cathédrale St-Léonce,** completed in the 16th century after many generations of laborers had worked on it. It was begun in the 10th century, and parts of it date from the 12th and 13th centuries. Its most striking features are from the Renaissance—ornately carved walnut doors depicting scenes from the Virgin's life and tableaux inspired by Saracen invasions. The 5th-century **baptistery ★★** is one of the oldest in France. Octagonal like many paleo-Christian baptisteries, it features eight black granite columns with white capitals. Most interesting are the two doors, which are different sizes. Catechumens would enter by the smaller of the two; inside, a bishop would wash their feet and baptize them by complete immersion in the center outdoor pool. The baptized would then leave through the larger door; this signified their enlarged spiritual stature.

The most beautiful of all the structures in the Episcopal quarter is the 12th-century **cloister ★★**. The colonnade's two slender marble pillars are typical of the Provençal style. Inside, the wooden ceiling is divided into 1,200 small panels decorated with animals, portraits, and grotesques by 15th-century artists. A bell tower rises above the cloister, its steeple covered with colored tiles.

58 rue de Fleury. ✆ **04-94-51-26-30.** Admission includes entrance to all sites, the museum, and (optional) guided tour of cloister and baptistery: 5€ adults, 3.50€ students 24 and under and children. June–Sept daily 9am–6:30pm; Oct–May Tues–Sun 9am–noon and 2–5pm.

MORE SIGHTS

The small, round **Chapelle Cocteau,** route de Cannes (✆ **04-94-53-27-06**), was designed by the artist, film director, social gadfly, and *prince des poètes* Jean Cocteau in 1961. After Cocteau's death in 1963, the ornate frescoes were completed by his adoptive son Edouard Dermit. It's open Tuesday to Sunday 9:30am to noon and 2 to 5pm (until 6pm April–Sept). Admission is 2€ for all ages.

Just outside Fréjus are two curiosities that reflect the cultural mixture of France's early-20th-century empire. Northeast of Fréjus, the **Pagode Hong-Hien,** 13 rue Henri Giraud (✆ **04-94-53-25-29**), was built in 1917 by soldiers conscripted from Indochina as a shrine to their fallen comrades. It's still used as a Buddhist temple. It's open April to October daily from 10am to 7pm, and November to March 10am to noon and 2 to 5pm. Admission is 2€ for all ages. Off D4 (route des Combattants-d'Afrique-du-Nord), leading to Bagnols-en-Fôret, you can see the striking red exterior of the **Mosquée Soudanaise** (no phone), built by Muslim soldiers conscripted from the French colony of Mali. It's open from June to September 9:30am to 1:30pm and 2 to 6pm.

The grand neoclassical **Villa Aurélienne,** avenue du Général-d'Armée Calliès (✆ **04-94-52-90-49**), was originally a holiday home for an English industrialist in the 1880s. It's a popular venue for photographic exhibitions and classical concerts. Admission prices and opening hours vary according to the event. Call for information. The park surrounding the villa also hosts occasional festivals.

Parc Zoologique, Zone du Capitou (✆ **04-98-11-37-37;** www.zoo-frejus.com), is off A8 about 5.5km (3½ miles) north of the center of Fréjus. This safari-style zoo is home to more than 250 species of animals and is best visited by car as the animals are spread out over a wide terrain. It's open daily June to August 10am to 6pm; March, April, May, September, and October daily 10am to 5pm; and November to February daily 10:30am to 4:30pm. Admission is 15€ for adults, 10€ for children 3 to 9, and free for children 2 and under.

Spread over 260 hectares (642 acres), **Etangs de Villepey** (www.frejus.fr), off the D1098 west of Fréjus, is a nature reserve that is often known as the "Petite Camargue" of the Var, due to the marshlands here. You'll also find dry zones and sand dunes. Here you can explore nature along the walking and cycling paths. It's particularly busy during migration season in spring and autumn, when you can find over 250 species of birds. There are no specific opening hours as entry is free at any time.

A former Naval airdrome, **Base Nature,** François Léotard (✆ **04-94-51-91-10;** http://base.nature.free.fr) is the East Var's largest public park, covering 135 hectares (334 acres) of coastal land. There's a kids' playground, a roller park, games, a snack bar, and a beach. Exhibitions take place in the 6,000-sq.-m (64,580-sq.-ft.) disused air hangar, while the former diving training pool has been turned into an indoor swimming pool. The mounted police force regularly patrol the park and keep some of their horses in the paddock. As well as rabbits, turtles, and frogs, Base Nature's grassy parkland houses 130 species of birds and rare beetles. The car park for the beach and park is open daily from 8am–10pm (until midnight July–Aug). For the swimming pool, opening hours vary throughout the year, so it's best to phone in advance (✆ **04-94-51-97-28**).

Aqualand, Quartier Le Capou along D1098 (✆ **04-94-51-82-51;** www.aqualand.fr), is a theme park with 19 water-based rides for kids of all ages, as well as snack bars and a shop. It's open every day from mid-June to mid-September from 10am to 6pm (until 7pm from early July to late Aug). Entry costs 25€ for adults and kids 13 years and over, 19€ for kids from 3 to 12 years, and free for kids under 1m tall (3 ft.).

A Day at the Beach

One of the best public sandy beaches is the Blue Flag beach of Plage Port Fréjus, situated by the new marina. Centrally located Fréjus Plage and Plage de la Galiote in St-Aygulf are both partly private sandy beaches where you can rent beach recliners and umbrellas. Further along from Plage de la Galiote is the public sandy beach Plage St-Aygulf—it's worth noting that there is a small nude beach (bordering the Etangs de Villepey). There is a well-maintained 1.5km (1 mile) beach at **Base Nature** (✆ **04-94-51-91-10;** http://base.nature.free.fr; see above), the Var's largest theme park bar; it's supervised during the summer months.

Where to Stay

Families often opt to stay along Fréjus's smart port area near the Blue Flag beach Plage Port Fréjus or in the nearby upscale neighborhood of St-Aygulf. Both are close to the **Aqualand** theme park, the **Etangs de Villepey** nature reserve, and **Base Nature.**

Hôtel L'Aréna ★★ On the doorstep of the old town center and next to the train station, this three-star hotel provides a convenient base to explore Fréjus's old town by foot. The staff is friendly, and the hotel is a good value for the area. Bedrooms are small, but well soundproofed and comfortably decorated with a Provençal ocher palate. In summertime, a gourmet table d'hôte dinner is served on the shaded garden terrace where tropical plants give the air a sweet smell. The hotel has a good-size outdoor pool. The hotel is now part of a well-run southern French boutique hotel group, Hôtels Ocre et Azur, with sister properties including Le Canberra in Cannes and Hôtel Suisse in Nice.

145 rue du Général-de-Gaulle, 83600 Fréjus. www.hotel-frejus-arena.com. ✆ **04-94-17-09-40.** Fax 04-94-52-01-52. 39 units. 85€–165€ double; triples from 115€; quadruples from 125€. AE, DC, MC, V. Parking 12€. Closed mid-Dec to mid-Jan. **Amenities:** Restaurant; bar; babysitting; pool (outdoor). *In room:* A/C, TV, hair dryer, Wi-Fi (free).

Mercure Thalassa Port Fréjus ★ Overlooking the port, this three-star hotel offers a well-priced stay in Fréjus with easy access to the beach and restaurants and to nearby attractions such as Base Nature and Aqualand. Guests are pampered in the thalassotherapy spa with its seawater swimming pool (accessed for a fee) or at the outdoor pool adjacent to the beach. Bedrooms have balconies overlooking the city, the pretty harbor, or the sea. City view rooms can be noisy. The restful sea-view rooms glimpse the sea beyond the garden and pool, but some sea views are partly obscured by palm trees. Space is tight for large cars in the car park: You may be better finding car parking nearby.

16 quai dei Caravello, Port Fréjus Ouest, 83600 Fréjus. www.mercure.com. ✆ **04-94-52-55-00.** Fax 04-94-52-55-01. 116 units. 125€–250€ double. AE, DC, MC, V. Parking 15€. **Amenities:** Restaurant; bar; babysitting; spa; 2 pools (outdoor and heated indoor). *In room:* A/C, TV, hair dryer, Wi-Fi (free).

Where to Eat

If you have time for a sit-down meal, see our recommendations below. If you're in a rush, head to rue Sieyès, where you can pick up spit-roast chickens and paella from **Maison Belu** (✆ **04-94-51-39-66**) and melt-in-the-mouth cheeses from **Mon Fromager** (✆ **04-94-40-67-99**).

Chocolathé ★★ CAFE/LIGHT FARE This restaurant is the best place in the pedestrianized old town for a reasonably priced lunchtime snack. Set up in 2009 by young Parisian Cécile as a teahouse offering 26 types of tea, it rapidly expanded into a restaurant serving panini and salads, plus a hot dish of the day. With coffee imported from Big Train (the manufacturer that supplies Starbucks) and cookie-filled jars lining the counter, it's the perfect place to relax for an hour or so between visiting sights. The decor is appropriately decorated in tones of chocolate and cream.

19 rue Général de Gaulle. ✆ **04-94-83-00-71.** Main courses 11€–16€. MC, V. Mon–Sat 8am–7pm (plus some Sun afternoons during school holidays).

L'Amandier ★ MEDITERRANEAN Chef Loïc Balanec and his wife Elisabeth welcome diners to this 16th-century town house with its vaulted second dining room. Balanec brings his experience as the Pourcel Brothers' deputy (at the Michelin-starred Le Jardin des Sens in Montpellier) to his southern French cuisine. Olive oil and rosemary are sprinkled liberally throughout his seasonally changing menus. Try the soft rack of lamb or the oven-baked sea bream. In summer, tables spill out onto the pedestrianized pavement.

19 rue Desaugiers. ✆ **04-94-53-48-77.** Main courses 16€–20€. Fixed-price midweek lunch menu 20€; fixed-price dinner menus 24€–37€. MC, V. Tues and Thurs–Sat 12:30–2pm; Mon–Sat 7–10pm. Closed early Jan.

SAINT-RAPHAËL

3km (2 miles) E of Fréjus; 43km (27 miles) SW of Cannes

Between the red lava peaks of the Massif de l'Estérel and the densely forested hills of the Massif des Maures, St-Raphaël was first popular during Roman times, when rich families came to the resort here. Barbaric hordes and Saracen invasions characterized the Middle Ages incarnation. Not until 1799, when a proud Napoleon landed at the small harbor beach on his return from Egypt, did the city once again draw attention.

Fifteen years later, that same spot in the harbor was the point of embarkation for the fallen emperor's journey to exile on Elba. In 1864, Alphonse Karr, a journalist and ex-editor of *Le Figaro,* helped reintroduce St-Raphaël as a resort. Dumas, Maupassant, and Berlioz came here from Paris on his recommendation. Gounod also arrived; he composed *Romeo et Juliet* here in 1866. Unfortunately, most of the Belle Époque–era villas and grand hotels were destroyed during World War II when St-Raphaël served as a key landing point for Allied soldiers.

Today some of the mansions have been rebuilt (many in the style of the 1970s apartment blocks) and others have been replaced by modern resorts and buildings. However, the city still offers the wide beaches and the coastal ambience of other Côte d'Azur resorts—at a fraction of the price. This is why St-Raphaël draws more families than couture-clad Parisians. The resort town is probably best known for its Santa Lucia Marina, the third largest on the Riviera.

Essentials

GETTING THERE St-Raphaël sits directly on the **rail** lines running parallel to the coast between Marseille in the west and the Italian border town of Ventimiglia in the east. Within some 3 hours you can take a fast **TGV train** from Paris to Marseille. For rail information and schedules, call © **36-35,** or visit www.voyages-sncf.com. Once at Marseille, it is another 1¾ hours by train to St-Raphaël. Trains leave Marseille every hour during the day, costing about 24€ one-way. Trains from Cannes head east to St-Raphaël every 30 minutes during the day (trip time 25 min.); one-way fare costs about 6€.

The **bus** station behind the train station provides local and regional services alike. There's a bus service from Fréjus to St-Raphaël every 30 minutes or so (one-way tickets cost 1.10€). From Nice to St-Raphaël takes approx 70 minutes and costs 15€ each way, while a bus to St-Tropez takes approx 90 minutes and costs just 2€ each way. For more information, call the St-Raphaël bus station at © **04-94-44-52-70.**

You can also arrive in St-Raphaël by **boat.** Between June and September, **Les Bateaux Bleus** (© **04-94-95-17-46**) provides daily waterborne transit between the Gare Maritime in St-Raphaël's Vieux Port and St-Tropez for 14€ each way. The rest of the year, the boat service runs on Tuesday and Saturday mornings only.

By **car** from St-Tropez in the west, take D98A northwest to N98, at which point you drive east toward St-Raphaël. To reach St-Raphaël from Nice or Cannes, head west along the A8 before cutting south at exit 38 on the D37 to Fréjus and then east on the D100 to St-Raphaël.

GETTING AROUND Normally, taxis line up at the bus station; if you can't find one, call © **04-94-83-24-24.** You can rent bikes and scooters from **Patrick Moto,** 260 av. du Général-Leclerc (© **04-94-53-65-99**). Bikes rent for 9€, with a 150€

deposit; mountain bikes rent for 13€, with a 300€ deposit; and scooters go for 30€, with a 900€ deposit. For scooter rentals, insurance documentation is required. (MasterCard and Visa can be used for the deposit.)

VISITOR INFORMATION The **Office de Tourisme** faces the train station on rue Waldeck-Rousseau (© **04-94-19-52-52;** www.saint-raphael.com).

SPECIAL EVENTS For the last 30 years, Dixieland-style musicians from around the world have congregated every July to display their talent at the **Festival de Jazz New Orleans;** call © **04-98-11-89-00,** or contact the tourist office, for exact dates and musical venues for this 3-day event. In mid-August, the **Festival St-Pierre des Pêcheurs** is conducted in and around the town center. Honoring the patron saint of fishermen, it features a night of fireworks, a brief medieval-style procession to and from the village church, music, dancing on platforms built beside the port, and a series of jutes (mock naval battles between competing boat teams) where everyone gets soaking wet.

Exploring the Town

St-Raphaël is divided in half by railroad tracks. The historical **Vieille Ville (Old Town)** lies inland from the tracks. Here you'll find St-Raphaël's only intact ancient structure, the **Eglise San Rafèu** (also known as Eglise des Templiers), rue des Templiers (© **04-94-19-25-75**). The 12th-century church is the third to stand on this site; two Carolingian churches underneath the current structure have been revealed during digs. A watchtower sits atop one of the chapels, and at one time, watchers were posted to look out over the sea for ships that might pose a threat. The church served as a fortress and refuge in case of pirate attack. In the courtyard are fragments of a Roman aqueduct that once brought water from Fréjus. You can visit the church June to September every Tuesday to Saturday from 9:30am to noon and 2 to 6:30pm (Thurs until 9pm); October to May, hours are Tuesday to Saturday 9am to noon and 2 to 5:30pm. Ironically, no Masses are conducted in this church on Sunday—it's a consecrated church, but one that's been relegated to something akin to an archaeological rather than religious monument.

Near the Eglise des Templiers, the **Musée d'Archéologie Sous-Marine (Museum of Underwater Archaeology),** rue des Templiers (© **04-94-19-25-75;** www.musee-saintraphael.com), displays amphorae, ships' anchors, ancient diving equipment, and other interesting items recovered from the ocean's depths. At one time, rumors circulated about a "lost city" off the coast of St-Raphaël. Jacques Cousteau came to investigate; instead of a sunken city, he discovered a Roman ship that had sunk while carrying a full load of building supplies. The museum is open Tuesday to Saturday from 9am to noon and 2 to 6pm. Admission is free.

You'll also find **flower and fruit markets** in the old city. Every morning, you'll find a fish market in the Vieux Port. Also, check out the **Marché Alimentaire de St-Raphaël,** where carloads of produce, fish, meat, wines, and cheeses are sold Tuesday to Sunday from 8am to 1pm in place Victor-Hugo and place de la République—a 5-minute walk apart. Every Tuesday from 9am to 6pm in place Coullet, there's a *brocante* (flea market).

A Day at the Beach

Of course, most visitors come to St-Raphaël for its beaches. The best ones (some rock, some sand) are between the Vieux Port and Santa Lucia. Here you'll find plenty of stands that rent watersports equipment on each beach. The closest beach to the

hiking IN THE MASSIF DE L'ESTÉREL

One of the best places for hiking along the Côte d'Azur is in the Massif de L'Estérel. Stretching for 39km (24 miles) along the Mediterranean coast from St-Raphaël to Mandelieu, this mass of twisted red volcanic rock is a surreal landscape of dramatic panoramas. Repeated forest fires have devastated much of the area's cork oak—today a more rugged *maquis* (shrubland) of brooms, cistus, rosemary, euphorbia, and heather prevails. This was once the stamping ground of colorful characters such as 19th-century highwayman Gaspard de Besse, nicknamed *Robin des Bois Provençal* (Robin Hood of Provence), and 5th-century hermit Saint-Honorat, who dwelt in the Grotte de la Sainte Baume before founding the Lérins monastery on Île Saint-Honorat.

Following the path of the ancient Roman Aurelian Way, D237 traces the area's northern edge, running through the Estérel Gap between Fréjus and Cannes. This route offers the massif's most stunning vistas. You may prefer to start by car from Fréjus along the busy voie Aurélienne and then veer onto D237 towards the quiet village of Les Adrets-de-L'Estérel. Here, you can stop off at the tourist office in Les Adrets, where you can get maps marking hiking trails; hikes can last a couple of hours or longer, depending on the route you choose.

For information on hiking trails in the Estérel hills, contact the tourist offices in St-Raphaël (✆ **04-94-19-52-52;** www.saint-raphael.com) or Les-Adrets-de-l'Estérel, place de la Mairie (✆ **04-94-40-93-57**).

town center is the **Plage du Veillat,** a long stretch of sand that's crowded and family friendly. Further east in Agay, you'll find the sandy beaches of **Plage d'Agay** and **Plage de la Baumette;** these are partly private beaches where you can rent recliners and umbrellas for a fee. Within a 5-minute walk east of the town center is **Plage Beau Rivage,** whose name is misleading because it's covered with a smooth and even coating of light-gray pebbles that might be uncomfortable to lie on without a towel. History buffs will enjoy a 7km (4½-mile) excursion east of town to the **Plage du Dramont,** a public pebble stretch with watersports and a restaurant that was hurled into world headlines on August 15, 1944, as one of the main sites of the Allied Forces' Provence Landings. Today expect relatively uncrowded conditions, except during the midsummer crush.

Where to Stay

St-Raphaël has plenty of accommodations, but during summer even the less-than-desirable places fill up fast. Reserve well in advance.

Best Western Hôtel La Marina Overlooking the yacht-basin harbor at Santa Lucia, this four-star hotel provides comfortable accommodations in a setting a bit removed from the crowded beaches. Most of the well-furnished rooms have private balconies. The restaurant serves well-prepared regional food on a sunny terrace overlooking sailboats and yachts.

Nouveau Port Santa Lucia, 83700 St-Raphaël. www.bestwestern-lamarina.com. ✆ **800/528-1234** in the U.S. and Canada, or 04-94-95-31-31. Fax 04-94-82-21-46. 100 units. 110€–205€ double. AE, DC, V. Parking 9€. **Amenities:** Restaurant; bar; babysitting; concierge; fitness room; pool (outdoor). *In room:* A/C, TV, hair dryer, minibar, Wi-Fi (free).

Hôtel Continental This seafront hotel is a good choice for a cost-conscious beach vacation. Spread over the first floor of a smart residence, it's deceptively small with only 44 rooms. Rooms come in a wide variety, ranging from compact (relatively cramped) to spacious, with rates charged according to view (seascape or urban). All have well-maintained tiled bathrooms. No meals are served other than breakfast, but two well-recommended restaurants lie within a short walk. Located 200m (656 ft.) from the train station, it's also convenient for travelers arriving by train.

101 promenade René-Coty, 83700 St-Raphaël. www.hotels-continental.com. ✆ **04-94-83-87-87.** Fax 04-94-19-20-24. 44 units. 79€–199€ double; family rooms 169€–239€. AE, DC, MC, V. Parking 13€. **Amenities:** Lounge; babysitting. *In room:* A/C, TV, hair dryer, minibar, Wi-Fi (free).

Hôtel Excelsior This hotel, on the beachfront promenade, is a charming family-run place. The small to medium-size guest rooms are comfortably appointed, with tidy bathrooms; most have views of the ocean. A sand beach is directly across the street. The hotel is best known for its restaurant whose terrace is usually chockablock with locals and tourists alike.

193 promenade René-Coty, 83700 St-Raphaël. www.excelsior-hotel.com. ✆ **04-94-95-02-42.** Fax 04-94-95-33-82. 40 units. 135€–205€ double; 175€–210€ family suite. AE, DC, MC, V. **Amenities:** Restaurant; pub; room service. *In room:* A/C, TV, hair dryer, minibar, Wi-Fi (free).

L'Estirado des Andrets & Auberge Panoramique ★ In the heart of the Estérel hills lies a combined hotel and restaurant that's worth a detour. The village of Les Andrets is between St. Raphaël and Mandelieu, between sea and hills. A stay, or even a stopover for lunch, is like a journey back to old-time Provence. Everything is traditional in style, with cozy, well-furnished bedrooms with private bathrooms. On hot summer days, guests congregate at the outdoor swimming pool or lounge in the sun against a scenic backdrop of forested hills. The food here is among the best in the area, highlighting a *provençale* and French cuisine that changes with the seasons. Dining can be in the shade of a straw hut in summer or close to a roaring fireplace in winter.

83600 Les Andrets de l'Estérel. www.estirado.com. ✆ **04-94-40-90-64.** Fax 04-94-40-98-52. 21 units. 75€–100€ double; 130€–150€ suite. MC, V. Free parking. Closed mid-Nov to late Jan. **Amenities:** Restaurant; babysitting; pool (outdoor). *In room:* TV, hair dryer, Wi-Fi (free).

Villa Mauresque ★ This posh address lies 30 minutes from either Cannes or St-Tropez, and the little village of Boulouris itself is only a 5-minute drive from St-Raphaël. The two neo-Moorish castles that make up the villa have been converted into an elegant B&B framed by lush century-old palms and umbrella pines. Even though furnishings don't live up to the fabulous grandeur of the villa and its setting, the villas were freshly renovated in 2010. Rooms range from small to medium size, some with terraces. The Picasso room has a large terrace overlooking the park and the sea.

1792 rte. de la Corniche, Boulouris, 83700 St-Raphaël. www.villa-mauresque.com. ✆ **04-94-83-02-42.** Fax 04-94-83-02-02. 15 units. 175€–450€ double; from 450€ suite. AE, DC, MC, V. Free parking. **Amenities:** Breakfast room; Jacuzzi; 2 pools (outdoor); restaurant; sauna; watersports equipment/rentals. *In room:* A/C, TV, hair dryer, Wi-Fi (free).

Where to Eat

La Brasserie ★ FRENCH/PROVENÇALE Chef Philippe Troncy has started a new culinary chapter with the opening of La Brasserie in 2010 (on the same spot as his L'Arbousier restaurant). A new contemporary decor, a more affordable menu, and an all-day-dining concept have ensured a loyal following for his traditional Provençal cuisine. Typical dishes include asparagus and Iberian ham, *brandade de morue* (cod stew), and roasted lamb.

6 av. de Valescure/angle rue Marius Allongue. ✆ **04-94-95-25-00.** Reservations recommended. Main courses 13€–20€; fixed-price lunch menu 19€. AE, DC, MC, V. Mon–Sat 8:30am–11pm.

Les Charavins FRENCH/WINE BAR Just behind the town hall lies this jolly wine bar–cum-bistro. Garlic and ham hocks hang from the ceiling, while the walls are lined with wine bottles and gastronomy-related pictures. You can keep an eye on your food in the open-plan kitchen. Most of the year you'll find all the classics of hearty French cuisine, such as foie gras and snails and frogs' legs, although summer menus tend to be lighter with more fish dishes. Tempting desserts include Rum Baba and chocolate cake. The 300-strong wine list offers many Provençal wines and a generous selection of wines by the glass.

36 rue Charabois. ✆ **04-94-95-03-76.** Main courses 17€–29€; fixed-price menu 29€. MC, V. Mon–Tues and Thurs–Sat 12:30–2pm and 7–10pm.

St-Raphaël After Dark

As this is a family vacation spot, the after-dark scene is a little sparse. Nights at the **Casino Barrière de St-Raphaël,** square de Grand (✆ **04-98-11-17-77**), feature slot machines and gambling, plus a bar and restaurant. The slot machines are open daily from 10am to 4am (until 5am Sat); gambling begins at 9pm.

One of our favorite clubs is **La Réserve** (✆ **04-94-95-02-20** or 06-09-97-25-58) on promenade René Coty, a popular disco with a punk-rock crowd between 16 and 25.

DRAGUIGNAN

80 km (49 miles) NE of Toulon; 62 km (38 miles) NW of Cannes; 56km (34 miles) W of Grasse.

The former capital of the Var, Draguignan has a faded charm that is evident in its grand town hall and elegant townhouses. Although there's little to do in the town center, the surrounding countryside offers plentiful attractions, from the intriguing Pierre de la Fée stone table to numerous picturesque villages, such as restaurant-filled Flayosc, medieval Tourtour, and Villecroze, with its troglodyte caves.

Essentials

GETTING THERE The train station, Le Arcs-Draguignan, is actually in neighboring Les-Arcs-sur Argens, on avenue de la Gare. **Trains** from Cannes take 40 minutes with one-way tickets costing 10€, and from St-Raphaël trains take under 20 minutes with one-way tickets at 5.20€. For information and schedules, call ✆ **36-35,** or visit www.voyages-sncf.com. If you're **driving,** take A8 west from Cannes, turning off at exit 36 pour Draguignan on N555 past Le Muy, before arriving into Draguignan.

VISITOR INFORMATION The **Office de Tourisme** is on 28 rue Georges Cisson (✆ **04-94-60-31-00;** www.villedraguignan.com).

Exploring the Town

The Pierre de la Fée ("fairy stone") is an extraordinarily large Neolithic (2,500–2,000 B.C.) stone table. The columns supporting the dolmen weigh more than 20 tons and contain bone fragments. Legend tells that a fairy, disguised as a shepherdess, accepted a young man's wedding proposal on the condition that he made her a table from three huge stones. After much toil, he maneuvered two stones into place but

Gastronomic Villages

Gourmands should fit in a visit to Lorgues to dine at Bruno (✆ 04-94-85-93-93; www.restaurantbruno.com), where truffles reign supreme. Dine on a truffle-infused feast on the shaded terrace of this Michelin-starred restaurant—it's an unforgettable experience. Also in Lorgues, foodies will want to visit Château de Berne (✆ 04-94-60-48-88; www.chateauberne.com), the luxury Relais & Châteaux hotel and vineyard, where you can taste the estate's excellent wines over a meal at one of its three restaurants.

Nearby, the tiny hilltop village of Flayosc is bustling with dining options: We'd recommend L'Oustaou ✆ 04-94-70-42-69) on place Joseph Brémond.

couldn't budge the third, so the fairy used her magical powers to help him. Struck down by her superior talent, the young man died and was turned to stone. You'll find the Pierre de la Fée on route de Montferrat on the outskirts of Draguignan about 1.5 km (nearly a mile) from the town center.

For table-top views over the surrounding countryside, the 17th-century clock tower is worth a visit. Nearby, the **Musée des Arts et Traditions Populaires,** 15 rue Joseph Roumanille (✆ **04-94-47-05-72;** fax 04-94-47-39-49; www.villedraguignan.com), is a well-designed ethnographic museum that charts the history of Provençal life through reconstructions and audio-visual guides.

Where to Stay

Four Seasons Provence at Terre Blanche ★★★ ☺ Set in the Var countryside between Draguignan and Grasse, this is one of the plushest resorts in southern France. The location is 32km (20 miles) north of the Cannes-Mandelieu airport. It's also the only resort in the region with two 18-hole golf courses, each designed by Wales-born Dave Thomas, a big name in course design. Its look emulates one of the "perched villages" of medieval Provence.

The hotel's layout evokes an isolated cluster of masonry-sided villas, each painted ocher, capped with a terra-cotta roof, and connected by undulating brick walkways that snake across manicured lawns and gardens. Villas are artfully decorated with airy postmodern furnishings vaguely influenced by the traditions of Provence. Even the smallest of the accommodations here is a suite suitable for up to four occupants. The largest is a full-blown private villa for up to eight guests.

As well as golf, guests are pampered with a luxurious health club and spa. There are several high-end restaurants in this property, including Faventia (see below). A new kids' pool was added in 2011.

Domaine de Terre Blanche, 3100 Route de Bagnols-en-Fôret, 83440 Tourrettes. www.fourseasons.com/provence. ✆ **04-94-39-90-00.** Fax 04-94-39-90-01. 115 units. Suites 380€–1,150€; 1-bedroom villas from 800€. AE, DC, MC, V. **Amenities:** 5 restaurants (2 summer only, and 3 in winter); bar; babysitting; kids' club; concierge; 2 golf courses; health club and spa; 3 pools (indoor, outdoor, and kids); room service. *In room:* A/C, TV, kitchenettes (in some villas), minibar, Wi-Fi (12€).

Where to Eat

Faventia ★★★ PROVENÇALE/MEDITERRANEAN If you're driving up from the coast into the hills of the Var, stop to enjoy Faventia's great charm and sublime cuisine made with the best of market-fresh ingredients. In an elegantly modern setting, the restaurant showcases a contemporary Mediterranean cuisine with a heavy *provençale* influence. Dishes are relatively simple and filled with flavor, backed up by a regional wine list. From the restaurant's hilltop perch, panoramic views open onto the nearby villages. In summer guests dine alfresco on a shaded terrace. The menu is forever changing and seasonally adjusted.

In the Four Seasons Resort Provence at Terre Blanche. ✆ **04-94-39-90-00.** Reservations required. Main courses 44€–46€. AE, DC, MC, V. Tues–Sat 7:30–10:30pm.

Lou Galoubet ★ PROVENÇALE Chef Philippe Rousselot trained with the Côte d'Azur's best Michelin-starred chefs before opening up this pistachio-colored restaurant located in Draguignan's town center. Market-fresh ingredients combine with sophisticated Provençale flavors for a pleasurable meal. Try king prawns in a grilled zucchini salad or lamb shank with roasted polenta.

23 bd. Jean-Jaurès. ✆ **04-94-68-08-50.** www.lougaloubet.fr. Fixed-price menus 22€–34€. MC, V. Sun–Tues and Thurs–Fri 12:30–2:30pm; Mon and Thurs–Sat 7:30–10:30pm.

7

THE FRENCH RIVIERA

by Louise Simpson

Stretching from Mandelieu-La Napoule near the Var to Menton near the Italian border, the French Riviera coastline—known as the Côte d'Azur—is a sunny playground for writers, artists, and sun-kissed aristocrats. Glamour is epitomized in the Belle Époque palaces that lie beside sun-drenched shores, and have lured so many admirers from Coco Chanel to F. Scott Fitzgerald.

You don't have to raise your head from your beach towel to enjoy some of the area's best natural attractions: 300 days of sunshine a year and the bright-blue Mediterranean Sea. When you do leave the sun-drenched beaches, there's much to explore. Michelin-starred restaurants, five-star hotels, theme parks, luxury spas, and private beaches offering watersports galore are the upside of this coastline's overdevelopment. Art lovers can head straight to art museums dedicated to legendary Riviera residents: Chagall and Matisse in Nice, Renoir in Cagnes-sur-Mer, and Picasso in Antibes and Vallauris. Aquariums along the coast offer not-to-be-missed days out, such as Monaco's 100-year old Oceanographic museum and Europe's largest marine park, Marineland. The latest arrivals at Marineland are two polar bears in a 3.5-million€ refrigerated home complete with year-round snow, 24-hour surveillance, and a maternity den.

The Riviera's capital, Nice retains a scruffy earthiness while impressing with its state-of-the-art tramway and its splendid turn-of-the-twentieth-century squares. West of Nice lie the fun-filled and family-friendly resorts of Antibes and Juan-les-Pins, which are renowned for their natural sand beaches, while festival-famed Cannes draws crowds all year around. Resorts east of Nice, such as Villefranche-sur-Mer, Saint-Jean-Cap-Ferrat, and Beaulieu-sur-Mer are more agreeable, serene, and much more expensive. Monaco is awash with royal romance, glamorous nightlife, and gambling; this tiny principality is smaller than New York's Central Park and London's Hyde Park. And sleepy Menton, on the border with Italy, feels more Italianate than French.

As sun-bathing beauties annex the Riviera's beaches all summer long, locals escape the heat to their country farmhouses and await quieter winter days. Here in the back-country, you'll find medieval hilltop towns and villages such as perfumed Grasse; art-filled St-Paul de Vence; violet-strewn Tourrettes-sur-Loup; gastronomic Mougins; and exotic-planted

Eze. Nature reserves abound from Valbonne's La Valmasque park, with its lotus-strewn lake to the undisturbed beauty of the Mercantour National Park, with its gorges, *grottes* (caves), and mountain goats.

MANDELIEU-LA NAPOULE ★

901km (560 miles) S of Paris; 8km (5 miles) W of Cannes

The prettiest part of Mandelieu-La Napoule is the secluded waterside community La Napoule-Plage on the sandy beaches of the Golfe de la Napoule. In 1919, the once-obscure fishing village was a paradise for the eccentric sculptor Henry Clews, son of a New York banker, and his wife, Marie, an architect. Clews fled America's "charlatans," whom he believed had profited from World War I. His house is now a museum. One of the biggest draws of Mandelieu-La Napoule is the two Michelin-starred Oasis restaurant, where Stéphane Raimbault and his brothers Antoine and François have added an informal bistro to their mini-empire of gastronomic excellence.

Essentials

GETTING THERE Mandelieu–La Napoule lies on the **bus** and **train** routes between Cannes and St-Raphaël. The one-way fare, for the train, from Cannes to Mandelieu–La Napoule is 2.10€ and for the bus is 1€. For information and schedules, call ✆ **36-35,** or visit www.ter-sncf.com. If you're **driving,** take A8 west from Cannes.

VISITOR INFORMATION The **Office de Tourisme** is at 806 av. de Cannes (✆ **04-93-93-64-64;** fax 04-93-93-64-66; www.ot-mandelieu.fr).

The Main Attraction

Château de la Napoule/Musée Henry-Clews ★★ An inscription over the entrance to this fairy tale–like château reads: ONCE UPON A TIME. The château, a brooding, medieval-looking fortress whose foundations begin at the edge of the sea, was rebuilt from the ruins of a real medieval château. Clews covered the capitals and lintels with his own grotesque menagerie—scorpions, pelicans, gnomes, monkeys, lizards—the revelations of a tortured mind. Women and feminism are recurring themes in the sculptor's work; an example is the distorted suffragette depicted in his *Cat Woman.* The artist was preoccupied with old age in men and women alike, and admired chivalry and dignity in the man represented by Don Quixote—to whom he likened himself. Clews died in Switzerland in 1937, and his body was returned to La Napoule for burial. Marie Clews later opened the château to the public as a testimonial to the inspiration of her husband. Visitors can enjoy the Salon de Thé (tea room) with its rampart views over the Bay of Cannes from April to September (11am–5pm). The museum also organizes kids' workshops and artists-in-residence programs.

Bd. Henry Clews. ✆ **04-93-49-95-05.** www.chateau-lanapoule.com. Admission 6€ adults; 4€ children 7–18; free for children 6 and under. Mid-Feb to mid-Nov daily 10am–6pm; mid-Nov to mid-Feb Mon–Fri 2–6pm, Sat–Sun 10am–6pm.

Where to Stay

La Calanque The foundations of this two-star hotel date from the Roman Empire. The present hotel, run by the same family since 1942, looks like a hacienda, with salmon-colored stucco walls and shutters. Register in the bar in the rear (through the dining room). Plainly furnished bedrooms range from small to medium, each with a comfortable mattress. Those who take the cheapest bathroomless units will find the corridor bathrooms adequate and well maintained. The hotel's restaurant spills onto a terrace and offers some of the cheapest meals in La Napoule.

404 av. Henry Clews, 06210 Mandelieu-La Napoule. www.hotel-restaurant-lacalanque.fr. ✆ **04-93-49-95-11.** Fax 04-93-49-67-44. 17 units. 35€–87€ double. MC, V. Closed mid-Oct to Feb. Free parking. **Amenities:** Restaurant; bar; smoke-free rooms; Wi-Fi (free). *In room:* A/C (in some), TV.

L'Ermitage du Riou ★ This tranquil, old-fashioned Provençal house is a seaside four-star hotel bordering the Riou River and the Cannes-Mandelieu golf club. The rooms are furnished in regional style, with authentic furniture and ancient paintings, although the upholstery is worn in places. Rooms range in size from medium to spacious with views of the sea, the Riou River, or the golf course. It's worth upgrading to a sea-view room with a balcony. One of the highlights of the hotel is its Mediterranean restaurant Le Riou, which serves wine from the owners' vineyard.

26 av. Henry Clews, 06210 Mandelieu-La Napoule. www.ermitage-du-riou.fr. ✆ **04-93-49-95-56.** Fax 04-92-97-69-05. 41 units. 126€–331€ double; 375€ suite. AE, DC, MC, V. **Amenities:** Restaurant; bar; pool (outdoor). *In room:* A/C, TV, hair dryer, minibar, Wi-Fi (free).

Pullman Cannes Mandelieu Royal Casino ★ A member of the Accor group, this Las Vegas–style hotel is on the beach near a man-made harbor, about 8km (5 miles) from Cannes. It was the first French hotel with a casino and the last (before building codes changed) to have a casino directly on the beach. The hotel has one of the most contemporary designs on the Côte d'Azur. The big plus of the hotel are the spacious rooms—choose one angling toward a sea view as those facing the street are likely to be noisy, despite soundproofing. The restaurant, Le Royal Bay Restaurant, serves modern Mediterranean and Asian fusion cuisine. Service can be hit and miss.

605 av. du Général de Gaulle, 06212 Mandelieu-La Napoule. www.pullmanhotels.com. ✆ **04-92-97-70-00.** Fax 04-93-49-51-50. 213 units. 2119€–455€ double; from 500€ suite. AE, DC, MC, V. Parking 12€. **Amenities:** 2 restaurants; 2 bars; babysitting; casino; concierge; 2 tennis courts (lit). *In room:* A/C, TV, hair dryer, minibar, safe, Wi-Fi (9€).

Where to Eat

Note that the restaurant in **La Calanque** (p. 231) is open to nonguests.

La Brocherie II SEAFOOD The way this restaurant curves along the shoreline gives the impression that you're riding out to sea on a floating houseboat. You'll enter its precincts by crossing a gangplank lined with flaming torches. Specialties include virtually every fish that can be found in local waters—the freshest and best are grilled and served as simply as possible. Your choices of sauce include a rich hollandaise or béarnaise, or an herb-flavored version of white wine, butter, or vinaigrette. The heady version of bouillabaisse is priced at 50€ per person, and a selection of (very expensive) lobsters is chosen from the establishment's bubbling holding tank. Meat dishes include succulent brochettes of Provençal lamb with rosemary and red wine.

Au Port. ✆ **04-93-49-80-73.** Reservations recommended. Main courses 23€–50€; fixed-price menu 38€. MC, V. Daily noon–2:30pm and 7–11pm.

L'Arbre Jaune ★★ MEDITERRANEAN With memorable views over the golf course towards the Esterel hills, this restaurant attracts golfers, gourmands, and art lovers from around the region. Chef Michaël Morel, formerly at Comme Chez Soi in Cannes, has transformed the all-day menu with mouth-watering additions such as lobster prepared three ways, paella, and market-fresh fish at weekends. L'Arbre Jaune is part of the 1,300-hectare (526-acre) Domaine de Barbossi estate that juggles

The French Riviera

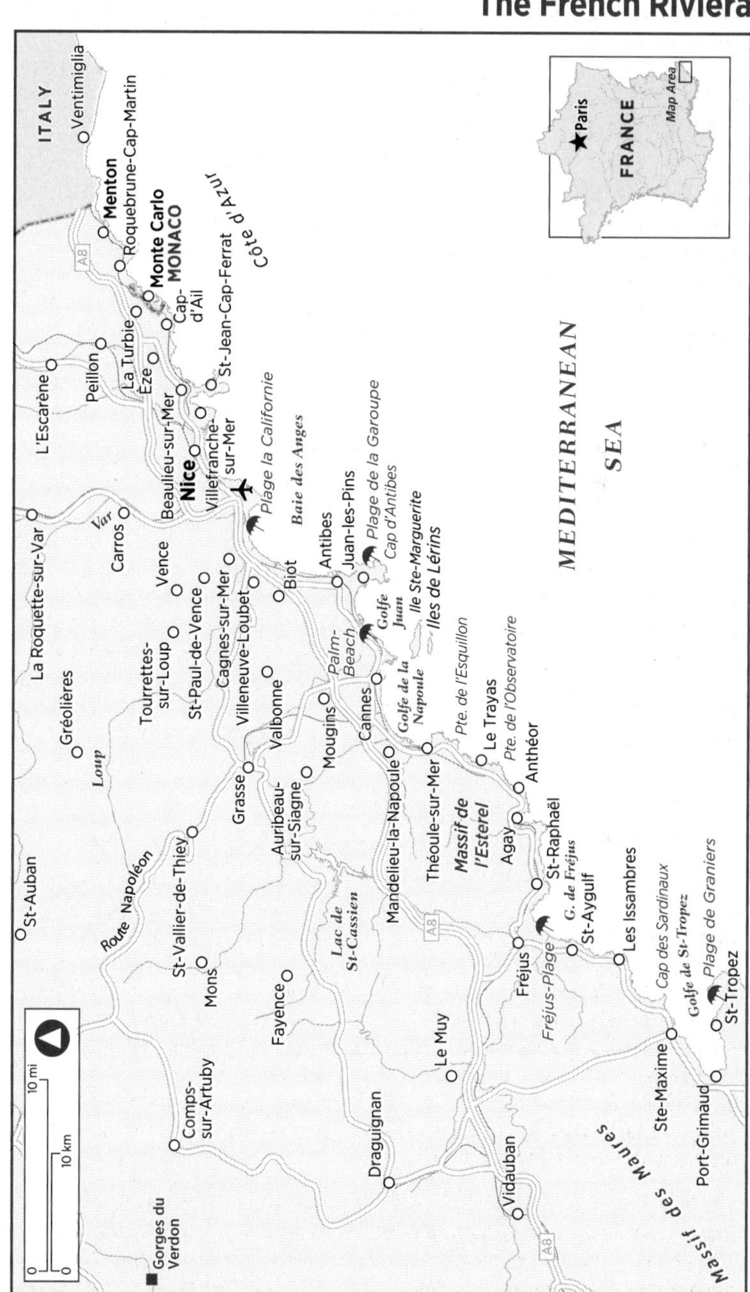

ITALY
Ventimiglia
Menton
Roquebrune-Cap-Martin
Monte Carlo
MONACO
Cap-
d'Ail
St-Jean-Cap-Ferrat
Côte d'Azur
L'Escarène
Peillon
La Turbie
Èze
Beaulieu-sur-Mer
Villefranche-
sur-Mer
Nice
Plage la Californie
Baie des Anges
La Roquette-sur-Var
Var
Carros
Vence
Cagnes-sur-Mer
Villeneuve-Loubet
Biot
Antibes
Juan-les-Pins
Plage de la Garoupe
Cap d'Antibes
Golfe
Juan
Ile Ste-Marguerite
Iles de Lérins
Gréolières
Tourrettes-
sur-Loup
St-Paul-de-Vence
Valbonne
Palm-
Beach
Mougins
Cannes
Golfe de la
Napoule
Pte. de l'Esquillon
Le Trayas
Pte. de l'Observatoire
Anthéor
Loup
Grasse
Auribeau-
sur-Siagne
Mandelieu-la-Napoule
Théoule-sur-Mer
Massif de
l'Esterel
Agay
St-Raphaël
G. de Fréjus
St-Aygulf
Les Issambres
Cap des Sardinaux
Golfe de St-Tropez
Plage de Graniers
St-Tropez
St-Auban
Route Napoléon
St-Vallier-de-Thiey
Mons
Lac de
St-Cassien
Fayence
A8
Fréjus
Fréjus-Plage
Le Muy
Ste-Maxime
Port-Grimaud
Comps-
sur-Artuby
Draguignan
Vidauban
Massif des Maures
Gorges du
Verdon
0
10 mi
0
10 km
MEDITERRANEAN
SEA
Paris
FRANCE
Map Area

golf, viticulture, and a contemporary sculpture collection (installed in spring 2011). Products from the estate such as wine, honey, and olive oil can be purchased at the pro shop.

Domaine de Barbossi, 802 av. des Amazones, Mandelieu-La Napoule. ✆ **04-92-97-49-49.** Reservations recommended. Main courses 16€–26€. MC, V. June–Sept daily 11:30am–11pm; Oct–May daily 11:30am–4:30pm.

FOLLOWING la route napoleon

On March 1, 1815, having escaped from a Senate-imposed exile on Elba that began in April 1814, Napoleon, accompanied by a small band of followers, landed at Golfe-Juan. The deposed emperor was intent on marching northward to reclaim his throne as emperor.

Though the details of his journey have been obscured by time, two versions of a local legend about one of his first mainland encounters exist. The first version claims that shortly after landing at Golfe-Juan, Napoleon and his military escort were waylaid by highwaymen unimpressed by his credentials. The other turns the story around, claiming that Napoleon's men, attempting to build a supply of money and arms, waylaid the coach of the prince de Monaco, whose principality, stripped of independence during the Revolution, had just been restored by Louis XVIII. When the prince told Napoleon that he was on his way to reclaim his throne, the exiled emperor stated that they were in the same business and bid his men to let the coach pass unhindered.

In the 1930's, the French government recognized Napoleon's positive influence on internal affairs by building Route 85, **La Route Napoleon,** to roughly trace the steps of the exiled emperor in search of a throne. It stretches from Golfe-Juan to Grenoble, but the most scenic stretch is in Provence, between Grasse and Digne-les-Bains. The route is well marked with commemorative plaques sporting an eagle in flight, though the "action" documented south of Grenoble revolves around simple stops made for food and sleep along the way.

After embarking from Cannes on the morning of March 2, the group passed through Grasse and halted just beyond St Vallier de Thiey, spending the night. From this point to the end destination at Digne-les-Bains, the route touches only a handful of small settlements; the most notable is Castellane and the village of Barrème, where an encampment was set up on the night of March 3. The next day, the group stopped for lunch in Digne-les-Bains before leaving the region to continue north toward the showdown at Grenoble. Although the relais where he dined is long gone, you can stop at **Restaurant Le Préjoly,** place du Cavalier Fabre, in St Vallier de Thiey (✆ **04-93-42-60-86**). Cozy and historic, with a staff that's consciously tied into the travails and tribulations of Napoleon during his transit through their town, it serves tasty set-price menus for between 19€ and 35€. From May to August, it's open daily for lunch and dinner; but the rest of the year, it's closed on Mondays.

The **Office de Tourisme** at 10 place du Tour, St Vallier de Thiey (✆ **04-93-42-78-00**), can provide you with a detailed account of the trek, a map of the three campsites where Napoleon and his men slept, and a map indicating where the road deviates from Napoleon's actual route, now maintained as a hiking trail where you can follow in his footsteps. The office is open Monday to Saturday 9am to noon and 3 to 6pm.

L'Oasis ★★★ MODERN FRENCH There's no more wonderful cuisine in this corner of the French Riviera than at L'Oasis. At the entrance to the harbor of La Napoule, in a mid-20th-century house with a lovely garden and a re-creation of a medieval cloister, this two-Michelin-starred restaurant became world famous under now-retired Louis Outhier. Today, his protégé, Stéphane Raimbault, prepares sophisticated cuisine alongside his brothers Antoine and François. Because Raimbault cooked in Japan for 9 years, many of his dishes are of the "East meets West" variety. The cuisine falls roughly into modern French or Mediterranean, with a touch of Japanese. The cellar houses one of the finest collections of Provençal wines anywhere. In summer, meals are served under the plane trees in the garden. Along with a cooking school and a boutique selling Raimbault's homemade fine foods and pastries, a delightful informal bistro, serving hearty Mediterranean dishes, was added in 2009.

Rue Jean Honoré Carle. ✆ **04-93-49-95-52.** www.oasis-raimbault.com. Reservations required. Main courses 18€–95€; fixed-price lunch 70€–89€, dinner 95€–180€. AE, DC, MC, V. Tues–Sat noon–3:30pm and 7–11pm.

CANNES ★★★

905km (562 miles) S of Paris; 164km (102 miles) E of Marseille; 26km (16 miles) SW of Nice

When Coco Chanel got a suntan here, she startled the milk-white ladies of Parisian society. Today, there's hardly an inch of sand along La Croisette's beaches that isn't covered with bronzing bodies in the summer. Cannes's whitewashed luxury hotels, designer shops, and Michelin-starred cuisine all embody Riviera glamour. But away from the flashing cameras and Hollywood starlets who come for May's International Film Festival, a tamer city charms all year round.

Things to Do Strolling along glamorous seaside promenade **La Croisette** is a requisite activity. Follow the celebrity handprints of **Allée des Etoiles** on the palm-lined La Croisette, climb the medieval slopes of the old town of **Le Suquet,** or smell the salty breeze as you admire the yachts along the **Vieux Port. Forville Market** is the place to fill your picnic basket with freshly caught fish, pungent cheeses, and tapenade (olive paste).

Relaxation Sun worshippers head to sandy private beaches along **La Croisette.** If you relax with retail therapy, you're in luck: There are designer labels along La Croisette, high-street fashion along the **rue d'Antibes,** and bargain finds on **rue Meynadier.** On summer evenings, watch fireworks light up the Bay of Cannes or listen to open-air classical concerts in La Castre museum's courtyard.

Restaurants & Dining Cannes is the city for spring-to-autumn alfresco dining and coffee drinking in pavement cafes. Splash out on Michelin-starred restaurants along **La Croisette,** try *bouillabaisse* (fish stew) on **Quai Saint Pierre** and **rue Félix Faure,** or sample traditional French cuisine in **place du Suquet.** For dining on the hoof, grab a filled baguette from **rue Meynadier.**

Nightlife & Entertainment From high rollers to celebrity chic, La Croisette's hotel bars and casinos, including those at the **Majestic** and **Carlton,** have seen it all. On the streets around **rue du Commandant André,** you'll find kitten-heeled Cannoises sipping mojitos at cafe-bars. For summertime nightspots where you can ogle the Mediterranean as you boogie until dawn, head for the jutting peninsula of the **Pointe Croisette.**

Cannes

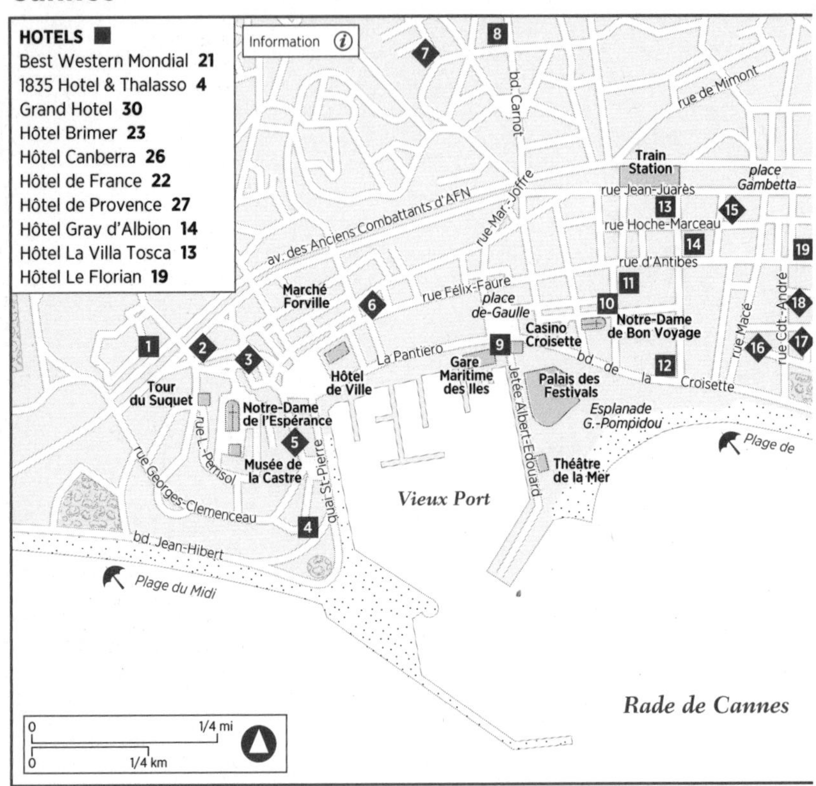

Essentials

GETTING THERE **Nice international airport** (✆ **08-20-42-33-33;** www.nice.aeroport.fr) is a 30-minute drive northeast. Buses pick up passengers at the airport every 30 minutes during the day and drop them at the bus station, place de l'Hôtel de Ville; the fare is 16€.

Trains from the other Mediterranean resorts, Paris, and the rest of France arrive frequently throughout the day. By train, Cannes is 15 minutes from Antibes and 35 minutes from Nice. The TGV from Paris via Marseille reaches Cannes in about 5½ to 6 breathless hours. The one-way fare from Paris is about 50€ to 100€. For rail information and schedules, call ✆ **36-35,** or visit www.voyages-sncf.com.

There's a **bus** service from Cannes bus station, place de l'Hôtel de Ville to Nice and back approximately every 15 minutes during the day (trip time 1½ hr.). The one-way fare is 1€. A bus service from Antibes operates every half-hour. For more information, contact **Lignes d'Azur** (✆ **0810-06-10-06;** www.lignesdazur.com).

By **car** from Marseille, take A51 north to Aix-en-Provence, continuing along A8 east to Cannes. From Nice, follow A8 southwest to Cannes.

VISITOR INFORMATION The **Office de Tourisme** is at Palais des Festivals, 1 bd. de la Croisette (✆ **04-92-99-84-22;** www.cannes.com).

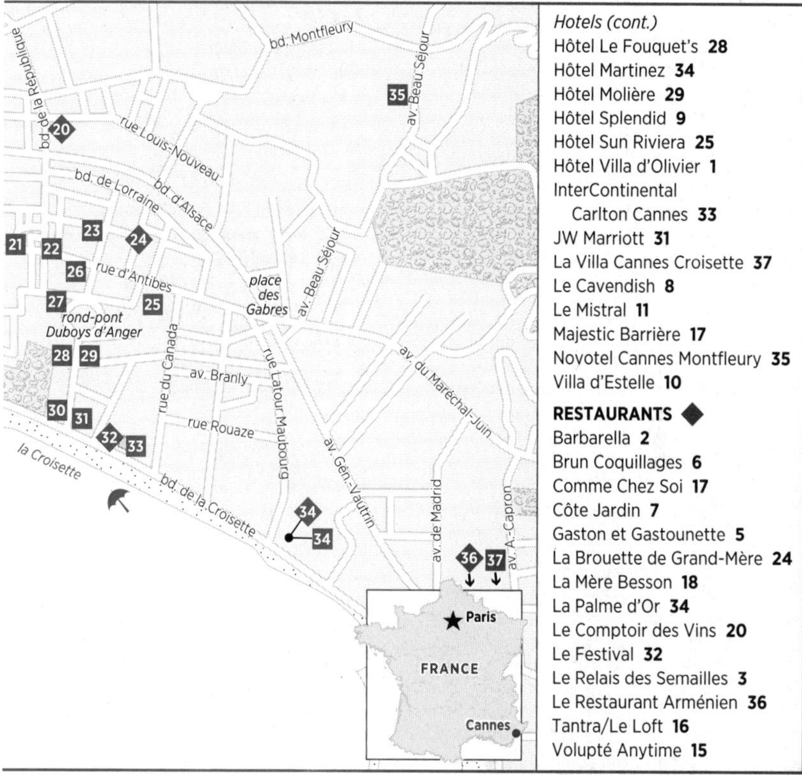

SPECIAL EVENTS Cannes is a popular venue for festivals and conventions. The most famous is the **Festival de Cannes,** the international film festival that transforms this city every May into the kingdom of the media deal, with daily melodramas acted out in cafes, on sidewalks, and in hotel lobbies. Admission to some of the prestigious films is by invitation only, but there are box-office tickets for the less important films, which play 24 hours. For information, contact the **Association Française du Festival International du Film,** 3 rue Amélie, 75007 Paris (✆ **01-53-59-61-00;** www.festival-cannes.com). In July and August, the skies above La Croisette are lit up by the **Festival d'Art Pyrotechnique,** a flashy fireworks spectacle that's completely free for spectators. There's an elastic 9:30pm start, depending on whether it's dark enough; relax at a neighboring restaurant or cafe while you wait. For more information, visit the website www.festival-pyrotechnique-cannes.com.

Exploring the City

For many, Cannes consists of only one street, **boulevard de la Croisette ★★** (or just La Croisette), curving along the coast and split by islands of palms and flowers. It's said that Edward, Prince of Wales (before he became Edward VII), contributed to its

SEEING Cannes FROM A PETIT TRAIN

One of the best ways to get your bearings in Cannes (and to get an idea of the difference between the city's new and old neighborhoods) is to board a white-sided *petit train.* The diesel-powered vehicles roll through the streets on rubber tires. They operate every day from 9am to between 7 and 11pm, depending on the season (there's no service in Nov). Choose from two itineraries: Croisette Tour for views of glittery modern Cannes along La Croisette and Palm Beach, or History Tour for a ride through the narrow streets of Vieux Cannes (Le Suquet). Both tours depart every hour from Palais des Festivals along La Croisette. They last around 35 minutes, depending on traffic, and cost 7€ for adults, 3€ for children ages 3 to 9, and free for 2 years and under. A combination ticket to both tours (good on separate days, if you prefer) costs 10€ for adults, 5€ for children ages 3 to 9, and free for 2 years and under. For details, call ✆ **06-22-61-25-76** or visit www.cannes-petit-train.com.

original cost. But he was a Johnny-come-lately to Cannes. In 1834, Lord Brougham, a lord chancellor of England, set out for Nice and was turned away because of an outbreak of cholera. He landed at Cannes and liked it so much that he built a villa here. Returning every winter until his death in 1868, he proselytized it in London, drawing a long line of British visitors. In the 1890s, Cannes became popular with Russian grand dukes (it's said that more caviar was consumed here than in all of Moscow).

A port of call for cruise liners, the seafront of Cannes is lined with hotels, apartment houses, and chic boutiques. Many of the bigger hotels, some dating from the 19th century, claim part of the beach for the private use of their guests, but public areas do exist. Above the harbor, the old town of Cannes sits on Suquet Hill, with its 14th-century tower, the **Tour du Suquet,** which the English dubbed "the Lord's Tower."

Nearby is the **Musée de la Castre ★**, in the Château de la Castre, Le Suquet (✆ **04-93-38-55-26**). It contains paintings, sculpture, and works of decorative art. The ethnography section includes Peruvian and Maya pottery; one gallery is devoted to relics of Mediterranean civilizations, from the Greeks to the Romans, the Cypriots to the Egyptians. Five rooms hold 19th-century paintings. Don't miss the Chapelle Sainte-Anne section of the museum, which contains a fascinating collection of musical instruments from around the world. The museum is open daily in July and August 10am to 7pm; October to March Tuesday to Sunday 10am to 1pm and 2 to 5pm; and April to June and September Tuesday to Sunday 10am to 1pm and 2 to 6pm. Admission is 3.50€ adults, 2.20€ ages 18 to 25, and free for ages 17 and under.

Though nobody plans a trip to Cannes to see churches, the city does contain some worthy examples. The largest and most prominent is **Notre-Dame de Bon Voyage,** square Mérimée, opposite the Palais des Festivals; it was built in a faux Gothic style in the late 19th century. The most historic church, **Notre-Dame de l'Espérance,** place de la Castre, was built between 1521 and 1641 and combines both Gothic and Renaissance elements. The town's most unusual church is the **Eglise Orthodoxe Russe St-Michel Archange,** 36–40 bd. Alexandre-III (✆ **04-93-43-00-28**), built in 1894 through the efforts of Alexandra Skrypitzine, a Russian in exile; it's capped with a cerulean-blue onion dome and a gilded triple cross. It is usually locked, except for services on Saturday at 5pm and Sunday between 9:30am and noon.

Outdoor Pursuits

BICYCLING & MOTORSCOOTERING Despite the roaring traffic, the flat landscapes between Cannes and satellite resorts such as Mandelieu-La Napoule are well suited for riding a bike or motorscooter. At **Mistral Location,** 4 rue Georges Clémenceau (✆ **06-20-33-87-64;** www.mistral-location.com), *vélos tout terrain* (mountain bikes) cost 16€ a day. Motorized bikes and scooters cost from 26€ per day; renters must be at least 14 years old. For larger scooters, you must present a valid driver's license.

BOATING Several companies rent boats of any size, with or without a crew, for a day, a week, or a month. An outfit known for short-term rentals of small motorboats is **Elco Marine,** 110 bd. du Midi (✆ **04-93-47-12-62;** www.elcomarine.fr). For larger boats, including motor-driven and sailing yachts, try **International Yacht Charter,** Les Jardins du Grand Hôtel, 45 bd. de la Croisette (✆ **04-92-99-39-93;** www.yachtcharters.fr).

GOLF One of the region's most challenging courses, **Golf Country Club de Cannes-Mougins,** 175 av. du Golf, Mougins (✆ **04-93-75-79-13;** www.golf-cannes-mougins.com), 6.5km (4 miles) north of Cannes, is a 1977 reconfiguration by Allis and Thomas of a 1920s-era course. Noted for the olive trees and cypresses that adorn the flat terrain, it has many water hazards and technical challenges. For many years, the par-72 course played host to the Cannes-Mougins Open, a stop on the PGA European Tour. The course is open to anyone (with proof of handicap of 28 or under) willing to pay greens fees from 70€ for 9 holes and from 100€ per person for 18 holes. An electric golf cart rents for 40€. Reservations are recommended.

SWIMMING Cannes probably has more privately owned swimming pools per capita than anywhere else in France. If your hotel doesn't have one, consider an excursion to the **Piscine Pierre de Coubertin,** avenue Pierre Poési, Cannes-La-Bocca (✆ **04-93-47-12-94**). Its length of almost 25m (82 ft.) makes this outdoor pool ideal for swimming laps. Because it's used for a variety of civic functions, including practices for local swim teams, hours are limited, so call ahead. Entrance costs 3€ for adults and 2€ for children 4 to 17.

TENNIS Some resorts have their own courts. The city of Cannes also maintains 16 courts (six clay-topped, six synthetic resin, and four synthetic indoor courts); you'll pay 12€ to 16€ per hour per court for two to four players, depending on the court and the time you want to play, plus 3.50€–4.50€ per hour for lighting. You should book by telephone a day in advance. They're at **Cannes Garden Tennis Club,** 99 av. Maurice Chevalier, Cannes-La-Bocca (✆ **04-93-47-29-33;** www.cannes-tennis.com).

A Day at the Beach

Beachgoing in Cannes has more to do with exhibitionism and voyeurism than with actual swimming. **Plage de la Croisette,** with its imported golden sand, extends between the Vieux Port and the Port Canto. Though the beaches along this billion-dollar stretch of sand aren't in the strictest sense private, they're *payante,* meaning entrance costs 15€ to 35€. You don't need to be a guest of the Martinez, Carlton, or Majestic to use the beaches associated with those hotels, though if you are you'll usually get a 50% discount outside peak season. A wooden barricade that stops close to the sea separates each beach from its neighbors, making it easy for you to stroll from one to another.

Why should you pay a fee at all? Well, it includes a full day's use of a mattress, a chaise longue, and a parasol, as well as easy access to freshwater showers and kiosks selling beverages. You can also dine at outdoor restaurants where no one minds if you appear in your swimsuit. The merits of each of the 20 or so beaches vary daily depending on the crowd. And because every beach allows topless bathing (keep your bottom covered), you're likely to find the same forms of décolletage along the entire strip.

One of the most sought-after private beaches is the **Z-Plage,** which is associated with the Martinez (see "Where to Stay" below), and has 400 beach recliners, an excellent restaurant, and a bar serving refreshing Bellinis. However, such luxury doesn't come cheap: Beach recliners on the exclusive pontoon of this private beach go for up to 53€ per day in peak season. Meanwhile, **Vegaluna** (**© 04-93-43-67-05;** www.vegaluna.com) is our favorite beach for families because of its kids' play area and summertime baby club. For both beaches, it's worth booking in advance to ensure a place.

Looking for a free public beach where you'll have to survive without renting chaises or parasols? Head for **Plage du Midi** along boulevard du Midi just west of the Vieux Port (no phone), or **Plage du Mourre Rouge** (often called Plage Gazagnaire), on boulevard Eugène Gazagnaire just east of the Port Canto (no phone). Here you'll find families with children and lots of mobile home–type vehicles parked nearby.

Shopping

Cannes competes more successfully than many of its neighbors in a highly commercial blend of resort-style leisure, luxury glamour, and media glitz. So you're likely to find branch outlets of virtually every stylish Paris retailer. Every big-name designer you can think of (Saint Laurent, Rykiel, Hermès) as well as big-name designers you've never heard of (Claude Bonucci, Basile, and Durrani) are here—but, more important, real-people shops (shops for gently worn star-studded cast-offs; flea markets for fun junk; and a fruit, flower, and vegetable market) thrive.

ANTIQUES In the Palais de Festivals on La Croisette, Cannes stages one of France's most prestigious **antiques salons** in mid-July and late December or early January. Its organizers refuse to include low- or even middle-bracket stock. This is serious, with lots of 18th- and early-19th-century merchandise. Admission is 10€. Shipping services are available. For dates and information, visit www.spat.fr/antiquairesdecannes.

BOOKS A year-round bookstore, **Ciné-Folie,** 14 rue des Frères Pradignac (**© 04-93-39-22-99**), is devoted entirely to films. It's called *La Boutique du Cinema.* The outlet is the finest film bookstore in the south of France and also sells vintage film stills and movie posters.

CHOCOLATE & CANDIES Several famous chocolatiers keep chocolate lovers in Cannes happy. **Confiserie Bruno,** 13 rue Hoche (**© 04-93-39-26-63**), opened in 1929 and is maintained by a descendant of its founder; the shop is famous for *fruits confits* (dried, candied fruits), chocolates, and *marrons glacés* (glazed chestnuts), made fresh daily.

DEPARTMENT STORES Just off the rue d'Antibes, **Galeries Lafayette** has a small branch at 6 rue du Maréchal Foch (**© 04-97-06-25-00;** www.galerieslafayette.com). It's noted for the upscale fashion in its carefully arranged interiors.

DESIGNER SHOPS Most of the big names in fashion, for men and women alike, line **boulevard de la Croisette,** known as La Croisette, the main drag facing the sea. Among the most prestigious is **Dior,** 38 bd. de la Croisette (**© 04-92-98-98-00;**

ferrying to the ÎLES DE LÉRINS

Across the bay from Cannes, the Lérins Islands are the major excursion from the port. Ferries depart daily from quai Laubeuf opposite Cannes's Hôtel 1835. You have to choose which island to visit as island politics decrees that no ferry company visits both. **Trans-Côte d'Azur** (✆ **04-92-98-71-30;** www.trans-cote-azur.com) operates ferries to Île Sainte-Marguerite between 7:30am (9am on Sun in wintertime) and 4:30pm for 12€ for adults, 6.50€ for children 5 to 10, and free for children 4 and under. Compagnie Planaria offers round-trips to Île Saint-Honorat daily between 8am and 5pm for 12€ for adults, 6€ for children 5 to 10, and free for children 4 and under.

ÎLE SAINTE-MARGUERITE The first island is named after Saint Honorat's sister, Sainte Marguerite, who lived here with a group of nuns in the 5th century. Today it is a youth center whose members (when they aren't sailing and diving) are dedicated to the restoration of the fort. From the dock where the boat lands, you can stroll along the island (signs point the way) to the **Fort Royal** (✆ **04-93-43-18-17**). Leonardo DiCaprio fans flock to this 17th-century fortress prison to see where the unlucky man immortalized in *The Man in the Iron Mask* was imprisoned.

One of French history's most perplexing mysteries is the identity of the man who allegedly wore the ***masque du fer,*** a prisoner of Louis XIV who arrived at Ste-Marguerite in 1698. Dumas popularized the legend that he was a brother of Louis XIV. However, the most common theory is that the prisoner was a servant of the superintendent, Fouquet, named Eustache Dauger. He might have earned his fate by aiding Fouquet in embezzling the king's treasury. At any rate, he died in the Bastille in Paris in 1703. You can visit his cell at Ste-Marguerite, where it seems that every visitor has written his or her name. As you stand listening to the sound of the sea, you realize what a forlorn outpost this was.

Musée de la Mer, at Fort Royal, traces the history of the island, displaying artifacts of Ligurian, Roman, and Arab civilizations, plus the remains discovered by excavations, including paintings, mosaics, and ceramics. The fort and museum are open April to May Tuesday to Sunday 10:30am to 1:15pm and 2:15 to 5:45pm, June to September daily 10am to 5:45pm, and October to March Tuesday to Sunday 10:30am to 1:15pm and 2:15 to 4:45pm. Admission is 3.50€ for adults, 2.20€ for ages 18 to 25, and free for students and children 17 and under.

ÎLE SAINT-HONORAT Less than 2km (only a mile) long, but richer in history than any of its sibling islands, the beautiful Île St-Honorat is the site of a working monastery whose origins go back to the 5th century. Today the **Abbaye Notre Dame de Lérins** (✆ **04-92-99-54-00**) maintains a combination of medieval ruins and early-20th-century ecclesiastical buildings, inhabited by a permanent community of about 30 Cistercian monks. The monks produce their own olive oil, lavender, wine, and colorful liqueurs—the green liqueur looks like the green fairy, Absinthe. If space is available, outsiders can visit, for prayer and meditation only, and spend the night. However, most visitors come to wander through the pine forests on the island's western side and sun themselves on its beaches.

www.dior.com). The stores are in a row, stretching from the Hôtel Carlton almost to the Palais des Festivals, with the best names closest to the **Gray d'Albion,** 38 rue des Serbes (✆ **04-92-99-79-79**), which is both a mall and a hotel (how convenient);

Mammillary Tribute to a Courtesan

The twin cupolas of the InterContinental Carlton were modeled on the breasts of the most fabled local courtesan, La Belle Otéro. The hotel's main restaurant also carries her name.

inside the Gray d'Albion mall, you'll find **Hermès,** 17 bd. de la Croisette (✆ **04-93-39-08-90;** www.hermes.com). The two-section mall serves as a cut-through from the primary expensive shopping street, La Croisette, to the less expensive shopping street, **rue d'Antibes.**

FLEA MARKETS Cannes has two regular flea markets. Casual, dusty, and increasingly filled with castaways from estate sales, the **Marché Forville,** conducted in the neighborhood of the same name near the Palais des Festivals, is a stucco structure with a roof and a few arches but no sides. Monday is *brocante* (second-hand goods) day, when the market fills with dealers selling everything from *grandmère's* dishes to bone-handled carving knives. The rest of the week from Tuesday to Sunday, it's the fruit, vegetable, and flower market that supplies dozens of grand restaurants.

On Saturdays, a somewhat disorganized and busy **flea market** takes place outdoors along the edges of the allée de la Liberté, across from the old port. Hours depend on the whims of whatever dealer happens to haul in a cache of merchandise, but it usually begins around 8am and runs out of steam by around 4:30pm. ***Note:*** Vendors at the two flea markets may or may not be the same.

FOOD The street with the greatest density of emporiums selling wine, olives, herbs, cheese, bread, and oils is the appealing **rue Meynadier.**

A charming old-fashioned shop, **Cannolive,** 16–20 rue Vénizelos (✆ **04-93-39-08-19**), is owned by members of the Raynaud family, which founded the place in 1880. It sells Provençal olives and their byproducts—tapenades that connoisseurs refer to as "Provençal caviar," black *olives de Nice,* and green *olives de Provence,* as well as three grades of olive oil from regional producers. Oils and food products are at no. 16; gift items (fabrics, porcelain, and Provençal souvenirs) are sold next door.

MARKETS At the edge of the Quartier Suquet, the **Marché Forville** is the town's primary fruit, flower, and vegetable market. On Monday it's a *brocante* market. See "Flea Markets," above.

PERFUME The best shop is **Bouteille,** 59 rue d'Antibes (✆ **04-93-39-39-28**). Its prices are higher than its competitors' because it stocks more brands, has a wider selection, and gives away occasional samples. Other shops dot rue d'Antibes. For reasonably priced perfumes, head opposite to the boutiques associated with the Hôtel Gray d'Albion.

Where to Stay

Cannes is one of the most popular places to stay on the Côte d'Azur. Although lodgings are often expensive, the quality of two- and three-star places for those on a budget is high, and renovations are frequent.

If you're splashing out on one of the grand dames of La Croisette, remember that you're paying for the view and the location, so room sizes don't necessarily match the size of the price. To avoid disappointment, you can check the exact room size on the hotel website. Exceptional low-season deals can be found at even the most glamorous hotels, so it's worth checking out websites for the latest offers. ***Warning:*** Look out for hidden extra charges for beach recliners, chaise longues by the pool and beach, gym access, and even Wi-Fi. During conventions and high season, you should make hotel car parking, restaurant, and even beach lounge chair reservations when you book your room.

More and more hotels in Cannes are joining Green Globe's world-wide certification label for sustainable tourism. For more information on environmentally friendly hotels in Cannes, contact **Green Globe** (✆ **06-15-09-27-21;** www.greenglobe.com).

VERY EXPENSIVE

Hôtel Martinez ★★★ Built in 1929, this hotel stands proudly as one of the grand dames of La Croisette. You'll see traces of its history in the Art Deco interiors, from the grand decorative spiral staircase to the loud geometric carpeting and wallpaper that permeate the hotel. The hotel underwent a renovation in 2011, which updated many of the guest rooms and suites, as well as some public areas. Guest rooms range in style, but many pay tribute to the Art Deco era, with luxe fabrics, geometric shapes, and wood furniture; other rooms are more subdued, with neutral tones. The luxury suites are sprawling, and most overlook the sea. The Martinez is home to La Palme d'Or (see p. 249), the only two-star Michelin restaurant in Cannes, serving creative French cuisine that takes advantage of the region's bounty. The Martinez is also home to Z-Plage, the biggest private beach in Cannes. The hotel holds a Green Globe certification for its environmentally friendly initiatives.

73 bd. de la Croisette, 06400 Cannes. www.hotel-martinez.com. ✆ **04-92-98-73-00.** Fax 04-93-39-67-82. 409 units. 610€–1,250€ double; from 2,900€ suite. AE, DC, MC, V. Parking 39€. **Amenities:** 3 restaurants; 2 bars; beach club; concierge; fitness center; kids' club (in summer); pool (outdoors); room service; spa. *In room:* A/C, TV, hair dryer, minibar, Wi-Fi (free).

InterContinental Carlton Cannes ★★★ Cynics say that one of the most amusing sights in Cannes is watching vehicles drop off huge amounts of baggage and numbers of fashionable (and sometimes not-so-fashionable) guests at the Carlton's grand gate. Built in 1912, the Carlton once attracted the most prominent members of Europe's *haut monde.* Today this legendary hotel is more democratic, booking lots of conventions and tour groups; however, in summer (especially during the film festival) the public rooms still fill with all the voyeuristic and exhibitionistic fervor that seems so much a part of the Riviera. Guest rooms are plush and a bit airier than you may expect. Make sure you book one of the renovated bedrooms, as some classic rooms at the back of the hotel could do with a refurbishment. The most spacious rooms are in the west wing, and many upper-floor rooms open onto waterfront balconies.

58 bd. de la Croisette, 06400 Cannes. www.ichotelsgroup.com. ✆ **04-93-06-40-06.** Fax 04-93-06-40-25. 343 units. 195€–1,165€ double; from 850€ suite. AE, DC, MC, V. Parking 38€. **Amenities:** 2 restaurants (1 summer only and 1 year-round); 2 bars; concierge; health club; room service. *In room:* A/C, TV, hair dryer, minibar, Wi-Fi (free for 30 min., then 24€).

Majestic Barrière ★★★ At the west end of La Croisette, the Majestic stands for glamour and has done so since 1926. It's a favorite with celebs during the annual film festival and beloved by the Parisians as part of the exclusive Lucien Barrière group. A 72-million€ hotel renovation along with the arrival of a new spa and La Petite Maison restaurant in 2010 has given it the stylistic edge over its rival, the friendlier InterContinental Carlton. Constructed around an overscale front patio, the hotel opens directly onto the esplanade and the sea. Inside, the setting is one of marble, crystal chandeliers, Oriental carpets, Louis XV silk furniture, and potted palms. The guest rooms are furnished with more of the same. All rooms are fitted with bedside controls and luxury amenities; the most special of the lot are seaview suites with private terraces. Bathrooms are sumptuous, with deluxe toiletries.

10 bd. de la Croisette, 06407 Cannes. www.lucienbarriere.com. ✆ **04-92-98-77-00.** Fax 04-93-38-97-00. 369 units. 199€–1,300€ double; from 558€ suite. AE, DC, MC, V. Parking 40€. **Amenities:** 2 restaurants; bar; babysitting; concierge; private beach; pool (outdoor); room service; spa and fitness room. *In room:* A/C, safe, TV, hair dryer, minibar, Wi-Fi (15€).

JW Marriott This hotel has changed ownership several times in the past decade alone—past guests may know it as the Palais Stéphanie or the Noga Hilton. Whether it's current incarnation (since late 2010) as a Marriott will last is yet to be seen. Further renovations are currently underway. Unlike the period architecture of its Croisette compatriots, this four-star hotel is a gleaming glass-and-steel construction with a white marble atrium-style lobby. Guest rooms are carefully soundproofed, each decorated with black-and-white wallpaper friezes of film festival stills. There's no private beach, but it does have a rather stark rooftop pool and Jacuzzi. The hotel has an adjacent casino, owned by the Lucien Barrière group, with table games and 150 slot machines.

50 bd. de la Croisette, Cannes 06414. www.marriott.com. ✆ **04-92-99-70-00.** 261 units. 320€–1,200€ double; from 650€ suite. AE, DC, MC, V. Parking 38€. **Amenities:** 2 restaurants (1 summer only and 1 year-round); bar; concierge; pool (outdoor); room service. *In room:* A/C, TV, hair dryer, minibar, Wi-Fi (15€ per hr.).

EXPENSIVE

1835 Hotel & Thalasso ★ Part of the Radisson Blu hotel chain, this seven-story hotel on the harborfront of Cannes offers views that extend over some of the most expensive private yachts in the Mediterranean. A remake of an older hotel, it has a well-designed, bright interior, offering contemporary-looking upscale bedrooms, some with views over the sea. There are impressive 360° views from the rooftop terrace and restaurant. However, it's worth noting that hotel guests have to pay 25€ per day to access the adjoining thalassotherapy spa with its indoor and outdoor seawater pool. External guests can also use the spa if they book spa treatments. Service is friendly, but there should be more staff on check-in and concierge.

2 bd. Jean Hibert, 06414 Cannes. www.1835-hotel.com. ✆ **04-92-99-73-00.** Fax 04-92-99-73-25. 134 units. 145€–750€ double; from 265€ suite. AE, DC, MC, V. Parking 35€. **Amenities:** 2 restaurants; bar, babysitting; concierge; seawater pool (indoor and outdoor); room service; thalassotherapy spa. *In room:* A/C, TV, DVD, CD player, hair dryer, minibar, Wi-Fi (free).

Grand Hôtel ★★ Tall date palms and a lawn sweeping down to the waterfront esplanade lend this hotel a gracious air. It's a great option for those wanting a four-star hotel with fewer amenities (and at times less professional service) than its sumptuous five-star neighbors, but with all the drama of staying on La Croisette. A renovated structure of glass and marble, it is part of a complex of adjoining apartment-house wings and encircling boutiques. Eleven floors of rooms (with wall-to-wall picture windows) open onto wooden terraces. Vibrant colors are used throughout: sea blue, olive, sunburst red, and banana. Those rooms with sea views are the most expensive. As well as the private beach, one of the hotel's highlights is its restaurant **Park 45:** Its gastronomic French cuisine was rewarded with a Michelin star in 2010.

45 bd. de la Croisette, 06140 Cannes. www.grand-hotel-cannes.com. ✆ **04-93-38-15-45.** Fax 04-93-68-97-45. 76 units. 200€–1,300€ double; from 700€ suite. AE, MC, V. Parking 25€. Closed mid-Dec to mid-Jan. **Amenities:** 2 restaurants (1 summer only and 1 year-round); bar; babysitting; private beach; room service. *In room:* A/C, TV, hair dryer, high-speed Internet (15€), minibar.

Hôtel Gray d'Albion ★ The smallest of the major hotels, this four-star hotel occupies a contemporary building. Now part of the Lucien Barrière chain, it enjoys a respectable though somewhat staid image. Groups form a large part of its clientele, but it caters to individual travelers as well. The medium-size rooms blend contemporary and traditional furnishings. Most units have a balcony, but the views aren't notable, except for some executive suites which overlook the Mediterranean. The hotel's restaurant, Le 38, features the simple yet refined French cuisine of respected chef Alain Roy. The hotel has its own shopping mall on the ground floor (p. 241).

38 rue des Serbes, 06408 Cannes. www.lucienbarriere.com. ✆ **04-92-99-79-79.** Fax 04-93-99-26-10. 199 units. 210€–549€ double; from 280€ suite. AE, DC, MC, V. **Amenities:** 2 restaurants (1 summer only and 1 year-round); bar; babysitting; concierge; room service. *In room:* A/C, TV, hair dryer, minibar, Wi-Fi (15€).

Novotel Cannes Montfleury This hotel has carved out a good market for itself among independent travelers, although it can't compete with the big guns reviewed above. Its quiet residential location seems distant from the buzz of Cannes, but a complimentary shuttle service takes guests to the seafront—it's best to reserve a place in advance. The modern palace shares a 4-hectare (10-acre) park with a sports complex. The open-air curved outdoor pool is surrounded by palms. The guest rooms are stylishly filled with all the modern conveniences, including bedside controls.

25 av. Beauséjour, 06400 Cannes. www.novotel.com. ✆ **04-93-68-86-86.** Fax 04-93-68-87-87. 182 units. 129€–209€ double. AE, DC, MC, V. From Cannes, follow the signs to Montfleury or the blue-and-white signs to the Novotel Montfleury. Free covered parking. **Amenities:** 2 restaurants (1 summer only and 1 year-round); bar; babysitting; concierge; health club; pool (outdoor); room service. *In room:* A/C, TV, hair dryer, minibar, Wi-Fi (free).

MODERATE

Best Western Mondial Just a 3-minute walk from the beach, this well-located modern hotel sits above stores on Cannes' main shopping street, the rue d'Antibes. It's recently been awarded four stars, although its lack of amenities suggests a well-maintained three-star hotel. Three-quarters of its rooms have views of the water, and the others overlook the mountains and a street. The soft Devonshire-cream facade has a few small balconies. The attractive rooms are the draw here, with matching fabrics for the comfortable beds and draperies, and hand-painted wall friezes. One downside is that the hotel has no parking lot.

77 rue d'Antibes and 1 rue Teisseire, 06407 Cannes. www.bestwestern.com. ✆ **04-93-68-70-00.** Fax 04-93-99-39-11. 49 units. 110€–410€ double; from 255€ suite. Rates include breakfast. AE, DC, MC, V. **Amenities:** Babysitting; room service. *In room:* A/C, TV, hair dryer, minibar, Wi-Fi (free).

Hôtel Canberra ★ 🎁 This low-profile boutique hotel occupies a marvelous location on Cannes' main shopping street and near the Palais des Festivals. It's often booked during the festival by independent producers hoping to hit the big time. This four-star hotel was recently redesigned along the theme of 1950s glamour, with signature white leather and curved pink armchairs. Rooms are well maintained, with attractive black-and-white-tiled bathrooms; those with southern exposure are sunnier and cost more. Size ranges from small to medium, but each comes with a good mattress. Limited parking is available so book in advance. As well as a lounge bar, restaurant, and patio, this popular hotel has the added bonus of a pretty bougainvillea-clad garden with a pool.

120 rue d'Antibes, 06400 Cannes. www.hotel-cannes-canberra.com. ✆ **04-97-06-95-00.** Fax 04-92-98-03-47. 35 units. 140€–500€ double; from 310€ suite. AE, DC, MC, V. Parking 25€. **Amenities:** Restaurant; bar; babysitting; fitness room; pool (outdoor); sauna. *In room:* A/C, TV, hair dryer, minibar, Wi-Fi (free).

Hôtel Le Fouquet's ★ This intimate four-star hotel draws a discreet clientele, often from Paris, who'd never think of patronizing the grand hotels. Riviera French in design and decor, it lies several blocks from the beach. Each of the cozy guest rooms is outfitted individually: some with bold Provençal colors and furniture, others with a pastel contemporary design. The owner is often on-site, making the hotel feel like an intimate B&B. There's no car park, but they offer discounted parking at an underground garage nearby.

2 rond-point Duboys d'Angers, 06400 Cannes. www.le-fouquets.com. ✆ **04-92-59-25-00.** Fax 04-92-98-03-39. 12 units. 140€-280€ double. AE, DC, MC, V. Closed Nov to mid-Apr. Parking 17€. **Amenities:** Babysitting. *In room:* A/C, TV, hair dryer, minibar, Wi-Fi (free).

Hôtel Splendid ★ Opened in 1871, this has long been a favorite haunt of scholars, politicians, actors, and musicians. Three minutes from the Palais des Festivals, the ornate white Belle Époque building with wrought-iron accents looks out onto the sea, the old port, and a park. The rooms are decorated with antique furniture and paintings: Some are showing their age, but are still comfortable in a shabby chic way. There are also 15 rooms with kitchenettes. Most rooms from the second floor upwards have sea views. However, standard town-side rooms overlooking the side street can be noisy due to a late-night bar below.

4-6 rue Félix Faure, 06400 Cannes. www.splendid-hotel-cannes.fr. ✆ **04-97-06-22-22.** Fax 04-93-99-55-02. 62 units. 115€-264€ double; from 164€ room with kitchenette. Rates include breakfast. AE, MC, V. **Amenities:** Babysitting; room service. *In room:* A/C, TV, hair dryer, kitchenettes (in some), Wi-Fi (6€).

Hôtel Sun Riviera This genteel hotel is set at the end of busy shopping street rue d'Antibes, near shops and downtown bars and restaurants. The discreetly opulent decor is tired and worn in places, but the bedrooms are generously medium size. The hotel benefits from an outdoor garden and pool.

138 rue d'Antibes, 06400 Antibes. www.sun-riviera.com. ✆ **04-93-06-77-77.** Fax 04-93-38-31-10. 42 units. 134€-267€ double; from 240€ suite. AE, DC, MC, V. **Amenities:** Bar; babysitting; pool (outdoor). *In room:* A/C, TV, hair dryer, safe, minibar, Wi-Fi (9.90€).

Hôtel Villa de l'Olivier Charming and personal, this family-run hideaway is the only hotel in the pretty old town, Le Suquet. In the 1930s, it was a private villa, and in the 1960s it became a hotel, with a wing extending deep into its garden. Today, you'll find old-fashioned decor combining the French colonial tropics with late 19th-century Provence. Some bedrooms and bathrooms are showing their age. There is a kidney-shaped swimming pool.

5 rue des Tambourinaires, 06400 Cannes. www.hotelolivier.com. ✆ **04-93-39-53-28.** Fax 04-93-39-55-85. 21 units. 69€-300€ double; 108€-175€ triple; from 118€ suite. AE, DC, MC, V. Parking 10€. Closed mid-Jan to mid-Feb and late Nov-late Dec. **Amenities:** Bar; pool (outdoor). *In room:* A/C, TV, hair dryer, Wi-Fi (free).

La Villa Cannes Croisette ★ At the far end of La Croisette from the Palais des Festivals, this boutique hotel is set in a garden with lemon and olive trees. An outdoor pool is available if you don't want to take the free shuttle to the beach. The hotel also offers boat tours of offshore islands, plus free van rides around town. Handmade furniture, paintings from a local artist, and the tasteful Pierre Frey fabrics lend to the charm. Breakfast is served; for other meals many restaurants are nearby.

8 Traverse Alexandre III, 06400 Cannes. www.hotel-villa-cannes.com. ✆ **04-93-94-12-21.** Fax 04-93-43-55-17. 33 units. 109€-295€ double. AE, DC, MC, V. Parking 15€. **Amenities:** Pool (outdoor). *In room:* TV, Wi-Fi (free).

Le Cavendish ★ 🎁 Originally an 1897 private residence, this self-proclaimed "boutique hotel" is one of the best midpriced hotels in Cannes. The original elevator, marble stairways, and the facade (a historical monument) have all been stylishly renovated. The bedrooms have also been rejuvenated, with contemporary Provençal furniture and Egyptian cotton linen. This hotel feels like home, replete with a lounge that doubles as a breakfast room and an open bar offering free drinks and nibbles from 6 to 9pm every evening. The beachfront and the Palais des Festivals are a 5-minute walk down the hill, so this may inconvenient for guests with limited mobility.

11 bd. Carnot, 06400 Cannes. www.cavendish-cannes.com. ✆ **04-97-06-26-00.** Fax 04-97-06-26-01. 34 units. 150€–330€ double. AE, DC, MC, V. Parking 25€. **Amenities:** Lounge/bar. *In room:* A/C, TV, minibar, Wi-Fi (free).

Villa d'Estelle ★★ 🎁 Minutes from La Croisette, this self-catering apartment hotel is one of Cannes' best-kept secrets. What this 19th-century hotel lacks in sea views (except from the four-bedroom penthouse suite), it makes up for with its reasonable prices and convenient location. Each of its apartments has an American-style kitchen including a microwave, washing machine, and dishwasher. Sizes vary from studio apartments with a double bed and sofa bed to three-bedroom apartments. Apartments in the new building have a fresher, contemporary decor. Breakfast can be provided on request. There's no night porter, but there is an emergency number if you forget your keys. Prices are discounted for longer stays of 3 nights or more.

12–14 rue des Belges, 06400 Cannes. www.villadestelle.com. ✆ **04-92-98-44-48.** 23 units. 135€–265€ studio. MC, V. **Amenities:** Restaurant; pool (outdoor). *In room:* A/C, TV, kitchenette, hair dryer, Wi-Fi (free).

INEXPENSIVE

Hôtel Brimer On a quiet street about 4 blocks from the seafront, this is one of the best two-star hotels in Cannes for those on a small budget. It has been renovated and upgraded by charming owner Laurent Pichot, who runs a tight ship. Bedrooms are small, but well-maintained with fresh linen and bright paintings. Breakfast is the only meal served, although the neighborhood has many bistros.

9 rue Jean Daumas, 06400 Cannes. www.hotel-brimer-cannes.com. ✆ **04-93-38-62-91.** Fax 04-93-39-49-71. 15 units. 55€–82€ double. AE, DC, MC, V. Parking free on street. **Amenities:** Breakfast room. *In room:* TV, hair dryer, minibar, Wi-Fi (free for 24 hr., then 15€ for whole stay).

Hôtel de France This centrally located Art Deco hotel is 2 blocks from the sea and is a reliable and affordable three-star hotel with friendly staff. Rooms are functional, well maintained, and reasonably comfortable, with good beds. You can sunbathe on the rooftop.

85 rue d'Antibes, 06400 Cannes. www.hotel-de-france-cannes.com. ✆ **04-93-06-54-54.** Fax 04-93-68-53-43. 33 units. 71€–142€ double; 108€ suite. AE, DC, MC, V. **Amenities:** Bar; babysitting. *In room:* A/C, TV, hair dryer, minibar (in some), Wi-Fi (free except during conventions).

Hôtel de Provence 🎁 Built in the 1930s, this small three-star hotel offers courteous service and a convenient location minutes from La Croisette. The public areas and most of the guest rooms have been renovated in 2011 with plush contemporary furnishings. The chicest rooms have private balconies overlooking the shrubs and palms of the hotel's walled garden. For Cannes, this is a remarkable bargain. In warm weather, breakfast is served under the flowers of an arbor.

9 rue Molière, 06400 Cannes. www.hotel-de-provence.com. ✆ **04-93-38-44-35.** Fax 04-93-39-63-14. 30 units. 105€–215€ double; from 210€ suite. AE, MC, V. **Amenities:** Bar; room service. *In room:* A/C, TV, hair dryer, minibar, Wi-Fi (5€).

Hôtel La Villa Tosca This former Beaux Arts–style villa lies a minute's walk from the railway station and a 5-minute walk from the beach. Inside you'll find a wide assortment of rooms and room sizes, with the biggest having soaring ceilings and a sense of monumental spaciousness, and the smallest being cramped but with manageable beds. Seven of the rooms have tiny balconies overlooking the street. Expect a polite staff and a clientele that includes gay men and—to a lesser extent—women, many of whom are involved with aspects of the film industry.

11 rue Hoche, 06400 Cannes. www.villa-tosca.com. ✆ **04-93-38-34-40.** Fax 04-93-38-73-34. 22 units. 82€–144€ double; 109€–161€ triple; 153€–183€ suite. AE, MC, V. *In room:* TV, hair dryer, minibar, Wi-Fi (free).

Hôtel Le Florian This hotel is on a pedestrianized, densely commercial street that leads directly into La Croisette, near the beach and the Palais des Festivals. Three generations of the Giordano family have maintained it since the 1950s. The hotel is basic but comfortable, and most rooms are rather small, with Provençal styling. There are 15 studios with kitchenettes that are practical for longer stays. The hotel has a lift—a boon in a two-star hotel. Breakfast is the only meal available.

8 rue du Commandant André, 06400 Cannes. www.hotel-leflorian.com. ✆ **04-93-39-24-82.** Fax 04-92-99-18-30. 35 units. 62€–98€ double; studio with kitchenette from 300€. AE, MC, V. Parking 15€ nearby. Closed Dec to mid-Jan. Bus: 1. **Amenities:** Breakfast room. *In room:* A/C, TV, hair dryer, kitchenettes (in some), Wi-Fi (free).

Hôtel Molière ★ Although it dates from around 1990, this three-star hotel gives the distinct impression that it's one of the solidly established old-timers. The hotel lies just 100m (328 ft.) from the Croisette; you approach through a long garden studded with cypresses and flowering shrubs, in which tables and chairs are set out for gossip and contemplation. The neighborhood is quieter than you expect, just behind both the JW Marriott and the Carlton. Clean contemporary bedrooms with lots of dark wood and fresh white linen give the impression of well-upholstered comfort. The staff works hard and is generally polite and cooperative.

5 rue Molière, 06400 Cannes. www.hotel-moliere.com. ✆ **04-93-38-16-16.** Fax 04-93-68-29-57. 24 units. 123€–190€ double. AE, MC, V. Closed Nov. **Amenities:** Room service. *In room:* A/C, TV, hair dryer, Wi-Fi (free).

Le Mistral This two-star hotel may be named for the harsh wind that blows across Provence, but inside the renovated premises is a cool oasis. The great location is just a minute's walk from le Palais des Festivals and La Croisette, and only a 3-minute walk from the train and bus stations. Rooms are small, but soundproofed and well furnished, each with a private bathroom with shower. The rooms are spread across four floors, and there is no elevator. Only breakfast is served, but many restaurants and cafes are nearby.

13 rue des Belges, 06400 Cannes. www.mistral-hotel.com. ✆ **04-93-39-91-46.** Fax 04-93-38-35-17. 10 units. 69€–139€ double. AE, MC, V. **Amenities:** Breakfast room. *In room:* A/C, TV, hair dryer, Wi-Fi (free).

Where to Eat

Cannes offers everything from Michelin-starred gourmand fare to Armenian cuisine—but such variety comes with a price tag. For a cheap snack on the run, head to **rue Meynadier,** where you'll find filled baguettes aplenty.

Screen idols and sex symbols flood the front terrace of **Le Festival** restaurant, 52 bd. de la Croisette (✆ **04-93-38-04-81**) during the film festival. Sadly, the food doesn't live up to the prices or to its fabulous Croisette location. Rather than the run-of-the-mill fish and meat dishes, we'd recommend soaking up the glamorous atmosphere in this all-day-long venue with a simple panino, coffee, or a glass or two of bubbly.

VERY EXPENSIVE

The premier two-Michelin-starred restaurant in Cannes is La Palme d'Or (see below), but there is a new high-end culinary kid on the block: **Mon Rêve de Gosse,** 11 rue Louis Blanc (✆ **04-93-39-68-08;** www.monrevedegosse.com), near Marché Forville. Set up by Ludovic Ordas (the ex-number-two chef from La Palme d'Or), this diminutive French restaurant won its first Michelin star in 2011, and has been crowded with gastronomy-loving locals ever since.

La Palme d'Or ★★★ MODERN FRENCH Movie stars on the see-and-be-seen circuit head here to enjoy Cannes's only two-star Michelin restaurant. The Taittinger family (of champagne fame) set out to establish a restaurant that could rival the competition—and succeeded. The result is this chocolate-and-crimson Art Deco marvel with bay windows, a winter-garden theme, and outdoor and enclosed terraces overlooking the pool, the sea, and La Croisette. Chef Christian Sinicropi awakens the dreaming diner with a playful nod to the film world: Those who are happy to go with the chef's choice can opt for tasting menus ranging from a 90€ *Metteur en Scène* (director) menu to a 260€ *Compositeur* (composer) menu. Sinicropi serves up complex dishes that combine up to a dozen subtle flavors, as well as classics such as a whole fish of the day, lobster, or Black Angus chateaubriand. Diners' every whims are catered to by the attentive staff—women will even find a pull-out ledge for their handbag.

In the Hôtel Martinez (p. 243), 73 bd. de la Croisette. ✆ **04-92-98-74-14.** www.hotel-martinez.com. Reservations required. Main courses 48€–95€; fixed-price meals 95€–128€; tasting menus 90€–260€. AE, DC, MC, V. Tues–Sat 12:30–2pm and 8–10pm. Closed Jan–Feb.

EXPENSIVE

Brun Coquillages ★★ SEAFOOD Well-heeled seafood lovers crowd this informal restaurant serving the freshest oysters on the Côte d'Azur. It's been going since 1953 and attracts a loyal following (both local and international) who are happy to pay top dollar for their daily crustacean catch, including oysters, mussels, and prawns. There is a fish shop attached to the restaurant, so you can be assured that the seafood is delivered fresh every morning. The seafood platter is heaven on a plate. Expect a certain sang-froid (coolness) from the waiters if you don't speak French.

2 rue Louis Blanc (at rue Félix Faure), 06400 Cannes. ✆ **04-93-39-21-87.** Main courses 30€–79€. AE, DC, MC, V. Daily noon–2:30pm and 7–11pm. Shop daily 8am–11pm

Comme Chez Soi ★ FRENCH/PROVENÇALE In the achingly trendy epicenter of Cannes, which is occupied by the young and beautiful set, lies this surprising oasis of Provençal style and French gastronomic cuisine. With its upholstered chairs and large comfy sofas, it truly makes you feel *comme chez soi* ("at home"). With the departure of up-and-coming chef Michaël Morel in 2010, the restaurant seemed to lose its grasp. Yet a recent visit reassures us that the famously fiery owner Sophie Meissonier is back on track with a classic French menu featuring foie gras and lobster. Those in the know ring up 24 hours in advance to dine on Bresse roast chicken.

4 rue Batéguier, Cannes ✆ **04-93-38-20-65.** Main courses from 24€. AE, MC, V, DC. Tues–Sun 6pm–12:30am.

Gaston et Gastounette ★ SEAFOOD If you'd like to try *bouillabaisse* (*provençale* fish stew), this is your best bet. Located along the old port, this fish restaurant has a stucco exterior, oak moldings, big windows, and a sidewalk terrace surrounded by flowers. It serves two different bouillabaisses: a full-blown authentic stewpot prepared only for two diners at a time, and a less daunting, individualized version designed as an appetizer. Other cooked fish and seafood dishes on the menu are fine, but better fare can be found elsewhere. Profiteroles with hot chocolate sauce make a memorable dessert. Ask for a first-floor table to make the most of views over the yachts in the old port.

7 quai St-Pierre. ✆ **04-93-39-49-44.** Reservations required. Bouillabaisse 68€; main courses 25€-39€. AE, DC, MC, V. Daily noon-2pm and 7-10:30pm.

Le Tantra/Le Loft ★ FRENCH/ASIAN An enduring favorite on the city's dine-then-dance circuit is this duplex-designed restaurant and disco on a lively side street just behind La Croisette. On the street level, you'll find a Tao-inspired dining room. The arguably overpriced menu focuses on a French adaptation of Asian cuisine, with lots of sushi, grilled fish, and meat. Be warned in advance that the 8pm seating is relatively calm; the 11pm seating is more linked to the disco madness going on in Le Loft nightclub (p. 250) upstairs.

13 rue du Dr. Monod. ✆ **06-20-79-46-81.** www.tantra-cannes.com. Reservations recommended. Main courses 20€-40€. AE, DC, MC, V. Daily 8pm-2:30am. Dance club (no cover) nightly 11pm-5am.

MODERATE

Barbarella ★ FRENCH/FUSION This chic restaurant has taken the old town, Le Suquet, by storm since opening in 2002, and it's now the most popular gay restaurant in Cannes. The Philippe Starck furnishings and soft lighting set the scene for the inventive French fusion cuisine. Try signature dishes with an Asian twist, such as the scallop satay with a vegetable chop suey or the lobster in spinach leaves with a tandoori-flavored sauce.

16 rue Saint-Dizier. ✆ **04-92-99-17-33.** Reservations required. Main courses 22€-43€. AE, DC, MC, V. Tues-Sun 7-11:30pm.

Côté Jardin ★ FRENCH/PROVENÇALE Set near the courthouse (Palais de Justice) in the heart of commercial Cannes, this restaurant attracts loyal locals because of its unpretentious ambience and its reasonably priced and generous portions. You're offered three different choices as seating options: the glassed-in veranda on the street level, the garden terrace amid flowering shrubs, or upstairs within the cozy Provençal dining room. The best menu options include goat cheese and avocado with lavender honey, tomato-flavored *osso buco,* and caramel rice pudding.

12 av. Saint-Louis. ✆ **04-93-38-60-28.** www.restaurant-cotejardin.com. Reservations required, especially in summer. Fixed-price menus 23€-38€. AE, DC, MC, V. Tues-Sat noon-2pm and 7:30-10pm. Closed 1 week in Oct.

See & Be Seen

Sister restaurant to the legendary Villa Romana in St-Tropez, Villa Romana (✆ 04-93-83-84-53; www.villa-romana.com) has been rocking on La Croisette since its opening in 2009. You don't go there for the food, but for the decadent baroque furnishings and for celeb spotting amongst the party crowd.

La Brouette de Grand-Mère ★ TRADITIONAL FRENCH Few other restaurants in Cannes work so successfully at establishing a testimonial to the culinary skills of old-fashioned French cooking. For over 30 years, it has revitalized the recipes that many Cannois remember from their childhoods, such as *pot-au-feu* (a savory meat-and-potato stew), duck breast roasted in honey, and chicken casserole cooked with beer. A change of ownership in 2009 has changed little of this homey Cannes institution. Set in the heart of town just behind the JW Marriott and the InterContinental Carlton, the place offers two dining rooms, each outfitted in Art Deco style, and an outdoor terrace.

9 bis rue d'Oran/place Lamy. ✆ **04-93-39-12-10.** Reservations recommended. Fixed-price menu, including aperitif and half bottle of wine 35€. MC, V. Tues–Sun 7–10pm; Sun noon–2pm. Closed Dec.

La Mère Besson ★ TRADITIONAL FRENCH The culinary traditions of the late Mère Besson endure in one of Cannes's favorite dining spots. The specialties are prepared with respect for Provençal traditions. Most delectable is *estouffade provençale* (beef braised with red wine and rich stock flavored with garlic, onions, herbs, and mushrooms). Every Friday, you can sample a platter with codfish, fresh vegetables, and dollops of the famous garlic mayonnaise (aïoli) of Provence. Other specialties are fish soup, *bourride provençale* (thick fish-and-vegetable stew), and roasted rack of lamb with mint. This family-run restaurant is set on rue des Frères Pradignac with its lively cafe-bars and nocturnal haunts spilling onto wide pavements.

13 rue des Frères Pradignac. ✆ **04-93-39-59-24.** Reservations required. Main courses 20€–29€; fixed-price dinner 22€–34€. AE, MC, V. Mon–Sat 7–10:30pm. Bus: 1.

Le Comptoir des Vins 🎁 TRADITIONAL FRENCH The owners first established this as a wine shop with bottles from 450 to 500 wine producers from throughout France, some of them very obscure. Today the restaurant in the back of the store charms local diners with white marble tables, bistro-style chairs, and sunlight flooding in from an overhead skylight. You can order any of 25 kinds of wine by the glass, but if you're intrigued by something in the store, they will uncork it for you for the retail price and a surcharge of 10€. Menu items include an extensive selection of charcuteries and cheeses, piled high upon olive-wood planks, as well as a savory collection of meats, fish, and vegetarian dishes. All of these are designed to go well with wines, and with a vast inventory of vintages to choose from, the composition of a savory meal here is ripe with gastronomic possibilities.

13 bd. de la République. ✆ **04-93-68-13-26.** Reservations recommended. Main courses 17€–22€. MC, V. Mon–Fri noon–2pm and 6pm–1am; Sat 6pm–1am. Closed July.

Le Relais des Semailles ★ TRADITIONAL FRENCH This long-enduring favorite is reason enough to visit Le Suquet, Cannes's old town. The casual atmosphere is complemented by the food, based on available local ingredients. Dishes such as zucchini flowers stuffed with crab and breast of duck pan-fried with herbs and spices are always beautifully prepared. Depending on what looked good at the market that day, the chef might be inspired to, say, whip up a rabbit salad with tarragon *jus*. The old-fashioned setting is intimate, offering casual dining out on the terrace or in air-conditioned comfort.

9 rue St-Antoine. ✆ **04-93-39-22-32.** Reservations required. Main courses 19€–43€; fixed-price lunch 22€, dinner 34€. AE, DC, MC, V. Tues–Fri noon–2pm; Mon–Sat 7:30–10:30pm.

Le Restaurant Arménien ★ ARMENIAN/TURKISH/GREEK Cannes has always been one of the most cosmopolitan cities along the Riviera, and the success of this Armenian culinary outpost seems to prove it. It has no menu; for a set price, a medley of dishes is brought to your table in quantities you might find staggering. There are lots of braised eggplants, tomatoes (stewed and raw alike), cracked wheat in the form of such dishes as *kechkeg* (stewed beef served on a bed of cracked wheat), cabbage stuffed with mint, grilled meatballs with fresh herbs, and many others. According to owners Christian and Lucie Panossian, about 80% of the dishes served here are steamed rather than fried, establishing this as one of the most health-conscious eateries in town. You'll find this place directly on the coastal boulevard, a short walk from the Hôtel Martinez.

82 La Croisette. ✆ **04-93-94-00-58.** www.lerestaurantarmenien.com. Reservations recommended. Fixed-price menu 42€. DC, MC, V. Sun noon–2:30pm (reservations required); daily 7:30–10:30pm. Closed Mon in winter.

INEXPENSIVE

Parallel to the rue d'Antibes, **rue Hoche** is a popular local haunt for cheap snacks. Go to this pretty pedestrian street for a cheap baguette and coffee.

Situated between rue d'Antibes and the train station, a favorite cafe with the locals is **New Monaco,** 15 rue 24 Août (✆ **04-93-38-37-76**). You'll be won over by the Parisian bistro ambience and by the reasonably priced and delicious cuisine. Try the couscous or *bouillabaisse* (fish stew).

Volupté Anytime ★ CAFE Of all the pavement cafes spilling along rue Hoche, Volupté is my favorite. Set up 9 years ago by tea connoisseur Philippe Vasseur, this cafe-cum–tea salon was taken over in April 2011 by a young Antibes couple, Bruno and Francesca Estève. Since they've taken over, not much has changed because, as Bruno said, "It's a wonderful concept, so why change it?" As well as a wide selection of teas and juices, the all-day menu offers filled baguettes for just 5€ and salads, plus tempting cakes and brioches. The Volupté boutique opposite (still run by Philippe and his wife Theresa) sells 160 varieties of teas from Japan, India, China, and Vietnam, including impressive selections of oolong, rooibos, and green teas.

41 rue Hoche. ✆ **04-93-39-60-32.** www.volupte-cannes.com. Main courses 5€–18€. MC, V. Mon–Sat 8am–8pm.

Cannes After Dark

Cannes is invariably associated with permissiveness, filmmakers celebrating filmmaking, and gambling. If gambling is your thing, Cannes has some world-class casinos, each loaded with addicts, voyeurs, and everyone in between; to enter, you must be 18 or over. The best established is the **Casino Croisette,** in the Palais des Festivals,

Star Struck

The **International Film Festival** at the Palais des Festivals on La Croisette takes place at the end of May. It attracts not only film stars but also seemingly every photographer in the world. You have a better chance of being named prime minister of France than you do of attending one of the major screenings. (Hotel rooms and tables at restaurants are equally scarce during the festival.) But the people-watching is fabulous. If you find yourself here at the right time, you can join the thousands who line up in front of the Palais des Festivals, where the premieres are held. With paparazzi shouting and gendarmes holding back fans, the guests parade along the red carpet, stopping for a moment to strike a pose. *C'est Cannes!*

You may be able to get tickets for some of the lesser known films, which play for 24 hours. For information, visit www.festival-cannes.org.

1 jetée Albert-Edouard (✆ **04-92-98-78-00**). Run by the Lucien Barrière group, it has been a well-respected fixture in town since the 1950s and has 270 slot machines, as well as table games such as roulette, blackjack, and craps. There is also a dedicated poker room. It's open from 8pm to 3am (4am Fri–Sat and 5am during summertime). A second gambling den owned by the Barrière group, **Casino des Princes,** occupying the subterranean levels of the JW Marriott, Cannes, 50 bd. de la Croisette (✆ **04-97-06-18-50**), is more intimate. With just 125 slot machines, it focuses more on table games such as roulette, blackjack, stud poker, and punto banco. There is also a VIP salon for high rollers. It is open nightly 8pm to 4am (5am during summertime). A government-issued photo ID is necessary, and jackets for men are requested. Adjoining the casino is the upscale Restaurant/Bar des Jeux, open for dinner nightly from 8pm to 1am. A newer competitor is the **Palm Beach Casino,** place F-D-Roosevelt, Pointe de la Croisette (✆ **04-97-06-36-90;** www.lepalmbeach.com), on the southeast edge of La Croisette. Inaugurated in 1933 and rebuilt in 2002, it features a restaurant and Art Deco decor and attracts a young, sometimes gay crowd. Suites of rooms devoted to *les grands jeux* (blackjack, roulette, and stud poker) open nightly from 8pm to 3am (5am during summertime).

The aptly named **Bar des Stars,** in the Restaurant Fouquet's in the Hôtel Majestic Barrière, 10 bd. de la Croisette (✆ **04-92-98-77-29**), is where deals go down during the film festival. Directors, producers, stars, press agents, and screenwriters crowd in here at festival time. Even without the festival, it's a lively place for a drink.

The hip summertime hangout is **Le Bâoli** on Port Canto, La Croisette (✆ **04-93-43-03-43;** www.lebaoli.com). This nightclub occupies a waterfront site outfitted like a temple garden in Thailand, complete with lavishly carved doorways, potted and in-ground palms, and hints of the Spice Trade scattered artfully in the out-of-the way corners. With space for up to 350 diners, the place morphs from Asian-inspired dining into a dance venue where at least some of the clients might be dancing on the tables. The name of the restaurant, incidentally, derives from a well in Indonesia with reputed mystical powers. It's open nightly April to October (and during conventions) and at weekends from November to March from 8pm–5am (dancing from around midnight).

A cozier place in colder months, **Le Loft,** 13 rue du Dr. Monod (✆ **06-21-02-37-49**), is lined with plush sofas and exposed stone. Here you'll witness all the gyrations and mating games of a scantily clad crowd of hipsters from across the wide, wide range of social types inhabiting Cannes.

In the old town, **Le Vogue,** 20 rue du Suquet (✆ **04-93-39-99-18**), is a mixed bar open Tuesday to Sunday from 7:30pm until 2am. Nearby is the diminutive **Disco Le Sept,** 7 rue Rouguière (✆ **04-93-39-10-36**), where drag shows appear nightly at 1:30am. Entrance is free, except on weekends, when its 12€ cover includes one drink. It's open nightly from midnight to 5am.

Gays and lesbians will feel comfortable at **3.14 Bar,** attracting a lively crowd over cocktails. The bar is attached to the hedonistic **3.14 Hotel,** 3 rue François Einesy (✆ **04-92-99-72-00;** www.hotel314cannes.com), where guest room goodies include a love box. The most visible gay clientele in Cannes tends to gravitate toward **Le Night,** 52 bd. Jean-Jaurès (✆ **04-93-39-20-50**), which was reoutfitted as a 1950s retro venue that includes red vinyl banquettes, white walls, a busy bar, occasional drag shows, and lots of randomly scheduled and somewhat flippant theme parties. Open for drinks and dining daily 6pm to 2:30am, with fixed-price meals priced at 32€, it's a popular and convivial spot for same-sex socializing.

GRASSE ★★

906km (563 miles) S of Paris; 18km (11 miles) N of Cannes; 10km (6 miles) NW of Mougins

Grasse, a 20-minute drive from Cannes, is the most fragrant town on the Riviera, where some three-quarters of the world's essences are produced from foliage that includes violets, daffodils, wild lavender, and jasmine. Surrounded by jasmine and roses, it has been the capital of the perfume industry since the days of the Renaissance. It was once a famous resort, attracting such royalty as Queen Victoria and Princess Pauline Borghese, Napoleon's promiscuous sister. Though Grasse has never been picture-postcard perfect, after being sidelined in the 1970s and '80s as investment concentrated on the coastline, it's now back in fashion. Its restored train link with Cannes brings day-trippers seeking respite from the beach to wander around the historic perfume factories and museums or dine on Michelin-starred cuisine at **La Bastide Saint-Antoine** (see below).

Essentials

GETTING THERE **Trains** run to Grasse from Nice, Cannes, or Antibes. One-way tickets cost 3.80€ from Cannes, 5.90€ from Antibes, and 8.80€ from Nice. For train schedules and more information, call ✆ **36-35,** or visit www.ter-sncf.com. **Buses** pull into town every 30 to 60 minutes daily from Cannes (trip time 50 min.). The one-way fare is 1€. About 14 buses run every day from Nice (1 hr.). The one-way fare is around 1€. They arrive at the gare routière, place Notre Dame des Fleurs (✆ **04-93-36-37-3708-44**), a 5-minute walk north of the town center. Visitors arriving by **car** take A8, which funnels in traffic from Monaco, Aix-en-Provence, and Marseille.

VISITOR INFORMATION The **Office de Tourisme** is at 22 cours Honoré Cresp (✆ **04-93-36-66-66;** fax 04-93-36-86-36; www.grasse.fr).

SPECIAL EVENTS Perfumed Grasse is renowned for its flower festivals, including the **Expo Rose** festival, with rose-strewn events and showcases for specialist rose producers in May, and the **Jasmine Festival,** celebrating the start of the jasmine harvest with flower parades and a "Miss Jasmine" competition on the first weekend in August. For more information on both festivals, call ✆ **04-93-36-66-66** or visit www.ville-grasse.fr. A market for fruits and vegetables from the surrounding hills, **Marché aux Aires,** is conducted in the place aux Aires every Tuesday to Sunday 8am to noon.

Exploring the Town

PERFUME FACTORIES

Parfumerie Fragonard ★★ One of the best-known perfume factories is named after the famous 18th-century French painter Jean-Honoré Fragonard (see "Painted Creation," box on p. 256). This factory has the best villa, the best museum, and the best tour. An English-speaking guide will show you how "the soul of the flower" is extracted. After the tour, you can explore the perfume museum, which displays bottles and vases that trace the industry back to ancient times. You can also skip the tour and just shop for perfume.

Pricey Petals

It takes 10,000 flowers to produce 2.2 pounds of jasmine petals; almost a ton of petals is needed to distill 1½ quarts of essence. Keep these figures in mind when looking at that high price tag on a bottle of perfume.

Scented Formula

If you'd like to design your own perfume, consider taking the hour-long *atelier tarinologie* (perfume-making workshop) at Parfumerie Molinard (see above). English-speaking Céline will help you choose up to a dozen essences for your perfume from a collection of around 100 *eau de parfum* smells. Your secret formula joins an archive of 15,000 secret formulas so that you can reorder your perfume whenever you want.

20 bd. Fragonard. ✆ **04-93-36-44-65.** www.fragonard.com. Feb–Oct daily 9am–6pm; Nov–Jan daily 9am–12:30pm and 2–6pm.

Parfumerie Molinard This firm is well known in the United States, where its products are sold at Saks, Neiman Marcus, and Bloomingdale's. In the factory you can witness the extraction of the essence of the flowers. You can also admire a collection of antique perfume-bottle labels and see a rare collection of perfume *flacons* by Baccarat and Lalique.

60 bd. Victor-Hugo. ✆ **04-92-42-33-11.** www.molinard.com. Free admission. Apr–Sept daily 9:30am–6:30pm; Oct–Apr Mon–Sat 9am–12:30pm and 2–6:30pm.

MUSEUMS

Musée d'Art et d'Histoire de Provence ★ This museum is in the Hôtel de Clapiers-Cabris, built in 1771 by Louise de Mirabeau, the marquise de Cabris and sister of Mirabeau. Its collections include paintings, four-poster beds, marquetry, ceramics, brasses, kitchenware, pottery, urns, and archaeological finds.

2 rue Mirabeau. ✆ **04-93-36-80-20.** www.museesdegrasse.com. Admission 3€ adults, under 18 free. Oct to mid-Nov and mid-Feb to Mar Wed–Mon 11am–6pm; Apr daily 11am–6pm; May–Sept daily 10am–7pm.

Musée International de la Parfumerie ★★ ☺ Looking splendid after its 5-year-long face-lift, which was overseen by celebrated architect Frédéric Jung, Grasse's new Perfume Museum is the place to discover ancient Egyptian embalming vases and learn about the process of perfume making in a laboratory filled with copper perfume distillers and decanting jars. There's also a greenhouse where you can sniff raw materials such as jasmine, bergamot, and vanilla. The museum is good for families, offering buggies, kids' interactive tours, and even a supervised kids' play area. The perfume museum works well for a day-trip combination with the Fragonard perfume factory next door. If you're coming by car, you can park in the multistory lot beneath cours Honoré Cresp.

2 bd. du Jeu de Ballon. ✆ **04-97-05-58-00.** www.museesdegrasse.com. Admission 3€ adults, 17 and under free. Oct to mid-Nov and mid-Feb to Mar Wed–Mon 11am–6pm; Apr daily 11am–6pm; May–Sept daily 10am–7pm.

Shopping

One of the best shopping streets in Grasse is pedestrianized rue Jean Ossola, where shops are generally open from 10am to 7pm with a lunchtime closure during winter. Here again Fragonard leads the crowd. **Parfumerie Fragonard,** 20 boulevard Fragonard (at rue Jean Ossola; ✆ **04-93-36-44-65**), greets customers with the hazy scents of jasmine, green tea, and bergamot. After you've finished browsing soaps shaped like roses or ducks, you can walk further along the street to find **Confidentiel,** 3 rue Jean

Painted Creation

The fact that there are not one but two museums dedicated to the paintings of Jean-Honoré Fragonard is an indication of the esteem in which this great 18th-century painter is held. A private collection of his paintings can be viewed at **Musée Fragonard** in Hôtel de Villeneuve, 14 rue Jean Ossola (✆ **04-93-36-02-07**) in the pedestrianized zone around the corner from the perfume factory. Alternatively, you can visit this 18th-century aristocrat's town house, **Villa-Musée Jean-Honoré Fragonard,** 23 bd. Fragonard (✆ **04-93-36-52-98;** www.museesdegrasse.com), with a magnificent garden at the back. The collection displayed here includes the paintings not only of Jean-Honoré, but also his sister-in-law, Marguerite Gérard; his son, Alexandre; and his grandson, Théophile. As you gaze up at the grand staircase painted by Alexandre, you cannot help but marvel at the talent of this creative family.

Ossola (✆ **04-93-36-40-62**). This recently opened treasure trove is filled with antique jewelry, quilted Provençal boutis, and embroidered linen clothes. At nearby **Fragonard Maison,** 2 rue Amiral de Grasse (✆ **04-93-40-12-04**), you'll find glassware, embroidered tablecloths, and handmade souvenirs. Just opposite, **Maroquinerie Monique,** 5 rue Jean Ossola (✆ **04-93-36-23-29**), is the place to buy chic Parisian Longchamp handbags and fold-up tote bags.

Where to Stay

Grasse provides a convenient base for exploring the back country. Accommodations are generally reasonably priced, and you'll find plenty of budget options, but you should avoid the ragged hotels in Grasse town center. Instead, head to the well-maintained suburbs of Grasse and to neighboring villages such as Cabris (see "Whistle-stop Tour from Grasse," p. 258), Magagnosc, and Auribeau-sur-Siagne.

In addition to the suggestions below, **La Surprise** (✆ **06-77-86-86-38;** www.lasurprise.co.uk), in Magagnosc, is an appealing B&B run by a charming English couple Steve and Clare Dance.

Bastide Saint-Mathieu ★★ This exclusive country house is one of the best places to stay in the Grasse area. Lying just to the southeast of Grasse, this restored 18th-century house provides beautiful suites and personal service. Each of the spacious suites is individually decorated and furnished to a high standard, with luxurious bathrooms with tub and shower. Thoughtful touches abound, including such extras as cashmere blankets and Ralph Lauren bathrobes. The staff will guide you to the area's finest restaurants. The only downside is that it's often booked out for exclusive use during the summer season.

35 chemin de Blumenthal, 06130 St. Mathieu (Grasse). www.bastidestmathieu.com. ✆ **04-97-01-10-00.** Fax 04-97-01-10-09. 8 units. 250€–330€ double; 330€–380€ suite. Rates include breakfast. AE, MC, V. **Amenities:** Pool (outdoor). *In room:* A/C (in most rooms), TV, Wi-Fi (free).

La Bastide St-Antoine ★★★ This Relais & Châteaux hotel is one of our favorite places to stay in the Riviera back country. This 200-year-old Provençal farmhouse has been tastefully transformed into a luxury hotel. Its nine rooms and seven suites are decorated in Provençal or contemporary style with upscale furnishings and comfortable beds. Try out the Michelin-starred cuisine by chef Jacques Chibois (see below), relax in the library with a book, or wander around the 2.8 hectares (7 acres) of parkland dotted with sculptures and old olive trees. You can also take a tour of the vegetable garden or the 1,600-strong wine cellar. As well as an outdoor pool, there's a Jacuzzi where you can survey the panoramic hinterland views.

48 av. Henri-Dunant. www.jacques-chibois.com. ✆ **04-93-70-94-94.** Fax 04-93-70-94-95. 16 units. 240€–415€ double; from 460€ suites. AE, DC, MC, V. **Amenities:** Restaurant; fitness center; Jacuzzi; library; pool (outdoor). *In room:* A/C, TV, minibar, Wi-Fi (free).

Parc des Monges ★ Bargain hunters looking for a peaceful spot will love this campsite on the riverfront below the *village perché* of Auribeau-sur-Siagne. Framed by winter-flowering mimosa and summer-flowering oleander flowers, this site offers three-person caravans, six-person mobile homes, and five-person chalets for weekly rental (or 3-night minimum stays out of high season) and camping/caravan sites for nightly stays. Everything is spotlessly clean, from the cream-and-green paintwork of its chalets to the communal washing facilities and the outdoor pool. You'll need to bring your own sheets, and organize a bank transfer in advance if you don't want to pay in cash.

635 chemin du Gabre, 06810 Auribeau-sur-Siagne. www.parcdesmonges.com. ✆ **04-93-60-91-71.** Fax 04-93-60-91-71. 15 units plus camping/caravan sites. From 10€ camping/caravan site per night. From 200€ caravan/chalet/mobile home per week. No credit cards. Closed Oct–Mar. **Amenities:** Children's play area; games (table tennis and *pétanque*); outdoor pool and baby pool. *In room:* TV, kitchenette.

Where to Eat

With the exception of **La Grignote** (see below), it's best to avoid the tourist traps around the central square, place aux Aires. Head around the corner to **Les 3 Garçons** (see below) or to the diminutive **rue des Fabreries,** where cuisine spans from tasty Indian curries at **Le New Punjab** (✆ **04-93-36-16-03;** www.lenewpunjab.com) to bargain-priced Creole cuisine at **Chez Doudou** (✆ **04-93-42-07-31;** www.restaurant-chez-doudou.com). Another reasonably priced option is the interior-designed **Café des Musées** (✆ **04-92-60-99-00**) at 1 rue Jean Ossola.

VERY EXPENSIVE

La Bastide St-Antoine (Restaurant Chibois) ★★★ FRENCH/PROVENÇALE Chef Jacques Chibois might have lost one of his two Michelin stars in 2011, but La Bastide St-Antoine still offers one of the grandest culinary experiences along the Riviera. In a 200-year-old Provençal farmhouse surrounded by parkland, Chibois serves a sophisticated array of dishes sprinkled with rich helpings of foie gras, truffles, and lobsters. The menu changes with the seasons, but we enjoyed a splendid meal here recently of scallop risotto and slow-cooked chicken with zucchini and truffle gnocchi followed by a wild strawberry soufflé and sorbet. The wine list is set to impress with over 1,600 wines.

48 av. Henri-Dunant. ✆ **04-93-70-94-94.** Fax 04-93-70-94-95. www.jacques-chibois.com. Reservations required. Main courses 39€–90€; fixed-price lunch Mon–Sat 59€–190€, Sun 145€; fixed-price dinner 160€–190€. AE, DC, MC, V. Daily noon–2pm and 8–10pm.

INEXPENSIVE

Les 3 Garçons FRENCH Metallic walls and red leather seating set the upbeat scene. Opened in February 2011 by three young Parisians (two of whom worked in Les Deux Garçons in Aix-en-Provence), this funky eatery serves no-nonsense food at reasonable prices. Steak and chips or salad with goat cheese are the order of the day in a menu filled with grilled meat, fish, and salads.

Whistle-stop Tour from Grasse

Hilltop Cabris (✆ 04-93-60-55-63; http://cabris.voila.net) is one of the back-country's hidden gems. This immaculate village is bursting with places to feast on Provençal cuisine, as well as dramatic Riviera panoramas. For the best views, climb up to the cypress-shaded gravel courtyard beside the 10th-century château ruins. From here, you can see all the way from the jutting coastline of Cap-Ferrat to the St-Cassien lake. For a simple room with a view, you'll find no better place on the Côte d'Azur than L'Horizon Hotel, 100 promenade St-Jean Cabris (✆ 04-93-60-51-69; fax 04-93-60-56-29; www.relaisdusilence.com). From here, you can gaze down upon the memorable vista between sea and sky, as the young Antoine de Saint-Exupéry did during his childhood holidays in Cabris.

10 place des la Foux. ✆ **04-93-60-15-49.** Main courses 13€–17€; fixed-price menus 16€–28€. MC, V. Tues–Sat noon–3pm and 7–11pm.

La Grignote ★ PROVENÇAL This miniature cafe is a cut above the restaurants that border Grasse's central square. Dishes include fresh fettuccini and organic lamb and goat cheese, although we usually opt for the dish of the day (around 14€). With its tables spilling out onto the flagstones, lunchtime diners are rewarded with ringside seats to the daily food and flower market.

2 rue Thouron (overlooking place aux Aires). ✆ **09-61-46-37-30** or 04-93-09-91-45. Main courses 10€–20€. MC, V. June–Sept Mon–Sat noon–2pm and 7:30–10pm; Oct–May Mon–Sat noon–2pm.

VALBONNE ★

903km (561 miles) S of Paris; 11km (7 miles) S of Grasse; 8km (5 miles) N of Cannes

The photogenic medieval village of Valbonne looks serene and tranquil, but it's actually a hub for the 30,000-strong international community that live and work at nearby Sophia Antipolis, a well-landscaped technological park where more than 1,000 national and international companies have offices. It's so Anglophone that it has an English bookshop, grocery store, and cinema. The pretty town square is packed with locals dining outside all year around. It's also next door to two of the Riviera's largest nature parks: La Valmasque and La Brague.

Essentials

GETTING THERE Valbonne lies halfway between Antibes and Grasse. A train from Nice to Antibes is 4€. From Antibes, a bus service connects you to Valbonne-Sophia Antipolis bus station for just 1€. For more information on **trains,** call ✆ **36-35,** or visit www.ter-sncf.com. For **bus** information, contact **Envibus** (✆ **04-89-87-72-00;** www.envibus.fr). Given the complexities of a bus transfer from Antibes, it's a lot easier just to pay 30€ for a **taxi** to haul you and your luggage north from Antibes.

However, the best way to get to Valbonne is to **drive.** From Nice, follow the A8 to motorway exits at either Antibes or Cannes, then take signs to Sophia Antipolis and then to village of Valbonne.

VISITOR INFORMATION The **Office de Tourisme** is at 1 place de l'Hôtel de Ville (✆ **04-93-12-34-50;** fax 04-93-12-34-57; www.tourisme-valbonne.com).

Exploring the Town

Parc Départemental de La Valmasque covers 561 hectares (1,386 acres) of parkland stretching from Valbonne to Mougins. You can spot wild boar or foxes as you walk and bike around the oak-pine forests and open prairies and admire the 5-hectare **Font Merle** lake where you'll find Europe's largest colony of lotus plants, including *Nelumbo nucifera* (sacred lotus). There are plenty of bird-watching hiding spots, picnic tables, and children's play areas. This nature reserve is easily accessible with car parks spread along the RD 35 Route de la Valmasque near Sophia Antipolis.

Nearby is the **Parc Départemental de la Brague** that follows the meandering River Brague between Valbonne and Biot. Listen to the warblers and fieldfares as you discover waterfalls and aromatic Mediterranean plants. Car parks and picnic tables are available along RD (minor roads) 604, 4, and 198. Avoid the lower part of the river near Sophia Antipolis, where detergents have begun polluting the water.

Shopping

Valbonne is a popular place for locals shopping in the backcountry. The old village is dotted with interior design shops where you'll find everything from Provençal quilts to leather cushions. **La Gourmandine,** 17 bis rue Emile Pourcel (✆ **04-93-42-19-69**), is the place to buy well-priced wine, champagne, and spirits chosen by wine expert and ex-sommelier Thierry. **La Malle à Jouets,** 17 rue Eugène Giraud (✆ **04-93-12-25-94**), is a kids' toy shop filled to the gills with puzzles and traditional wooden toys. The **English Book Center,** 12 rue Alexis Julien (✆ **04-93-12-21-42;** www.englishbookcentre.com), sells English books, DVDs, and kids' games. Up next to the parking lot (to the west of the village center near the bus station), you'll find everything from a pharmacy and a news agent to a butcher shop, bakery, delicatessen, and greengrocer.

You can stock up on British favorites at **Brittain's Home Stores,** Forum roundabout, 1913 rte. de Cannes, on the outskirts of Valbonne (✆ **04-93-42-01-70;** www.brittains-stores.com), set up by the eponymous John and Caroline Brittain in 2004. Heinz baked beans, steak-and-onion pasties, peanut butter, curries, and classic ale can all be found here. They've even opened a restaurant nearby where you can enjoy a full English breakfast, cream tea with scones, and fish and chips.

Where to Stay

Chateau de la Begude ★ This 17th-century farmhouse offers the best hotel accommodation near Valbonne. It's essentially a golf hotel, but does offer a convenient base for a night or two. Rooms are clean and tidily furnished. Offering splendid views over the verdant fairway, the restaurant serves competent, though not outstanding, Mediterranean cuisine. Thursday is the night for summertime jazz while you dine.

Rte. de Roquefort les Pins, Golf d'Opio Valbonne, 06650 Opio. www.chateauxhotels.com. ✆ **04-93-12-37-00.** 34 units. 190€–310€ double; 220€–540€ suite. MC, V. Closed mid-Nov to mid-Dec. **Amenities:** Restaurant; bar; golf course; pool (outdoor); room service. *In room:* A/C, TV, hair dryer, minibar, Wi-Fi (free).

Where to Eat

With a multitude of informal dining options offering everything from crêpes to sushi, Valbonne has something for most taste buds. Place aux Arcades is filled year-round with local Anglophone families dining at cafes under the stone archways as their children run around this pedestrianized village square.

La Pigeot ★ MOROCCAN Taste the sweet-and-savory flavors here and you'll be transported to the souks of Morocco. Our favorite dishes include couscous with a seven-vegetable sauce and lamb tagine with almonds and prunes. This popular haunt has a rich North African decor of hand-painted furniture and colorful fabrics. During summertime, this restaurant is only open at night.

16 rue Alexis-Julien. ✆ **04-93-12-17-53.** Main courses 16€–27€. MC, V. June–Sept daily 7:30–10pm; Sept–May Wed–Fri and Sun noon–1:30pm, daily 7:30–10pm.

MOUGINS ★

903km (561 miles) S of Paris; 11km (7 miles) S of Grasse; 8km (5 miles) N of Cannes

This once-fortified town on the crest of a hill provides an alternative for those who want to be near the excitement of Cannes but not in the midst of it. Picasso and other artists appreciated these rugged, sun-drenched hills covered with gnarled olive trees. Picasso arrived in 1936 and, in time, was followed by Jean Cocteau, Paul Eluard, and Man Ray. Picasso decided to move here permanently, choosing as his refuge an ideal site overlooking the Bay of Cannes near the Chapelle Notre-Dame de Vie. Here he continued to work and spent the latter part of his life with his wife, Jacqueline. Fernand Léger, René Clair, Isadora Duncan, and even Christian Dior have lived at Mougins.

Nowadays, Mougins has expanded into one of the mainstays of the Riviera's backcountry. It's chockablock with gastronomic restaurants—some with Michelin stars. It's also a foodie heaven for self-catering visitors with the best fish shop (Poissonnerie Develay) and butcher (Boucherie Lerda) in the region.

Essentials

GETTING THERE In 2005, the French railways, **SNCF,** reactivated an antique **rail** line stretching between Grasse (the perfume capital) and Cannes, linking the hamlet of Mouans-Sartoux en route. The village of Mouans-Sartoux lies only 457m (1,500 ft.) from the center of Mougins. Rail service costs 2.80€ one-way from Cannes or 1.90€ from Grasse to Mouans-Sartoux. There are several trains per day. For more information call ✆ **36-35,** or visit www.ter-sncf.com. **Société Tam** (✆ **08-00-06-01-06**) runs **buses** between Cannes and Grasse. Bus no. 600 stops in Val-de-Mougins, a 10-minute walk from the center of Mougins. One-way fares from either Cannes or Grasse cost 1€. Given the complexities of a bus transfer from Cannes, it's a lot easier just to pay 30€ to 40€ for a **taxi** to haul you and your luggage north from Cannes.

However, by far the best way to get to Mougins is to **drive.** From Nice, follow E80/A8 west, then cut north on Route 85 into Mougins. From Cannes, head north of the city along N85. From La Napoule–Plage, head east toward Cannes on N7, then north at the turnoff to Mougins up in the hills.

VISITOR INFORMATION The **Office de Tourisme** is at 18 bd. Courteline (✆ **04-93-75-87-67;** fax 04-92-92-04-03; www.mougins.fr).

SPECIAL EVENTS Each year in mid-September, Mougins celebrates international culinary talent with its own weekend-long gastronomy festival, **Les Etoiles de Mougins.** During this festival, chefs from around the globe come to participate in workshops and competitions. For more information, call ✆ **04-93-75-87-67** or visit http://blog.lesetoilesdemougins.com.

Exploring the Town

For a look at the history of the area, visit the **Espace Culturel,** place du Commandant-Lamy (✆ **04-92-92-50-42**), in the St. Bernardin Chapel. It was built in 1618 and traces area history from 1553 to the 1950s. It's open December to October, Monday to Friday 9am to 5pm, Saturday and Sunday from 11am to 6pm (closed Nov). Admission is free.

You can also visit the **Chapelle Notre-Dame de Vie,** chemin de la Chapelle, 1.5km (1 mile) southeast of Mougins. The chapel, once painted by Winston Churchill, is best known for the priory next door, where Picasso spent his last 12 years. It was built in the 13th century and reconstructed in 1655; it was an old custom to bring stillborn babies to the chapel to have them baptized. The priory is still a private home occupied intermittently by the Picasso heirs. Alas, because of a series of break-ins and ongoing renovations, the chapel is open only during Sunday Mass from 9 to 10am.

Where to Stay

Note that **Le Moulin de Mougins** (p. 262) offers charming and well-priced rooms and suites.

Hôtel de Mougins ★ This 18th-century bastide has been turned into a stylish yet reasonably priced hotel. Chef Alessio Gove took over the running of the gastronomic restaurant in 2010. In summertime, meals are served in the sweet-smelling Mediterranean garden. Decorated with contemporary Provençal furniture and fabrics, rooms are spread over four Provençal-style houses. All bedrooms look onto the garden and pool: Ground-floor rooms have terraces, while first-floor rooms have balconies. Superior rooms are lighter, but no larger than classic rooms. Tennis lessons and massages are available on request.

205 av. du Golf, 06250 Mougins. www.hotel-de-mougins.com. ✆ **04-92-92-17-07.** Fax 04-92-92-17-08. 51 units. 195€–375€ double; from 550€ suite. AE, DC, MC, V. **Amenities:** Restaurant; bar; pool (outdoor); room service. *In room:* A/C, TV, hair dryer, minibar, Wi-Fi (free).

Le Mas Candille ★★★ This 200-year-old Provençal *mas* is the place for guests who'd like a taste of the countryside with the pampered trappings of a five-star hotel complete with a Shiseido spa and Michelin-starred restaurant. The public rooms contain many 19th-century furnishings, and some open onto the gardens. Rooms are individually decorated in French colonial (Indochina), and Provençal style, plus there are six new contemporary suites. As well as the gastronomic restaurant, Candille, with its pretty terrace shaded by orange trees, there's a summertime restaurant beside the pool. The staff at times might be just a bit too easygoing.

Bd. Clément Rebuffel, 06250 Mougins. www.lemascandille.com. ✆ **04-92-28-43-43.** Fax 04-92-28-43-40. 46 units. 295€–695€ double; from 650€ suite. AE, DC, MC, V. **Amenities:** 2 restaurants (1 summer and 1 year-round); bar; 3 pools (outdoor); room service; spa. *In room:* A/C, TV, hair dryer, minibar, Wi-Fi (free).

Where to Eat

L'Amandier de Mougins Café-Restaurant ★ PROVENÇALE This relatively inexpensive bistro was founded about a decade ago by the world-famous chef Roger Vergé. Today the restaurant carries on admirably under new owners who completed an extensive renovation of this Mougins institution in 2011. This restaurant serves simple platters in an airy stone house. The specialties, based on traditional recipes, may include gilt-head sea bream with lemon; roast chicken with gnocchi in a tomato and olive sauce; or *magret* of duckling with honey sauce and lemons, served with deliberately undercooked polenta.

Place du Vieux Village. ✆ **04-93-90-00-91.** www.amandier.fr. Reservations recommended. Main courses 19€–28€; fixed-price menu 18€–34€. AE, DC, MC, V. Daily noon–2pm and 7–9:30pm.

La Place de Mougins ★★ FRENCH It's worth a detour to this sophisticated restaurant in the heart of Mougins' old village. With its Cecil Beaton black-and-white prints and tasteful contemporary decor, it's almost unrecognizable from its previous life as the simply furnished eatery, Le Feu Follet. Since taking over in 2010, Denis Fétisson has been quietly adding the guts back into Mougins' gastronomic crown. After all, any chef who can transform calf's head into a tasty appetizer has to be a culinary genius. The menu changes seasonally with a collection of rich ingredients, such as North Sea king crab with cocoa-bean cream and quail eggs, or Iberian pork à la plancha served in a lentil-and-pancetta stew. For dessert, you can choose from a range of mouth-watering patisseries from the restaurant's boutique. The a la carte menu is expensive, so it's best to opt for its well-priced lunch, dinner, and seasonal fixed-price menus.

Place du Commandant Lamy. ✆ **04-93-90-15-78.** Reservations required. Main courses 32€–45€; fixed-price menus 25€–65€. AE, MC, V. Tues–Sat 12:15–2:45pm and 8:15–11:45pm; Sun 12:15–2:45pm.

Le Moulin de Mougins ★★★ FRENCH After a rocky ride under the helm of Alain Lorca, Le Moulins de Mougins is back on its historic Michelin-starred track with chef Sébastien Chambru. His cuisine brings a contemporary twist to the flavors of the South, with dishes such as spring vegetable French toast flavored with cardamom, mussels, and olive tapenade, or pan-fried, Grenobloise-style trout fillets with caramelized chicory and lemon curd. Budding amateur chefs can also sign up for cooking lessons at the new Moulins cookery school. Prices have come down in this legendary inn, so that accommodations here now represent excellent value in this expensive back-country village. The rooms were redesigned in 2008 and there are now six themed rooms and three fabulous suites; rooms cost 150€ to 200€ double, with suites from 200€.

Notre-Dame de Vie, 06250 Mougins. ✆ **04-93-75-78-24.** Fax 04-93-90-18-55. www.moulindemougins.com. Reservations required. Main courses 59€–95€; fixed-price menu 39–49€ lunch, 90€–120€ dinner. AE, DC, MC, V. Daily 12:30–2pm and 8–10pm.

GOLFE-JUAN ★ & VALLAURIS

913km (567 miles) S of Paris; 6km (4 miles) E of Cannes

Napoleon and 800 men landed at Golfe-Juan in 1815 to begin his Hundred Days. Protected by hills, Golfe-Juan was also the favored port for the American navy, though today it's primarily a family resort known for its beaches. It contains one notable restaurant: Chez Tétou.

The 2km (1¼-mile) RN 135 leads inland from Golfe-Juan to Vallauris. Once merely a stopover along the Riviera, Vallauris (now noted for its pottery) owes its reputation to Picasso, who "discovered" it. The master came to Vallauris after World War II and occupied a villa known as "the Woman from Wales."

Essentials

GETTING THERE The sleepy-looking rail station in Golfe-Juan is on avenue de la Gare. To get here, you'll have to transfer from a **train** in Cannes. The train from

Cannes costs 1.80€ each way. For railway information, call ✆ **36-35,** or visit www.ter-sncf.com. **Buses** operated by **Envibus** (✆ **04-89-87-72-00;** www.envibus.fr) make frequent trips from Cannes; the 20-minute trip costs 1€ each way.

You can **drive** to Golfe-Juan or Vallauris on any of the Riviera's three east-west highways. Although route numbers are not always indicated, city names are clear once you're on the highway. From Cannes or Antibes, N7 east is the fastest route. From Nice or Biot, take A8/E80 west.

VISITOR INFORMATION The **Office de Tourisme** (www.vallauris-golfe-juan.fr) is on avenue Aimé Berger, Golfe-Juan (✆ **04-93-63-86-93**), with another on place Jacques Cavasse, Vallauris (✆ **04-93-64-24-24**).

Exploring the Towns

On the place du Marché in Vallauris, near the site where Aly Khan and Rita Hayworth were married, you'll see Picasso's ***Homme et Mouton (Man and Sheep).*** The town council of Vallauris had intended to ensconce this statue in a museum, but Picasso insisted that it remain on the square "where the children could climb over it and the dogs water it unhindered."

Bordering place de la Libération is a chapel shaped like a Quonset (Nissen) hut, containing the **Musée Picasso La Guerre et La Paix** ★ (✆ **04-93-64-71-83;** www.musee-picasso-vallauris.fr), and also the entrance to the 16th-century **Château de Vallauris** (same phone). Inside the château is a two-in-one museum, **Musée Alberto Magnelli** and the **Musée de la Céramique Moderne.** This trio of museums developed after Picasso decorated the chapel with two paintings: *La Paix (Peace)* and *La Guerre (War),* offering contrasting images of love and peace on the one hand, and violence and conflict on the other. In 1970, a house painter gained illegal entrance to the museum one night and, after whitewashing a portion of the original, substituted one of his own designs. When the aging master inspected the damage, he said, "Not bad at all." In July 1996, the site was enhanced with a permanent exposition devoted to the works of the Florentine-born Alberto Magnelli, a pioneer of abstract art. The third section showcases ceramics, traditional and innovative alike, from regional potters. All three museums are open July to August daily 10am to 7pm, and September to May Wednesday to Monday 10am to 12:15pm and 2 to 5pm. Admission costs 2€ for adults and free for children 17 and under.

A Day at the Beach

Because of its position beside the sea, Golfe-Juan long ago developed into a warm-weather resort. The town's twin strips of beach are **Plages du Soleil** (east of the Vieux Port and the newer Port Camille-Rayon) and **Plages du Midi** (west of those two). Each stretches 1km (⅔ mile) and charges no entry fee, with the exception of small areas administered by concessions that rent mattresses and chaises and have snack kiosks. Regardless of which concession you select (on Plages du Midi they sport names such as Au Vieux Rocher, Passoa Beach, and Corail Plage; on Plages du Soleil you'll find Plage Nounou and Plage Tétou), you'll pay 12€ to 20€ for a day's use of a mattress. Plage Tétou is associated with the upscale **Chez Tétou** (p. 264). If you don't want to rent a mattress, you can cavort unhindered anywhere along the sands, moving freely from one area to another. Golfe-Juan indulges bathers who remove their bikini tops, but it forbids nude sunbathing.

Shopping

A popular art gallery is **Galerie Sassi-Milici,** 65 bis av. Georges Clemenceau (✆ **04-93-64-65-71;** www.sassi-milici.com), which displays ceramics and works by contemporary artists.

Market days in Vallauris are Tuesday to Sunday 7am to 12:30pm at **place de l'Homme au Mouton,** with its flower stalls and local produce. For a souvenir, you may want to visit a farming cooperative, the **Cooperative Nérolium,** 12 av. Georges Clemenceau (✆ **04-93-64-27-54**). It produces such foods as bitter-orange marmalade and quince jam, olive oils, and scented products such as orange-flower water. Another unusual outlet for local products is the **Parfumerie Bouis,** 50 bis av. Georges Clemenceau (✆ **04-93-64-38-27**).

Landlocked Vallauris depends on the sale of tourist items and ceramics. Merchants selling the colorful wares line both sides of **avenue Georges Clemenceau,** which begins at a point adjacent to the Musée Picasso and slopes downhill and southward to the edge of town. Some of the pieces displayed in these shops are in poor taste. In recent years, the almost-universal emphasis on the traditional rich burgundy color has been replaced with a wider variety geared to modern tastes.

Where to Stay

Villa Le Port d'Attache This popular B&B offers sweeping views over the Bay of Nice. Its four bedrooms are well maintained with pretty Provençal linens and spotlessly clean bathrooms. We'd recommend the Sirocco room with its seaview terrace. From the DVD library at your disposal to the Fragonard bathroom products, attentive owners Gillian and Daniel excel in the details. They also rent out an apartment in Juan-les-Pins by the week. There's little to do here but chill by the pool, but you're a short drive away from Cannes and Antibes. The driveway was improved during 2011.

1909 Voie Julia, Quartier de Riquebonne, 06220 Vallauris. www.portdattache.com. ✆ **04-93-64-90-64.** 4 units. 85€–120€ double. MC, V. Free parking. **Amenities:** Breakfast room; pool (outdoor). *In room:* A/C, TV, hair dryer, minibar, Wi-Fi (free).

Where to Eat

Café Marianne ★★ 🎁 MEDITERRANEAN Much gossip surrounded the takeover of Café Llorca by Marianne Estène-Chauvin of the Belles Rives group at the end of 2009. Despite the departure of celebrity chef Alain Lorca, this upbeat cafe remains a breath of fresh air for Vallauris. A pretty terrace and contemporary decor set the scene for all-day-dining, from a coffee-and-croissant breakfast to dinner of Mediterranean snacks such as crab spring rolls or cod served with *aïoli* (garlic mayonnaise). Our preferred time to go is for tea with mouth-watering homemade pastries.

Place Paul Isnard. ✆ **04-93-64-30-42.** Reservations required. Main courses 16€; fixed-price menus 19€–30€. AE, DC, MC, V. Daily 8:30am–10pm.

Chez Tétou ★ SEAFOOD In its own amusing way, this is one of the Côte d'Azur's most famous restaurants, capitalizing on the beau monde that came here in the 1950s and 1960s. Retaining its Provençal earthiness despite its ludicrously high prices, it has thrived in a white-sided beach cottage for 95 years. Appetizers are limited to platters of charcuterie or several almost-perfect slices of fresh melon. Most diners order the house specialty, bouillabaisse. Also on the limited menu are grilled sea bass with tomatoes *provençale,* sole meunière, and king prawns.

8 av. des Frères-Roustan, sur la Plage, Golfe-Juan. ✆ **04-93-63-71-16.** Reservations required. Main courses 80€–150€; bouillabaisse 98€. No credit cards. Thurs–Sun and Tues noon–2:30pm; Thurs–Tues 7:30–10:30pm. Closed Nov to early Mar.

ANTIBES ★★★ & JUAN-LES-PINS ★

913km (567 miles) S of Paris; 21km (13 miles) SW of Nice; 11km (7 miles) NE of Cannes

On the other side of the Baie des Anges (Bay of Angels) across from Nice, Antibes and Juan-les-Pins boast the best natural-sand beaches on the French Riviera. In 1923, these twin resorts became the Riviera's first summertime playground when the Grand Hôtel du Cap (now the Hôtel du Cap Eden-Roc) stayed open all year round, attracting guests as illustrious as Cole Porter and F. Scott Fitzgerald. There are five ports here, including Antibes's Port Vauban—the largest yachting port in Europe.

Juan-les-Pins is the epitome of family fun, while Antibes is famous for having been home to Picasso and for the young, yachting crowd who hang out in its bars and restaurants. Spiritually divorced from Antibes, Cap d'Antibes (a peninsula lying between Antibes and Juan-les-Pins) is studded with the villas and outdoor pools of the superrich. If you come in mid-July, you'll hear blues in the air around La Pinède Gould during Jazz à Juan (below).

Essentials

GETTING THERE Antibes and Juan-les-Pins are connected by **rail** to most other Mediterranean coastal resorts. Multiple trains arrive from Nice each day to avenue Robert-Soleau in Antibes (trip time 18 min.; one-way fare 4€) and to place de la Gare in Juan-les-Pins (trip time 30 min.; one-way fare 4.40€). For rail information, call ✆ **36-35,** or visit www.voyages-sncf.com. **Buses** arrive from Nice and its **airport** (www.nice.aeroport.fr) at 40-minute intervals throughout the day to Antibes and Juan-les-Pins; one-way bus tickets cost 8€.

If you're **driving** from Nice, take A8 west until you come to exit 47 for Villeneuve-Loubet. Take D2D in the direction of Grasse/Villeneuve-Loubet, then D6007 in the direction of A8 Nice. Turn left for central Antibes or turn right onto the D6107 for Juan-les-Pins.

VISITOR INFORMATION The **Office de Tourisme** is at 11 place du Général-de-Gaulle, Antibes (✆ **04-97-23-11-11;** fax 04-97-23-11-12; www.antibesjuan lespins.com) and 51 bd. Charles Guillaumont, Juan-les-Pins (✆ **04-97-23-11-10;** fax 04-97-23-11-09).

SPECIAL EVENTS The town offers some of the best nightlife on the Riviera, and the action reaches its height during the annual jazz festival. The 10- to 12-day **Jazz à Juan** (www.jazzajuan.fr), in mid-July, attracts international jazz masters and their fans. Concerts are in a temporary stadium, custom-built for the event in La Pinède Gould park. Tickets cost 38€ to 72€ and can be purchased at the tourist offices in Antibes and Juan-les-Pins alike.

Exploring the Towns

Hans Hartung & Anna-Eva Bergman Foundation ★ 🎁 Devotees of modern art can now visit the former home of this German abstract painter and his wife, also an artist. You must reserve space, as only 30 visitors are allowed on the weekly tour because of security reasons. The stark-white villa was designed by Hartung himself, who lived here until his death in 1989. The couple left 16,000 paintings, photographs, and engravings, and you get to see only a fraction on one visit. Exhibitions are rotated throughout the year.

173 chemin du Valbosquet, Antibes. ✆ **04-93-33-45-92.** www.fondationhartungbergman.fr. Admission 5€ adults, 3€ students, free for ages 15 and under. Guided tours Fri at 2pm. Bus: Line 7 to chemin du Valbosquet.

Marineland ★ ☺ Europe's largest marine park is Antibes' most popular attraction. This isn't the place to explore animals in their natural environment, but the impressive spectacle of dolphins and sea lions somersaulting through the air or through hoops is a sure-fire winner for most children. After you've watched the whale, sea lion, and dolphin shows, you can admire the park's latest arrivals: two polar bears in a new 3.5€ million refrigerated home. You can even wade in the dolphin tank and meet the dolphins (with an escort). You'll need at least half a day to visit Marineland, although there's plenty of entertainment for a whole day out, as the park is surrounded by its mini-empire of attractions, including Aquasplash (with wave pools and waterslides), Adventure Golf, and La Petite Ferme du Far West (an adventure farm suitable for young families). Bring dry T-shirts for the whale show as those on the front row are sprayed with water.

306 av. Mozart, Antibes (off RN 7). ✆ **08-92-30-06-06.** www.marineland.fr. Admission 36€ adults, 2€ children 3–12. July–Aug daily 10am–11pm; Apr–Sept daily 10am–7pm; Feb–Mar and holidays daily 10am–6pm.

Musée Napoléonien In this stone-sided fort and tower, built in stages in the 17th and 18th centuries, resides a collection of Napoleonic memorabilia, naval models, and paintings. A toy-soldier collection depicts various uniforms, including one used by Napoleon in the Marengo campaign. A wall painting on wood shows Napoleon's entrance into Grenoble; another shows him disembarking at Golfe-Juan on March 1, 1815. In contrast to Canova's Greek-god image of Napoleon, a miniature pendant by Barrault reveals the general as he really looked, with pudgy cheeks and a receding hairline. In the rear rotunda is one of the many hats worn by the emperor. You can climb to the top of the tower for a view of the coast that's worth the admission price.

Batterie du Graillon, bd. J.-F.-Kennedy, Antibes. ✆ **04-93-61-45-32.** Admission 3€ adults, 1.50€ seniors and students, free for children 17 and under. Mid-June to mid-Sept Tues–Sat 10am–6pm; mid-Sept to mid-June Tues–Sat 10am–4:30pm.

Musée Picasso ★★★ On the ramparts above the port is the Château Grimaldi, once the home of the princes of Antibes of the Grimaldi family, who ruled the city from 1385 to 1608. Today it houses one of the world's great Picasso collections. Picasso came to town after the war and stayed in a small hotel at Golfe-Juan until the museum director at Antibes invited him to work and live at the museum. After spending the autumn of 1946 painting here, he gave the museum all the paintings and drawings he'd done. This collection has been enriched over the years with numerous Picasso ceramics, lithographs, oils on paper, sculptures, and even tapestries. In addition, a gallery of contemporary art exhibits Léger, Miró, Ernst, and Calder, among others.

Place du Mariejol, Antibes. ✆ **04-92-90-54-20.** Admission 6€, 3€ seniors and students, free for children 17 and under. Mid-June to mid-Sept Tues–Sun 10am–6pm (Wed and Fri until 8pm); mid-Sept to mid-June Tues–Sun 10am–noon and 2–6pm.

Outdoor Pursuits

There are lots of watersports here. If you're interested in scuba diving, contact **Easy Dive,** Port Gallice (✆ **04-93-61-41-49;** www.easydive.fr). A one-tank dive costs 45€, including all equipment. **Water-skiing** is available at virtually every beach in Juan-les-Pins. Concessionaires include one outfit that's more or less permanently located on the beach of the Hôtel des Belles-Rives. Ask any beach attendant or bartender, and he or she will guide you to the water-skiing representatives who station themselves on the sands. A 1-hour session costs 30€ to 110€.

A Day at the Beach

People flock to Antibes and Juan-les-Pins for their natural-sand beaches. Extending over 25km (15 miles) of coastline, there are over 48 beaches to choose from. **Plage de Juan-les-Pins** is a Blue Flag eco-labeled public beach that's popular with families. Nearby are private beaches: **La Voile Blanche** (www.plagevoileblanche.com), with its restaurant and blue-and-white-striped recliners, and **Bijou Plage** (see "Sunbathing & Dining," p. 271).

In Old Antibes, there's a small, sheltered Blue Flag beach called **Plage de la Gravette** towards Port Vauban, while further towards the Cap lie the large and often-crowded Blue Flag public beaches of **Plage de la Salis** and **Plage du Ponteil.** On the tip of the Cap d'Antibes peninsula lies the exclusive **Plage de la Garoupe,** with both public and private sections where you can rent beach recliners. Along Plage de la Garoupe, you'll find private beaches with restaurants including the ultrasmart **Garoupe Beach** (www.garoupe.com) and **Plage Keller** (www.plagekeller.com), the down-to-earth **La Joliette,** and **Le Rocher,** famed for its Breton crêpes. Topless sunbathing is permitted, but total nudity isn't.

Where to Stay

VERY EXPENSIVE

Hôtel du Cap-Eden-Roc ★★★ Legendary for the glamour of its setting and its clientele, this Second Empire hotel is like a country estate. Opened in 1870 and surrounded by masses of gardens, it boasts spacious public rooms, marble fireplaces, paneling, chandeliers, and upholstered armchairs. Everything about this place is lavish—including the prices. The guest rooms are among the Riviera's most sumptuous, with deluxe beds, although it's worth pushing the boat out on your room choice if you really want to enjoy the feeling of Belle Époque grandeur. Even though the guests snoozing by the pool—blasted out of the cliffside at enormous expense—appear artfully undraped during the day, evenings are upscale, with lots of emphasis on clothing and style. The world-famous Pavillon Eden Roc, near a rock garden apart from the hotel, has a panoramic sea view. Venetian chandeliers, Louis XV chairs, and elegant draperies add to the Pavillon's drama. Lunch is served on a terrace, under umbrellas and an arbor.

Bd. J.-F.-Kennedy, 06601 Cap d'Antibes. www.hotel-du-cap-eden-roc.com. ✆ **04-93-61-39-01.** Fax 04-93-67-76-04. 130 units. 490€–1,200€ double; 1,100€–1,820€ suite. No credit cards. Closed mid-Oct to mid-Apr. **Amenities:** 2 restaurants; 2 bars; babysitting; concierge; exercise room w/sauna; private jetty; pool (outdoor); room service; spa; tennis courts. *In room:* A/C; TV; hair dryer; safe; Wi-Fi (free).

EXPENSIVE

Hôtel des Belles-Rives ★★★ This five-star hotel is one of the Riviera's fabled addresses, on par with its equally famous sister Hôtel Juana (see below). Once it was

Beachside Lounging

With its splendid views over the Garoupe Bay, the private beach of La Baie Dorée hotel, 575 bd. de la Garoupe (✆ 04-93-67-30-67; www.baiedoree.com), is open to non-hotel guests. For 20€ per day, you can lounge on the beachside deck and jetty, as well as enjoy the hotel's indoor and outdoor pools and Jacuzzi.

a holiday villa occupied by Zelda and F. Scott Fitzgerald, and the scene of many a drunken brawl. It later played host to such luminaries as the duke and duchess of Windsor, Josephine Baker, and Edith Piaf. A 1930s aura lingers through recent renovations, although the double-glazing and air-conditioning bring a welcome touch of modern amenities. As befits a hotel of this age, rooms come in a variety of shapes and sizes, from small to spacious. The lower terraces hold garden dining rooms, a waterside aquatic club with a recently renovated restaurant and lounge, and a jetty. The whole complex has its own private beach and dock.

33 bd. Edouard Baudoin, 06160 Juan-les-Pins. www.bellesrives.com. ✆ **04-93-61-02-79.** Fax 04-93-67-43-51. 43 units. 150€–755€ double. AE, DC, MC, V. Free parking; covered parking 25€. Closed Jan–Feb. **Amenities:** 2 restaurants (1 summer only and 1 year-round); bar; private beach and watersports club; babysitting; room service. *In room:* A/C, TV, hair dryer, minibar, Wi-Fi (18€).

Hôtel Juana ★★★ This balconied Art Deco hotel, beloved by F. Scott Fitzgerald, is separated from the sea by the park of pines that gave Juan-les-Pins its name. The hotel is constantly being refurbished, as reflected in the attractive rooms with mahogany pieces, well-chosen fabrics, tasteful carpets, and large bathrooms in marble or tile. The rooms often have such extras as balconies. The hotel has its own health club and pool, but you can also use the Belles Rives' private sandy beach. Overlooking the white marble terrace shaded by palm trees, its Café Marianne restaurant serves well-priced Mediterranean snacks and a range of 25 wines by the glass.

La Pinède, av. Gallice, 06160 Juan-les-Pins. www.hotel-juana.com. ✆ **04-93-61-08-70.** Fax 04-93-61-76-60. 40 units. 161€–528€ double; from 350€ suite. AE, MC, V. Parking 25€. Closed Nov–Dec. **Amenities:** Restaurant; bar; babysitting; health club; pool (outdoor). *In room:* A/C, TV, hair dryer, minibar, Wi-Fi (18€).

MODERATE

Castel Garoupe Located 300m (984 ft.) from the beach, this old-fashioned Mediterranean villa was built in 1968 on a private lane in the center of the cape. The spacious rooms are outdated, but many rooms have private balconies; some units also have air-conditioning and kitchenettes. A tranquil garden with a pool and tennis court is also on the premises. Although there are beach restaurants nearby, it's a trek to the restaurants and shops of central Juan-les-Pins or Antibes.

959 bd. de la Garoupe, 06160 Cap d'Antibes. www.castel-garoupe.com. ✆ **04-93-61-36-51.** Fax 04-93-67-74-88. 29 units. 132€–174€ double; 149€–188€ studio apt with kitchenette. AE, MC, V. Free parking. Closed mid-Nov to mid-Mar. Bus: A2. **Amenities:** 2 bars; babysitting; pool; tennis court. *In room:* A/C (some), hair dryer, kitchenette (in some), Wi-Fi (10€ per day).

Hôtel Beau Site ★ This white-stucco villa with a tile roof and heavy shutters is surrounded by eucalyptus trees, pines, and palms. Located off the main road, a 7-minute walk from the beach, it has a low wall of flowers and wrought-iron gates. The interior is like a country inn, with oak beams and Provençal furniture. The guest rooms are comfortable, and superior rooms on the third floor were beautifully refurbished in 2010. Studios with kitchenettes can also be booked by the week. Breakfast is the only meal served, but the friendly staff will bring hot and cold drinks to your room until 11pm. We'd recommend hiring a car to drive into central Juan-les-Pins and Antibes.

141 bd. J.-F.-Kennedy, 06160 Cap d'Antibes. www.hotelbeausite.net. ✆ **04-93-61-53-43.** Fax 04-93-67-78-16. 30 units. 85€–175€ double; 180€–235€ suite. AE, DC, MC, V. Free parking. Closed Nov–Feb. Bus: A2. **Amenities:** Bar; babysitting; bike rentals; pool (outdoor); room service. *In room:* A/C, TV, hair dryer, kitchenette (in some), Wi-Fi (free).

Hôtel des Mimosas This elegant 1870s-style villa sprawls through a tropical garden on a hilltop, a 10-minute walk to a good beach. The decor is a mix of high-tech and Italian-style comfort, with antique and modern furniture. Guest rooms come in a variety of shapes and sizes—some are quite small. Try for one of the four rooms with a balcony or the nine rooms with a terrace. A pool sits amid a verdant lawn dotted with palm trees. This well-priced three-star hotel is usually fully booked in summer, so reserve far in advance. Breakfast is the only meal served.

Rue Pauline, 06160 Juan-les-Pins. www.hotelmimosas.com. ✆ **04-93-61-04-16.** Fax 04-92-93-06-46. 34 units. 120€–150€ double. AE, MC, V. Free parking. Closed Oct–Apr. From the town center, drive 4km (¼ mile) west, following N7 toward Cannes. **Amenities:** Bar; pool (outdoor); Wi-Fi (free). *In room:* A/C, TV, hair dryer, minibar.

Hôtel Le Pré Catelan In a residential area near the town park, 200m (656 ft.) from a sandy beach, this 1920s Provençal villa features a garden with rock terraces, towering palms, lemon and orange trees, large pots of pink geraniums, and outdoor furniture. The atmosphere is casual, the setting uncomplicated and unstuffy. Furnishings are durable and basic. As is typical of such old villas, guest rooms come in a variety of shapes and sizes. Some have kitchenettes, and more expensive units have terraces. Despite its setting in the heart of town, the garden lends a sense of tranquility. There's no restaurant, but summertime snacks are served on the outdoor terrace. The hotel has no elevator.

27 av. des Palmiers, 06160 Juan-les-Pins. www.precatelan.com. ✆ **04-93-61-05-11.** Fax 04-93-67-83-11. 24 units. 92€–172€ double; from 158€ suite. AE, MC, V. Parking 8€–10€. **Amenities:** Bar; babysitting; pool (outdoor). *In room:* TV, hair dryer, kitchenette (in some), minibar, Wi-Fi (free).

INEXPENSIVE

Eden Hôtel Just 50m (164 ft.) from the beach, this centrally located two-star hotel is a bargain for Juan-les-Pins. Charming owner Patricia, aided by her mother and her daughter, is on hand to advise you on the best restaurants nearby. Most of the simply furnished bedrooms have sea views. Breakfast is served in the jaunty blue-and-yellow dining room or on the shaded terrace. The hotel has no elevator, but the friendly staff help with heavy luggage.

16 av. Louis-Gallet, 06160 Juan-les-Pins. www.edenhoteljuan.com. ✆ **04-93-61-05-20.** Fax 04-92-93-05-31. 17 units. 69€–105€ double. AE, DC, MC, V. Covered parking 9€–11€. **Amenities:** Lounge; terrace. *In room:* A/C, TV; Wi-Fi (free).

La Jabotte Bargain hunters will love this diminutive B&B overlooking sandy Salis beach on the Cap d'Antibes, within walking distance of Antibes' old town. Its 10 tastefully furnished rooms look onto a leafy courtyard. A generous breakfast is served in a breakfast room scattered with cerise chairs and colorful canvases painted by owner Yves. He and his partner Claude have just celebrated 10 years in business.

13 av. Max Maurey, 06160 Cap d'Antibes. www.jabotte.com. ✆ **04-93-61-45-89.** Fax 04-93-61-07-04. 10 units. 82€–135€ double; 139€–180€ suite. AE, MC, V. Free parking. Closed Nov–Jan. **Amenities:** Breakfast room; terrace. *In room:* TV (some).

La Place Hôtel Set in the historic town center, my favorite hotel in Antibes is a 5-minute walk to the Marché Provençal. With its sought-after location and its stylish contemporary decor, La Place has taken Antibes by storm since it opened in 2009. Rooms are small but well-equipped, and mattresses are comfortable. The hotel has the added bonus of a restaurant serving delicious French brasserie food. Downsides are that there's no elevator and no on-site parking (although there's public parking nearby).

1 av. du 24 Août, 06600 Antibes. www.la-place-hotel.com. ✆ **04-97-21-03-11.** Fax 04-93-34-44-07. 14 units. 89€-140€. AE, MC, V. Free parking. **Amenities:** Restaurant. *In room:* A/C, TV, hair dryer, Wi-Fi (free).

Where to Eat

EXPENSIVE

Le Vieux Murs ★ FRENCH/SEAFOOD The arrival of Stéphane Arnal (who used to work under Alain Lorca at the Moulin de Mougins) has transformed this gastronomic address, but perhaps resulted in the loss of some of its Provençal charm and service standards along the way. The location could not be better: set within the 17th-century ramparts that used to fortify the old seaport, not far from the Musée Picasso. Deep-red paint complements soaring stone vaults, and a glassed-in front terrace overlooks the water. They use market-fresh ingredients, especially fish and seafood, which is prepared with flavor and served with style. Menu staples include fish of the day with risotto and beef Rossini.

25 promenade de l'Amiral-de-Grasse, Antibes. ✆ **04-93-34-06-73.** www.lesvieuxmurs.com. Reservations recommended. Main courses 17€-35€; fixed-price menu 29€-60€. AE, DC, MC, V. Tues-Sun noon-2:30pm; Tues-Sat 7:30-10:30pm (also Sun during summertime).

Les Pêcheurs-Restaurant Le Cap ★ MEDITERRANEAN Everything about this private beach resort is satisfying, from the car valet service that greets you as you arrive to the professional but easygoing staff and the comfy recliners to flop onto after lunch. You can even swim before lunch to work up an appetite, changing into your swimming gear in one of the rows of beach huts. A luxuriant, if expensive, lunch of grilled meat, fish, and salads is served beneath a canopy of pine trees, with views over Cap d'Antibes. Advanced booking is recommended for restaurant and recliners in peak season.

10 bd. Maréchal Juin, Cap d'Antibes. ✆ **04-92-93-13-30.** www.lespecheurs-lecap.com. Reservations recommended. Main courses 18€-40€. AE, DC, MC, V. Daily 10am-7pm. Closed Oct-Apr.

Restaurant de Bacon ★★★ SEAFOOD The Eden Roc restaurant at the Hôtel du Cap is more elegant, but Bacon serves the best seafood around. Surrounded by ultraexpensive residences, this restaurant on a rocky peninsula offers a panoramic coastal view. Bouillabaisse aficionados claim that Bacon offers the best in France. In its deluxe version, saltwater crayfish float atop the savory brew; we prefer the simple version—a waiter adds the finishing touches at your table. If bouillabaisse isn't to your liking, try fish soup with garlic-laden rouille sauce; fish terrine; sea bass; John Dory; or a little-known Mediterranean fish such as sar, pageot, or denti.

Bd. de Bacon, Antibes. ✆ **04-93-61-50-02.** www.restaurantdebacon.com. Reservations required. Main courses 45€-145€; fixed-price menus 49€-79€. AE, DC, MC, V. Wed-Sun noon-2pm; Tues-Sun 8-10pm. Closed Nov-Feb.

MODERATE

Le Perroquet PROVENÇALE Open since 1927, this Juan-les-Pins institution is in synch with the resort's carnival-like summer aura. Located across from the Parc de

Sunbathing & Dining

Although the gastronomic brasserie of Bijou Plage on boulevard du Littoral (✆ 04-93-61-39-07; www.bijouplage.com) may be resting on its attractive laurels, the beach is still an excellent place to relax in central Juan-les-Pins. From April to September, you can hire a recliner and beach umbrella for 10€ for a half day or 14€ for a full day. During summertime, a simple menu of salads and sandwiches is served on the beach.

la Pinède, it's decorated with depictions of every imaginable form of the restaurant's namesake parakeet. Look for savory versions of fish, at its best when grilled simply with olive oil and basil, and served with lemons. A worthwhile appetizer is the *assortiment provençale,* which includes tapenade of olives, marinated peppers, grilled sardines, and stuffed and grilled vegetables. Steaks may be served with green peppercorns or béarnaise sauce, and desserts include three types of pastries on the same platter. Service can be hit and miss.

Av. Georges Gallice, Juan-les-Pins. ✆ **04-93-61-02-20.** Reservations recommended. Main courses 20€–45€; fixed-price menu 18€–36€. MC, V. Daily noon–2pm and 7–11pm. Closed early Nov to Dec 26.

INEXPENSIVE

Mamalu ITALIAN This miniature restaurant serves the best Italian food in Antibes. The setting is informal with mismatching brocante-style tables and chairs, but the pasta is tasty and the service friendly. Considering its location in the historic town center, prices are surprisingly reasonable. Try the tiramisu for dessert. You'll have to book in advance as it's always full.

11 cours Masséna, Antibes. ✆ **04-93-34-40-07.** Reservations recommended. Main courses 15€–20€. MC, V. Tues–Sun 7:30–10pm; Sat–Sun noon–2pm.

Antibes & Juan-les-Pins After Dark

With its vaulted stone walls and jazz-and-blues ambience, **Café Cosy,** 3 rue du Migrainier (✆ **04-93-34-81-55;** www.cafecosy.com), is a relaxed place for a glass of wine or two in the heart of Old Antibes. Nearby in rue Lacan is the friendly **Le Blue Lady Pub,** where you can watch football and rugby matches over beers. For a faux-tropical experience, head to the long-established **Le Pam Pam,** route Wilson (✆ **04-93-61-11-05**), where you can sip rum drinks until 2:30am in an atmosphere that celebrates reggae, Brazilian, and African music and dance.

Try your luck at the roulette wheel at the **Eden Casino,** boulevard Edouard Baudouin in central Juan-les-Pins (✆ **04-92-93-71-71**). The area with slot machines is open every day 10am to 4am. *Les grands jeux* are open every evening 9pm to 4am. A photo ID is required, preferably a passport.

If you prefer high-energy reveling, check out the town's discos. Nuits Blanches owns several venues in Juan-les-Pins around Carrefour de Nouvelle-Orléans off boulevard de la Pinède, including the long-established **Whisky à Gogo** (✆ **04-93-61-26-40**), with its '70s disco atmosphere, and **Le Village** (✆ **04-92-93-90-00**), with its action-packed dance floor and DJs spinning to salsa, soul, and house music.

BIOT ★

917km (570 miles) S of Paris; 10km (6 miles) E of Cagnes-sur-Mer; 6km (4 miles) NW of Antibes

Biot has been famous for its pottery ever since merchants began to ship earthenware jars to Phoenicia and destinations throughout the Mediterranean. Biot was first settled by Gallo-Romans and has had a long, war-torn history. The potters and other artists still work at their ancient crafts today. Biot is also the place Fernand Léger chose to paint until the day he died.

Essentials

GETTING THERE Biot's **train** station is 3km (2 miles) east of the town center in the Quartier de la Brague near the seafront. Frequent services connect Nice and Antibes. For rail information and schedules, call ✆ **36-35,** or visit www.voyages-sncf.com. To **drive** to Biot from Nice, take A8 west. From Antibes, follow D704 north.

VISITOR INFORMATION The **Office de Tourisme** is at 46 rue St-Sébastien (✆ **04-93-65-78-00;** www.biot.fr).

Exploring the Town

To explore the village, begin at the much-photographed **place des Arcades,** where you can see the 16th-century gates and the remains of the town's former ramparts. The **Eglise de Biot,** place des Arcades (✆ **04-93-65-00-85**), dates from the 15th century, when it was built by Italian immigrants who arrived to resettle the town after its population was decimated by the Black Death. The church is known for two stunning 15th-century retables: the red-and-gold *Vierge au Rosaire* by Louis Bréa, and the restored *Ecce Homo* by Guillaume Canavesio. The church is open daily from 8am to 7:30pm year-round. The church holds regular concerts, Les Heures Musicales, wherein the ceiling vaults resonate with the sounds of classical music.

Finally, fit in a free visit to a working glass-blowing factory, where the sight of guys in shorts and sandals blowing on molten glass down the end of long metal pipes is entertainment for all ages. The artists at **Verrerie de Biot,** chemin de Combes (✆ **04-93-65-03-00;** www.verreriebiot.com) turn red-hot molten blobs into glassware of surprising beauty and complexity. Have a look at the one-of-a-kind collector pieces in the adjoining **Galerie International du Verre,** where the beautifully displayed glass is for sale. You may even find a souvenir worth taking home.

Musée d'Histoire et de Céramique Biotoises This museum displays the historical and contemporary work of local glass-blowing artists, potters, ceramists, painters, and goldsmiths of the area. The museum, which can be visited in less than an hour, is mainly of interest to the serious collector, although it does help the casual visitor understand why Biot is the capital of glass blowing on the Riviera. Local craftsmen revived the old methods of making oil lamps and carafes in 1956, and have been working that way since. Local soils provide the best sand for glass blowing. Look for the narrow-spouted *pontons* from which a jet of liquid, such as wine, can be poured straight into one's mouth.

9 rue Saint-Sébastien. ✆ **04-93-65-54-54.** Admission 2€ adults, 1€ children 6-16, free for children 5 and under. July-Sept Wed-Sun 11am-7pm; Oct-June Wed and Sat-Sun 2-6pm, Thurs-Fri 10am-6pm.

A Biotour

If you'd like to rest your legs while taking in the sights, take an eco-friendly tour in an electric car with Biot resident, Guy Bitchko. You can choose from several 20-minute tours around the old village to longer 50-minute tours that take in the local countryside. Tour prices start at 3.50€ per person. You'll usually find his electric car parked up on the rue St Sébastien opposite the tourist office. For more information, contact Biotour at ✆ 06-78-37-94-25.

Musée National Fernand-Léger ★★ Following a 4-year renovation, this museum (created by the artist's widow Nadia Léger) celebrated its 50th anniversary in 2010, looking better than ever. Léger's mosaic-and-ceramic mural enhances the stone facade. On the grounds is a polychrome ceramic sculpture, *Le Jardin d'enfants;* inside are two floors of geometrical forms in pure, flat colors. The collection includes paintings, ceramics, tapestries, and sculptures showing the artist's development from 1905 until his death in 1955. His paintings abound with cranes, acrobats, scaffolding, railroad signals, buxom nudes, casings, and crankshafts. The most unusual work depicts a Léger Mona Lisa (*La Joconde aux Clés*) contemplating a set of keys, a wide-mouthed fish dangling over her head.

Chemin du Val-de-Pôme (on the eastern edge of town). ✆ **04-92-91-50-20.** www.musee-fernandleger.fr. Admission 5.50€, free for children 17 and under. May–Oct Wed–Mon 10am–6pm; Nov–Apr Wed–Mon 10am–5pm.

Shopping

Glass, pottery, and other crafts are your best bet in Biot. In the late 1940s, glassmakers created a bubble-flecked glass known as *verre rustique*. It comes in brilliant colors such as cobalt and emerald and is displayed in many store windows on the main shopping street, **rue Saint-Sebastien.** Interesting stores are also found in the pedestrian zone in Biot's historic center. Stroll along some of the oldest streets, such as **place des Arcades.** Most of the glassworks, and many shops selling glass, are at the lower (southern) side of town, beside the **Route de la Mer.**

Pascal Guyot shows off his colorful creations at the **Verrerie du Village,** 2 rue St-Sébastien (✆ **04-93-65-06-50;** www.verrerieguyot.com), where you can watch glass being blown in the neighboring atelier.

Glass artist Jean-Claude Novaro is known as the "Picasso of glass artists"; visit his gallery, **Galerie Jean-Claude Novaro** (also known as Galerie LePatrimoine Lea Novaro), 2 place des Arcades (✆ **04-93-65-60-23** or 06-12-78-27-27) to see his creations. His works are pretty and colorful, though sometimes lacking the diversity and intellectual flair of the artists displayed at the Galerie International du Verre.

Stop by **Le Mas des Orangers** (✆ **04-93-65-18-10;** www.lemasdesorangers.com) on rue Roses (just off rue St-Sébastien) for olive oils, jams, candles, and other citrus-scented goodies.

Where to Stay

Inter-Hotel Le Domaine du Jas Set at the base of the hill on which sits medieval Biot, this well-managed B&B was built in the early 1990s in the form of three villa-inspired low-rise buildings clustered within a palm-studded garden around a swimming pool. Each unit has its own terrace or balcony, views of the pool or garden, and, in some cases, panoramas of medieval Biot rising dramatically on the slopes above. The hotel was taken over by the group Inter-Hotels in 2010.

625 rte. de la Mer, 06410 Biot. www.domainedujas.com. ✆ **04-93-65-50-50.** Fax 04-93-65-02-01. 19 units. 95€–180€ double. AE, MC, V. Free parking. Closed Dec–Jan. **Amenities:** Babysitting; pool (outdoor); Wi-Fi (free). *In room:* A/C, TV, hair dryer.

Where to Eat

Along rue Sébastien, the road widens around the village fountain to form a square lined with restaurants. Here, you'll find a reliable option for an informal hot snack or salad at **Le Piccolo** (✆ **04-93-65-16-91**).

Les Terraillers ★★★ MEDITERRANEAN With its vine-shaded terrace, this stone-vaulted restaurant is worth a detour. Less formal than some if its Michelin-starred compatriots, this family-run restaurant offers sophisticated yet robust French cuisine. Chef Michaël Fulci changes his menu with the seasons but always includes plenty of Mediterranean fish and poultry dishes. From the mouth-watering cheese dome to the tea trolley with its pots of fresh herbs for you to concoct your own blend, the key to its success is in the detail.

11 Chemin-Neuf. ✆ **04-93-65-01-59.** www.lesterraillers.com. Reservations required as far in advance as possible. Main courses 33€–48€; fixed-price lunch 39€, dinner 65€–110€. AE, MC, V. Fri–Tues noon–2pm and 7–10pm.

TOURRETTES-SUR-LOUP ★

929km (577 miles) SE of Paris; 29km (18 miles) W of Nice; 6km (4 miles) W of Vence; 21km (13 miles) NE of Grasse

Often called the "City of Violets" because of the small purple flowers that abound beneath the olive trees, Tourrettes-sur-Loup sits atop a sheer cliff overlooking the Loup valley. Though violets are big business for the town (they're sent to the perfume factories in Grasse, made into candy, and celebrated during a festival held each March), you'll probably find the many shops lining the streets much more interesting. These small businesses are often owned by artisans who sell their own art—most notably hand-woven fabrics and unique pottery. Even if you're not interested in buying, walking through the Old Town is worth the trip up the hill. The unusual city was built so that the walls of the outermost buildings form a rampart; three towers rising above the village give it its name.

Essentials

GETTING THERE The nearest **rail** junction is at Cagnes-sur-Mer; buses run about every 45 minutes from Cagnes to Vence, where you must change to another bus to arrive in Tourrettes (about six a day; trip time from Cagnes-sur-Mer to Tourrettes via Vence: at least 1 hr.). The town has no bus station; the bus disembarks in the place du Village. For **bus schedules** and information, visit www.lignesdazur.com or call ✆ **0810 06-10-06.** It's more convenient to take a taxi from Cagnes-sur-Mer. **R.E.I.S.** taxis (✆ **06-07-10-65-38**) line up at the train station and cost around 30€ to 35€ each way. If you're **driving** from Nice, take the A8 west turning off at Cagnes-sur-Mer (exit 48). Head north towards Vence on the D336, then continue on the D2210 towards Tourrettes-sur-Loup.

VISITOR INFORMATION The Office de Tourisme is at 2 place de la Libération (✆ **04-93-24-18-93**).

SPECIAL EVENTS Every March, Tourrettes-sur-Loup hosts a weekend-long violet festival with a flower parade, violet-strewn events, and stalls selling violet-infused trinkets from soaps to sweets. For more information, call ✆ **04-93-24-18-93** or visit www.tourrettessurloup.com.

Exploring the Town

Tourrettes-sur-Loup is chockablock with **arts and crafts;** if you wander down Grand'Rue, you'll find jewelers, woodworkers, sculptors, painters, and fabric designers. Stop by **Poterie Arnaud Chassaing,** no. 1 Ferrage (✆ **04-93-59-27-92**), for Chassaing's signature deep blue-glazed ceramics, and long-established **La Paësine,** no. 14 Ferrage (✆ **04-93-24-14-55**), for silver jewelery. The **violet museum** at La Bastide aux Violettes, Quartier de la Ferrage (✆ **04-93-59-06-97;** www.tourrettes surloup.com), follows the history of violets for perfume production in the Grasse area. It's open 10am to 12:30pm and 1:30 to 5pm from Tuesday to Saturday.

Shopping

Tourrettes-sur-Loup is home to more crafts studios than any other village its size in Provence. Nearly 30 artisans, including a handful of noted ones from as far away as Paris, have set up their studios and outlets, often in stone-sided buildings facing the town's main street, **Grand'Rue.** The best way to sample their offerings is to wander and window-shop.

You'll find jewelry, in designs ranging from old-fashioned to contemporary, at **La Paësine,** 14 Grand'Rue (✆ **04-93-24-14-55**). Original clothing—in natural fibers including mohair and silk—for men and women, as well as draperies, bed linens, and tablecloths, usually in creative patterns, is available at the **Atelier Arachnée,** 8 Grand'Rue (✆ **04-93-24-11-42**). Ceramic signposts crafted from local clay in patterns inspired by the many civilizations that have pillaged or prospered in Provence are sold at **Poterie Tournesol,** 7 Grand'Rue (✆ **04-93-59-35-62**).

Looking for a pick-me-up after a day of shopping? Head for one of the region's best candy shops, **Confiserie Florian des Gorges du Loup** in Le Pont du Loup on the route from Tourrettes-sur-Loup to Grasse (✆ **04-93-59-32-91;** www.confiserie florian.com). Here, age-old techniques are used to layer fresh fruit with sugar. The result is an ultrachewy, ultrasweet confection that gradually melts as it explodes flavor—the taste has been called "angelic." Sample chocolate-covered orange peel, rose-petal jam, and sugar-permeated sliced apricots, tangerines, plums, cherries, and grapes. Even the local violets are transformed into edible, sugary treats.

Where to Stay & Eat

One of the most reliable dining options in Tourrettes-sur-Loup is **Le Relais des Coches** at 28 rte. de Vence (✆ **04-93-24-30-24;** www.lerelaisdescoches.com), owned by Lyonnaise chef Gérard. With its terrace looking towards the Vieux Village, this Mediterranean restaurant is open for lunch and dinner.

Les Belles Terrasses This Logis de France hotel offers views of the faraway peninsula of Antibes and the sea beyond. Its boxy shape and terra-cotta roof were inspired by an architect's fantasy of an old Provençal manor house, and it was named after the terraces that are angled for maximum exposure to the view. The rooms are simple, traditional, and comfortable. Much of the allure of this hotel is its restaurant. Menu items include fillet of sole and *magret de canard* (duck breast). Fixed-price menus range from 23€ to 28€.

1315 rte. de Vence, 06140 Tourrettes-sur-Loup. www.bellesterrasses.fr. ✆ **04-93-59-30-03.** Fax 04-93-59-31-27. 18 units. 45€–66€ double. AE, MC, V. Closed mid-Nov to mid-Dec. From town, drive about a kilometer (½ mile), following the signs toward Vence. **Amenities:** Restaurant. *In room:* TV, Wi-Fi (free).

SAINT-PAUL DE VENCE ★★

925km (575 miles) S of Paris; 23km (14 miles) E of Grasse; 27km (17 miles) E of Cannes; 31km (19 miles) N of Nice

One of the back country's most exclusive and priciest places to stay, the postcard-perfect hilltop village of Saint-Paul de Vence is home to artists' workshops and to the exalted Fondation Maeght.

Essentials

GETTING THERE The nearest **rail** station is in Cagnes-sur-Mer. Take ligne 400 from Nice's Gare Routière via Nice Airport and Cagnes-sur-Mer, dropping passengers off in St-Paul de Vence (one-way fare: 1€), then in Vence. For information, contact **Lignes d'Azur** (✆ **0810-06-10-06;** www.lignesdazur.com). If you **drive** from Nice, take coastal A8 east, turn inland at Cagnes-sur-Mer, and follow signs north to St-Paul-de-Vence.

VISITOR INFORMATION The **Office de Tourisme** is at 2 rue Grande (✆ **04-93-32-86-95;** fax 04-93-32-60-27; www.saint-pauldevence.com).

Exploring the Town

Except for local residents and service-related deliveries (such as dropping your luggage off at your hotel), driving a car within the center of St-Paul de Vence's Old Town is prohibited. The pedestrians-only **rue Grande** is the most interesting street, running the entire length of St-Paul de Vence. Most of the stone houses along it are from the 16th and 17th centuries, many still bearing the coats of arms placed here by the original builders. Today most of them are antiques shops, arts-and-crafts galleries, and souvenir and gift shops—some are still artists' studios.

Fondation Maeght ★★★ This avant-garde building houses one of the most modern art museums in Europe. Nature and the creations of men and women blend harmoniously in this unique achievement of the architect Josep Lluís Sert. Its white concrete arcs give the impression of a giant pagoda rising from a hill in a pine forest.

A stark Calder rises like some futuristic monster on the lawn. In a courtyard, the bronze works of Giacometti and marble statues by Miró and mosaics by Chagall form a surrealistic garden. Built on several levels, the museum creates links between indoors and out with glass walls and terraces. The foundation, a gift "to the people" from Aimé and Marguerite Maeght, also provides a showcase for new talent. Enjoy the works of 20th-century artists: mosaics by Chagall and Braque, Miró ceramics in the "labyrinth," and Ubac and Braque stained glass in the chapel. On the property are a library, a cinema, and a cafeteria. In one showroom, you can buy original lithographs by artists such as Chagall and Giacometti, and limited-edition prints.

Montée des Trious, outside the town walls. ✆ **04-93-32-81-63.** www.fondation-maeght.com. Admission 14€ adults, 9€ students and ages 10–18, free for children 9 and under. July–Sept daily 10am–7pm; Oct–Mar 10am–1pm and 2–6pm; Apr–June daily 10am–6pm.

L'Eglise Collégiale This church was constructed in the 12th and 13th centuries, though it was much altered over the years. The Romanesque choir is the oldest part, containing remarkable stalls carved in walnut in the 17th century. The bell tower was built in 1740, but the vaulting was reconstructed in the 1800s. Although the facade today isn't alluring, the church is filled with art, notably a painting of Saint Catherine of Alexandria attributed to Tintoretto. The Trésor de l'Eglise is one of the most beautiful in the Alpes-Maritimes, with a spectacular ciborium. Look also for a low relief of the Martyrdom of St-Clément on the last altar on the right. In the baptismal chapter is a 15th-century alabaster Madonna.

3 Montée de l'Eglise. No phone. Free admission. Daily 9am–6pm (until 7pm July–Aug).

Musée d'Histoire de St-Paul Located near the church, this museum in a village house dates to the 1500s. It was restored and refurnished in 16th-century style, with artifacts illustrating the history of the village.

Place de l'Eglise. ✆ **04-93-32-41-13.** Admission 3€ adults, 2€ students and children 5–18, free for children 4 and under. Apr–Sept daily 11am–1pm and 3–6pm; Oct–Mar daily 2–5pm.

Shopping

Climb down some steep steps to a 14th-century wine cellar to visit **La Petite Cave de St-Paul,** 7 rue de l'Etoile (✆ **04-93-32-59-54**), which stocks an excellent selection of regional wine. As well as wine from the Lérins monastery on the Ile St-Honorat off the coast of Cannes, he also stocks Clos Saint-Paul (formerly known as Le Mas Bernard owned by Adrien Maeght). This famous vineyard was taken over in 2010 by young vintner Julien Bertaina who runs the nearby Domaine St-Joseph in Tourrettes-sur-Loup. The bottles no longer boast wine labels designed by celebrated artists such as Georges Braque and Joan Miró, but the quality of the wine has improved.

The village streets are chock-full of expensive boutiques and galleries. Well-renowned artist Christian Choisy even has two outlets: the **Choisy Atelier** on 5 rue de la Tour and **Choisy La Galerie** on 104 rue Grande (✆ **04-93-32-19-06;** www.christianchoisy.com); they're open daily 9:30am to 7pm.

Where to Stay

St-Paul de Vence is one of the most popular villages along the Côte d'Azur and prices reflect this. Many "hotels" do not have restaurants, although some offer lunchtime snacks. Unless you're staying in the village center, such as at **Hôtel Le St-Paul** or **La Colombe d'Or** (see "Where to Dine"), we'd recommend you rent a car. This is especially true if you're staying in any of the B&Bs near route de la Colle as you may dislike walking along this traffic-laden road into the old village.

In addition to our recommendations below, we recommend **Le Mas de Pierre** (✆ **04-93-59-00-59;** www.lemasdepierre.com), a Relais & Châteaux hotel on the outskirts of St-Paul de Vence. Every possible creature comfort is on tap from a spa, two restaurants, poolside bar, and private poolside cabanas to an orchid greenhouse.

VERY EXPENSIVE

Hôtel Le St-Paul ★★★ Converted from a 16th-century Renaissance residence and retaining many original features, this member of Relais & Châteaux is in the heart of the village. The guest rooms are decorated with luxurious fabrics, antiques, sumptuous beds and bowls of fruit, chocolates or flowers. One woman wrote us that while sitting on the balcony of room no. 30 she understood why Renoir, Léger, Matisse, and Picasso were inspired by Provence. Many rooms enjoy a view of the valley with the Mediterranean in the distance. The restaurant has a flower-bedecked terrace sheltered by the 16th-century ramparts and a superb dining room with vaulted ceilings.

86 rue Grande, 06570 St-Paul de Vence. www.lesaintpaul.com. ✆ **04-93-32-65-25.** Fax 04-93-32-52-94. 16 units. 300€–520€ double; 440€–650€ suite. AE, DC, MC, V. Free parking. Closed Nov to Mar. **Amenities:** Restaurant; bar; babysitting; room service; Wi-Fi (free). *In room:* A/C, TV, hair dryer, minibar.

EXPENSIVE

Hôtel Les Vergers de Saint-Paul ★ 🎁 This contemporary hotel is a small *hôtel de charme,* as the French say. Bedrooms are tasteful, comfortable, and elegantly refined. All the accommodations come with a balcony or a terrace overlooking the large pool. The only downside is the 20-minute walk into St Paul village centre.

940 rte. de la Colle, 06570 St-Paul de Vence. www.hotel-vergers-saint-paul.cote.azur.fr. ✆ **04-93-32-94-24.** Fax 04-93-32-91-07. 17 units. 150€–165€ double; 250€ suite. AE, MC, V. **Amenities:** Bar; babysitting; pool (outdoor). *In room:* A/C, TV, Wi-Fi (free).

La Grande Bastide ★★ This 18th-century country home has been lovingly turned into a *hôtel de charme*. The midsize bedrooms are artfully decorated in a traditional Provençal style with pastel fabrics. All of the rooms open onto views of St-Paul (many also have a view of the sea). More panoramic views are visible from the terrace, where breakfast and lunchtime snacks are served. Staff is attentive to small details, whether it's providing plenty of pool towels or lighting the walkway to the pool at night with candles. The hotel is a 25-minute walk from the village center, but the hotel provides a shuttle service.

1350 rte. de la Colle, 06570 St-Paul de Vence. www.la-grande-bastide.com. ✆ **04-93-32-50-30.** Fax 04-93-32-50-59. 14 units. 140€–245€ double; from 255€ suite. AE, DC, MC, V. **Amenities:** Bar; pool (outside). *In room:* A/C, TV, minibar, Wi-Fi (free).

Villa St. Maxime ★★ Set on beautifully landscaped grounds, this B&B features a large panoramic terrace and garden beneath the ramparts of this old fortified town. While the town is ancient, the villa is like a work of contemporary art, built with Provençal stone sculpted in bold lines, with a retractable and glass-enclosed reception atrium. Vaulted and pillared halls are architectural grace notes, as is the sleek marble flooring. Views extend from almost every window, even of the faraway Mediterranean. Accommodations open onto private balconies or terraces. Guests are served complimentary evening aperitifs and digestifs.

390 rte. de la Colle, 06570 St-Paul de Vence. www.villa-st-maxime.com. ✆ **04-93-32-76-00.** Fax 04-93-32-93-00. 6 units. 155€–195€ double; 190€–380€ suite. AE, MC, V. **Amenities:** Babysitting; pool (outdoor). *In room:* A/C, TV, hair dryer, minibar, Wi-Fi (free).

Orion Bed & Breakfast ★★ With its treehouses scattered around the forested garden, the Orion is an eco-friendly paradise: Natural fabrics are used in the treehouses and the outdoor pool is filtered through stones and aquatic plants. Guests are lulled by the sound of birds and frogs as they doze in a hammock on their tree-house terrace. If you prefer *terra firma,* there's a two-bedroom house with a fully equipped kitchen. Owner Diane and her daughter Aina are charming hosts who speak fluent English and will bring your breakfast to your treehouse. There's no restaurant and it's a 10-minute drive into the village center, so the communal microwave, fridge, and kitchenware are very useful. There's a 2- to 4-night minimum stay depending on the season. Another drawback is that they don't accept credit cards, so you have to organize an advance bank transfer or pay cash.

Impasse des Peupliers, 2436 chemin du Malvan, 06570 St-Paul de Vence, www.orionbb.com. ✆ **04-93-24-87-51** or 06-75-45-18-64. 5 units. Treehouse for 2-night midweek stay from 400€ or 3-night weekend from 700€. Rates include breakfast. Cash only. **Amenities:** Kitchen (fridge, microwave); pool (outdoor). *In room:* Kettle. Wi-Fi (free).

MODERATE

Auberge Les Orangers ★ A verdant garden with a long pool and vegetable garden awaits at this highly personalized bed and breakfast. Decorated with dark antique furniture and white Provençal *boutis* (bedspreads), each bedroom has a balcony or terrace. M. Franklin and his wife are conscientious hosts. The only drawback is that the bedrooms aren't air-conditioned.

Quartier les Fumerates, rte. de la Colle (D107), 06570 St-Paul de Vence. www.lesorangers.fr. ✆ **04-93-32-80-95.** Fax 04-93-32-00-32. 5 units. 104€–150€ double; 148€–185€ suite. Rates include breakfast. MC, V. Free parking. **Amenities:** Babysitting. *In room:* Hair dryer.

Le Hameau ★ Set in a garden of citrus trees and jasmine, this is a reliable address in Saint-Paul de Vence. Since they've been in business for over 40 years, it's clear that we're not the only fans. Perhaps it's the reasonable prices in this unreasonably priced area that keep guests coming back. The converted 18th-century stables remind us of haciendas, with their white-washed walls, but the interiors have a distinctly Provençal flavor: Flowered *boutis* (quilts) and heavy wooden furniture predominate. Every one of its 17 air-conditioned rooms and apartments is different. If you want to self-cater, No. 15 is an apartment, with a kitchen. As well as an infinity pool, you can enjoy the use of a spa with a sauna, *hammam,* and Jacuzzi. In summertime, there are breakfast buffets on the flower-strewn terrace and lunchtime snacks around the pool.

528 rte. de la Colle (D107), 06570 St-Paul de Vence. www.le-hameau.com. ✆ **04-93-32-80-24.** Fax 04-93-32-55-75. 17 units. 120€-170€ double; 220€-280€ suite. MC, V. Closed mid-Nov to mid-Feb. **Amenities:** Jacuzzi; pool (outdoor); spa. *In room:* A/C, TV, hair dryer, kitchenette (in some).

INEXPENSIVE

Hôtel Marc Hély ★ Adrian and Christel welcome you to their family-managed *hotel de charme.* Although it's situated in nearby La Colle sur Loup, this B&B still commands a panoramic view of the St-Paul de Vence village. Each of the tasteful and well-equipped bedrooms contains a balcony or a private patio. The garden helps ensure serenity, even in this touristy part of France. Breakfast is served on the patio in the garden or on a veranda with a view of St. Paul. Families can rent the two-bedroom family suite.

535 rte. de Cagnes, 06480 La Colle-sur-Loup. www.hotel-marc-hely.com. ✆ **04-93-22-64-10.** Fax 04-93-22-93-84. 11 units. 70€-130€ double; 110€-210€ family suite. AE, DC, MC, V. Free parking. **Amenities:** Pool (outdoor); Wi-Fi (free). *In room:* A/C, TV, hair dryer, minibar.

Where to Eat

La Colombe d'Or ★ PROVENÇALE For many decades, the "Golden Dove" has been St-Paul's most celebrated restaurant—not for cutting-edge cuisine or exotic experiments, but for its remarkable art collection. You can dine amid Mirós, Picassos, Dufys, Signacs, and Calders. In fair weather everyone tries for a seat on the terrace. You can start with a basket of crudités (raw vegetables) or a summer truffle salad before venturing for a rack of lamb or an oven-baked beef with *gratin dauphinois* (potato). The rustic cuisine acts as a subtle foil to this mythical place.

La Colombe also runs several guest rooms (13 doubles, 12 apartments) in an original 16th-century stone house; two wings were added in the 1950s, one of which stretches into the garden next to the pool. Some units have exposed stone and ceiling beams; all are comfortable, with air-conditioning, minibars, and TVs. Prices are 250€–430€.

1 place du Général-de-Gaulle, 06570 St-Paul de Vence. ✆ **04-93-32-80-02.** Fax 04-93-32-77-78. www.la-colombe-dor.com. Reservations required. Main courses 17€-35€. AE, DC, MC, V. Daily noon-2pm and 7:30-10pm. Closed Nov to mid-Dec.

VENCE ★

925km (575 miles) S of Paris; 31km (19 miles) N of Cannes; 24km (15 miles) NW of Nice

Often overlooked in favor of its photogenic sister Saint-Paul de Vence, Vence is the Arrière-Pays's second town after Grasse. Travel up into the hills northwest of Nice, across country studded with cypresses, olive trees, pines, and banks of roses and oleanders to this quietly prosperous town. Visitors invariably have themselves photographed on place du Peyra in front of the urn-shaped Vieille Fontaine, a background shot in several motion pictures.

Essentials

GETTING THERE The nearest **rail** station is in Cagnes-sur-Mer, about 10km (6¼ miles) southwest from Vence. For train information, call ✆ **36-35,** or visit www.voyages-sncf.com. Frequent **buses** (no. 400 or 94) originating in Nice (from bus station and from Nice Airport) take approximately 1 hour to reach Vence; the one-way fare is 1€. For information, contact **Lignes d'Azur** (✆ **0810-06-10-06;** www.lignesdazur.com). If you **drive** from Nice, take coastal A8 east, turn inland at Cagnes-sur-Mer, and follow signs north on D336 and then D236 to Vence.

VISITOR INFORMATION The **Office de Tourisme** is on place Grand-Jardin (✆ **04-93-58-06-38;** fax 04-93-58-91-81; www.ville-vence.fr).

Exploring the Town

If you're wearing the right kind of shoes, the narrow, steep streets of the Old Town are worth exploring. Dating from the 11th century, the cathedral on place Godeau is unremarkable except for a Mark Chagall mosaic, *Moses Saved from the Waters,* and some 15th-century Gothic choir stalls. Most visitors quickly pass through the narrow gates of this once-fortified walled town to where the sun shines more brightly.

Chapelle du Rosaire ★★ When the great Henri Matisse was 77, he set out to design and decorate his masterpiece—"the culmination of a whole life dedicated to the search for truth," he said. Matisse created the Chapelle du Rosaire for the Dominican nuns of Monteils. (Sister Jacques-Marie, a member of the order, had nursed him back to health after a serious illness.) From the front you might find it unremarkable and pass it by—until you spot a 12m (39-ft.) crescent-adorned cross rising from a white-and-blue-tiled roof.

Matisse wrote: "What I have done in the chapel is to create a religious space . . . in an enclosed area of very reduced proportions and to give it, solely by the play of colors and lines, the dimensions of infinity." The light picks up the subtle coloring in the simply rendered leaf forms and abstract patterns in the stained-glass windows: sapphire blue, aquamarine, and lemon yellow. In black-and-white ceramics, St. Dominic is depicted in only a few lines. The most remarkable design is in the black-and-white-tile Stations of the Cross, with Matisse's self-styled "tormented and passionate" figures.

The price of admission includes entrance to **L'Espace Matisse,** a gallery devoted to the documentation of the chapel's design and construction from 1949 to 1951. It also contains lithographs and religious artifacts that concerned Matisse.

466 av. Henri-Matisse. ✆ **04-93-58-03-26.** Admission 3.50€ adults, 1.50€ children under 18; contributions to maintain the chapel are welcome. Mon, Wed, and Sat 2–5:30pm; Tues and Thurs 10–11:30am and 2–5:30pm. Closed mid-Nov to mid-Dec.

Where to Stay

VERY EXPENSIVE

Le Château Saint-Martin & Spa ★★★ If you're heading into the hills above Nice and you seek luxury and refinement, this Relais & Châteaux hotel is your address. The château, in a 14-hectare (36-acre) park with terraced gardens, was built in 1936 on the foundations of a 12th-century Templar castle. The main building holds the standard units, while suites are housed in the tile-roofed villas. You can walk through the gardens on winding paths lined with tall cypresses and olive trees, and past the ruins of a chapel. The two-Michelin-starred restaurant has a view of the coast and offers superb French cuisine. In summer, many guests prefer the poolside grill.

2490 av. des Templiers B.P. 102, 06142 Vence. www.chateau-st-martin.com. ✆ **04-93-58-02-02.** Fax 04-93-24-08-91. 40 units, 6 villas. 360€-570€ double; from 450€ suite. AE, DC, MC, V. Closed mid-Nov to mid-Feb. From the town center, follow signs toward Coursegoules and Col-de-Vence for 1.5km (1 mile) north. **Amenities:** Restaurant; bar; babysitting; pool (outdoor); room service; spa; 2 tennis courts (lit). *In room:* A/C, TV, hair dryer, Wi-Fi (free).

EXPENSIVE

Hôtel Le Cantemerle ★ One of the most appealing places in Vence is this cluster of Provençal buildings designed to resemble an old-fashioned compound. Capped with rounded terra-cotta roof tiles, they stand on a lawn dotted with old trees, surrounding a pool. Public areas, stylishly outfitted with contemporary furniture and accessories, include a paneled bar and a sun-flooded flagstone terrace where meals are served. Rooms aren't overly large but duplex rooms have balcony-style sleeping lofts with comfortable beds. The gourmet restaurant serves worthwhile regional and mainstream French cuisine, while midweek lunchtime snacks are served on the shaded terrace.

258 chemin Cantemerle, 06140 Vence. www.cantemerle-hotel-vence.com. ✆ **04-93-58-08-18.** 27 units. 210€-260€ double; 475€-525€ suite. AE, MC, V. Closed late Oct to mid-Mar. **Amenities:** Restaurant; bar; babysitting; exercise room; 2 pools (indoor and outdoor). *In room:* A/C, TV, hair dryer, minibar, Wi-Fi (free).

EXPLORING THE gorges du loup

After paying your respects to Matisse at the Chapelle du Rosaire in Vence, you can take D2210 through some of the Riviera's most luxuriant countryside. The **Gorges du Loup** isn't as dramatic as the **Gorges du Verdon** (p. 189), but it still features a scenic 13km (8-mile) drive that loops along the gorge's eastern and western edges. This drive showcases waterfalls, most notably the **Cascades des Demoiselles,** with its partially fossilized plant life, and the 39m (130-ft.) **Cascade de Courmes.** Jagged glacial holes, best exemplified by the **Saut du Loup,** can also be found at the valley's northeastern end. The Gorges du Loup are a popular point for aquatic hiking and canyoning. For more information, contact **Destination Nature** (✆ **06-86-66-35-49;** www.loisirs-explorer.com/destination-nature).

Gourdon, the only village along the gorge's western rim, has a year-round population of only 60 (100 if you include the population of the region immediately nearby), but in summer, its population swells into something approaching a honky-tonk tourist trap. It's worth a visit for its dramatic views alone.

If you're coming from Cannes, take A85 for 21km (13 miles) northwest to Grasse, and then travel east for 6km (3¾ miles) on Route 2085, where you'll turn north at Magagnosc, following D3 for 8km (5 miles) north to Gourdon, at the edge of the gorge. Once in Gourdon, continue north on D3 along the western rim of the gorge; after 6km (4 miles), turn right onto D6 to return south along its eastern lip. Turn east on D2210 at Pont-du-Loup for a 8km (5-mile) drive to Tourrettes-sur-Loup, or continue on to Vence, another 3km (2 miles), where you can turn south on Route 36 for a 9km (5½-mile) drive back to the coast.

For more information, contact the **Office de Tourisme,** 22 cours Honoré Cresp, 06130 Grasse (✆ **04-93-36-66-66**); place Grand-Jardin, 06140 Vence (✆ **04-93-58-06-38**); or 2 place de la Libération, 06140 Tourrettes-sur-Loup (✆ **04-93-24-18-93**).

Maison du Frêne ★★ Charm and serenity greet you in this grandly restored 18th-century building that stands next to a famous ash tree from the 5th century. It is decorated with baroque and Pop art, attracting devotees of art and design to its central location. The lounge library's wonderful collection of original art books is at your disposal. The comfortable suites with wonderful views are spacious, well maintained, and beautifully furnished. In the Pop Art Suite, you return to the '60s with Marilyn Monroe and Andy Warhol as your "hosts." The main floor is the social area. A good French breakfast is served in the large pink kitchen.

1 place du Frêne, 06140 Vence. www.lamainsondufrene.com. ✆ **04-93-24-37-83.** 4 units. 150€–185€ double. Rates include breakfast. MC, V. **Amenities:** Lounge. *In room:* A/C, TV, hair dryer, Wi-Fi (free).

INEXPENSIVE

Auberge des Seigneurs ★ This 400-year-old stone hotel gives you a taste of old Provence. The guest rooms are well maintained, but the family-run team dedicates its energy to the restaurant. Nevertheless, the Provençal-style rooms are comfortable, with lots of exposed paneling and beams. Two have nonworking fireplaces. The restaurant is in a stone building that used to be the kitchen of the Château de Villeneuve, where François I spent part of his youth. The house specializes in grills prepared on an open spit in view of the dining room, which holds a long wooden table and an open fireplace with a row of hanging copper pots and pans.

1 rue du Docteur Binet, 06140 Vence. ✆ **04-93-58-04-24.** Fax 04-93-24-08-01. 6 units. 85€–95€ double. DC, MC, V. Closed mid-Dec to mid-Jan. **Amenities:** Restaurant; bar. *In room:* Hair dryer.

Best Western Hôtel Le Floréal On the road to Grasse, this pleasant, comfortable hotel offers a view of the mountains and a refreshing lack of pretension. Many of the well-furnished rooms look out into the garden, where orange trees and mimosa add fragrance to the breezes. Most accommodations are medium size, and each is comfortable, with quality mattresses and fine linens.

440 av. Rhin-et-Danube, 06140 Vence. www.hotel-floreal-vence.com. ✆ **04-93-58-64-40.** Fax 04-93-58-79-69. 41 units. 78€–112€ double. AE, DC, MC, V. Free parking. **Amenities:** Restaurant; bar; pool (outdoor); sauna. *In room:* A/C, TV, hair dryer, Wi-Fi (free).

Where to Eat

Auberge des Seigneurs (see above) is an excellent place to dine at reasonable prices.

La Farigoule PROVENÇALE In a century-old house that opens onto a mulberry tree–shaded garden, this restaurant specializes in *provençale* cuisine. Menu items are conservative but flavorful: They include lamb shank with tapenade and pan-fried sea bream with sun-dried tomatoes. In the summer, you can dine in the garden.

15 rue Henri-Isnard. ✆ **04-93-58-01-27.** Reservations recommended. Fixed-price menus 29€ and 40€. MC, V. Wed–Sun noon–2pm and 7:30–10pm. Closed mid-Nov to mid-Dec.

Les Bacchanales ★★★ TRADITIONAL FRENCH In a villa close to the Chapelle Matisse, chef Christophe Dufau attracts diners with his Michelin-starred take on traditional French cuisine. On the ground level is a contemporary art gallery, with the restaurant upstairs. In summertime, meals are served in a garden amongst meadow flowers. Choose from several fixed-price menus that change throughout the year. Superior-quality and often difficult-to-source ingredients might include Corsican tiger veal, Camargue crayfish, or goat cheese from Courmettes. Friday nights are Jazz nights.

247 av. De Provence. ✆ **04-93-24-19-19.** Reservations recommended. Weekday lunch menus 35€-60€; fixed-price dinners 55€-80€. MC, V. Sept-June Thurs-Mon noon-2pm and 7-10pm; July-Aug Wed-Mon noon-2pm and 7-10pm.

CAGNES-SUR-MER & VILLENEUVE-LOUBET

917km (570 miles) S of Paris; 21km (13 miles) NE of Cannes

Cagnes-sur-Mer, like the Roman god Janus, has two faces. Perched on a hill in the "hinterlands" of Nice, **Le Haut-de-Cagnes** is a charming, historic village that has inspired many to creativity—from Simone de Beauvoir, who wrote *Les Mandarins* here, to Renoir, whose last home here has been turned into an art museum. At the foot of the hill is the rapidly developing beach resort called **Cros-de-Cagnes.**

The stretch of cheap seaside resorts around Cagnes-sur-Mer have been dubbed Concrete-on-Sea by Anglophone locals. This is not helped by the fact that the train line runs next to the sea at this point, so you have to find a rail-track crossing point every time you want to paddle.

Essentials

GETTING THERE The **train** depot, Gare SNCF, lies in Cros-de-Cagnes (the more commercial part of town). It serves trains that run along the Mediterranean coast, with several arrivals an hour from both Nice (trip time under 15 min.; one-way fare 2.60€) and Cannes (trip time 25 min.; 4€). For rail information, call ✆ **36-35,** or visit www.voyages-sncf.com. There are several buses per hour from Nice to Cagnes-sur-Mer. Take the no. 200 or 400 (trip time 30 min.; 1€). For information, contact **Lignes d'Azur** (✆ **08-10-06-10-06;** www.lignesdazur.com). The climb from Cagnes-Ville to Haut-de-Cagnes is strenuous; a free minibus runs daily about every 30 minutes year-round from place du Général-de-Gaulle to Haut-de-Cagnes. By **car** from any of the coastal cities of Provence, follow the A8 coastal highway, exiting at Cagnes-Sur-Mer/Cros-De-Cagnes.

VISITOR INFORMATION The **Office de Tourisme** is at 6 bd. Maréchal-Juin, Cagnes-Ville (✆ **04-93-20-61-64;** fax 04-93-20-52-63; www.cagnes-tourisme.com).

SPECIAL EVENTS Every July, Cagnes-sur-Mer holds a weekend-long festival dedicated to country music. Stetsons and boots are de rigueur, as would-be cowboys swing to the honky-tonk sounds of country music. For more information, contact the Cagnes-sur-Mer tourist office at ✆ **04-93-20-61-64** or visit www.frenchriviera festival.com.

Exploring the Towns

Narrow cobblestone streets and 17th- and 18th-century homes greet you in Haut-de-Cagnes. Drive your car to the top, where you can enjoy the view from place du Château and have lunch or a drink at a sidewalk cafe.

While in Le Haut-de-Cagnes, visit the **Château-Musée Grimaldi** on place Grimaldi. It was built in 1309 by Rainier Grimaldi, a lord of Monaco and a French admiral (see his portrait inside). Charts reveal how the defenses were organized. In the early 17th century, the dank fortress was converted into a more gracious Louis XIII–style château.

A Family-Friendly Side Trip to Villeneuve-Loubet

Neighboring beachside resort **Villeneuve-Loubet** (www.ot-villeneuveloubet.org) is easy to spot from a distance: Its landmark apartments on the **Marina Baie des Anges** curve back and forth like huge white, crested waves. It's one of only 32 destinations in France to have been awarded the official "Station Kid" designation, meaning it's particularly family-friendly. This town pays tribute to the *haute cuisine* of **Auguste Escoffier,** the greatest chef ever to run a kitchen in a nation with a rich culinary heritage. His former birthplace has been turned into a museum dedicated to French gastronomy, at 3 rue Auguste Escoffier (✆ **04-93-20-80-51;** www.fondation-escoffier.org).

The château contains two interconnected museums, the **Musée de l'Olivier (Museum of the Olive Tree)** and the **Musée d'Art Moderne Méditerranéen (Museum of Modern Mediterranean Art),** 7 place Grimaldi (✆ **04-92-02-47-30**). The modern art gallery displays works by Kisling, Carzou, Dufy, Cocteau, and Seyssaud, among others, with temporary exhibitions. In one salon is an interesting *trompe l'oeil* fresco, *La Chute de Phaeton.* From the tower, you get a panoramic view of the Côte d'Azur. The museums are open Wednesday to Monday 10am to noon and 2 to 5pm (May–Sept until 6pm). Admission to both museums is 4€ for adults and free for children 17 and under.

The Main Attraction

Musée Renoir & Les Collettes ★★ Les Collettes has been restored to appear as it did when Renoir lived here, from 1908 until his death in 1919. Although crippled by arthritis, he continue to sculpt here; in order to paint, he used assistants and tied the brush to his hands.

The house was built in 1907 in an olive and orange grove. A bust of Mme Renoir graces the entrance room. You can explore the drawing room and dining room on your own before going up to the artist's bedroom. In his atelier are his wheelchair, easel, and brushes. The terrace of Mme Renoir's bedroom has a stunning view of Cap d'Antibes and Haut-de-Cagnes. On a wall hangs a photograph of one of Renoir's sons, Pierre, as he appeared in the 1932 film *Madame Bovary.*

19 chemin des Collettes. ✆ **04-93-20-61-07.** Admission 4€ adults, 2€ children 12–18, free for children 11 and under. Wed–Mon 10am–noon and 2–5pm (May–Sept until 6pm). Ticket sales end 30 min. before lunch and evening closing hours.

A Day at the Beach

Cros-de-Cagnes, a part of Cagnes-Sur-Mer, is known for its 4km (2½ miles) of seafront, covered with light-gray pebbles smoothed by centuries of waves. These beaches are **Plages de Cros-de-Cagnes.** As usual, toplessness is accepted but full nudity is not. Concessions, such as **Le Cigalon** (✆ **04-93-07-74-82**), along this expanse rent beach mattresses and chaises for 10€ to 15€.

Where to Stay

IN CAGNES-SUR-MER

Hôtel Le Chantilly Just 50m (164 ft.) from the Côte d'Azur race course, this two-star hotel is the best bargain for those who prefer to stay near the beach and the train station. Built in a boxy and angular style in 1960, it won't win any architectural awards, but the owners have landscaped the property and made the interior as homey and inviting as possible, with Oriental rugs and potted plants. Most rooms are small but cozily furnished and well kept, often opening onto balconies. In fair weather you can enjoy breakfast, the only meal served, on an outdoor terrace. One drawback is the lack of air-conditioning.

31 chemin de la Minoterie, 06800 Cagnes-sur-Mer. www.hotel-lechantilly.fr. ✆ **04-93-20-25-50.** Fax 04-92-02-82-63. 17 units. 68€–77€ double. AE, DC, MC, V. Free parking. **Amenities:** Babysitting; room service. *In room:* TV, minibar, Wi-Fi (free).

IN LE HAUT-DE-CAGNES

Villa Estelle ★★ 🎁 Jean Cocteau, Renoir, and even Modigliani used to pass by the front door of this authentic Provençal mansion. The restored 14th-century villa opens onto a large terrace with Florentine-inspired columns set in a Mediterranean garden with terraces. The bougainvillea lends extra color to palm and orange trees, while white laurel blooms half the year. The five small to midsize bedrooms and suites are furnished with a personal touch and decorated with antiques and works of art alike. Some rooms open onto sea views, and old-fashioned charm is found around every corner. It's almost like staying in a private Provençal home. Guests convene in the living room with its old paintings, fine linen curtains, and rich velvet draperies. A self-catering apartment is available for weekly rentals. The only drawback is the lack of on-site parking.

5 montée de la Bourgade, 06800 Cagnes-sur-Mer (Haute-de-Cagnes). www.villa-estelle.com. ✆ **04-92-02-89-83.** Fax 04-92-02-88-28. 5 units. 100€–130€ double; 125€–175€ suite. Rates include breakfast. AE, DC, MC, V. **Amenities:** Wi-Fi (free). *In room:* A/C, TV, minibar.

Where to Eat

A former nose for the perfume industry, Catherine Armandi has breathed new life into Loulou-La Réserve since taking over this classic Cagnes-sur-Mer gourmet enclave in 2010. The restaurant, at 91 promenade de la Plage, has been renamed as **Catherine** (✆ **04-93-31-00-17;** www.catherine-lareserve.com).

IN LE HAUT-DE-CAGNES

Fleur de Sel FRENCH/PROVENÇALE Energetic owners Philippe and Pascale Loose run this charming restaurant in the center of the old village. In two ocher-toned dining rooms outfitted with Provençal furniture and oil paintings, you'll enjoy the kind of cuisine that Philippe learned during stints at some of the grandest restaurants of France, including a brief time with Marc Meneau at L'Espérance in Vézelay. Recommendations include foie gras pâté, goat cheese with truffle oil, and free-range guinea fowl.

85 Montée de la Bourgade. ✆ **04-93-20-33-33.** www.restaurant-fleurdesel.com. Reservations recommended. Fixed-price menu from 30€. MC, V. Thurs–Tues noon–2pm and 7:30–10pm. Closed 10 days in Nov.

Josy-Jo ★★ TRADITIONAL FRENCH This restaurant is the class act of Cagnes-sur-Mer. Behind a 200-year-old facade covered with vines and flowers, this restaurant was the home and studio of Modigliani and Soutine during their hungriest years. Paintings cover the walls, and the Bandecchi family runs everything smoothly. The Michelin-starred menu specializes in charcoal-grilled meats and Mediterranean fish.

2 rue du Planastel. ✆ **04-93-20-68-76.** Reservations required. Main courses 22€–45€; fixed-price lunch 30€–42€. AE, MC, V. Tues–Sat 12:30–2pm and 7:30–9:30pm.

NICE ★★★

929km (577 miles) S of Paris; 32km (20 miles) NE of Cannes

France's fifth-largest city and the French Riviera's capital, earthy Nice carries its Belle Époque heritage lightly. Turn-of-the-century mansions lord over the unceasing procession of fashionistas, rollerbladers, and beachgoers on the seafront promenade des Anglais. Brightly colored blooms greet passersby in cours Saleya, while a state-of-the-art tramway sweeps past majestic place Massena. Terra-cotta-clad buildings crowd the narrow streets of the Vieille Ville (Old Town), which is filled with antique shops and bistros. The city brims with artistic talent from Impressionists at the Beaux-Arts museum to contemporary stars at MAMAC.

Things to Do Admire the gracious palm-lined **promenade des Anglais** from the **Colline du Château's** (Castle Hill's) grassy summit, the perfect spot to see the bay sweep round to the distant Cap d'Antibes. Postcard-pretty Cimiez is home to the **Musée Matisse** and **Musée National Marc Chagall,** while the suburb's Roman amphithéâtre provides an idyllic back-drop to Nice's summertime **Jazz Festival.**

Shopping Fur-coated dames lead their diamante-collared dogs along **rue Paradis,** home to France's great fashion houses such as Chanel and Sonia Rykiel. Lose yourself among dazzling flowers or dig out a bargain at Monday's antique market in the open-air **cours Saleya.** Centuries-old chocolatier, **Confiserie Auer,** is the place to buy sweet Provençal treats, *fruits confits* (dried candied fruits).

Nightlife & Entertainment Start your evening in the unruly patchwork of bars along the **cours Saleya,** where you can sip pastis as you watch street performers dazzle with acrobatic escapades. Classical music fills the **Opéra de Nice,** while international pop stars perform at **Palais Nikaïa.** Serious partygoers head to **High Club** on Promenade des Anglais. The roulette ball clatters in the Art Deco hotel **casinos** on the waterfront.

Restaurants & Dining Tuck into ***socca*** (chickpea pancake) in the **cours Saleya. Vieux Nice** is the place for lovers of Niçoise cuisine, while beautifully restored **Place Garibaldi** excels in French bistro food. The **Nice Etoile** area is a hot spot for up-and-coming young chefs and for gastronomic wine shops where you can sip wine with the locals over nibbles. Local favorite dishes include **Provençal lamb** stuffed with fragrant garlic and rosemary or a salty **salad Niçoise,** which marries local olives and anchovies with Dijon vinaigrette.

Essentials

GETTING THERE Transatlantic and intercontinental flights land at **Aéroport Nice–Côte d'Azur** (✆ **08-20-42-33-33;** www.nice-aeroport.fr). From there, municipal bus no. 98 departs at 20-minute intervals for the central Nice; the one-way fare is 1€. Bus nos. 23 and 99 go to the train station Gare SNCF. A **taxi** from the airport into the city center will cost at least 22€ to 32€ each way. Trip time is under 30 minutes.

Trains arrive at Gare Nice-Ville, avenue Thiers (✆ **36-35;** www.voyages-sncf.com). From there you can take trains to Cannes (6.30€), Monaco (3.50€), and Antibes (4.10€), with easy connections to anywhere else along the Mediterranean coast. The train station has a small tourist center, open Monday to Saturday 8am to 8pm and Sunday 10am to 5pm (9am–7pm during peak season). If you face a long delay, you can eat at the cafeteria and even shower at the station.

The central bus station in Nice closed in 2011 to make way for an urban park. Buses for other resorts along the French Riviera now depart from two main terminals: **Station JC Bermond** (near the old bus station along bd. Jean-Jaurès) and **Vauban** tramway terminal (in the Saint-Jean d'Angély suburb). For more information, contact **Lignes d'Azur** (© **0810-06-10-06;** www.lignesdazur.com).

VISITOR INFORMATION Nice maintains three tourist offices, the largest and most central of which is at 5 promenade des Anglais, near place Masséna (© **08-92-70-74-07;** fax 04-92-14-46-49; www.nicetourisme.com). Additional offices are in the arrivals hall of the Aéroport Nice–Côte d'Azur and the railway station on avenue Thiers. Any office can make a hotel reservation (but only for the night of the day you show up) for a modest fee that varies according to the classification of the hotel.

GETTING AROUND Many local buses serve the railway station on avenue Thiers. Municipal buses charge 1€ for a ride within greater Nice. To save money, consider buying an unlimited day pass for 4€ or a 7-day pass for 15€.

No point within downtown Nice is more than about a 10-minute walk from the seafronting promenade, site of such well-known *quais* as the promenade des Anglais and the quai des Etats-Unis.

Nice Tramway (© **08-11-00-20-06;** www.tramway-nice.org), with 21 stations, runs from Comte de Falican in north Nice south to the city center, including place Masséna. All tickets cost 1€ and are available at ticket-dispensing machines located in all tram stations.

The best place to rent **bikes** and mopeds is **Nicea Rent,** 12 rue de Belgique (© **04-93-82-42-71**). It charges from 35€ per day for a moped with a deposit of at least 800€, depending on the value of the machine you rent. You can also take a bike taxi ride from **Cyclopolitain** (© **04-93-81-76-15;** www.cyclopolitain.com); you'll find these cycle-taxis at place Magenta or place Masséna. A public bike-sharing rental scheme runs throughout town with 1,200 bikes and 120 bike stations; the best place to pick up or drop off bikes is on the promenade des Anglais. Prices start at just 1€ per day. Find out more about the scheme by visiting www.velobleu.org.

SPECIAL EVENTS The **Nice Carnaval** draws visitors from all over Europe and North America. The "Mardi Gras of the Riviera" begins sometime in February, usually 12 days before Shrove Tuesday, celebrating the return of spring with 3 weeks of parades, *corsi* (floats), *veglioni* (masked balls), confetti, and battles in which young women toss flowers. Only the most wicked throw rotten eggs instead of carnations. The climax, a fireworks display on Shrove Tuesday, lights up the Baie des Anges (Bay of Angels). King Carnival goes up in flames on his pyre but rises from the ashes the following spring. For information, contact the tourist office (see above).

The **Nice Jazz Festival** (© **08-92-68-36-22;** www.nicejazzfestival.fr) runs for a week in mid-July, when jazz artists perform in the ancient Arènes de Cimiez.

Exploring the City

In 1822, the orange crop at Nice was bad and the workers faced a lean time, so the English residents put them to work building the **promenade des Anglais ★★**, a wide boulevard fronting the bay. Split by "islands" of palms and flowers, it stretches for about 6km (4 miles). Fronting the beach are rows of grand cafes, villas, and hotels—some five-star palaces, others decaying. Just off the promenade lies the magnificent 19th-century **Villa Masséna** (© **04-93-91-19-10**) on rue de France with its landscaped gardens and museum. Admission to the museum is free. It's open Wednesday to Monday 10am to 6pm.

Nice

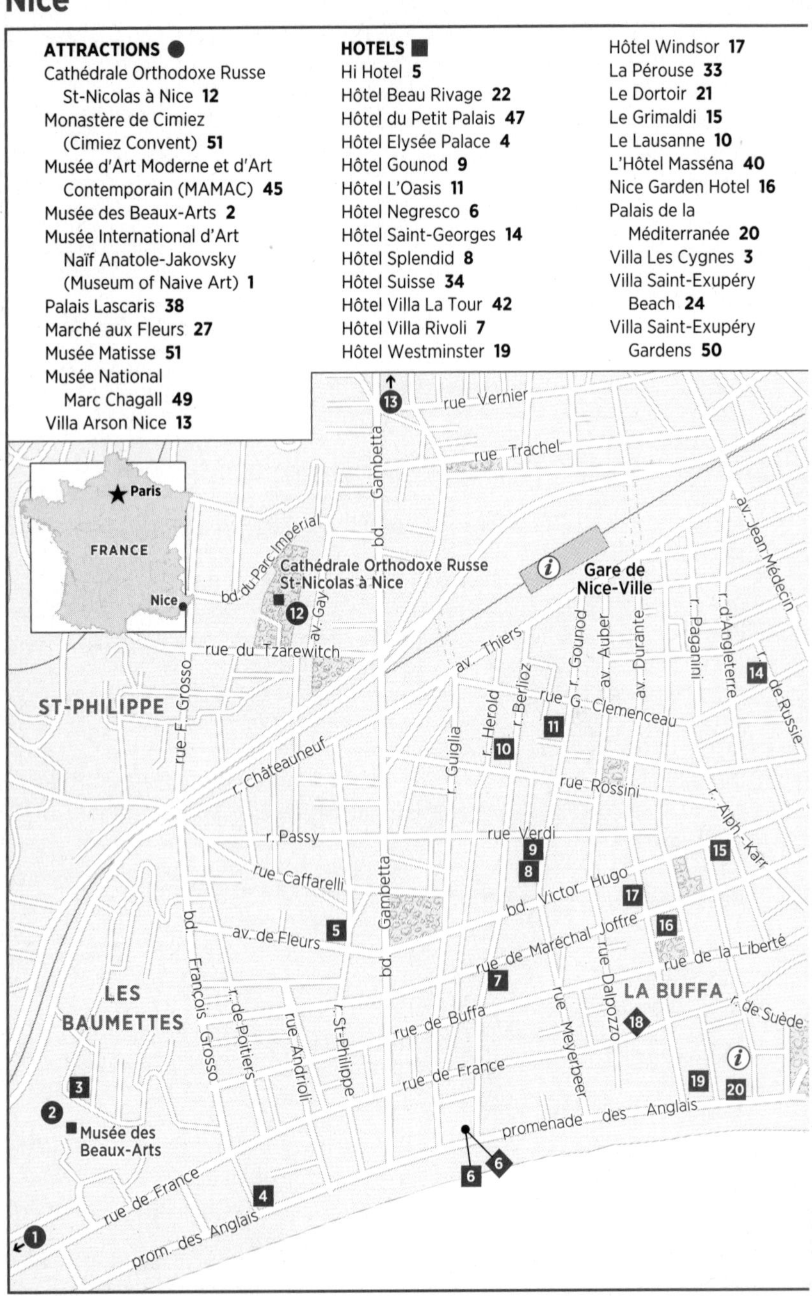
ATTRACTIONS
Cathédrale Orthodoxe Russe St-Nicolas à Nice 12
Monastère de Cimiez (Cimiez Convent) 51
Musée d'Art Moderne et d'Art Contemporain (MAMAC) 45
Musée des Beaux-Arts 2
Musée International d'Art Naïf Anatole-Jakovsky (Museum of Naive Art) 1
Palais Lascaris 38
Marché aux Fleurs 27
Musée Matisse 51
Musée National Marc Chagall 49
Villa Arson Nice 13
HOTELS
Hi Hotel 5
Hôtel Beau Rivage 22
Hôtel du Petit Palais 47
Hôtel Elysée Palace 4
Hôtel Gounod 9
Hôtel L'Oasis 11
Hôtel Negresco 6
Hôtel Saint-Georges 14
Hôtel Splendid 8
Hôtel Suisse 34
Hôtel Villa La Tour 42
Hôtel Villa Rivoli 7
Hôtel Westminster 19
Hôtel Windsor 17
La Pérouse 33
Le Dortoir 21
Le Grimaldi 15
Le Lausanne 10
L'Hôtel Masséna 40
Nice Garden Hotel 16
Palais de la Méditerranée 20
Villa Les Cygnes 3
Villa Saint-Exupéry Beach 24
Villa Saint-Exupéry Gardens 50
Paris
FRANCE
Nice
rue Vernier
rue Trachel
bd. Gambetta
bd. du Parc Impérial
Cathédrale Orthodoxe Russe St-Nicolas à Nice
av. Gay
rue du Tzarewitch
Gare de Nice-Ville
av. Thiers
av. Jean Médecin
r. Gounod
av. Auber
av. Durante
r. Paganini
r. d'Angleterre
r. de Russie
ST-PHILIPPE
rue F. Grosso
r. Châteauneuf
r. Berlioz
r. Herold
rue G. Clemenceau
r. Guiglia
rue Rossini
r. Alph.-Karr
r. Passy
rue Verdi
rue Caffarelli
bd. Victor Hugo
av. de Fleurs
rue de Maréchal Joffre
rue Dalpozzo
rue de la Liberté
LES BAUMETTES
bd. François Grosso
r. de Poitiers
rue Andrioli
r. St-Philippe
rue de Buffa
rue Meyerbeer
LA BUFFA
r. de Suède
rue de France
promenade des Anglais
Musée des Beaux-Arts
prom. des Anglais

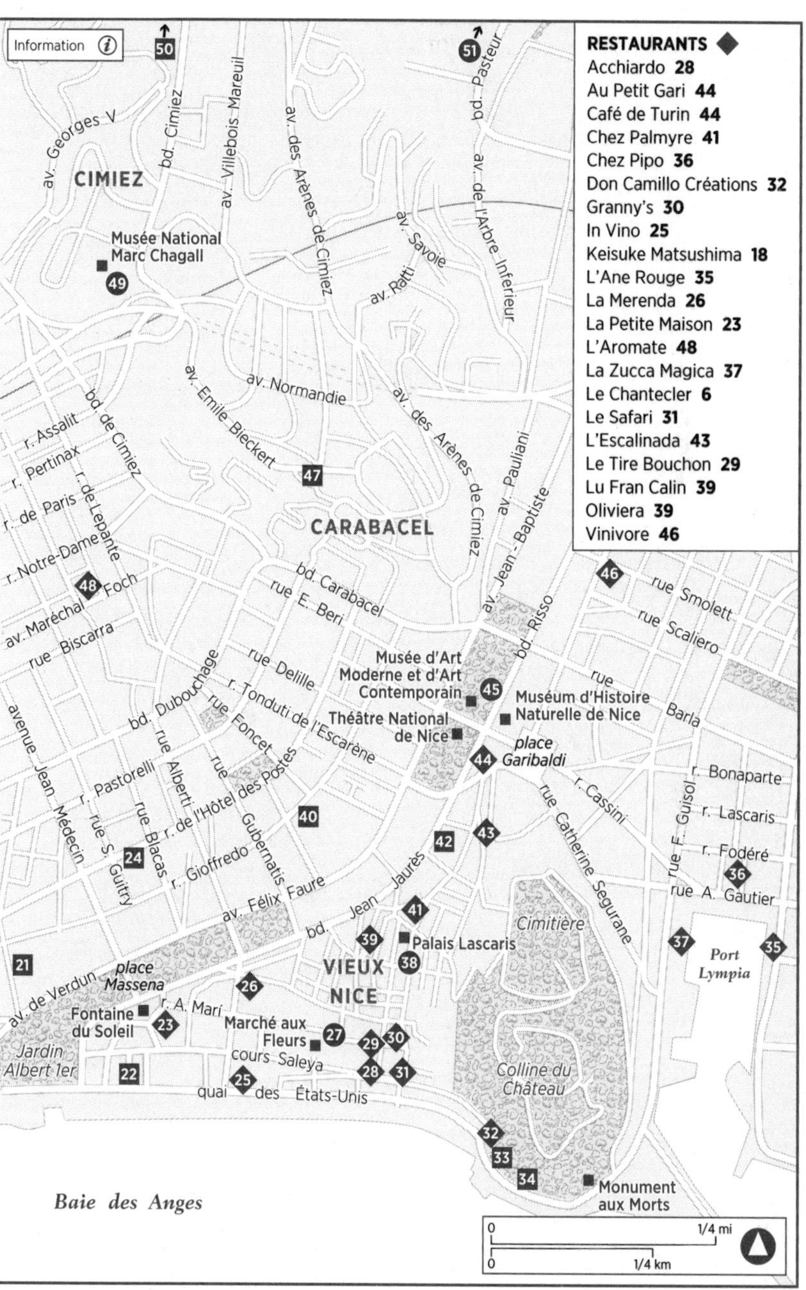
RESTAURANTS
Acchiardo 28
Au Petit Gari 44
Café de Turin 44
Chez Palmyre 41
Chez Pipo 36
Don Camillo Créations 32
Granny's 30
In Vino 25
Keisuke Matsushima 18
L'Ane Rouge 35
La Merenda 26
La Petite Maison 23
L'Aromate 48
La Zucca Magica 37
Le Chantecler 6
Le Safari 31
L'Escalinada 43
Le Tire Bouchon 29
Lu Fran Calin 39
Oliviera 39
Vinivore 46
Information
CIMIEZ
CARABACEL
VIEUX NICE
Musée National Marc Chagall
Musée d'Art Moderne et d'Art Contemporain
Théâtre National de Nice
Muséum d'Histoire Naturelle de Nice
place Garibaldi
Palais Lascaris
place Massena
Fontaine du Soleil
Marché aux Fleurs
Jardin Albert 1er
Cimitière
Colline du Château
Monument aux Morts
Port Lympia
Baie des Anges
av. Georges V
bd. Cimiez
av. Villebois-Mareuil
av. des Arènes de Cimiez
bd. Pasteur
av. de l'Arbre-Inferieur
av. Savoie
av. Ratti
av. Normandie
av. Emile Bieckert
av. des Arènes de Cimiez
av. Pauliani
av. Jean-Baptiste
bd. de Cimiez
r. Assalit
r. Pertinax
r. de Paris
r. de Lepante
r. Notre-Dame
av. Maréchal Foch
rue Biscarra
bd. Carabacel
rue E. Beri
rue Delille
r. Tonduti de l'Escarène
bd. Dubouchage
rue Foncet
bd. Risso
rue Smolett
rue Scaliero
rue Barla
avenue Jean Médecin
r. Pastorelli
rue Alberti
rue Gubernatis
r. de l'Hôtel des Postes
rue S. Guitry
rue Blacas
r. Gioffredo
av. Félix Faure
bd. Jean Jaurès
rue Catherine Segurane
r. Cassini
r. Bonaparte
r. Lascaris
r. Fodéré
rue F. Guisol
rue A. Gautier
av. de Verdun
r. A. Marí
cours Saleya
quai des États-Unis
0
1/4 mi
0
1/4 km

In the east, the promenade becomes **quai des Etats-Unis,** the original boulevard leading to the start of Nice *Vieille Ville* (Old Town) and the famous **Marché aux Fleurs** flower market in cours Saleya (see below). Rising sharply on a rock at the end of the quai des Etats-Unis is the site known as **Colline du Château (Castle Hill),** the spot where the ducs de Savoie built their castle, which was torn down in 1706. All that remains are two or three stones—even the foundations have disappeared in the wake of Louis XIV's deliberate destruction of what was viewed at the time as a bulwark of Provençal resistance to his regime. The hill has been turned into a garden of pines and exotic flowers. To reach the panoramic site, you can take a free elevator. The park is open daily from 9am to 8pm.

At the north end of Le Château is the famous old **graveyard** of Nice, visited primarily for its lavishly sculpted monuments that make their own enduring art statement. It's the largest in France and the fourth largest in Europe.

Continuing east from Le Château and "the Rock," you reach the harbor, where you'll find the restaurants galore serving bouillabaisse. While sitting here lingering over an aperitif at a sidewalk cafe, you can watch the boats depart for Corsica (or perhaps take one yourself). The port was excavated between 1750 and 1830. Since then, an outer harbor—protected by two jetties—has also been created.

The "authentic" Niçoise live in **Vieille Ville ★**, beginning at the foot of "the Rock" and stretching out from place Masséna. Sheltered by sienna-tiled roofs, many of the Italianate facades suggest 17th-century Genoese palaces. The Old Town is a maze of narrow streets, many of them teeming with local life. Some, including the rue Droite and the rue Pairolière, are reserved exclusively for pedestrians. On these narrow streets, you'll find some of the least expensive restaurants in Nice. Buy *la pissaladière* (an onion pizza) or *socca* (a crepe made with chickpea flour) from one of the local vendors. Many of the old buildings are painted a faded Roman gold, and banners of multicolored laundry flaps in the sea breezes.

While here, try to visit the **Marché aux Fleurs,** the flower market at cours Saleya. The vendors set up their stalls Tuesday to Saturday 6am to 5:30pm (until 6:30pm Wed and Sat) and Sunday 6am to 1:30pm. A flamboyant array of carnations, violets, jonquils, roses, and birds of paradise is hauled in by vans or trucks and then displayed in the most fragrant market in town. There's also a morning fruit and vegetable market further along in the cours Saleya.

Nice's commercial centerpiece is **place Masséna,** with pink buildings in the 17th-century Genoese style and the **Fontaine du Soleil (Fountain of the Sun)** by Janoit, from 1956. Stretching from the main square to the promenade are the **Jardins Albert-1er,** with an open-air terrace and a Triton Fountain. With palms and exotic flowers, this is the most relaxing oasis at the resort.

MUSEUMS

Musée d'Art Moderne et d'Art Contemporain (MAMAC) ★★ French and American avant-garde art from the 1960s until the 21st century is displayed in this quartet of square towers with rooftop terraces. Each section is linked by a glass passageway. We know of no other museum that so dramatically reveals the growth of parallel art movements in two countries. In the '60s, it was called American pop art, whereas on the Riviera it was known as Nouveau Réalisme, but the results are very similar. All the big names in pop art, including Andy Warhol, Roy Lichtenstein, and Robert Rauschenberg, are featured. One entire section of the museum is devoted to the French artist Yves Klein (1928–92). His two major works, *Garden of Eden* and *Wall of Fire,* can be seen on the rooftop terraces. Some of the outstanding works

Museum Freebies

When you get tired of relaxing at the beach and need a break from the heat, check out one of Nice's excellent museums—for free. All of the museums in Nice are free to enter.

displayed are by artists of the Nice School, including Sacha Sosno, Robert Malavaal, Ben Vautier, and Jean-Claude Farhi.

Promenade des Arts. ✆ **04-97-13-42-01.** www.mamac-nice.org. Free admission. Tues-Sun 10am–6pm. Bus: 1, 2, 3, 5, 6, 16, or 25.

Musée des Beaux-Arts ★★ The collection is in the former residence of the Ukrainian Princess Kotchoubey. It has an important gallery devoted to the masters of the Second Empire and the Belle Époque, with an extensive collection of 19th-century French experts. The gallery of sculptures includes works by J. B. Carpeaux, Rude, and Rodin. Note the important collection by the Dutch Vanloo family, a dynasty of painters. One of its best-known members, Carle Vanloo, born in Nice in 1705, was Louis XV's premier *peintre*. A fine collection of 19th- and 20th-century art includes works by Ziem, Raffaelli, Boudin, Monet, Guillaumin, and Sisley.

33 av. des Baumettes. ✆ **04-92-15-28-28.** www.musee-beaux-arts-nice.org. Free admission. Tues–Sun 10am–6pm. Bus: 3, 9, 12, 22, 24, 38, 60, or 62.

Musée International d'Art Naïf Anatole-Jakovsky (Museum of Naive Art) ★ This museum is in the beautifully restored Château Ste-Hélène in the Fabron district. The museum's namesake, for years one of the world's leading art critics, once owned the collection. His 600 drawings and canvases were turned over to the institution and opened to the public. Artists from more than two dozen countries are represented in everything from primitive painting to 20th-century works.

Château St-Hélène, av. de Fabron. ✆ **04-93-71-78-33.** Free admission. Wed-Mon 10am–6pm. Bus: 9, 10, 12, or 23; 10-min. walk. Closed Dec 25, Jan 1, and May 1.

Villa Arson Nice ★ This complex—which includes a restored 18th-century building, and a concrete-and-stone structure from 1970—houses both the Art School of Nice and the National Center for Contemporary Art (Centre National d'Art Contemporain). The museum section stages special exhibitions of young, emerging French artists. The exhibitions are always changing. Chances are that all the art will be daringly avant-garde.

20 av. Stephen Liégeard. ✆ **04-92-07-73-73.** www.villa-arson.org. Free admission. Wed-Mon 2–6pm (until 7pm July–Aug). Bus: Ligne 7 (stop at Deux Avenues).

MORE SIGHTS

Cathédrale Orthodoxe Russe St-Nicolas à Nice ★ Built by the Russian royal family in honor of the 20-year-old Grand Duke Nicolas Alexandrovitch who died in Nice of tuberculosis, this is the most beautiful religious edifice of the Orthodoxy outside Russia, and a perfect expression of Russian religious art abroad. It dates from the Belle Époque, when a few of the Romanovs and their entourage turned the Riviera into a stamping ground (everyone from grand dukes to ballerinas walked the promenade). The cathedral is richly ornamented and decorated with icons. You'll spot the building from afar because of its collection of ornate onion-shaped domes. During church services on Sunday morning, the building closes to tourist visits.

Av. Nicolas-II (off bd. du Tzaréwitch). ✆ **04-93-96-88-02.** www.acor-nice.com. Admission 3€ adults, 2€ students, free for children 11 and under. May–Sept daily 9am–noon and 2:30–6pm; Oct–Apr daily 9:30am–noon and 2:30–5pm. From the central rail station, head west along av. Thiers to bd. Gambetta, then go north to bd. du Tzaréwitch.

Palais Lascaris The baroque Palais Lascaris in the city's historic core is associated with the Lascaris de Vintimille family, whose recorded history predates the year 1261. Built in the 17th century, it contains elaborately detailed ornaments. An intensive restoration by the city of Nice in 1963 brought back its original beauty, and the palace is now classified as a historic monument. The most elaborate floor, the *étage noble,* retains many of its 18th-century panels and plaster embellishments. A pharmacy, built around 1738 and complete with many of the original delftware accessories, is on the premises.

15 rue Droite. ✆ **04-93-62-72-40.** www.palais-lascaris-nice.org. Free admission. Wed–Mon 10am–6pm. Bus: 1, 2, 3, 5, 6, 14, 16, or 17.

NEARBY SIGHTS IN CIMIEZ

In the once-aristocratic hilltop quarter of **Cimiez ★★**, Queen Victoria wintered at the Hôtel Excelsior and brought half the English court with her. Founded by the Romans, who called it Cemenelum, Cimiez was the capital of the Maritime Alps province. Recent excavations have uncovered the ruins of a Roman town, and you can wander among the diggings. The arena was big enough to hold at least 5,000 spectators, who watched contests between gladiators and wild beasts shipped in from Africa. To reach this suburb, take bus no. 15 or 17 from place Masséna.

Monastère de Cimiez (Cimiez Convent) ★ The convent embraces a church that owns three of the most important works by the locally prominent Bréa brothers, who painted in the late 15th century. See the carved and gilded wooden main altarpiece. In a restored part of the convent where some Franciscan friars still live, the Musée Franciscain is decorated with 17th-century frescoes. Some 350 documents and works of art from the 15th to the 18th centuries are on display, and a monk's cell has been re-created in all its severe simplicity. Also visit the 17th-century chapel. From the magnificent gardens, you'll have a panoramic view of Nice and the Baie des Anges. Matisse and Dufy are buried in the cemetery.

Place du Monastère. ✆ **04-93-81-00-04.** Free admission. Museum Mon–Sat 10am–noon and 3–6pm. Church daily 9am–6pm.

Musée Matisse ★★ This museum honors the artist, who died in Nice in 1954. Seeing his nude sketches today, you'll wonder how early critics could have denounced them as "the female animal in all her shame and horror." Most of the pieces in the museum's permanent collection were painted in Nice, and many were donated by Matisse and his heirs. These include *Nude in an Armchair with a Green Plant* (1937), *Nymph in the Forest* (1935–43), and a chronologically arranged series of paintings from 1890 to 1919. The most famous of these is *Portrait of Madame Matisse* (1905), usually displayed near a portrait of the artist's wife by Marquet, painted in 1900. An assemblage of designs prepared as practice sketches for the Matisse Chapel at Vence are on display along with *The Créole Dancer* (1951), *Blue Nude IV* (1952), and around 50 dance-related sketches drawn between 1930 and 1931. The artist's last work, *Flowers and Fruit* (1953), is made of cut-out gouache.

In the Villa des Arènes-de-Cimiez, 164 av. des Arènes-de-Cimiez. ✆ **04-93-81-08-08.** www.musee-matisse-nice.org. Free admission. Wed–Mon 10am–6pm. Closed Jan 1, May 1, and Dec 25.

Musée National Marc Chagall ★★★ In the hills of Cimiez, this handsome museum, surrounded by pools and a garden, is devoted to Marc Chagall's treatment of biblical themes. Born in Russia in 1887, Chagall became a French citizen in 1937. The artist and his wife donated the works—the most important Chagall collection ever assembled—to France in 1966 and 1972. On display are over 300 of his oils, gouaches, drawings, pastels, lithographs, sculptures, and ceramics; a mosaic; three stained-glass windows; and a tapestry. Chagall decorated a concert room with brilliantly hued stained-glass windows. Temporary exhibits each summer feature great periods and artists of all times.

Av. du Dr.-Ménard. ✆ **04-93-53-87-20.** www.musee-chagall.fr. Admission 7.50€ adults, free for students/children 25 and under. May–Oct Wed–Mon 10am–6pm; Nov–Apr Wed–Mon 10am–5pm.

Outdoor Pursuits

BEACHES Along Nice's seafront, beaches extend uninterrupted for more than 7km (4⅓ miles), from the edge of *Vieux Port* (the Old Port) to the international airport, with most of the best bathing spots subdivided into public beaches and private concessionaires. Beach lovers may find Nice's pebble beaches a disappointment; they're all covered with gravel (often the size of golf balls). The rocks are smooth but can be mettlesome to people with poor balance or tender feet. Tucked between the public beaches are the private beaches of such hotels as the Beau Rivage. Most of the public beaches consist of two sections: a free area and one where you can rent chaise lounges, mattresses, and parasols, use changing rooms, and take freshwater showers. For that, you'll pay 10€ to 14€ for a half-day, 12€ to 20€ for a full day. Nude sunbathing is prohibited, but toplessness is common.

GOLF The oldest golf course on the Riviera is about 16km (10 miles) from Nice: **Golf de Biot,** 1379 rte. d'Antibes, Biot (✆ **04-93-65-08-48;** www.golfdebiot.com). Open daily, this is a flat, not particularly challenging seafronting course. (Golfers must cross a highway twice before completing the full 18 holes.) Tee times are 8am to 6pm; you can play until the sun sets. Reservations aren't necessary, though on weekends you should probably expect to wait. Greens fees are 45€ to 61€.

HORSEBACK RIDING **Club Hippique de Nice,** 368 rte. de Grenoble (✆ **04-93-83-15-04;** www.nicecheval.com), rents about a dozen of its horses. About 5km (3 miles) from Nice, near the airport, it's hemmed in on virtually every side by busy roads and highways, and conducts all activities in a series of riding rings. Riding sessions should be reserved in advance; they last 2 hours and cost 19€ to 26€.

SCUBA DIVING The best outfit is the **Centre International de Plongée (CIP) de Nice,** 2 ruelle des Moulins (✆ **06-09-52-55-57** or 04-93-55-59-50; www.cip-nice.com), adjacent to the city's Old Port, between quai des Docks and boulevard Stalingrad. A *baptême* (dive for first-timers) costs 45€. An appropriate diver's certification is required.

TENNIS The oldest tennis club in Nice is the **Nice Lawn Tennis Club,** Parc Impérial, 5 av. Suzanne-Lenglen (✆ **04-92-15-58-00;** www.niceltc.com). It's open daily 9am to 8pm from mid-October to mid-April (closed winter) and charges 15€ to 32€ per person for 2 hours of court time. The club has a cooperative staff, a loyal clientele, 16 outdoor clay courts, and 2 paddle tennis courts. Reserve the night before.

Shopping

You may want to begin with a stroll through the streets and alleys of Nice's historic core. The densest concentrations of boutiques are along **rue Masséna, place Magenta, avenue Jean-Médecin,** and on the streets around them, where you'll find popular French high-street brands. Expensive boutiques and designer brands including Louis Vuitton and Hermès cluster around **avenue de Suède, avenue de Verdun,** and **rue Paradis.**

Façonnable, 7–9 rue Paradis (✆ **04-93-87-88-80;** www.faconnable.com), is the original site of an upscale chain with several hundred branches around the world. This is one of the largest, with a wide range of men's suits, raincoats, overcoats, sportswear, and jeans. The look is youthful and conservatively stylish, and cut for French bodies. An outlet for women's clothing and sportswear (Façonnable Sport) and the main line of Façonnable women's wear (Façonnable Femmes) is across the street at 10 rue Paradis (✆ **04-93-88-06-97**).

Opened in 1949 by Joseph Fuchs, the grandfather of the present English-speaking owners, the **Confiserie Florian du Vieux-Nice,** 14 quai Papacino (✆ **04-93-55-43-50;** www.confiserieflorian.com), is near the Old Port. Their specialty is glazed fruit crystallized in sugar or artfully arranged into chocolates. Look for exotic jams (rose-petal preserves, mandarin marmalade), candied violets, verbena leaves, and rosebuds, as well as a free recipe leaflet. One of the oldest chocolatiers in Nice, **Confiserie Auer,** 7 rue St-François-de-Paule, near the opera house (✆ **04-93-85-77-98;** www.maison-auer.com), was established in 1820. Since then, few of the original Belle Époque–era decorative accessories have changed. The shop specializes in chocolates, candies, and *fruits confits,* the signature Provençal goodies.

If you're thinking of indulging in a *provençale pique-nique,* **Nicolas Alziari** (✆ **04-93-85-76-92;** www.alziari.com.fr) at 318 bd. Madeleine and 14 rue St François de Paule, will provide everything from olives, anchovies, and pistous to tapenades. It's one of Nice's oldest purveyors of olive oil, with a house brand that comes in two strengths: a light version that aficionados claim is vaguely perfumed with Provence, and a stronger version suited to the earthy flavors and robust ingredients of a Provençal winter. Numerous regional and flavored olive oils are also for sale.

La Couqueto, 8 rue St-François-de-Paule (✆ **04-93-80-90-30**), sells *santons,* the traditional Provençal figurines. The best selection of Provençal fabrics is at **Le Chandelier,** 7 rue de la Boucherie (✆ **04-93-85-85-19**), where you'll see designs by the region's best-known producers of cloth, including Valdrôme.

In addition to the flower market, **Marché aux Fleurs** (see "Exploring the City," earlier), the main flea market, **Marché à la Brocante,** also at cours Saleya, takes place Monday 8am to 5pm. Another flea market on the port, **Les Puces de Nice,** place Robilante, is open Tuesday to Saturday 10am to 6pm.

Where to Stay

Hotels in Nice are a mix of the good, the bad, and the ugly. For those who can afford to splash out, seafront hotels such as the palatial **Palais de la Méditerranée** or the discreet **La Pérouse** are bound to impress. If you're traveling outside peak season, you may find five-star hotels offering website deals that are cheaper than standard tariffs of midrange hotels.

Accommodations are often disappointing: Expect three-star quality from four-star hotels. If you want to find value, you may have to compromise on a location further away from the Vieille Ville. There are exceptional places here, including contemporary **Le Dortoir,** art-loving **Hôtel Windsor,** well-priced **Villa La Tour,** and peaceful **Villa Les Cygnes** (all reviewed below). Chain hotel brands can provide a reliable bet, although those along the beachside promenade des Anglais sometimes abuse their premium location. Worth a look are **Best Western** (www.bestwestern.fr; Hôtel Roosevelt and Hôtel Riviera) and **Mercure** (www.mercure.com; Nice Promenade des Anglais and Nice Marché aux Fleurs). The **Holiday Inn** (www.holidayinn.com) at 20 bd. Victor Hugo is also a good bet.

VERY EXPENSIVE

Hôtel Negresco ★★★ The Negresco, on the seafront in the heart of Nice, is one of the Riviera's superglamorous hotels. The Victorian wedding-cake hotel is named after its founder, Henry Negresco, a Romanian who died a pauper in Paris in 1920. The country's châteaux inspired the interior and the exterior alike, with its mansard roof and domed tower. The hotel's decorators scoured Europe to gather antiques, tapestries, and art. Some of the accommodations, such as the Coco Chanel room, are outfitted in homage to the personalities who stayed here. Suites and public areas are even grander; they include the Louis XIV salon, reminiscent of the Sun King, and the Napoleon III suite, where swagged walls, a leopard-skin carpet, and a half-crowned pink canopy create a sense of majesty. The most expensive rooms with balconies face the Mediterranean and the private beach. The sumptuous decor is looking tired in places, but a much-needed room refurbishment was completed in 2010. Ask for one of the refurbished rooms when booking. One of the two restaurants, **Le Chantecler** (p. 301), is one of the Riviera's greatest. Service standards can be hit or miss.

37 promenade des Anglais, 06000 Nice. www.hotel-negresco-nice.com. ✆ **04-93-16-64-00.** Fax 04-93-16-64-40. 146 units. 245€–615€ double; from 690€ suite. AE, DC, MC, V. Free parking. **Amenities:** 2 restaurants; bar; babysitting; concierge; room service. *In room:* A/C, TV, hair dryer, minibar, Wi-Fi (free).

Palais de la Méditerranée ★★★ This glittering seaside palace on the promenade des Anglais reigned from 1929 to 1978 and is now back as the "Queen of the Nice Riviera" since its reopening in 2004. During its heyday, the hotel theater hosted everybody from Maurice Chevalier to American chanteuse Josephine Baker, who performed wearing high heels, a skirt of bananas, and nothing else. Its Art Deco facade was left intact after a restoration, but the interior was gutted. Nowadays there's no theater, but the hotel's casino (p. 307) has been restored to its 1930s splendor. Monumental chandeliers and stained-glass windows, among other architectural features, were spared in the renovations. Bedrooms, midsize to grandly spacious, are outfitted in a tasteful modern decor, with luxurious bathrooms. Ninety of the bedrooms also open onto sea views. Executive rooms and suites have added extras such as iPod docks, DVD players, and espresso coffee machines.

13 promenade des Anglais, 06011 Nice. www.palais.concorde-hotels.com. ✆ **04-92-14-77-00.** Fax 04-92-14-77-14. 188 units. 228€–830€ double; from 348€ suite. AE, DC, MC, V. **Amenities:** Restaurant; bar; casino; concierge; exercise room w/Turkish bath; 2 pools (indoor and outdoor); room service. *In room:* A/C, TV, DVD, hair dryer, iPod docks, minibar, Wi-Fi (free).

EXPENSIVE

Hi Hotel ★ An architectural and decorative statement, this hotel occupies a former boardinghouse that dates to the 1930s. Spearheaded by Matali Crasset, a onetime colleague of Philippe Starck, a team of architects and engineers created one of the most aggressively avant-garde hotels in the south of France. Each of the nine high-tech room "concepts" is different. They range from hospital white-on-white to birch-wood veneer and acid green to cool violet and gray. The unconventional layouts may include a bathtub tucked behind a screen of potted plants or elevated to a position of theatrical prominence. It's worth checking the layout when you book as many rooms are completely open plan—including the toilet. The Japanese word *hi* describes the black mottling on the back of an ornamental carp, which has traditionally been associated with good luck. There is a sushi restaurant at the hotel's plush beach club. Prices are steep considering it has a less convenient location than its four-star competitors.

3 av. des Fleurs, 06000 Nice. www.hi-hotel.net. ✆ **04-97-07-26-26.** Fax 04-97-07-26-27. 38 units. 269€-369€ double; 489€ suite. AE, DC, MC, V. Parking 24€. Bus: 23. **Amenities:** Beach club; restaurant; bar; Turkish bath. *In room:* A/C, TV, Wi-Fi (free).

Hôtel Beau Rivage ★ This four-star hotel across from the beach is famous for having housed both Matisse and Chekhov during its heyday around the turn of the 20th century. The hotel received a makeover in 2004 by prestigious French architect Jean-Michel Wilmotte with a contemporary Niçoise theme reflected in the imaginative pebble-shaped sofas and black-and-white pebble photos in the lounge-bar Les Galets. The staff seems to make a point of appearing overworked regardless of how few guests there might be. The tastefully decorated, soundproofed rooms are on the cramped side given the prices. Around the corner on quai des Etats-Unis, the hotel has the added bonus of its own private beach with a year-round restaurant for lazy lunches (and dinners May–Sept).

24 rue St-François-de-Paule, 06300 Nice. www.nicebeaurivage.com. ✆ **04-92-47-82-82.** Fax 04-92-47-82-83. 118 units. 250€-470€ double; 380€-750€ suite. AE, DC, MC, V. Bus: 1, 2, 5, or 12. **Amenities:** Restaurant; beach; bar; babysitting; concierge; room service. *In room:* A/C, TV, hair dryer, minibar, Wi-Fi (free).

Hôtel Elysée Palace Views sweep out over the sea from most of rooms of this modern four-star hotel. Decor is conservative and contemporary. The seafront rooms, of course, are the more desirable. Rooms on the fifth, sixth, and seventh floors overlook the Mediterranean. Bathrooms are clad in marble with bidets, but you have to request robes and hair dryers from reception. Despite its seafront location, it's a 20-minute walk to the old town.

59 promenade des Anglais, 06005 Nice. www.elyseepalace.com. ✆ **04-93-97-90-90.** Fax 04-93-44-50-40. 143 units. 143€-219€ double; 251€-329€ suite. AE, DC, MC, V. Parking 19€. Bus: 9, 10, or 12. **Amenities:** Restaurant; bar; babysitting; pool; room service. *In room:* A/C, TV, hair dryer, minibar, Wi-Fi (free).

Hôtel Splendid This modern four-star hotel was built in the 1960s on the site of the original Hôtel Splendid (ca. 1881). On the corner of a wide tree-lined boulevard, it lies 400m (1,312 ft.) from its private beach and (in the opposite direction) from the railway station. You don't come here for its old-fashioned bedrooms, but for its convenient location and facilities: including roof terrace, pool, private beach, spa, and even a hairdresser. The small bedrooms could do with an update. They have nondescript city views, but deluxe rooms have a balcony or terrace.

50 bd. Victor-Hugo, 06048 Nice. www.splendid-nice.com. ✆ **04-93-16-41-00.** 128 units. 175€-270€ double; 265€-395€ suite. AE, DC, MC, V. Parking 22€. Bus: 9 or 10. **Amenities:** Restaurant; bar; pool; babysitting; health club w/sauna; room service, hairdresser. *In room:* A/C, TV, hair dryer, minibar, Wi-Fi (9.80€).

Hôtel Westminster The reason to stay at this four-star hotel is its location along the famous promenade near the Hôtel Negresco. Among many renovations, its elaborate pink Belle Époque facade has been restored to its former grandeur. The public areas feature high frescoed ceilings and ornate balustraded staircases. The contemporary rooms are comfortable and have soundproof windows. It's worth paying more to have a room overlooking the Baie des Anges. Although there's no pool, the hotel faces the beach.

27 promenade des Anglais, 06000 Nice. www.westminster-nice.com. ✆ **04-92-14-86-86.** Fax 04-93-82-45-35. 99 units. 185€–310€ double; from 323€ junior suite. AE, DC, MC, V. Parking 24€–26€ in public lot next door. Bus: 9, 10, or 11. **Amenities:** Restaurant; bar; babysitting; concierge; room service. *In room:* A/C, TV, hair dryer, minibar, Wi-Fi (free).

La Pérouse ★★★ Minutes from the Old Town's famous flower market, this four-star boutique hotel is one of my favorite Nice hotels. No grand reception greets you as you arrive, but a modest reception desk followed by a maze of corridors and lifts. Your patience will be rewarded with a spacious room furnished with contemporary Provençal fabrics and a dreamy sea and coastline view—be sure to ask for one with a loggia overlooking the Baie des Anges. Set back from the beachfront on a cliff, bedrooms are chiseled into the gardens of the ancient *château-fort*. It's quieter than other grand hotels along the promenade and the sound of birdsong rather than traffic greets you over breakfast on your loggia. There's a pretty poolside restaurant that serves excellent French food, as well as a rooftop Jacuzzi.

11 quai Raubà-Capéù, 06300 Nice. www.hotel-la-perouse.com. ✆ **04-93-62-34-63.** Fax 04-93-62-59-41. 60 units. 180€–550€ double; 600€–1,300€ suite. AE, DC, MC, V. Parking 15€. **Amenities:** Restaurant (Feb–Nov); bar; babysitting; health club w/Jacuzzi; pool; room service. *In room:* A/C, TV, hair dryer, minibar, Wi-Fi (free).

MODERATE

In addition to the recommendations below, peace seekers and romantics with a car may want to consider the luxurious **Villa Kilauea** (✆ **04-93-37-84-90;** www.villakilauea.com) in the hills behind Nice, near prestigious vineyard Château Bellet.

Hôtel du Petit Palais This whimsical three-star hotel occupies a mansion built around 1890; in the 1970s it was the home of the actor and writer Sacha Guitry (a name that's instantly recognized in millions of French households). It lies about a 10-minute drive from the city center in the pretty northern suburb of Cimiez near the Musée Chagall, the Musée Matisse, and the Roman ruins where the Nice Jazz Festival is held every July. Many of the Art Deco and Italianate furnishings and Florentine moldings and friezes remain intact. The preferred rooms, and the most expensive, have balconies that afford sea views during the day and sunset views at dusk. Breakfast is served in a small but pretty salon. There's no restaurant, but the hotel offers a limited room service.

17 av. Emile-Bieckert, 06000 Nice. www.petitpalaisnice.com. ✆ **04-93-62-19-11.** Fax 04-93-62-53-60. 25 units. 130€–220€ double. AE, DC, MC, V. Parking 10€. **Amenities:** Bar; babysitting; room service. *In room:* A/C, TV, hair dryer, minibar, Wi-Fi (free).

Hôtel Gounod Several blocks from the train station and from the sea, this three-star hotel offers an ideal stopover for those arriving by train. Built around 1910 in a neighborhood where the street names honor composers, the Gounod boasts ornate balconies, a domed roof, and an elaborate canopy of wrought iron and glass. The attractive lobby and adjoining lounge are festive and stylish, with old prints, copper flowerpots, and antiques. The high-ceilinged guest rooms are quiet, and most overlook the gardens of private homes. The two-bedroom suites are a good-value option for families. The hotel website offers spa packages with free unlimited use of the pool, cafe-bar, and Jacuzzi at its more expensive neighbor, the Hôtel Splendid (p. 296).

3 rue Gounod, 06000 Nice. www.gounod-nice.com. ✆ **04-93-16-42-00.** Fax 04-93-88-23-84. 45 units. 110€–160€ double; 140€–260€ suite. AE, DC, MC, V. Parking 15€. Closed late Nov–late Dec 20. Bus: 8. **Amenities:** Bar; babysitting; Wi-Fi (free). *In room:* A/C, TV, hair dryer.

Hôtel Suisse ★★ If La Pérouse is booked up or slightly beyond your budget, try its charming neighbor Hôtel Suisse. Part of the well-run boutique hotel chain, Hôtels Ocre et Azur, this three-star hotel is minutes from the Marché aux Fleurs. Most bedrooms offer sea views; the best views across the Baie des Anges and the Promenade des Anglais are from the Privilege rooms. There are few facilities, but there is a pretty cocktail bar on the ground floor. Single-occupancy rooms start at just 73€.

15 quai Raubà-Capéù, 06300 Nice. www.hotel-nice-suisse.com. ✆ **04-92-17-39-00.** 42 units. 120€–209€ double; from 235€ suite. AE, DC, MC, V. **Amenities:** Bar; Wi-Fi (free). *In room:* A/C, TV.

Le Dortoir ★★ This is our favorite B&B in Nice. In a town where high prices often are met with mediocre and tired furnishings, it's a welcome relief to find these designer-perfect, spacious suites. In each of the three suites, you'll find chic interiors, Philippe Stark–designed bathroom fittings, and excellent mattresses. The B&B is located on a quiet, pedestrian street in the heart of the posh shopping district. If you expect hotel services, this isn't the place to come as there's no reception and suites are accessed by a key pad code sent to you in advance of your stay. A continental breakfast is served every morning. The one downside is that the B&B is on the fourth floor and there's no elevator.

11 rue Paradis, 06000 Nice. www.ledortoir.net. ✆ **04-93-88-93-63.** 3 units. 100€–200€ suite. Rates include breakfast. AE, DC, MC, V. *In room:* A/C, TV, fridge, Wi-Fi (free).

Le Grimaldi Not far from the place Masséna, this hotel offers excellent value in central Nice. Housed in two gorgeous Belle Époque buildings sharing an inner courtyard, this old-fashioned hotel makes up for its lack of four-star facilities with its friendly staff. Bedrooms have been modernized, using glass, wrought iron, and fabrics. Bedrooms on the upper floors overlook the rooftops of Nice. Among the best features of the place are its generous breakfast offerings: homemade Provençal jams, fresh fruit, and crusty pastries made by one of the town's best bakers.

15 rue Grimaldi, 06000 Nice. www.le-grimaldi.com. ✆ **04-93-16-00-24.** Fax 04-93-87-00-24. 46 units. 95€–205€ double; 200€–240€ junior suite. AE, DC, MC, V. **Amenities:** Bar. *In room:* A/C, TV, minibar, Wi-Fi (free).

L'Hôtel Masséna ★ This graceful Belle Époque hotel is perfect for those who want to be in the Vieille Ville. The owners have upgraded the bedrooms, transforming the hotel into a well-orchestrated bastion of calm and comfort. Rooms are decorated in rich red and orange fabrics. Classic and tradition bedrooms are cramped, while deluxe rooms are spacious and most have balconies or terraces. Although all units have soundproofing, the ones that are the quietest are those overlooking the interior courtyard. The hotel offers few four-star facilities, but does provide room service.

58 rue Gioffredo, 06000 Nice. www.hotel-massena-nice.com. ✆ **04-92-47-88-88.** Fax 04-92-47-88-89. 110 units. 159€–339€ double; 659€ suite. AE, DC, MC, V. Parking 25€–30€. Bus: 15. **Amenities:** Bar; babysitting; room service. *In room:* A/C, TV, hair dryer, minibar, Wi-Fi (free).

Villa Les Cygnes ★★ For graceful living on the Rivera, this reasonably priced hotel is a find. Beautiful fabrics and Provençal antiques adorn this 1920s villa. Its six rooms over three floors feature (nonworking) marble fireplaces and well-designed bathrooms. Bedrooms on the first floor have balconies, while one of the ground-floor rooms opens onto the garden. Close to the Musée des Beaux-Arts and to the promenade des Anglais, this hotel is situated in the quiet western suburb of Les Baumettes. It's a 10-minute drive to Nice Vieille Ville.

6 avenue Château de la Tour, 06000 Nice. www.villalescygnes.com. ✆ **06-32-11-91-52.** ✆ 04-93-44-60-87. 6 units. 100€–135€ double. AE, MC, V. Parking 8€. **Amenities:** Garden. *In room:* A/C, TV, hair dryer, Wi-Fi (free).

INEXPENSIVE

Hôtel l'Oasis This three-star hotel reopened in 2010 after an extensive renovation, but summertime prices have stayed reasonable. In the semitropical garden here, you can imagine the ghosts of the influential people who stayed here during the first half of the 20th century when the place was a boardinghouse with a good number of Russians. They included Anton Chekhov, who composed part of *Three Sisters* here, and Lenin, who spent a holiday here in 1911. Although an air of old-fashioned manners remains intact, bedrooms have been modernized many times since, most recently in a contemporary, vaguely Provençal motif, and they are well maintained. The location, close to the railway station, is convenient for central Nice. It's a pity that staff can be rather officious at times.

23 rue Gounod, 06000 Nice. www.hoteloasis-nice.com. ✆ **04-93-88-12-29.** 38 units. 65€–99€ double. AE, MC, V. Parking 8€. **Amenities:** Bar service in garden; babysitting. *In room:* A/C, TV, hair dryer, fridge, Wi-Fi (free).

Hôtel Saint-Georges Originally built during the grand days of Niçoise tourism, this two-star hotel dates from around 1900 and still retains a few of its original architectural grace notes. A verdant patio and garden are set with clusters of iron chairs and tables, a perfect spot to enjoy breakfast or an afternoon read. Inside the motif is less nostalgic: It's angular and contemporary, and has mirrored, sometimes stark walls and efficient modern furnishings. Most bedrooms have high ceilings and casement doors that open onto tiny porches hemmed in with wrought-iron railings. The rooms are fairly small. Given its central Nice location, this hotel is good value for winter stays, but prices double in summer.

7 av. Georges Clémenceau, 06000 Nice. www.hotelsaintgeorges.fr. ✆ **04-93-88-79-21.** Fax 04-93-16-22-85. 30 units. 54€–110€ double; 72€–130€ triple. AE, DC, MC, V. Bus: 1 or 4. **Amenities:** Lounge; garden. *In room:* A/C, TV, hair dryer, Wi-Fi (free).

Hôtel Windsor ★ This is a long-standing favorite for art-loving and budget-conscious travelers who are bored of cookie-cutter hotels. Built by disciples of Gustav Eiffel in 1895, this *maison bourgeoise* lies near the Negresco and the promenade des Anglais. Each unit is a unique decorative statement by a different artist. In the "Ben" room, for example, a Provençal artist of the same name painted verses of his own poetry. Bedrooms range from small to medium size with small bathrooms. You can take your chances or select a room based on the photos on the hotel website. We'd recommend a garden-facing room with a balcony. The fifth floor holds the health club, steam room, and sauna. The garden contains scores of tropical and exotic plants, and the recorded sounds of birds singing in the jungles of the Amazon.

11 rue Dalpozzo, 06000 Nice. www.hotelwindsornice.com. ✆ **04-93-88-59-35.** Fax 04-93-88-94-57. 54 units. 78€–185€ double. MC, V. Parking 11€. Bus: 9, 10, or 22. **Amenities:** Restaurant; bar; babysitting; pool (outdoor); sauna. *In room:* A/C, TV, hair dryer, minibar, Wi-Fi (free).

Hôtel Villa La Tour ★ This well-run, two-star hotel in the heart of Vieille Ville offers exceptional value. The owner of Villa La Tour once worked at the legendary Hôtel Negresco, and she has brought her savvy to this former 18th-century convent, creating one of the most atmospheric little hotels in the ancient city. Outside the door are many authentic old Provençal bistros and bars, and you are only a 10-minute walk from the beach. All of the comfortable rooms are tastefully furnished, with designer fabrics on the walls and chic lighting, but some are a bit cramped. If you need more space, ask for one of the *supérieure* units. The hallways are rather narrow, but the rooms themselves open onto views of the Old Town, a few containing small balconies. The little roof garden is a grace note. The hotel has no elevator.

4 rue de la Tour, 06300 Nice. www.villa-la-tour.com. ✆ **04-93-80-08-15.** Fax 04-93-85-10-58. 14 units. 48€–139€ double; 118€–150€ triple. AE, MC, V. *In room:* A/C, hair dryer, Wi-Fi (free).

Hôtel Villa Rivoli 🎁 The younger and arguably prettier sister of the renowned Hôtel Villa La Tour, this boutique hotel has become a sought-after address since opening in 2007. Set in a Belle Époque mansion just off the promenade des Anglais, it's slightly more expensive than Villa La Tour but still offers exceptional value for Nice. The bedrooms have been individually decorated with white furnishings and Provençal fabrics; some have a small balcony, while *supérieure* rooms are lighter and more spacious.

10 rue de Rivoli, 06300 Nice. www.villa-rivoli.com. ✆ **04-93-88-80-25.** Fax 04-93-858-96-28. 24 units. 79€–175€ double; 155€–190€ triple. AE, MC, V. *In room:* A/C, TV, hair dryer, Wi-Fi (free).

Le Lausanne This is a solid, three-star hotel in a commercial neighborhood in central Nice. It was radically renovated in the mid-1990s and retains very few of its original architectural embellishments. Views from the windows look out over the street, and its small bedrooms are well kept. The friendly hotel staff is a bonus.

36 rue Rossini, 06000 Nice. www.lausannehotelnice.com. ✆ **04-93-88-85-94.** Fax 04-26-30-38-09. 35 units. 59€–165€ double. MC, V. Parking 11€. Bus: 8. **Amenities:** Babysitting. *In room:* A/C, TV, hair dryer, Wi-Fi (free 1st hr., then 1€ per hr.).

Nice Garden Hotel ★ With its flower-filled garden, this aptly named two-star hotel is an oasis in the heart of Nice. The bedrooms are well kept, although standard rooms are on the cramped side; ask for a room facing the garden. Charming owner Marion lends a warm ambience to this simple hotel. It's worth noting that the reception is open 8am until 9pm only and that the hotel is completely nonsmoking. The hotel has no elevator.

11 rue de Congrés 06000 Nice. www.nicegardenhotel.com. ✆ **04-93-87-35-62.** Fax 04-82-15-80. 9 units. 65€–110€ double; 90€–135€ triple. MC, V. **Amenities:** Garden; smoke-free rooms. *In room:* A/C, TV, Wi-Fi (free).

Villa Saint-Exupéry 🏷 You won't find a better-priced or friendlier place to stay than these twin Nice hostels. The main branch is **Villa Saint-Exupéry Gardens,** a former Carmelite monastery in Cimiez that has been completely renovated and turned into one of the Rivera's best hostels. As well as immaculately clean dormitory accommodations, there are en suite singles, doubles, and triples. Furnishings are modern and selected more for comfort than style. Echoing its past life, the Chapel Bar, which serves pizza and 1€ beer, retains its beautiful stained-glass windows. Guests are also welcome to use a fully equipped kitchen. There is a small shop on the premises, but a supermarket lies just down the steep hill. Luckily shuttle buses are on hand to take you to and from the local tram stop. The downtown branch of the youth hostel, **Villa Saint-Exupéry Beach** (✆ **04-93-16-13-45**), can be found at 6 rue Sacha-Guitry.

22 av. Gravier, 06100 Nice. www.villahostels.com. ✆ **04-93-84-42-83.** 60 units. 27€–90€ per person in a single or twin-bedded room; 18€ per person for dormitory bed. Rates include continental breakfast. MC, V. Parking 18€–30€. **Amenities:** Restaurant; bar; kitchen; Internet (free). *In room:* Wi-Fi (free).

Where to Eat

Nice is a mecca for gourmands with every budget and every culinary taste. The gastronomic competition is such that fixed-price menus at top restaurants around Nice are surprisingly reasonable and often cheaper than dining at moderate restaurants in the Old Town. With over 700 restaurants, the challenge is sorting out the local finds from the tourist chaff.

Vieux Nice is the place for lovers of Niçoise cuisine, while beautifully restored place Garibaldi is a reliable destination for French bistro food. The area around Nice Etoile is a hot spot for up-and-coming young chefs such as Mickaël Gracieux at **L'Aromate** (p. 302) and for gastronomic wine shops where you can sip wine with the locals over nibbles, like **Part des Anges,** 17 rue Gubernatis (**04-93-62-69-80**)—sister restaurant to **Vinivore** (p. 306). A traditional bouillabaisse (fish soup) is the order of the day in restaurants lining the Old Port.

VERY EXPENSIVE

La Petite Maison ★★★ NIÇOISE Housed in a 19th-century former grocery store, this restaurant is a Niçoise institution. Indeed, such is its success that La Petite Maison has offspring in London, Cannes, Moscow, and Dubai. Try the town's finest zucchini-blossom fritters, and finish with a dessert that will send you rushing to the phone to call *Gourmet* magazine: homemade ice cream flavored with pine nuts and candied orange blossoms. In between, you may enjoy a succulent array of grilled fish, pastas, and steaks, all prepared with the right Mediterranean touches and just enough garlic. Always packed to the gills, it's the perfect place to enjoy the pantomime of local and international glitterati (including Elton John, who owns a villa nearby). Your dining experience can depend upon the whim of its mercurial owner Nicole: She can be by turns charismatic and rude. If you make Nicole's grade, you'll be treated like a king and lavished with complementary limoncello digestifs.

11 rue St-Francois de Paule. ✆ **04-93-92-59-59.** www.lapetitemaison-nice.com. Reservations recommended. Main courses 20€–45€. AE, V. Mon–Sat noon–2:30pm and 7:30pm–midnight.

Le Chantecler ★★★ 📷 MODERN FRENCH This Michelin-starred fantasy is Nice's most prestigious restaurant. Located inside the Hotel Negresco, the dining room walls are sheathed with panels removed from a château in Pouilly-Fuissé; a Regency-style salon is available for before- or after-dinner drinks; and a collection of 16th-century paintings decorates the premises. A much-respected chef, Jean-Denis Rieubland, takes his diners on a gastronomic voyage of French and Mediterranean flavors using the highest-quality ingredients. The menus change almost weekly but may include roast fillet of cod with flakes of pata negra (Iberian ham) served on Carnaroli risotto with red Bellet wine; pigeon with ox-tongue cooked in Vallauris clay; and tantalizing half-cooked chocolate cake with Sicilian roasted-pistachio ice cream.

In the Hôtel Negresco (p. 295), 37 promenade des Anglais. ✆ **04-93-16-64-00.** Reservations required. Main courses 52€–70€; fixed-price dinner 90€–130€. AE, MC, V. Wed–Sun 7–10pm; Sun 12:30–2pm. Closed Jan to mid-Feb. Bus: 8, 9, 10, or 11.

EXPENSIVE

Don Camillo Créations ★★ ITALIAN/PROVENÇALE Named in the 1950s after its founder, Camille, a Niçoise patriot (who preferred the Italian version of his name), this nine-table gastronomic restaurant delivers some of Nice's most authentic Provençal food at surprisingly competitive prices. Just off cours Saleya, the dining room is adorned with pleasant, light colors and modern paintings, many of which are for sale. Supervised by chef Marc Laville, the menu changes with the seasons, but can include John Dory fillet lacquered with seaweed butter and foie gras ravioli served on a bed of green lentils with truffles. Caribbean influences from his time as a chef in St. Barths are seen in his desserts, such as small bananas candied in rum with coconut biscuits.

5 rue des Ponchettes. ✆ **04-93-85-67-95.** www.doncamillo-creations.fr. Reservations recommended. Fixed-price lunch 20€, dinner 33€–75€. MC, V. Tues–Sat noon–1:30pm and 7:30–9:30pm. Bus: 8.

Keisuke Matsushima ★★ MODERN MEDITERRANEAN The Japanese chef Keisuke Matsushima became the second Japanese chef in France to be awarded the Michelin star. Against a backdrop of a beige-and-black minimalist decor, he serves his imaginative creations. Guests are greeted with an amuse bouche that usually includes a candied cherry tomato—just make sure to eat it in one bite. His inventive and intensely flavored concoctions may include Mediterranean sea bream with roasted, spiky artichokes and mussels in a vegetable broth with carrot foam; pigeon breasts caramelized and served with a wasabi emulsion; Sisteron lamb roasted and served with a Parma ham foam; and Brittany scallops with turnip carpaccio and a sweet-and-sour vinaigrette.

22 Ter rue de France. ✆ **04-93-82-26-06.** www.keisukematsushima.com. Reservations required. Fixed-price lunch 25€–35€, dinner 35€–111€. AE, MC, V. Tues–Sat noon–2:30pm; Mon–Sat 7:30–10pm.

La Merenda ★ NIÇOISE Because they don't have a phone, you have to go by this place twice: once to make a reservation and once to dine. It's worth the effort. Forsaking his chef's crown at Le Chantecler (above), Dominique Le Stanc opened this tiny bistro where diners are packed in at simple trestle tables with red-checkered tablecloths. Le Stanc never knows what he's going to serve until he goes to the market—look for specials on a chalkboard. Perhaps you'll find stuffed cabbage, fried zucchini flowers, or oxtail flavored with fresh oranges. Lamb from the Sisteron is cooked until it practically falls from the bone.

4 rue Raoul Bosio. No phone. Reservations required. Main courses 36€–52€. No credit cards. Mon–Fri noon–2pm and 7–10pm (seatings at 7:15 and 9:15pm). Closed Aug 1–15. Bus: 8.

L'Ane Rouge PROVENÇALE Known as one of Nice's best-known seafood restaurants, L'Ane Rouge seems to be resting on its laurels. Facing the magnificent old port and occupying an antique building with old ceiling beams and stone walls, this restaurant has many natural advantages. The service and food quality may not be hitting their former sublime highs, but you can still have a pleasing and well-priced meal if you stick with the cheaper options. In the two modern yet cozy dining rooms, you can enjoy traditional specialties such as bouillabaisse, pesto soup with stuffed tomato, and sea bream on a bed of fennel and mussels.

7 quai des Deux-Emmanuels. ✆ **04-93-89-49-63.** www.anerougenice.com. Reservations required. Lunch menu 23€; fixed-price dinner 35€–49€. AE, DC, MC, V. Fri–Tues noon–2pm; Thurs–Tues 7–10:30pm. Closed Feb. Bus: 30.

L'Aromate ★★★ 🎁 FRENCH When an up-and-coming chef sets up his own restaurant, two secret ingredients will add to his success: an exceptional culinary imagination and an intelligent, dedicated wife to run the front of house. Mickaël Gracieux has both. He and his wife Elise run this restaurant, located in a former peanut factory, with meticulous precision. With its bare stone walls and springlike green tones, the dining room sets the scene for a four- or six-course gastronomic adventure that will impress even the well-seasoned diner. Dishes such as a crab jelly starter served in a huge oyster shell and then brought to the table under a museum-style glass container have no doubt contributed to his 2010 awarding of a Michelin star. The lighter lunchtime menu is a la carte.

20–22 av. Maréchal Foch. ✆ **04-93-62-98-24.** www.laromate.fr. Main courses 13€–17€; fixed price dinner menus 55€ or 75€. MC, V. Tues–Sat noon–2:30pm and 7:30–10:30pm.

MODERATE

Au Petit Gari BISTRO Set beneath the arcades of the place Garibaldi, this restaurant features a hip and friendly staff and a distinctly and deliberately old-fashioned decor and menu. The setting evokes an early-20th-century bistro, replete with banquettes, etched glass, and a fast pace that keeps clients well fed and briskly moving in and out of available seats. The menu is written on blackboards and can include a gratin of scallops and shrimp served on braised leeks; a terrine of rabbit with prunes; oven-baked Camembert; and an old-fashioned *magret* (grilled breast of duck). We'd recommend the lunchtime dish of the day, glass of wine, and coffee for just 13€.

2 place Garibaldi. ✆ **04-93-26-89-09.** www.aupetitgari.com. Reservations recommended. Main courses 17€–30€; set lunch 13€; fixed-price dinner 37€–40€. MC, V. Mon–Fri noon–2pm and 7–10pm. Closed 2 weeks in Jan.

Café de Turin ★★ CONTINENTAL/SEAFOOD This all-day-dining seafood legend overlooks Nice's finest square, place Garibaldi. The origins of this place began in 1900, when it served carafes of wine to local office workers and laborers. In the 1950s, it added a kitchen to its premises, and ever since, it's churned out the kinds of hearty, bistro-style platters that go well with wine and beer. Much of the energy is expressed outside, under the arcades of the central plaza, where local hipsters strut their stuff, people table-hop, and harassed but well-intentioned waiters do their best to keep the food and beverages flowing. The place is celebrated for its *coquillage* (raw shellfish), attracting the likes of Princess Caroline, who drives over from Monaco. Other items include whatever species of grilled fish is available that day, pâtés, terrines, salads, pastas, and a satisfying selection of ice creams and pastries.

5 place Garibaldi. ✆ **04-93-62-29-52.** Reservations recommended weekends at night; otherwise, not necessary. Main courses 12€–35€. MC, V. Daily 8am–10pm. Bus: 9 or 10.

In Vino BISTRO Owned by a husband-and-wife team from southeast France, this atmospheric bistro is minutes from the cours Saleya. Christian cooks up market-fresh ingredients, while his sommelier wife Nathalie gives advice on her 80-vintage wine list. Listen to low-volume jazz as you order such tasty, alcohol-infused dishes as Andouillette sausage cooked in chablis wine and scallop risotto with Noilly Prat vermouth. Once a month it's jazz night here with a live band.

2 rue de l'Hôtel-de-Ville. ✆ **04-93-80-21-64.** Reservations recommended. Main courses 13€–23€. MC, V. Mon–Sat noon–3pm and 6pm–midnight. Closed first 2 weeks in Jan. Bus: 1, 2, or 5.

La Zucca Magica ★ ☺ VEGETARIAN/ITALIAN The chef at this popular harborside restaurant has been named the "best Italian chef in Nice." That this honor should go to a vegetarian restaurant was the most startling part of the news. Chef Marco, who opened his restaurant in 1997 after cooking for many years in Rome, certainly has a fine pedigree—he's a relative of the late Luciano Pavarotti. He serves refined cuisine at reasonable prices, using recipes from Italy's Piedmont region and updating them with no meat or fish. The year-round Halloween decor of wall-to-wall pumpkins will put you in the mood for the creative cuisine. You'll have to trust Marco, though, because everyone is served the same three-course meal. You can count on savory cuisine using lots of herbs, Italian cheeses, beans, and pasta. Lasagna is a specialty. Kids 10 and under eat for free—an extra course or two is usually thrown in so kids can pick and choose from the dishes they like.

4 bis quai Papacino. ✆ **04-93-56-25-27.** www.lazuccamagica.com. Reservations recommended. Fixed-price lunch 17€, dinner 29€. No credit cards. Tues–Sat 12:30–2pm and 7pm–midnight.

Le Safari ★ PROVENÇALE/NIÇOISE Le Safari is a cut above the culinary competition lining the flower-laden cours Saleya. The decor couldn't be simpler: a black ceiling, white walls, and an old-fashioned terra-cotta floor. The youthful staff is fashionable and relaxed, sometimes in jeans. Many diners prefer the outdoor terrace overlooking the Marché aux Fleurs, but all appreciate the reasonably priced meals that appear in generous portions. Menu items include a pungent *bagna cauda,* which calls for diners to immerse vegetables in a sizzling brew of hot oil and anchovy paste, as well as the unfortunately named *merda de can* (dog poop), a type of gnocchi stuffed with spinach that is a lot more appetizing than it sounds.

1 cours Saleya. ✆ **04-93-80-18-44.** Reservations recommended. Main courses 12€–30€; fixed-price menu 27€. AE, DC, MC, V. Daily noon–midnight. Bus: 1.

L'Escalinada ★ NIÇOISE For more than half a century, diners have flocked to this Provençal nest on a side street in Vieux Nice. You can dine inside under old beams or out on a sunny terrace. The moment you sit down, the waiter arrives with a bowl of chickpeas (garbanzos to some), and you help yourself, enjoying a glass of kir and a square of *pissaladière,* the Niçoise, onion-enriched version of pizza. For an appetizer, the *encornets* (squid stuffed with Swiss chard and rice) is a winner, as are the sautéed zucchini flowers or the roast red peppers. For the main course, we recommend *porchetta* (pork roast), *cochon de lait farci* (stuffed suckling pig), or suckling pig rolled around various cuts of meats. You can try other classics such as beef carpaccio, veal kidneys, or even the stuffed sardines of the house (a favorite of ours).

22 rue Pairolière. ✆ **04-93-62-11-71.** Reservations recommended. Main courses 14€–23€; fixed-price menu 25€. No credit cards. Daily noon–2:30pm and 7–11pm.

Le Tire Bouchon BISTRO With its deep-red decor and candlelit alfresco tables, this cozy restaurant ("the Corkscrew") is designed for a romantic dinner. Chef Jonathan Fonteneau (who trained at the two-Michelin-starred Bastide Saint Antoine in Grasse) has introduced Provençal flavors to the solid French menu at this popular haunt near cours Saleya in Nice's Old Town. Tuck into rich classics such as homemade foie gras with a chocolate and apricot marmalade followed by lamb shank cooked in red wine, or opt for a lighter Mediterranean fish soup with garlic bread and then salmon in a creamy sorrel sauce. A la carte dishes are pricey, but the three-course Menu Découverte is reasonable at just under 27€. The dining area is split in two by the kitchen: Tables at the rear are quieter.

19 rue de la Préfecture/7 rue de L'Abbaye. ✆ **04-93-92-63-64.** www.le-tire-bouchon.com. Reservations recommended. Main courses 15€–25€; set menu 27€–31€. AE, MC, V. Daily 7am–10:30pm. Bus: 9 or 10.

Oliviera ★ PROVENÇALE/NIÇOISE Olive-infused cuisine is the order of the day at this Provençal restaurant in the heart of Vieux Nice. Knowledgeable owner Nadim Bérouji greets diners with olive oil tastings, while his wife Regine cooks up local specialties. As well as homey delights such as lasagna and Niçoise ravioli, there are well-seasoned salads—the Avocat Loco, served with apple, broccoli, tomato, and fennel, is particularly delicious. With its open-plan kitchen overflowing with fresh vegetables and myriad olive oil canisters, the pretty dining room is small but welcoming. Outdoor tables are usually snapped up by early birds or those who book in advance. Expect eccentricities such as clambering through the upstairs storage room to find the toilet. The restaurant doubles as an olive oil shop, open from 10am to 11pm.

8 bis, rue du Collet. ✆ **04-93-13-06-45.** www.oliviera.com. Main courses 10€–24€. MC, V. Tues–Sat 12:30–2:30pm and 7:30–9:30pm.

INEXPENSIVE

Acchiardo ★ PROVENÇALE This down-to-earth place cooks up good-value Provençal cuisine in the heart of Vieux Nice. Local workers are packed together in this bustling restaurant that has been run by the Acchiardo family since the end of World War II. Drinking is pursued as avidly as eating here. The recipes are time twisted and include a classic Niçoise version of gnocchi, which is prepared with Swiss chard and served with a choice of three different sauces, including pistou, Gorgonzola, and tomato. Many locals also begin their meal with *soupe au pistou.* Book in advance and ask for a table in the more atmospheric front room.

38 rue Droite. ✆ **04-93-85-51-16.** Reservations 2 days in advance. Main courses 6€–15€. No credit cards. Mon–Fri noon–2pm and 7–10pm. Closed weekends in Aug.

Chez Palmyre NIÇOISE/PROVENÇALE The owner of Chez Palmyre informed us, "We don't care about food fashions or decoration, only local home cooking like my grandmother's." She shops daily for locally sourced food and changes her menu depending on her inspiration that morning. Located in Vieux Nice, Chez Palmyre caters to regular diners, who come here for some of the best fried sardines in the old city. Try the rolled veal scallops filled with cheese and ham and served with a sauce of fresh tomatoes laced with wine. Many patrons come here to order *tripes á la niçoise,* although this is an acquired taste for some. This place has been a virtual institution in Nice since 1925, and we expect it'll be around at least until the dawn of the next century.

5 rue Droite. ✆ **04-93-85-72-32.** Reservations recommended. Fixed-price menu (the only choice) 14€. MC, V. Mon–Sat noon–2pm and 7–10pm.

Chez Pipo NIÇOISE No trip to Nice is complete without a taste of *socca* (chickpea pancake) from Chez Pipo, which has been in business since 1923. The format couldn't be simpler: bargain-priced Provençal snacks cooked in the huge Biot stone oven and served at trestle tables. Since Steve Bernardo has taken over, nothing has changed and the place is still as crowded as ever. As well as *socca* (2.50€), the menu features *pissaladières* (onion pizza); anchovy tapenades (olive paste); and the bizarre-sounding but delicious *tourtes de blettes* (sweet Swiss chard pastries).

13 rue Bavastro. ✆ **04-93-55-88-82.** Main courses 2.50€–15€. Cash only. Tues–Sun 5:30–10pm.

Granny's ☺ BRETON This informal crêperie is the perfect option for a bargain-priced lunch in Vieux Nice. With tables spilling onto a pretty pedestrianized square, local families flock here for Breton galettes and salads. Appropriate for a restaurant named after Granny Smith apples, the sweet crepe with apples and cream is especially delicious. Kids can play with the train set outside the toy shop next door owned by the same Antibes family that runs Granny's.

5 place de l'Ancien Sénat. ✆ **06-14-25-10-92.** Main course 3.50€–8.50€. Cash only. Thurs–Tues 8:30am–6:30pm.

Ice Cream Break

Nice's masterful ice cream maker Fenocchio (© 04-93-62-88-80; www.fenocchio.fr) is so successful that it has two Vieille Ville outlets, on rue de la Poissonerie and place Rossetti. There are over 90 flavors of ice cream and sorbet to choose from, including the unusual-tasting chewing gum, tomato and basil, jasmine, and Irish coffee, as well as the traditional flavors you'd expect.

Lu Fran Calin NIÇOISE/PROVENÇALE Here you'll find hearty Niçoise food and simple pasta dishes at local prices. Tourists rarely find their way to this homey bastion of traditional family cooking, but you'll find plenty of locals enjoying Niçoise favorites, such as *panisse* (chickpea fritters) and *petits farcis* (stuffed vegetables) as well as the tastiest lasagna in town. It's best to come on a sunny day so you can dine outside on the place Halle aux Herbes next to place Rossetti.

5 rue Francis Gallo. © **04-93-80-81-81.** Fixed-price menu 12€–26€. MC, V. Mon–Sat noon–2:30pm and 7:30–10pm.

Vinivore FRENCH Tucked away behind the Old Port, this wine shop–restaurant is a must for wine lovers. Olivier Labarde's latest adventure combines a 400-strong wine list with excellent bistro cuisine. A market-fresh daily menu includes grilled meats and salads, as well as unadorned cold cuts and cheese platters. During a recent wintertime visit to Nice, we grabbed the last available table inside. While we savored a truffled Brie de Meaux with a lightly oaked chardonnay in the cozy dining room, a young Niçoise crowd braved the frosty outdoor terrace warmed only by bowls of cured pork with lentils and bottles of robust red.

32 av. de la République. © **04-93-26-90-17.** Main course 12€–20€. Mon–Fri 9am–7pm; Fri–Sat 7–10:30pm.

BEYOND NICE

Restaurant Parcours Live ★ MEDITERRANEAN This is the kind of place that Niçoise gastronomes talk about in one-upmanship conversations with other locals. In a village just outside Nice, this restaurant's appeal derives from a combination of sweeping views, fabulous food, and the three monitors that provide real-time views of the food preparation rituals going on within the kitchens. Expect a century-old *mas* (farmhouse) Provençal, radically upgraded into a glossy, high-tech interior with seats for 85 diners at a time. Menu items, as supervised by two generations of the Galland family (son Fréderic capably handles the kitchens, *mamam* Danielle choreographs the dining rooms) vary with the seasons, but might include lobster risotto and stuffed courgette flowers. Try the Mexican chocolate soufflé for dessert.

1 place Marcel Eusebi, 06950 Falicon. © **04-93-84-94-57.** www.restaurant-parcours.com. Reservations recommended. Fixed-price lunches (Mon–Fri only) 23€–27€; fixed-price dinners 42€–75€. AE, MC, V. Tues–Sat 8am–9:30pm (also Mon July to mid-Sept). From downtown Nice, drive north along the av. De Cimiez, then turn right onto the bd. Aire St-Michel, following the signs to the hamlet (pop. 2,000) of Falicon. In Falicon, signs clearly indicate the location.

Nice After Dark

Nice has some of the most active nightlife along the Riviera. Evenings usually begin at a cafe. At kiosks around town, pick up a copy of *La Semaine des Spectacles,* which outlines the week's diversions.

The major cultural center on the Riviera is the **Opéra de Nice,** 4 rue St-François-de-Paule (✆ **04-92-17-40-00;** www.opera-nice.org), built in 1885 by Charles Garnier, fabled architect of the Paris Opéra. It presents a full repertoire, with emphasis on serious, often large-scale operas, as well as ballet and a *saison symphonique,* dominated by the Orchestre Philharmonique de Nice. The opera hall is also the major venue for concerts and recitals. Tickets are available (to concerts, recitals, and full-blown operas) a day or two prior to any performance. You can show up at the box office (Mon–Thurs 9am–5:45pm, Fri 9am–7:45pm, and Sat 9am–4:30pm; opening times can alter June–Aug) or buy tickets in advance by calling ✆ **04-92-17-40-79.** Opera tickets run from 12€ for nosebleed (and we mean it) seats to 78€ for front-and-center seats on opening night.

Near the Hôtel Ambassador, **Le Before,** 18 rue des Congrès (✆ **04-93-87-85-59**), is an aperitif bar—called *apero-bar*—where a stylish all-ages crowd goes before heading off to more dance-oriented places. The decor is "New York inspired," with lots of brick like you'd find in a Gotham cellar. It's open daily from 6pm to midnight, with cold platters served until 10pm.

The **Palais de la Méditerranée's** historic casino, 15 promenade des Anglais (✆ **04-92-14-68-00;** www.casinomediterranee.com), reopened in 2004, and today it is Nice's answer to the more ostentatious glitter of Monte Carlo and Las Vegas. Its sumptuous decor is influenced by Egypt, Greece, and the Riviera's Golden Age. As well as 200 slot machines, there are 17 game tables, 6 American roulette tables, and 2 French roulette tables. It's open daily from 10am to 3am (until 4am Fri–Sat). A passport or government-issued photo ID is required for admission; you must be 18 or over to enter. Dress code is smart-casual: Avoid jeans and sneakers.

Further along the promenade des Anglais lies the tacky **Cabaret du Casino Ruhl,** in the Casino Ruhl, 1 promenade des Anglais (✆ **04-97-03-12-22**), where shows include just enough flesh to titillate; lots of spangles, feathers, and sequins; a medley of cross-cultural jokes and nostalgia for the old days of French *chanson;* and an acrobat or juggler. The casino contains an area exclusively for slot machines, open daily from noon to 4am, with no admission fee. A more formal gaming room (jacket required, but not a tie), offers blackjack, baccarat, and chemin de fer. It's open Sunday to Thursday 8pm to 4am, Friday and Saturday 5pm to 5am.

Le Relais, in the Hôtel Negresco, 37 promenade des Anglais (✆ **04-93-16-64-00;** p. 295), is the most beautiful museum-quality bar in Nice, with an oxblood-red ceiling, Oriental carpets, English wooden paneling, and Italianate chairs. It was once a haunt of the actress Lillie Langtry. With its piano music and white-jacketed waiters, the bar still attracts a chic crowd sipping champagne or postdinner whiskies. But you pay dearly for the privilege of imbibing there.

Many bars in the Old Town cater to an Anglophone crowd of expats and tourists. They include the **Scarlett O'Hara Irish Pub,** at the corner of rue Rossetti and rue Droite (✆ **04-93-80-43-22**); sports bar **Chez Wayne's,** 15 rue de la Préfecture (✆ **04-93-13-46-99;** www.waynes.fr); and **William's Pub,** 4 rue Centrale (✆ **04-93-62-99-63** or 04-93-85-84-66). Of the three, Chez Wayne's is the liveliest, with a busy calendar of live band nights and sporting events on TV.

If you'd rather hang out with French people, try **La Civette,** 29 rue de la Préfecture (✆ **04-93-62-35-51**), a popular spot for aperitifs. A young local crowd can be found sipping champagne at **Effervescence,** 10 rue de la Loge, between place Rossetti and place St. François (✆ **04-93-80-87-37;** www.leffervescence-nice.com). This richly painted, cavernous champagne bar is the place to come for a glass or two of bubbly to start off your evening (happy hour is 6–7:30pm). The extensive champagne and wine list is accompanied by delicious nibbles from foie gras to sushi.

Later on, head to one of Nice's longest-standing nocturnal venues: **La Bodeguita del Havana,** 14 rue Chavin (✆ **04-93-92-67-24**), where you can soak up the Latin atmosphere over drinks or dance the night away to salsa and reggae.

The hottest ticket is Nice for late-night action at weekends only is **High Club** (✆ **06-16-95-75-87;** www.highclub.fr), which opened in 2007. This club is divided into two venues at 45/47 Promenade des Anglais: the High Club for the 20- to 30-something crowd and the adjoining club Studio 47 for older rockers. There's an entrance charge of 10€. Another popular club is **White Lab,** 26 quai Lunel (✆ **04-93-26-54-79**), attracting a 20-plus crowd to its elegant confines. Everybody looks pink at night, helped in no small part by the bubble-gum decor. On most nights a cover of 15€ is imposed.

VILLEFRANCHE-SUR-MER ★

935km (581 miles) S of Paris; 6km (4 miles) E of Nice

According to legend, Hercules opened his arms and Villefranche-sur-Mer was born. Sitting on a big blue bay that looks like a gigantic bowl, this serene fishing village boasts one of the deepest natural ports in the Mediterranean.

Once popular with such writers as Katherine Mansfield and Aldous Huxley, it's still a haven for artists, many of whom take over its apricot-colored houses—reached by narrow alleyways—that climb the hillside. Two of the more recent arrivals who have bought homes in the area are Tina Turner and Bono.

Essentials

GETTING THERE **Trains** arrive from most towns on the Côte d'Azur, especially Nice (every 30 min.), but most visitors **drive** via the Corniche Inférieure (Lower Corniche). For more rail information and schedules, call ✆ **36-35,** or visit www.voyages-sncf.com. Villefranche does not have a formal **bus** station. Lignes d'Azur company (✆ **08-10-06-10-06;** www.lignesdazur.com) maintains service at 15-minute intervals aboard line no. 100 from Nice and from Monte Carlo and no. 81 from Nice to St-Jean port—both services go via Villefranche-sur-Mer. One-way bus transit from Nice costs 1€. Buses deposit their passengers in the heart of town, directly opposite the tourist information office.

VISITOR INFORMATION The **Office de Tourisme** is on Jardin François-Binon (✆ **04-93-01-73-68;** www.villefranche-sur-mer.com).

Exploring the Town

The vaulted **rue Obscure** is one of the strangest streets in France. In spirit it belongs more to a North African casbah than to a European port. People live in tiny houses, and occasionally there's space enough for a courtyard. To get there, take rue de l'Eglise.

Jean Cocteau, the painter, writer, filmmaker, and well-respected dilettante, spent a year (1956–57) painting frescoes on the 14th-century walls of the Romanesque **Chapelle St-Pierre,** quai de la Douane/rue des Marinières (✆ **04-93-76-90-70**). He presented it to "the fishermen of Villefranche in homage to the Prince of Apostles, the patron of fishermen." One panel pays tribute to the Gypsies of the

Stes-Maries-de-la-Mer. In the apse is a depiction of the miracle of St. Peter walking on the water, not knowing that an angel supports him. Villefranche's women, in their regional costumes, are honored on the left side of the narthex. The chapel charges 2€ admission for everyone (adults and children). It is open December 15 to November 15 Tuesday to Sunday 10am to noon and 4 to 8pm.

Where to Stay

MODERATE

Hôtel Versailles Several blocks from the harbor and outside the main part of town, this three-story hotel gives you a perspective of the entire coast. The family-run hotel offers rooms and suites (suitable for up to three) with big windows and panoramas, as well as contemporary furnishings and comfortable beds. Guests can order breakfast or lunch on the roof terrace. The on-site restaurant offers excellent French food.

7 av. Princesse-Grace, 06230 Villefranche-sur-Mer. www.hotelversailles.com. ✆ **04-93-76-52-52.** Fax 04-93-01-97-48. 46 units. 130€–170€ double; 250€–300€ suite. AE, DC, MC, V. Free parking. Closed Nov to mid-Mar. **Amenities:** Restaurant; pool (outdoor). *In room:* A/C, TV, Wi-Fi (10€ for 3 hr.).

Hôtel Welcome ★ Situated on the harborfront near restaurants galore, this is as good as it gets in Villefranche. The Welcome was a favorite of poet and filmmaker Jean Cocteau. In this six-story villa hotel outfitted with shutters and balconies, everything has been modernized and extensively renovated. Try for a fifth-floor room overlooking the water. All the midsize to spacious rooms are comfortably furnished. The sidewalk cafe is the focal point of town life. There's no restaurant, but there's a Cocteau-inspired wine bar where they also serve generous buffet breakfasts. The hotel has its own yacht that you can hire for the day.

3 quai Amiral-Courbet, 06230 Villefranche-sur-Mer.www.welcomehotel.com. ✆ **04-93-76-27-62.** Fax 04-93-76-27-66. 36 units. 105€–280€ double; 215€–425€ suite. AE, DC, MC, V. **Amenities:** Bar; babysitting. *In room:* A/C, TV, hair dryer, minibar, Wi-Fi (free).

Villa Vauban Your hosts, Alan and Brenda, are a British couple who have invested a lot of time and money in restoring this once-neglected property, turning it into a cozy nest for today's visitors. The location is adjacent to the old citadel, and the hotel opens onto a secluded garden. Five of the units are in the older main building with the remaining rooms in a wing with direct access to the garden, where breakfast can be taken. This hotel isn't recommended for families.

11 av. Général de Gaulle, 06230 Villefranche-sur-Mer. www.hotelvillavauban.com. ✆/fax **04-93-55-94-51.** 9 units. 70€–165€ double; 115€–190€ suite. MC, V. Free parking. **Amenities:** Breakfast room; Wi-Fi (free). *In room:* A/C, TV.

INEXPENSIVE

Hotel de la Darse With its wonderful location overlooking the famous Port de la Darse, this simple hotel offers exceptional value. The original proprietors, who've owned the hotel since 1925, took control of the day-to-day management several years ago, and standards have risen. All the rooms now have air-conditioning and many have sea views. Only breakfast is served, but there are several restaurants close by. Alas, there's no elevator.

Port de la Darse, 32 av. du Général-de-Gaulle, 06230 Villefranche-sur-Mer. www.hoteldeladarse.com. ✆ **04-93-01-72-54.** 21 units. 57€–87€ double; 79€–89€ triple and quadruple. MC, V. **Amenities:** Breakfast room. *In room:* A/C; TV.

Where to Eat

La Mère Germaine ★ SEAFOOD This pricey restaurant is the class act among the string of restaurants on the port. Plan to relax over lunch while watching fishermen repair their nets. Mère Germaine opened the place in the 1930s. These days a descendant, Remy Blouin, handles the cuisine, producing bouillabaisse celebrated across the Riviera. We recommend thyme-infused Label Rouge sea bass, pan-fried sole with almonds, beef filet with garlic and seasonal vegetables, and perfectly roasted *carré d'agneau* (lamb). As well as valet parking, those staying on a yacht are offered a free boat shuttle to and from the restaurant.

9 quai Courbet. ✆ **04-93-01-71-39.** www.meregermaine.com. Reservations recommended. Main courses 28€–84€. Fixed-price menu 42€; bouillabaisse 70€. AE, DC, MC, V. Daily noon–2:30pm and 7:30–9:30pm. Closed mid-Nov to Christmas.

L'Aparté ★ MODERN FRENCH With its vaulted ceiling and autumn-colored walls, this tiny restaurant has a young, informal ambience. You'll find the restaurant on a narrow medieval street parallel to the harbor. The young chef Béatrice has culinary skills in her blood as her father was a renowned Niçoise chef. The food is dreamily good. Try tuna carpaccio, red mullets with olive tapenade, or the flambéed duck breast. A wonderful meal is complete with a complimentary digestif of homemade rum.

1 rue Obscure. ✆ **04-93-01-84-88.** www.restaurant-laparte.fr. Reservations recommended. Main courses 17€–24€. AE, DC, MC, V. Tues–Sun 6–10:30pm.

SAINT-JEAN-CAP-FERRAT ★

938km (583 miles) S of Paris; 10km (6 miles) E of Nice

This place has been called "Paradise Found"—of all the oases along the Côte d'Azur, none has quite the snob appeal of Cap-Ferrat. It's a 15km (9-mile) promontory sprinkled with billionaires' villas and outlined by sheltered bays, beaches, and coves. The vegetation is lush. From the immaculate gardens of the legendary Villa Ephrussi de Rothshchild, you can gaze upon a Riviera coastline that lives up to your imagination. The surprisingly earthy harbor of St-Jean accommodates yachts, fishing boats, and numerous bistros.

Essentials

GETTING THERE Most visitors drive or take a **bus** or **taxi** from the rail station at nearby Beaulieu. A frequent **bus service** runs from Nice to St-Jean Port via Beaulieu on line no. 81; it costs just 1€ one-way. For more information, contact **Lignes d'Azur** (✆ **0810-06-10-06;** www.lignesdazur.com). By **car** from Nice, take the D6098 to Villefranche-sur-Mer, then turn right onto the D125 and right again onto the D25 before arriving in St-Jean-Cap-Ferrat.

VISITOR INFORMATION The **Office de Tourisme** is on 59 av. Denis-Séméria (✆ **04-93-76-08-90;** fax 04-93-76-16-67; www.ville-saint-jean-cap-ferrat.fr).

Exploring the Town

One way to enjoy the scenery here is to wander on some of the public paths. The most scenic goes from **Plage de Paloma** to **Pointe St-Hospice,** where a panoramic view of the Riviera landscape unfolds. Everyone tries to visit the **Villa Mauresque,** avenue Somerset-Maugham, but it's closed to the public. Near the cape, it's where

Maugham spent his final years. When tourists tried to visit him, he proclaimed that he wasn't one of the local sights. One man did manage to crash through the gate, and when he encountered the author, Maugham snarled, "What do you think I am, a monkey in a cage?"

La Villa Ephrussi de Rothschild ★★★ Built by Baronne Ephrussi de Rothschild, this pink palace is one of the Côte d'Azur's legendary villas. Born a Rothschild, the baronne married a Hungarian banker and friend of her father, about whom even the museum's curator knows little. She died in 1934, leaving the Italianate building and its gardens to the Institut de France on behalf of the Académie des Beaux-Arts. The museum preserves the wealth of her collection: 18th-century furniture; Tiepolo ceilings; Savonnerie carpets; screens and panels from the Far East; tapestries from Gobelin, Aubusson, and Beauvais; Fragonard drawings; Boucher canvases; Sèvres porcelain; and more. The gardens contain fragments of statuary from churches, monasteries, and palaces. There are nine themed gardens, including a rose garden with around 100 rose varieties. There is a *salon de thé* serving lunchtime snacks and teatime cakes.

Off av. Denis-Séméria. ✆ **04-93-01-33-09.** www.villa-ephrussi.com. Admission 12€ adults, 9€ students and children 7–17, free for children 6 years and under. Mar–Oct daily 10am–6pm (until 7pm July–Aug); Nov–Feb Mon–Fri 2–6pm, Sat–Sun 10am–6pm.

Where to Stay

VERY EXPENSIVE

Grand Hôtel du Cap-Ferrat ★★★ One of the best features of this early-1900s palace is its location at the tip of the peninsula in the midst of a 5.6-hectare (14-acre) garden of semitropical trees and manicured lawns. It has been the retreat of the international elite since 1908 and occupies the same celestial status as La Réserve and the Métropole in Beaulieu. Its Michelin-starred restaurant is in the capable hands of Didier Aniès. Parts of the exterior have open loggias and big arched windows; you can also enjoy the views from the elaborately flowering terrace over the sea. Accommodations are now luxuriously contemporary with Art Deco touches and gadgets that include a mobile phone for every guest during their stay. Rooms are generally spacious and open to sea views. The beach is accessible by funicular from the main building. There's a new spa with outdoor pavilions opening onto the hotel gardens. After an extensive refurbishment, the hotel was nominated in 2011 for the elite "palace" label; so far it's the only hotel in Southern France to receive this distinction under the new hotel categorization, which distinguishes the most prestigious French hotels from their five-star competitors.

71 bd. du Général-de-Gaulle, 06230 St-Jean-Cap-Ferrat. www.grand-hotel-cap-ferrat.com. ✆ **04-93-76-50-50.** Fax 04-93-76-04-52. 72 units. 265€–1,550€ double; from 580€ suite. AE, DC, MC, V. Indoor parking 35€. Closed Dec–Apr. **Amenities:** 3 restaurants; bar; babysitting; bikes; concierge; health club and spa; pool (outdoor); room service; tennis court. *In room:* A/C, TV, hair dryer, minibar, Wi-Fi (free).

Hôtel La Voile d'Or ★★ Established in 1966, the "Golden Sail" is a tour de force. This four-star hotel offers intimate luxury in a converted 19th-century villa at the edge of the little fishing port and yacht harbor, with a panoramic coast view. It's not in the same league as the Grand Hôtel, but its portside location is unmatchable. The guest rooms, lounges, and restaurant open onto terraces. Accommodations are individually decorated, with hand-painted reproductions, carved gilt headboards, baroque paneled doors, parquet floors, antique clocks, and paintings. Guests gather on the canopied outer terrace for lunch and in a stately room with Spanish armchairs and white wrought-iron chandeliers for dinner. If you're not staying here, try to book a table at the main restaurant for its fine cuisine and even finer views. There's also an informal beach restaurant in summer months.

31 av. Jean-Mermoz, 06230 St-Jean-Cap-Ferrat. www.lavoiledor.fr. ✆ **04-93-01-13-13.** Fax 04-93-76-11-17. 45 units. 360€–890€ double; 665€–890€ suite. Rates include breakfast. AE, MC, V. Parking 25€. Closed mid-Oct to mid-Apr. **Amenities:** 2 restaurants; bar; babysitting; fitness room Internet (free); 2 pools (outdoor); room service. *In room:* A/C, TV, hair dryer, minibar.

EXPENSIVE

Hôtel Royal Riviera ★★★ Rising five graceful stories above the thin line that separates the quietly prestigious towns of St.-Jean-Cap-Ferrat and Beaulieu-sur-Mer, this 1904 hotel evokes the Riviera's Gilded Age. Fans of Zelda and F. Scott Fitzgerald know they frolicked here in the '30s, creating pages that might have been torn from *Tender Is the Night.* In 1988, an unfortunate modernization destroyed much of the Belle Époque charm of the palace, but Grace Leo-Andrieu, one of France's most inventive hoteliers, arrived from Paris to help the hostelry regain its old reputation. She can't help the location near the train tracks, which makes some of the front rooms noisy, but she's done everything else in her power to make the hotel ever more chic. It occupies a 4-hectare (1-acre) tract with a beach of its own, to which tons of sand are added at regular intervals. Bedrooms are posh and plush, with big windows, private balconies, deep sofas, and fruitwood armoires. The largest and most appealing are the corner units (any room ending in "16") with splendid views over the peninsula. Regardless, each is charming and elegant.

3 av. Jean Monnet, 06230 St-Jean-Cap-Ferrat. www.royal-riviera.com. ✆ **04-93-76-31-00.** Fax 04-93-01-23-07. 96 units. 250€–870€ double; 700€–2,800€ suite. Rates include half board. AE, DC, MC, V. Free parking. Closed Dec to mid-Jan. **Amenities:** 2 restaurants; bar; babysitting; pool (outdoor); room service. *In room:* A/C, TV, hair dryer, minibar, Wi-Fi (free).

MODERATE

Hôtel Brise Marine The reason for staying at this 19th-century villa is its exceptional location on the Cap-Ferrat peninsula, near St-Jean port and Paloma Beach. A long rose arbor, beds of subtropical flowers, palms, and pines provide an attractive setting. The atmosphere is casual and informal, and the rooms are comfortably but simply furnished. You can have breakfast in the beamed lounge or on the shaded terrace. The little corner bar serves afternoon drinks.

58 av. Jean-Mermoz, 06230 St-Jean-Cap-Ferrat. www.hotel-brisemarine.com. ✆ **04-93-76-04-36.** Fax 04-93-76-11-49. 16 units. 145€–185€ double. AE, DC, MC, V. Parking 14€. Closed Nov–Jan. **Amenities:** Bar; Wi-Fi (free). *In room:* A/C, TV, hair dryer, minibar.

Hôtel Le Panoramic This three-star hotel, built in 1958 with a red-tile roof, is one of the more affordable choices here. You'll reach the hotel by passing over a raised bridge lined with colorful flowers. The small, simply furnished rooms have a sweeping view of the water and the forested hills leading down to it. Breakfast is the only meal served. Free parking is a boon.

3 av. Albert-1er, 06230 St-Jean-Cap-Ferrat. www.hotel-lepanoramic.com. ✆ **04-93-76-00-37.** Fax 04-93-76-15-78. 20 units. 145€–175€ double. AE, DC, MC, V. Free parking. Closed mid-Nov to Dec 26. **Amenities:** Room service. *In room:* TV, Wi-Fi (free).

A Memorable Walk

If you're staying at the Royal Rivera, make time for a stroll along the Promenade Maurice Rouvier to St-Jean port. Halfway along this beautiful coastal path, you'll find the late David Niven's sugar-pink palace.

Where to Eat

The most memorable places to dine in St-Jean-Cap-Ferrat are both hotel restaurants: the Michelin-starred **Le Cap** at the Grand Hôtel Cap-Ferrat and the idyllic **La Voile d'Or** (see "Where to Stay"). The earthy fishing port of Saint-Jean is the place for fish. With its blue-and-white decor, portside **Le Sloop** (✆ **04-93-01-48-63;** www.restaurantsloop.com) is best known for the dubious accolade that film director and food critic Michael Winner loves it. However, you'll find better value elsewhere.

Capitaine Cook ★ PROVENÇALE/SEAFOOD Next door to the fancy La Voile d'Or hotel (see above), a few blocks uphill from the village center, this family-run restaurant specializes in hearty portions of seafood. You'll have a panoramic view of the coast from the terrace; inside, the decor is maritime and rugged. Roasted catch of the day is the mainstay, but salmon ravioli and grilled sea bass are also popular. The staff speaks English.

11 av. Jean-Mermoz. ✆ **04-93-76-02-66.** Fixed-price menus 26€-31€. MC, V. Fri-Tues noon-2pm; Thurs-Tues 7:15-11pm. Closed mid-Nov to Dec.

Restaurant La Goëlette ★ SEAFOOD Overlooking the yachts and fishing boats, this colorful portside restaurant is our favorite place to dine in St-Jean port. Owner Jean-Pierre and his Portuguese wife Paola have been tempting local diners with their bouillabaisse (fish stew) and its Spanish equivalent *zarzuela* for 2 decades. The menu mingles Southern French with Italian and Spanish dishes.

Port Saint-Jean. ✆ **04-93-76-14-38.** Fixed-price menus 23€-30€. MC, V. July-Aug daily 12:30-2:30pm and 7-10pm; Sept-June Fri-Sat 12:30-2:30pm, Mon-Sat 7-10pm.

BEAULIEU-SUR-MER ★

938km (583 miles) S of Paris; 10km (6 miles) E of Nice; 11km (7 miles) W of Monte Carlo

Protected from the cold north winds blowing down from the Alps, Beaulieu-sur-Mer is often referred to as "La Petite Afrique" (Little Africa). Like Menton, it has the mildest climate along the Côte d'Azur and is especially popular with the wintering wealthy. Beaulieu-sur-Mer is graced with lush vegetation, including oranges, lemons, and bananas, as well as palms.

Essentials

GETTING THERE **Trains** connect Beaulieu-sur-Mer with Nice, Monaco, and the rest of the Côte d'Azur. For rail information, call ✆ **36-35,** or visit www.voyages-sncf.com. **Buses** no. 100 and no. 81 leave Nice several times per hour stopping at Beaulieu-sur-Mer (trip time 20 min.). Tickets cost 1€. For information, contact **Lignes d'Azur** (✆ **0810-06-10-06;** www.lignesdazur.com). Most visitors **drive** from Nice on the Moyenne Corniche or the coastal highway.

VISITOR INFORMATION The **Office de Tourisme** is on place Georges-Clemenceau (✆ **04-93-01-02-21;** fax 04-93-01-44-04; www.beaulieusurmer.fr).

Exploring the Town

Villa Kérylos ★★, Impasse Gustave-Eiffel (✆ **04-93-01-01-44;** www.villa-kerylos.com), is a replica of an ancient Greek residence, painstakingly designed and built by the archaeologist Théodore Reinach, who mimicked ancient Grecian life here for 20 years. Inside the cabinets are filled with a collection of Greek figurines and ceramics. But most interesting is the reconstructed Greek furniture, much of which would be fashionable today. One curious mosaic depicts the slaying of the Minotaur and provides its own labyrinth (if you try to trace the path, expect to stay for weeks). It is open March to October daily 10am to 6pm (until 7pm July–Aug); hours November to February are Monday to Friday 2pm to 6pm and Saturday and Sunday 10am to 6pm. Admission is 9€ adults, 7€ for children 7 to 17, and free for children 6 and under.

The town boasts an important church, the late-19th-century **Eglise de Sacré-Coeur,** a quasi-Byzantine, quasi-Gothic mishmash at 13 bd. du Maréchal-Leclerc (✆ **04-93-01-18-24**). With the same address and phone is the 12th-century Romanesque chapel of **Santa Maria de Olivo,** it's used mostly for temporary exhibits of painting, sculpture, and civic lore. Both sites are open daily from 8am to 7pm.

As you walk along the **seafront promenade,** you can see many stately Belle Époque villas that evoke the days when Beaulieu was the very height of fashion. Although you can't go inside, you'll see signs indicating Villa Namouna, which once belonged to Gordon Bennett, the owner of the *New York Herald,* who sent Stanley to Africa to find Livingstone; and Villa Leonina, former home of the marquess of Salisbury.

A Day at the Beach

Don't expect soft sands. Some seasons might have more sand than others depending on tides and storms, but usually the shore surface is covered with light-gray gravel that has a finer texture than beaches at other resorts nearby. The longer of the town's two free public beaches is **Petite Afrique,** adjacent to the yacht basin; the shorter is **Baie des Fourmis. Africa Plage** (✆ **04-93-01-11-00**) rents mattresses for 25€ per day and sells snacks and drinks.

Where to Stay

Despite its premium location, Beaulieu-sur-Mer has plenty of cheaper accommodation for those on a budget.

VERY EXPENSIVE

La Réserve de Beaulieu & Spa ★★★ A member of the Small Leading Hotels of the World group, this pink-and-white *fin de siècle* palace is one of the Riviera's most famous hotels. Here you can sit, have an aperitif, and watch the sunset while a pianist plays Mozart. A number of the lounges open onto a courtyard with grass borders and urns of flowers. The social life revolves around the main drawing room. The individually decorated guest rooms range widely in size and design; most overlook the Mediterranean, and some have a view of the mountains. Some have private balconies. The dining room has a frescoed ceiling, parquet floors, chandeliers, and windows facing the Mediterranean.

5 bd. du Maréchal-Leclerc, 06310 Beaulieu-sur-Mer. www.reservebeaulieu.com. ✆ **04-93-01-00-01.** Fax 04-93-01-28-99. 39 units. 180€–1,240€ double; 620€ suite. AE, DC, MC, V. Parking 36€. Closed mid-Oct to mid-Dec. **Amenities:** 2 restaurants (1 summer and 1 year-round); bar; babysitting; concierge; room service; spa. *In room:* A/C, TV, hair dryer, minibar, Wi-Fi (free).

INEXPENSIVE

Hôtel Le Havre Bleu This two-star hotel is a great little bargain if you don't need a lot of services and amenities. Le Havre Bleu has one of the prettiest facades of any inexpensive hotel in town. In a former Victorian villa, the hotel has arched ornate windows and a front garden dotted with flowering urns. The guest rooms are comfortable and functional. Standard rooms are small, so it's worth paying more for a superior room with terrace. The in-room amenities are few, except for a phone; the compact bathrooms have showers. There's also a self-catering studio for rentals by the week. Breakfast is the only meal served.

29 bd. du Maréchal-Joffre, 06310 Beaulieu-sur-Mer. www.lehavreblue.com. ✆ **04-93-01-01-40.** Fax 04-93-01-29-92. 20 units. 65€–85€ double; studio from 330€ per week. AE, MC, V. Free parking. **Amenities:** Room service; babysitting; Wi-Fi (free). *In room:* A/C, TV, Wi-Fi (in some; free).

Hôtel Marcellin The early-20th-century Marcellin is a good budget selection in an otherwise high-priced resort. Built around 1900 for a local family, the sprawling, much-altered villa was divided into two about 25 years ago, and half was converted into this pleasant, cost-conscious hotel, while the other half remains a private home. The restored rooms come with homelike amenities and southern exposure. They're small to midsize, but comfortably furnished. There's also a self-catering studio for rentals by the week. The location isn't bad, either: It's only a 5-minute walk from the Baie des Fourmis beach. Breakfast is the only meal served, but many restaurants are nearby.

18 av. Albert-1er, 06310 Beaulieu-sur-Mer. www.hotel-marcellin.com. ✆ **04-93-01-01-69.** Fax 04-93-01-37-43. 21 units. 65€–99€ double; studio from 280€ per week. MC, V. **Amenities:** Bar; babysitting; room service. *In room:* A/C, TV, fridge, hair dryer, Wi-Fi (free).

Inter-Hôtel Frisia ★ The best thing about this three-star hotel is its location overlooking the Port de Plaisance. Bedrooms are decorated in a simple modern style. The rooms with harbor views are the most expensive, but we'd also recommend the cheaper mountain-view rooms. Two spacious suites with kitchenettes are in freestanding villas near the hotel's main building. Public areas include a sunny garden and inviting lounges. English is widely spoken here, and the management makes foreign guests feel especially welcome. Breakfast is the only meal served, but many reasonably priced restaurants are nearby.

2 bd. Eugène-Gauthier, 06310 Beaulieu-sur-Mer. www.frisia-beaulieu.com. ✆ **04-93-01-01-04.** Fax 04-93-01-31-92. 35 units. 60€–139€ double; from 110€ suite. AE, DC, MC, V. Parking 9€. Closed Nov to mid-Dec. **Amenities:** Bar; babysitting; Internet (free). *In room:* A/C, TV, hair dryer, kitchenette (in some), minibar.

Where to Eat

For Michelin-starred cuisine, look no further than **La Réserve** (see "Where to Stay"). Lovers of Moroccan cuisine won't be disappointed by **Le Petit Darkoum** (✆ **04-93-01-48-59**) on 18 bd. Maréchal-Leclerc, near La Réserve hotel. The shabby exterior belies the colorful Moorish ambience inside and the flavorsome Moroccan cuisine, which ranges from seven-vegetable couscous to pigeon-filled pastillas.

La Pignatelle FRENCH/PROVENÇALE There's no sea view, but La Pignatelle makes up for this with its fresh ingredients, olive-infused *provençale* cuisine and its pretty garden terrace. Fish is the order of the day with the chef's specialties including *Marimite du Pecheur* (fish stew).

10 rue de Quincenet. ✆ **04-93-01-03-37.** Reservations recommended. Main courses 9€–27€; fixed-price menus 15€–32€. MC, V. Fri–Tues noon–2pm; Thurs–Tues 7–9:30pm. Closed Nov.

Les Agaves TRADITIONAL FRENCH With its soft lighting and intimate ambience, Les Agaves is a reliable address for a romantic meal. Of note are curry-enhanced scallops rockfish soup, filet of sea bass with truffles and champagne sauce, and rum-and-coconut-flavored duck. You'll find the restaurant across the street from the railway station in an early-1900s villa.

4 av. Maréchal Foch. ✆ **04-93-01-13-12.** Reservations recommended. Fixed-price menu 36€. AE, MC, V. Daily 7:30–10pm.

The African Queen INTERNATIONAL Named for the Hollywood classic by its movie-loving founders, this hip and popular restaurant is filled with posters of Hepburn and Bogie and has a jungle-inspired decor. You don't come here for the cuisine, but to people watch and to enjoy the yachts in the Port de Plaisance. Over the past 40 years, numerous celebrities have passed through its doors during the Cannes Film Festival, from Jack Nicholson to Leonardo DiCaprio and Blake Lively. Menus items vary from pizzas and salads to Provençal fish and meat dishes. The check is presented in a video-cassette case labeled—what else?—*The African Queen*. Service can be patchy.

Port de Plaisance. ✆ **04-93-01-10-85.** www.africanqueen.fr. Reservations recommended. Main courses 10€–38€. MC, V. Daily noon–midnight.

EZE & LA TURBIE ★

941km (585 miles) S of Paris; 11km (7 miles) NE of Nice

The hamlets of Eze and La Turbie, though 6.4km (4 miles) apart, have so many similarities that most of France's tourist officials speak of them as if they were one. Both boast fortified feudal centers high in the hills overlooking the Provençal coast built during the early Middle Ages to stave off raids from corsairs. Clinging to the rocky hillsides around these hamlets are upscale villas, many of which were built in the 1950s by retirees. Culturally and fiscally linked to nearby Monaco, both Eze and La Turbie have a full-time population of fewer than 3,000. The defining difference between the two is that Eze Village has its own satellite Eze Bord de Mer clinging to the coastline, whereas La Turbie does not.

Essentials

GETTING THERE Eze is connected to Nice by train and bus. A Corniche **train** leaves Nice twice an hour during the day, stopping at Eze just 15 minutes later; a one-way fare is 2.40€. **Bus** no. 82 from Nice departs once per hour for Eze, Monday to Saturday (with 13 departures on Sun); the 20-minute trip costs 1€. For information, contact **Lignes d'Azur** (✆ **0810-06-10-06;** www.lignesdazur.com).

By **car,** Eze is accessible via the Moyenne Corniche (D6007) road; La Turbie is accessible via the Grande Corniche (D2564). Signs are positioned along the coastal road indicating the direction motorists should take to reach either of the hamlets.

The walk from Eze to the promontory of La Turbie is a steep climb of 6km (4 miles). You can also take a taxi from Eze. Most visitors travel to La Turbie by car.

VISITOR INFORMATION The **Office de Tourisme** is on place du Général-de-Gaulle, Eze-Village (✆ **04-93-41-26-00;** www.eze-riviera.com) and 2 place Detras, La Turbie (✆ **04-93-41-21-15;** www.ville-la-turbie.fr).

Exploring the Towns

The medieval cores of both towns contain restored galleries, boutiques, and artisans' shops. Art galleries of particular note within Eze are **Jean Eric Garnier** (✆ **04-93-41-23-58;** www.jean-eric-garnier.com) on rue du Barri for history-inspired art, **Galerie Sevek** (✆ **04-93-41-06-22**) on rue du Barri for abstract art, and **Galerie**

Marc Ferrero (✆ **04-92-10-82-92;** www.comitive.com) at 7 rue de la Paix for a New York perspective.

The leading attraction in Eze is the **Jardin d'Eze ★**, boulevard du Jardin-Exotique (✆ **04-93-41-10-30**), a showcase of exotic plants in Eze-Village, at the pinnacle of the town's highest hill. The renowned sculptor Jean-Philippe Richard has a permanent exhibition around the garden. Admission is 5€ for adults, 2.50€ for students and ages 18 to 25, 1€ for children 11 to 17, and free for children 10 and under. In July and August, it's open daily 9am to 8pm; the rest of the year, it opens daily at 9am and closes between 5 and 7pm, depending on the time of sunset.

La Turbie boasts a ruined monument erected by Roman emperor Augustus in 6 B.C., the **Trophée d'Auguste ★**. It's near a rock formation known as La Tête de Chien, at the highest point along the Grand Corniche, 450m (1,476 ft.) above sea level. The Roman Senate ordered the creation of the monument, which many locals call La Trophée des Alps (Trophy of the Alps), to celebrate the subjugation of the people of the French Alps by the Roman armies.

A short distance from the monument is the **Musée du Trophée d'Auguste,** rue Albert-1er, La Turbie (✆ **04-93-41-20-84**), a minimuseum containing finds from digs nearby and information about the monument's restoration. It's open mid-May to mid-September daily 9:30am to 1pm and 2:30 to 6:30pm, mid-September to mid-April daily 10am to 1:30pm and 2:30 to 5pm. Admission is 5€ for adults; it's free for EU residents aged 18 to 25 and for children 17 and under.

Where to Stay

EXPENSIVE

Château Eza ★★★ This château is the former Riviera home of Prince William of Sweden. It stands at the edge of a cliff at 396m (1,300 ft.) looking out over the resort of St-Jean-Cap-Ferrat. Entered on a narrow cobblestone street, this boutique hotel offers sumptuous bedrooms, a celebrated gourmet cuisine, and service fit for royalty. The elegant bedrooms are spread over a cluster of restored buildings dating from the Middle Ages. Each of the guest rooms is reached by walking under stone passageways past cavelike shops. Although the setting is ancient, the rooms are thoroughly modernized, with private bathrooms, charming fireplaces, and private balconies opening onto panoramic views. Modern gadgets such as iPod docks and DVD players are on hand. Canopied beds, art objects, beautiful carpets, and valuable tapestries set the tone. This is as close as the Riviera gets to fantasy living.

Rue de la Pise, 06360 Eze Village. www.chateaueza.com. ✆ **04-93-41-12-24.** Fax 04-93-41-16-64. 11 units. 278€–600€ double; 720€–1,200€ suite. AE, DC, MC, V. Closed Nov to mid-Dec. **Amenities:** Restaurant; bar; babysitting. *In room:* A/C, TV, DVD, hair dryer, iPod dock, minibar, Wi-Fi (free).

Le Château de la Chèvre d'Or ★★★ One of the French Riviera's grandest resort hotels, this five-star miniature-village retreat was built in the 1920s in neo-Gothic style. The Relais & Châteaux property is a complex of village houses, all with views of the coastline. But unlike most villages in the area, this one doesn't have a beach. The decor of the "Golden Goat" maintains its character while adding modern comfort. The spacious guest rooms are filled with quality furnishings. Even if you don't spend the night, try to visit for a drink in the lounge to take in the panoramic view.

Rue du Barri, 06360 Eze-Village. www.chevredor.com. ✆ **04-92-10-66-66.** Fax 04-93-41-06-72. 37 units. 280€–760€ double; 660€–2,900€ suite. AE, DC, MC, V. Closed Nov–Feb. Valet parking 15€. **Amenities:** 3 restaurants; bar; babysitting; exercise room w/sauna; Internet (free); massage room; pool (outdoor); room service. *In room:* A/C, TV, hair dryer, minibar.

MODERATE

Domaine Pins Paul ★★★ With its fairy-tale views over the Mediterranean, this is one of our favorite B&Bs along the French Riviera. The bougainvillea-clad, stone-built farmhouse has been imaginatively restored with luxurious fabrics and furniture. Each of the well-furnished rooms is spotlessly clean. At 450m (1,476-ft.) altitude, the house lies in 1 hectare (2½ acres) of pine-forested gardens with fruit and olive trees and a tiled pool that looks down upon the panorama of medieval Eze and the Mediterranean. Charming hosts Philippe and Marie Josée provide generous breakfasts and advice on local restaurants.

4530 av. des Diables Bleus, 06360 Eze. www.domainepinspaul.fr. ✆ **04-93-41-22-66.** 4 units. 130€–160€ double; 230€–260€ suite. Rates include breakfast. MC, V. **Amenities:** Breakfast room. *In room:* No phone, TV, Wi-Fi (free).

La Bastide aux Camelias ★ Set in the middle of the park of the Grande Corniche, the little inn lies close to Eze Village, opening onto panoramic views in all directions. After a lovely French breakfast on the veranda, the day is yours. The swimming pool, surrounded by greenery, is a magnet, and there are such luxuries as a Jacuzzi, sauna, and a little spa. You can even play a game of boules in the shade of sherry trees. Each bedroom is individually decorated with softly draped fabrics, making for a comfortable, intimate atmosphere. The one-bedroom suite is situated in the heart of the old village, but guests can still enjoy the facilities at the Bastide.

23C Rte. De l'Adret, 06360 Eze. www.bastideauxcamelias.com. ✆ **04-93-41-13-68** or 06-22-33-15-45. 5 units. 110€–150€ double; 200€–200€ suite. Rates include continental breakfast. Credit cards not accepted. **Amenities:** High-speed Internet (free); Jacuzzi; pool (outdoor); sauna. *In room:* Fridge, hair dryer, no phone.

La Vielle Bergerie ★ Those who'd like to go the B&B route along the coast between Nice and Monaco could do no better than this miniature lodging near the village of Eze. Roselyne Carpentier is the gracious innkeeper; living here is like being a guest in an old-fashioned Provençal home where everything is immaculate and beautifully decorated with traditional styling. The one bedroom comes with a small private bathroom. You approach the old house at the entrance to the forest park, De La Revère, at the bend of a small road. The house is surrounded by terraces and wildflower gardens, including olive trees, and umbrella-shaded tables and chairs are placed out next to an old stone bread oven.

585 rte. de la Revère, 06360 Eze. www.lavieillebergerie.com. ✆ **04-93-41-10-22** or 06-89-33-68-08. 1 unit. 110€–130€ double. Rates include breakfast. No credit cards. **Amenities:** Breakfast room. *In room:* No phone, Wi-Fi (free).

INEXPENSIVE

Hostellerie Jérôme Famed for its two Michelin-starred restaurant, this 12th-century presbytery is the perfect overnight stopover for dedicated foodies. The rooms are simply furnished, and prices reflect this. A vaulted dining room decorated with frescoes and 18th-century furniture sets the scene for sublime French cuisine. Chef Bruno Cirino makes daily trips across the Italian border to source the freshest produce from Ventimille market. With tasting menus for 65€ to 120€ per head, you'll undoubtedly pay more for the food

Staying Cool in Eze's B&Bs

Despite the high quality of B&Bs in Eze, most don't offer air-conditioning as the altitude helps to guard against the outdoor heat.

than for the rooms. Note that the restaurant is closed on Mondays and Tuesdays (except July–Aug).

20, rue Comte-de-Cessole, La Turbie. ✆ **04-92-41-51-51.** Reservations recommended. 95€–150€ double. MC, V. Closed Nov to mid-Feb. **Amenities:** Restaurant. *In room:* AC, TV, Wi-Fi (free).

Where to Eat

Neighboring bastions of gastronomic excellence, the Michelin-starred **Château de la Chèvre d'Or** and **Château Eza** (see both above) vie for top position in the old village of Eze. If you want to relax beside the beach over a seafood lunch, we'd recommend the restaurant and private beach **Anjuna** (✆ **04-93-01-58-21;** www.anjunabay.com) in Eze Bord de Mer.

Le Café de la Fontaine ★★ FRENCH/PROVENÇALE Not far from Hostellerie Jérôme, chef Bruno Cirino also runs this informal cafe-bistro. It may not have the same vaulted ceilings as its Michelin-starred compatriot, but it offers exceptional value. High-quality ingredients and hearty French flavors ensure a loyal local following. Dishes include pea-filled ravioli and herb-crusted cod. Finish with a bitter-chocolate tart.

4 av. Du Général-de-Gaulle, La Turbie. ✆ **04-93-28-52-79.** Reservations recommended. Main courses 6€–13€. MC, V. Daily noon–2:30pm and 7–11pm (closed Mon in winter).

Le Troubadour SOUTHWESTERN FRENCH The stone-fronted medieval house that contains this well-known restaurant often receives diners such as local athletes and drag-race drivers from nearby Monaco. Within three dining rooms, you can order succulent and flavorful dishes that include millefeuille of snails, duck breast with truffles, and other dishes that showcase some aspect of the Southwestern French diet. You'll find the place close to the village church in the upper heights of Eze Village.

4 rue du Brec, Eze Village. ✆ **04-93-41-19-03.** Reservations recommended. Main courses 26€–38€; fixed-price menu 39€. MC, V. Tues–Sat 1–2:30pm and 7:30–10pm. Closed mid-Nov to mid-Dec.

PEILLON ★★

19km (12 miles) NW of Nice

This fortified medieval town is one of the most spectacular "perched villages" along the Côte d'Azur. At 300m (1,000 ft.) above the sea, it's also unspoiled, unlike those other towns filled with day-trippers and souvenir shops. The main incentive to visit Peillon is the town itself; its semifortified architecture makes you feel that even today it could lock its doors, bar its windows, and keep any intruder at bay.

Essentials

GETTING THERE Public transport to Peillon is tricky, so you're best relying on a car. Several **trains** a day link Nice with the dilapidated train station Peillon-Saint-Thècle (journey time approx. 25 min.; one-way ticket 2.80€), but it's still a 3km (10-mile) journey into the old village of Peillon so some backpackers end up hitchhiking. For rail information and schedules, call ✆ **36-35,** or visit www.voyages-sncf.com.

Few other towns in Provence are as easy to reach by **car** and as inconvenient to reach by public transportation. Peillon is an easy 25-minute drive (depending on traffic) northeast from Nice; take D2204 to D21.

VISITOR INFORMATION The Peillon tourist office is located on the very short rue Centrale in Peillon-Village (✆ **06-24-97-42-25**), and is open for limited hours throughout the year. If the staff happens to not be open at the time of your call, the tourist office in Nice (✆ **08-92-70-74-07**) is usually well informed about the attractions and allures of Peillon. Barring that, you can always contact the Town Hall (La Mairie) of Peillon (✆ **04-93-79-91-04**), where staff members have in the past been extraordinarily helpful. Additionally, the receptionists at the town's most colorful inn, Auberge de la Madone (see below), are usually informative about the layout and attractions within their town.

Exploring the Town

Specific sites of interest include the town's severely dignified parish church, the **Eglise Saint-Sauveur,** open daily from 8am to around 6pm. Built in a simple country-baroque style, it's the site of many marriages, baptisms, and wedding ceremonies. Another site of interest is the 15th-century **Chapelle des Pénitents Blancs,** on place Auguste Arnulf. It's usually locked, so visits require that you first drop by the Tourist Office on rue Centrale in Peillon-Village (✆ **06-24-97-42-25**)—if it's convenient and if he or she isn't busy, an employee will accompany you with a key and wait for you while you admire the interior. The service is free, but a gratuity is appreciated. If you plunk .20€ into a machine near the gate, lights will illuminate the interior's noteworthy frescoes. Painted at the end of the 15th century by Jean Cannavesio, they represent the eight stages of the Passion of Christ.

The narrow streets radiate outward from the town's "foyer," **place Auguste-Arnulf,** which is shaded by rows of plantain trees centered around a fountain that has splashed water from its basin since 1800. Some of the streets are enclosed with vaulting and accented with potted geraniums and strands of ivy.

If you're in the mood for walking, consider a 2-hour, 12km (7½-mile) northward hike across the dry and rocky landscape to Peillon's remote, smaller sister, Peille.

Where to Stay & Eat

Auberge de la Madone ★★ This hotel has thrived since it opened back in the 1930s. The oldest section of the stone-sided complex of buildings dates from the 12th century. Evocative of a sprawling Provençal *mas,* it gives you a real glimpse of a Provence from long ago. It's capped with terra-cotta tiles and draped with a small version of the hanging gardens of Babylon. On the opposite side of place Auguste Arnulf from the rest of the village, its wide terrace opens onto a great view of the town's vertical, angular architecture. The small guest rooms are outfitted with bright and flower-patterned fabrics. The annex's accommodations are much simpler than those in the main building; rates depend on the plumbing and views. It's worth booking a room with a terrace to make the most of the views.

Most guests come for its famous restaurant (be aware it's closed Wed). Its Michelin star can be misleading, as the food and ambience are unashamedly rustic. Menu items include pan-fried foie gras and *civet* (stew) of rabbit followed by chard-flavored macaroon and orange-blossom ice cream. Fixed-price menus cost 32€ to 62€.

2 place Auguste Arnulf, 06440 Peillon. www.auberge-madone-peillon.com. ✆ **04-93-79-91-17.** Fax 04-93-79-99-36. 20 units. Main building 98€–200€ double; 235€–350€ suite. AE, MC, V. Free parking. **Amenities:** Restaurant; bar. *In room:* TV, hair dryer, minibar, Wi-Fi (free).

MONACO ★★★

954km (593 miles) S of Paris; 18km (11 miles) E of Nice

Hemmed in by France and fronting the Mediterranean, sparkling Monaco staunchly maintains its independence (and a tax-free policy) that has attracted international glitterati for more than a century. Its capital, Monte Carlo, is a world-famous symbol of glamour, with a grand casino, luxury shops, and chandeliered palace hotels. But there's history here, too. Beyond the sleek yachts bobbing in the port, the Grimadi's Palais Princier, on "the Rock," watches over the principality like a wise old patriarch—a stone-clad reminder that the Grimaldi clan has controlled Monaco since 1297.

Things to Do Watch the perfectly synchronized changing of the guards at 11:55am outside the **Palais Princier;** then head inside to admire the opulent **State Apartments** or to gaze at diaphanous moon jellies in the world-class aquarium at the nearby **Musée Océanographique.** Monaco's newest museum, **Villa Paloma,** puts modern art on the agenda.

Restaurants & Dining Much like its residents, the cuisine in Monaco is a fusion of French and Italian with a slice of true Monégasque. Michelin stars abound in central Monte-Carlo. **Larvotto** is home to family-friendly beachside food, while **Port Hercule** is the place to eat fish. Pizza and pasta restaurants crowd old town, **Monaco-Ville,** where you'll also find Monegasque *barbajuans* (chard-filled pastries) at **Castelroc.**

Nightlife & Entertainment Put on your glad rags for a night at the glorious Charles Garnier–designed **Opéra de Monte-Carlo.** When the last note has sounded, head next door to raise the stakes in the Belle Époque **Casino de Monte-Carlo,** where tuxedoed international types play blackjack beneath 19th-century frescoed ceilings. For a Monégasque-style boogie, miniskirts lead the way to chic nightclubs along avenue **Princess Grace.** Or head to **Quai Jean-Charle Rey** on the other side of **the Rock** to down ice-cold *bière* in English-style pubs.

Relaxation When the superyachts and designer labels get to be too much, find solace in the turquoise seas ringing Larvotto's pristine sandy beaches. Breathe in the perfume of 400 roses at Fontvieille's **Roseraie Princesse Grace** or explore prickly flora at the **Jardin Exotique.** An algae-infused hydromassage at the **Thermes Marins** will also help you unwind.

Essentials

GETTING THERE Monaco has rail, bus, and highway connections from other coastal cities, especially Nice. **Trains** arrive every 30 minutes from Cannes, Nice, Menton, and Antibes. For rail information, call ✆ **36-35,** or visit www.voyages-sncf.com. Monaco's railway station (Gare SNCF) has several access points: pont Sainte-Dévote (with elevators up to street level), place Sainte-Dévote, and an underpass from the old railway entrance on avenue Prince Pierre. If you'd rather take a **taxi** but can't find one at the station, call ✆ **0820-20-98-98.** Be prepared for a wait; we've waited up to 30 minutes for taxis to arrive in the past. Instead, we'd recommend taking one of the very efficient city **buses** from the bus stop outside the station on pont Sainte-Dévote or **walking**—nothing is far in Monte Carlo. You will face no border formalities when entering Monaco from mainland France.

A frequent **bus service** (every 15 min.) runs to Nice, Villefranche, and Menton on line no. 100 of the French bus company **Lignes d'Azur** (✆ **0810-06-10-06;** www.lignesdazur.com). The trip from Nice to Monaco by bus takes 40 minutes and costs just 1€ one-way. The times and prices are the same to Menton. The easiest place to catch a bus is in front of the gardens that face the Casino, but it also stops in front of the port (on bd. Albert-1er at the Stade Nautique stop) and at several other spots around town.

If you're **driving** from Nice to Monaco, take A8 motorway east. Turn off the motorway at exit 56 for Monaco.

VISITOR INFORMATION The **Direction du Tourisme et des Congrès** office is at 2a bd. des Moulins (✆ **377-92-16-61-16;** fax 377-92-16-60-00; www.monaco-tourisme.com).

GETTING AROUND The best way to get around Monaco is by **bus** (www.cam.mc). You can buy bus cards, which cost 1€ per ride, directly on the bus. Bus stops are set up every few blocks on the main streets in town and buses are scheduled every 5 to 10 minutes. Buses go to all the major tourist sights; just look at the front of the bus to see the destination.

For a **taxi,** call ✆ **0820-20-98-98.** Taxi stands are in front of the Casino on avenue de Monte-Carlo, at place des Moulins in Monte Carlo, at the Port de Monaco on avenue Président J. F. Kennedy, and in front of the post office on avenue Henry-Dunant. A **Hertz** car-rental office is at 27 bd. Albert-1er (✆ **377-93-50-79-60**), and an **Avis** office is at 9 av. d'Ostende (✆ **377-93-30-17-53**).

SPECIAL EVENTS Two of the most-watched **car-racing events** in Europe are in January (Le Rallye) and May (the Grand Prix; www.formula1monaco.com). For more information, call ✆ **377-93-15-26-50.** In June, Monte Carlo is home to a week-long convention that attracts media moguls from virtually everywhere, **Monte-Carlo Television Festival,** Grimaldi Forum, avenue Princesse-Grace (✆ **377-99-99-30-00;** www.tvfestival.com). Shows from all over the world are broadcast and judged on their merits.

Exploring the Principality

The second-smallest state in Europe (Vatican City is the tiniest), Monaco comprises five main parts. The Old Town, **Monaco-Ville,** on a promontory, "the Rock," 60m (200 ft.) high, is the seat of the royal palace and government building, as well as the Oceanographic Museum. To the west, **La Condamine** is at the foot of the Old Town, forming its harbor and port sector. Up from the port (walking is steep in Monaco) is **Monte Carlo,** once the playground of European royalty and still the center for the wintering wealthy, the setting for the casino, gardens, and deluxe hotels. The fourth part, **Fontvieille,** is a neat industrial suburb. To the east of Monte-Carlo is **Larvotto,** the beachside suburb towards the French border that attracts a chic crowd, including movie stars in scanty bikinis and thongs.

No one used to go to Monaco in summer, but now that has totally changed—in fact, July and August tend to be so crowded that it's hard to get a room. Although Monaco is developing a broader base of tourism (you can stay here moderately—but it's misleading to suggest that you can stay cheaply), the Monégasques very frankly court the affluent visitor. And at the casinos here, you can also lose your shirt. "Suicide Terrace" at the casino, though not used as frequently as in the old days, is still a real temptation to many who have foolishly gambled away family fortunes.

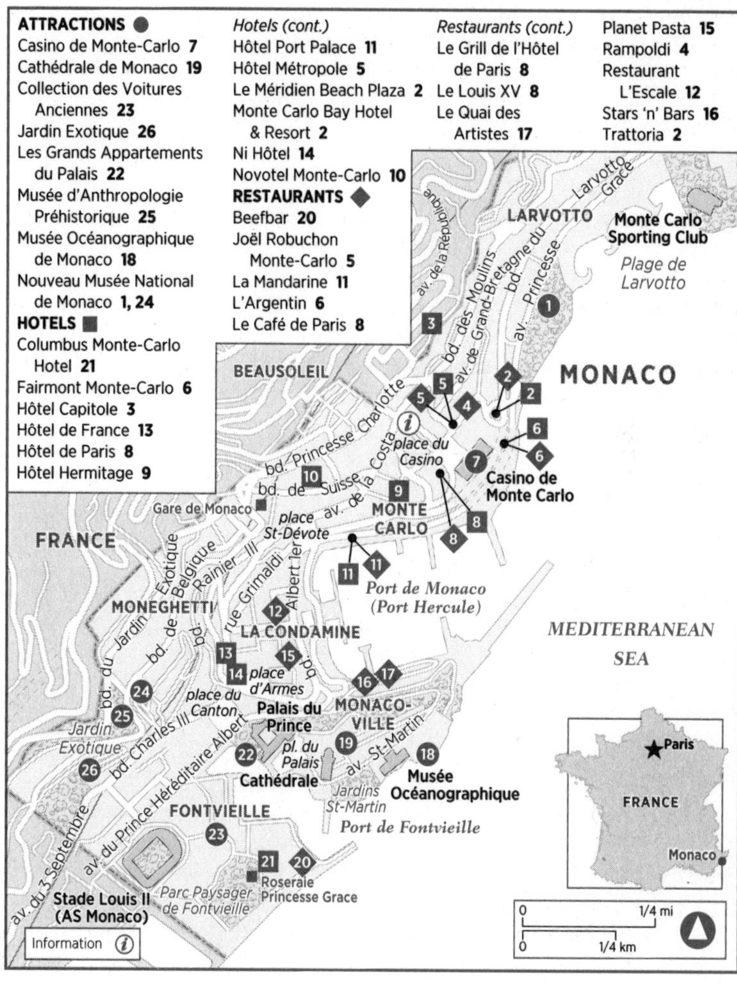

Life still focuses on the **Casino de Monte-Carlo** ★, which has been the subject of countless legends and the setting for many films (remember poor Lucy Ricardo and the chip she found lying on the casino floor?). Depending on the era, you might have seen Mata Hari shooting a tsarist colonel with a jewel-encrusted revolver when he tried to slip his hand inside her bra to discover her secrets—military, not mammary. The late King Farouk, known as "the Swine," used to devour as many as eight roast guinea hens and 50 oysters before losing thousands at the table. Richard Burton presented Elizabeth Taylor with the obscenely huge Kohinoor diamond here. Surrounded by cultivated gardens, the casino stands on a **panoramic terrace** ★★, offering one of the grandest views along the entire Riviera.

number, please: MONACO'S TELEPHONE SYSTEM

Since 1996, Monaco's phone system has been independent of France.

To call Monaco from within France and the European Union, dial 00 (the access code for all international long-distance calls from France), followed by the **country code (377),** then the eight-digit local phone number. (Don't dial the 33 code; that's the country code for France.)

To call Monaco from North America, dial the international access code, 011; the country code, 377; then the eight-digit Monaco number.

To call any other country from within Monaco, dial 00 (the international access code), then the applicable country code, and the number. For example, to call Cannes, you would dial 00, 33 (France's country code), 4 (the city code, without the zero), and the eight-digit number.

Cathédrale de Monaco This is one of the most visited attractions in the principality, primarily because it contains the tomb of the former princess of Monaco, Grace Kelly, who first gained fame as an American film actress, winning an Oscar for *The Country Girl*. Many of the ruling Grimaldis are also buried here, mostly recently Prince Rainier III.

Dedicated to Saint Nicholas, the cathedral was consecrated in 1911. It stands on the site of the first parish of Monaco dating from 1252. In addition to the Grimaldi tombs, seek out the huge organ containing almost 5,000 pipes and the white Carrara marble altar.

Av. St-Martin. ✆ **377-93-30-87-70.** www.cathedrale.mc. Free admission. Apr–Oct daily 8am–7pm; Nov–Mar daily 8am–6pm.

Collection des Voitures Anciennes de S.A.S. le Prince de Monaco ☺ Prince Rainier III opened a showcase of his private collection of more than 100 vintage autos, including the 1956 Rolls-Royce Silver Cloud that carried the prince and princess on their wedding day. Monaco shopkeepers gave it to the royal couple as a wedding present. A 1952 Austin Taxi on display was once used as the royal "family car." Other exhibits are a "woodie" (a 1937 Ford station wagon Prince Louis II used on hunting trips); a 1925 Bugatti 35B, winner of the Monaco Grand Prix in 1929; a 1903 De Dion Bouton; and a 1986 Lamborghini Countach.

Les Terrasses de Fontvieille. ✆ **377-92-05-28-56.** www.palais.mc. Admission 6€ adults, 3€ students and children 8–14, free for children 7 and under. Daily 10am–6pm. Closed Dec 25.

Jardin Exotique ★★ Built on the side of a rock, these gardens are known for their cactus collection. They were begun in the 19th century by Prince Albert I, who was a naturalist and scientist. He spotted some succulents growing in the palace gardens and created this garden from them. The garden was later opened to the public in 1933. You can also explore the grottoes here, as well as the **Musée d'Anthropologie Préhistorique.** The view of the principality is splendid.

62 bd. du Jardin-Exotique. ✆ **377-93-15-29-80.** www.jardin-exotique.mc. Admission (includes museum) 7€ adults, 3.70€ children 6–18, free for children 5 and under. Mid-May to mid-Sept daily 9am–7pm; mid-Sept to mid-May daily 9am–6pm (or until dusk).

Les Grands Appartements du Palais ★★ Most summer day-trippers from Nice want to see the home of Monaco's royal family, the **Palais Princier de Monaco,** which dominates the principality from "the Rock." A tour of the Grands Appartements allows you a glimpse of the Throne Room and some of the art (including works by Bruegel and Holbein), as well as Princess Grace's state portrait. The palace was built in the 13th century, and portions date from the Renaissance. The ideal time to arrive is 11:55am to watch the 10-minute **Relève de la Garde** (changing of the guard).

In a wing of the palace, the **musée (Souvenirs Napoléoniens et Archives du Palais)** holds a collection of mementos of Napoleon and Monaco. When the royal residence is closed, this museum is the only part of the palace the public can visit.

Place du Palais. ✆ **377-93-25-18-31.** www.palais.mc. Combination ticket 8€ adults, 3.50€ children 8-14, free for children 7 and under. Palace Apr–Oct 10am–6pm. Museum Apr–Oct 10am–6pm and Dec–Mar 10:30am–5pm.

Nouveau Musée National de Monaco ★★ The national museum now extends over two properties: the Villa Sauber at 17 av. Princesse-Grace and the Villa Paloma at 56 bd. du Jardin Exotique. The splendid turn-of-the-century Villa Paloma opened in 2010 after 2 years of restoration; here you'll find impressive and constantly changing modern art exhibitions of paintings, sculptures, and art installations. Meanwhile, the Charles Garnier–designed Villa Sauber pushes the boundaries with its modern art exhibitions fusing art and fashion; exhibitions here are often linked to creative workshops for local children. It also contains a rather freaky collection of antique mechanical toys and dolls—if you ask nicely they'll wind them up for you.

17 av. Princesse-Grace/56 bd. du Jardin Exotique. ✆ **377-98-98-91-26** or 377-98-98-48-60. www.nmnm.mc. Admission 6€ adults, free for children and students aged 26 and under. Daily 10am–6pm.

Musée Océanographique de Monaco ★★★ ☺ The highlight of this museum is the basement aquarium, a darkened sub-aqua world of diaphanous moon jellies, circling sea bass, and floaty seahorses. There are more than 90 tanks to explore, including a shark tank. Upstairs are collections amassed by Prince Albert I during 28 research trips he made aboard his four yachts between 1885 and 1915 around the Mediterranean and the North Atlantic. You'll see models of the ships and scientific prototypes used on his voyages, such as Jules Richard's *bouteille à renversement* (used to measure seawater temperatures at different depths). There is also a large collection of maritime artworks, including paintings, drawings, and sculptures. Founded in 1910 by Albert I, Monaco's Oceanographic Museum recently celebrated

The Principality's New Princess

The year 2011 marked the beginning of a new chapter for Monaco. The painful gap left by the death of American actress Grace Kelly was finally filled as Olympic swimmer Charlene Wittstock married SAS Le Prince Albert II on July 1st 2011. More than 400 events over 4 days were held around the municipality as Monégasques and international residents alike celebrated the couple's wedding nuptials. With her curled blonde locks and elegant sense of style, Princess Charlene's uncanny resemblance to her former mother-in-law has brought many parallels. How she'll fare as a princess in the world's most famous principality is anyone's guess.

its 100th anniversary with the purchase of a 150 million-year-old reptile called Anna and an installation designed by Huang Yong Ping. Ping's huge octopus-like fantasy straddles the main rotunda with one tentacle stretching towards a statue of Albert in his favorite costume: that of a sea captain.

Av. St-Martin. ✆ **377-93-15-36-00.** www.oceano.mc. Admission 14€ adults, 7€ children 4–18, free for children 3 and under. Apr–Sept daily 9:30am–7pm (until 7:30pm July–Aug); Oct–Mar daily 10am–6pm.

Outdoor Pursuits

GOLF The prestigious **Monte Carlo Golf Club,** Route N7, La Turbie (✆ **04-92-41-50-70**), on French soil, is a par-72 course with scenic panoramas. Certain perks (including use of electric carts) are reserved for members. In order to play, nonmembers are asked to show proof of membership and a handicap of at least 35 in another club. Greens fees for 18 holes are 120€ Monday to Friday, 150€ Saturday and Sunday. Clubs rent for 20€. The course is open daily 8am to sunset.

SPA TREATMENTS In 1908, the Société des Bains de Mer launched a seawater (thalassotherapy) spa in Monte Carlo, inaugurated by Prince Albert I. It was bombed during World War II and didn't reopen until 1996. With its splendid views over the port, **Les Thermes Marins de Monte-Carlo,** 2 av. de Monte-Carlo (✆ **377-98-06-69-00;** www.thermesmarinsmontecarlo.com), is one of the largest spas in Europe. Spread over four floors are a pool, Turkish *hammam* (steam bath), diet restaurant, juice bar, fitness center, hair and beauty salons, and private treatment rooms. A day pass, giving access to the sauna, steam rooms, fitness facilities, and pools, costs 90€. Massages cost 98€ for a 30-minute session, and start at 135€ for a 60-minute session.

SWIMMING Overlooking the yacht-clogged harbor, the **Stade Nautique Rainier-III,** quai Albert-1er, in La Condamine (✆ **377-93-30-64-83**), a pool frequented by the Monégasques, was a gift from Prince Rainier to his subjects. It's open May to October daily 9am to 6pm (until 8pm July–Aug). Admission for a one-time visit costs 5.10€ per person; discounts are available if you plan to visit 10 times or more. Between November and April, it's an ice-skating rink. If you want to swim in winter, try the indoor **Piscine du Prince Héréditaire Albert,** in the Stade Louis II, 7 av. de Castellane (✆ **377-92-05-42-13**). It's open Monday, Tuesday, Thursday, and Friday 7:30am to 2:30pm; Saturday 1 to 6pm; and Sunday 8am to 1pm. Admission is 2.30€.

TENNIS & SQUASH The **Monte Carlo Country Club,** 155 av. Princesse-Grace, Roquebrune-Cap-Martin, France (✆ **04-93-41-30-15;** www.mccc.mc), has 21 clay and 2 concrete tennis courts. The 42€ fee provides access to a restaurant, health club with Jacuzzi and sauna, putting green, squash courts, and the well-maintained tennis courts. Guests of the hotels administered by the Société des Bains de Mer (Hôtel de Paris, Hermitage, Mirabeau, and Monte Carlo Beach Club) pay half price. Plan to spend at least half a day, ending a round of tennis with use of any of the other facilities. It's open daily 8am to 8 or 9pm, depending on the season.

A Day at the Beach

Just outside the border, on French soil, the **Monte-Carlo Beach Club** adjoins the Monte-Carlo Beach Hôtel, avenue Princesse-Grace (✆ **04-93-28-66-66;** www.monte-carlo-beach.com). The beach club has thrived for years; it's an integral part of Monaco's social life. Princess Grace used to come here in flowery swimsuits, greeting her friends and subjects with humor and style. The sand is replenished at regular intervals. You'll find two large pools (one for children), cabanas, a restaurant, a cafe, and a bar. As the temperature drops in late August, the beach closes for the winter. The admission charge of 65€ Monday to Friday and 80€ on weekends grants you access to the changing rooms, toilets, restaurants, and bar, and use of a mattress for sunbathing. A fee of 160€ will get you a day's use of a private cabana. Most socializing occurs around the pool's edges. As usual, topless is de rigueur but bottomless isn't.

Monaco, the quintessential kingdom by the sea, offers swimming and sunbathing at the **Plage du Larvotto,** off avenue Princesse-Grace. This strip of beach is free, and the surface is frequently replenished with sand hauled in by barge. Part of it is open; other sections are private and owned by beachside restaurants.

Shopping

If you insist on ultrafancy stores, you'll find them around the Hôtel de Paris and the casino, lining the streets leading to the Hôtel Hermitage, and across from the gardens at the Park Palace minimall. Streets including **place du Casino, avenue des Beaux-Arts,** and **avenue Monte-Carlo** are all within Monte Carlo's Carré d'Or (Golden Square), where you'll find top designers such as Dior, Céline, Louis Vuitton, Hermès, Gucci, Chanel, and Prada.

However, you don't have to be Princess Caroline to shop in Monaco, especially now with **FNAC** (**© 377-93-10-81-81**) in the heart of town. A branch of the big French chain that sells CDs, tapes, and books, it's at the **Métropole Shopping Center,** 17 av. des Spélugues, next to the Hôtel Métropole and across from the casino gardens. The ornate Métropole Shopping Center also has a few specialty shops worth visiting. Check out **Segraeti Five Senses** (**© 377-97-77-34-30;** www.segraeti.com) for the coolest candles and its sister shop **Segraeti Home Collection** for designer kitchen utensils, or **Manufacture de Monaco** (**© 377-93-50-64-63;** www.mdpm.com) for glorious bone china and elegant tabletop items. If the prices make you want to take to your bed, two doors away is a branch of the chic French linen house **Yves Delorme** (**© 377-93-50-08-70**). **Spar Royal Food** (**© 377-93-15-05-04**) is a gourmet grocery store down a set of curving stairs hidden in the side entrance of the mall; here you can buy food from France, Lebanon, and the United States, or stock up for *le pique-nique* or for day trips. This shopping center is open Monday to Saturday 10am to 7:30pm.

For real-people shopping, stroll **rue Grimaldi,** the principality's most commercial street, near the fruit, flower, and food market (see below); and **boulevard des Moulins,** closer to the casino, where you'll see glamorous boutiques. **Rue Princesse-Caroline** is a pedestrian thoroughfare with shops less forbiddingly chic than those along boulevard des Moulins, and it's loaded with bakeries, flower shops, and the closest thing you'll find to funkiness in Monaco. Also check out the **Formule 1** shop, 15 rue Grimaldi (**© 377-93-15-92-44**), where everything from racing helmets to specialty key chains and T-shirts celebrates the roaring, high-octane racing machines. The best place to buy tea in Monaco is **Prince's Tea** at 35 bd. Princesse-Charlotte. The centuries-old Mariage Frères tea range is sold here, as well as a delectable selection of chocolates. You can also stop off here for a quick cup of tea between visiting sites. There's another outlet of this tea shop on avenue de la Costa. For a look at the heart and soul of the real Monaco, head to place d'Armes for the **fruit, flower, and food market,** which starts daily at 7:30am. The indoor and outdoor market has a fountain, cafes, and hand-painted vegetable tiles beneath your feet. The outdoor market packs up at noon, and some dealers at the indoor market stay open to 2pm. If you prefer bric-a-brac, a small but funky (especially for Monaco) flea market, **Les Puces de Fontvieille,** is open on Saturdays 9:30am to 5:30pm on the quai Jean-Charles Rey, immediately adjacent to Port de Fontvieille.

Where to Stay

Accommodations in Monaco are sumptuous in every respect—including the price. A less exciting but cheaper option is to look at midrange hotel chains. Since opening in 2007, **Novotel Monte-Carlo** (✆ **377-99-99-83-00;** www.novotel.com) has flourished on boulevard Princesse-Charlotte near Monte-Carlo's train station. More luxurious is the popular **Le Méridien Beach Plaza** (✆ **377-93-30-98-80;** www.lemeridienmontecarlo.com) on avenue Princesse-Grace overlooking Larvotto Beach.

Alternatively, you'll find prices come down as you literally step across the French border to Beausoleil and Cap d'Ail. The **Rivera Marriott Hotel La Porte de Monaco** (✆ **04-92-10-67-67;** www.marriott.fr) overlooks Cap d'Ail's yachting port and is across the street from Monaco's football stadium.

VERY EXPENSIVE

Fairmont Monte Carlo ★ This modern deluxe four-star hotel hugs the coast below the terraces that support the famous casino, on one of the most valuable pieces of real estate along the Côte d'Azur. Architecturally daring when built (some of its foundations were sunk into the sea bed, and some of the principality's busiest highways roar beneath it), the resort completed a 46€ million renovation in 2009, which added a new spa and roof-top restaurant, **Horizon.** The guest rooms are conservatively furnished with a pastel decor and flooded with light from big windows with views over the town or the sea. The hotel's second restaurant, **L'Argentin** (p. 332), serves grilled steaks, Argentine style.

12 av. des Spélugues, 98000 Monaco. www.fairmont.com/montecarlo. ✆ **377-93-50-65-00.** Fax 377-93-30-01-57. 602 units. 279€–689€ double; from 809€ suite. AE, DC, MC, V. Parking 42€. **Amenities:** 2 restaurants; 2 bars; babysitting; casino; concierge; health club w/sauna; room service. *In room:* A/C, TV, hair dryer, minibar, Wi-Fi (20€).

Hôtel de Paris ★★★ In Monaco's main plaza, opposite the casino, this is one of the world's most famous hotels. The ornate facade has marble pillars, and the reception hall (renovated in 2011) has an Art Nouveau rose window at the peak of the dome. The decor includes marble pillars, statues, crystal chandeliers, sumptuous carpets, Louis XVI chairs, and a wall-size mural. Elegant fabrics, rich carpeting, classic accessories, and an excellent restaurant make this hotel a favorite of the world's most discerning travelers. The guest rooms come in a variety of styles, with period or contemporary furnishings. Some units are enormous. Bathrooms are large, with marble and elegant brass fittings. ***Note:*** The rooms opening onto the sea aren't as spacious as those in the rear. Of the hotel's three restaurants, **Le Grill de l'Hôtel de Paris** and **Le Louis XV** (p. 332) are two of Monaco's most highly respected establishments. With its live piano and jazz, the **American Bar** (p. 334) is always buzzing. When you want to relax, head to the illustrious **Thermes Marins** (p. 326) to swim or indulge in some thalassotherapy.

Place du Casino, 98007 Monaco. www.hoteldeparismontecarlo.com. ✆ **377-98-06-30-00** Fax 377-98-06-59-13. 182 units. 344€–1,250€ double; from 580€ suite. AE, DC, MC, V. Valet parking 38€. **Amenities:** 3 restaurants; bar; babysitting; concierge; health club and spa; pool (indoor); room service; wine cellar. *In room:* A/C, TV, hair dryer, minibar, Wi-Fi (29€).

Hôtel Hermitage ★★★ Picture yourself sitting in an armchair, enjoying a drink under an ornate stained-glass dome with an encircling wrought-iron balcony. You can have all this at the discreet Hôtel Hermitage, just minutes from the place de Casino. The "palace," with its wedding-cake facade, was the creation of Jean Marquet (who also created marquetry). Most rooms have large brass beds and decoratively framed doors that open onto balconies. Even the smallest rooms are medium size, and the largest one is fit for the biggest movie star with the most luggage. Large mirrors, elegant fabrics and upholstery, deluxe bathrooms, and sumptuous beds make living here idyllic. Two floors were recently added to its century-old main building. Guest rooms are modern and sleek in styling. High-season rates apply during Christmas, New Year's, Easter, and July and August. Like its sister Hôtel de Paris, the Hermitage has a direct access to the **Thermes Marins** (p. 326) spa and health club.

Sq. Beaumarchais, 98005 Monaco Cedex. www.hotelhermitagemontecarlo.com. ✆ **377-98-06-40-00.** Fax 377-98-06-59-70. 280 units. 390€–1,080€ double; from 655€ junior suite; from 1,640€ suite. AE, DC, MC, V. Parking 34€. **Amenities:** Restaurant; 2 bars; babysitting; concierge; health club and spa; pool (indoor); room service. *In room:* A/C, TV, hair dryer, minibar, Wi-Fi (20€).

Hôtel Métropole ★★★ In the heart of Monaco, this is the only five-star hotel not owned by the Société des Bains de Mer. Built on the site of the original Métropole, it lies in a leafy oasis on Monte Carlo's *Carré d'Or* (golden square). The hotel is superb in every way and has an array of handsomely furnished and beautifully decorated rooms. Each includes a radio, hypoallergenic pillows, and a full line of toiletries. Spaces are generous and furnishings are classical, including occasional antiques; all come with double-glazing and soothing pastel color schemes. Marble bathrooms have robes and often a whirlpool tub. One of the highlights of this hotel is its cuisine designed by two-Michelin-starred chef Joël Robuchon. The upscale main restaurant serves world-renowned French and international cuisine, while Yoshi features gastronomic Japanese cuisine in a trendy setting. The hotel also has one of Monaco's finest spas with a *hammam*, sauna, caldarium, and scented showers.

4 av. de la Madone, BP 19, 98007 Monaco. www.metropole.com. ✆ **377-93-15-15-15.** Fax 377-93-25-24-44. 146 units. 290€–690€ double; from 490€ suite. AE, DC, MC, V. Parking 35€. **Amenities:** 2 restaurants; bar; babysitting; concierge; pool (outdoor); room service; spa; Wi-Fi (free). *In room:* A/C, TV, hair dryer, minibar, Wi-Fi (free).

Monte Carlo Bay Hotel & Resort ★★★ Occupying a 4-hectare (10-acre) Mediterranean garden, this is the finest hotel in the beachside suburb of Larvotto. It doesn't have the age or tradition of other Société des Bains de Mer properties, such as the Hôtel de Paris and the Hermitage, but it seemingly offers everything else. With a touch of Las Vegas in its styling, it's the most stunningly modern resort Monaco has ever seen.

Built right on the seashore, this is the first time in 75 years the society has launched a new hotel. Its aim is to recapture some of the splendor of the 1920s. Its neoclassical architecture, with arcades and colonnades, has created a new landmark in Monaco. The sumptuous nature of the resort is reflected in its waterfalls, terraces, spacious bedrooms, exotic woods, and lavish marble. Rooms are decorated with white-oak furnishings, often sandstone floors, and soft Mediterranean pastels, and more than three-quarters of them open onto sea views. The pool facilities are second to none, with both an outdoor sandy-bottomed lagoon and an indoor pool within a monumental glass dome. The casino and the famous Jimmy'z Disco have made the hotel one of the hot addresses for after-dark diversions.

40 av. Princesse-Grace, 98000 Monaco. www.montecarlobay.com. ✆ **377-98-06-02-00.** Fax 377-98-06-00-03. 334 units. 215€–950€ double; from 553€ suite. AE, DC, MC, V. Parking 30€. **Amenities:** 3 restaurants; 2 bars; babysitting; casino; concierge; health club and spa; nightclub and disco; 3 pools (indoor, outdoor, children's); room service. *In room:* A/C, TV, DVD player, hair dryer, minibar, Wi-Fi (20€).

EXPENSIVE

Columbus Monte-Carlo Hotel ★★ In the modern Fontvieille suburb of Monaco, this stylish, contemporary hotel faces Princess Grace's rose garden and the sea. Guest rooms are done in what owner Ken McCulloch calls "hybrid hip," a style that evokes Miami and London alike. Elegant touches include Lartigue photos of the Riviera, high-tech cabinets filled with video games, and chocolate-leather furnishings. Guest rooms have deluxe linens and Frette bathrobes. The main disadvantage is that the hotel is in a condo complex whose residents share the pool. The cocktail bar and brasserie are popular with guests and locals alike.

23 av. des Papalins, 98000 Monaco. www.columbushotels.com. ✆ **377-92-05-90-00.** Fax 377-92-05-91-67. 181 units. 160€–300€ double; from 240€ suite. AE, MC, V. Parking 23€. **Amenities:** Brasserie; bar; babysitting; concierge; exercise room; pool (outdoor); room service. *In room:* A/C, TV, hair dryer, minibar.

Hôtel Port Palace ★ Although not quite as grand as the Paris or the Hermitage, this—the first boutique hotel in Monaco—also helps define luxury in the principality. Overlooking the yacht-clogged Port Hercule marina, this four-star hotel is excessively opulent, while prices remain sensible. All units are spacious and elegantly furnished, with state-of-the-art private bathrooms, some of which contain a private steam room. Only first-class materials went into the suites, including rare woods, refined silks, Carrara marble, and premium leather, along with all the modern amenities such as 42-inch plasma TV screens. The hotel's restaurant, **Mandarine,** is one of the finest in Monaco, without offering too serious a challenge to the gourmet citadels at the Hôtel de Paris or the Métropole. Sadly the service rarely lives up to its plush surroundings.

7 av. John F. Kennedy, 98000 Monte-Carlo. www.portpalace.com. ✆ **377-97-97-90-00.** Fax 377-97-97-90-01. 50 suites. 207€–387€ double; from 399€ suite. AE, DC, MC, V. **Amenities:** Restaurant; bar; concierge; health club and spa; room service. *In room:* A/C, TV, hair dryer, Jacuzzi, minibar, Wi-Fi (free).

Ni Hôtel Near place d'Armes, this three-star hotel combines contemporary design with a central location and reasonable prices. Since opening in 2008, its trendy bar has become a nocturnal fixture for the cool Monégasque crowd. Single rooms and some Standard double rooms don't have windows, so check this before you book. All Superior rooms have windows. The suites have rooftop terraces and kitchenettes. Port Hercule and the *Rocher* (the rock where the Old Town lies) are all within a 5-minute walk.

1 bis, rue Grimaldi, Monaco-Ville. www.nihotel-nibar.com. ✆ **377-97-97-51-51.** 17 units. 150€–260€ double; 350€–480€ suite. DC, MC, V. Parking 7.50€. **Amenities:** Bar; fitness room; rooftop terrace. *In room:* A/C, TV, minibar, Wi-Fi (free).

MODERATE

Hôtel Capitole Located in Beausoleil (on French soil literally across the road from Monte Carlo), this hotel is the perfect no-frills option for those wanting to explore central Monaco. Small to medium-size clean bedrooms overlook a quiet street. The friendly staff serves a good-size breakfast. Parking is an additional bonus.

19 bd. Général Leclerc, 06240 Beausoleil. www.hotel-capitole.fr. ✆ **04-93-28-65-65.** Fax 04-93-28-65-69. 56 units. 115€–145€ double. DC, MC, V. Parking 10€. **Amenities:** Babysitting. *In room:* A/C, TV, minibar, Wi-Fi (free).

INEXPENSIVE

Hôtel de France Not all Monégasques are rich, as a stroll along rue de la Turbie will convince you. Here you'll find some of the cheapest accommodations and eateries in the high-priced principality. This 19th-century hotel, 3 minutes from the rail station, has modest furnishings but is well kept and comfortable. The guest rooms are small.

6 rue de la Turbie, 98000 Monaco. www.monte-carlo.mc/france. ✆ **377-93-30-24-64.** Fax 377-92-16-13-34. 24 units. 85€–135€ double. MC, V. Parking 7.50€. **Amenities:** Bar. *In room:* TV, hair dryer, Wi-Fi (1€).

Where to Eat

Each district in Monaco has a distinct ambience. Michelin-starred sophistication glitters in Monte-Carlo's Carre d'Or; Larvotto Beach is lined with informal and family-friendly beach restaurants and the Old Town on the Rocher is chockablock with touristy pizza and pasta restaurants. Meanwhile, Port Hercule is the place to dine on fish: Try **Le Quai des Artistes** at 4 quai Antoine 1er (✆ **377-97-97-97-77**, www.quaidesartistes.com) and the long-standing **Restaurant L'Escale** at 17 bd. Albert 1er (✆ **377-93-30-13-44;** www.restaurant-escale-monaco.com).

VERY EXPENSIVE

Joël Robuchon Monte-Carlo ★★★ MODERN FRENCH Joël Robuchon vies with Ducasse for top position within the pantheon of Michelin-starred Monaco restaurants. His buttery mashed potatoes with truffles attract a loyal following in this conservatively contemporary dining room in the landmark Hôtel Métropole. The menu changes regularly, but dishes likely to remain long-term include grilled filets of John Dory seasoned with "perfumes of the Mediterranean," some of the best lamb chops in France (from the Sisteron region), and crayfish served with crisp-cooked pasta and basil sauce. If you're in the mood for dessert, the "chocolate temptation" is an alluring choice. If you're cutting costs, choose the fixed-price lunch rather than dinner. It includes two glasses of wine per person as part of the all-inclusive price.

In Hôtel Métropole, 4 av. Madone. ✆ **377-93-15-15-10.** Reservations required. Main courses from 34€; fixed-price lunch menus 49€–84€, 7-course dinner without wine 195€. AE, DC, MC, V. Daily 12:15–2pm and 7:30–10:30pm.

Le Grill de l'Hôtel de Paris ★★★ MODERN FRENCH In the flood of publicity awarded to this hotel's street-level restaurant, Le Louis XV (see below), it's been easy to overlook the equally elegant contender on the rooftop. The view alone is worth the expense, with the turrets of the fabled casino on one side and the yacht-clogged harbor of Old Monaco on the other. The decor is gracefully modern, with an ambience somewhat less intense than that in the self-consciously cutting-edge Ducasse citadel downstairs. Despite that, the place is undeniably elegant, with exceptional grilled and spit-roasted meats such as Charolais beef and roasted lamb from the foothills of the nearby Alps. In summer and fair weather, the ceiling opens to reveal the starry sky. The cuisine is backed up by one of the Riviera's finest wine lists, with some 600,000 bottles; the wine cellar is carved out of the rock below. Service is faultless but never intimidating or off-putting.

In the Hôtel de Paris (p. 328), place du Casino. ✆ **377-98-06-88-88.** Reservations required. Main courses 45€–120€. AE, DC, MC, V. Daily noon–2pm and 8–10pm. Closed mid-Jan to early Feb.

Le Louis XV ★★★ FRENCH/ITALIAN Nothing about star chef Alain Ducasse's legendary three-Michelin-starred restaurant in Hôtel de Paris is modest—including its prices. The 17th-century Versailles-style golden chic of Le Louis XV sets the scene for a memorable culinary feast. Star chef Alain Ducasse protégé Franck Cerutti creates elaborate cuisine, served by the finest staff in Monaco. Everything is light and attuned to the seasons, with intelligent, modern interpretations of *provençale* and northern Italian dishes. You'll find everything from imaginative vegetarian dishes such as "Cookpot" (winter vegetable and fruits with Muscat grape juice) to the best oven-roasted blue lobster on the coast. The wine list reads like a who's who of French vineyards—the hotel keeps its collection of rare fine wines in a dungeon chiseled out of the rocks.

In the Hôtel de Paris (p. 328), place du Casino, 98000 Monaco. ✆ **377-98-06-88-64.** www.hoteldeparis montecarlo.com. Reservations recommended. Jacket and tie required for men. Main courses 70€–116€; fixed-price lunch 140€, dinner 210€–280€. AE, MC, V. Thurs–Mon 12:15–1:45pm and 8–9:45pm; also late July to early Sept Wed 8–9:45pm. Closed late Feb to early Mar and late Nov to late Dec.

EXPENSIVE

La Mandarine FRENCH/MEDITERRANEAN Part of the chic Port Palace Hotel, this sixth-floor restaurant lets down its Michelin star and glittering vista of Monte Carlo's harbor with mediocre service. This gourmet restaurant serves cuisine that specializes in fresh, natural ingredients, mostly fashioned into familiar Mediterranean dishes. You can feast on such expensive produce as lobster, tender veal, or a risotto studded with truffles. The ever-changing menu is backed up by one of the best-stocked wine cellars in Monaco, with some 20,000 bottles awaiting your selection—wine lovers can head straight down to the beautiful cellars for a tasting

7 av. John F. Kennedy, 98000 Monte-Carlo. ✆ **377-97-97-90-00.** www.portpalace.com. Main courses 21€–47€; fixed-price lunch 37€–49€; wine tasting (booking required) from 32€. AE, MC, V. Daily noon–2pm and 7:30–10:30pm.

L'Argentin ★ STEAKS/GRILLS Decorated like a very upscale version of what you might have found on the Argentine plains, this stylish restaurant is on the lobby level of the Fairmont Hotel. Within an environment loaded with autumn colors and big windows overlooking the sea, diners enjoy some of the best grilled-meat dishes in town. One of the specialties on which this place has built its name is a *tampiqueña*, a much-marinated spicy filet of beef served with guacamole, salsa, tortillas, and a purée of string beans. An equally succulent choice is a standing hunk of roast beef presented on a wheeled trolley and carved at tableside.

In the Fairmont Monte Carlo (p. 328), 12 av. des Spélugues. ✆ **377-93-50-65-00.** www.fairmont.com/montecarlo. Reservations recommended. Main courses 17€–98€. AE, DC, MC, V. Daily 7–11:30pm.

Rampoldi ★ FRENCH/ITALIAN More than any other restaurant in Monte Carlo, Rampoldi is linked to the charming but somewhat dated interpretation of *la dolce vita.* Opened in the 1950s at the edge of the Casino

Ice Cream Stop

The best place for an ice-cream sundae in Monaco is Le Café de Paris (✆ 377-92-16-20-20) in the place du Casino, the plaza adjacent to the casino and the Hôtel de Paris. Make sure you bag a table outside so you can watch the comings and goings of Monte Carlo's nerve center as you eat.

Gardens and staffed with a mix of old and new, it's more Italian than French in spirit. It also serves the most authentic Italian cuisine in central Monte Carlo. Menu items include an array of pastas, such as tortellini with cream and white-truffle sauce, sea bass roasted in a salt crust, ravioli stuffed with crayfish, and veal kidneys in Madeira sauce. Crêpes Suzette make a spectacular finish.

3 av. des Spélugues. ✆ **377-93-30-70-65.** www.rampoldi.restaurants-montecarlo.com. Reservations required. Main courses 30€–60€. AE, MC, V. Daily 12:15–2:30pm and 7:30–11:30pm.

Trattoria ★★ ITALIAN/TUSCAN Trattoria offers posh Italian fare and splendid views over the sea. Alain Ducasse's newest creation in Monaco has replaced Bar & Boeuf, but still attracts the same international glitterati crowd. The grand master of French cuisine, Ducasse has been in love with Tuscan cooking ever since his first Italian venture (Trattoria Toscana) in 2005. Style comes before authenticity, but you can't fail to be impressed by details such as its focaccia oven, its 1907 Berkel meat slicer, and its huge wine cellar. Culinary highlights include the Salumeria course of Italian cured meats such as black pork Culatello, and ravioli stuffed with aubergine and San Marzano tomatoes.

Le Sporting, Monte Carlo, av. Princesse-Grace, 98000 Monaco. ✆ **377-98-06-71-71.** Reservations recommended. Main courses 19€–39€. AE, DC, MC, V. Mid-May to mid-Sept daily 8pm–1am.

MODERATE

Beefbar ★ 🎁 STEAK/FRENCH One patron said that this restaurant buzzes with a "polyglot crowd of dealmakers, socialites, and preclub beauties," and so it does. A chic crowd comes to this elegant salon overlooking the Mediterranean in Fontvieille to feast on beef from America, Argentina, and Holland. The chef's Black Angus beef from Kansas is some of the best you are likely to find in the south of France. For the noncarnivore, there are many other choices, such as tuna carpaccio and tagliolini with cherry tomatoes and caviar. You can also order lighter fare such as chicken Caesar salad. The carefully sourced menu is backed up by a well-chosen collection of Bordeaux wines. Although you can spend a lot here, the restaurant has bargain-priced lunchtime menus from 14€.

42 quai Jean-Charles Rey. ✆ **377-97-77-09-29.** www.beefbar.com. Reservations required. Main courses 19€–139€. Fixed-priced menus 14€–28€. AE, MC, V. Daily 11:30am–3pm and 7–9:30pm.

INEXPENSIVE

Planet Pasta ★ ITALIAN In a principality where the best restaurants can demand a gold-plated checkbook, this no-nonsense Italian restaurant is a find. Away from the tourist track in a quiet square behind Port Hercule, it's also a popular local haunt. There's a wide choice of pasta, from Trofie pasta quills with basil pesto to artichoke ravioli. It's best to go in summer months when tables spill onto the paving stones overlooking the garden square with its bandstand.

6 rue Imberty. ✆ **377-93-50-80-14**. Reservations recommended. Main courses 9€–14€. MC, V. Mon–Sat noon–2pm and 7:30–11pm.

Stars 'n' Bars ☺ AMERICAN/PACIFIC RIM Modeled on the sports bars popular in the U.S., this place features two dining and drinking areas devoted to American-style food, as well as a bar decorated with memorabilia of notable athletes. No one will mind if you drop in just for a drink, but if you're hungry, the fast food-style menu reads like an homage to the American experience. Try an Indy 500, a Triathlon salad, or the Breakfast of Champions (eggs and bacon and all the fixings). Teenagers are kept happy with plentiful video games, while a staffed play room provides entertainment for toddlers and younger kids.

The owners also operate **Fusion on the Port** (same address, phone, hours, and owners) in a space upstairs from the main dining room with platters inspired by the cuisines of the Pacific Rim such as sushi, tempura, rice-based dishes, and fast-wok-fried dishes of meats and seafood.

6 quai Antoine-1er. ✆ **377-97-97-95-95.** www.starsnbars.com. Reservations recommended. Main courses 11€–39€. AE, DC, MC, V. June–Sept daily 11am–midnight; Oct–May Tues–Sun 11am–midnight.

Monaco After Dark

CASINOS François Blanc developed the **Casino de Monte-Carlo,** place du Casino (✆ **377-98-06-21-21**), into the most famous in the world, attracting the exiled aristocracy of Russia, Sarah Bernhardt, Mata Hari, King Farouk, and Aly Khan. The architect of Paris's Opéra Garnier, Charles Garnier, built the oldest part of the casino, and it remains an example of the 19th century's most opulent architecture. The building encompasses the casino and other areas for different kinds of entertainment, including a theater (Opéra de Monte-Carlo; see below) presenting opera and ballet. Baccarat (chemin de fer and punto banco) and roulette are the most popular games, though you can play craps, blackjack, and thirty and forty as well.

The casino opens at 2pm Monday to Friday, noon on weekends. Doors for the **Salle Blanche**, with its slot machines, for the **Salon Europe,** with its thirty and forty, roulette, and punto banco, and for the **Salle des Amériques,** with its blackjack, craps, and American roulette, open at 2pm daily. Private rooms open Thursday to Sunday at 4pm with more roulette, blackjack, chemin de fer, and punto banco. The gambling continues until very late or early, depending on the crowd. The casino classifies its "private rooms" as the more demure, nonelectronic areas without slots. To enter the casino, you must show a passport or other photo ID, and be at least 18. After 8pm, the staff will insist that men wear jackets and neckties for entrance to the private rooms.

The brightly lit **Sun Casino,** in the Fairmont Monte Carlo, 12 av. des Spélugues (✆ **377-98-06-12-12**), feels more Vegas than Monte Carlo. As well as poker, it also features blackjack, craps, American roulette, and war game (based on the kids game Battleship). Slot machines operate daily noon to 4am, and gaming tables are open daily 5pm to 4am. Admission is free.

The **Opéra de Monte-Carlo** is headquartered in the lavish, Belle Époque **Salle Garnier** of the casino. Tickets to the operas start at 40€. Tickets to events within the Salle Garnier are available from a kiosk in the Atrium du Casino (✆ **377-98-06-28-28;** www.opera.mc), located within the casino; tickets can be purchased Tuesday to Saturday 10am to 5:30pm.

At the **Grimaldi Forum,** 10 av. Princesse-Grace (✆ **377-99-99-30-00** for tickets and information; www.grimaldiforum.com), you can see classical and pop concerts. If tickets are hard to come by, ask your hotel concierge for assistance.

BARS & CLUBS The arrival of **Buddha Bar** in the place de Casino (✆ **377-98-06-19-19**) has brought extravagant bar chic to Monaco's nightlife. East meets west in this high-ceilinged venue that replaces the Cabaret beside the Monte Carlo casino. You can unwind with a cocktail while you gaze upon Monaco's beautiful young crowd or at the extravagant red-and-gold furnishings complete with enormous Buddha. On the other side of the casino square, the **American Bar** (✆ **377-98-06-38-38**) at the Hôtel de Paris is the classic place for a glass of champagne and *barbajuans* (fried ravioli), listening to jazz tinkling on the grand piano. Other hotel bars that are popular with a chic Monégasque crowd include the übertrendy **NiBar** (✆ **377-97-97-51-51;** www.nihotel-nibar.com) at 1 bis rue Grimaldi and the **Columbus** bar (✆ **377-92-05-90-00;** www.columbushotels.com) in Fontvieille. A more informal place to unwind is **La Rascasse** (✆ **377-98-06-16-16;** www.larascassemontecarlo.com), overlooking Port Hercule, which reopened in May 2011 after an extensive refurbishment. In the day it's a place for coffee and Wi-Fi, but at night it transforms into a bar (after 5pm) and later into a nightclub (after 11pm). A relaxed Anglophone crowd can be found drinking beer at **McCarthy's** Irish pub (✆ **377-93-25-87-67**) on rue Portier.

If you'd like a late-night, postdinner boogie squeezed between and even on tables, then you'll like restaurant-cum–piano bar **Le Sass Café,** 11 av. Princesse-Grace (✆ **377-93-25-52-00**). With its deep-red brothel-like decor, it's always packed to the gills with Monaco partygoers. Drinks start at around 15€. A cooler contemporary decor and younger vibe can be found across the street at **Zelos** in the Grimaldi Forum, 10 av. Princesse-Grace (✆ **377-99-99-25-50**). In summertime, ask for a reservation on the outdoor terrace with its sea views.

Grooving at the miniature-size **Le Living Room,** 7 av. des Spélugues near place du Casino (✆ **377-93-50-80-31**), feels like dancing in your own living room. With its retro mirrored decor, it's more sedate than other Monégasque night clubs, but its central location attracts a steady stream of patrons over 35. There's no cover and it's open every night from 10:30pm until dawn.

The summertime showstopper of Monaco's nightlife is **Jimmy'z,** in the Sporting d'Eté, avenue Princesse-Grace (✆ **377-98-06-70-68**), open nightly 11:30pm to dawn from May to September and from Wednesday to Sunday in wintertime. With its roof opened to the skies, you'll be able to spot multiple stars of the stellar and celebrity variety.

Black Legend, quai Albert 1er (✆ **377-93-30-09-09**), is sprawling, ultracontemporary, and bigger than any nightlife venue ever before seen in Monte Carlo. From daytime portside restaurant, the venue is transformed into a nightclub that pays tribute to the Motown era, R&B, and funk. It's open Monday to Saturday year-round until 5am.

ROQUEBRUNE-CAP-MARTIN ★★

953km (592 miles) S of Paris; 5km (3 miles) W of Menton

The coastal resort of Roquebrune-Cap-Martin has been associated with the rich and famous since Empress Eugénie wintered here in the 19th century. In time the resort was honored by the presence of Sir Winston Churchill, who came here often in his final years. Two famous men died here—William Butler Yeats in 1939 and Le Corbusier, who drowned while swimming off the cape in 1965. Don't look for a wide sandy beach—you'll encounter plenty of rocks against a backdrop of pine and olive trees. Along the Grande Corniche lies the medieval hilltop village of Roquebrune. It has been extensively restored, and not even the souvenir shops can spoil its charm. Steep stairways and alleys lead up to its feudal castle crowning the village.

Essentials

GETTING THERE Cap-Martin has **train** and bus connections from the other cities on the coast, including Nice and Menton. For railway information and schedules, call ✆ **36-35,** or visit www.voyages-sncf.com. Trains from Nice to Cap-Martin take 25 minutes and a one-way train ticket costs 3.50€. A frequent **bus service** runs from Nice to Cap-Martin on line no. 100 of the French bus company **Lignes d'Azur** and costs just 1€ one-way. For information, contact **Lignes d'Azur** (✆ **0810-06-10-06;** www.lignesdazur.com).

If you're **driving** from Nice to Roquebrune-Cap-Martin, take A8 motorway east. Turn off the motorway at exit 59 for Menton. Turn onto the D2566 to Menton, then take D6007 through Menton and towards Monaco before arriving into Roquebrune-Cap-Martin.

VISITOR INFORMATION The **Office de Tourisme** is at 218 av. Aristide-Briand (✆ **04-93-35-62-87;** fax 04-93-28-57-00; www.roquebrune-cap-martin.com).

Exploring the Town

Exploring Roquebrune's old village will take about an hour. You can stroll through its colorful covered streets, which retain their authentic look even though the buildings are now devoted to handicrafts, gift and souvenir shops, and art galleries.

Château de Roquebrune (✆ **04-93-35-07-22**) was originally a 10th-century Carolingian castle; the present structure dates in part from the 13th century. Dominated by two square towers affording a panoramic view of the coast, today the Château houses a museum. The interior is open in July and August daily 10am to 12:30pm and 3 to 7:30pm; April to June and September daily 10am to 12:30pm and 2 to 6:30pm; February, March, and October daily 10am to 12:30pm and 2 to 6pm; November to January daily 10am to 12:30pm and 2 to 5pm. Admission is 3.70€ for adults, 1.60€ students and children 7 to 11, and free for children 6 and under.

Rue du Château leads to place William-Ingram. Cross this square to rue de la Fontaine and take a left. This leads you to chemin de Menton, where you'll find the **Olivier Millénaire (Millenary Olive Tree),** one of the oldest trees in the world—it's at least 1,000 years old.

On rue du Grimaldi is **Eglise Ste-Marguerite,** which hides behind a relatively common baroque facade that masks the 12th-century church. It's not entirely from that time, however, having undergone many alterations over the years. The interior is of polychrome plaster. Look for two paintings by a 17th-century local artist, Marc-Antoine Otto, who painted a Crucifixion (in the second altar) and a Pietà (above the entrance door). It's open Monday to Saturday 2 to 5pm.

The coastal satellite of Roquebrune-Cap-Martin is a rich town. At the center of the cape is a feudal tower that's now a telecommunications relay station. At its base you can see the ruins of the **Basilique St-Martin,** a priory constructed by the monks of the Lérins Islands in the 11th century. Privately owned, it is not open to visitors. After pirate raids in later centuries, notably around the 15th century, it was destroyed and abandoned. If you follow the road (by car) along the eastern shoreline of the cape, you'll be rewarded with a view of Menton against a backdrop of mountains. In the far distance looms the Italian Riviera, and you can see as far as the resort of Bordighera.

You can take one of the most interesting walks along the Riviera here. It lasts about 3 hours. The coastal path, **Sentier Touristique ★**, leads from Cap-Martin to the border with Monte-Carlo beneath the **Monte-Carlo Country Club** (tennis club) along boulevard du Larvotto. If you have a car, you can park in the lot at avenue Winston-Churchill and begin your stroll. A sign labeled PROMENADE LE CORBUSIER marks the path. As you go along, you'll take in a view of Monaco set in a natural amphitheater. In the distance, you'll see Cap-Ferrat and even Roquebrune.

If you have a car, you can take a **scenic 9.5km (6-mile) drive ★**. Leave the town on D23, following signs to Gorbio, a village on a hill reached by this winding road. Along the way you'll pass homes of the wealthy and view a verdant setting with pines and silvery olives. The site is wild and rocky, and the buildings were constructed to withstand pirate attacks. The most interesting street is rue Garibaldi, which leads past an old church to a panoramic belvedere.

Where to Stay

Hôtel Victoria ★ This rectangular low-rise building is behind a garden in front of the Roquebrune-Cap-Martin beach. Built in the 1970s, it was renovated in the mid-1990s in a neoclassical style that weds tradition and modernity. Traditionally it's the second choice in town for those who can't afford the Vista Palace (below). Each of the midsize rooms is well furnished with contemporary furniture; some open onto balconies fronting the sea. The casual bar and lounge sets a stylishly relaxed tone. Breakfast is the only meal served.

7 promenade du Cap, 06190 Roquebrune-Cap-Martin. www.hotel-victoria.fr. ✆ **04-93-35-65-90.** Fax 04-93-28-27-02. 32 units. 109€–174€ double. AE, DC, V. Limited free parking outdoors; 10€ indoors. **Amenities:** Bar. *In room:* A/C, TV, minibar.

Hôtel Vista Palace ★ This extraordinary hotel and restaurant stands above Cap-Martin on the outer ridge of the mountains running parallel to the coast, giving it a spectacular "airplane view" of Monaco. The design of the Vista Palace is just as fantastic: Three levels are cantilevered out into space so every unit seems to float. Nearly all the rooms have balconies facing the Mediterranean. Sadly, the interior decor does not live up to the grandeur of its surroundings: The tired bedroom furnishings could do with an upgrade. Guests are pampered with leisure facilities such as a pool, health club, and private beach.

1551 rte. de la Grande Corniche, 06190 Roquebrune-Cap-Martin. www.vistapalace.com. ✆ **04-92-10-40-00.** Fax 04-93-35-18-94. 70 units. 212€–382€ double; from 467€ suite. Rates include breakfast. AE, DC, V. Free parking. **Amenities:** 2 restaurants; bar; babysitting; private beach; health club w/Jacuzzi; pool (outdoor); room service. *In room:* A/C, TV, hair dryer, minibar, Wi-Fi (8€).

Les Deux Frères ★ "The Two Brothers" (its English name) hangs over the Mediterranean with Monaco in the distance. This is a *restaurant avec chambres* (restaurant with guest rooms) and offers some of the best room deals in this pricey resort area. The hotel/restaurant was created from an 1854 schoolhouse, and each of the small to medium-size bedrooms has a different theme, opening onto the square, the sea, or a mountain view. A mahogany bar takes up much of the lobby, and a narrow staircase leads up to the bathrooms. In addition to the celebrated restaurant, a cafe named *Fraise et Chocolat* (Strawberry and Chocolate) stands next to the hotel and serves a choice of sandwiches and drinks.

1 place Deux Frères, 06190 Roquebrune-Cap-Martin. www.lesdeuxfreres.com. ✆ **04-93-28-99-00.** Fax 04-93-28-99-10. 10 units. 75€–110€ double. MC, V. **Amenities:** Restaurant; cafe; bar. *In room:* A/C, TV, Wi-Fi (free).

Where to Eat

Les Deux Frères (see above) is well known for its gastronomic French cuisine. If you're bored of overpriced and overfussy French cuisine, head to **Zapp** (✆ **04-93-52-20-20;** www.zappmonaco.com) on avenue de France. With its wide menu that ranges from Tex-Mex to Swedish specialties to Ben & Jerry's ice cream, this fast-food restaurant delivers quality.

Au Grand Inquisiteur ★ TRADITIONAL FRENCH This 28-seat restaurant occupies a two-room vaulted cellar near the top of the medieval mountaintop village of Roquebrune. On the steep, winding road to the château, the building is made of rough-cut stone, with large oak beams. The cuisine, though not the area's most distinguished, is good, including the chef's duck special and the beef fillet chateaubriand. The wine list is exceptional—some 150 selections, most at reasonable prices. Curiously, the kitchen is situated in a separate village house across the street from the restaurant.

18 rue du Château. ✆ **04-93-35-05-37.** www.augrandinquisiteur.com. Reservations required. Fixed-price menu 25€–38€. AE, MC, V. Sat–Sun noon–2pm; Tues–Sun 7:30–9:30pm. Closed Jan.

MENTON ★★

959km (596 miles) S of Paris; 63km (39 miles) NE of Cannes; 8km (5 miles) E of Monaco

Menton feels more Italianate than French. Right at the border of Italy, Menton marks the eastern frontier of the Côte d'Azur. Its climate is the warmest on the Mediterranean coast, and in winter it attracts a large crowd of British seniors.

According to a local legend, Eve was the first to experience Menton's glorious climate. When she and Adam were expelled from the Garden of Eden, she tucked a lemon in her bosom, planting it at Menton because it reminded her of her former stamping grounds. Lemons still grow in profusion here, and the fruit is given a position of honor at the Lemon Festival held over a 2-week period in February. Actually, the oldest Menton visitor might have arrived 30,000 years ago. He's still around—or, at least, his skull is—in the Musée de Préhistoire Régionale (see below).

Essentials

GETTING THERE Menton has good **rail** and **bus** connections. Two trains per hour pull in from Nice (trip time 35 min.; one-way fare 4.60€), and two trains per hour arrive from Monte Carlo (trip time 10 min.; 2€ one-way). For rail information and schedules, call ✆ **36-35,** or visit www.voyages-sncf.com. **Buses** run every 15 minutes from Nice via Monaco to Menton on line no. 100 of the French bus company **Lignes d'Azur** (✆ **08-10-06-10-06;** www.lignesdazur.com).

Many visitors arrive by **car** on one of the corniche roads. The drive on N7 east from Nice takes 45 minutes.

VISITOR INFORMATION The **Office de Tourisme** is in the Palais de l'Europe, 8 av. Boyer (✆ **04-92-41-76-76;** www.villedementon.com).

SPECIAL EVENTS Menton is famed for its lemons. Each February to March, these citrus fruits are celebrated in a 2-week **Fête du Citron** where thousands of lemons and oranges are piled up in zesty creations around the Jardin Biovès (opposite the Menton tourist office). For tickets and information, call ✆ **04-92-41-76-95** or visit www.feteducitron.com.

Exploring the Town

Menton is situated on the Golfe de la Paix (Gulf of Peace) on a rocky promontory that divides the bay in two. The fishing town, the older part with its narrow streets, is in the east; the tourist zone and residential belt are in the west.

The filmmaker, poet, and artist Jean Cocteau liked this resort, and in the **Musée Jean-Cocteau,** Bastion du Vieux Port, quai Napoleon-III (✆ **04-93-57-72-30**), you can see his death portrait, sketched by MacAvoy. Some of the artist's memorabilia is here—stunning charcoals and watercolors, brightly colored pastels, ceramics, and signed letters. The museum is open Wednesday through Monday from 10am to noon and 2 to 6pm. Admission is 3€; it's free for children 17 and under.

At **La Salle des Mariages,** in the Hôtel de Ville (Town Hall), rue de la République (✆ **04-92-10-50-00**), Cocteau painted frescoes depicting the legend of Orpheus and Eurydice, also the subject of his film *Orphée*. A tape in English helps explain them. The room, with its red-leather seats and leopard-skin rugs, is used for civil marriage ceremonies. It's open Monday to Friday 8:30am to 12:30pm and 2 to 5pm. Admission is 2€; it's free for children 17 and under. Advance reservations are necessary.

Musée de Préhistoire Régionale, rue Lorédan-Larchey (✆ **04-93-35-84-64**), presents human evolution on the Côte d'Azur for the past million years. It contains the 25,000-year-old head of the *Nouvel Homme de Menton* (sometimes known as "Grimaldi Man"), found in 1884 in the Baousse-Rousse caves. Audiovisual aids, dioramas, and videocassettes enhance the exhibition. The museum is open Wednesday to Monday 10am to noon and 2 to 6pm. Admission is free.

Musée des Beaux-Arts, Palais Carnolès, 3 av. de la Madone (✆ **04-93-35-49-71**), contains 14th-, 17th- and 18th-century paintings from Italy, Flanders, Holland, and the French schools, as well as modern paintings by Dufy, Valadon, Derain, and Leprin—all acquired by a British subject, Wakefield-Mori. The museum is open Wednesday to Monday 10am to noon and 2 to 6pm. Admission is free.

A Day at the Beach

Menton's beaches stretch for 3.2km (2 miles) between the Italian border and the city limits of Roquebrune and are interrupted only by the town's old and new ports. On the western side of Menton, you'll find the free public beach **La Plage de la Promenade du Soleil.** Don't expect soft sands or even any sand at all: This beach is narrow, covered with gravel (or, more charitably, big pebbles), and notoriously uncomfortable to lie on. Don't expect big waves or tides, either. Who goes there? In the words of one nonswimming resident, mostly Parisians or residents of northern France, who are grateful for any escape from their urban milieu. To the right of the Vieux Port, sand has been imported for the private sandy beaches of Menton Garavan, home to beach restaurants with mattresses and parasols to rent. Private beach restaurant **Les Sablettes** (✆ **04-93-35-44-77**) serves great fish and charges around 10€ for use of a mattress. Further east is a small, pebble beach off Promenade Reine Astrid that's usually quieter than those in the centre of town. Topless bathing is widespread, but complete nudity is forbidden.

Where to Stay

Despite some splendid period architecture, many hotels and B&Bs around Menton are badly in need of updating. Happily, there are some notable exceptions.

Hôtel Méditerranée This white-and-salmon-colored hotel is 3 short blocks from the sea, and as a result it's further from the busy beachfront promenade. A raised terrace with a view of the water, chaise longues, and potted plants are on the premises. The rooms are attractively decorated and include private balconies opening onto the sea. Most rooms are spacious, with comfortable beds (usually twins). The hotel also has a restaurant, which offers a veranda for dining in fair weather.

5 rue de la République, 06500 Menton. www.hotel-med-menton.com. ✆ **04-92-41-81-81.** Fax 04-92-41-81-82. 89 units. 76€–112€ double. Children 4 and under stay free in parent's room. AE, DC, MC, V. Parking 15€. **Amenities:** Restaurant; bar. *In room:* A/C, TV, hair dryer, minibar, Wi-Fi (free).

Hôtel Napoléon 🎁 This three-star hotel is one of the best in Menton. It sits on a palm-shaded avenue, just across from a beach, where it maintains an excellent restaurant and a scattering of parasols and chaise longues. There's also a well-maintained outdoor pool and fitness area. Guest rooms have contemporary furniture, vivid, colors and comfortable beds, and some have balconies overlooking the sea. The cheapest and quietest rooms face the back garden. As well as free Wi-Fi, each bedroom has its own iPod dock.

29 Porte de France, 06503 Menton. www.napoleon-menton.com. ✆ **04-93-35-89-50.** Fax 04-93-35-49-22. 44 units. 104€–179€ double; 209€–299€ suite. AE, DC, MC, V. Free parking. **Amenities:** Bar; exercise room; pool (outdoor); private beach. *In room:* A/C, TV, hair dryer, iPod dock, minibar, Wi-Fi (free).

Hôtel Princesse & Richmond Since the opening of its reasonably priced restaurant Le Galet in 2008, the reputation of this well-run hotel has been enhanced. The building is a 1970s-style boxy structure with an angular design. The comfortable, soundproof, midsize rooms have modern and French traditional furnishings and balconies. With its Jacuzzi and fitness room, the roof terrace offers views of the curving coastline.

MERCANTOUR: THE lungs OF SOUTHERN FRANCE

The 70,000-hectare (173,000-acre) **Mercantour National Park** (www.mercantour.eu) is a sparsely populated haven for endangered fauna and flora, including wild orchids, bearded vultures, and golden eagles. Since 1992, it has been a hiding place for wolves: You can visit the wolf packs and listen to the fierce debate between ecologists and shepherds at **Scénoparc** (✆ **04-93-02-33-69;** www.alpha-loup.com) in Saint-Martin Vésubie.

In the **Vallée des Merveilles** (www.tendemerveilles.com) near Tende, you can trek through springtime meadows dotted with wild orchids and rhododendrons on your way to visit Europe's largest collection of prehistoric rock engravings. From June to September, you can board the themed **Train des Merveilles** (✆ **04-93-04-92-05;** www.royabevera.com), which runs daily at 9am from Nice to Tende with an onboard tour guide (English-language guides are available). If you're driving from Menton, cross the border into Italy. Take the SS1DIR and SP1 to Ventimiglia, then north on the SS20 towards Colle di Tenda. You cross back onto French soil on the D6204/E74 towards Breuil-sur-Roya and then Tende.

Mercantour is also a mecca for adventurous travelers for everything from trekking to watersports. The **Gorges de Saorge** near Breuil-sur-Roya are popular for canoeing, tubing, kayaking, rafting, and canyoning. Tour outfitters here include Roya Evasion (✆ **04-93-04-91-46;** www.royaevasion.com) and Mat & Eau (✆ **06-81-56-21-56;** www.mat-et-eau.com). When the waters are fuller in springtime, the papercut-thin **Gorges de Daluis** in the Vallée de la Tinée are the place to go for canoeing and aquatic hiking (hiking through water) with Les Eskimos à L'Eau (✆ **06-11-38-02-82;** www.eskimosaleau.com), based in Nice.

617 promenade du Soleil, 06500 Menton. www.princess-richmond.com. ✆ **04-93-35-80-20.** Fax 04-93-57-40-20. 46 units. 90€–138€ double; 183€–231€ suite. AE, DC, MC, V. Parking 6€–9€. Closed Nov to mid-Dec. **Amenities:** Restaurant; bar; exercise room; Jacuzzi; room service. *In room:* A/C, TV, hair dryer, minibar, Wi-Fi (free).

Hotel Riva ★ A few steps across the seafront boulevard from the beach, this three-star hotel has an angular design punctuated with balconies and multileveled terraces. Bedrooms are small to medium in size but are elegantly furnished with quality mattresses and fine linens. High-quality materials such as marble and granite are used throughout, complementing dignified beechwood furniture. Other than breakfast and brunch, no meals are served, but considering the proximity of many restaurants, no one seems to mind.

600 promenade du Soleil, 06500 Menton. www.rivahotel.com. ✆ **04-92-10-92-10.** Fax 04-93-28-87-87. 40 units. 90€–131€ double. AE, DC, MC, V. Parking 10€. **Amenities:** Bar; babysitting; Jacuzzi; sauna; Wi-Fi (free). *In room:* A/C, TV, minibar, hair dryer, Wi-Fi (free).

Where to Eat

Le Mirazur ★ FRENCH The lofty molecular cuisine served at this Michelin-starred restaurant matches its lofty location; located on a hilltop, the dining room offers dramatic views over the coastline towards Roquebrune-Cap-Martin. The midweek lunchtime menu, at 29€, is the best way of being introduced to chef Mauro Colagreco's complicated tapas-style food. The a la carte menu offers a choice of three mysterious starters: *chlorophylle* (vegetarian), *terra* (meat), or *acqua* (fish). Despite its grandeur and Michelin status, the service here can be hit or miss; however, Le Mirazur is still Menton's classiest restaurant.

30 av. Aristide Briand. ✆ **04-92-41-86-86.** Main courses 39€; fixed-price lunch 29€–55€, dinner 55€–105€. AE, MC, V. Mid-Feb to Oct Wed–Sun 12:30–2pm and 7–10pm; mid-July to mid-Aug Sat–Sun 12:30–2pm and Tues–Sun 7–10pm.

Petit Port FRENCH Small and charming, with enough Italian overtones to make you believe that you've finally crossed the border, this restaurant occupies a cozy, partially paneled dining room in a century-old house near the medieval port of Menton. Surrounded by nautical accents and oil paintings of the wide, blue sea, you'll enjoy a menu that is strong on fish and seafood. Tasty specialties include grilled sardines, fish soup, and many different kinds of grilled fish. The kitchen will prepare the day's catch in whatever way your taste dictates.

4 rue Jonquier, at place Fontana. ✆ **04-93-35-82-62.** Reservations recommended. Main courses 20€–50€. AE, MC, V. Thurs–Mon noon–2:30pm and 7–11pm (daily July–Aug).

PLANNING YOUR TRIP TO PROVENCE & THE RIVIERA

8

In the following pages you will find all the information you need on traveling to Provence and the Riviera. There are tips on transport to and within the region, information on the various types of accommodation available, as well as essential facts about Provence that will help you to make the most of your visit to this part of France.

GETTING THERE

From North America

BY PLANE

THE MAJOR U.S. CARRIERS All major airlines fly to Paris from the U.S. cities listed below. Once you fly into Orly (ORY) or Roissy-Charles-de-Gaulle (CDG), you can fly **Air France** (✆ **800/237-2747;** www.airfrance.com) or **KLM** (✆ **800/618-0104;** www.klm.com) to reach your destination in Languedoc, Provence, or the Riviera. From Orly or Charles de Gaulle, there are flights to Marseille, Nice, Perpignan, and Avignon.

American Airlines (✆ **800/433-7300;** www.aa.com) offers daily flights to Paris from Dallas–Fort Worth, Chicago, Miami, Boston, and New York. **Delta Airlines** (✆ **800/241-4141;** www.delta.com) flies nonstop to Paris from Atlanta, Cincinnati, and New York. Note that Delta is the only American airline offering nonstop service from New York to Nice, although Air France also has direct flights.

Continental Airlines (✆ **800/231-0856;** www.continental.com) flies nonstop to Paris from Newark and Houston. **US Airways** (✆ **800/428-4322;** www.usairways.com) offers nonstop service from Philadelphia to Paris.

THE FRENCH NATIONAL CARRIER **Air France** (✆ **800/237-2747;** www.airfrance.com) offers nonstop flights between New York and Nice and also offers regular flights between Paris and such North American cities as Newark; Washington, D.C.; Miami; Atlanta; Boston; Cincinnati; Chicago; New York; Houston; San Francisco; Los Angeles; Montreal; Toronto; and Mexico City.

THE MAJOR CANADIAN CARRIER Canadians usually choose the **Air Canada** (✆ **888/247-2262** in the U.S. and Canada; www.aircanada.com) flights to Paris from Toronto and Montreal that depart every evening.

From Paris

BY PLANE

From Paris, if you're heading for the French Riviera, your connecting flight will probably land you in Nice's international airport, **Aéroport Nice–Côte d'Azur** (✆ **08-20-42-33-33;** www.nice.aeroport.fr) There are also airports at Avignon, Marseille, Montpellier, Nîmes, and Perpignan.

BY TRAIN

The world's fastest trains link some 50 French cities, allowing you to get from Paris to just about anywhere else in the country in hours. With 39,000km (24,233 miles) of track and about 3,000 stations, **SNCF** (French national railroads; www.voyages-sncf.com) is known for its on-time performance. You can travel in first or second class by day and in couchette by night. Many trains have dining facilities.

INFORMATION If you plan to travel a lot on European railroads, get the latest copy of the *European Rail Timetable.* This 500-plus-page book documents all of Europe's main passenger rail services with detail and accuracy. It's available online at www.raileurope.com.

In the United States: For more information and to purchase rail passes before you leave, contact **Rail Europe** (✆ **1-800/622-8600;** www.raileurope.com).

In Canada: Contact **Rail Europe** (✆ 1-800/361-RAIL [7245]; www.raileurope.com).

In London: Contact **Rail Europe,** 179 Piccadilly, London W1V 0BA (✆ **0844/848-4064;** www.raileurope.com).

In Paris: For information or reservations, go online (www.voyages-sncf.fr) or call ✆ **36-35.** You can also go to any local travel agency. A simpler way to buy tickets is to use the *billetterie* (ticket machine) in every train station. If you know your PIN, you can use a credit card to buy your ticket.

FRANCE RAIL PASSES Working cooperatively with SNCF, Air Inter Europe, and Avis, Rail Europe offers flexible rail passes that can reduce travel costs considerably. The **France Railpass** (www.railfrance.com) provides unlimited rail transport in France for between 3 and 9 days within 1 month. The **France Rail 'n' Drive Pass,** available only in North America, combines good value on both rail travel and Avis or Hertz car rentals, and is best used by arriving at a major rail depot and then exploring the countryside by car. It includes the France Railpass and use of a rental car. You have 1 month to complete your travel on this pass that grants 2 days of unlimited train travel and 2 days of car rental with unlimited mileage in France.

EURAIL **Eurail** (www.eurail.com) has a variety of different passes that are valid for travel throughout France and other European countries. It is strongly recommended that you purchase passes before you leave home, as not all offers are available in Europe.

BY CAR

For more information on getting to each city and town in this book from within France, see the "Getting There" section of the town of interest.

From Elsewhere in Europe

BY EUROTUNNEL & FERRY FROM GREAT BRITAIN

Ferries and Eurotunnel trains operate day and night in all seasons, with only the occasional ferry cancellation during storms. **Eurotunnel** (✆ **0844/335-3535;** www.eurotunnel.com) trains take cars, buses, trucks, and passengers from Folkestone through the Channel Tunnel to the Coquelles terminal just outside Dover. The crossing takes 35 minutes, and fares vary considerably depending on how far in advance you book.

The leading operator of ferries across the channel is **P&O Ferries** (✆ **0871/664-6464;** www.poferries.com). The fastest route is the 90-minute crossing between Dover and Calais, of which there are 23 a day. Fares start at £35 each way for a car and up to nine passengers.

BY PLANE

Although **Air France** (✆ 0870/142-4343; www.airfrance.com) and **British Airways** (✆ 0844/493-0787; www.ba.com) fly frequently to Paris and further south, many people traveling from the United Kingdom choose the budget airlines. **Ryanair** (✆ 0871/246-0000; www.ryanair.com), **easyJet** (✆ 0843/104-5000; www.easyjet.com), **bmi** (✆ 0844/848-4888; www.flybmi.com), **Flybe** (✆ 0871/700-2000; www.flybe.com), and **Jet2** (✆ 0871/226-1737; www.jet2.com) have flights to Languedoc and Provence destinations from airports all over the United Kingdom, including Manchester, Birmingham, Leeds, Southampton, and Edinburgh.

BY TRAIN

Eurostar (✆ **0843/218-6186;** www.eurostar.com) operates regular trains from St. Pancras International station in London to numerous destinations in Provence and Languedoc. Passengers change trains either in Paris or Lille, and in the summer there are direct trains from London to Avignon.

The south of France is connected to Spain and Italy by rail. Trains from Montpellier go to Barcelona, Spain, and you can reach Milan, Italy, from Marseille and Nice. Check the timetables on the **SNCF** website (www.voyages-sncf.com), and the websites of the national railways of Spain (www.renfe.es) and Italy (www.ferroviedellostato.it).

GETTING AROUND

The most charming Provençal villages and best country hotels always seem to lie away from the main cities and train stations. Renting a car is usually the best way to travel once you get to the south of France, especially if you plan to explore in depth and not stick to the standard route along the coast.

The south of France also has one of the most reliable bus and rail transportation systems in Europe. Trains connect all the major cities and towns, such as Nice and Avignon. Where the train leaves off, you can most often rely on local bus service.

By Bus

While the trains are faster and more efficient if you are traveling between major cities, if you are traveling between the towns and villages of Languedoc and Provence, including the French Riviera, you may want to take the bus. You can use the network of buses that link the villages and hamlets with each other and the major cities to get off the beaten path.

Plan to take advantage of the bus services from Monday to Saturday when they run frequently; very few buses run on Sunday. **Sodetrav** (✆ **08-25-00-06-50** or 04-94-12-55-12; www.sodetrav.fr) has some of the best bus routes, and is especially strong in the western Riviera, taking in stopovers at such destinations as St-Raphaël, St-Tropez, Arles, Grasse, Avignon, Marseille, Nîmes, and Hyères. One of its most popular routes is the run between Toulon and St-Tropez.

Contact information for buses to specific towns can be found in the "Getting There" section of each individual town and city.

By Car

Driving in France can be a pleasure, thanks to its large and efficient network of highways, or autoroutes, which are prefixed by A. Apart from certain days in July and August when the entire country decamps to the south and traffic jams lasting 10 hours are not uncommon, the autoroutes are relatively empty. This comes at a price, however, as they are toll roads and cost money. The 7-hour journey between Paris and Marseille, for example, could cost about 40€ in tolls. The *routes nationales,* or RNs, are free but usually cluttered with slow-moving trucks and caravans.

CAR RENTALS To rent a car, you'll need to present a passport, a driver's license, and a credit card. You'll also have to meet the minimum-age requirement of the company. (For the least expensive cars, this is 21 at Hertz, 23 at Avis, and 25 at Budget. More expensive cars might require that you be at least 25.) Be aware that the excess you have to pay if the car is damaged can be extremely high. Car-rental companies will offer you insurance against that, but their policies are generally expensive. Check with your travel insurance policy or credit card to see if you're covered. Note also that automatic transmission is not common in Europe, so cars that come with it are among the most expensive.

For rentals of more than 7 days, in most cases cars can be picked up in one French city and dropped off in another, but there are additional charges. **Budget** (www.budget.com) has numerous locations in southern France, including those in **Avignon** at the airport (✆ 04-90-87-17-75); in **Marseille** at the airport (✆ 04-42-14-24-55) and at 40 bd. de Plombières (✆ 04-91-64-40-03); and in **Nice** at the airport (✆ 04-93-21-36-50).

Hertz (www.hertz.com) is also well represented, with offices in **Avignon** at the airport (✆ 04-90-84-19-50) and at the train station (✆ 04-32-74-62-80); in **Marseille** at the airport (✆ 08-25-09-13-13) and at 15 bd. Maurice-Bourdet (✆ 04-91-14-04-24); in **Montpellier** at the airport (✆ 04-67-20-04-64); and in **Nice** at the airport (✆ 08-25-34-23-43). When making inquiries, be sure to ask about promotional discounts.

Avis (www.avis.com) has offices in **Avignon** at the airport (✆ 04-90-87-17-75) and at the railway station (✆ 04-90-27-96-10); in **Marseille** at the airport (✆ 04-42-14-21-67) and at 267 bd. National (✆ 04-91-50-70-11); in **Montpellier** at the airport (✆ 04-67-20-14-95) and at the railway station (✆ 04-67-92-92-00); and in **Nice** at the airport (✆ 04-93-21-36-33) and at place Masséna, 2 av. des Phocéens (✆ 04-93-80-63-52).

National (www.nationalcar.com) is represented in France by Europcar, with locations in **Avignon** at the train station (✆ 04-90-27-30-07); in **Marseille** at the airport (✆ 04-42-14-24-90) and at the St-Charles train station, 96 bd. Rabatau (✆ 04-91-83-05-05); in **Montpellier** at the airport (✆ 04-67-15-13-47); and in **Nice** at the airport (✆ 04-93-21-80-90). You can rent a car on the spot at any of these offices, but lower rates are available by making advance reservations from North America.

Two United States–based agencies that don't have offices in France but act as booking agents for France-based agencies are **Kemwel Drive Group** (✆ **877/820-0668** or 207/842-2285; www.kemwel.com) and **Auto Europe** (✆ **888/223-5555;** www.autoeurope.com). These can make bookings in the United States only, so call before your trip.

GASOLINE Known in France as *essence,* gas is expensive for those accustomed to North American prices. Most rental cars will run on the octane rating of 95, so look for pumps marked *sans plomb* 95. Diesel is known as *gazole.*

Note: Sometimes you can drive for miles in rural France without encountering a gas station, so don't let your tank get dangerously low. More and more stations are unstaffed and customers have to use their card to pay at the pump. If you're paying with cash, make certain you see that someone is in the payment office, called a *caisse.* If you don't want to pay the high prices at the stations on the autoroutes, look for supermarket stations such as Auchan, Leclerc, Intermarché, or SuperU in the *centres commercials* zones of superstores that ring towns and cities.

DRIVING RULES Everyone in the car, in both the front and the back seats, must wear seat belts. Children 11 and under must ride in the back seat. Drivers are supposed to yield to the car on their right, except where signs indicate otherwise, as at traffic circles.

If you violate the speed limit, expect a big fine. Those limits are about 130kmph (81 mph) on expressways, about 110kmph (68 mph) on major national highways, and 90kmph (56 mph) on country roads. All of these speeds are reduced by 10kmph (6 miles) when it rains. In towns, don't exceed 50kmph (31 mph). Speed cameras are a common sight, as are speed traps.

MAPS The Michelin series of yellow road atlases is the best for driving in France. They are clearly laid out, and include rest stops, service stations, restaurants, and toll road payment stops, known as *péages.* They also contain useful information about road safety in France, as well as maps of the major cities. Big travel-book stores in North America carry these maps, and they're commonly available in France (at lower prices).

BREAKDOWNS/ASSISTANCE A breakdown is called *une panne* in France. Call the police at ✆ **17** anywhere in France to be put in touch with the nearest garage. If the breakdown occurs on an expressway, find the nearest roadside emergency phone box, pick up the phone, and put a call through. You'll be connected to the nearest breakdown service facility.

By Plane

Air France (✆ **800/237-2747;** www.airfrance.com) serves about eight cities in France. Air travel time from Paris to almost anywhere in France is about an hour.

By Train

Rail services between the large cities of Languedoc-Roussillon and Provence and the French Riviera are excellent. If you don't have a car, you can tour all the major cities by train. Of course, with a car you can also explore the hidden villages, but for short visits with only major stopovers on your itinerary, such as Nice and Avignon, the train should suffice. Service is fast and frequent.

Montpellier is a major transportation hub for the Languedoc-Roussillon area, and it's on the TGV route from Paris. Montpellier also has good rail connections to Avignon. The ancient city of Nîmes, one of the most visited in the area, also is a major rail terminus, a stop on the rail link between Paris and Perpignan.

Marseille, the largest city in the south of France, has rail connections with all major towns on the Riviera as well as with the rest of France.

The major rail transportation hub along the French Riviera is Nice, although Cannes also enjoys good train connections. Nice and Monaco are linked by frequent service with the rapid TGV train from Paris to Marseille. In winter, the schedule is curtailed depending on demand. Monaco also has excellent rail links along the Riviera.

The website for the national rail service is www.voyages-sncf.com. Otherwise, call ✆ **36-35,** or 08-92-35-35-35 when outside France.

TIPS ON ACCOMMODATIONS

The French government rates hotels on a one- to five-star system. In 2011, a new rating of "palace" (or *palais*) rating was given to a small number of luxury hotels, which takes them beyond the five-star rating. Only one is in Provence and the Riviera, the Grand Hôtel du Cap Ferrat in St-Jean-Cap-Ferrat, and all hotels will have their "palace" rating reviewed after 5 years. Generally speaking, one-star hotels are budget accommodations; two-star lodgings are good tourist hotels; three stars go to high-quality hotels; and four and five stars are reserved for deluxe accommodations. Travelers will notice that the number of stars often bear little resemblance to the quality of the hotel. A three-star could have just slipped into the category and needs a more polish, while a two-star might be missing a vital ingredient that takes it to the next level, usually something as simple as the lack of an elevator. The French tourism industry is in the process of standardizing all of the criteria, but this is still a work in progress. In some of the lower categories, the rooms might not have private bathrooms; instead, many have a sink and maybe a bidet. Not all private bathrooms have a bathtub/shower combination; ask in advance if it matters to you.

More and more hotels in France are joining Green Globe's worldwide certification label for sustainable tourism. For more information on environmentally friendly hotels in Provence and the Riviera, contact **Green Globe** (✆ **06-15-09-27-21;** www.greenglobe.com). In Cannes, the Hotel Martinez and the InterContinental Carlton hold a Green Globe certification.

RELAIS & CHÂTEAUX This organization of deluxe hotels began in France in 1954 when a group of hoteliers joined together to set the highest standards for luxurious hotel living and dining. Initially the hotels were along the route of the Paris-Riviera train. These *relais de campagne* offered travelers an unforgettable gastronomic experience as they made their way south. Not surprisingly, it wasn't long before this route was christened *La Route du Bonheur* (the road of happiness). Relais & Châteaux establishments are former castles, abbeys, manor houses, and town houses converted into elegant hotels. All have a limited number of rooms, so reservations are imperative. Many of these owner-run establishments have pools, tennis courts, and spa facilities. For information and reservations, call ✆ **800/735-2478,** or check out the website www.relaischateaux.com.

LOGIS DE FRANCE This collection of mainly two- and three-star hotels is a good bet for those on a budget who want to sample French hospitality and high-quality cooking (www.logishotels.com). Accommodations vary widely, but a Logis de France hotel guarantees a certain level of comfort, and many of the restaurants offer very good regional cuisine for reasonable prices. The distinctive yellow-and-brown logo will show the hotel's rating in the number of fireplaces, from one (quite basic) to three (very good).

BED-AND-BREAKFASTS Called *chambres d'hôtes* in France, these could be one or several bedrooms in anything from a farm or a village home to a wing in a château. Many offer one main meal of the day as well (lunch or dinner), known as *table d'hôte,* which are usually communal affairs. Although simpler houses in rural locations offer low rates, others can be quite expensive. But the experience is a world away from a night in a chain hotel. In some towns that lack decent hotels, a B&B is the best choice. You can search the directory at www.chambresdhotes.org.

In the United States, a good source for this type of accommodations is the **French Experience** (www.frenchexperience.com), which also rents furnished houses. Another U.S. agency is **Provence West** (www.provencewest.com), which has connections with some of the best accommodations in the region. You can also contact **France: Homestyle** (www.francehomestyle.com), whose upscale repertoire in Provence includes more than 300 properties.

VILLAS, HOUSES & APARTMENTS If you can stay for at least a week (sometimes even less) and don't mind doing your own cooking and cleaning, you might want to rent long-term accommodations. The possibilities are practically endless. To begin with, there are simple ***gîtes,*** which are often outbuildings on farms that have been turned into rental accommodation. You can find a list of suitable properties at www.gites-de-france.com. There are companies that hold thousands of rental accommodations on their books, which could be anything from a seaside studio apartment in Collioure to a luxurious villa in St-Tropez.

HomeAway (www.homeaway.co.uk) is a major holiday rental agency with about 75,000 properties in France, almost 30,000 of which are in Provence, the Riviera, and Languedoc-Roussillon. Other U.K.-based companies include **French Connections** (www.frenchconnections.co.uk), **Vintage Travel** (www.vintagetravel.co.uk), **Interhome** (www.interhome.com), and **Holiday Lettings** (www.holidaylettings.co.uk).

In the United States, **At Home Abroad** (www.athomeabroadinc.com) specializes in villas on the French Riviera and in the Provençal hill towns. Rentals are usually for 2 weeks. **Barclay International Group** (www.barclayweb.com), can give you access to about 3,000 apartments and villas throughout Languedoc, Provence, and the Riviera, ranging from modest modern units to those among the most stylish.

HOLIDAY VILLAGES France, and Provence in particular, has a large number of self-contained holiday villages that offer self-catered apartments in residences with a large range of facilities. They are very popular with French families who want a safe environment for their children, with swimming pools and play areas on-site, for a reasonable weekly rent. Some of the best known operators are **Lagrange Holidays** (www.lagrange-holidays.co.uk), **Pierre & Vacances** (www.pv-holidays.com), and **Madame Vacances** (www.madamevacances.co.uk).

Hotel Chains

Accor Hotels (www.accor-hotels.com) is made up of a wide range of chain hotels within France and around the world. There is a type of hotel to suit all budgets. **Formule 1** (www.hotelformule1.com) is the most basic, with purely functional rooms that can sleep four. They are almost always situated in out-of-town shopping areas, and are useful for breaking up a long car journey. The next step up is **Etap** (www.etaphotel.com), which has a few more frills than a Formule 1 and more often can be found a little closer to the center of town. **Ibis** (www.ibishotel.com) is the first step out of the budget category but is still an economical choice, as it can be found in central locations and has modern rooms of a decent size. **Mercure** (www.mercure.com) and **Novotel** (www.novotel.com) jump another level towards the four-star category, and many have extra facilities such as swimming pools. **Pullman** (www.pullmanhotels.com) are the deluxe hotels favored by well-to-do business people, while **Sofitel** hotels (www.sofitel.com) are among the most luxurious to be found.

At the least expensive end, **Hostelling International USA,** 8401 Colesville Rd., Silver Springs, MD 20910 (✆ **301/495-1240;** www.hiusa.org), offers a directory of low-cost accommodations and hostels around the country.

[FastFACTS] PROVENCE & THE RIVIERA

Area Codes All French telephone numbers consist of 10 digits, the first two of which are like an area code. If you're calling anywhere in France from within France, just dial all 10 digits—no additional codes are needed. If you're calling from outside of France, drop the initial 0 (zero). Area code in Provence for land lines is generally 04; for mobile phones it's 06. See also "Telephones" later in this chapter.

Business Hours Business hours can be erratic. Most banks are open Monday to Friday from 9:30am to 4:30pm. Many, particularly in smaller towns or villages, take a lunch break at varying times. Hours are usually posted on the door. Most museums close 1 day a week (Mon or Tues), and they're generally closed on national holidays. Usual hours are from 9:30am to 5pm. Many museums close for lunch from noon to 2pm and are open on weekends. Some museums offer free admission the first Sunday of the month (refer to the individual museum listings).

Generally, offices are open Monday to Friday from 9am to 5pm, but always call first. In larger cities, stores are open from 9 or 9:30am (often 10am) to 6 or 7pm without a break for lunch. Most shops, even in cities of a substantial size, will close at noon and won't reopen in many cases until 3 or 4pm.

Car Rentals See "Getting Around: Car Rentals," earlier in this chapter.

Cellphones See "Mobile Phones" later in this section.

Crime See " Safety" later in this section.

Customs **What You Can Bring into France:** Customs restrictions for visitors entering France differ for citizens of European Union (E.U.) and non-E.U. countries. Non-E.U. nationals can bring in duty-free either 200 cigarettes, 100 cigarillos, 50 cigars, or 250 grams of smoking tobacco. This amount is doubled if you live outside Europe. You can also bring in 2 liters of wine and 1 liter of alcohol over 22%, and 2 liters of wine 22% or under. In addition, you can bring in 60cc of perfume and a quarter liter of eau de toilette. Visitors ages 15 and over can bring in other goods totaling 175€; for those under 15, the limit is 90€. Customs officials tend to be lenient about general merchandise as the limits are very low. Citizens of E.U. countries can bring in any amount of goods as long as the goods are intended for their personal use and not for resale.

What You Can Take Home from France:

Australian Citizens The duty-free allowance in Australia is A$900 or, for those under 18, A$450. Citizens can bring in 250 cigarettes or 250 grams of loose tobacco, and 2.25 liters of alcohol. If you're returning with valuables you already own, such as foreign-made cameras, you should file form B263.

A helpful brochure available from Australian consulates or Customs offices is *Know Before You Go.* For more information, call the **Australian Customs Service** at ✆ **1300/363-263,** or log on to www.customs.gov.au.

Canadian Citizens Canada allows its citizens a C$750 exemption, and you're allowed to bring back duty-free one carton of cigarettes, one can of tobacco, 40 imperial ounces of liquor, and 50 cigars. In addition, you're allowed to mail gifts to Canada from abroad valued at less than C$60 a day, provided they're unsolicited and don't contain alcohol or tobacco (write on the package UNSOLICITED GIFT, UNDER C$60 VALUE). All valuables, including those you already own, such as expensive foreign cameras, should be declared on the Y-38 form before departure from Canada. ***Note:*** The C$750 exemption can be used only once a year and only after an absence of 7 days.

For a clear summary of Canadian rules, write for the booklet *I Declare,* issued by the **Canada Border Services Agency** (✆ **800/461-9999** in Canada, or 204/983-3500; www.cbsa-asfc.gc.ca).

New Zealand Citizens The duty-free allowance for New Zealand is NZ$700. Citizens 18 and over can bring in 200 cigarettes, 50 cigars, or 250 grams of tobacco (or a mixture of all three if their combined weight doesn't exceed 250g), plus 4.5 liters of wine and beer, or 1.125 liters of liquor. New Zealand currency does not carry import or export restrictions. Fill out a certificate of export, listing the valuables you are taking out of the country; that way, you can bring them back without paying duty.

Most questions are answered in a free pamphlet available at New Zealand consulates and Customs offices: *New Zealand Customs Guide for Travellers, Notice no. 4.* For more information, contact **New Zealand Customs Service,** the Customhouse, 17–21 Whitmore St., Box 2218, Wellington (✆ **04/473-6099** or 0800/428-786; www.customs.govt.nz).

U.K. Citizens Citizens of the U.K. returning from an E.U. country such as France go through a Customs exit especially for E.U. travelers. In essence, there is no limit on what you can bring back from an E.U. country, as long as the items are for personal use (this includes gifts) and you have already paid the duty and tax. However, Customs law sets out guidance levels. If you bring in more than these levels, you may be asked to prove that the goods are for your own use. Guidance levels on goods bought in the E.U. for your own use are 3,200 cigarettes, 200 cigars, 400 cigarillos, 3 kilograms of smoking tobacco, 10 liters of spirits, 90 liters of wine, 20 liters of fortified wine (such as port or sherry), and 110 liters of beer.

For information, contact **HM Revenue & Customs** at ✆ **0845/010-9000** (from outside the U.K., 02920/501-261), or consult their website at www.hmrc.gov.uk.

U.S. Citizens Returning U.S. citizens who have been away for 48 hours or more are allowed to bring back, once every 30 days, $800 worth of merchandise duty-free. You're charged a flat rate of duty on the next $1,000 worth of purchases, and any dollar amount beyond that is subject to duty at whatever rates apply. On mailed gifts, the duty-free limit is $200. Have your receipts or purchases handy to expedite the declaration process. ***Note:*** If you owe duty, you are required to pay on your arrival in the United States, using cash, personal check, government or traveler's check, or money order; some locations also accept Visa or MasterCard.

To avoid having to pay duty on foreign-made personal items you owned before your trip, bring along a bill of sale, insurance policy, jeweler's appraisal, or receipt of purchase. Or you can register items that can be readily identified by a permanently affixed serial number or marking—think laptop computers, cameras, and MP3 players—with Customs before you leave. Take the items to the nearest Customs office, or register them with Customs at the airport from which you're departing. You'll receive, at no cost, a certificate of registration, which allows duty-free entry for the life of the item.

You cannot bring fresh foodstuffs into the U.S.; canned foods are allowed. For specifics on what you can bring back and the corresponding fees, download the invaluable free pamphlet *Know Before You Go* online at **www.cbp.gov**. (Click on "Travel," and then click on "Know Before You Go.") Or, contact the **U.S. Customs & Border Protection (CBP),** 1300 Pennsylvania Ave. NW, Washington, DC 20229 (✆ **877/287-8667**), and request the pamphlet.

Disabled Travelers Nearly all modern hotels in the south of France now provide rooms designed for persons with disabilities. However, many hotels that are in historic buildings might not have elevators, special toilet facilities, or ramps for wheelchair access. Always ask before making a reservation. People with limited mobility might find it difficult to navigate some of the steep cobbled lanes of hilltop villages, and wheelchair users might not be able to get around some ancient monuments.

The high-speed **TGV trains** are wheelchair accessible; older trains have special compartments for wheelchair boarding. Guide dogs ride free. Be aware that some older stations don't have escalators or elevators.

Association des Paralysés de France, 17 bd. Auguste-Blanqui, 75013 Paris (✆ **01-40-78-69-00;** www.apf.asso.fr), is a privately funded organization that provides wheelchair-bound individuals with documentation, moral support, and travel ideas. In addition to the central Paris office, it maintains an office in each of the 90 *départements* of France and can help you find accessible hotels, transportation, sightseeing, house rentals, and (in some cases) companionship for paralyzed or partially paralyzed travelers. It's not, however, a travel agency.

Doctors If you get sick, consider asking your hotel concierge or manager to recommend a local doctor—even his or her own. Also try the emergency room at a local hospital; many have walk-in clinics for emergency cases that are not life-threatening. You might not get immediate attention, but you won't pay the high price of an emergency room visit. Also see "Health" later in this chapter.

Drinking Laws The legal age for the purchase and consumption of alcohol is 18. You'll rarely be asked to show ID, although everyone should carry some form of identification as it is a legal requirement in France. The police are very strict about driving while intoxicated. If convicted, you face a high fine and possibly jail time.

Driving Rules See "Getting Around" earlier in this chapter.

Electricity French voltage is 220 volts, 50 cycles. Adapters are needed to fit sockets.

Embassies & Consulates All embassies are in Paris, but several cities in Provence and the Riviera have consulates.

The Embassy of **Australia** is at 4 rue Jean-Rey, 15e (✆ **01-40-59-33-00;** www.france.embassy.gov.au), open Monday to Friday 9:15am to noon and 2:30 to 4:30pm.

The Embassy of **Canada** is at 35 av. Montaigne, 8e (✆ **01-44-43-29-00;** www.international.gc.ca/canada-europa/france/menu-en.asp), open Monday to Friday 9am to noon and 2 to 5pm. There is a consulate of Canada in Nice at 2 place Franklin (✆ **04-93-92-93-22**).

The Embassy of **Ireland** is at 4 rue Rude, 16e (✆ **01-44-17-67-00;** www.embassyofireland.fr), open Monday to Friday 9:30am to 1pm and 2:30 to 5:30pm. There are Irish consulates in Cannes at 69 av. Roi Albert (✆ **06-77-69-14-36**) and in Monaco at 5 av. des Citronniers (✆ **377-93-15-70-45**).

The embassy of **New Zealand** is at 7 ter rue Léonard-de-Vinci, 75116 (✆ **01-45-01-43-43;** www.nzembassy.com), open Monday to Friday 9am to 1pm and 2:30 to 6pm.

The Embassy of the **United Kingdom** is at 35 rue du Faubourg St-Honoré, 8e (✆ **01-44-51-31-00;** http://ukinfrance.fco.gov.uk), open Monday to Friday 9:30am to 1pm and 2:30 to 5pm. There is a British consulate in Marseille at 24 Avenue du Prado (✆ **04-91-15-72-10**).

The Embassy of the **United States,** 2 av. Gabriel, 8e (✆ **01-43-12-22-22;** http://france.usembassy.gov), is open Monday to Friday 8:30am to 5pm. There are U.S. consulates in Marseille at place Varian Fry (✆ **04-91-54-92-00**) and in Nice at 7 av. Gustave V (✆ **04-93-88-89-53**).

Emergencies In an emergency while at a hotel, contact the front desk. Most staffs are trained in dealing with a crisis and will do whatever is necessary. If the emergency involves something like a stolen wallet, go to the police station in person. Otherwise, you can get help anywhere by calling ✆ **17** for the police, ✆ **18** for the fire department *(sapeurs pompiers),* or ✆ **15** for medical emergencies.

Gasoline (Petrol) See "Getting There" earlier in this chapter.

Health In general, France is viewed as a "safe" destination. You don't need to get shots, most food is safe, and the water is drinkable. It is easy to get a prescription filled in French towns and cities, Provence and the Riviera have some of the best medical facilities in Europe, and finding an English-speaking doctor is generally no problem in most of the top resorts of the Riviera or major cities in Provence such as Avignon.

Contact the **International Association for Medical Assistance to Travelers (IAMAT;** ✆ **716/754-4883** or, in Canada, 416/652-0137; www.iamat.org) for tips on travel and health concerns in France, and for lists of local, English-speaking doctors. The United States **Centers for Disease Control and Prevention** (✆ **800/232-4636;** www.cdc.gov) provides up-to-date information on health hazards by region or country and offers tips on food safety. **Travel Health Online** (www.tripprep.com), sponsored by a consortium of travel medicine practitioners, may also offer helpful advice on traveling abroad. You can find listings of reliable medical clinics overseas at the **International Society of Travel Medicine** (www.istm.org).

Check the following government websites for up-to-date health-related travel advice: **Australia** (www.smartraveller.gov.au), **Canada** (www.hc-sc.gc.ca), **U.K.** (www.nathnac.org), and **U.S.** (www.cdc.gov/travel).

Hospitals In **Nice** there is the Hôpital St-Roch, 5 rue Pierre Dévoluy (✆ 04-92-03-33-75); in **Monaco,** Centre Hospitalier Princesse Grace, av. Pasteur (✆ 377-97-98-99-00); in **Antibes,** Chemin des Quatres Chemins (✆ 04-92-91-77-77); and in **Cannes,** Hôpital des Broussailles, 13 av. des Broussailles (✆ 04-93-69-70-00).

Insurance Although travel medical insurance is not a must in France, it is highly recommended.

Canadians should check with their provincial health plan offices or call **Health Canada** (✆ **866/225-0709;** www.hc-sc.gc.ca) to find out the extent of their coverage and what documentation and receipts they must take home in case they are treated overseas.

Travelers from the U.K. should carry their **European Health Insurance Card (EHIC)** as proof of entitlement to free/reduced-cost medical treatment abroad (✆ **0845/606-2030;** www.ehic.org.uk). Note, however, that the EHIC covers only "necessary medical treatment," and a separate travel insurance policy should be bought to cover repatriation costs, lost money, baggage, or cancellation.

For travel overseas, most U.S. health plans (including Medicare and Medicaid) do not provide coverage, and the ones that do often require you to pay for services upfront and reimburse you only after you return home. As a safety net, you may want to buy travel medical insurance. If you require additional medical insurance, try **MEDEX Assistance** (✆ **410/453-6300;** www.medexassist.com) or **Travel Assistance International** (✆ **800/821-2828;** www.travelassistance.com; for general information on services, call the company's **Worldwide Assistance Services, Inc.,** at ✆ **800/777-8710**).

For information on traveler's insurance, trip cancellation insurance, and medical insurance while traveling, please visit www.frommers.com/planning.

Internet & Wi-Fi More and more hotels, resorts, airports, cafes, and retailers are going Wi-Fi (wireless fidelity), becoming "hot spots" that offer free high-speed Wi-Fi access or charge a small fee for usage. You will see the recognized Wi-Fi logo in the entrance. Most hotels offer Wi-Fi for free, although there are still a number, particularly in the luxury hotels, that charge high fees.

Language English is widely understood in France, especially among young people who have studied it in school and residents of larger cities. Hotel staff members tend to speak English, at least at the front desk, as do workers in many restaurants. However, any attempt at the language is appreciated, even just *"bonjour"* and, just as importantly, *"merci."* After that, French people will often switch to English as a courtesy. It's best to carry a phrase book, however, and not rely on finding someone who speaks English. For some basic vocabulary, see chapter 9. It's a common courtesy to say *"Bonjour"* when entering a store or a cafe, and to say *"Au revoir"* when leaving. When you want to get a waiter's attention, it's polite to say *"S'il vous plaît"* (please) or *"Excusez-moi"* (excuse me).

Legal Aid The French government advises foreigners to consult their embassy or consulate (see above) in case of an arrest or similar problem. The staff can generally offer advice on how you can obtain help locally and can furnish you with a list of local attorneys. If you are arrested for illegal possession of drugs, the U.S. Embassy and consular officials cannot interfere with the French judicial system. A consulate can advise you only of your rights.

LGBT Travelers
France is one of the world's most tolerant countries toward gays and lesbians, and no special laws discriminate against them. "The Gay Riviera" boasts a large gay population, with dozens of gay clubs and restaurants. **Gay Provence,** 42 rue du Coq, Marseille (✆ **04-91-84-08-96;** www.gay-provence.org), is operated by a group of gays and lesbians, each native to Provence, who offer tours to American and European gays and lesbians. Various activities can be preplanned or customized according to interests, and tours range from 1 day to 1 week. Participants are welcomed into the private homes of gay or gay-friendly locals. Attractions include such outdoor excursions as hiking, biking, or horseback riding, or cultural activities such as Mediterranean cooking lessons or meetings with artists and artisans.

The **International Gay & Lesbian Travel Association (IGLTA;** ✆ **800/448-8550** or 954/776-2626; www.iglta.org) is the trade association for the gay and lesbian travel industry, and offers an online directory of gay- and lesbian-friendly travel businesses. Many agencies offer tours and travel itineraries specifically for gay and lesbian travelers. **Above and Beyond Tours** (✆ **800/397-2681;** www.abovebeyondtours.com) is a gay Australian tour specialist. **Now, Voyager** (✆ **800/255-6951;** www.nowvoyager.com) is a well-known San Francisco–based gay-owned and -operated travel service. **Olivia Cruises & Resorts** (✆ **800/631-6277;** www.olivia.com) charters entire resorts and ships for exclusive lesbian vacations and offers smaller group experiences for both gay and lesbian travelers.

Gay.com Travel (✆ **415/644-8044;** www.gay.com/travel or www.outandabout.com) is an excellent online successor to the popular ***Out & About*** print magazine. It provides regularly updated information about gay-owned, gay-oriented, and gay-friendly lodging, dining, sightseeing, nightlife, and shopping establishments in every important destination worldwide. British travelers should click on the "Travel" link at **www.gay.com** for advice and gay-friendly trip ideas. The Canadian website **GayTraveler** (**http://gaytraveler.ca**) offers ideas and advice for gay travel all over the world.

Mail Most post offices in France are open Monday through Friday from 8am to 7pm, and Saturday from 8am to noon. Some in smaller towns will close at lunch. Allow 5 to 8 days to send or receive mail from your home. Airmail letters to North America cost .89€ for 20 grams. Letters to the U.K. cost .77€ for up to 20 grams. You can exchange money at post offices. Many hotels sell stamps, as do local post offices and cafes displaying a red TABAC sign outside.

Medical Requirements See "Health" earlier in this section.

Mobile Phones The three letters that define much of the world's wireless capabilities are GSM (Global System for Mobile Communications), a big, seamless network that makes for easy cross-border cellphone use throughout Europe and dozens of other countries worldwide. GSM phones function with a removable plastic SIM card, encoded with your phone number and account information. If your cellphone is on a GSM system and you have a world-capable multiband phone, you can make and receive calls across much of the globe. Just call your wireless operator and ask for "international roaming" to be activated on your account. Unfortunately, per-minute charges can be high.

Using your phone or mobile device abroad can be very expensive, and you usually have to pay to receive calls or use the internet. Check with your phone supplier to see if you can buy a data package for overseas use. It's also a good idea to get your phone "unlocked" before you leave for France. This means you can buy a SIM card from one of the three French providers—**Bouygues Télécom** (www.bouygestelecom.fr), **Orange** (www.orange.fr), or **SFR** (www.sfr.fr)—and simply insert it into your phone. A SIM card with 5€ call credit costs about 10€. Alternatively, if your phone isn't unlocked, you could buy a cheap mobile phone. To top up your phone credit, buy a Mobicarte from *tabacs*, supermarkets, and mobile phone outlets. Prices range from 5€ to 100€.

Money & Costs France, and especially the Riviera, is an expensive destination. Part of the problem is the value-added tax (VAT—called TVA in France), which tacks between 6% and 33% onto everything. If you need to exchange currency, do so at a bank, not a currency exchange desk, hotel, or shop. The easiest and best way to get cash away from home is from an **ATM (automated teller machine),** also known as a cash machine or a cashpoint. In French they are called a *guichet automatique* or a *distributeur de billets.* ATMs are very common and easy to find in all cities, towns, and major villages in Provence and the Riviera. As they are outside of banks, they can be accessed at all hours. The **Cirrus** (✆ **800/424-7787;** www.mastercard.com) and **PLUS** (✆ **800/843-7587;** www.visa.com) networks span the globe. Go to your bank card's website to find ATM locations at your destination. Be sure you know your personal identification number (PIN) and your daily withdrawal limit before you depart. ***Note:*** Fees for international transactions can be extortionate. For international withdrawal fees, ask your bank.

THE VALUE OF THE EURO VS. OTHER POPULAR CURRENCIES

Euro (€)	Aus$	Can$	NZ$	UK£	US$
1€	A$1.32	C$1.36	NZ$1.69	£0.88	$1.40

WHAT THINGS COST IN NICE	EUROS
Taxi from the airport to central Nice	22.00–32.00
Bus ride within the city center	1.00
Double room, very expensive (Hôtel Negresco)	245.00–615.00
Double room, moderate (Le Dortoir)	100.00–200.00
Double room, inexpensive (Villa La Tour)	48.00–139.00
Lunch for one without wine, expensive	25.00
Lunch for one without wine, inexpensive	13.00
Dinner for one without wine, very expensive	90.00
Dinner for one without wine, inexpensive	14.00
Glass of wine in a cafe	4.00
Cup of espresso	3.50
Admission to most museums	free
Admission to the Opéra de Nice	12.00–78.00

Frommer's lists exact prices in the local currency. The currency conversions quoted above were correct at press time. However, rates fluctuate, so before departing consult a currency exchange website such as **www.oanda.com/currency/converter** to check up-to-the-minute rates.

Credit cards are another safe way to carry money and they generally offer relatively good exchange rates. Visa (known as Carte Bleue in French) is the most common credit card in France, but most international credit cards are widely used. In an attempt to reduce credit card fraud, French credit cards are issued with an embedded chip and a PIN to authorize transactions. Most credit card transactions are done with handheld machines which might not be able to read U.S. and Canadian cards. Non-French cards (which don't have a chip) do work but they print a slip that requires a signature. You can withdraw cash advances from your credit cards at banks or ATMs but high fees make credit card cash advances a pricey way to get cash. Keep in mind that you'll pay interest from the moment of your withdrawal, even if you pay your monthly bills on time. Also, note that many banks assess a 1% to 3% "transaction fee" on all charges you incur abroad (whether you're using the local currency or your native currency).

There are still shops, restaurants and bars, often family run, that don't accept credit or debit cards, so it's always good to both check in advance and have cash on you. The minimum amount you have to spend to use a credit or debit card is slowly decreasing, but in some shops and bars, again often smaller businesses, it can be as high as 15€.

For help with currency conversions, download Frommer's convenient Travel Tools app for your mobile device. Go to www.frommers.com/go/mobile and click on the Travel Tools To Go icon.

Multicultural Travelers Anti-Semitism has been on the rise in Europe, especially in France, which has registered a significant increase in incidents against Jews. French Jews (not visitors from abroad) have suffered assaults and attacks against synagogues, cemeteries, schools, and other Jewish property. Officially, the government of France welcomes Jewish visitors and promises a vigorous defense of their safety and concerns. The French Government Tourist Office website (www.franceguide.com) has a *FranceGuide for the Jewish Traveler* in the "Publications" section with more information.

Newspapers & Magazines France's main national daily newspapers are *Le Monde, Le Figaro,* and *Libération.* The regional newspapers for the Languedoc region are *L'Indépendant* and *Midi Libre,* while Provence is served by *La Provence* and *Nice Matin.* The French also like weekly news magazines such as *Le Nouvel Observateur* and *L'Express,* while gossip hounds get their fix of celebrity photos in *Paris-Match.* An English-language monthly newspaper, *The Connexion,* is available by subscription, and many shops also sell the *International Herald Tribune* in addition to British newspapers such as *The Daily Telegraph* and *The Independent.*

Packing Resist the urge to take a large suitcase and fill it to the brim. Provence and Languedoc are filled with pretty villages that often have traffic-free centers, so you will find yourself lugging heavy suitcases along bumpy cobbled streets and up and down hills. Many hotels are too old to be able to install elevators, so be prepared to walk several flights of stairs with heavy bags. If you haven't got room for your purchases, you can always mail them home.

For more helpful information on packing for your trip, download our convenient Travel Tools app for your mobile device. Go to www.frommers.com/go/mobile and click on the Travel Tools icon.

Passports All travelers entering France are required to carry a passport. Visas are not required for U.S., Canadian, U.K., Australian, and New Zealand citizens. To prevent international child abduction, E.U. governments have initiated procedures at entry and exit points. These often (but not always) include requiring documentary evidence of relationship and permission for the child's travel from the parent or legal guardian not present. Having such documentation on hand, even if not required, facilitates entries and exits. Go to the following agencies to acquire a passport or for information about passports:

Australia Australian Passport Information Service (✆ **131-232,** or visit www.passports.gov.au).

Canada **Passport Office,** Department of Foreign Affairs and International Trade, Ottawa, ON K1A 0G3 (✆ **800/567-6868;** www.ppt.gc.ca).

Ireland **Passport Office,** Setanta Centre, Molesworth Street, Dublin 2 (✆ **01/671-1633;** www.foreignaffairs.gov.ie).

New Zealand **Passports Office,** Department of Internal Affairs, 47 Boulcott Street, Wellington, 6011 (✆ **0800/225-050** in New Zealand or 04/474-8100; www.passports.govt.nz).

United Kingdom Visit your nearest passport office, major post office, or travel agency or contact the **Identity and Passport Service (IPS),** 89 Eccleston Square, London, SW1V 1PN (✆ **0300/222-0000;** www.ips.gov.uk).

United States To find your regional passport office, check the U.S. State Department website (http://travel.state.gov/passport) or call the **National Passport Information Center** (✆ **877/487-2778**) for automated information.

Petrol See "Getting Around" earlier in this chapter.

Police Call ✆ **17** anywhere in France.

Safety France is a generally safe country, although travelers should always be on the lookout for thieves and pickpockets. They frequent tourist attractions such as museums, monuments, restaurants, hotels, beaches, trains, train stations, airports, and subways. Passports should be carried on the body when necessary, and it's safer to wear a bag diagonally across the chest rather than on one shoulder.

Crimes involving vehicles with nonlocal license plates can occur. Car doors should be kept locked and windows closed while traveling in cities to prevent incidents of "snatch and grab" thefts. Similar incidents have also occurred at tollbooths and rest areas. Special caution is advised when entering and exiting the car because that offers opportunity for purse snatchings. There have also been a number of thefts at Nice Airport, particularly at car-rental parking lots where bags have been snatched as drivers have been loading luggage into rental cars. Also, try not to leave valuables in a parked car.

The loss or theft of a passport should be reported immediately to local police and your nearest embassy or consulate, where you can obtain information about passport replacement.

Senior Travel Many discounts are available for seniors. At any rail station in France, seniors 60 and over (with proof of age) can get a **Carte Senior.** The pass costs 56€ and is good for a 50% discount on unlimited rail travel throughout the year. The *carte* also offers reduced prices on some regional bus lines and half-price admission at state-owned museums. Check to see if there are restrictions on certain days.

Air France offers seniors a 10% reduction on its regular nonexcursion tariffs on travel within France. Some restrictions apply. Discounts of around 10% are offered to passengers 62 and over on selected Air France international flights. Be sure to ask for the discount when booking.

Members of **AARP** (✆ **888/687-2277;** www.aarp.org) get discounts on hotels, airfares, and car rentals. AARP offers members a wide range of benefits, including *AARP The Magazine* and a monthly newsletter. Anyone over 50 can join.

Road Scholar (formerly **Elderhostel;** ✆ **800/454-5768;** www.roadscholar.org) arranges study programs for those 55 and over (and a spouse or companion of any age). Most courses last 2 to 4 weeks abroad, and many include airfare, accommodations in university dormitories or modest inns, meals, and tuition. **ElderTreks** (✆ **800/741-7956;** www.eldertreks.com) offers small-group tours to off-the-beaten-path or adventure travel locations, restricted to travelers 50 and older.

Smoking France banned smoking in public places, including restaurants and bars, in 2007. It doesn't seem to have dented the national enthusiasm for smoking, however, as it's still a popular occupation. Visitors used to smoke-free environments need to be aware that cigarette smoke is still very much a part of outdoor cafe life.

Student Travel Students get reduced admission to museums, galleries, and other attractions. Always ask if there is a student discount. There are also substantial savings for students on rail travel, so check with companies such as **Rail Europe** (see "Getting There"). **STA Travel** in the U.S. (www.statravel.com) and the U.K. (www.statravel.co.uk) offers special deals for students on flights, accommodation, and insurance.

Taxes Every visitor, regardless of nationality, who spends a night in a French hotel, B&B, rented accommodation, or campsite is subject to a ***taxe de séjour.*** This could be as little as 0.70€ per person per day in a two-star hotel and easily rises to more than 1.50€ in a luxury hotel. This also varies from region to region. It's effectively a tourist tax, and the money goes into the local town or village towards communal events such as annual festivals. Hotels rarely include it in their costs when quoting room rates, so be prepared to pay a little extra when presented with the bill. Many tour operators and holiday rental companies absorb the tax into the cost of the holiday.

French sales tax, or **VAT** (value-added tax), is a hefty 19.6%, but you can get most of that back if you spend 175€ or more at any participating retailer. The name of the refund is *détaxe,* meaning exactly what it says. You never really get the full 19.6% back, but you can come close. After you spend the required minimum amount, ask for your *détaxe* papers; fill out the forms before you arrive at the airport and allow at least half an hour for standing in line. All refunds are processed at the final point of departure from the E.U., so if you're going to another E.U. country, apply for the refund there. If you're considering a major purchase, especially one that falls between 175€ and 304€, ask the store policy before you get too involved—or be willing to waive your right to the refund.

Telephones To call France:

1. Dial the international access code: 011 from the U.S. and Canada; 00 from the U.K., Ireland, or New Zealand; or 0011 from Australia.
2. Dial the country code 33.
3. Dial the city code and then the number. Most of the numbers in this guide are prefaced with the city code of 04, which must be dialed.

For information on calling Monaco, see p. 324.

To make international calls: To make international calls from France, first dial 00 and then the country code (U.S. or Canada 1, U.K. 44, Ireland 353, Australia 61, New Zealand 64). Next you dial the area code and number. For example, if you wanted to call the British Embassy in Washington, D.C., you would dial 00-1-202/588-7800.

For directory and operator assistance: Dial 12 for assistance in French; in English, dial 0-800/364-775. For international inquiries, dial 08-36-59-32-12. This will link you with a bilingual (French and English) phone operator. You are allowed to request only two numbers for which you pay a service charge of 3€. However, if you wish to use an operator to call your home country, you dial the toll-free number of ✆ **08-00-99-00** plus the following 10 digits of your country code: 08-00-99-00-11 for the U.S. and Canada, and 08-00-99-00-44 for the U.K., or 08-00-99-00-61 for Australia.

Toll-free numbers: For France, numbers beginning with 08 and followed by 00 are toll-free. But be careful. Numbers that begin with 08 followed by 36 carry a surcharge per minute.

Time France is on Central European Time, which is 1 hour after Greenwich Mean Time. It moves an extra hour ahead in the spring and returns back in the autumn for daylight savings. The use of the 24-hour clock (16:00 instead of 4pm) is very common.

Tipping France's tipping culture is very different from North America's. For a start, French **restaurants** are legally obliged to add an automatic 15% service charge to your bill. You will see *"service compris"* on the menu and/or check. There is no need to add an additional tip unless you are exceptionally happy with the service. A few extra euros will do, not necessarily another 10% or 15%. Very occasionally, you might find an unscrupulous restaurant that has written *"pourboire non inclus"* on the menu. That translates as "tip not included," which is patently wrong and cynically misleading. If you see this, leave immediately and find another restaurant. In cafes and bars, it's fine to round up an amount from, say, 2.70€ to 3€. **Cab drivers** don't need a percentage, just a couple of extra euros. Staff at luxury **hotels,** such as those who carry your bags or park your car, should be tipped a few euros, but this depends on the number of bags and the number of stars in the hotel.

Toilets Most towns and villages will have public toilets, many of them free. The level of cleanliness ranges wildly, though, so carry some tissues with you. France is notorious for sticking to *les toilettes à la turque,* an evil creation that forces the user to stand on two plates with a hole between the feet. Be aware the flush sometimes works automatically once it senses movement. Restaurants and cafes expect you to be a customer before you use the facilities. Toilets in train and bus stations are often payable, about 0.20€ to 0.50€, but some merely require a token from the staff in the ticket office.

VAT See "Taxes" earlier in this chapter.

Visas See "Passports" earlier in this chapter.

Visitor Information Your best source of information before you go is **Atout France,** the French government tourist office; visit its website at www.franceguide.com. In the United States, call ✆ **514/288-1904** to request information. In Canada, call ✆ **514/288-2026;** in the United Kingdom, ✆ **09068/244-123** (60p per min.) or fax 020/7493-6594; in Ireland, ✆ **015/60-235-235;** and in Australia, ✆ **02/9231-5244.** There's no representative in New Zealand—you will have to call the Australian office.

The regions of **Languedoc-Roussillon** (www.sunfrance.com) and Provence and the **Côte d'Azur** (www.52coupsdecoeur.com) are divided into separate *départements,* each of which has its own tourism website. They are an excellent source of information in addition to individual city websites. See each town or city section for more specific information on the local tourist boards.

Water Drinking water is safe in France. In fact, many of France's beautiful fountains can be safely drunk from when there is an EAU POTABLE sign visible. Some restaurants will automatically bring out a bottle of chilled tap water. If the water doesn't appear, and you don't want to pay for bottled water, ask for *une carafe d'eau.* Tap water translates as *l'eau du robinet,* but you won't need to say this. When ordering bottled water, sparkling water is *l'eau gazeuse,* and still water is *l'eau plate* (pronounced "platt").

Wi-Fi See "Internet & Wi-Fi," earlier in this section.

USEFUL TERMS & PHRASES

If nothing else, learn basic greetings, and—above all—the phrase, *Parlez-vous anglais?* ("Do you speak English?"). Many people speak passable English and will use it liberally, if you show the basic courtesy of greeting them in their language. Go out, try a few phrases from this chapter, and don't be bashful. *Bonne chance!*

9

FRENCH-LANGUAGE TERMS

BASICS

English	French	Pronunciation
Yes/No	**Oui/Non**	wee/noh
Okay	**D'accord**	*dah*-core
Please	**S'il vous plaît**	seel voo *play*
Thank you	**Merci**	*mair*-see
You're welcome	**De rien**	duh ree-*ehn*
Hello (during daylight)	**Bonjour**	bohn-*jhoor*
Good evening	**Bonsoir**	bohn-*swahr*
Goodbye	**Au revoir**	o ruh-*vwahr*
What's your name?	**Comment vous appellez-vous?**	kuh-*mahn* voo za-pell-ay-voo?
My name is	**Je m'appelle**	*jhuh* ma-pell
How are you?	**Comment allez-vous?**	kuh-*mahn* tahl-ay-voo?
I'm sorry/excuse me	**Pardon**	pahr-*dohn*

GETTING AROUND & STREET SMARTS

English	French	Pronunciation
Do you speak English?	**Parlez-vous anglais?**	par-lay-*voo* ahn-glay?
I don't speak French	**Je ne parle pas français**	jhuh ne parl pah frahn-*say*
I don't understand	**Je ne comprends pas**	jhuh ne kohm-*prahn* pas
Could you speak more loudly/more slowly?	**Pouvez-vous parler plus fort/plus lentement?**	Poo-*vay* voo par-lay ploo for/ploo lan-te-*ment?*
What is it?	**Qu'est-ce que c'est?**	kess kuh *say?*

English	French	Pronunciation
What time is it?	**Quelle heure est-il?**	kel uhr eh-*teel?*
What?	**Quoi?**	kwah?
How? *or* What did you say?	**Comment?**	ko-*mahn?*
When?	**Quand?**	kahn?
Who?	**Qui?**	kee?
Why?	**Pourquoi?**	poor-*kwah?*
Where is?	**Où est?**	ooh eh?
here/there	**ici/là**	ee-*see/*lah
left/right	**à gauche/à droite**	a goash/a drwaht
straight ahead	**tout droit**	too drwah
Fill the tank (of a car), please	**Le plein, s'il vous plaît**	luh plan, seel-voo-*play*
I'm going to . . .	**Je vais à . . .**	jhe vays ah
I want to get off at . . .	**Je voudrais descendre à . . .**	jhe voo-*dray* deh-son drah-ah
. . . the airport	**. . . l'aéroport**	la-air-o-*por*
. . . the bank	**. . . la banque**	lah bahnk
. . . the bridge	**. . . le pont**	luh pohn
. . . the bus station	**. . . la gare routière**	lah gar roo-tee-*air*
. . . the bus stop	**. . . l'arrêt de bus**	lah-*ray* duh boohss
. . . the cathedral	**. . . la cathédrale**	lah ka-tay-*dral*
. . . the church	**. . . l'église**	lay-*gleez*
exit (from a building or a freeway)	**la sortie**	lah sor-*tee*
gasoline	**de l'essence**	de leh-*sahns*
hospital	**l'hôpital**	low-pee-*tahl*
museum	**le musée**	luh mew-*zay*
no smoking	**défense de fumer**	day-*fahns* de fu-may
one-way ticket	**aller simple**	ah-*lay sam*-pluh
round-trip ticket	**aller retour**	ah-*lay* re-*toor*
first floor (U.S.) ground floor (U.K.)	**rez-de-chaussée**	ray duh show-*say*
second floor (U.S.) first floor (U.K.)	**premier étage**	prem-ee-*ehr* ay-*taj*
slow down	**ralentir**	rah-lahn-*teer*
street	**rue**	roo
subway	**le métro**	le *may*-tro
telephone	**le téléphone**	luh tay-lay-*phone*
ticket	**un billet**	uh *bee*-yay
toilets	**les toilettes/les WC**	lay twa-*lets*/les vay-*say*

NECESSITIES

English	French	Pronunciation
I'd like . . .	**Je voudrais . . .**	jhe voo-*dray*
. . . a room	**. . . une chambre**	ewn *shahm*-bruh
. . . the key	**. . . la clé (la clef)**	la clay
How much does it cost?	**Ça coûte combien?**	sah coot comb-bee-*ehn?*
That's expensive.	**C'est cher/chère**	Say share
That's inexpensive.	**C'est raisonnable/C'est bon marché**	Say ray-son-*ahb*-bluh/Say bohn mar-*shay*
Do you take credit cards?	**Est-ce que vous acceptez les cartes de credit?**	es-kuh voo zaksep-*tay* lay kart duh creh-*dee?*
I'd like to buy . . .	**Je voudrais acheter . . .**	jhe voo-dray ahsh-*tay*
. . . aspirin	**. . . des aspirines**	deyz ahs-peer-*een*
. . . a gift	**. . . un cadeau**	uh kah-*doe*
. . . a map of the city	**. . . un plan de ville**	uh plahn de *veel*
. . . a dictionary	**. . . un dictionnaire**	uh deek-see-oh-*nare*
. . . a newspaper	**. . . un journal**	uh zhoor-*nahl*
. . . a phone card	**. . . une carte télépho-nique**	ewn cart tay-lay-fone-*eek*
. . . a postcard	**. . . une carte postale**	ewn carte pos-*tahl*
. . . a road map	**. . . une carte routière**	ewn cart roo-tee-*air*
. . . a stamp	**. . . un timbre**	uh *tam*-bruh
. . . condoms	**. . . des préservatifs**	day pray-ser-va-*teef*

IN YOUR HOTEL

English	French	Pronunciation
balcony	**un balcon**	uh bahl-cohn
bathtub	**une baignoire**	ewn bayn-*nwar*
hot and cold water	**l'eau chaude et froide**	low showed ay fwad
Is breakfast included?	**Le petit déjeuner est inclus?**	luh peh-*tee* day-jheun-*ay* eh ehn-*klu?*
room	**une chambre**	ewn *shawm*-bruh
shower	**une douche**	ewn dooch
sink	**un lavabo**	uh la-va-*bow*

NUMBERS & ORDINALS

English	French	Pronunciation
zero	**zéro**	zare-*oh*
one	**un**	uh
two	**deux**	duh
three	**trois**	twah
four	**quatre**	*kaht*-ruh

English	French	Pronunciation
five	**cinq**	sank
six	**six**	seess
seven	**sept**	set
eight	**huit**	wheat
nine	**neuf**	nuf
ten	**dix**	deess
eleven	**onze**	ohnz
twelve	**douze**	dooz
thirteen	**treize**	trehz
fourteen	**quatorze**	kah-*torz*
fifteen	**quinze**	kanz
sixteen	**seize**	sez
seventeen	**dix-sept**	deez-*set*
eighteen	**dix-huit**	deez-*wheat*
nineteen	**dix-neuf**	deez-*nuf*
twenty	**vingt**	vehn
twenty-one	**vingt-et-un**	vehnt-ay-*uh*
twenty-two	**vingt-deux**	vehnt-*duh*
thirty	**trente**	trahnt
forty	**quarante**	ka-*rahnt*
fifty	**cinquante**	sang-*kahnt*
sixty	**soixante**	swa-*sahnt*
sixty-one	**soixante-et-un**	swa-sahnt-et-*uh*
seventy	**soixante-dix**	swa-sahnt-*deess*
seventy-one	**soixante-et-onze**	swa-sahnt-et-*ohnze*
eighty	**quatre-vingts**	kaht-ruh-*vehn*
eighty-one	**quatre-vingt-un**	kaht-ruh-vehn-*uh*
ninety	**quatre-vingt-dix**	kaht-ruh-venh-*deess*
ninety-one	**quatre-vingt-onze**	kaht-ruh-venh-*ohnze*
one hundred	**cent**	sahn
one thousand	**mille**	meel
one hundred thousand	**cent mille**	sahn meel
first	**premier**	*preh*-mee-ay
second	**deuxième**	*duhz*-zee-em
third	**troisième**	*twa*-zee-em
fourth	**quatrième**	kaht-ree-em
fifth	**cinquième**	*sank*-ee-em
sixth	**sixième**	*sees*-ee-em
seventh	**septième**	*set*-ee-em
eighth	**huitième**	*wheat*-ee-em
ninth	**neuvième**	*neuv*-ee-em
tenth	**dixième**	*dees*-ee-em

THE CALENDAR

English	French	Pronunciation
January	**Janvier**	*jhan*-vee-ay
February	**Février**	*feh*-vree-ay
March	**Mars**	marce
April	**Avril**	a-*vreel*
May	**Mai**	meh
June	**Juin**	jhwehn
July	**Juillet**	*jhwee*-ay
August	**Août**	oot
September	**Septembre**	sep-*tahm*-bruh
October	**Octobre**	ok-*toh*-bruh
November	**Novembre**	no-*vahm*-bruh
December	**Decembre**	day-*sahm*-bruh
Sunday	**Dimanche**	dee-*mahnsh*
Monday	**Lundi**	*luhn*-dee
Tuesday	**Mardi**	*mahr*-dee
Wednesday	**Mercredi**	*mair*-kruh-dee
Thursday	**Jeudi**	*jheu*-dee
Friday	**Vendredi**	*vawn*-druh-dee
Saturday	**Samedi**	*sahm*-dee
yesterday	**hier**	ee-*air*
today	**aujourd'hui**	o-jhord-*dwee*
this morning/this afternoon	**ce matin/cet après-midi**	suh ma-*tan*/set ah-preh-mee-*dee*
tonight	**ce soir**	suh *swahr*
tomorrow	**demain**	de-*man*

FOOD & MENU TERMS

English	French	Pronunciation
I would like . . .	**Je voudrais . . .**	jhe voo-*dray*
. . . to eat	**. . . manger**	mahn-*jhay*
. . . to order	**. . . commander**	ko-mahn-*day*
Please give me . . .	**Donnez-moi, s'il vous plait . . .**	don-nay-*mwah,* seel voo play
. . . a bottle of . . .	**. . . une bouteille de . . .**	ewn boo-*tay* duh
. . . a cup of . . .	**. . . une tasse de . . .**	ewn tass duh
. . . a glass of . . .	**. . . un verre de . . .**	uh vair duh
. . . a cocktail	**. . . un apéritif**	uh ah-pay-ree-*teef*
. . . the check/bill	**. . . l'addition**	la-dee-see-*ohn*
. . . a napkin	**. . . une serviette**	ewn sair-vee-*ett*

English	French	Pronunciation
Cheers!	**A votre santé!**	ah vo-truh sahn-*tay!*
fixed-price menu	**un menu**	uh meh-*new*
Is the tip/service included?	**Est-ce que le service est compris?**	ess-ke luh ser-*vees* eh com-*pree?*
Waiter!/Waitress!	**S'il vous plait!/Excusez-moi!**	seel voo *play*/ex-kyus-ay-*mwah!*
appetizer	**une entrée**	ewn en-*tray*
tip included	**service compris**	sehr-*vees* cohm-*pree*

MEATS

English	French	Pronunciation
beef stew	**du pot-au-feu**	dew poht o *fhe*
chicken	**du poulet**	*dew poo*-lay
chicken stewed with mushrooms and wine	**du coq au vin**	dew cock o vhin
ham	**du jambon**	dew jahm-*bohn*
lamb	**de l'agneau**	duh lahn-*nyo*
rabbit	**du lapin**	dew lah-pan
steak	**du bifteck**	dew beef-*tek*
veal	**du veau**	dew *voh*

FISH

English	French	Pronunciation
Mediterranean fish soup or stew	**de la bouillabaisse**	duh lah booh-wee-ya-*besse*
lobster	**du homard**	dew oh-*mahr*
mussels	**des moules**	day *moohl*
mussels in herb-flavored white wine with shallots	**des moules marinières**	day moohl mar-ee-nee-*air*
oysters	**des huîtres**	dayz hoo-*ee*-truhs
shrimp	**des crevettes**	day kreh-*vette*
tuna	**du thon**	dew tohn
trout	**de la truite**	duh lah tru-*eet*

FRUITS & VEGETABLES

English	French	Pronunciation
eggplant	**de l'aubergine**	duh loh-ber-*jheen*
grapes	**du raisin**	dew ray-*zhan*
green beans	**des haricots verts**	day ahr-ee-coh *vaire*
lemon/lime	**du citron/du citron vert**	dew cee-tron/dew cee-tron *vaire*
potatoes	**des pommes de terre**	day puhm duh *tehr*

English	French	Pronunciation
potatoes au gratin	**des pommes de terre dauphinoises**	day puhm duh tehr doh-feen-wahze
french-fried potatoes	**des frites**	day freet
spinach	**des épinards**	dayz ay-pin-*ards*
strawberries	**des fraises**	day *frez*

SOUPS & SALADS

English	French	Pronunciation
fruit salad	**une salade de fruit/une macédoine de fruits**	ewn sah-lahd duh *fwee*/ewn mah-say-doine duh fwee
green salad	**une salade verte**	ewn sah-lahd *vairt*
lettuce salad	**une salade de la laitue**	ewn sah-lahd duh la lay-*tew*
onion soup	**de la soupe à l'oignon**	duh lah soop ah low-*nyon*

BEVERAGES

English	French	Pronunciation
beer	**de la bière**	duh lah bee-*aire*
draft beer	**une pression**	ewn press-y-*ohn*
milk	**du lait**	dew *lay*
orange juice	**du jus d'orange**	dew joo d'or-*ahn*-jhe
water	**de l'eau**	duh lo
red wine	**du vin rouge**	dew vhin *rooj*
white wine	**du vin blanc**	dew vhin *blahn*
coffee (espresso)	**un café**	uh ka-fay *nwahr*
coffee (with milk)	**un café crème/café au lait**	uh ka-fay *krem/*ka-fay o *lay*
coffee (decaf)	**un café décaféiné** (slang: **un déca**)	un ka-fay day-kah-fay-*nay* (uh *day*-kah)
tea	**du thé**	dew *tay*
cola	**un coca**	uh ko-*kah*

SPICES/CONDIMENTS

English	French	Pronunciation
mayonnaise	**de la mayonnaise**	duh lah may-o-nayse
mustard	**de la moutarde**	duh lah moo-*tard*-uh
ketchup	**du ketchup**	dew ketch-up
pepper	**du poivre**	dew *pwah*-vruh
salt	**du sel**	dew *sel*
sour heavy cream	**de la crème fraîche**	duh lah krem *fresh*
sugar	**du sucre**	dew *sooh*-kruh

Index

A

B

C

D

E

F

G

H

Q

R

S